NORTHWEST
Readers

Oregon

Indians

VOICES FROM TWO CENTURIES

EDITED BY Stephen Dow Beckham

OREGON STATE UNIVERSITY PRESS

CORVALLIS, OREGON

A NORTHWEST READER

Robert J. Frank, *Series Editor:*

The paper in this book meets the guidelines for permanence and
durability of the Committee on Production Guidelines for Book
Longevity of the Council on Library Resources and the minimum
requirements of the American National Standard for Permanence
of Paper for Printed Library Materials z39.48-1984.

Library of Congress Cataloging-in-Publication Data

Oregon Indians : voices from two centuries / edited by Stephen
Dow Beckham.— 1st ed.

   p. cm.

   Includes bibliographical references and index.

   ISBN-13: 978-0-87071-088-9 (alk. paper)

   ISBN-10: 0-87071-088-5 (alk. paper)

   1. Indians of North America—Oregon—History—
Sources.   2. Indians of North America—First contact with
Europeans—Oregon.   3. Indians, Treatment of—Oregon—
History—Sources.   4. Whites—Oregon—Relations with
Indians.   5. Oregon—Discovery and exploration.   6. Oregon—
History—Sources.   I. Beckham, Stephen Dow.

   E78.O6O74 2006

   979.5004'97—dc22

                                        2005032426

Oregon State
UNIVERSITY

Oregon State University Press

500 Kerr Administration

Corvallis OR 97331-2122

541-737-3166 • fax 541-737-3170

http://oregonstate.edu/dept/press

Contents

Introduction

Forty years ago I began dropping bibliographical citations and copies of articles into files. The object was to find and preserve as far as was feasible a Native American commentary about the events affecting their lives in Oregon. The data came from many places: minutes of treaty councils, personal statements given to congressional committees or touring federal commissions, letters (sometimes written by a scribe assisting a non-literate person), comments captured by newspaper reporters, answers to deposition interrogatories, and testimony in court. These were the raw materials of history, but they were much more. They were first-person accounts of events threatening, changing, and shaping the lives of Oregon Indians. They were also the beginning of my work on this book.

This volume is organized topically and chronologically. It opens with "Encounters," the arrival of Euro-Americans and the consequences to the Native people of the new arrivals' technology, weaponry, clothing, foods, and diseases. Some of the selections address "first encounters," such as the moment when the Qua-to-mah, a band of Athabaskan-speakers living near Cape Blanco and the Port Orford headlands, paddled to sea on April 25, 1792, and encountered the Vancouver exploring expedition. This event is recounted through the narratives of a half-dozen British diarists and is revealing in the range of their reactions to the Indians. It is remarkable in its preservation of the words of greeting shouted across the waves by the Quah-to-mah to those sailing to their shores. I entered these accounts in my notebook on September 5, 1965, at the Public Record Office, London, and later that week at the Manuscript Division of the British Museum library. These notes were the genesis of this volume.

The next several selections—organized by topic—bring Oregon Native Americans into the context of federal Indian policy. The role of treaties, machinations of the Oregon Volunteers, efforts of the U.S. Army to protect the Indians but also to subdue and confine them, and the emergence of reservation programs to "civilize" them are recounted in a variety of documents.

These range from treaties to letters, minutes of councils, and to the ad hominem attacks on Sarah Winnemucca by those who feared her influence and honesty.

Euro-American attitudes toward Native Americans were of immense consequence. When members of the surrounding culture alleged that Oregon Indians lacked ambition and were not using reserved lands, they developed schemes to plunder and dismember reservations. They prosecuted Indians under the Trade and Intercourse Act of 1834; they summarily imprisoned Indian leaders without trial and sequestered them in reservation jails or at Alcatraz. These attitudes were sometimes promoted in the public schools. This volume includes a selection from the long-taught *History of Oregon*. The section on the First Oregonians opens with the message: "The Oregon Indians were true savages."

A number of tribal leaders and spokespersons expressed their views. They addressed the closure of the Alsea Sub-Agency on the Coast Reservation, the dispossession of the Northern Paiutes of the Malheur Reservation, and matters of hunting and grazing rights on the Umatilla Reservation. Some Oregon Indians shared their views nationally in lecture tours and in books. Others were featured in lectures or publications by John Beeson and Alfred Meacham, two remarkable champions of Indian rights who resided in Oregon.

Although Native Americans were romanticized and stereotyped in the first decades of the twentieth century—at a time when they were no longer an existential threat to others—they endured continuing loss of land, destruction of culture, and compulsory "civilization" for their children. These matters began to change during the New Deal in the 1930s, but the question of whether or not to accept the Indian Reorganization Act (1934) proved difficult for Oregon tribes. Part of the problem was that the officials of the Bureau of Indian Affairs only described the anticipated impacts of IRA; they did not circulate the legislation so that the tribes could study it carefully.

This volume addresses the terrible experiment of Termination. This post-World War II program hit Oregon tribes with a vengeance. By 1956 Congress had passed laws to sever relations with the Klamath Tribe and every tribe and band west of the Cascades in Oregon. A number of tribal leaders who endured those events and who sustained the hope that they might eventually secure reversal of this policy spoke to the "disastrous policy of Termination."

The final selections in this volume illustrate the success of tribes in securing protection of treaty rights, of gaining settlement for tribal land claims, in working with members of Congress, and in trying to protect their religious rights and ancestral remains. This course, while not always successful, has engendered hope. Oregon tribes have increasingly taken charge of their own destinies and, with economies powered by casino revenues, have started to diversify their investments and underwrite education, health care, housing, and care for their young and old. At Warm Springs and Umatilla reservations, they have constructed handsome museums to preserve their culture and history and present them to visitors.

Each section in this volume has a prefatory essay to establish the historical context of the era that the selections more fully illustrate. Each selection has a brief introduction, is cited to its source, and is followed by suggested related reading.

The challenge of this volume was what to exclude. In several instances the selections are the "tip of the iceberg." The fuller text contains additional voices and more material. The minutes of the Celilo Fish Committee, for example, vividly document the role of Chief Tommy Thompson and others in mediating conflicts among the fishers who gathered annually at this great crossroads of the Pacific Northwest. The oral histories collected from tribal elders for use by ethnohistorians in land claims cases are another source of first-person information. This volume has sought representative sources and makes no brief to be comprehensive. It is hoped, however, that it suggests the potentials for further exploration of materials that will contribute to the continuing reassessment of Indian history.

Acknowledgments

A number of friends, some now deceased, advised and suggested materials for this volume. Some, in fact, are represented in the selections. If there had been room, I would have included every line of testimony of the tribal witnesses who went to Washington, D.C., to argue for the restoration of Oregon's terminated tribes. Those people—many of them my friends—worked diligently on their statements, bunked at William Penn House or Davis House (bed and breakfast sites operated by the American Friends Service Committee), and confronted taxies, appointments at offices they had never before seen, and appearance in congressional hearing rooms. They were determined, a bit fearful, ever hopeful, and—at last—they prevailed.

The staffs of several libraries assisted in securing these materials. My appreciation goes to the archivists of the Public Record Office and Manuscript Division of the British Museum Library, London, where this volume had its beginning. It extends to the specialists at the National Archives who introduced me to the wide range of materials held in Washington, D.C., as well as in the branch depositories. I recall vividly the assistance of Laura Kelsay, Robert Kvashnicka, James Glenn, and Joyce Justice of the National Archives, Washington, D.C., and Seattle. Similarly I was aided in my research by the staff of the National Anthropological Archives, Smithsonian Institution, and the librarians of several divisions of the Library of Congress.

In Oregon my research labors ranged from the Watzek and Boley libraries at Lewis & Clark College to the Knight Library, University of Oregon; Millar Library, Portland State University; Oregon State Library, Salem; State Archives, Salem; and the Oregon Historical Society Library, Portland. This project consumed rolls and rolls of dimes and quarters, copy cards, and requests for retrieval of items from off-site storage.

In the early phase of this volume I was fortunate to have a faculty research grant from Lewis & Clark College. The project included a student collaborator, Laura Provinzino. Laura was zealous in her quest for sources and generous in her critiques of her professor's prose. Subsequently Laura graduated with double honors, secured a Rhodes Scholarship for study at Balliol College, Oxford, and earned a law degree from Yale University. Laura was truly remarkable in her efforts to launch this project. Had not the Lewis and Clark Expedition Bicentennial and two other books intervened, this volume might have been completed in a more timely way!

Robert Frank, Jeffrey Grass, Mary Braun, Jo Alexander, and Tom Booth were patient but persistent that this volume get done. The wonderful support of those associated with Oregon State University Press has helped drive this volume to completion. I consistently felt guilty about not getting the manuscript into their hands in a more timely manner.

To the many librarians and archivists who helped find what I was seeking, to tribal leaders such as Sue Shaffer or the late Bill Brainard, to my attorney friend Dennis J. Whittlesey who has helped chart a new course for many American Indian tribes over the past thirty years—I say thank you. Helen Sanders, lead plaintiff in *Mitchell v. United States* and longtime chair of the Quinault Allottees Association, has taught me much about the intricacies of federal Indian policy and BIA practices.

I am particularly appreciative of the endowment funds from the Cow Creek Band of Umpqua Tribe of Indians for the Indian Law Program at Lewis & Clark College, as well as for the support of the Spirit Mountain Community Fund of the college's summer programs in Indian Law and for the Helen Sanders and Nelson Terry Scholarship endowments from the Quinault Allottees Association. These programs have enabled me to work with generations of undergraduate and law students and have helped shape my thinking about the essays in this volume.

I am mindful of the special research projects I was retained to carry out for the Tribal Council, Confederated Tribes of Grand Ronde. In the course of those ventures I found some of the selections included in this volume. The same was also the case in my work as a witness in the U.S. Claims Court for the Karuk Tribe and the Cow Creek Band of Umpqua Tribe of Indians. My labors in the federal acknowledgment projects for the Cowlitz Tribe, Chinook Tribe, Duwamish Tribe, and Esselen-Oholone also led me to find materials that would not have come my way had I not been engaged in those ventures.

I also thank my family for patience and encouragement: my wife, Patti, my son, Andrew Dow, and my daughter Ann-Marie. They encountered this volume in various stages of construction and endured my commentary and enthusiasm about things I was finding, reading, or wanting to share with a willing victim. My father, Dow Beckham, and my mother, Anna Beckham, unleashed the interests that led my path toward Native American history. To all—thank you.

STEPHEN DOW BECKHAM
Pamplin Professor of History
Lewis & Clark College

Editorial Methodology

The selections in this volume are presented as written, with the following exceptions. A number of the accounts had no paragraphing. The editor has thus, in some instances, created paragraphs to facilitate the flow or reading. Material in brackets is the voice of the editor. I have attempted to provide modest clarification by inserting first names or, on occasion, a missing word lost in transcription or composition.

The selections have integrity but are not, in several instances, the complete transcription of the original material. The hearing record of Task Force No. 10 of the American Indian Policy Review Commission in Salem, Oregon, in 1976, for example, is a typescript of 250 pages. This volume presents only representative selections from the several voices raised about the impact of "Termination" on Oregon tribes.

Buried in the thousands of "Letters Received" by the Bureau of Indian Affairs subsequent to 1875 are many more voices of Oregon's native people. Those letters are exceedingly difficult to find because the Department of Interior ceased accessioning letters by jurisdiction—such as the Oregon Superintendency of Indian Affairs—and, instead, date-stamped each letter received each year. Although the letters in-coming were dutifully recorded in letter registers and preserved, the only way to find one is to know the name of the letter writer. Using the name in the letter register, the researcher finds a number for the letter for a specific year, such as 1898, Letter No. 73,224. The researcher has to fill out a call slip and wait for the archivist to pull the letter. Sometimes the result is a fascinating document; other times the file is empty or contains only the envelope. The staff of the National Archives is able to retrieve only about fifty letters per day in this system.

This volume is thus the result of purposeful research and fortuitous discovery of data. The net was cast wide; the catch is not complete, but, hopefully, is representative of an incompletely documented history.

One

Encounters

A View in Hancocks River · North end of Wasjingtons Ifslands

A VOYAGE ON DISCOVERIES

The *Columbia Rediviva* (left) crossed into the Columbia River in 1792 under Captain Robert Gray. Robert Haswell (1768–1801/02), a member of the crew, kept a detailed, illustrated journal of the expedition. His account documented first encounters with Oregon Indians (Courtest of the Massachusetts Historical Society).

FOR MILLENNIA the lives of Native Americans in the Oregon Country passed unnoticed by a larger world. Summer followed winter in endless succession. Villages grew, flourished, waned, and disappeared. The existence of the people moved like the great rivers of the region. The cultures of humankind in the Pacific Northwest ebbed and flowed with the forces of nature and time. The marks on the land were few: a trail etched by countless feet trekking to a fishing hole, a stone cairn stacked atop a lonely mountainside as part of a spirit quest rite, a pictograph painted in red ochre on the face of basalt rock, a lithic scatter of flakes where a man had patiently made a projectile point, a mortar etched into bedrock where a succession of women had ground seeds. The most notable imprint occurred in the annual burning of the region's valleys and headlands. Indian fire ecology shaped the landscape. These were the subtle signals of human existence that transcended time and memory.

Travelers from afar probably first spied the shores of Oregon in the late sixteenth century. Starting in 1565, Spanish mariners began sailing the Manilla Galleon, a trading ship monopoly that, for two hundred fifty years, plied the North Pacific once a year to carry porcelains, candlesticks, beeswax, silk, and spices of southeast Asia to Mexico and ports south along the west coast of Central and South America. Although Cape Mendocino was the usual landfall for the galleons sweeping the North Pacific on the Japanese Current, a number of these vessels probably fell in along the shore to the north. For the native peoples of coastal Oregon, their sightings of these heavily laden galleons were the first hint of other peoples from distant lands.

Among the oral traditions of the Indians of the coast of Oregon are accounts of shipwrecks, survivors, and salvaged goods. Precisely who these unfortunate mariners were or when their ships foundered is unknown. The native accounts speak of such events as do the pieces of beeswax washed out of the sands at the Nehalem spit near the base of Neahkahnie Mountain or the shards of blue and white porcelain in the middens of the Indian villages along that estuary.[1]

In 1774–75 the scrim of time began to lift. Spanish expeditions outfitted in Mexico sailed north to explore the region beyond Alta California. The Spanish were eager to learn the location of the Russian fur traders and trappers who, since the 1740s, had followed the Aleutian Islands eastward. The voyages of discovery of Juan Pérez, Juan Bodega y Quadra, Bruno de Hezeta, and Juan Martínez y Zayas logged information in ship ledgers and on charts.

Far more significant, however, was the impact of the Enlightenment and the quest of Europeans to record discrete information. In their attempt to ascertain natural law and find order in a disorderly world, European nation-states mounted voyages of discovery. The North Pacific was a great *terra incognita*. Its magnetism included the prospects of settling issues of mythical geography: finding the legendary Northwest Passage, the Kingdom of Quivera, or an alleged large body of water in the interior, the Sea of Ronquillo. More alluring was the prospect of staking claims to new lands for colonies, finding wealth in gold, silver, furs, or other commerce, or extending Christian missions to native peoples. The forces of curiosity, commerce, colonies, and conversion drew outsiders to the Oregon Country.

Embedded in the ship logs and travel diaries of the late eighteenth and early nineteenth centuries are brief accounts of first contacts. The story is one-sided, for it was penned by Europeans and Americans, not the native peoples. Nevertheless it documents the beginning of relationships. Of considerable interest are the repeated accounts of favorable first contacts. These occurred at sea at several locations along the Oregon coast in the eighteenth century. The multiple shipboard diaries of members of the Vancouver expedition in 1792 confirmed the different ways in which a half dozen visitors described an initial encounter with the native peoples. While many of these exchanges were positive, there was a notable exception. In 1788 Robert Gray's trading party raked the shore of Tillamook Bay with cannon fire and dubbed the port Murderers' Harbor.[2]

Following the first, brief accounts of encounter, another literature began to document the life ways of Oregon natives. These descriptions commenced with the journals of the Lewis and Clark Expedition, the American exploring party that sojourned during the winter of 1805–06 at the mouth of the Columbia River. It grew with the arrival of members of the Pacific Fur Company who, in 1811, established Astoria, the first, permanent Euro-American settlement in the region. The documentation took on another dimension when, in the 1840s, overland emigrants began settling in the valleys of western Oregon. Their accounts confirmed the preconceptions they carried with them about native peoples, a preface to the wars of conquest leading to Indian removal and confinement on reservations in the ensuing decades.

By the 1840s the initial contacts accelerated rapidly. The Oregon Trail and the Applegate Trail brought hundreds, and sometimes thousands, of emigrants across the Columbia Plateau or through the northern Great Basin into western Oregon. When the emigrants came, they brought pathogens—smallpox, measles, typhus and other calamitous diseases. The missionaries who had begun their labors in the 1830s among the tribes seemed incapable of saving Indian lives, yet the majority of the pioneer settlers survived. Seeds of distrust and conflict sowed by these events prompted Dr. Elijah White to try to impose laws and craft a hierarchy of chiefs among the Cayuse. Going one better than the dealings of Moses with God, White handed down eleven commandments to the Plateau Indians in 1843.

Throughout the period between the 1770s and 1849 the government of the United States exerted no policy or formal program for the Indians of the Oregon Country. Initially Spain, Russia, Great Britain, and the United States were all contenders for the region through the assertion of their respective "rights of discovery." Spain withdrew from contention in 1819; Russia dropped from active status in the 1820s. Finally on June 15, 1846, Great Britain and the United States agreed to the Oregon Treaty, setting the 49th parallel as the boundary between the United States and Canada.

The problematic nature of relations between Native Americans and the pioneer generation gained bloody confirmation in events on the Columbia Plateau in 1847–48. In November a few members of the Cayuse tribe, aggrieved by the wholesale deaths of their people and irked by the attitudes and actions of the missionaries at Waiilatpu, attacked the mission. The incident resulted in the deaths of more than a dozen Euro-Americans. In its wake settlers of the Willamette Valley invaded the Plateau to seek retribution, round up alleged perpetrators, and put the natives of that region on notice about the might and intention of the Americans moving into their country. These events created an interesting historical narrative, including voices of response from tribal leaders participating in the council of 1848 at Fort Nez Perces.

In the spring of 1849 Joseph Lane, Oregon's first territorial governor and ex-officio superintendent of Indian Affairs, arrived in Oregon City. The era of first encounters effectively ended. Henceforth the Indians of the Oregon Country were plunged into the morass of federal Indian affairs and the incomplete execution of policies and procedures established thousands of miles away.

The following accounts document a variety of encounters. They range from the prophecy of the coming of strangers to sightings of Indian villages along the shore. They include recording words of greeting from the tribal delegations who paddled out to sea to trade with mariners from distant lands. The perspectives range from Native American accounts of shipwrecks on the coast to the bizarre efforts of Dr. Elijah White to give laws to the Cayuse and Nez Perce. They deal with the tragic events of the incident at Waiilatpu in 1847 and the proceedings of the commission attempting the following year to resolve the Cayuse War.

NOTES

1. Warren L. Cook, *Flood Tide of Empire: Spain and the Pacific Northwest, 1543–1819*. New Haven, CT: Yale University Press, 1973, pp. 35–38.

2. J. Richard Nokes. *Columbia's River: The Voyages of Robert Gray, 1787–1793*. Tacoma, WA: Washington State Historical Society, 1991, pp. 52–57.

"A Prophecy of the Coming of the Whites"

In July and August 1905, Edward Sapir, a skilled linguist and field ethnographer, collected literary information from informants living on the Yakama Reservation. Peter McGuff, a man of mixed Indian and African-American ancestry, served as his interpreter. As a child living at the Cascades, McGuff learned a number of Wishram tales. He attended a Bureau of Indian Affairs school and mastered reading and writing English. Sapir was impressed with McGuff's "remarkable intelligence" and help to him both in the field and in correspondence about the development of Wishram Texts (1909). "As I had taught Pete the phonetic method of taking down Indian text followed in my own work," Sapir wrote, "the additional texts forwarded by him were all in strictly phonetic shape, and are published here with such comparatively slight revision as they seemed to demand."

An aged woman, Sophia Klickitat, resided at the Cascades of the Columbia, the rapids created by the massive Bonneville landslide. Approximately one thousand years ago the north shore of the Columbia River collapsed. The flow of mud, rock, and timber momentarily dammed the Columbia River, leaving a series of three major rapids. The following narrative, recalled by McGuff from Sophie Klickitat's oral tales, anticipated the encounter with Euro-Americans. Appropriately it is a story from the Columbia River—the artery of contact for mariners arriving by sea and for the Lewis and Clark Expedition by land.

Long ago, I believe, the people learned that now whites would soon come. One old man, I believe, learned of it at night. Then he dreamt; he saw strange people, they spoke to him, and showed him everything; and he heard something like three or four Indian songs. In the morning he spoke to all the people. And then everybody gathered together to hear him,—women, men, children, old men—everybody. He told the people what he had seen in his sleep at night. And then they gathered together to hear him; they danced every day and every night. They were made glad because of his story.

He said: "Soon all sorts of strange things will come. No longer (will things be) as before; no longer, as will soon happen, shall we use these things of ours. They will bring to us everything strange; they will bring to us (something which) you just have to point at anything moving way yonder, and it will fall right down and die." As it turned out, it was a gun of which he spoke.

"There will be brought to us a bucket for boiling-purposes; no longer will you use your old-fashioned bucket made out of stone." As it turned out, they really brought to us what he told the people of. "No longer will you make fire by drilling with sticks as before." Still more were they made glad, they danced with energy. "Certain small pieces of wood will be brought to us with which you will make a fire." As it turned out, it was matches whereof he spoke.

For days and nights they danced. They were not at all hungry, truly they did their best (in dancing). Everything they saw—ax, hatchet, knife, stove. "Strange people will bring us such things. White people with mustaches on their faces will come from the east. Do you people be careful!" Then indeed they would again jump up and down; they did their best strongly. And truly things are just so to-day; now surely the old man dreamt just that way. Up to that time there were no cattle at all. Presently white people brought them; only farther up there were buffaloes. Nor were there any horses either, only dogs. Thus long ago did it happen to the people dwelling along the river.

SOURCE

Sapir, Edward. *Wishram Texts.* Publications of the American Ethnological Society. Leyden, Netherlands: E. J. Brill, 1909, pp. 228–31.

RELATED READING

Jones, Suzi and Jarold Ramsey, eds. *The Stories We Tell: An Anthology of Oregon Folk Literature.* Corvallis, OR: Oregon State University Press.

First Ship Seen by the Clatsop

"A'l ta i'kta age'ElkEl. NaXLo'lEXa-it e'kole. Q!oa'p agia'xom. A'lta mokct tma'ktcXEma tigE'nxat. NaXLo'leXa-it: 'O nekct taL! E'kole. Eqctxe'Lau taL!'" ["Now something she saw it. She thought a whale. Now two spruce trees stood upright near her. She thought: 'Oh not behold a whale. A monster behold!'"] Thus went the tale recited by Charles Cultee to Franz Boas about the Clatsop encounter with a sailing ship and its surviving crew.*

A brilliant German-born Jewish scholar, Boas emigrated to the United States in 1887 when he perceived that his religion stood in the way of his academic advancement. Finding a position at Columbia University, where he taught for nearly fifty years, Boas began field work with Lower Chinookan informants during the summers of 1890 and 1891. He located a number of Clatsops, but he discovered that, as a consequence of extensive intermarriage with the Nehalem Tillamook, they had largely abandoned their language. His three informants could give only vocabulary words and a few sentences. They urged him to visit Bay Center on Willapa Bay to the north of the Columbia River and speak with their relatives who resided there.

Boas found that the Chinooks at Bay Center had also largely given up their language in preference to Chehalis. However, he did find two Chinookan informants—Charles Cultee and a woman identified only as Catherine (possibly Catherine Dawson). "Cultee (or more properly Q!Elte') proved to be a veritable storehouse of information," he recalled. Cultee, who had lived for several years in his mother's village at Kathlamet on the Oregon shore, spoke Chehalis with his wife. He had learned the Clatsop dialect from his father, a Tinneh (Athabaskan) dialect from his mother, and spoke regularly in Chinook with one of his relatives and with Catherine.

Cultee was a superb informant. Boas wrote about the man's "remarkable intelligence," and noted: "After he had once grasped what I wanted, he explained to me the grammatical structure of the sentences by means of examples, and elucidated the sense of difficult periods." Among the many texts Cultee dictated was the story

of a shipwreck on the Clatsop Spit. It told of an interesting encounter and how the
Clatsop "became rich."

The son of an old woman had died. She wailed for him a whole year and then she stopped. Now one day she went to Seaside. There she used to stop, and she returned. She returned walking along the beach. She nearly reached Clatsop; now she saw something. She thought it was a whale. When she came near it she saw two spruce trees standing upright on it. She thought, "Behold! It is no whale. It is a monster."

She reached the thing that lay there. Now she saw that its outer side was all covered with copper. Ropes were tied to those spruce trees and it was full of iron. Then a bear came out of it. He stood on the thing that lay there. He looked just like a bear, but his face was that of a human being. Then she went home.

Now she though of her son, and cried, saying, "Oh, my son is dead and the thing about which we heard in tales is on shore." When she nearly reached the town she continued to cry. [The people said,] "Oh, a person comes crying. Perhaps somebody struck her." The people made themselves ready. They took their arrows. An old man said, "Listen!" Then the people listened. Now she said all the time, "Oh, my son is dead, and the thing about which he heard in tales is on the shore."

The people said, "What may it be?" They went running to meet her. They said, "What is it?" "Ah, something lies there and it is thus. There are two bears on it, or maybe they are people." Then the people ran. They reached the thing that lay there. Now the people, or what else they might be, held two copper kettles in their hands. Now the first one reached there. Another one arrived.

Now the persons took their hands to their mouths and gave the people their kettles. They had lids. The men pointed inland and asked for water. Then two people ran inland. They hid themselves behind a log. They returned again and ran to the beach. One man climbed up and entered the thing. He went down into the ship. He looked about in the interior of the ship; it was full of boxes. He found brass buttons in strings half a fathom long. He went out again to call his relatives, but they had already set fire to the ship. He humped down. Those two persons had also gone down. It burnt just like fat.

Then the Clatsop gathered the iron, the copper, and the brass. Then all the people learned about it. The two persons were taken to the chief of the Clatsop. Then the chief of the one town said, "I want to keep one of the men with me." The people were almost began to fight. Now one of them was taken to one town. Then the chief was satisfied.

Now the Quenaiult, the Chehalis, the Cascades, the Cowlitz, and the Klickitat learned about it and they all went to Clatsop. The Quenaiult, the Chehalis, and the Willapa went. The people of all the towns went there. The Cascades, the Cowlitz, and the Klickitat came down the river. All those of the upper part of the river came down to Clatsop.

Strips of copper two fingers wide and going around the arm were exchanged for one slave each. A piece of iron as long as one-half the forearm was exchanged for one slave. A piece of brass two fingers wide was exchanged for one slave. A nail was sold for a good curried deerskin. Several nails were given for long dentalia. The people bought this and the Clatsop became rich. Then iron and brass were seen for the first time. Now they kept these two persons. One was kept by each chief; one was at the Clatsop town at the cape [Point Adams].

SOURCE

Boas, Franz, ed. Chinook Texts, *Bulletin of the Bureau of American Ethnology*, 20 (1894).

RELATED READING

Cook, Warren L. *Flood Tide of Empire: Spain and the Pacific Northwest, 1543–1819*. New Haven, CT: Yale University Press, 1973.

Ruby, Robert H., and John A. Brown. *The Chinook Indians: Traders of the Lower Columbia River*. Norman, OK: University of Oklahoma Press, 1976.

Treasure of Echanie (Neahkahnie) Mountain

Silas B. Smith (1840–1902) was a remarkable figure who delivered the first annual address on December 16, 1899, to the Oregon Historical Society. His mother, Celiast (or Helen), was the daughter of Clatsop chief Cobaway, whose people traded with the Lewis and Clark Expedition during the winter of 1805–06. His father, Solomon Smith (1809–76), was a school teacher who emigrated overland in 1832 with fur trader Nathaniel Wyeth. The elder Smith taught at Fort Vancouver and French Prairie before settling in 1840 on the Clatsop Plains. A doctor, store owner, and sawmill operator, Smith served in the Oregon legislature. He and Celiast had seven children.

Silas Smith was educated in Clatsop County, then studied at Dartmouth College, Hanover, New Hampshire, in its program that catered to outstanding, young Native Americans. After college, Smith read law in an apprenticeship to a lawyer and entered legal practice in Astoria. In 1899 he secured passage of the first jurisdictional act to permit Pacific Northwest tribes to sue the federal government for the taking of their lands. He served as attorney for the Clatsop, Chinook, Cathlamet, and Nehalem Band of Tillamook. The case slowly worked its way through the Claims Court in Washington, D.C., ultimately leading to a token financial settlement for the tribes a decade after Smith's death. Smith was active in public affairs, published articles on Indian history and culture, and was the first college-educated Native American in Oregon.

In the following selection Smith discussed Spanish exploration of the Northwest Coast and the wrecks of ships near the mouth of the Columbia. Historians believe today that Smith may have described the foundering of the San Francisco Xavier, *a Manilla Galleon bound for Mexico that beached on the Nehalem Spit in 1707. The identity of the other vessels he describes is unknown.*

The first authenticated recorded account of the exploration of the Pacific Northwest coast by white men—not considering the mythical voyages of Lorenzo Ferer Maldonado, Juan de Fuca, and Admiral Bartolome de Fonte, relating to their alleged discovery of the Straits of Anian—was that made by

Lieutenant Juan Perez, of the Spanish navy, on the sloop of war *Santiago*, from San Blas, Mexico, in 1774, leaving that port on January 25, of that year on her northern cruise.

But tradition among the Indian tribes at the mouth of the Columbia river and vicinity tell us that long prior to that time their shores had been visited by at least three other vessels; that is to say, the treasure ship at Echanie mountain, the bees-wax ship near the mouth of the Nehalem river and one other, just south of the mouth of the Columbia river. The two last becoming wrecks on the ocean beach at the places named, evidences of which facts of a more or less conclusive character can be adduced to establish the truthfulness of such statements.

The treasure ship did not become a wreck; she dropped anchor as she approached land and sent a boat ashore with several men and a large chest or box. The box was taken up on the southwest face of the mountain above the road and there buried. And some say that a man was then and there killed and buried with the chest. Then some characters were marked on a large stone which was placed on the spot of burial, and the men then returned to the vessel, when she again put to sea. The treasure character of the deposit is an inference of the whites and the alleged manner of entombment.

The natives have never pretended to know what was contained in the chest.

The above is the substance of the account of the treasure ship at Echanie mountain as given by the older Indians in the early settlement of the country.

Much has been told and written about the bees-wax wreck. It has gone into song and story.

It has developed a sort of literature peculiarly its own, and the end is not yet.

The Indian account is something like this: That sometime ago, before the coming of the whites, a vessel was driven ashore in the vicinity of where the beeswax is now found, just north of the mouth of the Nehalem river.

The vessel became a wreck, but all of most of her crew survived. A large part of her cargo was this bees-wax. The crew, unable to get away, remained there with the natives several months, when, by concerted action the Indians massacred the entire number, on account, as they claimed, that the whites disregarded their—the natives'—marital relations. The Indians also state in connection with the massacre, that the crew fought with slung-shots. It would appear from this that they had lost their arms and ammunition.

I think it not too hazardous to identify this wreck as the Spanish ship *San Jose*, which had left La Paz, Lower California June 16, 1769, loaded with mission supplies for the Catholic mission at San Diego, Upper California, and of which nothing was ever heard after she left port. Every circumstance connected with the vessel and her journey favors this solution. Her course on her voyage was towards the north. Her mission supplies would include bees-wax or some other kind of wax as an article that would be needed for images, tapers, candles, etc. We find that some of the blocks of bees-wax from this wreck are inscribed with the Latin abbreviations "I. H. S.," "Jesus Hominum Salvator," which abbreviation is, I believe, largely or commonly used in the Roman Catholic church.

And we also find candles and tapers with the wicks in some, still remaining. And I believe a piece of this wax has now been found with the body of a bee imbedded in the wax.

This vessel falling in, in all probability, with a storm at sea while on her northward course, was driven away from her point of destination and found her fate on the sands at the mouth of the Nehalem river. The matter of the finding of the wax some 200 yards from the sea is accounted for by the fact that the crew, perhaps, endeavored to save the cargo, and carried a part of it there, which afterwards became buried by the drifting sands.

The third vessel of which tradition speaks, and whose advent, I think, has priority of date to the others, came ashore about two miles south of the mouth of the Columbia river.

Two of the crew survived, one of whom was named Konapee. The orthography of this name is given here phonetically, as pronounced by the Indians. The vessel was cast far enough up on the beach as to be accessible at low tide. After being looted she was burned by the natives for her iron.

Konapee and his companion were taken prisoners and held as slaves. The former soon showed himself as a worker in iron, and could fashion knives and hatchets for his captors. The natives soon considered him too great a person to be held as a slave, and gave him and his friend their liberty. After their release they went up the river about a mile above the Indian village to a place now known as New Astoria, and there located their dwelling. After that the Indians called the place Konapee, and it was known by that name long after the country was being settled by the whites. These men always declared that their home was towards the rising sun. And after a year or two they started east up the Columbia river, but, after reaching the Cascades, they went no further and there intermarried with the natives.

This wreck I believe to be a Spanish galleon. Gabriel Franchere tells in his "Narrative" that, on their first voyage up the Columbia river, in 1811, at an Indian dwelling not far below the Cascades, they found a blind old man—-presumably blind from old age—who, their guide said, was a white man, and that his name was Soto. And Franchere goes on to say: "We learn from the mouth of the old man himself that he was the son of a Spaniard who had been wrecked at the mouth of the river; that a part of the crew on this occasion got safely ashore, but were all massacred by the Clatsops, with the exception of four, who were spared, and who married native women; that these four Spaniards, of whom his father was one, disgusted with the savage life and attempted to reach a settlement of their own nation toward the south, but had never been heard of since; and that when his father, with his companions, left the country, he himself was quite young." And then the editor of the second edition of the "Narrative" in a note says: "These facts, if they were authenticated, would prove that the Spaniards were the first who discovered the Columbia. It is certain that long before the voyages of Captain Gray and Vancouver they knew at least a part of the course of that river, which was designated in their maps under the name of 'Oregon.'"

My mother, Mrs. Helen Smith, used to tell that at Fort Vancouver, in the later [18]20s she met a Cascades woman who was reputed to be a descendant of Konapee; that she was already past middle life, and was much fairer in complexion than the other natives.

This, I would say, was Soto's daughter.

These two men, Konapee and his companion, I believe were the first white men ever seen by the Indians on the pacific Northwest coast, and they were, I further believe, the first of the white race who ever saw the majestic "River of the West," floated on its bosom, or navigated its crystal waters. This wreck was first discovered by a woman. The survivors who had built a fire among the driftwood above the tide, and who also must have been heavily bearded men, were roasting popcorn, and made signs to her for water to drink. The woman, as she neared the village on her way for succor, began to wail, and her cry was: "I have found people who are men, and yet are also bears," thus indicating that these were the first heavily bearded people that she had seen.

From the manner of the coming of these castaways the Clatsops and Chinooks named all white people, without respect to nationality, 'Tlon-hon-nipts"; that is, "of those who drifted ashore."

A name of first impression, suggested by the condition under which they first met that race of people, and which name ever afterwards, even unto this day, in conversations among themselves, is largely used to signify white people.

Soto is a Spanish name. I think that Konapee is a corruption of some other name. Just for an illustration, we will say Juan de Pay. The natives not being able to pronounce it according to the Spanish method, followed the sound as nearly as they could and called Juan, "Kon"; de, "a"; Pay, "pee." This is simply a suggestion that I make.

Indian corn was unknown to the Indians of the Northwest at that time. This vessel having corn would indicate, possibly that she had gone from Mexico, and that her supplies included corn, and that she had some on hand yet. She also had Chinese coin or money of that kind of denomination having a small, square hold in the center of the piece. The natives preserved these and used them as ornaments on their wampums and in other ways, and had them even in my day, and would always call them Konapee's money. I have some of these coins here which my mother had obtained from the Indians some 40 or 50 years ago.

Having this coin on board would indicate, probably, that the vessel had been to the Philippines, or to some port on the China coast. That on her return voyage she was driven away from her course and lost, as above described.

Soto was probably, at the time of meeting Franchere, in 1811, about 80 years of age, and then allowing five years for the wanderings of his parent after the wreck and before settling down to domestic life, would place the event of the loss of the ship at about 1725. It will be recalled that commerce of a permanent character had been established between the Philippines and Acapulco and other of the western ports of Mexico a century and a half prior to the last named date.

I have been thus circumstantial about this tradition in order to show that it related to an actual occurrence and also to approximately, at least, fix the date of the event. The facts given are from sources independent of each other, and yet they support each other.

Franchere is surely a disinterested witness. He meets Soto nearly 200 miles from the mouth of the river, who tells him of the wreck of his father's ship and of his marriage to the natives. This fits in with the story of the natives at the mouth of the river relative to Konapee's voyage and sojourn at the cascades, and not given to Franchere but to other persons not in any way connected with him. And then comes the name given to the whites expressive of the manner of the advent of these persons to these shores, which fact should be taken as evidence that these people were the first of the white race seen by these natives. All these facts are of such character, I believe, as to warrant me in claiming that Konapee and his companion were the first white people who had ever seen the Columbia river.

It will be noticed that there is a discrepancy between the tradition of the Clatsops and Soto's account of the number of survivors. The Clatsops always gave the number as two. Franchere may have misunderstood the number given by Soto, or Soto may have erred as to the number given by his father; but this is not very material; the main fact that there was a wreck and that these white people were here, still remains as an actual event.

As to whether any of these people ever reached civilization again, I, at present, have no means of determining.

SOURCE
Smith, Silas B. Tales of Early Wrecks on the Oregon Coast, and How the Bees-wax Got There, *Oregon Native Son*, 1(1899):443–46.

RELATED READING
Cook, Warren. Spanish Castaways at Nehalem, *Flood Tide of Empire: Spain and the Northwest Coast, 1543–1819*. New Haven, CT: Yale University Press, 1973, pp. 35–38.
Peterson, David del Mar. Intermarriage and Agency: A Chinookan Case Study, *Ethnohistory* 42:1(Winter, 1995):1–30.
Smith, Eugene O. Solomon Smith, Pioneer: Indian-White Relations in Early Oregon, *Journal of the West* 13(1974):44–58.
Smith, Silas B. Primitive Customs and Religious Beliefs of the Indians of the Pacific Northwest Coast," *The Quarterly of the Oregon Historical Society*, 2:255–65.

"There Came Along Side Two Indion Canoes," 1788

First contacts between Oregon's Native Americans and Europeans were rarely recorded. Those incidents, however, began in the mid-1770s when Spanish mariners—Juan Perez, Bodega y Quadra, and Bruno de Hezeta—fought against currents and winds to bring their sailing ships north along the shore from the new colony of Alta California. In 1778 Captain James Cook during this third voyage to the Pacific made a landfall at Cape Foulweather on the central Oregon coast. Cook sailed north, encountered numerous native peoples in British Columbia, and accidently discovered the wealth in fur-bearing animals of the region.

Within a few years, word of Cook's crewmen bartering sea otter pelts for the wealth of China spawned the maritime fur trade. Between 1774 and 1820, an estimated 450 voyages brought explorers and traders to the Northwest Coast. Coming from at least eight different countries, these newcomers introduced firearms, metal tools, glass beads, paint, alcohol, cotton and wool clothing, mirrors and glass, and other items that proved highly consequential to the lifeways of the region's Indians. So, too, did the new diseases that ravaged the coastal populations before passing to the tribes of the interior.

Robert Haswell sailed the Northwest Coast in 1788–89. The logs of his travels document numerous encounters with native peoples, including those of the coast of Oregon. Haswell was born in 1768, probably in Massachusetts. His father was a British loyalist and naval officer. The family was interned during the Revolutionary War, removed to Nova Scotia, and finally settled in Yorkshire, England. Haswell returned to Massachusetts in 1787 and at the age of nineteen signed on as third mate on the Columbia. *Tensions with the vessel's captain led to Haswell's transfer to a consort ship, the sloop* Washington, *under Captain Robert Gray. From September 1788 to July 1789, the two vessels were on the coast engaged in trade with the Indians.*

From August 4 to 18, 1788, the Washington *edged along the headlands from near the mouth of the Klamath River to the Columbia (not discerned by Gray until 1792). Although Haswell referred in his diary to "Cape Mendocin[o]," the latitude confirmed he was, in fact, near Cape Blanco in southwestern Oregon. The diary first described an encounter at sea with a shallow, truncated Klamath type double-ended canoe. Designed for use primarily on the swift Klamath, Smith, Chetco, and Rogue rivers, this craft also proved maneuverable at sea on calm days. Of special interest was the exploration of Tillamook Bay and its tragic consequences on August 16 and 18. What had begun as a positive, mutually satisfying trade degenerated into death and destruction for the Tillamooks.*

In spite of Haswell's irregular spelling—a reflection less of his education than of the lack of an American dictionary to standardize usage—his accounts vividly document encounters with coastal tribes in the vicinity of Cape Blanco and Cascade Head, and at Tillamook Bay.

On monday the 4th [of August, 1788] we had fresh brezes and pleasant Cariing a press of sail in with the land at 5 PM the breze grew light and weather foggy we sounded in 45 f[atho]m water over a bottom of black mud wore Ship and stood to the westward dewering the first part of the night with a light breze at 2 PM tacked and stood to the Eastward with a fresh breze at 8 AM in 15 f[atho]m water distant from the shore about 2 miles and a half it died away calm we were at this time within a quarter of a mile of a ledge of rocks in shore of us we were neceseated to Anchor but it was scarce to the ground when it began to blow a stiff Breze at North veared away 1/2 a Cable and it ridd her at this time we discovered a canoe with ten natives of the Countrey paddling towards us on there nigh aproach they made very expressive seigns of friendship.

These were the first inhabitance we had seen here I must add that a regular account of People manners and customs etca. of this vast coast is a task equell to the skill of an able Historian and what I am totaly inadequate to however as there are some few remarkable occurences I mention them without rule or form.

These people were in a canoe of a most singular shape it was hued from a tree of vast bulk it was very wide and caried its bredth nearly equell fore and aft its head and stern were but little different boath ending abruptly as flat as a board they rose some inches above the side of the boat in an arch which was neatly worked over with straw of various coulers the boat tho' of the most clumsey shape in the world yet so well was it finished that it looked very pasable there paddles were very rough wrought of ash wood. They were cloathed chiefly in deerskins and they were ornemented with beads of Europan manufactor.

I am apt to think they have sometimes intercorse with the Spaniards at Monteray which is but three or four degrees to the Southward of them they smoak tobacco out of a small wooden tube about the size of Childs wistle. they had some sweet sented Herbs. the countrey from whence these people came to me appeared the most pleasant I had ever seen the men in the Boat appeared to be well limed people about the middle size there bodies were punctuated in maney forms in all parts.

Capt. Gray made them several preasants but our attenton was called another way the wind by this time b[l]ew a gale. we hove up and stood off shore upon a wind to the westward.

Tuesday 5th [of August, 1788]. The 5th was accompaneyed with no remarkable occurence we coasted the shore along but saw no place where there was shelter even for a boat this Countrey must be thickly inhabited by the maney fiers we saw in the night and Culloms of smoak we would see in the Day time but I think they can derive but little of there subsistance from the sea but to compenciate for this the land was beautyfully divercified with forists and green verdent launs which must give shelter and forage to vast numbers of wild beasts most probable most of the natives on this part of the Coast live on hunting for they most of them live in land this is not the case to the Northward for the face of the Countrey is widly different I was in Latd. 42 3' N the Variation 13 50' E.

Wednesday 6th [of August, 1788]. On the 6 favourable brezes and pleasant in the morning about 8 Oclock we were abrest a cove where tolerable good shelter from a Northwardly wind may be had it is formed by a small bay to the Northward and a little Island to the Southward here wood and water may be procured but what sort of anchorage remains unknown the people were very ancious to come onboard they Paddled after us an amazing distance with great alacrity waving somthing I supose skins but we had at this time a good wind and pleas[an]t weather and it was judged best to seek a harbour while they continued we ran along shore with a Cloud of sail passing within a Quarter of a Mile of a Bould sanday shore in 5 and 6 f[atho]m water above the beach appeared a delightfull Countrey thickly inhabited and Cloathed with woods and verdure with maney Charming streems of water gushing from the vallies most of the inhabitance as we passed there scatered houses fled into the woods while others ran along shore with great swiftness keeping abrest of us maney miles. Cape Mendocin bore North distant about 5 Leagues.

Thursday 7th [of August, 1788]. we now ran for a place that looked like an inlett this place was in a large deep bay to the southward and Eastward of Cape Mendocin having ran in within about a Mile of a small Island we hove the Jolley Boat out and sent her to sound the Channel between the Island and Main and explore the Harbour if aney she soon made a signal that there was plenty of water within the Island we then followed her but soon discovered what we supposed to be an inlett to be no other than two hills seperated by a deep valey. we wore ship within 1/2 a Mile of the Land and found no bottom with a long scope of Line we now took the boat in and stood out on the other side the Island which could be compared to nothing elce but a hive with the beeas sworming the birds were so numerous. they were of maney speces but most of them Pelicons at 4 PM foggy at 6 Cape Mindocin bore NNE distant about 6 or 7 Leagues a long and very daingerous Reef of Rocks [Cape Blanco Reef] ran out 6 Leagues westward of this promontory we stood of a proper distance to give this Ledge a proper berth, and then stood to the North[war]d for the Land obs[erve]d in Latitude 43 20' No.

There is a very deep bay to the Northward of the Cape in which probably there may be some deep Sound and rivers but in the night we were imperceptabley drifted by a current from the Eastward far from the Shore this prevented us from exploreing this part of the Coast a knoledge of this Situation might be asential for if there should bee a harbour here no doubt there would be great numbers of sea otter skins its situation is by no meens too far to the Southward for these animels to exist in abundance of the Spanish misionares send anualy several thousand skins that are collected on the Coast of California to China by the way of Manilla.

About ten or eleven leagues to the Northward of the Cape we hoisted our boat out to more minutely examin the Coast while we sailed in the Sloop within a mile of the shore at 1/2 past 12 the 9th we passed a bared inlett where tho' there appeared not to be suffisent water for our vessell yett I am of opinion it is the enterence of a very large river where great commershal advantages might be reeped in a small vessell about 18 or 20 Tuns this harbour is in Latd. 44 20' No. and Longd. 122 0' W from Greenwich. The long boat in the evening returned alongside they had seen nothing remarkable except vast numbers of the natives they appeared to be a very hostile and warlike people they ran along shore waving white skins these are the skins of moose Deer three or four thicknesses compleatly taned and not penetrable by arrows these are there war armour. they would sometimes make fast there bows and quivers of arrows to there spears of incredable length and shake them at us with an air of defyence every jesture they accompaneyed with hideous shouting the Coast trented by the Compass N *b* W at 8 PM we hove too with our head to the northward at 2 wore ship and stood in shore at 4 AM Made sail along shore at 11 AM there came alongside two Indions in a small Canoe very differently formed from those we had seen to the Southward it was sharp at the head and stern and Extreemly well built to paddle fast they came very cautiously towards us nor would they come within pistol shot untill one of them a very fine look[in]g fellow had delivered a long oration accompaneying it with actions and Jestures that would have graced a Europan oritor the subject of his discorse was designed to inform us they had plenty of Fish and fresh water onshore at there habitations which they seemed to wish us to go and partake of we made them understand that skins was the articles we most wanted these as well as we could understand them they would bring the ensuing day we could proceve there Language was entierly different from those we had first fell in with to the southward. after viewing the vessell attentively some time they departed well pleased with some trifling preasants they had recieved the place these people came of from is in Latd. 45 0' No.

Sunday 10th [of August, 1788]. The first part of the tenth was pleasant but the wind hauling to the Northward it came in foggey and disagreable weather insued the middle part calm at 4 PM wore ship and stood in with the land at 9 we hove the boat out and she went in surch of a landing place duering her absence there came along side two Indion Canoes the one containing two and the other 6 people among them were our yesterdays friends they brought with them several sea otter skins and one of the best peces I ever saw. they were a smart sett of active fellows but like all others without one exception on this Coast are addicted to thefts and we allways found those who were the most mistrustfull were the most adicted to commit the offence.

They were armed with bows and arrows they had allso spears but would part with none of them they had both Iron and stone knives which they allways kept in there hands uplifted in readiness to strike we admited one of them onboard but he would not come without this weapen two or three of our visitors were much pitted with the small pox.

They were dexterous in the manegement of there Canoes they paddled with great velosity and tho' there canoes were long would turn them in there length there paddles were neatly made of Ash they run down of an equel bredth to the ent the Corners are pointed and End arched up like a swallows tail they departed promusing to return again soon. I observed in Latitude 45 02' No.

Monday 11th [of August, 1788]. The 11th was marked by no singular event we had light airs to the Northward and westward and frequently calm we had the small boat out and hoged the Ship the Coast we were abrest of looked pleasant I obs[erve]d in Latitude 44 58' No. having made 5 miles Southing.

Tuesday 12th [of August, 1788]. The 12th being pleasant weather at 3 PM we came to Anchor within half a mile of the shore hoisted the long boat and went to a small inlett where there was not suffishant water for the Sloop to enter we took of two loads of wood and then hove up and Came to sail with the wind favourable we saw while the boat was onshore one of the Natives who were of on Sunday last, the place had been inhabited but was deserted no doubt as late as when they saw the boat coming onshore. Light br[e]zes to the Southward and drizling rain all the latter part.

Wednesday the 13th [of August, 1788] there came alongside twelve Natives in a Canoe they had nothing to trafic but seemed enticed by curiosity off to view the vessell there Chief was the only person that was allowed to come onboard he observed every thing with great attention and was presented with a few preasants and departed well pleased with there entertainment at Noon I observed in Latitude 45 56' N about this time the wind hauled from the Northward with so rappid a current from the same quarter that we could not make aney way to the Northward on the contorary we could not hold our own.

Thursday 14th [of August, 1788]. Between the hours of 5 and 6 Last evening we passed a tolerable harbour but having a bar Where it broke pretty nigh all athort it looked as tho' we could with ease git into it this harbour was now 10 Leagues to leeward but in the afternoon it was determined to bear away and at 1 PM we lay her head to the Southward at 6 we hove too off and on and at 6 came too with the small bower in 7 f[atho]m water distant from the shore about 2 miles over a bottom of sand we now hoisted the boat out man'd and armed her and sent her to explore the Harbour and sound its enterence taking proper bearings and marks for sailing into it at 10 the boat returned with an account that the Harbour was tolerably Commodious and suffishent water for us in the proper Channel we immediately hove up with a commanding breze and went in without cuming into less than two fathom and a Quarter water we anchored half a mile distant from the shore in 3 f[atho]m in the Anchoring place I observed my Latd. to be 45 27' N and Longd. 122 19' W. the Variation by Asmith was 14 26' Et in the afternoon it was pleasant with a moderate breze to the Northward. t'was with great persuasion late in the Afternoon that one of there small Canoes came alongside and received maney trivial preasants this soon entised maney others off and Each Canoe brought with them large quantities of berries and Crabs ready boiled

Friday 15th [of August, 1788]. these they liberaly handed onboard as preasants seemingly without an Idea of payment, and these were the most acceptable things they could have brought to most of our seamen who were in a very advanced state of the scurvey and was a means of a restoration of health to 3 or four of our Company who would have found one months longer duration at sea fatal to them so advanced were they in this malignant distemper.

Trafic on a very friendly footing being thus established before Evening we had purchased a number of Good Sea otter skins for knives axes adzes etca. but had we had Copper a pece two or three inches square would have been far more valuable to them, they would hand there skins onboard without scruple and take with satisfaction whatever was given in return; this we very seldom found the case in any other part of the coast. the nesecery operations of wooding and watering were the pri[n]saple objects of our attention the watering place was situated at a very considerable distance from the Sloop and totaly out of the protection of her guns for this reason one turn of water was Judged suffishent to serve till some more safe place might be discovered at some other part of the Coast. we took off several boat load of wood which was handey to the vessell and of a very good quality the natives while we were at work onshore behaved with great propriety frequently bringing us frute but they allways kept themselves armed and never ventured nigh us but with there knives in there hands uplifted reddy to strike, this we imputed to there being such total straingers to Europeans.

Saturday 16 [of August, 1788]. On the 16 we had pleasant weather with a moderate breze to the eastward at this time an amazing number of the natives were alongside with boiled and roasted crabbs for sale which our people purchaced for buttons etca. they had allso dryed salmon and buries in abundance.

At noon we weighed and came to sail with a very moderate breze which soon died away to a purfect calm and the flud tide still setting strong swept us on a reef of rocks. the water was smooth as glass and the tide still flowing the vessell could receive no meterial Damage we run out our kedge with a small worp and hauled off the sea breze cuming in prevented our geeting out we veared ascope and moared with our two bowers.

About this time the old Chief who came onboard of us on the 13 about 6 Leagues to the Northward he had a great number of the natives with him all armed and they had no skins with them tho' they were well convinced it was them alone we wanted and he had promused to supply us with some however tho' he had not fullfilled his engagement he mett with a very polight reseption.

Having nothing else to do but wate for the next days tide to depart, Earley in the Afternoon I accompaneyed Mr. Coolidge onshore in the long Boat to amuse ourselves in taking a walk while our boat was loaded with grass and shrubbs for our stock we took all the people in the Boat who were affected by the Scurvey our number in all amounted to seven the disposition of the people seemed so friendly we went worse armed than ordinary we had two Muskets and three or four Cutlaces we boath took our swoards and each of us a pistol on our first landing we visated there Houses and such victles as they eate themselvs they offered us but they are so intolerable filthey there was nothing we could stumac except the frute.

They then amused us shewing there dexterity with there arrows and spears they then began a war dance it was long and hedious accompaneyed with frightfull howlings indeed there was somthing more horrid in there song and the jestures which accompanied it than I am capable of Discribing it Chilled the bludd in my vains. The dance over we left the natives to themselves and walked along the beach to the boat where the people were cutting grass and only one or two of the Natives with them we went past the boat a little way but within call to a small sand flatt in hopes to find some clams while we were digging for these shell fish a young Black man Marcus Lopius a native of the Cape de Verd Islands and who had shiped Captain Grays servant at St. Jago's being employed carieng grass down to the boat, had carelessly stuck his Cutlas in the sand one of the natives seeing this took a favourable oppertunity to snatch it at first unobserved and run off with it one of the people observing him before he was quite out of sight called vehemonantly thretening to shoot him in hopes he would abandon the stoln goods and make his escape but I had given posative orders to our people not to fier but in cases of the most absolute emmergence when for self defence it might be nesecery.

'Twas the hollowing of our people that first roused our attention and we immediately flew to know the cause, we were informed of the sircumstance adding that the Black boy had followed him in spite of every thing they could say to the contorary.

I was struck by the daingerous situation the ladd was in and feared its concequences doubting of there being a posability of saving him from the impending danger, but resolving no project should go untried without hesitation ordering the boat to keep abrest of us we ran toward the village we mett several Chiefs persons whose friendship we had taken every oppertunity to obtain by kind youseage and liberal preasants Indeed it seemed before this period we had fully effected it to these people Mr. Coolidge offered several articles to them of great value to bring back the man unhurt, this they refused intimating there wish for us to seek him ourselvs. I now remarked to Mr. Coolidge that all the natives we saw were unusualy well armed having with them there bows arrows and spears however we proceeded still further and on turning a clump of trees that obstructed our prospect the first thing which presented itself to our view was a very large groop of the natives among the midst of which was the poor black with the thief by the colour loudly calling for assistance saying he had cought the thief, when we were observed by the main boddy of the Natives to haistily aproach them they instantly drenched there knives and spears with savage feury in the boddy of the unfortunate youth. He quited his hold and stumbled but rose again and stagered towards us but having a flight of arrows thrown into his back and he fell within fifteen yards of me and instantly expiered while they mangled his lifeless cor[p]se.

We were now by our passing a number whom as I remarked before we supposed to be our friends situated between two formidable parties. Those we had passed being reinforsed by a great number from the woods they gave us the first salutation by a shower of arrows Our only method was to get to the boat as fast as posable for this purpos we turned leaving the dead body; for it would have been the highth of imprudence as our Number was so small to have attempted its rescue we made the Best of our way for the Boat assaulted on all sides by showers of arrows and spears—and at length it became absolutely nesecery to shoot there most dairing ringleader which I did with my pistol Mr. Coolidge and one man who was with us followed my example and Mr. Coolidge ordered those who were in the boat to fier and cover us as we waided off for the boat could not come within a considerable dist[ance] of the shore. But undaunted by the fate of there Companions they followed us up to the middle in water and slightly wounded both Mr. Coolidge and myself in the hand and totaley disabled the person who was with us onshore who fainting with loss of blud lay lifeless several hours and continued to bleed a torant till the barb of the arrow was extracted, we jumped into the Boat and pushed of and were soon out of arrow shot when we found this they launched there Canoes intending to cutt us off indeed they were well situated for it but some were timid some were bold and not half paddled but keeping a constant fier from the boat they came bairley within arrow shot before we were nigh the sloop, and they returned towards the shore as soon as we got onboard we discharged two or three swivel shot at them and in a few Moments not one Canoe was to be seen all having fledd, duering the whole of the night it was dismal to hear the hoops and houlings of the natives they had fiers on the beach near the spot where the ladd was killed and we could see great number of them passing too and froo before the blaze.

I must confess I should not have lett them enjoy there festervile so peasabley had I been Cap. Gray but his humanity was commendable.

Murderers Harbour for so it was named is I suppose the enterence of the river of the West it is by no meens a safe place for aney but a very small vessell to Enter the shoale at its enterence being so aucwardly situated the passage so narrow and the tide so rapid that it is scarce posable to avoid the dangers. It is provable whenever a vessel goes there they may procure twenty or thirty good sea otter skins. We know but little of the manours and customs of these people our stay among them was so short. the men ware no Cloathing but the skins of animels well dressed the women wore nothing but a petticoat of straw about as long as a highlanders kilt, there hutts were very small made of boards and a neat matt on the flore they appeared to be very indolent and were intolerably filthey. there Canoes were very well shaped for paddling and every yousefull purpus there language we attained no knoledge of and I am of opinion it was very Hard to lern.

I am posative it was a planed affair which first gave rise to Our quarrel seeing how fue we were they had hopes of overpowering us and making themselves masters of our Cloths and arms and had we been taken it would have been no difficult jobb to have made a prize of the Sloop for Captain Gray had but three people left onboard. It was folly for us to go onshore so ill armed but it prooved a suffishant warning to us to allways be well armed ever afterwards.

Indeed I think it prudent no boat should land among the midst of such numerous tribes without another well armed boat to protect her landing.

Sunday the 17th [of August, 1788] having a moderate breze to the Eastward at 4 AM we hove up and Came to sail making a second attempt to gett to sea haveing passed the sand point of the Harbour and Middle ground, the wind died and the tide setting with great rapidity over the outer shoal we were obliged to lett go our anchor in two fat[ho]m water, the tide ebbed and the surf rose to so vast a size that we struck a great maney times so violently hard we could scarce stand the Deack the surf breaking over our taffle stove in our cabbin windows and allmost filled it with water as soon as the tide began to slack we hoisted the longboat out and run a small anchor to the eastward which when hove taut on keept us clear of the ground till still water when we hove up and worped into deep water and came too with the small bower for the flud tide began to run so strong we could not gett out till the ebb returned while we lay on the bar we saw a large war canoe go out of the Harbour keeping at as great a distance from us as posable.

We received no damage from this accident except having the pintles and gudgins of our rudder bent so they would not admit it to come down into its proper berth.

Monday the 18th [of August, 1788] was calm and foggey. the natives of the Harbour all came down to the beach that was situated nearest our vessell with all there Canoes we continualy heard them shouting and it was answered by maney voises on the outside of the barr and at 1/2 past twelve we saw three large war canoes each containing upwards of thirty armed men it was so foggey that we did not see them untill they were within half a musquet shot we becken'd to them to keep there distance but they continued to paddle towards us and we could plainly see that the better part of them satt with there bows reddy bent and there spears in there hands there behaviour being very suspisious three swivels were discharged at them and they paddled off with great speed we then hove up and worped out without aney further difficulty.

Haswell's log is important to document the use of sea-going canoes along the coast of Oregon and the eagerness with which the region's natives sought encounters with newcomers. Robert Haswell returned to the Northwest Coast as first officer under Robert Gray on the Columbia Rediviva *in 1792. On May 12, Gray entered a great river and named it the Columbia in honor of his ship, the* Columbia Rediviva. *Haswell next sailed aboard the Adventure bartering with the Haida in the Queen Charlotte Islands and along the west coast of Vancouver Island. After his marriage in 1799, Haswell entered the U.S. Navy, but in 1801 returned to the fur trade, and in August of that year left Boston as captain of the* Louisa *for a trip to the Northwest Coast and China. Nothing was ever heard again of anyone aboard the ship.*

SOURCE

Howay, Frederic W., ed. *Voyages of the "Columbia" to the Northwest Coast 1787–1790 and 1790–1793.* Boston, MA: The Massachusetts Historical Society, 1941, pp. 29–41.

RELATED READING

Cook, Warren L. *Flood Tide of Empire: Spain and the Pacific Northwest, 1543–1819.* New Haven, CT: Yale University Press, 1973.

Nokes, J. Richard. *Columbia's River: The Voyages of Robert Gray, 1787–1793.* Tacoma, WA: Washington State Historical Society, 1991.

"Shi-lahsri, Shi-lahsri!" ["My Friends, My Friends!"]: Encounters at Sea, 1792

One of the remarkable documents of first encounters between Native Oregonians and Europeans is a single word recorded in the leather-bound manuscript diary of Dr. Archibald Menzies in the library of the British Museum. This log of travels of the Vancouver expedition to the North Pacific chronicled a meeting at sea on April 25, 1792, off the headlands near Port Orford. Two canoes of Indians paddled out from the shore and, as Menzies noted: "On their coming alongside & after they were on board they kept constantly repeating the word Slaghshee."

Athabaskan language scholar Victor Golla of Humboldt State University identifies the word as from the Tututni language of southwestern coastal Oregon. In Tututni the term lahsri *means "friend" and* shi *or* sh *is the emphatic pronoun meaning "my" or "mine." Thus, at the moment of contact at the end of the eighteenth century, the natives approached the Europeans with kindly words as well as eagerness. "My friends, my friends," they uttered over and over. This single word in the Menzies diary is the earliest recorded coastal Athabaskan term and may be one of the oldest from the large language family as spoken in what is now the United States.*

Both American maritime fur traders and British explorers converged in April 1792 on the coast of Oregon. The inducements for traders were the lustrous fur pelts that they bartered from the region's natives. The quest for Captain George Vancouver was the fabled Northwest Passage and the award of £20,000 offered by the British parliament to the mariner who found a route through North America by water. During the voyages that spring came encounters with the Kalawatset or Lower Umpqua Indians near the mouth of the Umpqua River and with the Quoto-mah, an Athabaskan-speaking people of the Tututni dialect with villages in the vicinity of Cape Blanco and the Port Orford headlands.

The first encounter with the natives was penned by John Boit, Jr., born in Boston in 1774. Boit shipped out at age sixteen on the second voyage of the Columbia Rediviva *under Captain Robert Gray. Probably educated at the Boston Latin School, Boit kept a log of the trading expedition to Oregon. He returned to the coast at age nineteen as master of the* Union. *Following his trading along the North Pacific, Boit sailed to China and then became the first American to circumnavigate the world. He returned on July 8, 1796, to Boston where he wrote: "Thank God, I found all my relations in health & the tender embraces of an affectionate & honored father made up for all the troubles & anzietys incident to such long voyages."*

The following passage is from Boit's log of the Columbia Rediviva *in 1792. The vessel was sailing south from the Straits of Juan de Fuca. The officers began looking for a good harbor in the vicinity of Cape Foulweather. On April 10 Indians came out from a "small inlett in the land," most likely the estuary of the Umpqua River. Boit's fears about cannibalism and the natives' possession of buffalo meat were unfounded. His remarks confirm how tentative he was about this first encounter. In the course of their sailing south to Cape Mendocino, the crew of the* Columbia *traded with several Indians who came out to meet the ship.*

[April] 7. N. Latt. 44 56' W. Long. 122 52'. Very blowing weather and quite cold. beating off the Coast, waiting for to find a good harbour. the weather grows pleasent.

[April] 9. N. Latt. 44 24' W. Long. 122 17'. Pleasent weather, wind NW. Runing along shoar to the South and Eastd. about 2 miles off the land trended N b E and N b W and look'd very pleasent. the Shore made in sandy beaches, and the land rose gradually back into the high hills, and the beautifull feilds of grass, interpersed among the wood lands, made itt delightfull.

[April] 10. N. Latt. 43 45' W. Long. 122 11'. Abrest a small inlett in the land, which had some the appearance of an harbour. Hove too for some canoes that where coming off these Natives talk'd a different language from any we have before heard. their Canoes had square Stems and the blades of the paddles oval. We purchas'd of them many fine Otter Skins for Copper and Iron. they had some raw *Buffaloe* in the Canoes, which they offer'd us for sale, and gredily devour'd some of it, in that state as a recommendation. I'm fearfull these fellows are Caniballs. Mr. *Smith*, 2d Officer, was sent in the Cutter to look for an harbour but was unsuccessful. bore off and made sail. Cape Gregory (so call'd by Capt. Cook) bore SE. Variation. Ampd. 15 57' East.

[April] 11. N. Latt. 42 50' W. Long. 122 3' Ampd. 16 42' E. Some Canoes came along side full of Indians and brought a few Otter and Beaver Skins. Cape Mendocin bore ESE, 2 leagues. Haul'd again to the Northward.

[April] 17. N. Latt. 44 54' W. Long. 122 23' Azi. 16 57' E. Sent the Boat, under charge of 2d officer, to examine an inlett, abrest the Ship, to see if there was safe anchorage, but was *unsuccessfull*. A large Canoe came along side full of the Natives. by their behaviour, the *Columbia* was the first ship *they* ever saw.

[April] 22. N. Latt. 46 39' W. Long. 122 50' Azi. 17 33' E. Still beating about, in pursuit of anchorage. Sent the boat in shore often, but cou'd find no safe harbour. The Natives frequently came along side and brought Otter furs and fish. their language to us was unintelligable. Experience strong currents setting to the southward. We have frequently seen many appearances of good harbours, but the Currents and squally weather hindered us from a strict examination however Capt. Gray is determin'd to persevere in the pursuit.

Later in April, 1792, the Chatham *and* Discovery *of the Vancouver expedition sailed along the coast of Curry County. Outfitted as a scientific exploration to chart the coast, discern its features, and collect useful information, the party contained a number of diarists. The following accounts, most never published, are in the holdings of the British Museum Library and the Public Record Office, London. The several different versions describe a highly positive encounter between these British mariners and the Qua-to-mah Indians in the vicinity of Port Orford and Cape Blanco.*

ROBERT PIGOT, April 25, 1792

Finding a current, setting us on the shore very fast, we came too, with the small Bower [anchor] in 36 fathm. water. Two canoes came off with 4 or 5 people in each. They willingly sold us every thing they had, which Consisted of a few skins & Bows & Arrows, for which they demanded Iron & Brass.

DR. ARCHIBALD MENZIES, April 25, 1792

Early on the 24th we again stood in for the land & fetching near to the place where we quitted it on the preceeding evening reassumed our course to the Northward examining & surveying the Coast. In the forenoon we passed on the outside of another group of naked rocks & breakers 4 or 5 miles from the shore in the Latitude of 42° 20' North & had Soundings in 45 fathoms about 2 miles from them. Our Latitude at noon was 42° 36' North & our Longitude 235° 44' East, the Northern extreme of the Land stretched out into a low hammoc point bore N 22 W 5 or 6 leagues which will be nearly the situation of Cape Blanco. In the afternoon we had it chiefly calm & finding the tide or a strong current setting us very fast on shore we dropped anchor in 36 fathoms till a breeze should spring up to favor our progress to the Northward which happened towards midnight when we both weighed & made Sail out from the Land.

When we anchored two Canoes came off from the Shore, one went along side of the Chatham & the other paddled towards us without shewing any kind of dread or apprehension. When she came along side we invited her Crew on board & the whole of them consisting of seven Men accepted very readily of the invitation, having first made their Canoe fast along side, which shewed a degree of confidence that indicated their mild & peaceable dispositions. Most of them appeared on our Decks naked having left their garments which were made from squirrel racoon & deer skins in their Canoe; they wore Caps on their heads made from the breast & belly parts of shag skins which fitted them very close & comfortable. Each of them had his ears & the septum of his nose perforated, in the latter some of them wore an ornament made of the tooth shell but which they readily parted with on thrusting a small nail in the place of it. Their bows & arrows were of an inferior sort, the latter were armed with a kind of flinty stone fastened in a slit in the end of the Arrow by means of hardend Rosin. We saw no Sea Otter Skins among them, nor did they bring or offer any thing to barter, but received with avidity whatever was offerd them. Their Canoe was by no means calculated to go far to sea or enduring much bad weather, it had some distant resemblance to a Butchers Tray being truncated at both ends short broad & shallow. It was about 10 feet long 4 feet & 1/2 broad in the middle but a little narrower towards the ends, & it was about 2 feet deep, formd of one piece of Pine Tree dug out & tolerably well finished, so that the wood on this part of the Coast must be pretty large. The blades of the paddles were narrow & cut square off at the end, the shafts ended with a small knob. These Natives remaind with us about an hour, & after leaving us paid a short visit to the Chatham, after which they went towards the shore & we saw no more of them. They were of a middling size with mild pleasing features & no-wise sullen or distrustfull in their behaviour, they were of a Copper colour but cleanly, as we observed no vestige of greasy paint or ochre about their faces or among their hair, some had their bodies marked with slight linear scars cross-ing each other in various directions & some were Tatooed in different parts.

On their coming alongside & after they were on board they kept constantly repeating the word *Slaghshee* the meaning of which we did not comprehend, some thought it was their word for friendship, others imagined they meant Iron a metal they were very desirous of posessing, for during the time they were on board their attention was so much engaged on other objects that all my endeavours proved fruitless in collecting any part of their language which appeared to us to be a very clattering jargon.

HARRY HUMPHREYS, April 25, 1792

finding there was a strong current setting us in shore we came too with the B[est] B[ower] in 39 f^m soft black muddy bott^m Soon after a canoe came on board with several of the Indian natives

LT. HEDDINGTON, April 25, 1792

Light air and clear weather. Remarks: At 2 ans^d sig^l to prepare to anchor 1/2 part 2 brought up with the Best Bower Anchor in 37 Inst. The Extn of the land from N 22 W to S 24 Et found Current setting ENE 1/2 mile f^m It. Some Indians cam off in large canoes like Butchers Trays they spoke a very unintelligible Guterel Language, were so then short in their persons & ill made; with tolerable good features. they had nothing to Barter but Bows & Arrows.

The record of subsequent encounters between Oregon coastal natives and marine traders remained silent until July 14, 1817, when Peter Corney, sailing along the coast of Curry County, wrote:

On the 14th it cleared up, and we saw Cape Orford, bearing S.E. seven leagues; the nearest land two miles, latitude 43° North; observed many smokes on shore. About noon, several canoes came off within hail of the ship; we waved to them to come closer, which they did, displaying green boughs and bunches of white feathers; they stopped paddling, and one man, whom we took to be a chief, stood up, and made a long speech, which we did not understand. We then waved a white flag, and they immediately pulled for the ship, singing all the way. When they came alongside we gave them a rope, and made signs for them to come on board, which nothing could induce them to do; they seemed quite terrified, and after handing some land-furs on board, for which we gave them beads and knives, they seemed well pleased, and made signs that if we came nearer the shore, they would bring us plenty. They also brought some berries, fish, and handsome baskets for sale. These men were tall and well formed, their garments made of dressed deerskins, with a small round hat, in the shape of a basin, that fitted close round the head; none of the women made their appearance. Their canoes do not seem to be so well constructed as the canoes in the Columbia, which cannot be occasioned by want of material, as the country appears to be well wooded. We observed a bay which looked well sheltered from the N.W. winds. About four o'clock the natives left the ship singing, and, when they got a certain distance, made another long speech.

We now stood along shore toward Cape Orford, sounding occasionally in from 30 to 70 fathoms; sandy bottom from four to six miles from shore; the wind increasing from N. W. stood off from the land under easy sail for the night. Next morning we ran in, and lay-to off an Indian village, to the southward of Cape Orford; saw many natives on the shore, but it blew too hard for them to launch their canoes; we intended to have anchored here, there being, apparently, a snug, well-sheltered bay, from all but the S.W., but it was too rough to send the boat from the ship to sound it; we therefore filled and ran along shore, at the distance of three miles. The land had a very fine appearance, the hills well wooded, and the plains covered with Indian huts. Towards night, the gale increased so much, that we were obliged to haul off under a close reefed main top-sail and fore-sail, and, before morning, had to lay-to under bare poles.

SOURCES

Baker, Joseph. A Log of His Majesty's Ship Discovery. Ad. 55, #32, Public Record Office, London, England, p. 142.

Corney, Peter. *Voyages in the Northern Pacific: Narrative of Several Trading Voyages from 1813 to 1818, Between the Northwest Coast of America, the Hawaiian Islands and China, With a Description of the Russian Establishments On the Northwest Coast.* Honolulu, HI: Thos. G. Thrum, 1890.

Heddington, Lt. Log of *HMS Chatham*, 1791 to 1793. MS Ad. 55, #15, Public Record Office, London, England, p. 82.

Howay, Frederic W., ed. *Voyages of the "Columbia" to the Northwest Coast, 1787–1790 and 1790–1793.* Boston, MA.: The Massachusetts Historical Society, 1941; Portland, OR: Oregon Historical Society Press, pp. 391–92.

Humphreys, Harry. Masters Log *HMS Discovery*, 1790–1794. MS Ad. 55, #26, Public Record Office, London, England.

Menzies, Archibald. A. Menzies Journal of Vancouver's Voyage, 1790–1794. British Museum Additional MS 32,641, Manuscript Division, British Museum, London, England, pp. 108–10.

Pigot, Robert. A Log of *HMS Discovery*, 1791–1795. MS Ad. 55 #30, Public Record Office, London, England, p. 82.

Puget, Peter. Log of *Discovery*, 1791–92. MS Ad. 55, #27, Public Record Office, London, England, p. 88.

RELATED READING

Anderson, Bern. *Surveyor of the Sea: The Life and Voyages of Captain George Vancouver.* Seattle, WA: University of Washington Press, 1960.

Cook, Warren L. *Flood Tide of Empire: Spain and the Pacific Northwest, 1543–1819*. New Haven, CT, and London: Yale University Press, 1973.

Gough, Barry M. *Distant Dominion: Britain and the Northwest Coast of North America, 1579–1809*. Vancouver and London; University of British Coloumbia Press, 1980.

Hayes, Edmund, ed. *Log of the 'Union': John Boit's Remarkable Voyage to the Northwest Coast and Around the World, 1794–1796*. Portland, OR: Oregon Historical Society and Massachusetts Historical Society, 1981.

Salmon in the Columbia River

If cedar was the wonder wood of Northwest Coast Indian technology, salmon was the staff of life. Bountiful runs surged into the region's streams, providing a certainty of food and leisure time that nourished the development of arts, ceremony, and oral literature. The silvery hordes of fish entering the Columbia traveled hundreds of miles into the interior to provide resources for the peoples of the Columbia Plateau and to shape the great trade depot that revolved around the fisheries at Five Mile Rapids and Celilo Falls.

The Clatsop and Chinook who resided at the mouth of the Columbia had first chance to intercept the fish runs. They prospered and became arbiters in the trade, which passed in and out of the river and along the nearby coasts of Oregon and Washington. Buried in the volumes of Proceedings of United States National Museum *are the Chinookan words for the salmon that sustained at least ten millennia of Indian life in this region. Silas B. Smith (1840–1902), son of Celiast "Helen" Smith and grandson of Cobaway, Clatsop chief in 1805–06, responded to questions posed by Charles J. Smith of Brookfield, Washington.*

The Chinnook names for the different varieties, following the order given by you, are as follows:

1st.   Chinook Salmon [*Oncorhynchus chouicha*], "*E-quinna*" (accent second syllable and give the "a" the broad sound).

2d.   Blue-back [*Oncorhynchus nerka*], "*Oo-chooya-ha*" (accent first syllable and give the broad sound to "a").

3d.   Silver-side [*Oncorhynchus kisutch*], "*O-o-wun*" (accent first syllable). Your next is "Dog Salmon (red)." My mother and all the other Indians I have spoken to on the matter, and some of the whites, maintain that the red-skinned salmon with hooked nose or beak is nothing more or less than the male silver-side, having turned red after inhabiting fresh water, and his nose assuming that shape upon its becoming poor.

They say that there is another species of Salmon that comes in the fall, having transverse dark spots, large teeth, and nose largely curved, but it does not turn red or but little at most. I will give the name and consider it in place of the "Dog Salmon."

4th. Spotted Fall Salmon [*Oncorhynchus keta*], "*O-le-arah*" (accent on first syllable).

5th. Steel-head [*Salmo gairdneri*], "*Quan-nesho*" (accent last syllable).

I have been unable to give the right sound in English to the last syllable of the last name. The above is as near as I can make it.

There is another salmon which you did not mention. It comes in the last of the summer run; it is as large if not larger than the spring salmon, but of a darker color and not so fat.

It will make number—

6th. [*Oncorhynchus chouicha*], "*Ek-ul-ba*" (accent first syllable).

SOURCE

Smith, Silas B. On the Chinnook Names of the Salmon in the Columbia River, *Proceedings of the National Museum, 1882. Smithsonian Miscellaneous Collections,* 4(1881):391–92.

RELATED READING

Gibbs, George. *Alphabetical Vocabulary of the Chinook Language.* New York, NY: Cramoisy Press, 1863.

Plumb, Har. A Happy Summer on Peacock Spit, *The Sou'wester: Quarterly of Pacific County Historical Society,* 13 (Summer–Autumn 1978):26–59.

Ruby, Robert H., and John A. Brown. *The Chinook Indians: Traders of the Lower Columbia River.* Norman, OK: University of Oklahoma Press, 1976.

Swan, James G. *The Northwest Coast; Or, Three Years Residence in Washington Territory.* New York, NY: Harper & Brothers, 1857.

The Cascades Chinookans, 1805

In the fall of 1805 the Lewis and Clark Expedition descended the Clearwater, Snake, and Columbia rivers by dugouts. Their crude pirogues, as the men dubbed their vessels, enabled the party to travel up to thirty miles per day in an eager rush toward the Pacific and the construction of their winter camp, Fort Clatsop, at the mouth of the Columbia River. The explorers found the banks of the rivers lined with Indian villages—mat lodges east of the Cascades and plank houses to the west. In spite of rapids and rocky islands, their journey proceeded swiftly except for the portages at Celio Falls and at the Cascades in the western end of the Gorge.

The following passage, written by William Clark, describes the transit of the wild rapids, later known as the Cascades, a site inundated in the 1930s by the backwaters of Bonneville Dam. The Indians residing in the area were speakers of Watlala, an Upper Chinookan dialect. The Upper Chinookan language reached from Gray's Bay on the lower Columbia estuary east to Five Mile Rapids and Celilo Falls. The Lewis and Clark party identified the E-nee-shur, E-chee-lute, Clah-cle-lah, and the Wah-clel-lah villages in the vicinity of the Cascades rapids. Clark described both the native burial vaults and plank houses. The natives' wood carving and use of sculptural images confirmed the imprint of the Northwest Coast culture on these people. The Watlala shared a lifeway that extended from the Tlingit in southeast Alaska to the Yurok at the mouth of the Klamath River in northwestern California.

October 31ˢᵗ Thursday 1805

A Cloudy rainey disagreeable morning I proceeded down the river to view with more attention we had to pass on the river below, the two men with me Jo. Fields & Peter Crusat proceeded down to examine the rapids the Great Shute which commenced at the Island on which we encamped Continud with great rapidity and force thro a narrow chanel much compressd. and interspersed with large rocks for 1/2 a mile, at a mile lower is a verry Considerable rapid at which place the waves are remarkably high, and proceeded on in an old Indian parth 2 1/2 miles by land thro a thick wood & hill Side, to the river where the Indians make a portage, from this place I dispatched Peter Crusat (our principal waterman) back to follow the river and examine the practibility of the Canoes passing, as the rapids appeared to continue down below as far as I could See, I with Jo. Fields proceeded on, at 1/2 a mile below the end of the portage passed a house where there had been an old town for ages past as this house was old Decayed and a plac of flees I did not enter it, about 1/2 a mile below this house in a verry thick part of the woods is 8 valuts which appeared Closely Covered and highly deckerated with orniments. Those vaults are all nearly the Same Sise and form 8 feet Square, 5 feet high, Sloped a little So as to convey off the rain made of Pine or Cedar boards Closely Connected & Scurely Covered with wide boards, with a Dore left in The East Side which is partially Stoped with wide boards curiously engraved. In Several of those vaults the dead bodies wre raped up verry Securely in Skins tied around with cords of grass & bark, laid on a mat, all east & west and Some of those vaults had as maney as 4 bodies laying on the Side of each other. the other Vaults Containing bones only, Some contained bones for the debth of 4 feet. on the tops and on poles attached to those vaults hung Brass kittles & frying pans pearced thro their bottoms, baskets, bowls of wod, Sea Shels, Skins, bits of Cloth, Hair, bags of Trinkets & Small peices of bone &c and independant of the curious ingraveing and Paintings on the boards which formed the vaults I observed Several wooden Images, cut in the figure of men and Set up on the (South) Sides of the vaults all round. Some of those So old and worn by time, that they were nearly out of Shape, I also observed the remains of Vaults rotted entirely into the ground and covered with moss. This must bee the burrying place for maney ages for the inhabitants of those rapids, the vaults are of the most lasting timber Pine & Cedar—I cannot Say certainly that those nativs worship those wooden idols as I have every reason to believe they do not; as they are Set up in the most conspicuous parts of their houses, and treated more like orniments than objects of aderation. at 2 miles lower & 5 below our Camp I passed a village of 4 large houses abandend by the nativs, with their dores bared up, I looked into those houses and observed as much property as is usial in the houses of those people which induced me to conclude that they wre at no great distance, either hunting of Collecting roots, to add to their winter Subsistance. from a Short distance below the vaults the mountain which is but low on the Stard. Side leave the river, and a leavel Stoney open bottom Suckeeds on the Said Std. Side for a great Distance down, the mountains high and rugid on the Lard Side this open bottom is about 2 miles a Short distance below this village is a bad

Stoney rapid and appears to be the last in view I observed at this lower rapid the remains of a large and antient Village which I could plainly trace by the Sinks in which they had formed their houses, as also those in which they had buried their fish—from this rapid to the lower end of the portage the river is Crouded with rocks of various Sizes between which the water passes with great velociety createing in maney places large Waves, an Island which is Situated near the Lard. Side occupies about half the distance the lower point of which is at this rapid. immediately below this rapid the high water passes through a narrow Chanel through the Stard. Bottom forming an Island of 3 miles (wide) Long & one wide, I walked through this Island which I found to be verry rich land, and had every apperance of haveing been at Some distant period Cultivated. at this time it is Covered with grass intersperced with Strawberry vines. I observed Several places on this Island where the nativs had dug for roots and from its lower point I observed 5 Indians in a Canoe below the upper ponit of an Island near the middle of the river Covered with tall timber, which indued me to believe that a village was at no great distance below . . . .

November 1st Friday 1805

Set all hands packing the loading over th portage which is below the Grand Shutes and is 940 yards of bad way over rocks & on Slipery hill Sides The Indians who came down in 2 Canoes last night packed their fish over a portage of 2–1/2 miles to avoid a 2d *Shute*. . . . .

We got our Canoes and baggage below the Great Shute 3 of the canoes being Leakey from injures recved in hauling them over the rocks, obliged us to delay to have them repaired a bad rapid just below us three Indian canoes landed with pounded fish for the &c., trade down the river arrived at the upper end of the portage this evening. I Can't lern whether those Indians trade with white people or Inds. below for the Beeds & copper, which they are So fond of—They are nearly necked, prefruing beeds to anything—Those Beeds they trafick with Indians Still higher up this river for Skins robes &c. &c. The Indians on those waters do not appear to be Sickly, Sore eyes are Common and maney have lost their eyes, Some one and, maney both, they have bad teeth, and the greater perpotion of them have worn their teeth down, maney into the gums, They are rather Small high Cheeks, women Small and homely, maney of them had Sweled legs, large about the knees,—owing to the position in which they Set on their hams, They are nearly necked only a piece of leather tied about their breech and a Small robe which generally comes to a little below their wastes and Scercely Sufficely large to cover arround them when confined—they are all fond of Clothes but more So of Beeds perticularly blue & white beeds. They are durty in the extreme both in their Coockery and in their houses.

Those at the last Village raise the beads [beds] about five feet from the earth—under which they Store their Provisions—Their houses is about 33 feet to 50 feet Square, the dore of which is about 30 Inc. high and 16 Inches wide in this form cut in a wide pine board they have maney imeges Cut in wood, generally, in the figure of a man—Those people are high with what they have to Sell, and Say the white people below Give them great Prices for what they Sell to them. Their nose are all Pierced, and the[y] wear a white Shell maney of which are 2 Inch long pushed thro the nose—all the women have flat heads pressed to almost a point at top The[y] press the female childrens heads between 2 bords when young—untill they form the Skul as they wish it which is generally verry *flat.* This amongst those people is considered as a great mark of buty—and is practised in all the tribes we have passed on this river more or less. men take more of the drugery off the women than is common with Indians—

SOURCE

Moulton, Gary E., ed. *The Journals of the Lewis & Clark Expedition. Vol. 5, July 28– November 1, 1805,* pp. 360–65. Lincoln, NE: University of Nebraska Press, 1988.

RELATED READING

Beckham, Stephen Dow. *"This Place Is Romantic and Wild": An Historical Overview of the Cascades Area, Fort Cascades, and the Cascades Townsite, Washington Territory.* Portland, OR: U.S. Army Corps of Engineers, Portland District, 1984.

Minor, Rick, Kathryn Anne Toepel, and Stephen Dow Beckham. *An Overview of Investigations at 45SA11: Archaeology in the Columbia River Gorge.* Heritage Research Associates Report No. 27 submitted to the U.S. Army Corps of Engineers, Portland District, 1984.

"They Possess Their Present Lands and Situation From Time Immemorial," 1811

The tenure of the Chinookans on the Columbia River reached from its mouth east through the Gorge to Five Mile Rapids and Celilo Falls. The great "River of the West" produced abundant food resources and opportunities for trade. The Columbia Gorge cut a sea-level cleft through the highest mountain range in the region. The tribes had a surplus of salmon, steelhead, sturgeon, smelt, and eels. They were the rich arbiters of trade and commerce in the Oregon country. Through their hands passed obsidian from quarries in central Oregon, slaves captured on raids into the northern Great Basin, dugout canoes and paddles eagerly desired by the natives on the largely treeless Columbia Plateau, marine shells, camas and wappato bulbs, and beargrass for manufacturing baskets.

Robert Stuart (1785–1848) visited the Chinookans in 1811–12. A partner with investor John Jacob Astor of New York City, Stuart had entered the fur trade in the employment of the North West Company of Canada. In 1810 he sailed on the Tonquin *around Cape Horn to help establish Astoria on the south shore of the Columbia. Stuart resided among the Clatsop and Chinook Indians for fifteen months before he set out overland for St. Louis. Stuart was an astute observer. An abridged version of his narrative was published in Paris in* Nouvelles Annales des Voyages, de la Geographie et de l'Histoire, *Volumes 10 and 12, April and October, 1821. Washington Irving acquired Stuart's "Travelling Memoranda" and drew heavily from it when writing* Astoria *(1836). A grandnephew of Irving found Stuart's manuscript in the author's papers and sold it at auction in 1930 to William Robertson Coe, who in 1948 gave the ledger to Yale University.*

The following selection is Stuart's overview of Chinookan lifeways observed during more than a year of residency in 1811–12 at the mouth of the Columbia River. The tone of Stuart's presentation is positive. He genuinely admired the skills of the men in manufacturing canoes, their prowess in hunting, and their attention to personal appearance. Stuart sketched the picture of a rich life, well-lived on the banks of the Columbia River.

The Chinooks and Clatsops are the only Tribes in the immediate vicinity, the former can bring 214 and the latter 180 fighting men into the field. About 40 miles to the Northward, along the Coast, live the Chi-hee-leesh [Chehalis], 234 men, and about the same distance to the southward are the Callemax [Tillamook], in number 200; these four nations generally come directly to the establishment, with what Furs &ct. they have to trade, which for the most part consist, of Sea Otter, Beaver, River Otter, Bear Skins, dressed Elk skins, Muskrats, Salmon, and Roots—but the Chinooks are more especially the intermediate traders between the whites and inland Tribes, particularly those to the northward.

The Religion or rather enthusiastic superstition of these people I have not sufficient opportunity, or knowledge of their language, to investigate fully, and notwithstanding my making the strictest enquiries, all I could collect was that they represent the supreme being, as an immense Bird, inhabiting the Sun (called by them Uth-lath-Gla-gla), being a benevolent spirit, and omnipotent,—to him they attribute the creation, and suppose him capable of assuming any shape or appearance at pleasure, but upon extraordinary occurances, he is believed to take the likeness aforesaid, occasionally ranging through the aerial regions, and in his wrath hurling down Thunder & lightning upon us guilty Mortals; to him they offer annual sacrifices, of their first Salmon, Venison &ct. &ct. A particular being is ascribed to the fire, of whom they are in perpetual dread, and constantly offer sacrifices, supposing him equally possessed of the power of good and evil: they are very desirous of being patronised by this gentleman, for it is he alone who has the power of interceding with their winged protector, and procure them all desirable things, such as male children, a plentiful fishing, an abundance of game, with comforts and riches of every description.

When any of their chief personages is supposed to be on his death bed, or any way in imminent danger of his life, all the Literati of the Nation are immediately convened, the High Priest and Physician, or *medicine Man*, brings and consults each his deity (i.e., the benevolent, or spirit of the air, and that of the Fire), which are made of wood and ingeniously carved, with a number of Beaver's teeth, Bear and Eagles claws suspended from them; they are capriciously formed, in shape of a Horse, Bear, Deer, Beaver, Swan, Fish &ct.: Those Idols, with their possessors, are placed in a remote corner of the Lodge for the purpose of consultation, but should they not agree regarding the patients malady, the owners, who are mostly always competitors for fame, power, and influence, beat them violently against each other, untill a tooth or claw falls off

Sculptural carving in cedar connected the Chinookans of the Columbia River with the Indian cultures of the Northwest Coast. In 1850 George Gibbs (1815–71) sketched the prow of a Chinook burial canoe in a cemetery on the banks of the river (National Anthropological Archives, Smithsonian Institution, 2854-F6).

one, which is always taken as a full proof of his confutation, consequently the advice, and prescriptions, of the other are implicitly attended to; should the sick person recover, a sacrifice is immediately made to the revered deity, and his adherent is liberally rewarded, but should he on the contrary make his exit, no offering or compensation is given, and the failure is entirely attributed to the displeasure of the offended deity. A day or two after his death, a few of the nearest relatives carry off the corpse, which, with his most valuable moveables, they deposit in a canoe prepared for the purpose and neatly covered with handsome matts, made of straw, they then lay it on a scaffold, or suspend it between two trees, in a retired part of the woods; all the deceased's well wishers cut of[f] their hair in token of grief, and for several days, neither eat nor drink, but mope about the village, howling and lamenting the departed; when the season of mourning is over (which generally lasts about one Month), a division of the slaves and other property takes place agreeably to the defuncts request on his death bed.

Their manner of courtship and marriage is somewhat singular; *when a fair one has the good fortune to kindle a flame in the bosom of a hero,* he watches for a private conference, and if favorably received, repairs soon after to her Father's lodge, with a considerable present, which he carelessly throws down at the old Gentleman's feet, then his intention is disclosed, generally by a friend he prefers on this important occasion; the Sire then enquires whether the proposal is agreeable to his daughter, and on being answered in the affirmative, demands so many slaves, Horses, Canoes, &ct. according to her beauty and accomplishments, and promises a certain return on her going into house-keeping; preliminaries thus settled, the remainder of the day is devoted to festivity and mirth,—at a late hour the party breaks up, and all retire to rest, except the lover, who steals to her Ladyship's couch, where he remains untill morning, when, if they are satisfied with each other's company, the match is finally settled; but should either be inclined to retract, they are at liberty so to do, as the present the lover has made his intended Father-in-law is thought a full equivalent for this breach in the maid's virtue or reputation. Both sexes seem incapable of forming any tender attachment, the women are very inconstant to their husbands, the worst of disorders is deeply rooted among them, having been first introduced by some of our country-men, probably from the Sandwich Islands, where it has been known, time immemorial, the effects however are not so destructive as might be expected.

Poligamy is not only allowed, but considered honorable, and the greater number of wives a man can maintain, the more power & influence has he in the Nation. The first wife is always respected as the real and legitimate one by all the others, who are called secondary wives; she has the management of all domestic concerns and regulates the interior of the house; the husband has sometimes much to do to keep harmony among so many women, who are not a little inclined to jealousy, the usual manner is, each night at supper, to make known his choice of her, who is to have the honor of sharing his bed, by directing her to prepare it.

The chieftainship is not hereditary, but he who exceeds in the number of his wives, male children, and slaves, is elected.

Their system of criminal jurisprudence, in a particular manner, is very imperfect: the offences that are deemed deserving of capital punishments are treachery, intentional homicide, and the robbery of any valuable article, nevertheless those found guilty of homicide can most generally screen themselves from punishment by a composition with the relatives of the murdered, but should the assassin be inclined to make no reparation or concession, the injured family often assume the right of pursuing and punishing him, or some of his kindred, considering themselves under the most sacred obligations of supporting, even by force, the rights of their relations—

Husbands and Fathers are not subject to any punishment for killing their wives or children, as they are declared by their laws to be natural masters of their lives. But most generally the power of deciding controversies and of punishing offences is intrusted to the chiefs—they being considered by the lower order as omniscient, and having an indisputable right to those privileges, however it cannot be supposed that a rugged proprietor of the forest or Rocks, unprincipled and unenlightened, can be a nice resolver of entangled claim, or very exact in proportioning punishments to offenses, but generally the more he indulges his own will, the more he holds his subjects in dependence, therefore innocence and forbearance, without the favor of the Chief, confer no security, and crimes however atrocious involve no danger when the judge is resolute to acquit.

Their arms are principally Bows and Arrows, Iron and bone Bludgeons, with a few muskets, which they are extremely fond of, and so much is their effect dreaded by the surrounding tribes (who have few or none) that a dosen on either side are sufficient to decide their most obstinate conflicts—when a quarrel arises between two tribes, a day and place are appointed, where the affair is settled in a *pitched battle,* which is their universal mode of warfare; they generally prefer the banks of a rivulet for the field of action, and post the adverse parties on either side of the stream; the number killed and wounded never exceed half a dosen, and should an equal number of each party fall, the war is ended, but otherwise the conquerors must make an equivalent compensation, in slaves, &ct., else hostilities are renewed on a future day; they seldom make prisoners, but when this is the case, they are always well treated and never reduced to slavery; these poor creatures are procured from the interior Tribes, who are of savage nations, their military power is an undiciplined rabble, unfit to content with 1/5 their number of Whites: They like the others seldom shed much blood in their engagements, and sometimes battles are fought which last 2 or 3 days, yet altho' 5 or 600 men may be engaged on each side, and the conflict terminated in a complete rout, the whole loss is seldom more than 12 or 15 killed and wounded,—predatory excursions are the favorite war like exploits of these people; consequently, many such plundering parties are formed who make frequent incursions on their enemies, and sometimes upon their friendly neighbors, they seldom exceed 50 or 60 in number, but when fortunate enough to fall on a small band, they massacre all the men, and carry away the women and children as slaves, the rest of their plunder is carried off on horses, each man being provided with two or three of these animals on all such expeditions.

There is perhaps no race of people in the world (for that they are of the same origin I have little doubt) who can exhibit a greater variety, with regard to size and appearance, than those of the tract we traverse. The affluent (as they may be termed) whose good fortune has placed them among the Buffalo plains, on the east side of the mountains, are generally from 5 feet 8 to 6 feet 2 inches in stature, well proportioned, extremely strong and active—while the indigent inhabitants of the western side are in general below the middle size, indolent, and of a very unhealthy complexion, evidently stunted by the badness of their food and the want of proper clothing; it is however very uncommon to find a crooked or deformed person among them, not from their pursuing, as some have maintained, the cruel custom of destroying such unfortunate children, but, in my belief, because they leave to nature the care of forming them, without obstructing her operations by the improper application of bandages, stays, corsets &ct. &ct.

They have very round faces, with small animated eyes, a broad flat nose, a handsome mouth, even and white teeth, well shaped legs and small flat feet. In their infancy the crown and forehead are flatened, by means of a small piece of board, shaped and tied on for that purpose; this in their opinion is a great acquisition to personal beauty, consequently whoever has the broadest and flatest head is esteemed by far the handsomest person. They have scarce any beard, and it is seldom the smallest hair is to be discerned on their faces; from the care they take to pluck out the little that appears, they esteem it very uncooth and impolite to have a beard, calling the whites by way of reproach the long beards; the same attention is paid to removing it from their bodies, where its growth is more abundant; that of their head is thick and black, but rather coarse; they allow it to grow to a great length, sometimes wearing it pleated, and sometimes fancifully wound round the head in tresses: of this they are as proud & careful as they are averse to beards, nor could a greater affront be offered them, than to cut it off. Those whose lot it is to inhabit the interior country depend chiefly on hunting, consequently lead a roving life through the plains, without any stationary habitation, whereas those who live near the sea subsist, I may say entirely, on Fish, and dwell in large scattering villages on the banks of the principal water courses: their lodges are constructed of cedar boards, a little sunk in the ground, and leaning against strong poles set erect, with cross spars which serve likewise as a support to the roof; these dwellings are generally large enough for the accommodation of 3 or 4 families, have a door in the gable end, made of a square piece of board or framed seal skin, a fire place (or places) in the middle, a hole over it in the roof of the house, which serves at once for the discharge of the smoke and the admission of light—the sides are partitioned off, for sitting and sleeping places, and covered with neat grass mats: the principal houses have a small apartment attached to them, which serves as a vapor bath, to prepare which stones must be heated and placed in a large hole, dug in the middle of the bath, or sweating house, where the heat may be encreased to any degree by the steam of the water which is poured on them.

They pass a great portion of their lives in revelry, and amusement, music, dancing, and play form their customary diversions; as to the first, it scarcely deserves the name, both from the defficiency of their instruments; and their manner of singing has something in it harsh & disagreeable to the ear, their songs being almost all extempore, on any triffeling object that strikes the imagination; they have several kinds of dancing, some of which are lively, pleasing and possess some variety; the women are rarely permitted to dance with the men, but form their companies a part, and dance to the sound of the same instrument and song.

Their games are numerous, and for the most part ingenious, and they sometimes indulge in play, to very great excess, indeed there have been instances of their losing everything they possessed in the world, even their Women, Children and Lodges. They are notorious thieves, and he who is so dextrous as on all occasions to elude detection is much applauded, acquires great celebrity and popularity; but the wretch who is unfortunate enough to be discovered is severely punished, and sometimes loses an ear &ct., which is thought so disgraceful as to reduce him to a level with the women, and disqualifies him ever after from becoming a warrior; some whose family have influence may be indulged with the privilege of being mogsan carrier to a war party.

Their general mode of hunting Elk and Deer is with the Bow and Arrow, very few possessing or knowing the use of Fire Arms; they frequently go in large parties, surround the game while grazing in a favorable place, such as a small prairie or meadow, environed by wood; they plant themselves in the different avenues or paths leading to this spot, then set in their dogs, which throws the affrighted animals in such confusion as to scatter in every direction, thereby giving the most, or all, a chance of exercising their skill, for let the consternation of these poor creatures be ever so great, they can, only escape by those

LT. JOSEPH BAKER, April 25, 1792

Finding a Current setting us in Shore, let go the small Bower Anchor in 36 F^ms over a bottom of fine black Sand. Unbent the F.F. Sail & bent another.

We were here visited by some of the Indians, who came alongside in 2 or 3 Canoes & ventured on board with great confidence, the Bear & otter skins of which their clothing was Composed, they bartered with great eagerness for Sails or any trifling pieces of Iron which was offer'd them; there people are of a middling stature, or rather below it. their countenance open & not unpleasant, their complexion when freed from dirt would be as fair as the Inhabitants of the Southern parts of Europe, they exercise the strictest honesty, in the little traffic which was carried on with them. their Language no one understood.

At 11 Made Sign^l. to the Chatham, weight & came to Sail under top sails. F. Galt. Sails & F. Sail at 1 Modt. Breezes Sounded 50 fms. No ground.

At Noon Modt. Breezes & Cloudy W North Extreme of the Land North. Nearest Land E^t. 4 or 5 miles. South extreme SSE, this pt. is called by Captain Vancouver Cape Orford. at a distance on each side of it, it appears much like an Island, & about WSS 3 or 4 miles from the Cape lies a cluster of Smale Rocks at the distance of a mile, they obtain'd the Name of Walpole Rocks. the Cape is situated in the Lat^d of 42 50 N.O. Long^d. 235° 21'.

LT. PETER PUGET, April 25, 1792

Calm Finding the ship drifting in bodily on the Shore & the water smooth. We let go the Small Bower [anchor] in 36 fths. water fine grey sand Northern Extreme

Southern Extreme off shore 3 Miles. Two Canoes came off—vide my Journal for an account of their Persons—in one was a Sea Otter Skin which was purchased after receiving a few Presents they returned apparently well pleased with their Reception. unbent the Fore topsail & bent another. At 11 a Breeze springing up from the SSE—fired 3 Guns made the Signal to weigh— weighed & made Sail Steering west to avoid some Rocks which lay off the Norther Extreme I sounded 50 fths no ground at 2 Imagining we had Run the Distance of the Above Rocks [at Cape Blanco] Shortned Sail & hawled to the wind on the Porsbord Tack at 3 made the Signal I wase 2 pt. Sounded 65 no Ground at 4 Sounded 60 fths. no ground 1/2 pt. Tacked W 1/2 pt. It coming on thick shortned sail I hauled to the wind on the Porsboard Tack Saw a Water Spout.

leading paths. Some of the best warriors shoot an arrow with such force as to send it thro' an Elk or Buffalo at the distance of 15 or 20 paces. On certain occasions they use darts, which are adapted with the greatest judgement to the different objects of the chase; for animals, a simple barbed point: for birds, they have them with three points of light bone, spread and barbed; for Seals & sea otter, they use a false point, inserted in a socket at the end of the dart, which parts on the least effort of the animal to dive, remaining in its body: a string of considerable length is fastened to this barbed point, and twisted round the wooden part of the dart; this serves as a float to direct them to the animal, which, having the stick to drag after it, soon tires and becomes an easy prey; (it however requires skill to humour it, perhaps equal to our angling.)—The boards used in throwing these darts are very judiciously fixed, in semblance of a *gutter,* which enables the natives to cast them with great exactness to a considerable distance.

Their Canoes for the most part are made of Cedar, and altho' possessed of no other instrument than a small chisel, it would be in vain for any White (with every tool he could wish) to set up a competition with them in this art; if perfect symmetry, smoothness, and proportion constitute beauty, they surpass anything I ever beheld: I have seen some of them as transparent as oiled paper, thro' which you could trace every formation of the insider and the natives of this river & its vicinity are the most expert paddle men any of us had ever seen; two or three of these fellows, in a small canoe, can with perfect security navigate in the most boisterous weather, for no sooner does their canoe fill or upset than they spring into the water (more like amphibious animals than human beings), right, and empty her, when with the greatest composure they again get in, and proceed. The men never wear any other garment than a small robe, made of Deer or musk-rat-skins, thrown loosly over the shoulders; and the Women have no other addition than a fringe of cedar bark tied round the waist and reaching about two inches below the knees. There are no two tribes who speak the same tongue, but most generally, each nation understands the tongue of the nearest neighbours on either side, so that each horde may be said to comprehend three different languages.

They possess their present lands and situation from time immemorial. They are never troubled with epidemic or contagious diseases, except the small-pox, which, from nation to nation, has found its way across the Rocky mountains, and sometimes its effects are so calamitous as to carry off three fourths of those who have the misfortune to be attacked therewith. Their method of life neither secures them perpetual health nor exposes them to any particular diseases; it is generally supposed that life is longer in places where there are few opportunities of luxury, but I found few or no instances among them of extraordinary longivety, *an indian grows old over his smoked salmon, just like a citizen over a turtle feast*: instances of long life are often related here, which (it appears to me) those who hear them are more willing to credit than to examine.

They informed us that Capt. Gray of the Ship *Columbia*, from Boston, was the first White who entered the River [on May 11, 1792]; on the vessels first appearance in the offing, they were very much surprised and alarmed, but after her entering and anchoring in the river, they were all seized with such consternation as to abandon their village, leaving only a few old people who could not follow; some imagined that the ship must be some overgrown monster come to devour them, while others supposed her to be a floating island inhabited by cannibals, sent by the great spirit to destroy them and ravage their country &ct. &ct. however a Boats crew soon went ashore, who by their mild behavior, and distributing a few trinkets, succeeded in assuring the old people of their friendly intentions, which they soon found means to communicate to the fugitives, thus a friendly intercourse was immediately entered into, which has never since been interrupted.

SOURCE

Spaulding, Kenneth A., ed. *On the Oregon Trail: Robert Stuart's Journey of Discovery*. Norman, OK: University of Oklahoma Press, 1953, pp. 28–29, 33–42.

RELATED READING

Franchere, Gabriel. *Adventure at Astoria, 1810–1814*. Hoyt C. Franchere, ed. Norman, OK: University of Oklahoma Press, 1967.

Irving, Washington. *Astoria; Or Anecdotes of an Enterprise Beyond the Rocky Mountains*. 2 vols. Philadelphia, 1836.

Ronda, James. *Astoria and Empire*. Lincoln, NE: University of Nebraska Press, 1990.

Ross, Alexander. *The Fur Hunters of the Far West*. Kenneth A. Spaulding, ed. Norman, OK: University of Oklahoma Press, 1956.

Ruby, Robert H., and John A. Brown. *The Chinook Indians: Traders of the Lower Columbia River*. Norman, OK: University of Oklahoma Press, 1976.

Swan, James Gilchrist. *The Northwest Coast; Or, Three Years Residence in Washington Territory*. New York: Harper & Brothers, Publishers, 1857.

Like God and Moses: Laws For the Cayuse, 1843

Arrogance reverberated through the actions of Dr. Elijah White (1806–79), first Indian agent in the Oregon Territory. A native of New York and graduate of a medical college in Syracuse, White traveled in 1836 to Hawaii, but in 1837 joined the Methodist mission in the Willamette Valley. Engaged in frequent quarrels with his associates, he returned to the East and in 1841 gained the appointment to deal with Indian affairs at a time when the claims of the United States to the region beyond the Rockies were, at best, tenuous. He returned overland in 1842 leading a wagon train of nearly one hundred emigrants.

The following account was recorded in the diary of Rev. Gustavus Hines (1809–73). Sailing on the Lausanne *with the "Great Reinforcement" of the Methodist Mission, Hines arrived in the Willamette Valley in 1840. Over the next two years Hines traveled with Rev. Jason Lee and Elijah White in explorations to find additional mission sites. In 1841 they journeyed to the Umpqua Valley and descended by canoe to the Pacific Ocean. In 1842 Hines visited Fort Vancouver to purchase supplies from the Hudson's Bay Company. In the spring of 1843 rumors of discontent among the Nez Perce, Cayuse, and Walla Walla suggested they might attack the settlements west of the mountains. The tribes were angered by killing of their game, opening of the Oregon Trail, and the news that Marcus Whitman, a missionary who had lived among them since 1836, would soon lead a large wagon train to Oregon.*

On April 25, 1843, Hines, Elijah White, George W. LeBreton, Sampson, an Indian boy, and John, a Hawaiian, departed for the interior. White had visited the Nez Perce the previous October, dictating laws and naming Ellis, a Nez Perce who had gone to school as a youth in the Red River Settlements in Canada, as chief. White's purpose on this second trip was to secure peace and establish a code of laws to govern Cayuse and Walla Walla society. The party obtained horses at Wascopam Mission at The Dalles and traveled as far east as the Spaldings' mission at Lapwai, Idaho, on the Clearwater River, where they persuaded hundreds of Nez Perce to return with them to the Walla Walla.

The following account from the Hines diary covers the events of late May 1843, when White attempted to persuade the tribal leaders to accept his law code. Several men responded. These included Ellis, Yellow Serpent, and Lawyer of the Nez Perce, and Tauitau, Telaukaikt, Five Crows, Prince, and Illutin of the Cayuse.

Tuesday, [May] 23d. The chiefs and principal men of both tribes came together at Dr. [Marcus] Whitman's [mission] to hear what we had to say. They were called to order by Tauitau, who by this time had got over his excitement, and then was placed before them the object of our visit. Among other things they were told that much had been said about war, and we had come to assure them that they had nothing to fear from that quarter; that the President of the United States had not sent the Doctor to their country, to make war upon them, but to enter into arrangements with them to regulate their intercourse with the white people. We were not there to catch them in a trap as a man would catch a beaver, but to do them good; and if they would lay aside their former practices and prejudices, stop their quarrels, cultivate their lands, and receive good laws, they might become a great and a happy people; that in order to do this, they must all be united, for they were but few in comparison to the whites; and if they were not all of one heart, they would be able to accomplish nothing; that the chiefs should set the example and love each other, and not get proud and haughty, but consider the people as their brothers and their children, and labor to do them good; that the people should be obedient, and in their morning and evening prayers they should remember their chiefs.

Liberty was then given for the chiefs to speak, and Ellis remarked that it would not be proper for the Nez Perce chiefs to speak until the Kayuse people should receive the laws. The Kayuse chiefs replied, "If you want us to receive the laws, bring them forward and let us see them, as we cannot take them unless we know what they are."

A speech was then delivered to the young men to impress them favorably with regard to the laws. They were told that they would soon take the places of the old men, and they should be willing to act for the good of the people; that they should not go here and there and spread false reports about war; and that this had been the cause of all the difficulty and excitement which had prevailed among them during the past winter.

The laws were then read, first in English, and then in the Nez Perce.

Yellow Serpent then rose and said: "I have a message to you. Where are these laws from? Are they from God or from the earth? I would that you might say, they were from God. But I think they are from the earth, because, from what I know of white men they do not honor these laws."

In answer to this, the people were informed that the laws were recognized by God, and imposed on men in all civilized countries. Yellow Serpent was pleased with the explanation, and said that it was according to the instructions he had received from others, and he was very glad to learn that it was so, because many of his people had been angry with him when he had whipped them from crime, and had told him that God would send him to hell for it, and he was glad to know that it was pleasing to God.

Telaukaikt, a Kayuse chief rose and said: "What do you read the laws for before we take them? We do not take the laws because Tauitau says so. He is a Catholic, and as a people we do not follow his worship." Dr. White replied that this did not make any difference about law; that the people in the States had different modes of worship, yet all had one law.

Then a chief, called the Prince, arose and said: "I understand you gave us liberty to examine every law—all the words and lines—and as questions are asked about it, we should get a better understanding of it. The people of this country have but one mind about it. I have something to say, but perhaps the people will dispute me. As a body, we have not had an opportunity to consult, therefore you come to us as in a wind, and speak to us as to the air, as we have no point, and we cannot speak because we have no point before us. The business before us is whole, like a body we have not dissected it. And perhaps you will say that it is out of place for me to speak, because I am not a great chief. Once I had influence but now I have but little."

Here he was about to sit down, but was told to go on. He then said,—"When the whites first came among us, we had no cattle, they have given us none; what we have now got we have obtained by an exchange of property. A long time ago Lewis and Clark came to this country, and I want to know what they said about us. Did they say that they found friends or enemies here?" Being told that they spoke well of the Indians, the Prince said, "that is a reason why the whites should unite with us, and all become one people. Those who have been here before you, have left us no memorial of their kindness, by giving us presents."

"We speak by way of favor. If you have any benefits to bestow, we will then speak more freely. One thing that we can speak about is cattle, and the reason why we cannot speak out now is because we have not the thing before us. My people are poor and blind, and we must have something tangible. Other chiefs have bewildered me since they came; yet I am from an honorable stock. Promises which have been made to me and my fathers, have not been fulfilled, and I am made miserable; but it will not answer for me to speak out, for my people do not consider me as their chief. One thing more; you have reminded me of what was promised me sometime ago, and I am inclined to follow on and see; though I have been giving my beaver to the whites, and have received many promises, and have always been disappointed. I want to know what you are going to do."

Illutin, or Big Belly, then arose and said, that the old men were wearied with the wickedness of the young men. That if he was alone, he could say yes at once to the laws, and that the reason why the young men did not feel as he felt was because they had stolen property in their hands, and the laws condemned stealing. But he assured them that the laws were calculated to do them good, and not evil.

But this did not satisfy the Prince. He desired that the good which it was proposed to do them by adopting the laws, might be put in a tangible form before them. He said that it had been a long time since the country had been discovered by whites, and that ever since that time, people had been coming along, and promising to do them good; but they had all passed by and left no blessing behind them. That the Hudson's Bay Company had persuaded them to continue with them, and not go after the Americans; that if the Americans designed to do them good why did they not bring goods with them to leave with the Indians? That they were fools to listen to what the Yankees had to say; that they would only talk, but the company would both talk and give them presents.

In reply to this the Doctor told them that he did not come to them as a missionary, nor as a trader.

It was now nearly night, but just before the meeting closed a gun was fired in one of the lodges, and directly John, the Hawaiian, came running to the house with his hand up to his head, and the blood running down his face, and as he came into the assembly he cried out with great agitation. "Indian, he kille me! Indian, he kille me!"

John had been to the lodge for the purpose of trading with the young Indians, and the Indians became angry at John and threatened to shoot him. John told them that they dare not do it, and one of them instantly seized a musket and lodged the contents of it in the side of John's head. Fortunately there was no ball in the gun, consequently the results were not serious, though a hole was cut to the bone, an inch in diameter.

In the evening Ellis and Lawyer came in to have a talk. They said they expected pay for being chiefs, and wished to know how much salary Dr. White was going to give them. Ellis said he had counted the months he had been in office, and thought that enough was due him to make him rich. They left at a late hour without receiving any satisfaction.

Wednesday, [May] 24th. Some hundreds again assembled to resume the business relative to laws; but the first thing investigated was the shooting of John. The Indian, immediately after committing the deed, had fled, but the chiefs took summary measures to bring him back. He was brought before the assembly and found guilty of the crime, but the sentence was postponed until they received the laws.

The Indians then continued to speak in reference to the laws, and their speeches were grave, energetic, mighty and eloquent, and generally in favor or receiving the laws. After all had spoken it was signified that they were ready for the vote whether they would take the laws or not, and the vote was unanimous in the affirmative. Having adopted the laws, it was now necessary to elect their chiefs, according to the provisions of the laws; and Tauitau was nominated to the high chieftainship. Some were opposed; a majority were in favor, and while the question was pending Tauitau rose and said: "My friends, my friends, I rise to speak to you, and I want you all to listen." He then adverted to their past histories, and told them how much they had suffered in consequence by their divisions and quarrels, and then inquired if they would lay aside all their past difficulties and come up and support him, if he would accept of the chieftainship.

It was now time to close for that day, and the vote being put, Tauitau was declared duly elected to the high chieftainship of the Kayuse tribe. Before the meeting adjourned, Dr. White presented the Indians with a fat ox which he bought of the mission, and Mrs. [Narcissa] Whitman gave them a fat hog. These they butchered directly, and feasted upon them till ten o'clock at night, when all was consumed.

Thursday, [May] 25th. A number of the chiefs came early in morning at our request, to settle a difficulty concerning some horses which they gave to Rev. Jason Lee, when he first came to Oregon, Mr. Lee having requested us to come to an arrangement with them, if possible. After a long talk, we succeeded in settling with them by proposing to give them a cow for each horse that they had given Mr. Lee. We found that the Indians always expect to be well paid for a present.

After this the Indians again assembled, and Tauitau came forward and certified that he had made up his mind that he could not accept of the chieftainship in consequence of the difference of his religion from that of the most of his people. He was accordingly excused from serving, and Five Crows, his brother, was immediately nominated. When the virtues and firmness of Five Crows were spoken of, the people exclaimed, "our hearts go towards him with a rush." His election was nearly unanimous, and highly pleasing to the whites, of whom he is a great friend, particularly of the Americans. He was so affected when his appointment was announced, that he wept. It required but a short time to elect the subordinate chiefs, after which Mr. [H. K. W.] Perkins and myself addressed the meeting on the subject of the discovery of the country by Americans, their settling in it, and the necessity of living together on friendly terms; and then the meeting, which had been continued for four days, and at some stages of which the utmost excitement had prevailed, came to a peaceful conclusion, and all went about preparing for the closing feast.

A second ox was butchered, cut into small pieces and boiled. It was then spread out upon the grass, and cut into mouthfuls, put on to plates, pail covers, and pieces of boards, and placed along in the center of a large temporary lodge, made of skins, and about seventy-five feet long. The people were then all called together, and took their seats on the ground, ourselves being conducted by the chiefs to some seats of skins prepared on the windward side of the lodge, so that we would be secure from the smoke, all, when seated, forming a lengthened ring around the food, three and four persons deep. Five Crows called the table to order, when a blessing was asked; then several Indians passed around the meat to all present, the number, as near as we could judge, being six hundred, embracing men, women and children. Fingers were used instead of forks, and the clattering of teeth and smacking of lips served as music while the process of mastication was going on. All seemed intent upon the business before them; laws, speeches, and war, were lost sight of, and the eating of the ox absorbed every other consideration. It was only necessary for each person to eat one pound, and all would be consumed. In twenty minutes the ox which, three hours before, was peacefully feeding on the prairie, was lodged in the stomachs of six hundred Indians.

After the feast Ellis arose and said that it was fashionable among the Indians for all the chiefs to unite with the whites at such a time as this, in smoking the pipe, in token of their alliance and friendship. Accordingly, the pipe of peace was brought forward. Its stem was one inch in diameter, and three feet long, and the bowl four inches long and two in diameter, and made out of a species of dark free-stone. Ellis passed it around, to the chiefs first, and then to the whites, after which speeches were delivered by Five Crows, Ellis, Lawyer, Brothers, Tauitau, and Yellow Serpent; a season of prayer followed and the scene was closed.

Next morning the Indians all came to give us the friendly hand before we parted; and the chiefs informed us that they had sentenced the Indian who shot John to a punishment of forty lashes on his bare back. Thus closed our negotiations, and the immense crowd of Indians, taking their leave, returned to their homes in the utmost order. In the evening all was still, and, walking out to the camping ground where the fires were still blazing, I found but one solitary old Indian, who was boiling up the feet of the ox for his next day's supplies.

LAWS OF THE NEZ PERCES.

Art. 1. Whoever wilfully takes life shall be hung.

Art. 2. Whoever burns a dwelling house shall be hung.

Art. 3. Whoever burns an outbuilding shall be imprisoned six months, receive fifty lashes, and pay all damages.

Art. 5. If any one enter a dwelling, without permission of the occupant, the chiefs shall punish him as they think proper.

Art. 6. If any one steal he shall pay back two fold; and if it be the value of a beaver skin or less, he shall receive twenty-five lashes; and if the value is over a beaver skin he shall pay back two-fold, and receive fifty lashes.

Art. 7. If any one take a horse, and ride it, without permission, or take any article, and use it, without liberty, he shall pay for the use of it, and receive from twenty to fifty lashes, as the chief shall direct.

Art. 8. If any one enter a field, and injure the crops, or throw down the fence, so that cattle or horses go in and do damage, he shall pay all damages, and receive twenty-five lashes for every offence.

Art. 9. Those only may keep dogs who travel or live among the game; if a dog kill a lamb, calf, or any domestic animal, the owner shall pay the damage, and kill the dog.

Art. 10. If an Indian raise a gun or other weapon against a white man, it shall be reported to the chiefs, and they shall punish him. If a white person do the same to an Indian, it shall be reported to Dr. White, and he shall redress it.

Art. 11. If an Indian break these laws, he shall be punished by his chiefs; if a white man break them, he shall be reported to the agent, and be punished at his instance.

Dr. White displayed no compunction about dictating laws to the tribes of the interior and attempting to narrow their leadership to selected head chiefs. White first took his law code to the Nez Perce on the Clearwater in December 1842, and later that month to the Wasco on the Columbia River near The Dalles. White's laws were included in Wilupupki 1842, Lapwai hipaina Takta Hwait tamalwi-awat himakespinih, suiapu-miohat-upkinih, *a printing of eight pages at the Lapwai Mission press in 1842. The code also appeared in the* Annual Report of the Commissioner of Indian Affairs *(1844), and in* Testimonials and Records, *together with* Arguments in favor of Special Action for our Indian Tribes *(Washington, D.C., 1861).*

White showed little understanding of these societies, which had sustained themselves for millennia, nor comprehension of a tribal structure where independent bands operated without benefit of an overarching government with a single leader. White's laws did nothing to quell the distress among the Cayuse. Their lands were bisected by the Oregon Trail and, in the fall of 1843, Dr. Whitman returned, followed by over twenty-five hundred emigrants. The newcomers brought smallpox and trouble. The stage was set for the Cayuse War of 1847.

SOURCE

Allen, A. J. *Ten Years in Oregon: Travels and Adventures of Doctor E. White and Lady West of the Rocky Mountains.* Ithaca, NY: Mack, Andrus, 1848, pp. 189–90.

Hines, Gustavus. *Oregon: Its History, Condition, and Prospects. . . .* Buffalo, NY: Geo[rge] H. Derby and Co., 1851, pp. 178–85.

RELATED READING

Haggert, Lester. The Nez Perce Tribe, *A Bibliography of The Constitutions and Laws of the American Indians.* Cambridge MA: Harvard University Press, 1947, pp. 96–97.

Ruby, Robert H., and John Brown. *The Cayuse Indians: Imperial Tribesmen of Old Oregon.* Norman, OK: University of Oklahoma Press, 1972.

Stern, Theodore. *Chiefs & Change in the Oregon Country: Indian Relations at Fort Nez Percés, 1818–1855.* 2 vols. Corvallis, OR: Oregon State University Press.

White, Elijah. *Concise View of Oregon Territory: Its Colonial and Indian Relations . . . .* Washington, DC: T. Bernard, 1846.

The Tragedy at Waiilatpu, 1847

Marcus Whitman was a stern missionary. Narcissa Prentiss Whitman, his wife and co-worker among the Indians, resented the invasions of her privacy by the Cayuse and considered Oregon Trail pioneers unwashed, unchurched, and foul-mouthed. In 1836 this couple, driven by personal religious zeal and underwritten by the American Board of Commissioners for Foreign Missions, traveled overland and founded a mission at Waiilatpu—the "Place of the Rye Grass." The setting was beautiful. The Walla Walla River meandered through lush bottom-lands fringed by cottonwoods and willows. Rich loess hills covered with bluebunch wheatgrass and sage rolled to the southern horizon to the foot of the conifer-clad Blue Mountains.

The Whitmans' choice of location was strategic. Located a day's ride upstream from Fort Walla Walla, a fur trade post standing near the Columbia River at the eastern end of Wallula Gap, the station was in the midst of the Cayuse homeland and the Hudson's Bay Company's great horse farm. Herds of Appaloosa and Cayuse ponies thundered across the countryside, signs of the wealth, mobility, and proud traditions of the native peoples. Whitman saw the site as ideal for a two-fold conversion. He would bring the Cayuse and Nez Perce, who lived nearby, to Christianity. He would transform these "benighted people" from nomadism to a sedentary, agricultural lifeway.

The Whitmans were sometimes impatient and vexed. They were lonely, over-worked, driven, and bereft when their only child, Clarissa, toddled into the river and drowned. Returning from the East in 1843, Whitman preceded a major emi-gration on the Oregon Trail. Already suffering from smallpox, measles, and other new illnesses, the Cayuse saw the pioneers as a great uninvited and menacing invasion. Hundreds of the newcomers passed by the Whitman station, where the doctor's medicine gave most restored health and life. But the Cayuse continued to die. Then, on a foggy November day in 1847, a group of Cayuse men attacked the Whitman mission, murdering the failed medicine man, his wife, and several others.

The station at Waiilatpu had become a relatively large community of more than fifty Americans, buttressed by seven orphans of the Sager family, children of fur trappers, lingering emigrants, and others who assisted the Whitmans. The reports of 1847 referred to some of these people as well as to the Cayuse alleged to have perpetrated the murders.

The following letters were the initial reports of the event. James Douglas (1803–77) was Chief Factor for the Hudson's Bay Company at Fort Vancouver. William McBean (ca. 1816–92), a Scotsman, was a long-time trader who lived with his Indian wife and family at Fort Nez Perces [Walla Walla]. Alanson Hinman (1822–1908) was a school teacher who joined the Whitman mission in 1844; he was living in 1847 at Wascopam Mission at The Dalles. George Abernethy (1807–77) was governor of the Oregon Provisional Government and sent on December 8 a special message to the legislature forwarding these communications.

Letter of William McBean, Fort Nez Perces, to Board of Managers,
Hudson's Bay Company, November 30, 1847

GENTLEMEN: It is My painful duty to make you acquainted with a horrible massacre which took place yesterday at Waiilatpu, about which I was first apprised early this morning by an American by the name of Hall, who had escaped, and who reached this place half naked and covered with blood, as he started at the outset; the information I received was not satisfactory. He, however, assured me that the Doctor and another man were killed, but could not tell us the persons who did it, and how it originated. I immediately determined on sending my interpreter and one man to Dr. Whitman's to find out the truth, and if possible, to rescue Mr. [Donald] Manson's two sons and any of the survivors. It so happened that before the interpreter had proceeded half-way, the two boys were met on their way hither, escorted by Nicholas Finley, it having been previously settled among the Indians that these boys should not be killed; as also the American women and children. Tilokaikt is the chief who recommended this measure.

I presume that you are well acquainted that fever and dysentery have been raging here in the vicinity, in consequence of which a great number of Indians have been swept away, but more especially at the Doctor's place, where he had attended upon the Indians. About thirty souls of the Cayuse tribe died, one after another, who evidently believed the Doctor poisoned them, and in which opinion they were, unfortunately confirmed by one of the Doctor's party. As far as I have been able to learn, this has been the sole cause of the dreadful butchery. In order to satisfy any doubt on that point; it is reported that they requested the Doctor to administer medicine to three of their friends, two of whom were really sick, but the third feigned sickness, and that the three were corpses the next morning. After they were buried, and while the Doctor's men were employed slaughtering an ox, the Indians came one by one to his house, with their arms concealed under their blankets, and, being all assembled, commenced firing on those slaughtering the animal, and in a moment the Doctor's house was surrounded; the Doctor, and a young lad brought up by himself, were shot in the house. His lady, Mr. [Andrew] Rogers, and the children had taken refuge in the garret, but were dragged down and dispatched (excepting the children) outside, where their bodies were left exposed.

It is reported that it was not the intention to kill Mr. Rogers, in consequence of an avowel to the following effect, which he is said to have made, and which nothing but a desire to save his life could have prompted him to do. He said "I was one evening lying down, and overheard the Doctor telling Rev. Mr. Spalding that it was best that you should all be poisoned at once, but that the latter told him it was best to continue slowly and cautiously, and between this and spring not a soul would remain, when they would take possession of your lands, cattle and horses." These are only Indian reports, and no person can believe the Doctor capable of such action without being as ignorant and brutish as the Indians themselves. One of the murderers, not having been made acquainted with the above understanding, shot Mr. Rogers.

It is well understood, that eleven lives were lost and three wounded. It is also rumored that they are to make an attack upon the fort; let them come if they will not listen to reason; though I have but five men at the establishment, I am prepared to give a warm reception; the gates are closed day and night, and bastions in readiness.

In company with Mr. Manson's two sons was sent a young half-breed lad brought up by Dr. Whitman; they are all here and have got over their fright.

The ringleaders in this horrible butchery are Tilokaikt, his son, Big Belly, Tamsaky, Istacus, Towmoulisk, etc. I understand from the interpreter that they were making one common grave for the dead. The houses were stripped of everything in the shape of property, but when they came to divide the spoils they all fell out among themselves, and all agreed to put back the property. I am happy to state the Walla Walla chief had no hand in the whole business. They were all the doctor's own people—the Cayuses. One American shot another and took the Indians' part to save his own life.

Allow me to draw a veil over this dreadful affair, which is too painful to dwell upon, and which I have explained conformably to information received and with sympathizing feelings.

I remain with much respect, your most obedient servant,

WILLIAM McBEAN,

N. B.—I have just learned that the Cayuses are to be here to-morrow to kill Serpen Juane, the Walla Walla chief.

W. McB.

Names of those who are killed: Dr. Whitman, Mrs. Whitman, Mr. Rogers, Hoffman, Sanders, Osborn, Marsh, John and Francis Sager, Canfield and a sailor, besides three that were wounded more or less—Messrs. Kimball and another whose name I cannot learn.

W. McBEAN.

Letter of James Douglas, Fort Vancouver, to George Abernethy,
December 7, 1847

Dear Sir.   Having received intelligence last night by special express from Walla Walla, of the destruction of the missionary settlement at Waiilatpu, by the Cayuse Indians of that place, we hasten to communicate the particulars of that dreadful event, one of the most attrocious which darkens the annals of Indian crime.

Our lamented friend, Dr. Whitman, his amiable and accomplished lady, with nine other persons, have fallen victims to the fury of those remorseless savages, who appear to have been instigated to this appalling crime by a horrible suspicion which had taken possession of their superstitious minds, in consequence of the number of deaths from dysentery and measles, that Dr. Whitman was silently working the destruction of their tribe by administering poisons under the semblance of salutary medicines. With a goodness of heart and benevolence truly his own, Dr. Whitman has been laboring incessantly since the appearance of the measles and dysentery among his Indian converts to relieve their sufferings: and such has been the reward of his generous labors.

A copy of Mr. McBean's letter herewith transmitted, will give you all the particulars known to us of this indescribably painful event. Mr. Ogden, with a strong party, will leave this place as soon as possible for Walla Walla, to endeavor to prevent further evil; and we beg to suggest to you the propriety of taking instant measures for the protection of the Rev. Mr. Spalding, who, for the sake of his family, ought to abandon the Clearwater mission without delay, and retire to a place of safety, as he cannot remain at that isolated station without imminent risk, in the present excited and irritable state of the Indian population.

I have the honor to be, sir, your most obedient servant.

JAMES DOUGLAS.

Letter of Alanson Hinman, Fort Vancouver, to George Abernethy, ca. December 7, 1847

DEAR SIR: A Frenchman from Walla Walla arrived at my place on Saturday, and informed me that he was on his way to Vancouver, and wished me to assist in procuring him a canoe immediately. I was very inquisitive to know if there was any difficulty above. He said four Frenchmen had died recently, and he wished to get others to occupy their places. I immediately got him a canoe and concluded to go in company with him, in order to get some medicine for the Indians, as they were dying off with measles and other diseases very fast. I was charged with indifference. They said we were killing in not giving them medicine, and I found if we were not exposing our lives, we were our peace, and consequently I set out for this place. This side of the Cascades I was made acquainted with the horrible massacre that took place at Waiilatpu last Monday. Horrible to relate! Dr. and Mrs. Whitman, Mr. Rogers, Mr. Osborn, Mr. Sanders, a school teacher, two orphan boys (John and Francis Sager), together with all the men at that place— eleven in all. Some are living at the sawmill, which is situated about twenty miles from the doctor's. A party set out for that place to dispatch them; also, a party for Mr. Spalding's to dispatch them; and they are not satisfied yet, but a party is said to have started for my place, and has, if true, reached there before this time. Oh! had I known it when I was at home. I can neither sleep nor take any rest on account of my family and those with them, viz.: my wife and child, the doctor's nephew, Dr. Saffron, and Mr. McKinney and wife. If I had ten men I could defend myself with perfect ease, by occupying the meetinghouse, which is very roomy and close. You see my situation, as well as Mr. Spalding's. I have perfect confidence in your doing all you can to get a party to come up and spend the winter there, and likewise to go to the women and children and Mr. Spalding if alive, which I think is very doubtful. Delay not a moment in sending a few men for my protection; a few moments may save our lives. I expect to leave to-morrow for home, and perhaps the first salutation will be a ball. My family is there and I must return if it costs me my life. We are in the hands of a merciful God, why should we be alarmed? I will close by saying again, send a small force immediately without the delay of one day. Farewell. Yours truly,

ALANSON HINMAN.

Letter George Abernethy to Provisional Legislature, December 8, 1847

GENTLEMEN: It is my painful duty to lay the enclosed communication before your honorable body. It will give you the particulars of the horrible massacre committed by the Cayuse Indians on the residents of Waiilatpu. This is of the most distressing circumstances that has occurred in our Territory, and one that calls for immediate and prompt action. I am aware that to meet this case funds will be required, and suggest the propriety of applying to the Hudson's Bay Company and the merchants of this place for a loan to carry out whatever plan you may fix upon. I have no doubt but the expense attending this affair will be promptly met by the United States Government.

The wives and children of the murdered persons, the Rev. Mr. Spalding and family, and all others who may be in the upper country, should at once be proffered assistance, and an escort to convey them to places of safety.

I have the honor to remain gentlemen, your obedient servant.

GEORGE ABERNETHY

On hearing these letters, the Oregon Provisional Legislature adopted the motion of James Nesmith:

Resolved That the Governor is hereby required to raise arms and equip a company of riflemen, not to exceed fifty men, with their captain and subaltern officers, and dispatched them forthwith to occupy the mission station at The Dalles, on the Columbia river, and to hold possession of the same until reinforcements can arrive at that point, or other means be taken as the Government may think advisable.

Thus began the Cayuse War of 1847–48 and the military invasion of the southern Columbia Plateau by companies of volunteers—soldiers raised by the Oregon Provisional Legislature.

SOURCE

Brown, John Henry. *Brown's Political History of Oregon: Provisional Government.* Vol. 1. Wiley B. Allen, Publisher; Press of The Lewis & Dryden Printing Co., 1892, pp. 322–25.

RELATED READING

Drury, Clifford Merrill. *Marcus Whitman, M.D.: Pioneer and Martyr.* The Caxton Printers, Ltd., Caldwell, ID., 1937.

———. *Marcus and Narcissa Whitman and the Opening of Old Oregon.* 2 vols. Arthur H. Clark Company, Glendale, CA, 1973.

Jeffrey, Julie Roy. *Converting the West: A Biography of Narcissa Whitman.* Norman, OK: University of Oklahoma Press, 1991.

Miller, Christopher. *Prophetic Worlds: Indians and Whites on the Columbia Plateau.* New Brunswick, NJ: Rutgers University Press, 1985.

Ruby, Robert H., and John A. Brown. *The Cayuse Indians: Imperial Tribesmen of Old Oregon.* Norman, OK: University of Oklahoma Press, 1972.

Thompson, Erwin N. *Shallow Grave at Waiilatpu: The Sagers' West.* Portland, OR: Oregon Historical Society, 1973.

Proceedings to Resolve the Cayuse War, 1848

Both military and diplomatic efforts arose during the winter of 1847–48 to try to resolve the tensions that flowed from the murder of the Whitmans and others at Waiilatpu. The initiatives included ransom of hostages from the mission by the Hudson's Bay Company, an offer from F. W. Pettygrove to travel to Salt Lake City to enlist the assistance of the Mormons in crushing the hostile Indians, dashing about of volunteer companies in search of the alleged Cayuse killers, and a delegation of peace commissioners sent out by the Provisional Government in Oregon City.

In February 1848, Governor George Abernethy named Capt. H. A. G. Lee, commander of the troops in the field; Robert Newell (1807–69), a former mountain man, legislator, and settler in the Willamette Valley; and Joel Palmer (1810–81), subsequently the government's superintendent of Indian Affairs, to hold a council "to avert a general war with the Indians of the upper country, and to prevent a union among the tribes as far as possible." The governor instructed the commissioners to demand the surrender of the murder suspects, delivery of all stolen property, and restitution of property stolen from emigrants during the previous year's migration. "I am aware the greatest difficulty will be in obtaining the persons of the murderers," he wrote, "but the Indians must be given to understand in the commencement of negotiations, that this must be done; that no compromise can be made."

The peace commissioners traveled east via the Columbia Gorge to the "upper country" and on March 7 held the council at Fort Nez Perces. The Walla Walla, Nez Perce, and "friendly" Cayuse, namely those who claimed they had no involvement in the Whitman incident or the ensuing conflicts with the volunteers, attended the council. The selections that follow include the report of the commissioners, the declaration of Governor Abernethy read at the meeting, the responses of several of the participating chiefs, Joel Palmer's remarks addressed specifically to Peo-peo-mox-mox and others to the council in general, and the speech of Robert Newell.

The council proceedings identified several of the Indian spokesmen by Christian names, a legacy of mission efforts and baptisms. Among those participating was Old Joseph, known as Tu-eka-kas to his people, who resided in the Wallowa and Imnaha region of northeastern Oregon. The minutes confirmed the geographical sophistication of the Plateau Indians. Not only did they travel annually to hunt buffalo and trade on the northern Plains, Kentuck, a Nez Perce chief, referred to his journey in 1847 to Sutter's Fort in the Sacramento Valley.

Report of H. A. G. Lee, Robert Newell, and Joel Palmer, March, 1848

On the receipt of our commissions and instructions, we proceeded immediately to Wascopam [The Dalles], where according to our instructions, we held a council with the field officers of the army, and it was agreed in counsel that we should go in advance of the army, taking with us Capt. [Thomas] McKay and his company, so soon as he should arrive at that place, with as many others as might be deemed necessary for a safe escort, including Mr. [Joseph] Meek and his party, first to Fort Walla Walla, and then if necessary, to the Nez Perces country, in order to prevent an alliance of those tribes with the Cayuses, in the war against the Americans. Capt. McKay did not arrive till the evening of Feb. 13th. In the meantime we saw and conversed with many of the Indians about that place. They were evidently alarmed at seeing so many armed men in their midst, and feeling guilty, perhaps, of having mistreated the emigrants. We made them acquainted with our business, as Commissioners, and Gen. Palmer was pointed out to them as Superintendent of Indians Affairs.

On the 14th, two Yakimas came to the fort, saying they were sent by their chiefs to learn the truth as to the intentions of the whites—that the Cayuses have been several times to see them since the massacre, and had offered them horses and cattle, if they would join them, telling them the whites were coming to kill them all. They had not joined the Cayuses, but wished to know the true intentions of the whites. They said, they had never troubled the whites—that the whites did not pass through their country, because it was not on the road traveled by the emigrants—and finally, they thought the Cayuses had done very badly in killing Dr. Whitman. We gladly embraced this opportunity to form an acquaintance with these people, and to give them correct information as to the object of the present campaign; and hearing they had a priest with them, we wrote to the chiefs—sent them a flag and some tobacco as a mark of friendship.

To-day the regiment was ordered to be in readiness to take up the line of march for Walla Walla to-morrow at 10 o'clock, and we were informed by the commander that he could not furnish us an escort to go in advance—as he thought it unsafe to divide his forces. On the morning of the 15th, before we marched from this place, two of the Des Chutes Indians came in for peace. They belong to Sue, Seletza's older brother—he is quite an old man and had not been in battle against us, though some of his people had; but said they were forced to do so in order to escape the same treatment from the Cayuses, that Seletza had received. We spoke to them about as we had done to the Yakimas the previous day, and sent the old chief a similar present, with a request that he should meet us on the road; as we could not wait at the fort.

Disappointed in our wish to go in advance of the regiment, and fearing the Nez Perces and Walla Wallas might be driven to hostilities, we determined to dispatch a messenger to them. Old Elijah, an Indian professing to be a Nez Perces, who had accompanied Messrs. Newell and Palmer from Oregon City, was thought to be the most suitable person at our command. Accordingly on the 20th, from the upper crossing of the John Day's river, he was sent forward with a letter from Rev. H. H. Spalding to the Nez Perces chief—a flag and some tobacco to them from us, and a letter to Mr. [William] McBean, to whom he was directed to deliver the package. He, however, unfortunately (or designedly) fell in with the Cayuses before he reached Walla Walla, and was retained as prisoner, the flag and tobacco appropriated to their own use, but the package, being directed to McBean, was sent to him by Young Chief, who afterwards intercepted and destroyed his reply to us. Fortunately, two Nez Perces, Timothy and Red Wolf, arrived at Walla Walla just as McBean received the package, he made known to them the contents of our letter to him, in which Mr. Spalding's letter to them was mentioned, he gave it to Timothy, who readily opened and read it aloud; after which, these two men immediately set out for their own country, bearing with them Mr. Spalding's letter and also the information they had gained through our letter to McBean, which was also communicated to Yellow Serpent (Walla Walla chief). To this fortunate occurrence we owe, perhaps, much of our success in preventing a general combination of the Indian tribes against us.

On the 23rd, Sue, the Des Chutes chief came to our camp on Willow Creek, bearing the flag we had sent him, accompanied by twelve of his men as escort. We had a friendly talk with him, and Capt. T. McKay, received by him a fine horse as a present from Waluptouleeky, from whom Col. [Cornelius] Gilliam received a message by the same, saying he would bring in all the property left with him and all that had been taken from the emigrants by his people, and deliver it up to the Colonel on his return to Wascopam, if it would make them friends. The Colonel replied it would. We all sent word to the same effect, and requested Sue to meet us again at Wascopam on our return, and to tell all the Indians to do the same, as we wished to talk to them. At daylight on the morning of the 24th, a boy of Seletza's came to us at the springs, bringing us an express at Wascopam, which proved to be a letter from Rev. Mr. [Augustin M. A.] Blanchet, missionary to the Yakimas, to whom we had written from Wascopam on the 14th. This letter had been sent to that place with some presents to us from the Yakima chief. . . .

The Cayuses met us in battle array a few miles from these springs with all their allied forces. We made every exertion in our power to get to speak with them, but could not. A battle ensued, the particulars of which you have from the proper source. After the battle, however, we succeeded in getting a talk with the Finlay's (half breeds), which opened the way for negotiating with all the tribes. On our approach to Walla Walla, we received the accompanying letter from McBean in reply to the one from us by one of the Finlay's.

To the Commissioners:
MESSRS. PALMER AND NEWELL.—GENTLEMEN. I have to acknowledge your esteemed favor of this date, which was handed me this evening. I am happy to learn that your success to effect peace, has so far rewarded your endeavours and that the Nez Perces are on your side. Previous to their visiting you, the most influential chiefs came to me to know your real intentions, which I fully explained and addressed them at length. They left me well disposed, and I am glad to learn they have acted up to their promise. I now forward letters to Fort Hall and Fort Boise, and have to request in behalf of the Company, that you be kind enough to get them forwarded by Mr. Meek. They are of importance—on their being delivered, depends loss or gain to the Company, and by so doing you will confer a favor on us,
   Your most obedient servant,
   WILLIAM McBEAN.
   P.S. Please present my best respects to Gen. Gilliam and Maj. Lee.

Our first interview with Yellow Serpent, was at Walla Walla on the 28th. We found him decidedly friendly and withal prudent and sensible. He visited our camp frequently afterwards furnished some beef cattle to the army, and was in the general council, which was held at Waiilatpu on March 7th. There were present also the Cayuse *War Chief* Coshmashpello, and the following Nez Perces,

Joseph (head chief during the absence of Ellis), Jacob, James, Red Wolf, Timothy, Richard, Kentuck, Luke, Stupetpenin, Youm-tama-laikin, Thomas and about 250 men. Col. Gilliam, C.W. Cook, Asst. Quartermaster, Capt. McKay, Mr. [William] Craig, and a few others of the regiment were with *us*. After the pipe of friendship had passed around till our hearts were all good and our eyes watery, we informed them that we had a communication to them from our head chief in the Willamette, and we wished them to break the seal, which they did, and we read it to them, which called out the feelings and views of nearly all the chiefs. The substance of the whole amounts to about this: They had no knowledge of an intention on the part of the Cayuses to murder the Doctor, till the deed was done. When they heard it they were grieved. Some of them came to see the chiefs, and enquire who had been guilty of so foul a deed—*they had a law amongst them*—that when one committed murder, he forfeit his own life. They had one head chief—they all listened to his words. Their old chiefs who were now dead, had told them to be friendly with the Americans, and they had not forgotten their words. The Cayuses had told them the Americans were coming to kill all the Indians and to take their lands, but they still came to see us. They had not killed Mr. [Henry H.] Spalding, but *protected* him. They asked him to stay with them, his property was still there. They would not join the murderers to fight us.

Declaration of Governor George Abernethy To the Great Chiefs of the Nez Perces, and other Tribes Read in Council

BROTHERS. I speak to you now on a subject of great importance to Americans, and I ask you to listen to what I have to say. Many years ago, a few Americans, came to your country; you received them gladly, and told them you wished them to stay with you and instruct you; they did so at your request; among these was Dr. [Marcus] Whitman and his lady. Many Americans have since that time passed through your country to join their brethren in the Willamette. At first they were permitted to pass without being molested. After a while some of your neighbors, without your knowledge, would steal from the Americans as they passed along. Soon they began to steal large things, and last summer much was stolen, very much. We did not want to be enemies to you, and our warriors were not sent up. If you will enquire into these things, you will find that they are as I tell you. We have borne a great deal, we believed that your chiefs did not know how much was stolen from the Americans, but we think your power ought to be exerted to prevent stealing altogether. But all this was nothing compared with what has since been done.

On the 27th of last November, the Cayuse Indians bathed their hands in the blood of their best friend, and in the blood of many of our brothers. Dr. Whitman had at your request remained among you. He has ever since been trying to do you good by teaching you many useful things, and above all, we know that he was teaching you to understand the Bible, the great Book that our Creator has given us, by which we may understand the way in which he wished all his creatures to live, that we may be happy in this world, and be happy after death. Dr. Whitman labored with you for a long time, what he told you was true, and had you listened to him, and all your neighbors listened to him, Dr. Whitman and our brothers would not have been killed, because one of the great commandments of our great Creator is "Thou shalt not kill"; another one is, "Thou shalt not steal."

I hear you say "Dr. Whitman was poisoning us"; you know better, sickness is sent by our Creator, it is in the world, and he has said all men must die, we cannot escape. Did you not see the Americans die with the same disease? Have not a great many of our people been buried this year? But if it was believed by our neighbors that Dr. Whitman poisoned them, why kill all Americans? But I tell you Dr. Whitman did not poison any one, he was giving medicine and advice to try to save you from dying; how many times has he healed your sick, that would have died, had he not given them medicine? He was your best friend, your great friend. He was always speaking of you and trying to do you good. But he is dead; his wife is dead; our brethren are dead. How did they die? How did he die? The men that asked him to stay among them, that had partaken of his hospitality, that have been the subjects of his kindness, stole upon him and murdered him. Our hearts bled when we heard of it. We cannot pass this by. We hope you sympathize with us, that your hearts say we will not protect such men.

Brothers, our warriors are on the war path, what shall be done, that we may all again be friends, and not enemies? I will tell you what we want, listen to me. We want the men that murdered our brother Dr. Whitman, and his wife, and the rest of our brothers; Tiloquoit, Tamsukie, and all that were engaged, and those that forced our young women to become their wives. We want all these to be given up to us, that they may be punished according to our law. And further, that restitution of the property stolen and destroyed be made, either by returning the property or giving an equivalent. If this is done, our hatchet will be buried, and the Indians and Americans will be friends and brothers. Every tribe that united with the murderers and protects them, we must look on as our enemies. On the other hand, every tribe that does not unite with and protect them, we shall look upon as our friends, and protect them if necessary. My brothers, consider this well. The Americans are a great people; a few, very few, have come to this country. Our Great Chief has always been told that the Indians in this country were all friendly; he has not sent any of his war chiefs here. We have now sent word to him, that our people have been killed, his war chiefs will come, and should you prefer war to peace, let me tell you, and listen to what I say, they will punish you until you shall be fully satisfied with war, and be glad to make peace. Consider this well, if your young men speak for war. My advice to you as a friend is, that you deliver up the murderers, or let the Americans go and take them, without your interfering with them. In this case do not let the murderers shelter among you, lest your people should get killed through mistake, for which I would be very sorry.

I have sent this news to California, and very soon one or more ships of war will be here, but if you are determined to be friendly with the Americans, this need not alarm you; Americans never injure their friends. We know our Great Chief wished the Americans and Indians to be as brothers. We wish to be so. Will you let us be as brothers, or will you throw us away. I could talk a great deal, but will say no more at this time. The three chiefs that I have sent up to meet you and talk to you, will tell you what is wanted, whatever they say to you, you can believe. In testimony that this is my writing, I sign my name, the second day of February, 1848.

GEO. ABERNETHY
Gov. of Oregon Territory.

Speeches of the Chiefs in Council

CAMASH-PELLO, CAYUSE WAR CHIEF: My people seem to have two hearts. I have but one. My heart is as the Nez Perces. I have had nothing to do with the murderers. Tamsuckie came to me to get my consent to the murder, before it was committed. I refused. I pointed to my sick child, and told him my heart was there, and not on murder. He went back and told his friends he had obtained my consent—it was false. I did not give my consent to the murder, neither will I protect or defend the murderers.

[OLD] JOSEPH, NEZ PERCE CHIEF: *Joseph acted as principal chief in the absence of Ellis, who was with many of the tribe hunting buffalo beyond the Rocky Mountains.*

Now I show my heart. When I left my home I showed my heart. I took the book (a Testament) in my hand and brought it with me—it is my *light.* I heard the Americans were coming to kill me. Still I held my book before me and came on. I am here. I have heard the words of your chief. I speak for all the Cayuses present, and all my people. I do not wish my children engaged in this war, although my brother is wounded. You speak of the murderers. I shall not meddle with them. I bow my head.

JACOB, NEZ PERCE CHIEF: It is the law of this country, that the murderer shall die. This law I keep in my heart, because I believe it is the law of God—the first law. I started to see the Americans, and when on the way, I heard the Americans were coming to kill all the Indians—still I came. I have heard your speech and am thankful. When I left home, I believed the Americans were coming for the murderers only. I thank the Governor for his good talk.

JAMES, NEZ PERCE CHIEF: I have heard your words and my heart is glad. When I first heard of this murder, our white brother Spalding was down here. I heard the Cayuses had killed him also, and my heart was very sad. A few days after, when he returned, I met him as one arisen from the dead. We spoke together. He said he would go to Willamette. I told him to tell the chiefs there, my heart. We have been listening for some word from them. All these chiefs are of one heart.

RED WOLF, NEZ PERCE CHIEF: You speak of Dr. Whitman's body. When I heard of the Doctor's death, I came and called for the murderers. I wished to know if it was the work of the chiefs. I went to Tawhatoe's and found it was not of all, but of the young men. I did not sleep. I went to Mr. Spalding and told him the chiefs were engaged in it. Mr. Spalding said I go to Willamette, and will say the Nez Perces have saved my life, and I go to Willamette and to save yours. We have been listening to hear from the white chiefs.

TIMOTHY, NEZ PERCE CHIEF: (This man repeated each sentence as spoken by the Indians; hence, probably the language: "I am as one in the air.") "You hear these chiefs, they speak for all. I am as one in the air. I do not meddle with these things. The chiefs speak. We are all of their mind."

RICHARD, NEZ PERCE CHIEF: I feel thankful for the kind words of your chief. My people will take no part in this matter. Our hearts cling to that which is good. We do not shed blood. This is the way our old chief (Cut Nose), talked. His last word were: "My children, I leave you—love which is good—be always on the side of right, and you will prosper." His children remember his words. He told us, "take no bad advice." Why should I take bad words from your enemies, and throw your good words away? Your chief's words are good. I thank him for them. My chief in the buffalo country, will be glad to hear I talked thus to you.

He would be sorry should I talk otherwise. This much I tell you of the hearts of my people . . . .

Remarks of Joel Palmer to Peo-peo-mox-mox, Walla Walla Chief and his people

Chief. We are glad to see you, and have an opportunity to talk with you. We have been sent here by the American people to find out who murdered Doctor Whitman, his wife, and the other Americans at Waiilatpu, and ask that justice be done. We are glad to hear that you had no hand in the matter, and that you would not unite the Cayuses. We believe this report, for we heard a long way off by Lieut. [John C.] Fremont, that you and your people had fought with the Americans in California, that you acted bravely, and that your hearts were good toward the Americans. Your conduct since the massacre convinces us that we judged rightly.

We now consider you a great, good chief—your conduct places you far above those around you. These things have been written down, and sent to our Great Chief, that all may know it. You are now getting old, why should you embroil yourself and people in a way with the Americans? You will not do it—you will listen to good. To separate the innocent from the guilty. Must we allow bad men to murder our brothers, and ill treat our women, and not punish them? All good people say no. The Great Master of life, orders that the guilty be punished. It is our duty to do it. It is the duty of every good man to aid in bringing the guilty to punishment. It is this, that brings us here. You express a desire to be with us in council with the Nez Perces, it is our wish that you should be present. For the present, I have nothing more to say.

Remarks of Joel Palmer to the Council

Chiefs and Friends. We are glad to see and hold a talk with you. We now believe that we shall reason like men, and that all the difficulties that exist between the whites and the Indians of this country can be settled without further fighting. With the Nez Perces we are and always have been at peace. I am glad to say we have not seen cause of war, and in this council I hope we shall strengthen the bonds which have heretofore existed between us and the Nez Perces and Walla Wallas. But with the Cayuses this cannot be said. The land of the Cayuses has been stained with the blood of our brothers—the Cayuses have done it. What shall be done? The great God orders that the guilty be punished. Is it not our duty to do it? Is it not the duty of all good men, to aid in punishing these murderers? But, we do not wish to injure the innocent.

We have been long coming. Mr. Newell, Mr. Lee and myself were sent to see, and talk with the chiefs. But when we reached Wascopam we were told that the road was closed, and that the Cayuses had been down and killed two of our men. That they had hired a great many Indians to join them. That if we came we would be killed. We then waited for our war chiefs, we came with him. Many met us on the road and made war. We wished peace, and went in advance of our war chief with a flag to hold a talk, but their young men were surrounding us, and made signs of war. We returned to the wagons with sickened hearts, for we could not prevent the fighting. We sent messengers with letters, telling them that we did not come to make war upon the innocent, it was the guilty that were to be punished. They would not listen to our talk, we were grieved. Some of their men were killed, and others wounded; some of our men were wounded, but none killed. Since then we have seen some of these chiefs; we know not whether they will listen to us; but we must punish these murderers, and all those who unite with them, we shall consider as an enemy.

The Cayuses have forfeited their lands by making war upon the Americans; but we do not want these lands, but we wish to open the road for Americans to travel, as they have done before; and if the Cayuses continue to make war upon us, we shall be compelled to drive them from their lands. We shall build a fort and station a number of men at Waiilatpu.

Our war chief will hunt these murderers as you hunt the deer, until he drives them from the face of the earth. It is no credit to be associated with murderers. Suppose you all were to unite with the Cayuses and kill us off; we are but a handful. Others would come with both hands full and wipe you out. We have not two hearts, not a forked tongue, we speak the truth. The Americans are many, and if the Cayuses were wise, they would listen to us, cease fighting and surrender the guilty, They must also return the property belonging to the mission and the individuals, as well as to Seletza, whom they have robbed, and in every case where the property has been destroyed, or injured, an equivalent must be given; when this is done, we will talk of peace with them. We have submitted to many wrongs whilst traveling to our country, the Willamette. We did not go to war with them, because our chief had told our people not to interrupt the Indians. We are slow to get angry, but when we begin war, we never quit until we conquer. These robbers must pay for the wrongs they have done our people; they need not expect to escape. Our war chief has a good heart, he wished the Indians well, but will punish the bad. We have sent word to our Great Chief of what has been done; we soon expect great ships.

Three years ago, when I was here, I saw many of these people; when I went home I wrote a book[1]; I sent it among our people. I spoke of these people, told them how well you all behaved. That the Nez Perces, Walla Walla, and Cayuses, were all good people, that you listened to good advice. O, how I was astonished when I heard what had been done! I did not believe it, but I see that it is so. I have lied, for I said your people were all good—it is not so, I am ashamed of what I said, but I am glad there are some good people, I esteem you. We must judge your hearts by your acts. I am told the Cayuses say, that Dr. Whitman was poisoning them. They know better, is it not the fate of all to die; do not the Americans die as well as the Indians? Do they charge the other Americans with poisoning them? No, why did they kill them? Because their hearts were bad, they listened to bad counsel. When men's hearts get bad, they are ready to give and take bad counsel. I learn they say they had ordered Dr. Whitman away. Did the chiefs do it in counsel, or did a few bad men wish to drive him off, so that they might get his property, and ill treat our women. If our people do a bad act, we punish them. If my brother commit murder, he is hanged by the neck until he is dead. We are sorry to do it, but the peace and safety of our people demand it. Our great God of heaven commands it and it must be done.

Was not Dr. Whitman doing them all the good he could, were the whites injuring them? How is it, who enabled them to be thus comfortably clothed. How came they to have cows, and cattle for beef, wheat, corn, peas, and potatoes for food; why are all these fields that we see along the streams; for whose benefit are they? Is the Indian's condition so much better than that of the whites that they wish to throw away our counsel. But I hope they will see their errors, will get good hearts and do well hereafter. When chiefs do wrong, what must we expect of the people? But we will not acknowledge these murderers as chiefs; none but good men should be chiefs. The chiefs should govern their people.

Remarks of Robert Newell to the Council

Brothers. I have a few words to say, call together all your men, old and young, women and children. This day I am glad to see you here, we have come to talk with you, and to tell you the duty we owe to our God and all good people. I have not come here to make peace with you, we never have been at war, but always friendly. This I know, this all our people know, I have fought with the Nez Perces, some of them I see here, but we were on the same side; we have lost friends on the same day and at the same battle together. But we did not lose those friends in trying to kill innocent people, but by trying to save our own lives. This I have told our people, our people believe it.

I have told them you are honest and good people, they believed it. Your hands are not red with blood. I am glad, my children are glad.

And now brothers hear me, never go to war with the Americans, if you do, it will be your own fault and you are done. I have come here to see you, the Nez Perces and other good people, no one else. I am not here to fight, but to separate the good from the bad, and to tell you that it is your duty to help make this ground clean. Thank God you have not helped to make it bloody. I was glad to hear the Nez Perces had no hand in killing Dr. Whitman, his wife and others. What have the Cayuses made, what have they lost! Everything, nothing left but a name. All the property they have taken, in a short time will be gone, only one thing left, that is a name, "the bloody Cayuses." They never will lose that, only in this war, obey the great God and keep his laws. And my friends this must be done, if you will obey God and do what is right, we must. This is what our war chief has come for. What is our duty to the Great God? This is his law. He who kills man, by man shall his blood be spilt. This is his law. This is what God says, and he must be obeyed, or we have no peace in the land. There are good people enough here among the murderers to have peace again in the land should they try. In a few days we could go about here as we have done, all friendly, all happy. Will you hear, or will you not. You have heard that we have come here to fight all the Indians, it is not so. The evil spirit has put bad words in the mouths of those murderers and they have told you lies.

My friends, one thing more let me tell you; we have come here because it was our duty. We are sorry to have to come, but the laws of God have been broken on this ground, look at these walls, see how black they are, look at that large grave; He is angry with those people who broke His laws, and spilt innocent blood. How can we have peace. This way my friends and no other. All join together, and with good hearts try to get those murderers and do by them as the great God commands, and by so doing, this land will be purified, and in no other way will we have peace. I am sorry to see people fight like dogs. People who love to kill and murder: they are bad people. We have come here to get those murderers, if good men puts themselves before those bad people, they are just as if they had helped to murder, and we will hold them as such. The most of the Cayuses have gone off, but a few are here, they have left their farms. Why is this, what have they done? Because some of their people have been foolish, all should not turn fools and be wicked. I am sorry, very sorry to see it so. What will they do if they fight us, and fight against our God, and break our laws. I will tell you, they will become poor, no place will they find to hide their heads, no place on this earth nor a place in heaven, but down to hell should they go if God's words are true. I hope you will be advised and take good council before it is too late.

Our war chief has waited a long time for the Cayuses to do what is right, he will wait no longer, and when he begins to fight, I do not know when he will stop. His heart is sore for Dr. Whitman and his wife, that have been slaves to these people, who done all they could to teach them how to work, and how to do all good things, that they might live like the whites and be Christians, but they have joined the evil one and become bad; they have murdered, they must not escape. My friends I am not angry, I am sorry. The other day over yonder where we fought the Cayuses, we saw people coming, I went with a flag, I had no gun, made signs of peace, waved the flag for them not to shoot, but stop and talk, but they would not. I went back sorry, I knew there were some people there who had done us no harm; but those bad people told them lies, and gave them horses to fight us. Bought them live slaves to fight. I knew they came blind, they knew not what they were doing; I wanted to tell them what we had come for but could not. I have done my duty. God knows my heart. If I do wrong, then the great God will punish me, and now I tell you the same as if you were my own children. Do not join with those murderers, not let them come in your country, or in your lodges, or eat with them; but try and bring them to justice.

My friends, I have no more to say to you now. I have come a long way to see you and talk with you, will you throw my words away? I hope not, I beg you to hear my words and be wise. I have brought this flag for the Nez Perces; take it, I hope you will keep clear of blood. Let the Nez Perces assemble and settle among yourselves who will keep the flag. Ellis is not here, and many other chiefs are gone to the buffalo country that I am acquainted with. Mr. Craig will tell you that we are your friends; he loves you; so do we all like him; he has told us many good things of you.

Closing of Report of the Peace Commissioners

After which Messrs. Lee, Gilliam and McKay, all spoke, corroborating in sub-stance what the first two had said. A social conversation then ensued, after which the Superintendent of Indian Affairs told them that Mr. Craig would remain with them for the present, as his agent, and would assist and instruct them in their efforts at agriculture. That as soon as the present difficulty was settled, he would send them a blacksmith, and if they wished it, a school teacher; that after this no other white man should settle upon their lands without their consent. But that those already settled and having families amongst them must be respected both in person and property—and others should be allowed to travel peacefully through their country for the purpose of trade, &c., and they should have the same privilege to travel through our settlements. That if any difficulty occurred between them and the whites, they should make it known to him through Mr. Craig, or otherwise, and he would have it fairly adjusted between them. To all of which they gave a sanction.

Mr. Newell then presented them a large American flag, as a national present, and requested them to preserve it as such—and to hoist it on all national occasions, which they received with evident good will. We also gave them some tobacco to smoke in friendship to the Americans, and we are happy to say the whole affair went off highly satisfactory to all parties. In the evening the Nez Perces gave us a *war dance*, which amused and delighted us much; and we do them the bare justice when we say the performance was well timed, the parts well acted, characters represented to the very life, and the whole *first rate*. We felt gratified with our success in our efforts to prevent a general war with the Indians, in saving the Nez Perces which had been a matter of much anxiety with us; in breaking the ranks of the enemy by calling off their allies; and especially in separating the innocent from the guilty.

On our return, we fell in with Yellow Serpent, who accompanied us to Walla Walla and there spent the evening with us in friendly conversation. He told us that the Walla Walla Indians who had been with the Cayuses, had left them, as most of the other allies had done. We inquired for the Indian who befriended Mr. [Josiah] Osborne and his family and found that he was a brother-in-law to Mr. McBean's interpreter. We expressed our appreciation of such praiseworthy conduct, and our wish to reward him. He was not present however, and the manifestation of our sincerity remains yet to be made, which it is hoped will not be neglected. It was a matter of much regret to us, that neither the Superintendent, nor the Commissioners were able to compensate such and similar services, in a manner becoming *Americans*. The boy whom Seletza sent on his own horse from Wascopam to our camp at the Springs, with dispatches to us, performed that trip of more than 100 miles through a hostile country, entirely alone, and in about twelve hours. A feat that perhaps few men in our regiment would have undertaken. We repeat our regret at not having the means to make them sensible of the estimate we place upon such services. In the absence of any appropriation made by law for the pay of contingent expenses in this department, we could only make them such presents as our private resources would allow.

SOURCE

Brown, John Henry. *Brown's Political History of Oregon: Provisional Government*. Vol. 1. Wiley B. Allen, Publisher; Press of The Lewis & Dryden Printing Co., 1892, pp. 387–97.

RELATED READING

Denny, Gertrude Hall. An Interview With A Survivor of the Whitman Massacre, *Oregon Native Son*, 1(2)[June, 1899]:63–65.

Drury, Clifford Merrill. *Marcus Whitman: Pioneer and Martyr*. Caldwell, ID: The Caxton Press, 1937.

Joseph, Alvin M. *The Nez Perce Indians and the Opening of the Northwest*. New Haven, CT: Yale University Press, 1965. (Reprinted: Boston: Houghton Mifflin, 1997).

Ruby, Robert H., and John A. Brown. *The Cayuse Indians: Imperial Tribesmen of Old Oregon*. Norman, OK: University of Oklahoma Press, 1972.

Stern, Theodore. *Chiefs & Change in the Oregon Country: Indian Relations at Fort Nez Percés, 1818–1855*. 2 vols. Corvallis, OR: Oregon State University Press.

Thompson, Erwin N. *Shallow Grave at Waiilatpu: The Sagers' West*. Portland, OR: Oregon Historical Society, 1969.

Victor, Frances Fuller. *The Early Indian Wars of Oregon Compiled From the Oregon Archives and Other Original Sources and Muster Rolls*. Salem, OR: Frank C. Baker, State Printer, 1894.

NOTE

1. *Journal of Travels Beyond the Rocky Mountains* was published in Cincinnati in 1847. Palmer's volume included word lists in Chinook Jargon and the Nez Perce language. It was intended for use as a guidebook for overland emigrants.

The Indians of Oregon: Customs, Habits and Character, 1848

Overland emigrants carried not only their food, clothing, tools, and personal possessions in their covered wagons; they also brought a heavy load of intellectual baggage. Attitudes toward Native Americans, honed by frontier tales, "captivity narratives" (more than three hundred books had been published by 1850 about "victims" of Indian kidnapping), and racism shaped their perceptions of Oregon Indians.

Riley Root set out on the Oregon Trail in 1848 in a train of thirty wagons. He left Illinois in April, visited St. Louis, and traveled by steamboat to St. Joseph to connect with fellow travelers. Root kept a careful account of his travels, sometimes punctuated by poetic passages. He logged days, miles of travel, and impressions. His intent was to record information so that he might publish a book useful for subsequent emigrants. Working under the maxim of Marcus Aurelius Antonius, "Look beneath the surface, let not the quality of a thing escape thee," Root penned his Journal of Travels from St. Josephs to Oregon With Observations of That Country, Together With a Description of California, Its Agricultural Interests, and a Full Description of Its Gold Mines. *The volume was published in 1850 in Galesburg, Illinois.*

Root arrived on September 13, 1848, in Oregon City, by his calculation a journey of 1,846 miles. Although he had but limited contact with the Indians of Oregon, he did not hesitate to write about their customs, habits, and character. Root's "Indians of Oregon" was representative of the preconceptions held by overland emigrants about the Native Americans. His choice of vocabulary, use of the image of the wily fox, depreciation of the Indian sweat lodge, misrepresentation of the impact of head-flattening, and rejection of the utility of missionary labors accorded with the attitudes of many who settled in the Oregon Territory in the 1840s and the 1850s.

The Indians of Oregon, notwithstanding the exertions that have been made to improve their condition, are still a degraded race of semi-human beings, rapidly approaching to total extinction. Such is the proneness of the human race to indolence and vice, that it requires the whole of a short life to make any considerable advances towards an improvement in his natural or mental condition, even amongst the most favord portions of the human family.

The Indian does not appear to have the most distant conceptions of any moral obligation towards another. He is prompted by tradition more than by a sense of duty, and the more he becomes enlightened, the more he becomes alive to vice.

The fox, taken from its lair in an infantile state, is only reard and shown to the lodgings of the domestic fowl of the barnyard, ere he escapes from the hands of his benefactor, with his prey, to his distant and secret abode, amongst the thicket of the forest. So the Indian. Point him to the comforts and enjoyments of a domestic life, and he looks up°n them with indifference and disdain. Teach him that from the plow is derivd his food, and that in due time time he may reap if he faint not, and yet if he is hungry he will resort to the potato patch of his neighbor and dig them all up so soon as they are planted, leaving his future well-being to the fates.

There is but little confidence reposd in each other respecting the safe-keeping of property, and it is impossible to make an Indian believe that it is morally wrong to steal. The only thing that prevents them from stealing, is the probability of being detected and punished for it, and that Indian is smartest, who is keenest at the business.

At present, the few remaining Indians of Oregon are in a worse condition than before the whites settled amongst them. Formerly, they depended entirely on furs to keep them warm during the inclement season of the year, but now they are partly clad in skins and partly in garments nearly worn out, sold them by the whites for a trifling amount of labor, or such other pay as is agreed upon. With these, they are often amusingly and fantastically dressd. A man is sometimes seen wearing a bonnet, wrong side before. Sometimes a woman is seen wearing a man's shirt, and others, again, are seen wearing a dress, reversed. Sometimes, in the summer season, it would puzzle a Philadelphia lawyer to tell what kind of a dress they do wear, or whether—

At present, there are probably not more than twenty-five Indians, who consider the Willamet valley their home, though others, from the upper country of the Columbia, resort to Oregon city to winter, because they can obtain support during that season more readily, where abundant supplies can be had at all times.

The mode of doctoring, when any prevalent disease is among them, has a tendency rapidly to depreciate their numbers. It is done by heating the system as hot as they can bear, in ovens made for the purpose, along the banks of streams, where the patient is shut in for several minutes, with heated pebbles, until he obtains a thorough sweat. He then rushes to the stream and plunges

In 1847 Paul Kane (1810–71) painted a powerful portrait of four Clackamas men with painted faces and flattened heads. Speakers of an Upper Chinookan dialect, the Clackamas maintained a major fishery at the Willamette Falls (Stark Foundation, 31.78/208, WOP 11).

into the water, which cools the system so suddenly, that hundreds live to try the experiment but a few times.

Another depopulating mode of conduct is practiced amongst some of the tribes, which is that of flattening the head. The opinion that the Great Spirit can better distinguish between the aristocrat and his slave, in another world, has led to the practice of flattening the heads of the aristocracy, and leaving the heads of their slaves natural. This practice is common only amongst some of the tribes of the Western valley. Those Indians of the upper country, nominally Flat Heads, are so only in derision.

The mode of flattening the head, is to take the infant, at the first dawn of its existence, and lash firmly to its back a board, somewhat longer than the child and of suitable width, probably eight or ten inches, for it to lie upon when placd in a prostrate position. Its arms are brought downward to this board, and lashd so firmly that the infant cannot stir them. The board at its back reaches two or three inches above the head, so that the board which serves for flattening the head, being fastened to the top of this, is brought over the head forward to the edge of the brow. To the edges of this are fastened small cords, that are brought back and fastend to the board behind. These cords are drawn so tight that the board on the head forms an acute angle at the top, with the board on its back. In this position the miserable infant is kept more than three months, languishing for want of action. Sometimes, the blood gushes out from the nostrils and ears, from the severe pressure of the board.

But few survive the operation. When the operation is fully accomplishd, the head is flattend from the brow to the top of the head, though sometimes, in after life, it becomes a little raisd at the fontanelle and cross sutures.

An Indian can be taught to pray, and, in fact, they do often pray to their Tyee, or Big Spirit, as they call him, that he will give them a supply of venison and other present supplies—but what may be considerd a change of heart, is entirely foreign to an Indian.

A few years ago, at the station of Mr. Lee, upon the Willamet river, there was a revival of religion, amongst whom were a considerable number of Indians. The whites succeeded in getting them to pray for awhile, but after they had prayd long enough, as they supposd, for a good lot of blankets, they began to call for them. The whites told them that they must not pray in that way. They replied, that they would not pray for them any more, if they would not pay them for what they had done.

The Indians at Dr. Whitman's station, on the Walla Walla river, have manifested, in their conduct towards him, what may truly be considerd traits of Indian character. Like a venomous serpent, that bites the hand that feeds it, so the

Indians of that country, after incessant toil of ten or twelve years, to teach them husbandry and the various comforts of domestic life, stretchd forth their cruel hands, upon the 29th of November, 1847, and murdered himself and family.

I have long been of the opinion, that it is useless to send missionaries to barbarous races of men, for the sake of Christianizing them, or even civilizing them. The only benefit arising from an operation of that kind, is to furnish a foothold for the enterprising white man, who may follow the steps of the missionary, to seek a new home, where he may display his wisdom, in beautifying and improving the face of nature. Whom God has cursd, and whom God has blessd, truly is blessd.

Soon after the massacre of Dr. Whitman, the authorities of Oregon advisd all the missionaries of the upper country to leave their fields of operation, which they did, with the exception of Roman Catholics, who have some localities there.

It is difficult to determine what brought events to such a crisis as that of the death of Dr. Whitman. It is supposd by some, that the Roman Catholics sought an advantage to break up the Protestants at that place, by making the Indians believe that the whites were endeavoring to exterminate them, by introducing disease among them.

On their way to the Western valley of Oregon, some of the emigrants, who were afflicted with the measles, passd through Dr. Whitman's place, and imparted them to the Indians, from which cause, many of them died.

The Indians are great believers in sorcery. They are of the opinion, that the man who has power to cure, has also power to kill, by means of witchcraft. From this belief, has arisen the custom amongst the Indians, of killing their doctors, when any of their patients do not recover.

SOURCE

Root, Riley. *Journal of Travels from St. Josephs to Oregon With Observations of That Country Together With A Description of California, Its Agricultural Interests, and a Full Description of Its Gold Mines.* Biobooks, Oakland, CA, 1955, pp. 58–61.

RELATED READING

Kane, Paul. *Wanderings of an Artist Among the Indians of North America From Canada to Vancouver's Island and Oregon Through the Hudson's Bay Company's Territory and Back Again.* Toronto: The Radisson Society of Canada, Ltd., 1925, pp. 117–43.

Tender Ties: Indian Wives and Fur Trading Husbands, 1850

Hundreds of Native American women in Oregon married fur trappers and traders between 1810 and the mid-1840s. Dozens more found husbands among the Euro-American settlers who arrived via the Oregon Trail. The parish registers of the Catholic missionaries as well as the marriage records in the early county records document the ties that developed as people of different cultures and languages met in the Oregon Country.

Dr. Elijah White, first Indian agent appointed by the United States to serve in Oregon, emigrated overland in 1842 with his commission. During his labors for the Methodist Mission in the Willamette Valley and subsequent travels, White had the opportunity to make many observations on the country and its inhabitants. In the following passage, White described the departure of a Hudson's Bay Company brigade that set out from Fort Vancouver for the Sacramento Valley, known to many as the Valley of the San Bonaventura. The brigades included trappers, Indian wives, children, company employees from Hawaii and Polynesia, and as many as a hundred horses. In this instance Michel LaFramboise (1790–1861?), who had arrived in Oregon in 1811 aboard Astor's Tonquin, *was in charge of the brigade. His wife was probably Emelie Picard, identified at their marriage in 1838 as the "daughter of Andree Picard, a farmer of the Willamette, and a woman, Okanogan of nation, now dead."*

White explained the role of inter-marriage in the functioning of the fur trade and quoted Washington Irving's assessment from Astoria; Or Anecdotes of an Enterprise Beyond the Rocky Mountains *(1836). Jean Baptiste Garnier, head trader at Fort Umpqua, had an Indian wife; so did William McBean, trader at Fort Nez Perces, as did Edouard Crete, director of Hudson's Bay Company bateaux carrying goods and furs up and down the Columbia from Kettle Falls to Fort Vancouver. Other company officials—John McLoughlin, James Douglas, and Peter Skene Ogden—likewise were tied to the country by their marriages to Indian women. James Douglas phrased the connection in a letter at Fort Vancouver in*

March, 1842: "There is indeed no living with comfort in this country until a person has forgot the great world and has his tastes and character formed on the current standard of the stage . . . habit makes it familiar to us, softened as it is by the many tender ties, which find a way to the heart."

They start in the spring for California, carrying with them merchandise and English goods, for barter with the natives, and return, laden with furs, principally of the beaver and otter. This company, just before entering the settlement, which was early in the morning, stopped to remove from their persons stains and traces of travel, and dress themselves carefully in their best attire. They then formed themselves in Indian file, led by Mr. La Fromboy, the chief of the party. Next him rode his wife, a native woman, astride—as is common with the females—upon her pony, quite picturesquely clad. She wore a man's hat, with long black feathers fastened in front, and drooping behind very gracefully. Her short dress was of rich broadcloth, leggins beautifully embroidered with gay beads, and fringed with tiny bells, whose delicate, musical tinkling, could be heard at several hundred yards distance. Next, the clerk and his wife, much in the same manner; and so on to the officers of less importance, and the men; and finally the boys, driving the pack horses, with bales of furs, one hundred and eighty pounds to each animal. The trampling of the fast-walking horses, the silvery tinkling of the small bells, rich, handsome dresses, and fine appearance of the riders, whose number amounted to sixty or seventy. The array was really patriarchal, and had quite an imposing appearance.

It is customary for the members of the party to take unto themselves Indian wives. It is their policy, considered by them necessary to conciliate the good will of the tribes. The officers set the example, and have ever encouraged the men to follow it, each taking to be his wife the daughter of a chief, whose grade corresponded with his own. For instance, Governor McLoughlin, and Mr. James Douglas, holding the highest offices in the company, selected the daughters of the first chiefs of the most important tribes in the country.

The *gentlemen* are at great pains to educate their wives and children, and they often become refined, pleasing, and engaging in their manners. The custom did not, however, originate with the Hudson's Bay Company, for one of the first accounts we have of a marriage of this kind, was that of McDougal, of the Astor Company, with the daughter of the one-eyed chief, Comcomly, "who held sway over the fishing tribe of the Chenooks, and had long supplied the factory with smelts and sturgeons."

The following is a brief relation of the affair from Washington Irving's "Astoria":

Some accounts give rather romantic origin to this affair, tracing it to the stormy night when McDougal, in the course of an exploring expedition, was driven by stress of weather, to seek shelter in the royal abode of Comcomly. Then and there he was first struck with the charms of this piscatory princess, as she exerted herself to entertain her father's guest. The "Journal of Astoria," however, which was kept under his own eye, records this union as a high state alliance, and a great stroke of policy. The factory had to depend in a great measure on the Chenooks for provisions. They were at present friendly, but it was to be feared they would prove otherwise, should they discover the weakness and exigencies of the post, and the intention of abandoning the country. This alliance, therefore, would infallibly rivet Comcomly to the interests of the Astorians, and with him the powerful tribe of the Chenooks. Be this as it may, and it is hard to fathom the real policy of governors and princes, McDougal despatched two of the clerks as embassadors extraordinary, to wait upon the one-eyed chieftain, and make overtures for the hand of his daughter. The Chenooks, though not a very refined nation, have notions that would not disgrace the most refined sticklers for settlement and pin money. The suitor repairs not to the bower of his mistress, but to her father's lodge, and throws down a present at his feet. His wishes are then disclosed by some discreet friend, employed by him for the purpose. If the suitor and his present find favor in the eyes of the father, he breaks the matter to his daughter, and inquires into the state of her inclinations. Should her answer be favorable, the suit is accepted, and the lover has to make further presents to the father, of horses, canoes, and other valuables, according to the beauty and merits of the bride; looking forward to a return in kind whenever they shall go to house keeping. The shrewdness of Comcomly was never exerted more adroitly than on this occasion. He was a great friend of McDougal, and pleased at the idea of having so distinguished a son-in-law; but so favorable an opportunity of benefitting his own fortune was not likely to occur a second time, and he determined to make the most of it. Accordingly, the negotiation was protracted with true diplomatic skill.

Conference after conference was held with the two ambassadors. Comcomly was extravagant in his terms; rating the charms of his daughter at the highest price, and, indeed, she is represented as having the flattest, most aristocratical head in the tribe. At length the preliminaries were all happily adjusted. On the 20th of July, early in the afternoon, a squadron of canoes crossed from the village of the Chenooks, bearing the royal family of Comcomly, and all his court. That worthy sachem landed in princely state, arrayed in a bright blue blanket, with an extra quantity of paint and feathers, attended by a train of half-naked warriors and nobles. A house was in waiting to receive the princess, who was mounted behind one of the clerks, and was thus conveyed, coy but compliant, to the fortress. Here she was received with devout, though decent joy, by her expecting bridegroom. Her bridal adornments it is true, at first caused some little dismay, having painted and adorned herself according to the Chenook toilet; by dint however of copious ablutions, she was freed from all adventitious tint and fragrance, and entered into the nuptial state, the cleanest princess that had ever been known of the somewhat unctuous tribe of Chenooks.

From that time forward, Comcomly was a daily visitor at the fort, and was admitted into the most intimate councils of his son-in-law. He took an interest in every thing that was going forward, but was particularly frequent in his visits to the blacksmith's shop, tasking the labors of the artificer in iron for every kind of weapon and implement suited to the savage state, insomuch that the necessary business of the factory was often postponed to attend to his requisitions. Comcomly was very proud of his son-in-law, till McDougal so traitorously gave to Black, an English commander, the possession of the fort, after which event the old chief would say but little about him, excepting that his daughter thought she had married a great brave, but she was mistaken, for he was nothing but a squaw.

SOURCE

Allen, A. J. *Ten Years in Oregon; Travels and Adventures of Doctor E. White and Lady West of the Rocky Mountains . . . .* Ithaca, N.Y.: Andrus, Gauntlett & Company, Ithaca, NY, 1850, pp. 118–22.

RELATED READING

Maloney, Alice Bay. Fur Brigade to the Bonaventura: John Work's California Expedition of 1832–33 for the Hudson's Bay Company, *California Historical Society Quarterly*, 22(3):193–222, 22(4):323–48; 23(1):19–40, 23(2):123–46.

Nunis, Doyce B., Jr. *The Hudson's Bay Company's First Fur Brigade to the Sacramento Valley: Alexander McLeod's 1829 Hunt.* Sacramento, CA: The Sacramento Book Collectors Club, Sacramento, CA., 1968.

Van Kirk, Sylvia. *Many Tender Ties: Women in Fur Trade Society, 1670–1870.* Norman, OK: University of Oklahoma Press, 1980.

Lifeways of the Cow Creek Band of Umpqua, 1851

In 1851 the family of William H. and Maximilla Riddle arrived in the south Umpqua Valley. Traveling overland, the Riddles had taken the Applegate Trail via northern Nevada and the Klamath Basin. They had crossed the southern Cascades and traveled north through the Rogue River Valley to the south Umpqua. The Riddles selected the open meadows along lower Cow Creek, an idyllic site nestled at the eastern base of the Coast Range, as their new home. It was an environment shaped by centuries of Native American fire ecology, the purposeful burning of the fields in the fall of the year to create open areas and to harvest seeds. The emigrants discovered as soon as they set up camp, however, that these lands belonged to the Miwaleta and Quintiousa bands of Cow Creek Indians. Speaking a Takelman-Kalapuyan language and related by dialect and culture to the Takelmans of the Rogue River Valley, the Cow Creeks were a peaceful people about to confront major assaults on their culture, lands, and lives.

George Riddle (1840–1927) was an eleven-year-old when his parents selected their claim. Riddle developed a cordial relationship and ability to communicate with the Cow Creeks, primarily through the Chinook Jargon, and a clear respect for native lifeways. In his old age, Riddle wrote thirty-three articles for the Riddle Enterprise. *These reminiscences were collected and reprinted as a paperbound booklet,* History of Early Days in Oregon *(1920). Because he lived among the Cow Creeks, Riddle observed both their lifeways and the emerging tensions with pioneer settlement, epidemics, and warfare.*

Riddle's account provides details about the traditional culture of the Indians of the Umpqua Valley not available elsewhere. He described fishing, hunting—especially the use of game drives and snares—and the employment of fires to facilitate the harvest of seeds as well as to keep the countryside open and productive. Although he was a pre-teenager when he encountered Cow Creek culture in its full development, Riddle was a skilled observer in crafting a partial ethnography of his new neighbors.

In a very short time [in October, 1851] our camp was surrounded by Indians who seemed to come from every direction. This caused us no alarm. They came from curiosity—old Indians, squaws, papooses and all came to the number of a hundred or more. They were curious about everything—the children were objects of interest, many of them never having seen a white child. A cook stove was setup and a fire started in it, which excited their wonder and curiosity. One young buck came in contact with the hot stove pipe on his naked shoulder which caused a leap and yell from the buck, but uproarious laughter on the part of the crowd. The Indians, although friendly and good-natured, were crowding so closely about the camp that my mother and sisters were unable to prepare the evening meal, and this situation was becoming embarrassing.

At that time we heard the words "Mi-wa-leta, Mi-wa-leta" and a hush fell upon the crowd as an Indian appeared whose presence and appearance showed that he was one in authority. He was a man between sixty and seventy years old, about six feet tall, of heavy build, with full, round face at least as I remember him, with none of the gnarled features of the moving-picture Indian. The Indians seemed to regard him with reverence, more than fear. My father advanced to meet him, and by signs made him understand that he wanted the Indians to stand back out of the way, which they did, forming a circle around our camp where they seated themselves upon the ground or squatted upon their heels. My mother offered the chief a chair, which he declined, but seated himself upon his blanket on the ground. My father proceeded to tell him by signs that we had come to live there, that he would build a house. Neither of them could speak a word that the other could understand, but they seemed to arrive at a mutual understanding and liking that endured during the lifetime of Mi-wa-leta.

During the sign language conference, an incident occurred which in a way will illustrate the character of Mi-wa-leta, and greatly impressed my mother. A very handsome Indian boy about eleven years old detached himself from the crowd and came near the chief, stretching himself at full length on his stomach near the chief. This boy, I afterwards learned, was a son of Mi-wa-leta's son, who was dead. The old man's hand went out and rested on the boy's head. My mother said she knew from that that he was a good Indian. At the close of the sign interview, my father offered the chief food, which he accepted, giving a portion to the boy. The boy, who was named Sam, and myself were afterwards boon companions, and in a few months had learned the Chinook jargon, Sam learning a great many English words while I learned the native Indian; and through this medium, with Sam and myself at interpreters, a perfect under-

Umpqua Indian

In 1841 Alfred T. Agate (1812–46) sketched an Umpqua Indian holding a musket but wearing a traditional fringed leather outfit and pantaloons. A member of the U.S. Exploring Expedition, Agate passed through the homeland of the Cow Creek Band of Umpqua Tribe (U.S. Navy Historical Center, 98–89–BR).

standing was had between the chief and my father, it being understood that any overt act of the Indians should be referred to the chief but so far as our family was concerned, there never was any trouble of any consequence.

At the time of which I write, Mi-wa-leta was the chief of five bands of Indians, all of whom comprised about two hundred souls, by far the strongest tribe of the Umpqua Valley. They spoke the same language as the Rogue River Indians, or Indians as far south as the Siskiyous. But the Rogue River Indians were the hereditary enemies of the Mi-wa-letas, and they termed all the southern Indians "Shastas."

The bands were divided about as follows, and each band and chief has the name of the locality where they made their home: All the north side of the creek in Cow Creek Valley was Mi-wa-leta's and the Indians numbered about seventy-five. The south side of the creek was Quintiousa, the head man took the same name, and was sometimes called Augunsah, the name of the country of the South Umpqua, east of Canyonville; the Quintiousas were about fifty strong. The Targunsans were about twenty-five. Their head man was called "Little Old Man." And in the Cow Creek country east of Glendale was a band of twenty-five or thirty whose head man was known as "Warta-hoo." In addition to the above there was a band known as the Myrtle Creek Indians, about forty in number but who their chief was I never knew. There were three of the number who were always making trouble. Curley, who was a large powerful, young Indian, and Big Ike, and Little Jim.

All the Indians north of Myrtle Creek spoke a different language and were considered a different people, although they had more or less intercourse.

Over the Myrtle Creek, Targunsaw, Warta-hoo and Quintiousa bands, Mi-wa-leta was the head chief, and although there was often trouble between these bands, they held together against the Shastas and Rogue River Indians.

Sam related to me some of the battles and the mighty deeds of his grandfather, Mi-wa-leta, and at one time the chief showed my father his war dress when I was present. The dress was made of two large elk's skins dressed soft, but left as thick as possible, then laced down the sides so as to hang loose about the body and leave the legs and arms free, the thickest part of the skins were back and front and were impenetrable for arrows. The elk skin armor was ornamented with Indian paints forming figures and designs of which I do not remember the meaning. I do not remember seeing the chief wearing a head dress, but have seen the younger Indians wear head dresses that seemed more for ornament than protection. In war times they wore a single white feather from the tail of the bald or white-headed eagle that was snow white.

Mi-wa-leta's war dress showed evidence that it had been of practical use, being pitted all over where arrow points had struck it, and the chief's arms, face and head showed many scars, which they claimed were made in the wars with the Shastas.

It has always been a question in my mind whether Mi-wa-leta had a genuine friendship for the white man or was wise enough to know the hopelessness of opposition. That he always counseled peace and was able to restrain his people from going to war with the whites, we had ample evidence. In the fall of 1852 there were runners from the Rogue River tribes who came to induce the Cow Creek Indians to join them in a war against the whites, and a great council it was. At this council I witnessed a sample of Indian oratory. When I arrived at the scene the Rogue River Indians had evidently submitted their petition, and Mi-wa-leta was making a reply. The older Indians were seated in a large circle, squaws and Indian boys forming the outer circle. The chief was also seated and talked without gesture in a moderate but oratorical tone. The Rogue River Indians sat in perfect silence, and the elder of Mi-wa-leta's people occasionally gave grunts of assent or approval. I, in company with Indian boys of my age, listened to the chief for some time the day he commenced to talk. I was there on the day following, the chief was still talking, and I was informed by the boys that he continued to talk until he fell asleep. Just what the chief could find to say in such a long talk was explained to me by the Indian boys. It appears that the history and legends are committed to memory and handed down from father to son through their chiefs. In this case the chief was reciting to the delegates the history of their tribal wars and remonstrating with some of his own people who were inclined to listen to the Rogue Rivers and join them in a war on the whites. The counsel of Mi-wa-leta prevailed, and when the Rogue River Indians went on the war path, Mi-wa-leta's Indians encamped near our house and remained at peace.

There were many things happening to irritate the Indians and to threaten the peace. There was a class of white men in the country who acted upon the principal that the Indian had no rights that a white man should respect. In the fall of 1852 a young man, a mere boy, wantonly stabbed an Indian boy, who lingered a few weeks and died. The white boy was hastily gotten out of the country and the Indians conciliated. The settlers' hogs rooted up the Kamas, a bulb upon which the Indians depended largely for food. In settlement of any kind of trouble, there would be a "pow-wow" in which Mi-wa-leta, John Catching and my father would be the mediators. I remember a young Indian, a kind of a runabout among the Indians, broke into the cabin of a settler named Chapin at Round Prairie and stole a lot of clothing. Capt. R. A. Cowles came to Mi-wa-leta's camp and reported the theft. The thief was apprehended with some of the clothing, his arms tied behind a tree, and was given a thorough whipping by the Indians.

Another time an Indian whose home was near Galesville, stole a horse and log chain from a traveler, came through the mountains, hid horse and chain in the timber and showed up in Quentiousa's camp, the white man coming to our house in search of his horse. My father reported the matter to Chief Mi-wa-leta, who immediately sent his young men out, who soon struck the trail and found the horse and chain, the Indian making his escape to his own band.

At this time no treaty had been made with these Indians. General [Joel] Palmer, Superintendent of Indian Affairs for the Territory of Oregon, at the solicitation of the settlers, had paid them a visit and promised to return, but before he did so an epidemic, a kind of slow fever broke out in Mi-wa-leta's camp, and the old chief was among the first to succumb. I well remember my chum, Sam, and several other Indians who came to our house and said the Indians would soon all be gone, that Chief Mi-wa-leta was dead. They lost all hope; in fact they were dying so fast that they were unable to bury their dead, but placed them upon drift wood and burned them.

After the death of the chief, the Indians who were not affected with the fever scattered into the mountains, leaving some of the sick who were unable to follow to shift for themselves. More than half of Mi-wa-leta's band died, and of his immediate family I can now recall but three young Indians that escaped the plague, Jackson, and Jim, sons of the chief, and John, a grandson of the chief. Sam, my chum, contracted the sickness and attempted to follow, but was unable to do so and was left to die alone. When his condition was reported to me I prevailed upon my mother to allow me to bring him to our house, and although my parents were afraid of infection, they allowed me to do so. We gave him the best care we could, but after lingering about two months he died. He was uncomplaining and grateful but seemed to have no hope of recovery. It is said to be characteristic of the Indian that if he makes up his mind that he is going to die that he is pretty sure to do it.

In the fall of 1852 [September 19, 1853] General Joel Palmer made a treaty with the remnants of Mi-wa-leta's band of Indians, establishing a reservation and allowed the Indians to elect their own chief. They chose Quentiousa head chief and his son, Tom, as second chief, thus passing over Jackson, the son of Mi-wa-leta, and hereditary chief, much to the dissatisfaction of the remnant of their band.

When the Rogue River Indians went upon the warpath against the whites in the fall of 1855, the wise counsel of Mi-wa-leta was forgotten and the young chief, Tom, carried his people into the war, joining their hereditary enemies, the Rogue Rivers, against the whites. From this war of 1855 and 1856 there was not a full-grown Indian man who survived. One, a boy, John, a grandson of Chief Mi-wa-leta, is said to have acted as messenger between whites in their preliminary arrangements for a treaty at the close of the war.

The Indians as we found them were dressed in the skins of wild animals, principally in dressed deer skins, in the tanning of which they were experts. Their process in treating skins so that they would remain soft and pliable may be interesting. The brains of the deer was the only thing used. The brains when taken from the deer were mixed with oak tree moss which was formed into balls and hung overhead in their huts to be smoked and dried to be used at any time. The grain and hair of the deer skin was removed with a sharp edge of a split bone after which the skins were soaked in a solution of brains and warm water for twenty-four hours or more. The skins were then wrung out and rubbed until thoroughly dry, then smoked until the yellow color desired was obtained. The smoke also prevented the skins from becoming hard when wet. Furs and deer skins were treated with the hair on in much the same manner.

In relation to what the Indians of this country subsisted upon—how they obtained their food and how they prepared it may be interesting. Nature seems to have furnished the Indians with a great variety of foods such as game fish, Kamas, acorns, seeds of various kinds. The deer was the principal game, which before they had guns, were taken with snares. To capture a deer in this manner they must have ropes and good ones. These were made from a fibre taken from a plant—a kind of flag [iris]—growing in the mountains. From each edge of the long flat leaves of the flag a fine threat of fiber was obtained by the squaws, stripping it with their thumb nails. This was a slow process and would require the labor of one squaw a year to make a rope five-eighths of an inch thick and fifteen feet long, but the rope was a good one and highly prized by the owner. In order to snare a deer miles of brush fences were made across the heads of canyons. The ropes were set at openings where experience had taught the Indians that the deer would likely go. Then a great drive was organized with Indians strung along the sides of the canyon. Those making the drive, with dogs, set up a great racket crying "ahootch, ahootch," and those stationed on the ridges would make the same sound, while their wolf dogs kept up a howling. All the noise was made to direct the deer to where the ropes were located. I never participated in one of these drives, but I have seen their fences and the manner of making the drives was explained to me by the Indian boys. They also set their snare ropes around salt licks and watering places. I remember at one time a great antlered buck came across the field with a rope around his neck with a piece of root on the end. The deer in plunging through the brush at the river's edge entangled the rope and being in swimming water was unable to pull loose. An Indian soon came running on the track and was greatly pleased at the capture of the buck and recovery of his valuable snare rope.

Grouse and waterfowl were also snared by twine made from the same fibre as the ropes.

The Indians had another method of hunting the deer—with bows and arrows—and in order to approach the deer to make the arrows effective they dressed themselves to resemble the deer by covering themselves with a deer skin with the head and neck mounted to look natural, keeping the deer to the windward and going through the motions of a deer feeding. At fifty yards the Indian arrow was as deadly as a bullet.

On our arrival most of the Indians were armed with bows and arrows. The bows were made of yew-wood, the backs covered by the sinews of the deer held by some kind of glue. The bows were about thirty inches long and very elastic. They could be bent until the ends could almost meet. The quiver holding the bow and arrows was made of the whole skin of the otter or fox and swung across the back so that the feather end of the arrow could be reached over the shoulder. They were so expert in reaching the arrows and adjusting to the bow that they could keep an arrow in the air all the time.

The Indians' manner of fishing was more simple than snaring deer. The silver salmon came in such multitudes in the fall runs that they were easily taken at the falls of Cow Creek. Dams of sticks were made across the small channels through the rocks and traps with hazel rods woven together with withes forming a basket about three feet in diameter at the upper or open end which come to a point at the closed or lower end. This trap was fastened in the rapid water in the narrow channel with twisted hazel withes fastened to the poles of the dam. The salmon in great numbers would pass up by the side of the trap and, failing to get above the dam, would be carried back into the open end of the trap and the weight of the water would hold them. The Indians would work two such traps and when the river began to raise in the fall they would take several hundred in a night. When the fall rains came sufficient to raise the river two or three feet the great run of salmon would come day and night. Crowding up under the falls hundreds of them being in sight at one time.

The successful fishing season of the Indians depended upon the raise of the water. When the river raised above a certain stage the salmon passed over the falls to their spawning grounds. Very few of them ever return to the salt water alive. The only salmon returning are those carried by the currents of winter freshets after they become too weak to resist. The salmon takes no food after leaving salt water.

The foregoing may appear to be something of a fish story. Commercial fishing is carried on at the present day to such an extent that few if any salmon reach the upper waters of our river.

Lamprey eels were highly prized by the Indians. They were a scaleless, snake-like fish which would hold to the rocks with their sucker mouth and the Indians would dive in the icy water, seize the eel with both hands and, coming to the top of the water, kill the squirming thing by thrusting its head in their mouth and crushing it with their teeth.

Hunting and fishing was the only work that I ever knew an Indian man to do, especially in providing food. The squaws were the workers. The greatest part of their winter food was the "kamass"—a small onion-shaped bulb about one inch in diameter which were plentiful in the low lands of the valley. In the early morning the squaws would be out in the Kamass field provided with a basket—a cone shaped affair wide open at the top, and swung across the forehead—a manner in which the Indians carried all their burdens and which left both arms free. Each squaw would be armed with a kamass stick made of Indian arrow wood fashioned to a point at one end by burning and rubbing the charred wood off leaving the point as hard as steel. At the top end was fitted a curved handle, generally a piece of deer horn. Locating the bulb by the seed top above ground they would insert the stick under the root with the weight of the body, prying up the kamass, which they would deftly throw over the shoulder into the basket. In this manner if the expert squaw worked all day she could bring home about one bushel. If she was the mother of a papoose she carried it along strapped on a board.

The kamass was cooked by excavating a pit, filling it with wood, with rocks on top. After the rocks were sufficiently heated they were covered with dry grass and then a great lot of kamass, covering them up with earth for several days; when they came out they would be of a reddish-brown color and were sweet and really good to eat.

The "soap tart," a large bulb with layers of coarse fibre all through, was treated in the same manner as the kamass, but was poor food.

The white acorn was used as food, but I do not think relished, and perhaps only used to appease hunger. The acorns were pounded in a mortar, the hulls separated and meat pounded into a meal. It was then spread out on clean sand and water poured over to take out the bitter taste. It was then boiled in a mush or porridge. Some of my readers may wonder how the Indians would boil food when they had neither pot nor kettle made of metal, yet they did boil much of their food.

They had vessels or baskets made of hazel twigs closely woven and lined with a blue clay, making them watertight. The boiling was by dropping hot rocks in the water. The squaws were experts at picking the heated rock from the fires, blowing the ashes from it and dropping it into the mush pot. The cooled rocks were renewed with hot ones until the mess was cooked.

During the summer months the squaws would gather various kinds of seeds of which the tar weed seed was the most prized. The tar weed was a plant about thirty inches high and was very abundant on the bench lands of the valley, and was a great nuisance at maturity. It would be covered with globules of clear tarry substance that would coat the head and legs of stock as if they had been coated with tar. When the seeds were ripe the country was burned off. This left the plant standing with the tar burned off and the seeds left in the pods. Immediately after the fire there would be an army of squaws armed with an implement made of twigs shaped like a tennis racket with their basket swung in front they would beat the seeds from the pods into the basket. This seed gathering would only last a few days and every squaw in the tribe seemed to be doing her level best to make all the noise she could, beating her racket against the top of her basket. All seeds were ground into meal with a mortar and pestle. The mortar was made by forming a hollow in the face of flat boulders, over which was placed a basket with a hold in the bottom to fit the depression of the rock, making a kind of hopper to hold the seeds, then with a stone fashioned about two inches in diameter at its lower end and tapered at the other end to a size easily grasped with the hand the operator would sit upon the ground with the mortar between her knees and would pound the seeds, using the pestle which was usually about ten inches long, and weighing five or six pounds, with one hand and stirring the seeds with the other, often changing hands, using right or left for pounding or stirring the seeds with equal skill.

For the Indian to fashion one of these pestles must have required time and patience. They were formed as round, straight and true as if they had been turned in a lathe.

SOURCE

Riddle, George W. *Early Days in Oregon: A History of the Riddle Valley.* Riddle, OR: Riddle Parent Teachers Association, 1953.

RELATED READING

Beckham, Stephen Dow. *Land of the Umpqua: A History of Douglas County, Oregon.* Roseburg, OR: Douglas County Commissioners, 1986.

Chandler, Stephen L. *Cow Creek Valley: From Mi-wa-leta to New Odessa.* Drain, OR: Drain *Enterprise*, 1981.

Cornutt, John M. *Cow Creek Memories: Riddle Pioneers Remembered in John M. Cornutt's Autobiography.* Eugene, OR: Industrial Publishing Company, 1971.

Two

Treaties and Warfare

A Clackamas Indian lodge, fish-drying rack, and canoe prow appeared in the foreground of Eugéne de Girardin's (1822–88) sketch of Oregon City and Willamette Falls, ca. 1854. For millenia this site was a major Indian fishery and trading location (Oregon Historical Society).

Several factors stimulated the flood of settlers into the Oregon Territory in the mid-nineteenth century. Lewis Linn and Thomas Hart Benton, senators from Missouri, had for several years urged the Congress to give "donation" lands to those who emigrated to Oregon and helped tip the tenure of the region to the United States. In 1850 the Congress granted a donation claim of 320 acres per person or a square mile for a married couple. Several thousand settlers, including avid land speculators and those who had been unable to sell out for a profit in "the states" because of economic conditions following the Panic of 1837, viewed free land in Oregon as a good reason for moving. Thousands had seized the opportunity by 1855, the year the amended law expired.

Other factors fostered interest in the Oregon Country. Reports by explorers, fur trappers, and travelers painted a favorable view of a land with open meadows, temperate climate, fine stands of timber, abundant fish, and navigable harbors. The reports of Meriwether Lewis, William Clark, John C. Frémont, Lieutenant Charles Wilkes, William Slacum, and Lieutenant Neil Howison— explorers sent to the region by the federal government—confirmed the promise of Oregon. Several years of flooding and recurring malaria fevers among those living in the bottomlands along the Ohio, Mississippi, and Missouri rivers were further reason to think about starting over in the Willamette Valley.[1]

Adventure beckoned to the young. Emigrant guidebooks painted a favorable picture of Oregon and its resources. The guides laid out routes, distances, conditions, seasons of travel, and suggested appropriate supplies. Some even provided handy phrases or vocabularies for communicating with natives along the trail.

The Indians of the Oregon Country were not consulted in the matter of their dispossession until thousands of pioneers had staked claims and driven them from their villages and fisheries. By 1855 7,437 settlers had filed on 2.5 million acres of Donation Land Claims in the Oregon Territory. These claims were recorded prior to the ratification of treaties with the tribes.[2]

The discovery of gold in the Sierras of California in January 1848 became another factor. The gold rush spread. By 1851 thousands of miners had poured into the Klamath River watershed of northwestern California. They carried with them negative attitudes about Indians and a will to exploit nature at any cost. Mining spread into southwestern Oregon in 1852 and 1853. It exacerbated the difficult problem of dispossession already begun by the Donation Land Act. A rough generation of men bent on finding quick wealth, many of them living recklessly with addictions to alcohol, brawling, and massacring Indians, poured into the territory. The stage was set for the Rogue River Indian Wars of 1852-56.

Part of the problem for Oregon Indians lay in the attitude and actions of the miners and settlers. Another factor was the incomplete carrying out of federal policy. The numbers of federal personnel, their lack of conviction to assert trust responsibility—a matter buttressed by the Supreme Court decision in *Cherokee Nation v. Georgia* (1832)—and the complexity of coming to terms with the tribes contributed to the difficulties.

Other parts of the problems lay in the ecological disruption of the means of native subsistence. Mining released torrents of mud that buried spawning gravels; fishing became increasingly difficult. Settlers constructed log cabins and split-rail fences, in this era prior to the invention of barbed wire. The newcomers also ordered the Indians to stop setting fire to the countryside to harvest tarweed and other seeds. The settlers used firearms to kill deer and elk; their hogs ate the acorns; their cattle and horses cropped off the camas bulbs and their plows turned under the meadows that had once produced life-sustaining foodstuffs for the native people. Starvation stalked the people who had once lived abundantly in a land whose resources they had used so well.

The following selections speak to the times of trial and tribulation besetting the Oregon Indians by the mid-1800s. They were subjected to starvation, dislocation, capricious treatment at the hands of self-styled protectors of "civilization," and massacre. They participated in treaty councils, only to find no action on the agreements except the taking of their lands. They endured assaults from "volunteers" who organized into companies and provoked warfare, then billed the federal government for their "services rendered."[3]

In some instances the Indians fought back, but their resistance was thwarted, in part, when on January 16, 1854, the territorial legislature prohibited the sale to them of weapons and ammunition.[4] Their champions were few. John Beeson and Frederick M. Smith dared to voice public condemnation of the murders of their Indian neighbors. Both had to flee Oregon in fear for their lives as a consequence of having spoken on a matter of conscience.

The federal government made several mis-steps in establishing a consistent Indian policy in the Pacific Northwest. After the Oregon Treaty (June 15, 1846), Congress took no action to set up a territorial government, station the U.S. Army at posts in the region, or name officials to handle Indian affairs. The murders at the Whitman Mission in November 1847 pressured Congress to pass the Organic Act (August 14, 1848). Section 14 of the law extended the provisions of the Northwest Ordinance (July 13, 1787) to the Pacific Northwest and set the stage for the delivery of federal services.

The mis-steps continued, however. Congress created the Willamette Valley Treaty Commission in 1850 and it began its work to secure treaties of land cession in the Willamette Valley in 1851, only to have its powers revoked. The Senate ignored the treaties the commission forwarded to Washington, D.C. Congress then gave treaty-making powers to Anson Dart, Superintendent of Indian Affairs. Dart negotiated six treaties with Oregon tribes at the Tansy Point Treaty Council at the mouth of the Columbia River in August 1851, and two additional treaties at Port Orford in September of the same year. Because Dart provided for reservations within the old tribal homelands and did not require removal to east of the Cascade Mountains, Congress also ignored all of the agreements he forwarded to Washington, D.C.[5]

The treaties proceeded under the assurances of the Organic Act, which created the Oregon Territory (1848) and Washington Territory (1853). This enabling legislation not only set up territorial governments, it extended provisions of the Ordinance of 1787 to the Pacific Northwest. Embedded in that ordinance was the philosophy of dealing with the Indian tribes in "utmost good faith." The federal government promised in each territory to acknowledge aboriginal land title, not to invade the tribes unless in "just and lawful wars declared by Congress," and from time to pass laws to prevent injustices being done to them.

But, many times, after the treaties were signed, nothing happened to sustain their promises. Only dispossession, death, and destruction continued.

The years following the Organic Act of 1848 were a nightmare for the Indians of Oregon. New diseases such as measles and tuberculosis took a heavy toll. The spread of venereal disease robbed countless adults of the ability to have children. Fevers broke out and swept through villages. The traditional means of curing by calling on a shaman or going to the sweat lodge did not stop the illnesses and deaths. Some bands and tribes vanished entirely. Many were reduced in population by 70 percent or more in a matter of a few years.[6]

For the native peoples the treaty councils, ceremonies, speeches, and promises of schools, sawmills, grist mills, and reservations with staff to assist them in coming to terms with cultural change must have seemed both alluring and confusing. The councils were staged with troops, flags, barbeques, and speeches. Communication, however, was woefully inadequate because of the poor quality of interpretation, the use of the Chinook Jargon as a means of common communication, and the subtly of such concepts as "vested title" and cession of lands.

Nowhere did the federal government act with the level of commitment and personnel necessary to bring the situation under control and mete out a humanitarian program consonant with the goals of federal policy articulated in the "utmost good faith" assurances of the Northwest Ordinance. The military presence was minuscule. During the worst years of conflict in southwestern Oregon, the army had only token forces stationed at Fort Orford on the coast, Fort Lane in the Rogue River Valley, and Fort Jones in the mining districts in the upper Klamath region of northwestern California. When the soldiers did act, they were usually compelled to go into the field to try to quell the troubles fomented by the volunteers. Their role was more to defend the Indians than to enforce standards of good conduct and the federal commitment in a frontier region.

The Indian agents and sub-agents were few in number and lacked support staff. They had desperate need for the military and federal courts to support them; this support seldom, if ever, happened. They had major problems in communication with the tribes, lacking interpreters and linguistic skills to deal effectively with problem-solving. Some of the agents—such as Benjamin Wright of Port Orford—were miscreants who had murdered and mutilated Indian victims only to secure appointment to federal office. Others, such as Samuel Culver, Indian agent in the Rogue River Valley, were self-seeking plunderers who tried to benefit financially from their appointments rather than meeting the needs of the Indians in their district. The information they had about the tribes was incomplete. In several instances the government negotiated treaties not knowing the extent of tribal territories, population, or needs.

The following accounts—several of them recording the words of Indian leaders—speak to times of turmoil. The world of Oregon Indians was coming undone. Few of the newcomers seemed to care. These were terrible times.

NOTES

1. John D. Unruh, Jr. *The Plains Across: The Overland Emigrations and the Trans-Mississippi West, 1840–60*. Urbana, IL.: University of Illinois Press, 1979, pp. 42–46.

2. Dorothy O. Johansen, The Roll of Land Laws in the Settlement of Oregon, *Genealogical Material in Oregon Donation Land Claims*, Vol. 1. Portland, OR.: Genealogical Forum of Portland, OR., 1957, pp. iii–viii.

3. Stephen Dow Beckham, History of Western Oregon Since 1846. *Handbook of North American Indians. Vol. 7, Northwest Coast*, Wayne Suttles, ed. Washington, D.C.: Smithsonian Institution, 1990, pp. 180–88.

4. *Statues of Oregon, Enacted and Continued in Force by the Legislative Assembly at the Session Commencing 5th December 1853*. Salem, OR.: Asahel Bush, Public Printer, 1854, p. 257.

5. Beckham, History of Western Oregon, p. 181.

6. Robert Boyd, *The Coming of the Spirit of Pestilence: Introduced Infectious Diseases and Population Decline Among Northwest Coast Indians, 1774–1874*. Seattle, WA.: University of Washington Press, 1999, pp. 231–61.

Peter Umpqua, Veteran of the Mexican War

Indian men from the Warm Springs and Umatilla reservations served as scouts for the U.S. Army in the Modoc and Bannock Indian wars of the 1870s. Peter Umpqua, who served in the Mexican War, however, was probably the first Oregon Native American to become a veteran of a military conflict on the side of the United States.

Umpqua, a resident of the Umpqua Valley in southwestern Oregon, served in 1846 in the California theater of operations of the Mexican War. Aware of his service, Indian Agent John B. McLane, Capt. H. S. Maloney of McMinnville, and C. H. Burch, his companion in arms in California, helped Umpqua secure his pension at the turn of the twentieth century—a scant $8.00 per month. In the following letter, C. H. Burch justified the award of the pension to the aged Indian veteran.

Umpqua also served on the side of the United States in the Rogue River Indian Wars and assisted government agents in the removal of the Indians of southwestern Oregon to the Grand Ronde Reservation. Umpqua and his wife Maria, also of the Umpqua tribe, resided with their children on the reservation on the South Yamhill River. Father Adrian Croquet entered the baptisms of their daughters in his missionary registers in the 1860s.

Umpqua Peter, bearer, has called on me with a note from Hon. S. C. Black, addressed to you, in which it says that his (Peter's) name is not borne on the rolls of Captain Ford, or on any of the companies of [John] Fremont's battalion. This would seem to settle the matter. But in justice to Peter, and at his request, I submit the following statements of facts: Mr. Andrew Baker and myself were members of Cameron's company en route for California in 1846; and when at South Umpqua. I think about the 1st of June, Peter, then a wild savage, with others of his tribe came into our camp, and on our march next morning he (Peter) and ten others joined our company and went through to California with us (our company was made up of Americans, Canadian-French and half-breeds.) Shortly after our arrival in California Baker and myself enlisted in the service, and in October, 1846, when we took up our line of march under Fremont, going south, I there found Peter with the command: he remained with us on our march and until the troops were discharged at San Gabriel, Cal. But I do not know as to whether he was enlisted or not, or, if so, whether he was honorably discharged. Besides Peter there were other Indians, probably a dozen Walla Wallas and two Delawares, whom I saw marshaled in battle array, and know that they were there for other purposes than sightseeing or their health; and I presume Peter was similarly circumstanced. I have known Peter since the date, to wit, 1846. Sir, Peter desires that you embody this statement in a letter to the honorable commission, and if such testimony as herein indicated will be of avail, then he will move in the matter; otherwise it would be useless. Trusting that you will do the friendly office of writing to the honorable commission, I subscribe myself, ever,

Your friend,
C. H. BURCH.

SOURCE
Rogers, Thomas Hesperian A Native Son, *Oregon Native Son*, 1(4)[August, 1899]: 195–96.

"To the Gallows," Trial and Punishment of the Cayuse, 1850

The deaths of Marcus and Narcissa Whitman and others at their mission station on the Walla Walla River in November 1847 plunged the Pacific Northwest into the Cayuse Indian War. Armed companies of volunteers tracked down, apprehended, and brought to trial those Indians believed to have perpetrated the "massacre." Historians for decades termed the event a massacre. More recent assessment, however, has examined the causes and resulted in a more neutral term, incident. The volunteer soldiers of 1847–48 interpreted the affair as a massacre. Eventually they delivered five men to the jail in Oregon City where slowly the "wheels of justice" began turning.

The accused murderers faced trial in the Oregon Territory in May 1850. "The trial was the Oregon frontier's first attempt to formalize and record judicial proceedings concerning an event of deep and abiding significance to the people of that time," observed legal historian Ronald Lansing. "It was a trial that today gives us some insight into the difficult beginnings of formal law, the opening struggles of a new judiciary, and the confrontation of civilizations in a place of wildness." The trial moved speedily toward a verdict of guilty with summary carrying out of the death sentences of those charged.

The following is the newspaper coverage from the Oregon Spectator *(Oregon City) of May 30, 1850, the week of the trial. Perhaps a thousand or more people gathered on Monday, June 3, to observe the executions at a gallows erected on the east bank of the Willamette River on Main Street. Sheriff Joseph Meek, whose daughter had died at Waiilatpu, carried out the executions. The* Oregon Spectator *noted: "The five Indians, whose trial and condemnation we recorded in our last paper, were hung on the 3d inst., according to the sentence of the court. The execution was witnessed by a large concourse of people. . . . This closes another act in the sad and terrible tragedy."*

Knowing that the public mind is deeply and universally interested in this trial we give below, a minute and careful report, which we prepared ourself, expressly for the Spectator. If we do not always express ourself with legal precision, our legal friends will kindly keep in mind that we are wholly unused to legal proceedings. Our report, as to the facts of it, may be relied on as minute and faithful. And we here tender our respectful acknowledgements to Judge [Orville C.] Pratt for his kindness in permitting us to occupy a seat within the bar, for the purpose of taking down the proceedings of Court.

District Court of the U.S., Clackamas Co., Oregon T'y. His Honor,
Judge Pratt, presiding.

May 21, 1850.

The Grand Jury came into court with an indictment against TELOKITE, TOMAHAS, (or THE MURDERER,) CLOKOMAS, ISIAASHELUCKAS, and KIAMASUMKIN.

The Indians thus indicted were brought into Court, and the indictment was read in their hearing; and its contents made known to them by two interpreters, appointed for that purpose. The Court assigned K. PRITCHETT, Esq., ROB'T B. REYNOLDS, ESQ., and THOMAS CLAIBORNE, Esq., as Counsel for the Indians.

AMORY HOLBROOK, Esq. District Attorney of the U.S., on behalf of the people.

The Court directed the Clerk to furnish the Indians, through their Counsel, with a copy of the indictment, and the witnesses names endorsed thereof, together with a list of the Petit Jury. Also, the Court ordered that they have said copies two days before they be required to plead.

Court adjourned till 9 o'clock, to-morrow morning.

Wednesday, May 22

9 o'clock, A.M. Court convened. The Counsel in behalf of the Indians appeared, and filed a "plea in bar of jurisdiction," which was verified by the affidavit of Counsel.

The District Attorney made his replication to the foregoing plea in form.

The substance of this plea was that at the time of the massacre the Laws of the United States had not been extended over the Territory of Oregon.

The replication to the plea set forth that all the territory West of the Mississippi, was by the Act of 1841 [actually, 1834], embraced within and declared to be Indian Territory; and as such, subject to the laws regulating intercourse with the Indians; and the Act of 1848, creating a Territorial Government for Oregon, gives jurisdiction to this Court to take cognisance of the offence.

His Hon. the Judge, gave a labored and very lucid opinion on the whole matter; and ordered the plea to be over-ruled.

The Counsel for the Indians entered their exceptions to this decision.

The Court demanded of the defendants what further they had to plead. They then made the general issue and plead "Not Guilty."

A petition was then presented to the Court asking a change of venue to Clark county, on the ground of public excitement in this county. This petition was verified by the affidavit of the Counsel for the Indians. Court over-ruled the application.

Two new indictments were here handed in against the same persons, one for the murder of Mrs. [Narcissa] Whitman, and the other for the murder of Mr.[L. W.] Saunders; and the same proceedings were had and orders issued as in the case of the other bill.

Court adjourned till 9 o'clock, to-morrow morning.

Thursday, May 23.

9 o'clock, A.M. Court convened. Prisoners at the Bar. Counsel for the Indians asked a continuance of the cause. An affidavit was filed, which being deemed insufficient, it was denied by the Court.

The Jury was then impanneled and sworn; twenty persons having been *peremptorily challenged* by the Counsel for the Indians, and two by the District Attorney.

The District Attorney then opened the prosecution with a brief review of the matters in the indictment.

Witnesses were called singly into Court and examined. (We will attempt merely in this place a statement of the most material points to which witnesses testified.)

MRS. ELIZA HALL——being sworn, stated that she was residing at Dr. Whitman's at the time of the massacre, (Nov. 27, 1847). Hearing the report of many guns, she went to the door of the Mansion house, and saw Telokite strike Dr. Whitman three times with a hatchet,—the blows falling on and about the Dr.'s face. They were in the backyard, about six feet from the door. The two houses were about one hundred yards apart and witness saw and recognized Telokite distinctly. Had resided there three months.

MISS ELIZABETH SAGER—being sworn, testified that she was residing with Dr. Whitman on the 27th of Nov., 1847, and was then about ten years of age. Saw Dr. Whitman while his wound was being dressed by Mrs. Hall and Mrs. Whitman and at the same time Mrs. W. was shot. Saw Dr. W. next morning, dead. Saw Isiaasheluckas attack and shoot Mr. Saunders, and saw Mr. S. fall where his dead body was found next morning. Saw Clokamas next day with a gun which he pointed at her sister, perhaps jocosely. Had lived at Dr. W.'s four years. There were many sick and dying.—Dr. W. gave medicine to the Indians.

MRS. LORINDA CHAPMAN—being sworn, testified that being at Dr. Whitman's on the 27th Nov., 1847, she was in bed sick above stairs. Heard loud and angry talking in the kitchen and recognized the speaker's voice distinctly as that of Telokite.—Knew his voice from hearing him rehearse for Dr. Whitman. Heard guns and confusion and went down stairs, and there saw Dr. W. wounded by a cut across the face. Started, in company with Mr. Rogers and Mrs. Whitman, to go to the Mansion House and at the kitchen door Mr. R. and Mrs. W. were killed. Could not stir with alarm. While standing there, saw the four prisoners at the Bar, armed—recollects them distinctly: did not see Telokite. Dr. Whitman was alive when she left. Saw the Indians rolling his dead body about next morning. There were many sick and Dr. W. gave medicine.

MR. JOSIAH OSBORN—being sworn, testified that he was at Waiilatpu on Nov. 27, 1847, was sick in Dr. W.'s house. Heard guns and went to the door and saw Mr. [Nathan L.] Kimble running and wounded, retreated inside and through the window saw Tomahas pursuing Mr. Saunders. While under the floor with his family heard murder going on. Dr. Whitman gave the same medicine to both Indians and Whites. Know Dr. W. was a white American citizen. Mansion House door was three feet high from the ground. The Indians knew that the Whites died as well as themselves. Dr. W. was anxious as to his safety, and spoke of it particularly in 1845. Does not know whether the Dr. anticipated immediate danger.

The District Attorney here said that he would call no more witnesses except to rebut testimony in the defence.

Testimony for the defence being called, *Dr. John McLaughlin*—being sworn, testified that he had warned Dr. Whitman of danger in 1840 and 1841, as the Indians did kill their own medicine men.

STICKAS—(a Cayuse Indian) called, and through two interpreters testified that Dr. W. left his lodge on the Utilla the day before the Massacre to go home, and after the Dr. was on his horse he told him to be careful for the bad Indians would kill him. The Dr. thanked him and left. Tomsuckee told Stickas they were going to kill Dr. W.

REV. HENRY H. SPAULDING—was sworn, and testified that he was at Stickas' lodge with Dr. W. and had similar warnings and the next day after the massacre became so fearful that he determined to go home to the Nes Perces country.

Here the testimony closed, and the District Attorney gave a brief summary of the evidence to the Jury.

Maj. R. B. Reynolds opened the defence in an address, the delivery of which occupied some 45 minutes.

Capt. T. Claiborne next addressed the Jury for one hour and thirty-seven minutes.

K. Prichette, Esq., closed the defence in an appropriate concluding appeal of some fifteen minutes' length.

The District Attorney then closed the prosecution in a neat, condensed, and forcible presentation of the whole subject. This address occupied twenty-five minutes.

Court adjourned till 9 o'clock, to-morrow morning.

Friday, May 24.

Court convened. Prisoners at the Bar, and the Jury in their place.

His Honor the Judge then gave his Charge to the Jury. The Charge was full, clear, and satisfactory, both in reference to the law and the testimony; and its delivery occupied one hour and ten minutes.

Jury retired and after an absence of one hour and fifteen minutes, returned a verdict against the prisoners—that they were guilty as charged.

Counsel for the Indians moved the Court in arrest of judgment—which was overruled.

A new trial was then moved for. Which was also overruled.

Court took a recess till 4 o'clock, P.M., at which time, having again convened, His Honor the Judge pronounced the final sentence of the law on the prisoners; and adjudged that they be hung on Monday, the 3d day of June, at the hour of 2 o'clock, P.M.

SENTENCE

You, *Telokite, Tomahas, Clokomas, Isiaasheluckas* and *Kiamasumkin*, having been duly convicted by the finding and verdict of the Jury, of the crime of wilful murder as alledged in the indictment, are therefore each adjudged to suffer death by hanging, and you and each of you are ordered and adjudged to be taken from hence to a place of security and confinement, and there kept until Monday the 3d day of June, A.D. 1850, and on that day at the hour of two o'clock in the afternoon, be taken by the Marshal of the District of Oregon, to the gallows or place of execution to be erected in Oregon City, and there by him be hung by the neck, until you are dead.

And may God in His Infinite Grace have mercy on your souls.

SOURCE

Oregon Spectator (Oregon City, OT.), May 30, 1850.

RELATED READING

Drury, Clifford Merrill. *Marcus and Narcissa Whitman and the Opening of Old Oregon.* 2 vols. Glendale, CA: Arthur H. Clark Company, 1973.

Jessett, Thomas E. *The Indian Side of the Whitman Massacre.* Fairfield, WA: Ye Galleon Press, 1971.

Lansing, Ronald B. *Juggernaut: The Whitman Massacre Trial, 1850.* Pasadena, CA: Ninth Judicial Circuit Historical Society, 1993.

Victor, Frances Fuller. *The Early Indian Wars of Oregon Compiled from the Oregon Archives and Other Original Sources With Muster Rolls.* Salem, OR: Frank C. Baker, State Printer, 1894.

"We Do Not Want Any Other Piece of Land," 1851

The resolve of the leaders of the Santiam Indians resounded loudly in their treaty council of April 11–12, 1851, at Champoeg. "We don't wish to remove," said Al-que-ma. "We wished to reserve the North half of all the land in the forks of the Santiam, but we agree only to reserve this," observed Ti-a-can. "Now you wish us to give up part of it. We want to keep it!" The minutes of the council document the resolute determination of the Indians of the Willamette Valley to remain in their traditional homeland in spite of the spread of Euro-American settlement and their wholesale dispossession.

The pressure was on. Thousands of pioneers, anticipating the Oregon Donation Land Act of 1850, had already filed provisional land claims. Belatedly Congress on June 5, 1850, created the Willamette Valley Treaty Commission. The president appointed John P. Gaines, former Oregon territorial governor; Col. Beverly S. Allen of Tennessee; and Alonzo A. Skinner, an Indian agent, to the commission. Their mission was to secure cession of the Willamette Valley to the United States and the removal of all the Kalapuyans and Molallans to east of the Cascade Mountains. The commissioners seemed oblivious to the tenure of the Wasco, Tenino, and Northern Paiute on the Columbia Plateau to the east. They failed to perceive, or thought it unimportant, that that region was an environment markedly different from the homeland of the Indians west of the mountains.

The commissioners hired George Gibbs, a graduate of Harvard and its law school, as commissary and secretary. Gibbs was preparing an alphabetical vocabulary of the Chinook language and a dictionary of the Chinook Jargon, both eventually published in 1863. Robert Newell, a former fur trapper and resident of Champoeg, served as interpreter. The Commission named Josiah L. Parrish, once an employee of the Methodist mission, to summon the Indians of the valley to Champoeg. Gaines, Allen, and Skinner opened dialog with Ti-a-can, Al-que-ma, and Sophan of the Santiam Band. The territory ultimately ceded reached from Champoeg and Aurora south along the eastern side of the Willamette River to the vicinity of Brownsville. It included the valley from the base of the western

Cascades to the Willamette and embraced the drainages of the Pudding, Santiam, and Calapooia rivers.

The following are the minutes of the Santiam treaty council. In spite of the promises made and the expenditure of nearly $20,000 to secure the agreements, Congress had revoked the treaty-making powers of the Commission before it held its first session. Not realizing they acted without authority, the commissioners negotiated, argued, and forwarded five treaties to Washington, D.C. Although there was widespread settlement and taking of the lands of the Kalapuyans by 1851, the Senate ignored the proposed treaties. Not until January 4, 1855, did Joel Palmer secure a treaty with the Santiam and other bands of Kalapuyans, Mollalans, and Chinookans in the watershed of the Willamette River; that treaty finally obtained Senate ratification and became binding.

The following text omits some of the over-punctuation in the original. It inserts quotation marks where verbatim comments were recorded by George Gibbs, the secretary.

Saturday morning [April 11, 1851] 11 o'clock, the Board met in council with the Santiam Band of the Kallapooya Tribe of Indians (the chiefs and the principal men having been assembled). They were introduced to the Commissioners by the Interpreter, Dr. [Robert] Newell. Gov. [John] Gaines, then, on the part of the Commissioners, proceeded to deliver the following speech.

"Brothers, I am happy to assure you of the pleasure, with which we meet you today, to tell you of the kindness of the heart of our Great Father, the President, toward you, and all our red Brothers in Oregon. We express the hope, that, you will be found ready, at all times, to prove your own good intentions, and friendly feelings toward the Gr[ea]t Father, and his white children.

"Your Gr[ea]t Father, the President, has sent us among you, in order to show his love and care for you; and to treat with you for your lands, which, you kindly allowed his white children to live upon and cultivate for many years. Circumstances beyond his control have made it impossible for him to send us sooner, which the feelings of his heart would have prompted him to have done, if not so prevented. Now, however, we have come to you, that it is the will of the G[rea]t Father and our wish to see you honestly and fairly dealt with; that you shall receive all that you are entitled to receive; and if you come today, as we hope you do, equally desirous of doing right, we have no doubt our present council will be equally pleasant and profitable to you, our Gr[ea]t Father, and his white children.

"If you have no regularly acknowledged chief or chiefs, we desire you will get together at once, and select such, who, for their honesty and good sense, you can rely upon to meet us in council and talk with us upon the subject of selling your lands to the Gr[ea]t Father."

It was, then, interpreted to the Tribe. Thereupon they acknowledged Ti-a-can alias Louis, their principal chief and Alquema, alias Joseph, and Sophan their Subordinate chiefs.

The three chiefs desired then some time to confer among themselves and the council adjourned until 3 o'clock P.M.

3 o'clock P.M. Council met persuant to adjournment. Ti-a-can said they were much pleased with the speech that had been delivered to them, that they were friendly to the whites and had always been and that they were willing to do as their G[rea]t Father wished and to part with all their lands, except a small portion, that they wished to reserve to live upon, feed their Horses and cattle and cultivate.

The Board asked if they would be willing to remove beyond the Cascade Mountains provided our Government would give them as good a piece of land there and pay all their expenses in the removal.

They all answered very decidedly "No." Alquema said they had once been a great people but now they had decreased to nothing, and in a short time the whites would have all their lands, without their removing.

The nature of the powers with which the Commissioners were invested was then explained to them, and they were told that the Commissioners were willing to treat with them fairly; but, that the Treaty, when made, would have to be sent to the President, and if He concurred in the terms, that it would be confirmed; if not, then, it would be the same as if no Treaty had been made.

To give the Chiefs further time for consideration, the council adjourned until 9 o'clock Monday morning.

Monday morning 9 o'clock Council met persuant to adjournment. The morning was pretty much consumed in trying to get the Exact bound[a]ries of the Territory claimed by this Tribe. It was finally defined, as clearly as it was possible on a map prepared by Mr. [George] Gibbs from information obtained both from the chiefs and whites, who are old Settlers.

They claim from a point on the Wallamette River called the Butte [at Butteville near Champoeg]; thence up the Wallamette River to a point about 15 miles above the mouth of the Kallapooya River, for a western bound[a]ry; thence East in a direct line to the foot of the Cascade Range, for a Southern boundary; thence, following the foot of the Cascade Range to a point about

East of the head waters of the Moo-lal-le River, for an Eastern bound[a]ry; thence, west in a line about midway between the Moo-lal-le river and Butte Creek that empties into Pudding River untill within about five miles of the mouth of the Moo-lal-le River, where the line turns, and runs about southwest to the place of beginning, for a Northern bound[a]ry.

This Tribe appeared willing to make a Treaty, selling all their lands, except that between the forks of the River Santiam, which they wished to reserve.

Gov. Gaines asked if a reserve could be made there without taking in the claims occupied by white Settlers.

It was said it could not be done.

Col. Allen told the chiefs: "For the good of your people it would be better for you to be entirely separated from the whites, and for that reason, it will be better for you to remove to a reserve beyond the Cascade Mountains, that would be selected for you, or that you might Select. There, your people would be furnished with Teachers to teach your children, and teach you how to farm. And with plows, Tools, &c. necessary in farming, building Houses &c. And Blankets to keep you warm. There our Government would protect you both from the encroachments of the whites as any neighboring Tribes of Indians, whereas, if you remain among the whites, it will inevitably end in your annihilation as a people."

Alquema objected to removing. Said that they could now see that they had thrown away their country; but that they wanted to keep this piece of land as their reserve.

Gov. Gaines, to the Interpreter [Robert Newell]: "Impress upon them the necessity of being separated from the whites, in making their reserve, and of going beyond the Cascade Range. He then explained to the chiefs the different influences of whites, the one acting by instruction from the Government, the other being citizens merely. The first would protect you, while the latter would be apt to encroach upon your rights."

Ti-a-can, Said their hearts were upon that piece of land, and they didn't wish to leave it.

Judge Skinner thought it would be better to give them further time to consult, and told the chiefs to reflect and consider upon what had been said to them. Whereupon Council adjourned until 2 o'clock P.M.

2 o'clock P.M. Council met persuant to adjournment.

A small Band called the Hanshoke [Ahantchuyuk] people, who have been partially separated from the main Tribe, and who claimed part of the land of this Tribe, had previously objected to coming under their control. This afternoon they, upon consultation among themselves, agreed to unite with the main Tribe, and to acknowledge the chiefs as their chiefs and to be governed by the Treaty that they might make with the commissioners.

Gov. Gaines asked if they had thought over what had been said to them this morning and if they did not think it would be better for them to go beyond the Cascades.

Al-que-ma said they had thought over it and they had determined to reserve the country lying between the forks of the Santiam and that all the Indians (included in the bound[a]ries above mentioned) would go together into this reserve.

Col. Allen, to the Interpreter: "I wish to know if they distinctly understand, that our Government will provide them with a reserve equally as good beyond the Cascades as this they wish to reserve, and that they will be paid for all the lands they claim here, and have their expenses paid in the removal."

Interpreter: "I have explained it to them fully, and they understand it. They don't seem to like its being pressed upon them." He then explained again the benefits that would arise from such removal to them.

Al-que-ma: "We don't want any other piece of land as a reserve than this in the Forks of the Santiam River. We do not wish to remove."

Gov. Gaines: "In the event of our Treating with the Band of Kallapooyas beyond your southern line, and they should be willing to live with you in the reserve, would you be willing that you should occupy it together?" Not distinctly answered. It was again asked.

Al-que-ma said that the people were not here. But, in the event of their Treating with you, and are willing to come with us, we have no objections.

Gov. Gaines: "Would you be willing for the whites who occupy claims between the Forks of the Santiam, still to live there? Would you give them the land they occupy?"

Ti-a-can said: "Some we would. Others we would not."

Gov. Gaines: "Would you be willing to buy the improvements the whites have made out of what is paid you for the rest of your lands of those you do not like, and let those you do like live there as Brothers?"

Ti-a-can said: "No."

Judge Skinner asked what portion of the land in the Forks of the Santiam do you wish to reserve.

Alquema said: "We wanted it all. But we will consent to divide it by a line commencing at the forks and running East to the Cascade Mountains, and we will take the south half."

JUDGE SKINNER: "Would it not be enough for your Tribe to reserve the land between the North fork of the Santiam and the first creek, not including the claims of the whites on the creek?"

ALQUEMA: "No! We would be content though to have the South branch of the Santiam and the Creek for our North and South bound[a]ries, and the forks of the Creek and North branch for our west, and the mountains for our East."

In the event of failing to persuade the Santiams to move east of the Cascades, the object of the commissioners is to get them to reserve a tract of country that was a swamp. On the south side of this marsh between it and the creek resided some fifteen pioneers whose claims they proposed to exclude from the reservation. The swampy land afforded fine grazing for livestock, a worthy consideration, the commissioners thought, for the Santiams.

GOV. GAINES: "If you would make your south bound[a]ry these settlements we would be willing to pay you well for the narrow Strip occupied by these whites, in Blankets, shoes, &c. If you should drive these settlers from their claims you would make them your enemies. If you let them remain, they will be your friends."

Tiacan objected to the Settlements being excluded. He wanted the Creek to be their southern bound[a]ry. He didn't wish the whites so close to them.

COL. ALLEN: "We are not at all indisposed to your having the creek for your southern bound[a]ry, if these Settlements were not there. It is for your good we advise you. By removing the whites from their claims, you make them your enemies, which you now is not well for you. We think you would be more happy and comfortable with the Blankets, Shoes &c. that we propose giving you than you would be with it; and you would then be friends with the whites there."

TIACAN: "We wished to reserve the South half of all the land in the forks of the Santiam. But we agree to retain only this. Now, you wish us to give up part of it. We wish to keep it."

GOV. GAINES: "We are willing to buy it of you and to pay you three times its value for your own good."

ALQUEMA: "It would tie us up into too small a space; it is no reserve at all."

JUDGE SKINNER: "This would be the Home of yourselves and families. You then have the right to go wherever you wish. You would be friends with the whites, you could travel without any fear of them if you would be honest and do right."

ALQUEMA: "The whites are not all alike. Some would say to them you have no rights on our lands. We have bought it of you. Clear out and go back to your reserve."

GOV. GAINES: "The stipulations of the Treaty we make with you would protect you in your rights."

ALQUEMA: "Some of the whites are foolish. They would whip and kick us and tell us to go Home."

COL. ALLEN to the Interpreter: "Let them understand that we are willing to pay them for all the land they claim except what they reserve and that we are willing to pay them more for this narrow strip between the swamp and creek in proportion than the other lands they claim. We don't wish to drive the whites off their claims. It would be injurious to the interest of the Indians."

ALQUEMA: "We want the whites on the other side of the creek. They would be too close to us if we let them be so near our homes. They would ill treat us."

GOV. GAINES: "The whites will not molest you after the Treaty. If one hurts you or misuses you without cause, our government will punish him. If they kill your people, our government will hang them. We think the country is large enough for your tribe without including the Settlement. Besides you will receive from year to year from our government the comforts of life and you will be protected in your rights and reserve. You will be much happier and better off, than you are now."

AL-QUE-MA excited: "We have been willing to throw away the rest of our country and reserve the land lying between the forks of the Santiam—you thought it was too much. Then we agreed to take only half of it and to take in the Kallapooyas beyond our south line, if they were willing—you thought it was too much. We then agreed to take this small piece between the Creek and north branch—you want us still to take less. We can not do it; it would be too Small; it is tieing us up into too small a space."

COL. ALLEN: "We are willing to pay you for all the land you do not reserve and we wish you to do this because we know it is best for you. We don't wish to force you to do anything. We tell you it is best for you because we think it is."

GOV. GAINES: "Think over it more and come in again in the morning."

Whereupon Council adjourned untill 10 o'clock tomorrow morning.

Tuesday morning 10 o'clock. Council met persuant to adjournment. The Board wished to obtain more accurate information of the piece of country this Tribe wished to reserve. They, therefore, sent for persons, old settlers in the country who are intimately acquainted with it. They adjourned untill the afternoon to await their arrival and to obtain the desired information before discussing the matter further with the Indians. Adjourned until 2 o'clock P.M.

2 o'clock P.M. Council met persuant to adjournment.

Gov. Gaines to the Interpreter: "We wish you again to explain to the chiefs the desire we have for them to remove beyond the Cascade Mountains. Tell them that it is the desire of the G[rea]t Father that they should go, that they will be provided there with a larger and as good a piece of country as this they wish to reserve; that they will be paid for all the country they claim here that they do not reserve; that they will have a military force to protect them in the rights stipulated by the Treaty we would make with them; that they and all of their families will be furnished with the comforts of life in the removal, and that they will be removed from among the whites entirely. Impress upon them the benefits that would arise to them by so doing, and that we are anxious for them to remove because we think it is much better for them." It was interpreted.

Alquema: "We understand fully what you mean and that it may be better for us, but our minds are made up. We wish to reserve this piece of land (placing his finger on the spot upon the map). We do not wish to leave this. We would rather be shot on it than to remove."

Seeing the great dislike they manifested to the proposition of removing beyond the Cascades and the impossibility of getting them to freely consent to it, the commissioners concluded to let them make the following reserve, to wit:

Commencing at the point where the road crosses the North Bank of the Santiam River at [William or Moses] Edgars, running thence, in a Southeastwardly direction so as to strike the first Creek south of said River, above the claim of [Nathaniel or Joseph] Cranks, then eastwardly up said creek to the base of the Cascade Range; thence south along the base of Said Range to the North fork of the Santiam River; thence down said River to the place of beginning, provided, however, that all citizens of the United States who have taken claims within said reservation agreeably to the provisions of an Act of Congress of the 27th September [1850] entitled "An Act to Locate the Office of Surveyor general of the Public Lands in Oregon, and to provide for the Survey and to make donations to settlers of Said Public lands" who may entitle themselves to a grant from Government under the provisions of said Act shall in all things be protected therein. But no other person will be allowed to settle or in any wise occupy any of the land above described."

Alquema wished to know if the Whites settled there, at present, would be allowed to build any more fences than what was at this time built.

Col. Allen: "We want you to distinctly understand that the whites must be allowed to retain the amount of land the law allows them. One mile square to [do] with as they choose."

ALQUEMA: "We understand." He wanted then to know if the whites would be allowed to cut the Timber off the lands and if ill disposed persons should ill treat them, what they were to do.

GOV. GAINES: "No one will be allowed to cut the Timber and if any one ill treats you the Superintendent of Indian Affairs, Dr. [Anson] Dart or the ag[en]ts under him will protect you."

JUDGE SKINNER: "Are you willing to let the Kallapooyas south of you, (a small band of this Tribe who claim Territory south of them) come with you, into the reserve."

They all objected very decidedly.

Alquema said the reserve was now too small and besides they did not agree very well; they were quarrelsome, mischievous fellows.

GOV. GAINES: "How many slaves have you in your tribe?"

TIACAN: "We have none."

Contrary to the custom generally with the Tribes in Oregon this Tribe has no slaves.

GOV. GAINES: "How many men, women, and children and female children are there?"

Tiacan said there were 65 men, 10 mail [male] children, and 80 women and female children, not knowing how many female children there were.

Col. Allen asked if they desired teachers among them to teach their children. They said they did not.

The Board then proposed if they would cede the lands they claimed (except the reservation discribed) to the Government of the United States, that they would pay them Fifty-thousand Dollars to be paid in twenty annual installments of twenty five Hundred Dollars cash Five hundred Dollars of which would be paid in cash and the remainder to be expended in the purchase of Two hundred and fifty Blankets: 150 p[ai]rs of Pants; 75 coats, woolen; 300 striped shirts; 230 p[ai]rs of shoes; 75 Hats or caps; 560 y[ar]ds calico; 560 y[ar]ds Linsey plaid; 500 y[ar]ds Domestick Shirting; 80 Blankets, shawls and seven dozen Pocket Handkerchiefs. All of which to be the good and substantial articles the first payment to be made as soon after the satisfaction of the Treaty as possible at the town of Salem in Marion Co[unty]. The distribution to be made by a disbursing officer of the Government, to the individuals of the Tribe . . . .

SOURCE

Bureau of Indian Affairs. Unratified Treaties, 1821–69, RG 75, Microcopy T-494, frs. 252-270, National Archives, Washington, DC.

RELATED READING

Beckham, Stephen Dow. The Myth of the Vanishing Kalapuyans. *What Price Eden? The Willamette Valley in Transition, 1812-1855*. Salem, OR: Mission Mill Museum Association, 1995.

Boyd, Robert. Kalapuya Disease and Depopulation. *What Price Eden? The Willamette Valley in Transition, 1812-1855*. Salem, OR: Mission Mill Museum Association, 1995.

Mackey, Harold, ed. *The Kalapuyans: A Sourcebook on the Indians of the Willamette Valley*. Salem, OR: Mission Mill Museum Association Inc., 1974.

Zenk, Henry B. Kalapuyans, *Handbook of North American Indians*. Vol. 7, Northwest Coast, pp. 547–553. Wayne Suttles, ed. Washington, DC: Smithsonian Institution, 1990.

The Case of Indian Tom, 1853

In an atmosphere replete with the wholesale dispossession of their lands, rapid cultural change, overt efforts by missionaries to undermine traditional religious practices, military losses, and contact with the rough-and-tumble residents of the American frontier, Native Americans repeatedly fell victim to use and abuse of alcohol. The problem emerged early and endured, tallying a terrible toll in lives, violence, and health. In 1834 Congress attempted to cut off sale of alcohol to Indians in provisions of the Indian Trade and Intercourse Act (4 Stat. 734). On June 5, 1850, Congress extended the provisions of the law to Oregon.

The 1834 act included a definition of "Indian Country." This concept, affirmed in the Supreme Court decision of Worcester v. Georgia *(1832), held that until the tribes had ceded their lands to the United States by ratified treaty, Indian law and custom prevailed. Thus in 1850 Congress affirmed that the entire Pacific Northwest was "Indian Country." In December 1853, the Supreme Court of Oregon Territory heard the case of Indian Tom, a resident of Clackamas County, who was indicted in county court "for selling liquor to the Indians." Although Indian Tom was not a citizen of the United States, the issue that became the focus of the court's attention was the argument that Oregon was not "Indian Country" and hence that the 1834 statute was not applicable.*

Chief Justice George H. Williams and Justice Cyrus Olney found the 1834 act, when extended to the Oregon Territory, posed several problems. The region was widely settled and traversed by non-Indians. They believed the Oregon Territory did not meet the definition of "Indian Country." Williams, in particular, argued that "whatever militates against the true interests of a white population is inapplicable." Justice Obadiah B. McFadden concentrated on Section 20 of the 1834 act. He argued that the enforcement of the clause forbidding sale of "spirituous liquors or wine to an Indian" was a matter of public interest and for the protection of the Indians.

Thus, though the justices had deep concerns about the extent to which the 1850 act conflicted with conditions in the Oregon Territory, they upheld its prohibition on sale of alcoholic beverages to Indians. Williams, in fact, argued the law was necessary for the protection of "defenceless white persons, women and children, who are exposed to the violence of drunken savages." The motion to quash Indian Tom's indictment was overruled.

C[HIEF] J[USTICE GEORGE H.] WILLIAMS. The question is not free from doubt or difficulty. Oregon is generally supposed to be a part of the Indian country named in the act of Congress of June 30th, 1834; but such is not the case.

Great Britain and the United States made a treaty in 1818 by which the northern boundary of the latter was extended west on the 49th parallel of north latitude to the Stony Mountains; and the territory beyond this was described as country to be held in the joint occupation of the two powers.

The Rocky Mountains then was the western boundary of the United States for legislative purposes, and so continued until 1846. The act of 1834 shows in terms, that it was intended as a country over which the general government had absolute and exclusive jurisdiction. Congress, by express enactment in 1850, extended said act to this territory, for the reason, as must be supposed, that it was not in force here before that time. The act of 1834 then has no vitality here, because Oregon is Indian country, but by virtue of the act of 1850, which gives it effect here so far as its provisions may be applicable. Is that provision prohibiting the sale of liquor to the Indians applicable? Very much of the act of 1834 is clearly unsuited to the present condition of the country. All which tends to prevent immigration, the free occupation and use of the country by whites, must be considered as repealed. Whatever militates against the true interests of a white population is inapplicable. Reference can be made to no law which, in express words, or by implication, repeals the provision in question; and no good reason can be assigned why it should be not held applicable to our condition. If required in a country wholly inhabited by Indians, how much greater the necessity for its enforcement here, where defenseless white persons, women and children, are exposed to the violence of drunken savages.

Selling liquor to Indians is not necessary to the welfare or prosperity of the people here; on the contrary, such a prohibition is a blessing to the Indians, and highly promotive to the safety, peace and good order of the whole community.

J[USTICE CYRUS] OLNEY. I concur with the Chief Justice, that no part of Oregon is Indian country as defined by the act of 1834, and that none of the provisions of that act were put in force here the law establishing the territorial government. It was a local statute, and was no more extended here by the last clause of section 14 of our organic act, than were the local laws of the District of Columbia. That clause extended over us the general laws of the United States, under which we possessed the right to import, and sell to all classes of customers, goods of any description, spirits and wine included. I arrive at the same conclusion with the Chief Justice, that up to June 5th, 1850, there were no restrictions or regulations on the sale of spirits, or other commodities to Indians. On that day Congress enacted, "that the law regulating trade and intercourse with the Indian tribes, east of the Rocky Mountains, or such provisions of the same as may be applicable, be extended over the Indian tribes in the territory of Oregon." The law referred to is the act of 1834; by omitting to declare which of its provisions, if any, are applicable, Congress has devolved this task upon the courts. No rule being given whereby to determine which are, and which are not applicable, our first and perhaps most difficult duty is to fix upon such a rule. The Chief Justice thinks this particular provision beneficial to the whites, and therefore applicable. He makes "the true interests of the white population," or in other words, *his* ideas of what is *expedient* for them, the test of applicability. In this I have not as yet been able to concur. Congress has declared that this Indian code, in its application to Oregon, shall adapt itself to the existing state of things. If, therefore, any of its provisions conflict with existing laws, or rights under those laws, the former and not the latter must give way; thus making the *rights* of the whites, under existing laws, the test of applicability; and as the, rights of unrestrained traffic with the Indians is admitted to have existed, the Indian code must adjust itself to, and not destroy that right.

J[USTICE OBEDIAH] McFADDEN. The opinions of Chief Justice Williams, and Justice Olney, as to whether the act of Congress of 1834, entitled "An act regulating trade and intercourse with the Indian tribes, and to preserve peace upon the frontiers," is applicable here, have been submitted to me with a request, that I should give an opinion on what seems to be a vexed question in this territory. Upon an examination of the several acts of Congress, and the treaties of joint occupation between the United States and Great Britain, I have no hesitation in stating the conclusions to which I have arrived.

It is proper to say in this connection, that this question came before the District Court of Clackamas County, on a motion to quash an indictment for the sale of liquor to the Indians. I was not present at the argument of the case, and cannot say anything on the facts involved in this particular case. On the abstract questions of law I will state my opinion. I concur in opinion that, that whenever vitality the act of 1834, entitled "An act to regulate trade and intercourse with the

Indian tribes" may have in this territory, is derivable from the act of Congress of June, 1850, which extends the act of 1834, or so much of it as may be applicable, to the situation of affairs in the territory of Oregon. This act is positive and explicit in its terms; and, however objectionable the exercise of the discretionary power conferred upon the judiciary of the territory of Oregon may be, it is not a conclusive objection to the exercise of the power, if it be clearly delegated, as I apprehend it is, by the act of Congress of June, 1850. If there be any portions of the act of Congress of 1834 not in contravention of a subsequent law of Congress, and not inapplicable to the existing state of affairs in this territory, so much of the act must be enforced here, until Congress shall see proper, by legislation, to direct otherwise. That the act of Congress of 1834 does contain some important provisions which may affect the welfare of the white settlers, as well as the peace and quiet of the Indians, I think cannot be well doubted. I might refer to sections 12 to 16 inclusive, which embrace important provisions, calculated to secure not only the peace and welfare of the Indian tribes, but their observance is necessary to the security of the white population. Section 20 provides, "that if any person shall sell, exchange, or give, barter or dispose, of any spirituous liquors or wine to an Indian, such person shall forfeit and pay," &c. The enforcement of this clause is important as prohibiting the sale, or giving of liquor to Indians. The enforcement of it here, as has been aptly remarked by the Chief Justice, is not only necessary to the protection of "defenseless white persons, woman and children, who are exposed to the violence of drunken savages," but to the Indians themselves. Indian prosperity lies in the path of temperance; the reverse is certain and unerring destruction. This provision of the act of 1834 is well suited to the state of affairs here. Its enforcement would have a salutary influence on the community. It would contribute to the peace and quiet of the Indians, and, as a consequence, prevent the commission of crimes. It would not be in contravention of any act of Congress, or in conflict with any of the laws of this territory. The question, it is true, is not free from difficulty; but believing that no violence is done to the well-known and established rules of law in the construction given to the act of Congress, I have been constrained to this conclusion. On this question, therefore, I concur with the opinion of Chief Justice Williams.

As to whether this be Indian country or not, I am not so well satisfied. For the important purposes connected with the civilization and settlement of the country, under the laws of Congress, it cannot well be regarded as Indian country. The settlement of this question, I think, is not necessary in determining whether the act of Congress of 1834, or any put thereof, be in force.

SOURCE

Wilson, Joseph G., ed. *United States of America v. Tom*, 1:26–31, *Reports of Cases Decided in the Supreme Court of The Territory of Oregon and of the State of Oregon*. San Francisco, CA: Bancroft-Whitney Company, 1906.

RELATED READING

Knuth, Priscilla, and Charles M. Gates, eds. Oregon Territory in 1849–1850, *Oregon Historical Quarterly*, 40(1)(January, 1949):3–23.

Prucha, Francis Paul. *American Indian Policy in the Formative Years: The Indian Trade and Intercourse Acts, 1790–1834*. Cambridge, MA: Harvard University Press, 1962.

"A Massacre Too Inhuman to Be Readily Believed," 1854

Tragedies befell Oregon Indians almost daily in the 1850s. Driven from ages-old village sites by settlers and miners, set upon by self-styled "volunteers" bent on missions of extermination, they suffered dislocation, cruelty, and loss of life. The inexorable course of demographic calamity resulting from the introduction of new illnesses also took its toll. In some instances, such as among the Cow Creek Band of Umpqua, as many as 50 percent of the tribe perished within a year.

Many of the bloody encounters occurred seasonally, especially in the mining districts. When ocean waves and tides were too high in winter or water too scarce in late summer to wash the gravels for gold, the miners formed volunteer companies to make war on the Indians. They then billed the federal government for services rendered, an interesting means of securing income when thwarted by nature. Such was the situation in January 1854, near the mouth of the Coquille River.

The Indians of the Coquille included the Athabaskan-speakers who occupied most of the watershed and a scattering of Miluk-speaking Coosan people in the villages at the river's mouth. Perhaps the remnant of a population that had once occupied the entire watershed prior to the migration of the Athabaskans across the Coast Range from the Umpqua Valley (an event addressed in the oral history of Coquel Thompson as occurring in the late eighteenth century), the Miluk-speakers were closely tied to villages north along the coast and to those on South Slough and lower Coos Bay.

The discovery of gold and platinum in the black sands north of the Coquille River in 1853 produced a gold rush drawing in more than a thousand miners. These men lived in a shanty town—Randolph—and worked the diggings along the shore at Whiskey Run Creek. The following letters speak to the massacre they perpetrated and what happened when the Indian agent, F. M. Smith, reported their actions. Included with Smith's report are the officious letters of the Coose County Volunteers attempting to justify their murders. The village they attacked was located near the present community of Bandon.

Letter of February 5, 1854, F. M. Smith, Sub-Indian Agent at Port Orford, to Joel Palmer, Oregon Superintendent of Indian Affairs.

Hon. Sir:

I grieve to report to you that a most horrid massacre or rather an out-and-out barbarous murder, was perpetrated upon a portion of the Na-son tribe, residing at the mouth of the Coquille river, on the morning of the 28th of January last, by a party of forty miners. Before giving you the result of my examination, and my own conclusions, I will give you the reasons which that party assign in justification of their acts.

They avow that for some time past the Indians at the mouth of the Coquille have been insolent: that they have been in the habit of riding the horses of white men without permission; that of late they have committed many thefts, such as stealing paddles and many other articles of the property of white men; that one of their number recently discharged his gun at the ferry-house; and that but few days prior to the attack upon the Indians, the chief, on leaving the ferry-house, where he had just been fed, fired his gun at a party of four white men standing near the door of the house. They further state, that on the 27th of January they sent for the chief to come in for a talk; that he not only refused to come in, but sent back word that he would kill white men if they came to his house; that he meant to kill all the white men he could; that he was determined to drive the white men out of his country; that he would kill the men at the ferry and burn their house. This communication with the chief, and his returning answers, was had through my interpreter, Chilliman, who happened to be there at the time on a visit. On the afternoon of the 17th January, immediately after this conversation with the chief, the white men at and near the ferry-house assembled and deliberated upon the necessity of an immediate attack upon the Indians.

The result of their deliberation, with the full proceedings of their meeting, is herein enclosed. (Document No. 2) At the conclusion, a courier was despatched to the upper mines for assistance. A party of about twenty responded to the call, and arrived at the ferry-house in the evening preceding the morning of the massacre. On the arrival of this reinforcement, the proceedings of the meeting first held were reconsidered and unanimously approved.

The upper mines, referred to above, are on the sea-beach, about seven miles north of the mouth of the Coquille. There are about 250 men at work there.

At the dawn of the day on the morning of the 28th of January, the party at the ferry, joined by about twenty men from the upper mines, organized under the command of George H. Abbott, with A. H. Soap as first lieutenant, and W. H. Packwood as second lieutenant, and in three detachments marched upon the Indian ranches and consummated a most inhuman slaughter. A full account of what they falsely term "a fight," you will find in the report which their captain, George H. Abbott, forwarded to me on the day of the massacre. Said report is marked [Document] No. 3, and is herein enclosed. The Indians were aroused from sleep to meet their death, with but feeble show of resistance; they were shot down as they were attempting to escape from their homes; fifteen men and one squaw were killed; two squaws were badly wounded. On the part of the white men, not even the slightest wound was received. The houses of the Indians, with but one exception, were fired and entirely destroyed. Thus was committed a massacre too inhuman to be readily believed. Now for my examination of this horrid affair.

Receiving information from Mr. Abbot, on the evening of the 28th of January, in letter form, bearing date January 27, that the Indians at the mouth of the Coquille river were disposed to be hostile, and that in consequence thereof the miners were arming, I immediately set about making preparation to start, at an early hour of the following day, for the scene of difficulty.

On the morning of the 29th of January I left Port Orford for the Coquille, accompanied by Lieutenant [August V.] Kants [Kautz], commanding Fort Orford. We arrived at the mouth of the Coquille, at the ferry-house, early in the evening of that day. On my arrival, Mr. Abbott handed me despatch [Document] No. 4, containing, as you will find, an account of the proceedings at the ferry-house during the day of the 28th January. Early in the morning of the day after my arrival, I sent for the chief, who immediately came in, attended by about thirty of his people. The chief, as well as those of his people present, were so greatly alarmed, and apparently so apprehensive that the white men would kill them, even in my presence, that it was with a good deal of difficulty that I could induce the chief to express his mind freely. He seemed only anxious to stipulate for peace and the future safety of his people, and to procure this he was willing to accept any terms that I might dictate. The chief was evidently afraid to complain of, or in any manner to censure the slaughterers of his tribe, and for some time replied to the charges made against him with a good deal of hesitancy. After repeated assurances of my protection, he finally answered to the point every interrogatory. I asked him if he had, at any time, fired at the men at the ferry-house. *No!* was his prompt reply. At the time he was said to have fired upon the white men, he declared, with great earnestness, that he *shot at a duck in the river*, at a distance of some two hundred yards from the ferry-house, when on his way home, and possibly the ball of his gun might have bounded from the water. My subsequent observation of the course of the river, and the point from which he was said to have fired, convinced me that his statement was entitled to the fullest credit. This statement of the chief is somewhat confirmed by the doubt expressed by one of the party, at whom he was said to have fired.

The white men making this accusation against the chief only heard the whiz-zing of a bullet. *This* was the *only* evidence adduced in proof of the chief having fired at them. I asked the chief if he, or if, to his knowledge, any of his people, had ever fired at the ferry-house. To this he answered *no*. The chief most em-phatically denied sending threatening language to the men at the ferry, but admitted that some of his people had. He also admitted that some of his tribe had stolen from white men, and that they had used their horses without per-mission. He did not deny that his heart had been bad towards white men, and that he had hoped they would leave his country; but all graver charges, such as shooting at white people, or at their houses, he stoutly denied. The chief prom-ised to do all I required of him. If I desired, he said he would leave the home of his fathers, and with his people would take to the mountains; but with my permission, and the assurance of my protection, he would prefer remaining in the present home of his people.

Everything I asked or required of him he readily assented to, promising most solemnly to maintain on his part permanent friendly relations with white men. My interview with the tribe occupied about two hours. During the entire coun-cil they listened with most profound attention, evidently being determined to fasten on their minds all that fell from my lips. At the conclusion of the council I requested the chief to send for all the guns and pistols in the possession of his men. You will be surprised when I tell you that *all* the *guns* and *pistols* in the hands of the Indians at the ranches at the time of the massacre *amounted to just five pieces,* two of which *were wholly unserviceable*; as to powder and ball, I do not believe they *had even five rounds.* Does this look like being pre-pared for war? Can any sane man believe that those Indians, numbering not over seventy-five men, women, and children, all told, with but *three serviceable guns,* had concocted a plan to expel from their country some three hundred white men! Such a conclusion is too preposterous to be entertained even for a moment. Sir, there was no necessity for resorting to such extreme measures. I regard the murder of those Indians as one of the most barbarous acts ever perpetrated by civilized men. But what can be done? The leaders of the party cannot be arrested, though justice loudly demands their punishment. Here we have not even a justice of the peace; and as to the *military force* garrisoned at Fort Orford, it consists of but *four* men. If such murderous assaults are to be continued, there will be no end of Indian war in Oregon.

The proceedings of the meetings held at the mines above the Coquille I herein enclose. Those meetings were held subsequent to the massacre. The action of the citizens present at these meetings was based upon the statements of those engaged in the affair at the mouth of the Coquille. I was assured by several gentlemen at the upper mines that word was sent up from the ferry-house that Mr. Abbott was acting upon my authority—specially deputed by a full commission from my hands, and that the government interpreter was with him. Upon this and other kindred reports were based the proceedings of their meetings. The very first intimation of there being any difficulty, or any misunderstanding whatever, between the Indians and white men at the mouth of the Coquille, I received by letter form Mr. Abbott on the 28th of January, late in the afternoon of that day. You will find by referring to the letter marked [Document] No. 1, that it bears date January 27th.

The distance from Port Orford to the Coquille ferry is about twenty-eight miles. I left Port Orford for the scene of difficulty, as before stated, on the morning of the 27th of January, the earliest possible moment after receiving Abbott's communication. Now, why could they not have awaited my arrival? I will tell you why; and it was so urged in the meeting at the ferry-house. They knew if they awaited the arrival of the Indian agent a treaty would be entered into, and friendly relations with the Indians would be established without the sacrifice of Indian life. In plainer words, and more in accordance with the spirit and acts of these men, if they awaited my arrival they would lose the pleasure and opportunity of settling the alleged difficulty in their own peculiar way. On reading the proceedings of the meeting at the "upper mines," you will observe that it had been reported there that a large quantity of fire-arms and powder was destroyed in the burning of the Indian ranches. This report, of course, was sent up by the party engaged in the measure. I do not hesitate to pronounce the statement false—false in every particular. *Bold, brave, courageous men!* to attack a friendly and defenceless tribe of Indians; *to burn, roast, and shoot sixteen of their number; and all on suspicion* that they were about to rise and drive from their country *three hundred white men!*

In justice to Mr. Abbott, I must add, that he wholly denies having sent word to the upper mines that he was acting upon authority delegated to him by me; on the contrary, he asserts that he openly declared in the meeting at the ferry-house, the night preceding the attack upon the Indian ranches, that he possessed no authority at my hands; that he acted, and should continue to act, upon his own responsibility, and such further authority as should be conferred on him by the people there assembled.

In conclusion, I am happy to inform you that the Indians throughout my district are disposed to live on friendly relations with white men. They evince no desire whatever to be hostile, nor do I believe that they will ever become so unless forced by *savage* white men.

I am, sir, your obedient servant, F. M. Smith, *Sub-Indian Agent.*

Letter of January 27, 1854, G. H. Abbott, Coquille Ferry, to F. M. Smith. [Document No. 1]

Dear Sir:

I arrived at this place yesterday at dark, and found difficulties existing between the whites and Indians, and my arrival (with Chilliman [the interpreter from Fort Orford]) was hailed as very fortunate.

I sent for the chief for the purpose of holding a council, (in your name, of course,) but he refused to come, and said that he was determined to kill as many whites as he could; and if any of us dared to go to the village to talk to him, that it would be the commencement of hostilities, or at least he would consider it as such, and act accordingly. He appears anxious to drive the whites out of his country.

The whites are collecting and arming themselves, and it is hard to guess what will be the issue. The Indians have committed some depredations, which as cutting the rope by which the ferry-boat is fastened, stealing canoe-paddles, shooting at the house, &c. I think the whites are justifiable; in fact, it is necessary, for their own protection, to take a decided step, sufficient at least to frighten them.

Yours, &c., G. H. Abbott

Minutes of January 27, 1854, A. F. Soap and William H. Packwood, Coquille Ferry-House, to F. M. Smith. [Document No. 2]

At a meeting of miners and citizens assembled at the Coquille ferry-house, for the purpose of investigating Indian difficulties, the following resolutions were adopted:

That a chairman and secretary be appointed.

On motion, A. F. Soap was called to the chair, and W. H. Packwood appointed secretary.

Circumstances are as follows:

Statement 1st. John A. Pension stated, that he discovered, on the 23d instant, an Indian riding a horse up and down the beach. I went over to the ranche[ria] to see whose it was; it proved to be a horse that Mr. [William] Whike rode up from Port Orford. I took the horse from the Indian, and went to the Indian chief; he attempted to take the trappings off the horse; I would not allow him to do so, wanting them as proof of his conduct. I expostulated with them in regard to their conduct; they laughed at me, and ordered me to *clat-a-wa* [go]. Mr. William Whike being present, corroborates the above statement.

Statement 2nd. John A. Pension stated that, on the 24th instant, there were three men on the other side of the river. I went over to them to ferry them across; they complained to me, and asked me the reason why the Indians wanted to drive us back to the mines, and not let us cross the river. An Indian, present at the time, seemed to be in a great passion, using the words *God damn American* very frequently. Mr. Thomas Lowe corroborates the above statement.

Statement 3d. Mr. [David] Malcom stated that, yesterday evening, the 26th instant, the Indian chief John shot at a crowd of men standing in front of the ferry-house at that time. Mr. Thomas Lowe and Mr. Whike corroborate the above statement.

Statement 4th. Mr. Whike and Thomas Lowe stated that, early this morning (the 27th) they discovered the rope by which the ferry-boat was tied up to be cut in two, having been done on the night of the 26th instant. The boat would have been lost had it not been buoyed out.

Statement 5th. Mr. George H. Abbott stated: I came here yesterday evening, (the 26th,) and finding difficulties existing between the whites and Indians, and having an explanation; he returned for an answer, that he would neither explain nor be friendly with the whites on any terms. I sent back the Indian the second time, insisting on an explanation. He sent back word by some friendly Indians that he would not come nor give any explanation whatever, and that he would kill every white man that attempted to come to him or go to his village; that he intended to kill the white men at the ferry and destroy their houses; that he was going to rid the country of all white men; that it was no use talking to him, and that if they (the whites) would take out his heart and wash it he would still be the same. Mr. George H. Abbott's interpreter's interpretation of the above statement is corroborated by John Grolonis [Grosluis].

Resolved, That the Indians in this vicinity are in a state of hostility towards the whites, from their own acknowledgment and declarations.

Resolved, That to-morrow morning, (the 28th,) as early as possible, we will move up and attack the Indian villages.

By vote, George H. Abbott is elected captain of this expedition, A. F. Soap first lieutenant, and William H. Packwood second lieutenant.

On this motion, this meeting adjourned. A. F. Soap, *Chairman,* William H. Packwood, *Secretary.*

Letter of January 28, 1854, G. H. Abbott, Coquille Ferry, to F. M. Smith, Sub-agent, Port Orford. [Document No. 3]

Dear Sir:

At a meeting of the miners and citizens, held at this place yesterday, a copy of the proceedings of which I send enclosed, it was resolved that the threatening attitude of the Indians of this place called for immediate proceedings. A company of forty volunteers was raised, of which I was chosen captain and intrusted with the command of the party—A. F. Soap first lieutenant, and William H. Packwood second lieutenant—for the purpose of chastising the Indians. The Indian village is in three different parts, situated on both sides of the river, about one and a half mile[s] from the mouth. I divided the company into three detachments, and attacked them at all three points simultaneously, this morning at daylight. We were perfectly successful in surprising them (the Indians,) although they have been making preparations for a stand for several days, and appeared to be very confident of their ability to fight the whites. From the accounts, and from my personal observation, fifteen Indians were killed, their houses destroyed, &c. We took all the women and children and old men prisoners, as far as possible.

I have sent out three squaws for the purpose of offering terms of friendship, if they wish it.

The greatest regularity was observed during the whole of the proceedings; the authority of the officers was fully observed, and I can say, to the credit of both officers and men, that they behaved themselves like soldiers, and avoided innocent bloodshed as much as possible.

I think hostilities will be suspended till your arrival, which I hope will be soon. I will detain Chilliman till you come. I had almost forgot to say that our loss was none, in either killed, wounded, or prisoners. The Indians are in sight, hovering around the ashes of their homes.

Yours, &c., G. H. Abbott, *Captain commanding Coose County Volunteers*

P.S. 3 o'clock. The chief is coming in to council.

Letter of January 29, 1854, G. H. Abbott, Coquille Ferry, to F. M. Smith, Sub-Indian Agent, Port Orford. [Document No. 4]

Dear Sir:

I am happy to inform you that hostilities are at an end, and friendly relations established, so far as it is in my power to proceed with negotiations. As I informed you in my report yesterday, I sent three of the squaws, that we had taken prisoners, among the Indians, offering terms of friendship if they chose it. The chief sent in word that if we would send the chief of Shix [Sixes] river to him, with assurance that he would not be killed by our people, he would be glad to come in and come to any terms that the whites might offer. I sent the chief accordingly, and after a short delay, the chief John, the principal chief of the tribe here, came in with two of his principal men. The chief was badly wounded in the left arm. His wound was dressed by some of our men, and we held a council.

He stated that fifteen of his people had been found dead, and some wounded. He also stated that few of his people were left, and he was anxious to renew friendly relations on any terms, taking on himself and his people to the responsibility, and acknowledging their conduct as the cause of the war. He (the chief) will be glad to meet you here to-day. All of the prisoners have been released, some of their canoes returned, &c. The Indians appear quite confident of the protection of the whites, and rely upon our word that they will not be interrupted further if they remain peaceable, showing that they have not been unfairly dealt with or deceived.

In haste, yours, &c. G. H. Abbott, Captain, Coose County Volunteers

After the massacre the miners at Randolph City held a meeting on January 28 and passed seven resolutions to justify their military action against the Coquille Indians. Again on January 30 the miners assembled to pass five resolutions, endorsing the "prompt and timely action of the citizens and miners" who "struck a decisive blow, which we believe has quelled at the commencement an Indian war . . . ." Superintendent Joel Palmer forwarded Smith's letter and its enclosures to Washington, DC., noting: "These miscreants, regardless of age or sex, assail and slaughter these poor, weak, and defenceless Indians with impunity, as there are no means in the hands of the agents to prevent those outrages, or bring the perpetrators to justice." When the reports were published, Smith found his life in jeopardy. He fled Port Orford and abandoned his position with the Bureau of Indian Affairs.

SOURCE

Bureau of Indian Affairs. Annual Report of the Commissioner of Indian Affairs . . . 1854, pp. 267–277. Washington, DC: A. O. P. Nicholson, 1855.

RELATED READING

Beckham, Stephen Dow. *The Indians of Western Oregon: This Land Was Theirs*. Coos Bay, OR: Arago Books, 1977.

"Utmost Good Faith": Walla Walla Treaty Council, 1855

In December 1854, Isaac I. Stevens initiated a treaty program to secure cessions of lands throughout Washington Territory, where he was simultaneously serving as governor and supervising the Northern Division of the Pacific Railroad Surveys. Having negotiated several treaties in the Puget Sound area, Stevens traveled to the Walla Walla River, where he joined Joel Palmer, Superintendent of Indian Affairs of Oregon Territory, to negotiate cessions of lands from the Yakama, Nez Perce, Walla Walla, Cayuse, and Palouse. These tribes held millions of acres in Washington, Idaho, and Oregon.

The Walla Walla Treaty Council opened on May 28, 1855, and continued for days. Hundreds of native peoples gathered to hear the presentations of Stevens and Palmer and to consider the treaties. The hosts offered food, friendship, presents, and promises of teachers, doctors, and annuity goods (clothing, tools, and food) if agreements could be made. The tribes argued that they wanted to retain their homes, traditional fisheries and hunting and gathering areas, and lands sufficient to graze their vast herds of horses and cattle.

After days of discussions and negotiations, the council moved toward conclusion. The following selection is from the minutes of June 9. On June 11 chiefs Lawyer and Old Joseph signed their treaty. As the council closed, the minutes included final remarks from Joel Palmer, and several of the chiefs. The minutes confirm the steadfastness of the chiefs in spite of the paternalism of the American negotiators, but also their determination to try to resolve the crisis from the mounting Euro-American incursion with a reasonable set of agreements. William McKay and James Doty served as secretaries recording the discussions as part of the formal record to submit to Washington, D.C.

Saturday, June 9th [1855]

The Council was opened at 2 o'clock P.M. when Gov. [ISAAC I.] STEVENS Said:

My Friends, Today we are all I trust of one mind. Today we shall finish the business which brought us together. Yesterday the Yakamas had not made up

Hundreds of tribal members gathered in May and June, 1855, for the Walla Walla Treaty Council. Governor Isaac Ingals Stevens negotiated for land cessions, reservations, and reserved subsistence rights (Washington State History Museum).

their minds fully. Today they and ourselfs agree; the papers have been drawn up. A paper for the Nez Perces: they live on one Reservation. A paper for the Walla Wallas, Cayuses and Umatillas, they have their Reservation on the Umatilla. And a paper for the Yakamas, they have their Reservation. These papers engage us to do exactly what we have promised to do.

My brother explained yesterday to the Walla Wallas, Cayuses and Umatillas what would be given in their paper. It has been given to them in the paper.

In the paper for the Yakamas we have included the tribes who acknowledge Kam-I-ah-kan for their head chief. The Piscouse, the Swan-wap-um and Palouse, the Yakamas and all the Bands on the Columbia below the Walla Walla down to the White Salmon River. *They have their reservation and fishing stations which I understand is satisfactory.*

The Nez Perces have their reservation as was shown them in Council and in the paper everything was set down which was promised them. They all know what was said.

The money, the payment intended for the Nez Perces, the Walla Wallas, the Cayuses and Umatillas has been divided. We have given two parts or a $150,000 to the Walla Walla, Cayuses and Umatillas. We have given the Nez Perces three parts or $200,000.

In the Yakama reservation we have not placed as many tribes as we expected. We have thrown out the Okan-ah-gaus and Colvilles and the Tribes below the White Salmon. Their numbers are about the same as the Nez Perces. We have given them the same amount. There is the paper for the Nez Perces (holding it up), here is the paper for the Yakamas. My brother will show the paper for the Walla Wallas, the Cayuses, the Umatillas.

It is stated first in all the papers the Indians who signed the paper, then your lands are described. We have got the descriptions from yourselfs. Then your reservations are pointed out, those you all know.

You will not be called according to the paper to move on the Reservation for two or three years; *then is secured to you your right to fish, to get roots and berries, and to kill game*: then your payments are secured to you as agreed; then your schools, your shops, and physician and the other things we have promised you are secured; then the salaries, the houses and the ten acre farms of your chiefs are secured to him.

Then there is another article if any of you get into debt then payments cannot be taken for your debts, every Indians must pay his own debts.

Then you promise to be friendly with other tribes and the whites.

Last you are to drink no whiskey and do all you can to prevent others doing it; and also those who drink whiskey will not be paid their annuities.

I have thus given the substance of the different Treaties. Shall it be read over in detail? You have already heard it not once but two or three times. It can be read over Article by Article and the Interpreters can state to you whether it is what you are promised. If there is anyone present who wishes to speak let him do so before we go on with this business. Let Looking Glass speak.

Looking Glass said: I am now going to speak. From those who have been speaking, they have been listening to us from above and from the ground. A long time ago the Great Spirit spoke to my children. I am from the body of my parents and I set on a good place. The Great Spirit spoke to his children the Laws, will track on the ground straight and after that there have been tracks on my ground and after that the big Chief, the President, his ground was stept on in the same way and for that reason I am not going there to trouble on his grounds and I do not expect anyone to tramp on mine.

I have great respect for my friends, he sees your eyes and your hearts, and that is the reason all this people are his children. Why do you want to separate my children and scatter them all over the country? I do not go into your country and scatter your children in every direction.

It is for me to speak for these people my children, that is what I say. The Big Chief speaks to his children and I also speak to my children and tell them what to do; and that is what we are talking about; you see where the Sun is. I never go where the whites are and mix with them and talk with them.

I am already named from above, by the Supreme Being, my heart is with the country. I live upon [it?] and head, that is the reason my heart tells me to say where my children shall go. I want you to look well to what I have shown you.

I want to know if an Agent will stay up in my country?

GOV. STEVENS: As long as there are people.

LOOKING GLASS: Will the Agent be there that long to keep the whites from pushing into our country?

GEN. PALMER said: Certainly.

LOOKING GLASS: Will you mark the piece of country that I have marked and say the Agent shall keep the whites out?

GEN. PALMER: None will be permitted to go there but the agent and the persons employed, without your consent.

LOOKING GLASS: It is not for nothing I am speaking to my chiefs, it is to talk straight, it is just as if I were to see the President and talk to him it would be straight, that is just what I want, that you talk straight from the President. Look at my talk. I am going to talk straight. When I hear your talk it goes to my heart. I am not like those people (pointing about) who hang their heads and say nothing. We will have a short talk, not a long one.

(After a silence of a few minutes the) YOUNG CHIEF said: That is the reason I told the Governor to let it be till another time, till we know what the Looking Glass would say. I heard that Looking Glass was coming.

GOVERNOR STEVENS. I will say to the Young Chief, let Looking Glass have time to think, he is thinking now in order that he may speak, he will speak straight and from his heart. We will wait now till we have heard Looking Glass speak.

LOOKING GLASS: The line of the Cayuse Reservation will be where the trail crosses the Walla Walla, there in a straight line to the Umatilla below Wm. McKay's house, from thence north of the butte, straight to John Day's River. The reason why that shall be the line is that they want more room for their horses and cattle. (After a pause of a few moments he continued) By what time will you build the mill?

GOV. STEVENS: The year they move on, when the President approved the Treaty.

LOOKING GLASS: Yes! Now we will talk. We have talked before, You said you would send this talk to the President and if he says yes, then it is right. Yes. And I will listen to what the President says and if he says yes, then we will talk.

BILLY: This is just putting it off further and making us more tired. You have no pity on us.

THREE FEATHERS: We cannot understand back here. Why don't he speak louder. Looking Glass is speaking, we look upon him as a Chief.

BILLY: I thought we had appointed Lawyer our head Chief and he was to do our talking, that is the reason why I have spoken.

GOV. STEVENS: I will say to my brother the Looking Glass that everything we say and do is sent to the President. What Looking Glass has said and what I say now goes to the President, but can I send anything to the President unless you agree to it? Can the President act? We have met that we may agree upon something then it goes to the President. The President has sent me and my brother to make this very agreement. We must agree upon something then it goes to the President and if he thinks it is good then he approves of it. I ask L[ooking] Glass to look upon it and see that it cannot be done any other way.

GEN. PALMER: Our great Chief, the President, directed me and my brother to come here. We have been here 19 days, we have been talking a great deal. That talk has been for your good. We came here to talk straight, we have shown you our hearts, we will not lie to you. Yesterday we made a bargain with the Cayuse the Walla Wallas and the Umatillas and the day before with the Nez Perces. The Looking Glass was not here but we did not forget him. We know that when he understands it all he will say yes. This morning we made a bargain with the Yakamas, they with these others all say yes. We expect the Looking Glass and his people will all say yes. We have told these people and it is so said in the paper that their horses and cattle would be allowed to graze outside of the reservation the same as our people when it was not occupied by whites. If we change the line to where he says we would have to stay here two or three days more to arrange the paper. We are all tired. You are tired. Shall we say one thing today and another thing tomorrow?

They have said yes! My heart says yes to the line that was shown yesterday and today. All things will be done as we told you. Shall we do so. My heart says yes. I have nothing more to say.

LOOKING GLASS: Yes! Let it be so.

EAGLE FROM THE LIGHT: When I spoke to you before I said that I should speak slowly and I have been thinking about what to say, but I don't know yet what to say. These people have been talking among themselfs as though there was two and when I heard what they had to say I said very well; let us go as two.

LOOKING GLASS: What I showed these people when I came here. I spoke beyond it (referring to the map) and you have said that this talk you would send to the President and he will see it.

You see my body it is not divided, it is one body as these are all my children (pointing about). They have all got horses and cattle that is the reason I made it larger.

I want you to talk plain just like the light and then I will say yes. That is all I have to say now.

GOV. STEVENS: I will ask of Looking Glass whether he has been told of our council. Looking Glass knows that in this reservation settlers cannot go, that he can graze his cattle outside of the reservation on lands not claimed by settlers, *that he can catch fish at any of the fishing stations, that he can kill game and can go to Buffalo when he pleases, that he can get roots and berries on any of the lands not occupied by settlers.* He knows what the Reservation is; that we promise him two mills, a saw and a grist mill, two schools and a blacksmith; that we give him a physician, and all the other things that have been spoken of; the people all know it, it has been read over two or three times.

This Reservation is in his own country. I ask Looking Glass is not this talking straight? We send all this to the President and besides this we pay a certain sum of which you all know; we have been looking for him ever since we have been here; Lawyer will recollect that I have been enquiring when will Looking Glass come? We wanted him to come.

Those who go to the Buffalo are all my children. I am going to see the Blackfeet next moon. The Blackfeet had stolen some of his horses, but he got them back again. I heard the story last night. He killed some of their men. I know that Looking Glass wants me to go and made peace in that country. Let us first agree here.

GEN. PALMER: We buy your country and pay you for it and give the most of it back to you again.

Looking Glass. You have said to me that the whites shall not go over that line, none shall go into that country and this you said and it *is* said: And you will show to the President what we *have* said.

GOV. STEVENS: I understand Looking Glass has consented with the other Chiefs. The papers are now ready to sign: here I will particularly speak to Kamahkan or the head Chief of the Yakamas. Are you ready?

YOUNG CHIEF: What the Looking Glass says, I say.

GOV. STEVENS: I ask you whether you are ready to sign? I stated that whatever the Looking Glass said and we said would go to the President. We agreed upon a line yesterday and the day before. The papers are drawn: we ask are you now ready to sign those papers and let them go to the President.

Looking Glass: That he said yes to his line.

Gov. Stevens: Looking Glass is satisfied with the Nez Perce line, the Young Chief and Pe-pe-mox-mox yesterday agreed to the Umatilla reserve.

Looking Glass: I said yes to the line I marked myself, not to your line.

Gov. Stevens: I will say to the Looking Glass, we cannot agree.

Gen. Palmer: I would say to the Looking Glass, what use is it to purchase his country and give it all back again. We did not come here to talk like boys. We don't wish to part with a misunderstanding.

The Nez Perces, the Walla Wallas, the Cayuses and the Umatillas agree to the boundaries as we have marked. Do you wish to throw all we have said to you behind you. Shall we like boys say yes today and no tomorrow? Pe-pe-mox-mox, Young Chief and the Nez Perces say yes! None of their people say no! Why do we talk so much about it? I have done.

Young Chief: The President is your Chief and you do what he tells you. That is the reason the Looking Glass marked out the line he wanted: he is the head Chief.

Looking Glass: It was my children that spoke yesterday and now I come and hear them speak. I asked my children what was their hurry? They knew that I was coming. Why did they run and speak till I came: that is the reason I marked it bigger. I wanted to talk with you and have you talk with me. And after that. Your talk and my talk will go to the President.

Gen. Palmer: I will say to my brother that I did not know that he was absent when we made our minds to come here, and set the time. My brother and myself come here and we come a long way. We have been here a long time. We were not in a hurry, these people wanted to go home, they had fields of wheat, and of potatoes, the weeds were growing up, they wanted to go home, there was no one at home to take care of the fields. We have other persons to see besides these.

My Brother has to go to the Blackfoot country and make peace. He wanted to say to them. You shall not steal these peoples horses: you shall not make war upon them; these are the reasons we talk. We talk because our Great Chief told us.

The papers have not been signed, they had not forgotten him nor had we. Shall all our efforts to protect them be destroyed? Shall our talk be thrown away? If the Looking Glass is a Chief I hope he will act as a Chief acts for the good of his people.

If we were to say yes to his line our Chief would say No! but if we shall say the line we have marked we believe our Chief will say Yes. Which will you do, take that line or have it all thrown away? Let us act like wise men and not part without doing good for each other.

LOOKING GLASS: I am not going to say any more today.

GEN. PALMER: If the Nez Perces are not ready they can talk among themselfs and come tomorrow.

If the Cayuses, the Walla Wallas and Umatillas are ready to do what yesterday they said they would, then the paper is ready for them to sign, and tonight they can get their goods and go home when they please.

The paper is also ready for the Yakamas if they choose to sign it they can do so.

GOV. STEVENS: The Council will now adjourn till Monday morning and I trust by that time Looking Glass will have thought the matter over and we will be able to agree.

The Council concluded on June 11, 1855, following the signing of the treaties. A number of the tribal leaders gave concluding remarks:

TIN-TIN-MEET-SEE: I understand you well. We are never the begin[n]ers in doing wrong to the whites. All Indians here understood well what has been said. When your white children come into this country they do things at random. (to the Indians) You have heard all that has been said and now let us go home and do right.

EAGLE FROM THE LIGHT: My forefathers are all dead, I only am left, there is but the encampment remaining, it is good to hear and think of each other. We have heard good words spoken from the President to take care of us poor people well. His children's way you have come here to see. For days our bodies have been together, also the night and also for years, also for winters. You have shown that he likes his red children. I do not want our hearts to come together wrong, but right, and remain so as long as we are a people, and we will stop the bad people on both sides. The Lord will reward us both when our hearts are good that we will look and care for each other,—The old and the young will go right and then all will be right—from little could come great difficulties—that is the reason we speak from small things to big ones that is all at present.

JAMES said: It is not from anything bad that I have not Spoken. It is as though the man I speak of is not of the party. When the white people came to my country Mr. See told me when he came there he was coming for good and not for bad. When the white people come and they would come in great numbers do not do anything bad to them. I have never done bad to them. I wish Mr. [William] Craig to stay with us and hear the Indians speak for he could speak to our people and they could understand him—therefore I wish him to stay.

RED GRIZZLY said: I like your talk—you talk well. When you have finished I like it still, this you have brought us from the President. I like that talk my friends. From the time I spoke here I have been sick at heart. This man who has just now spoken, he spoke a little longer because he knows how to speak and there is also another who has just come, the Looking Glass, they speak straight and friendly. You have also spoken friendly, and shown them your heart plainly—not that I am a good man that I like it. My heart is glad as though I see your heart when I hear your words. What I have good to speak I have not spoke yet. (Here he was interrupted by the Indians when the Red Owl said the young chief wished to say that he wanted you to stop the whites from taking their horses or cattle and if my horses go across the line of the reservation which is a small one I do not want these horses and cattle to be taken off because they are over the line).

GEN. PALMER said: My brethren. This man has said from little things grow great ones. It is true, it is so—a single word spoken unkindly leads to a difficulty. It would be better if we always would not do or say bad things, but if little things are done wrong we should try and forget them. I have been told that there are sometimes difficulties among the Indians in reference to their mode of worship. That is a thing that we do not interfere with. We are willing to let the people worship God as they please. We do not say do this or do that. If their heart is to sing or pray and preach it is good, if others say it is not our heart to pray and to preach it is good, but we want all people to be good people. If those who sing and pray think it is good, let them to try to convince others. Talk kindly, treat them kindly and convince them they will do right. Some will worship one way and some will worship another—do not quarrel about it but worship or not worship, we want you to have good hearts. I have done.

LOOKING GLASS says: As so many are now working, some other time you and I will have a heart. I have a good head and a good heart, by and by we will have a talk.

Council Adjourned *sine die* at three o'clock.

We hereby certify the above to be a true record of the proceedings.

SS James Doty
Secty. to Treaties in N. Terry.

SS W[illia]m McKay
Secty. to Treaties in O.T.

Approved
Isaac Stevens
Gov. & Supt. W.T.

Joel Palmer
Supt. Ind. Affairs
for O.T.

SOURCE

Swindell, Edward G., Jr. *Report on Source, Nature, and Extent of the Fishing, Hunting and Miscellaneous Related Rights of Certain Indian Tribes in Washington and Oregon Together with Affidavits Showing Locations of a Number of Usual and Accustomed Fishing Grounds and Stations.* Los Angeles, CA: U. S. Department of Interior, Office of Indian Affairs, Division of Forestry and Grazing, 1942.

RELATED READING

Josephy, Alvin M., Jr. *The Nez Perce Indians and the Opening of the Northwest.* New Haven, CT: Yale University Press, 1971.

Trafzer, Clifford E. *Indians, Superintendents, and Councils: Northwestern Indian Policy, 1850–1855.* Lanham, MD: University Press of America, 1986.

"Awful Hard Time When I'm Baby," 1855

John Adams, who was born between 1850 and 1852, endured the holocaust of the Rogue River Indian Wars when he was a boy. He and his family were swept up in the conflicts that erupted between 1852 and 1855 in southwestern Oregon. When Oregon Volunteers attacked and murdered twenty-nine Indians on the margin of the Table Rock Reservation in October 1855, the region erupted in conflict. Panic-stricken Indians fled west into the Rogue River Canyon or into the hills surrounding the Rogue, Umpqua, Applegate, and upper Klamath rivers.

John Adams identified his family as Shasta, suggesting that his mother was a Shasta-speaker from the Bear Creek watershed in the Rogue River Valley. His father was identified as "Rogue River," presumably a Takelman-speaker. To survive, remnants of his family hid out in the Rogue River canyon during the winter of 1855–56. The following spring the U.S. Army rounded up the refugees, collected them at Fort Orford, then shipped them on the sidewheeler Columbia *north along the Oregon coast to Portland. The Indians then had to walk to Dayton, home of Joel Palmer, Superintendent of Indian Affairs, and on through the Coast Range to their designated reservation on the Siletz River.*

Adams recalled these events of his childhood in 1910 or 1911 for Edward Sheriff Curtis, who probably recorded them on a wax cylinder, part of his technique when doing field enthnography. A documentary photographer of Native Americans, Curtis visited Siletz to collect cultural information and to take photographs for The North American Indian, *a twenty-volume work published over a period of thirty years. Although Curtis included information on the Tututni and Shasta removed in 1856 to the Coast Reservation, he published no portraits of them nor of his informant, John Adams. The fate of Curtis's Siletz photographs is unknown.*

In 1910 John Adams was living with his second wife at Siletz, Oregon. He was an employee of the Indian Police.

Pretty rough times! Awful hard time when I'm baby. Rogue River Injun war that time. Well, soldier come, everybody scatter, run for hills. One family this way, one family other way. Some fighting. My father killed, my mother killed. Well, my uncle he come, my grandmother. Old woman, face like white woman, so old. "Well, my poor mother, you old, not run. Soldier coming close, we have to run fast. I not help it. I sorry. Must leave you here. Maybe soldiers not find you, we come back. Now this little baby, this my brother's baby. Two children I got myself. I sorry, I not help it. We leave this poor baby, too." That's what my uncle say.

Course, I small, maybe two years, maybe nearly three years. I not know what he say. Somebody tell me afterwards. Well, old grandmother cry, say: "I old, I not afraid die. Go ahead, get away from soldiers."

Well, just like dream. I 'member old grandmother pack me round in basket on her back. All time she cry and holler. I say, "Grandmother, what you do?"

"I crying, my child."

"What is it, crying, grandmother?"

"I sorry for you, my child. Why I cry. I not sorry myself, I old. You young, maybe somebody find you all right, you live."

Then like I sleep long time. When I wake up, winter gone, spring time come. I 'member plenty flowers, everything smell good. Old grandmother sitting down, can't walk no more. Maybe rheumatism. She point long stick, say, "Pick that one, grandson."

I weak, can't walk. S'pose no eat long time. I crawl on ground where she point. "This one, grandmother?"

"No, that other one."

"This one?"

"No, no! That one no good. That other one."

Bimeby I get right one, she say, "Pull up, bring him here."

I crawl back, she eat part, give me part. Don't like it. Too sour. Well, she show me everything to eat, I crawl round, get roots. Pretty soon can walk. Old grandmother never walk. Just sit same place all time. One day she point big tree. "You go see. If hole in bottom, inside you find nice, sweet ball hanging up. That's good."

Well, I find hole, crawl inside. White stuff there, sweet, good. I like that. Every day go to that tree.

Grandmother say: "S'pose you hear something say 'Pow! Pow!' That's man. You holler, he come help us." But I can't holler, too small, just make squeak. She make new basket, tell me: "Put upside down out there, maybe somebody find it."

John Adams (seated left), survivor of the Rogue River Wars, and his family at Siletz posed in their church-going clothing. Adams became the first Indian minister of the Methodist Church at Siletz (Oregon Historical Society, OrHi 48,491).

One day hear something: "Pow! Pow!" She's too old to holler, me, I'm too small. Maybe I'm scared too. Well, I crawl inside tree and eat sugar. Pretty soon hear somebody talk. Then I'm 'fraid, hide in tree. Somebody coming! I lay down on ground, hide close. "Where are you? Where are you?" Well, there's my uncle. He pick me up one hand. I 'member hanging over his arm while he go back my grandmother.

"Well," that man say, "soldiers not stay long that time. Pretty soon come back, can't find you. Think some grizzly-bear eat you. Look for bones, can't find bones. All winter I cry. Then I say my wife: 'Maybe better go other side today. Maybe find something other side.' That's how I come find that new basket. Then I look close. Little grass been moved. Pretty near can't see it. Some kind little foot been there! That's how I find my old mother."

Pretty soon soldiers come again. That's the time they leave my old grand-mother cause she can't walk. Maybe she die right there, maybe soldiers kill her. She cry plenty when my uncle take me away. Well, all time going round in woods. After while my uncle get killed. Then I'm lone. Klamath Injun find me, bring me to new reservation.

Two my relations, they're married to Rogue River man. They take me, but pretty soon both dead. One Rogue River man he say: "Well, you're small. You can't do nothing. I keep you. Long as you like to stay, you stay with me." I can't talk his language, my mother's Shasta Injun. So we talk jargon. Few years after that, then he die. Then some woman hear about me, say she's my sister. Well, I don't know. I look at her. Don't know her. She take me in steamboat from Port Orford for Portland. It's like the ground falling under me, one side, other side. Can't eat, sick all time. Well, we get Portland, I'm glad. Eat lots. Then we stay Dayton good many years, come Siletz. I'm young fellow now.

All this Coast Injun say: "That fellow bad blood. His people make that Rogue River war. They start it. He's bad fellow." They keep talking that way, looking at me. Sometimes throw rocks. One day they start again, maybe twenty. I tired all that talking, get mad. When they throw rocks, I throw too. That's the time lose these front teeth. Got no teeth since then. Rock knock 'em out. When that rock hit me, I get crazy. I start for my house for get gun. They head me off. Can't run fast, feels like my head coming off. All time throwing rocks. One fellow's got knife. Says, "We get him!" I grab fence rail, hit him on the neck. He drop, squirm like fish in canoe. Next one come, hit him on the head. He drop too. Don't squirm. That rail too heavy, throw him away and run again. Can't get to my house, they head me off. What I going do? Well, I get in fence corner. What I going fight with?

Some white man on other side say, "Here, Johnny, some rocks." Push some rocks under fence. I say, "Well, you come over help me."

"No, I 'fraid. Here's more rocks."

I pick up rocks. Four men get close now. He's got knife, too. Thump! Hit him in ribs. Stagger like drunk. Next man, thump! Hit him in ribs. He go back. Others all stop. Then I jump fence, run home, get my gun. They go back. That's rough times!

SOURCE

Curtis, Edward S. *The North American Indian: Being a Series of Volumes Picturing and Describing the Indians of the United States, the Dominion of Canada, and Alaska.* Frederick Webb Hodge, ed. Vol. 13. Norwood, MA: Plimpton Press. (Reprinted: Johnson Reprint Corporation, New York, 1970).

RELATED READING

Beckham, Stephen Dow. *Requiem For a People: The Rogue Indians and the Frontiersmen.* Norman, OK: University of Oklahoma Press, 1971. (Reprinted, Oregon State University Press, 1994).

———. *The Indians of Western Oregon: This Land Was Theirs.* Coos Bay, OR: Arago Books, 1977.

Douthit, Nathan. *Uncertain Encounters: Indians and Whites at Peace and War in Southern Oregon, 1820s-1860s.* Corvallis, OR: Oregon State University Press, 2002.

Kasner, Leone Letson. *Siletz: Survival for an Artifact.* Dallas, OR: *Itemizer-Observer,* 1977.

Schwartz, E. A. *The Rogue River Indian War and Its Aftermath, 1850–1880.* Norman, OK: University of Oklahoma Press, 1997.

Youst, Lionel. *Coquelle Thompson, Athabaskan Witness: A Cultural Biography.* Norman, OK: University of Oklahoma Press, 2002.

A Plea for the Indians of Oregon, 1856–57

"I am afraid Father will have to leave this country. Public opinion is so strong against him some would as leave kill him as an Indian just because he has spoken the truth bold against the rascality of this Indian war, or rather, butchery of the Indians," wrote Welborn Beeson on May 22, 1856. Few on the frontier dared speak on behalf of the Indians. John Beeson (1803–89) was a rare Oregonian who risked his life and family's welfare in the midst of the Rogue River Indian wars to condemn the actions of the "Volunteers," companies of vigilantes who hunted down and murdered Indians. Beeson, in fact, attacked the barbarism of his neighbors and their use of a war against the Indians to bill the government for "services rendered." These convictions and his willingness to share them got Beeson into deep trouble.

An overland emigrant of 1853, Beeson, his wife, Ann, and son, Welborn, settled on a Donation Land Claim in the watershed of Bear Creek midway between Medford and Ashland. English by birth, the Beesons emigrated between 1828 and 1830 to the United States. They subsequently lived in La Salle County, Illinois, where Beeson labored as a farmer. In the Rogue River Valley, Beeson and his teenage son fenced fields, plowed, raised crops, and built a schoolhouse.

When John Beeson sensed the tragedy befalling the valley's native population, he dared speak about it. On May 22, 1856, Welborn Beeson wrote in his diary: "There was an indignation meeting at the school house against Father on account of his being opposed and writing and talking against the present Indian war. They passed several resolutions which will be published in the [Table Rock] Sentinel." The danger was great. On May 24 Beeson left his farm at eleven at night to go to Fort Lane where a U.S. Army escort accompanied him down Rogue River and north toward the Umpqua to protect him from the vigilantes. Beeson did not return to his home for many years, nor did he see his wife again; she died in 1866.

Beeson traveled to the Willamette Valley and San Francisco. He met with newspaper editors and challenged them on why they had not printed his letters explaining the causes and consequences of the Rogue River Indian War.

Finally he traveled via Panama to New York City, where he wrote A Plea for
the Indians *(1857). Beeson became a leading figure in humanitarian efforts to
help Native Americans. He traveled, lectured, met with Abraham Lincoln, and
for a time edited and published* The Calumet, *an Indian rights journal. This irregular publication began in 1859 with his essay "Are We Not Men and Brethren?
An Address to the People of the United States." Beeson's* A Plea for the Indians
*had three printings and was followed by a sequel that contained several essays
and speeches.*

*Beeson's stirring opinion piece, "Address to the Citizens of Rogue River Valley,"
published in the* Argus *(Oregon City) one of the largest-circulation papers in the
Willamette Valley, on June 28, 1856, put his views before the public during the
final weeks of the Rogue River Indian War of 1855–56. Tensions ran high as fearful
settlers "forted up" and volunteer companies scoured the countryside in pursuit of
"savages." The United States Army, badgered by newspapermen and politicians for
temporizing, played the role of quelling hostilities and rounding up the survivors
for removal to reservations.*

Fellow Citizens—As you have accused me of falsehood and slander, and some
of you have threatened personal violence, because I have protested against the
war as being unnecessary and aggressive; and as I am denied the freedom of
speech and of your press for self-defense; patriotism, equally with self-respect,
demands that I should speak to you from my retirement; for although the
occurrence has transpired in a remote corner of our vast Republic, yet in its
bearings it affects the interests and elicits the attention of the nation.—Permit
me then, fellow citizens, briefly to state the case as it stands between us.

For eight months the scourge and waste of war has been carried on in our
vicinity, and until quite lately there seemed little disposition and less prospect
for a speedy close, either by treaty or conquest. On the other hand, I have not
failed from its first inception and at every stage of its progress, both in public
and in private to declaim against it as a cruel injustice to the people against
whom it is waged, and its prosecution as a reckless and unnecessary waste of
the resources of our common country.

You have through your press and in public assembly attempted to justify
yourselves, not by explaining the facts or refuting the proof upon which opposition is based, but by impugning motives and aspersing character; and so far
as the authorities and the public at large can see to the contrary, you are unanimous, and they might therefore infer that you are correct. You have sought to
destroy the testimony by asserting that it is nothing but the "production of a

low and depraved intellect." Since you have made the matter to rest upon the credibility of the witness, I am necessitated to speak in vindication of self, and however reluctant I may feel to dwell on so small a point, yet it is the only one you have given me occasion to sustain, and I dare not by silence allow you to triumph in a matter in which the deepest interests of humanity and our national honor are alike involved.

I shall not go abroad for certification of character, but shall appeal to yourselves as the witnesses of my "course" and the hearers of my "assertions." I shall simply state the causes which operated as motives, and the occasions on which they found expression.

Having come to this country in acceptance of the Governmental offer of land for occupancy, I honestly believed that the original owners had received a fair compensation and that the treaty stipulation guarantying protection and forbidding private war, would be promptly fulfilled. And as I never looked with pleasure at the master brute monopolizing the crib and forcing his weaker mate to starve by his side, so when I saw that we had possessed ourselves of the fertile valleys and creeks and most of the pleasant homes of the Indian, and had exposed him to violence and outrage of the evil disposed and vicious, I could not but feel the injustice we were doing. And when so many of you frequently recited in my hearing cases of aggravated cruelty and wrong, and at the same time I read almost weekly in the Yreka *Herald* merciless appeals to the baser passions, exciting to still more destructive violence upon a people who had no hold upon public sympathy or governmental protection, I felt aroused to plead for justice.

And, moreover, when I beheld in one of your public restaurants, exposed to view with the usual glitter of wine and whisky, the voluptuous painting of an undressed, a naked woman, reclining upon a couch, and in the stores and in the streets comely Indian girls arrayed in silks and finery, and read in the "Sentinel," weekly paraded before the people under the caption, "*A Great Blessing to Mankind*," Dr. L. J. Czapkay's Prophilacticum, of self-disinfecting agent, which (the Dr. says) "every young man ought to have," and when I realized the appalling apathy that neither politician nor press nor priest offered rebuke to this ruinous licentiousness, and that virtue seemed driven from our midst, and moral principle and public honor seemed wasting away or merged in "*the root of all evil*," my soul was stirred from its depths, and before high Heaven I pledged myself to be true to my God, my conscience, and my country. Much rather would I that all this was hid in oblivion, and covered with impenetrable darkness, but as you have persisted in defense of wrong, and publicly aspersed my motive in its resistance, I am necessitated to unfold the secret cause of that course which you have (as I conceive) unjustly charged as being "the production of a low and depraved intellect."

Permit me, fellow citizens, to invite you to a calm review of some of the more prominent features of the past. In process of time, the evils to which I have above alluded produced their legitimate results. Mutual outrages and retaliatory murders between the races became frequent, and as the Indians were well supplied with ammunition and arms, (the price of crime,) excitement and panic seized the public mind, and what seemed to me the climax of wrong, was meditated and finally determined, instead of a civil of legal process for mutual redress, it was assumed that the Indians were the only sinners, and they alone should suffer. Kill the savages, exterminate the race, became the one idea, the ruling sentiment. Accordingly, the arrangements being made, the work was to be begun on Monday at early dawn of October 8th, 1855. During the previous week an earnest appeal had been made to the Grand Jury to present the state of affairs before the Court which was then sitting for investigation, but they decided it was not in their place. On Sabbath, the 7th, there being a Methodist quarterly meeting within two hours' ride of the intended scene of massacre, I attended, and improved a general invitation to speak by expressing myself somewhat as follows:

"My friends, is it enough that we should be content with mere feelings of present comfort and hopes of future heaven, 'to read our' (own) 'title clear,' then 'wipe our weeping eyes'? Are there not those in our vicinity, children of the same Father, heirs of the same immortality, entitled to the same enjoyments as ourselves, but doomed by our community to deprivation and death? Have we no sympathy, no fears, no effort in behalf of these our brethren? Could we not in some manner invoke the civil power, and prevent this contemplated wrong? My friends, if we allow these proceedings retribution will follow. As yet, out homes have not been molested, or our wives and children destroyed; but commence this wholesale slaughter, and some of us will become homeless, and some of our families be made desolate."

But no one making response, the meeting concluded as though there was nothing unusually wrong.

Three months afterward several gentlemen promised that if a meeting could be convened, they would attend and advocate measures of peace. I therefore caused a notice to be published, but the *Sentinel* proclaimed that there was not a man known in Jacksonville who desired such a meeting; but on the 22d of January, 1856, by getting handbills and posting them round town myself,

Coos and Lower Umpqua Indians held at Fort Umpqua, 1856–59 by the U.S. Army underwent rapid cultural change. A saw, cooking kettles, and cotton clothing confirmed the shift from traditional technologies and material culture. The view appeared in *Frank Leslie's Illustrated Magazine*, April 24, 1858 (Oregon Historical Society).

(some of which were torn down before my face,) a meeting was fathered in the Robinson House; but to my sorrow not one of my promised aids was present. I alone was left to declaim against the measures of war, and in favor of the practicability and necessity of peace. Several spoke in opposition. One said he was for treaty; he would invite all the Indians to sign it, and then take the opportunity to kill the whole. Another objected to that mode; he would rather continue the war until all were destroyed in honorable war. The Rev. Dr. K— said he was going to leave the valley, but advised the destruction of all the "red skins." So the meeting broke up without anything being done, except the remonstrance of a single voice; but in coming away a gentleman suggested to me the writing out in speech form of the remarks which had been presented, and sending to some eastern paper for publication.

And I am happy, fellow citizens, to perceive that though you were impervious and turned a deaf ear to a direct appeal, that you are nevertheless sensitive to its vibrations, since its echo has returned to you emphasized with a thousand sympathies from abroad.

Thus, gentlemen, you have not only allowed me to throw the first stone, but have left me alone to strain at the work. And now, that our fellow-citizens beyond the mountains are likely to overwhelm us with a shower, may we not hope that some chord will be struck, that the deep fountains of human sympathy may be broken up, and that the gushing and commingling streams will flow over the land as a wave of love and mercy, causing the evils we witness and lament to ultimate in blessings and the speedy advancement of that "good time coming," when "spears shall be beaten into pruning hooks, and swords into ploughshares; when nation shall not lift up sword against nation, and men shall learn war no more."

Fellow citizens, my interests and my home are in your pleasant valley. I appreciate your friendship, and mean to deserve your esteem, but I know that this can be only secured in the advocacy of "righteousness, which exalteth a nation"; and I doubt not that when the causes of danger and excitement, which have induced some of you to err and others passively to acquiesce, shall subside, we shall approximate in our views, and be more firmly united to "do justly, love mercy, and walk humbly with God." And be assured, gentlemen, no one more deeply regrets than myself the unfavorable position in which circumstances have made you to appear, and if the sentiment of *justice* has prompted me to plead for the Indian, and to vindicate the course I have taken, that sentiment is no less potent in its regards for the happiness and welfare of those whom I now address, and whatever of influence or position I possess shall be strenuously used for the prompt relief of these embarrassment under which you suffer. I am deeply sensible that the causes from which past and present wrongs have arisen are deep, and broad, and high, and for the existence as well as for the removal of which others as well as the people of Oregon are responsible. It has been foreign to my feelings to mar the pecuniary interests or to throw an evil shade over the character of any. I have tried to modify rather than exaggerate, but justice required the facts, and I have intended to present nothing more. And since the indemnity will not be paid until the facts are analized which have occasioned the difference between the two Generals and the two Governors, you have nothing to hope for from secrecy, or blaming me for exposure. All would have been examined, even if I had not lived.

I wish also to correct a mistake which some have entertained, viz: that I have acted under the direction of Gen. [John] Wool or Gen. [Joel] Palmer. The truth is, I have received no communication whatever, directly or indirectly, from one or the other; except what I have read in the newspapers; neither have I from any other public officer, except a call at my house by Capt. [Andrew J.] Smith, of Fort Lane, in company with Dr. [George] Ambrose. The life of the former was threatened, and from the extensive and deep feeling of disapprobation expressed against him, I had reason to believe he was in imminent danger, and simply because as a gentleman and soldier he declared his resolve to defend the defenseless who had fled to the Fort for protection. On Christmas I was impressed to write him a letter of sympathy. On the last of January he made the call as above, and stated that he had duly received the letter, but its contents being so novel and different from the general current, and not having previously heard the name of the writer, he concluded it was from an enemy and designed to mislead; but having heard of the effort for peace made in the Robinson House on the 22d, he was satisfied of its genuineness, and had come in person to make the acknowledgment. In that interview there was no plan proposed or agreement made; in fact it was the first and last and only interchange of thought with public functionaries, except volunteers and editors to the present time. My action has been the spontaneous prompting of the moment, and its operation intended directly upon the party addressed, but opposition has hightened zeal and enlarged the sphere.—You have connected my name with circumstances upon which our countrymen from the centre to the circumference of the land will look. I cannot hide if I would; so, my fellow-citizens, I am resolved to stand with all of you who will "do good, love truth, be just and fair to ALL, exalt the RIGHT, though every ism fall."

And believe me your friend and well wisher,

JOHN BEESON

Oregon City, June 23, 1856

The following selections are from Beeson's A Plea for the Indians of Oregon. *Beeson was a man of uncommon bravery to lay out for the American readers the atrocities that the miners and settlers perpetrated in the Rogue River Valley.*

Atrocities Get Common-place

During the following week [in October, 1855] all was intense excitement through the length and breadth of the Valley; but the prevailing hope was, that, as the work had commenced, it would be effectual, and soon accomplished. Numerous were the reports, as to individual cases, as well as the general progress of the enterprise; and it was difficult to obtain the exact details. The following is as near the truth as I could ascertain.

During the night of Sunday, the main body of the assailants approached as near to the Indians, on, or near the [Table Rock] Reserve, as they could without being perceived. They were found in several Ranches on the banks of the River. Three companies crept on their hands and knees through the chaparral, so as to obtain advantageous positions. With the first early dawn of morning they poured the deadly contents of their rifles through the frail tenements, under which were sleeping helpless men and women, little children, and nursing infants. Let fathers and mothers fancy themselves and their sleeping babes thus assailed; and they will realize better than I can describe the horrors of that occasion.

Being thus unprepared for war, and taken by surprise, the Indians fled for shelter to the surrounding chaparral, while their assailants continued, with their revolvers, to despatch all they could reach. They captured two or three Indian women alive; and when no man was in sight, it being something of a risk to creep after them in the brush, these women were compelled, under threats of instant death, to force out their husbands, and sons, and brothers, that they might be shot without danger to their destroyers. It was while thus employed that Major [James] L[upton], already spoken of, received an arrow from an unseen hand, which penetrated his lungs, and he fell. One of his companions was also mortally wounded by an arrow; and both of them died in the course of two or three days. Several others were slightly wounded, and thus their cowardly and outrageous proceedings were, for the time, suspended, if we except the *amusement* of stabbing and target-shooting at the bodies of the dead that were left on the ground.

I never ascertained how it was that on this occasion the Indians used only bows and arrows. It must have been that some strategy had been used to get possession of their guns; or else they had not time to load them; for in the various reports of this affair, fire-arms were not mentioned in my hearing.

Fort Lane, commanded by Captain [Andrew J.] Smith, was within a short distance. I can not think of this officer but with feelings of profound respect. His proximity to the Indians, and frequent intercourse with their Chiefs, afforded him facilities for knowing the nature and extent of their grievances. With the heroism of a soldier, and the magnanimity of a true man, he steadily, and to the utmost of the means at his command, resisted the popular torrent, and nobly pledged his life in protection of the weak and defenseless.

A detachment was sent from the Fort to bury the dead. They reported having found twenty-eight bodies, fourteen being those of women and children. But as many dead were undoubtedly left in the thickets, and no account was taken of the wounded, many of whom would die, or of the bodies that were afterward seen floating in the river, the above must be far short of the number actually killed.

Of those that escaped, eighty were received into the Fort; and had there been provision, and men enough for defense, more would have been admitted. For thus leaning favorably toward the poor fugitives from slaughter, the most bitter denunciations were poured upon the head of the Captain; and for many months his name was often coupled with the most ignominious and degrading epithets.

In another small valley, a few miles distant, there were a few Indians living on terms of intimacy with the Whites. These were assailed by surprise, and most of them put to death, according to previous arrangement. As might have been expected, the survivors who were not admitted into the Fort, fled beyond the settlements toward the coast. In passing down the valley, early on the morning of the 9th, they set fire to thirteen houses, and put to death ten or twelve white persons, among whom was Mr. Jones, with his wife and family. It seems either that his heart had failed him, or for some other reason he had not organized a party, as arranged when he was in town a few days before.

Owing to the firm stand taken by Captain Smith, and his utter refusal to aid or countenance these self-styled volunteers, a temporary check was given to their proceedings; and the constrained pugilists occupied themselves for a time in taking care of their wounded, and sometimes in short excursions for the purpose of shooting game or Indians. A number of these unfortunate people were living as domestics in different families; but even this could not protect them. They were in continual danger, and could not go abroad without being liable to provoke that wanton spirit of destruction, whose uncounted victims were left either dead or dying, to the final destruction of birds and beasts less ferocious and less cruel than their savage assassins. Even the sick and the wounded found no mercy and no quarter. For them there opened no city of refuge. Among the cases of this kind of which I heard most frequent mention, I will relate the following, given to me by one who participated in the affair:

"We found," said my informant, "several sick and famished Indians, who begged hard for mercy and for food. It hurt my feelings; but the understanding was that all were to be killed. So we did the work."

From another source I learned the following almost incredible atrocities: An Indian girl in the act of fetching water for her employers, was shot, and her body thrown into the creek. An Indian boy, scarce in his teens, who was in the habit of visiting the shanty of some miners, with whom he was a great favorite, and always welcome, was taken and hung upon the limb of a tree. Another was caught and had his throat cut. Two women and a man who had taken refuge upon Table Rock, which is high and very precipitous were pursued; and it was reported that they had killed themselves by jumping down its steep and craggy sides. But Dr. [George] Ambrose, who lived in the vicinity, informed me that they fell because they were shot, and could not avoid it. Their mangled, but yet living forms, as they lay on the loose rocks below, were so revolting a sight, that many began to declaim against such proceedings; and several prominent citizens wrote to Governor [George L.] Currey an account of what was doing, upon which the Governor issued a proclamation to the effect that the unauthorized companies who were committing outrages upon peaceable Indians, should immediately desist, as the Government would not sanction such proceedings.

How he came to this resolution against the very outrages which he had himself sanctioned and commissioned, it is difficult to surmise. Possibly some latent principle of human kindness, which was drawn from his mother's milk, and nursed at his mother's knee, might just then have revived within him. It is evident that he had reason to be shocked at the brutal outrages, which on every hand stared him in the face. There were deeds done which ought to have startled the conscience of any man or magistrate, and even policy might seem to demand a hearing.

Nor is this all. Let us suppose ourselves treated as the Indians were—that our property was taken away, our families scattered and destroyed, our people wantonly murdered, and ourselves made outlaws in our own land—should we not think that justice required something more than to be informed that Government did not approve of it? Should not we want and claim indemnification and more secure protection? The fact of these being a poor people, and unable to enforce their own claims, is surely no sufficient reason why they should not be protected. Their very weakness is an appeal which a truly magnanimous people could not resist.

But unfortunately the Chief Magistrate did not view the matter in this light; for instead of legal proceedings against those who had committed the outrages, or of redress for the sufferers, Governor Currey soon grew ashamed of his amiable weakness. Humanity was out of fashion, and he had not manliness enough to wear its colors, for fear that some human adder, which he ought to have felt strong enough to set his foot upon, might thrust forth its venomous tongue and hiss at him. This weakness is pitiful; but there is much of it to be found in the world, especially in high places, and the reason is, that the character and power of the man are so often set aside in the function and prerogative of the officer. In his zeal for acting officially, he utterly forgets that he either can, or ought, to act humanly—that humanity is, in fact, under all true law, the very basis of his official power; and without it his commission itself is null and void. Thus, insofar as he is not humane, he is a usurper, invading, by assumed and arbitrary action, the very authority that clothes him with his power, since this is avowedly for the good of the governed. To say that this wrong is common, does not justify or excuse it at all. It is time the people knew that there is no such thing as divorcing humanity from a true and righteous official power. In other words, the responsibility, character, and action of the man, can not be separated from those of the officer. Who ever attempts to do this, will entangle himself in an inextricable mesh of falsehoods and wrongs, and bring the blood of the guiltless upon his own head.

Soon after the proclamation already referred to, Governor Currey issued another, authorising the very men who had been denounced in the first to organize themselves in companies, elect officers, and prosecute the war against the Indians. We shall perceive the unfairness of these proceedings, if we compare them with what takes place between different Nations on occasions of disagreement. There is always investigation. Their respective claims are weighed; and war is not begun, until every reasonable effort to avoid it has been tried and fails. In common law the accused is not condemned and punished without a hearing; and if any nation, or individual, who happened to be our superior in power, should treat us on principles the reverse of these, we should esteem it unjust and tyrannical.

In defense of the measures pursued, it was reported that the Indians were false—pretending to desire peace, but still thieving and killing. But it should be remembered that they were obliged to take whatever they could lay their hands on, for present subsistence. The necessity of mutual protection required them to keep in company, so that they could not disperse themselves to fish, hunt, and gather seeds and roots, widely enough to obtain the necessary supplies. They did, therefore, only what every other people would have to do under similar circumstances. This they must have felt, and justly too, was only levying contributions on the enemies who had impoverished them.

Battles and Murders

No sooner had the war been authorized by the Governor, and some of each political party had got appointments of office, and prospective profit, than arrangements were made on the largest scale, which the great number of unemployed men and speculators could afford. As the drought had been continued late into the Fall, there were scores of Miners who, being deprived of work, for want of water, found an offer of employ, at such a time, acceptable; and many, from every point, were flocking to enroll. And besides these, men who were well to do, came out from almost every family to join the crusade; for it was considered unpatriotic not to do so. They also made a great speculation in Mules and ponies, gathering up every creature of the kind, except such as were really good and valuable. The more of these animals a man could muster, the more fortunate he was considered; for they were appraised at various estimates, from $100 to $350. Many of these were not worth more than $30 or $40; but if any were lost or injured in war, the owners looked to Government for pay, to the full amount of the appraisal. Oats, barley, and wheat were brought up at high prices—several thousand bushels of the latter, some of which was black with smut, bringing $2 a bushel. Farmers, teamsters, and packers, were all busy, hauling grain and provender a few miles down the Valley, or along the mountains. In some instances, the pack-mules ate all they carried before they got to their journey's end, and had to go back for more, for they were hired by the day. This, as may well be surmised, was a thriving business; but it was often said, that Uncle Sam could afford to keep fat horses.

The feed was crushed in the mill, and then fed on the ground so liberally, that several men, on seeing the waste and extravagance, left the service, believing that Government would never pay such unnecessary expenses. On one occasion, as the Newspapers reported, out of over a hundred horses, only thirty were able to travel the second day, the rest all being badly foundered.

Every thing was done on the assumption that all the settlements in the Valley were in danger from an invading foe; and every little shadow was made available by the Press and Propagandists, to keep up the excitement at home, and produce effect abroad. Several Forts were built, and crowded with families; and what was singular is, that in the thickest settlements, in the central part of the Valley, there were the most Forts, and the most terror, while others continued to occupy their houses, although situated at the outskirts, or near the base of mountains—the very place for Indians to attack, if so disposed. The latter doubtless believed the assertions of the Indians, who said that they did not consider themselves at war with the "good Americans," but only with the "Bostons." It may here pertinently be asked, if our people as generously made exceptions in favor of good Indians. The Volunteers, many of whom were from Pike county, Missouri, were, from this circumstance, known throughout Oregon and California as "Pikes," in addition to their more common soubriquet of "Bostons," which was solely applied to them by the Indians; though from what idea, or association, the latter name was derived, I have never been able to imagine, unless some villainous Yankee, from the City of Notions, earned for himself the questionable honor of establishing it. As the treatment which they have received from this class is so different from what they have been accustomed to have from the Fur Traders, they naturally enough entertain the idea that they are a different tribe both from the latter and the Government troops and Settlers, with all of whom they had long lived on friendly terms.

Had the Indians been disposed to destroy and slaughter all they could, there would have been hardly a house left in the Valley; and it was often a subject of remark, that they did so little damage. And so far as Volunteers and Forts were concerned, many thought that fifty determined Indians, bent on their object, could have overthrown and burned the whole in a week.

But the fact is, there were only a few Indians in a body. During the Fall and Winter, I made frequent enquiries of Volunteers, who had been in the service. Their estimates of those actually engaged in the Southern war were very indefinite, ranging from 150 to 400, including women and children. There were a few small, scattered bands, away in the mountains, who did all they could to keep out of the way, and after whom it was useless to follow.

The main body of the Indians evidently acted with the greatest discretion, keeping entirely on the defensive, so much so, that if details were given, the world might wonder how a professedly Christian people kept up for months, the semblance of war, against a few poor, starving men, destitute of homes, or stores, or allies, who fought only for existence, and not for territory or conquest. And yet, against these were arrayed, for months together, from three to five hundred men. At one time there were seven hundred in the field, armed and equipped with all the tents, stores, munitions, and weapons of modern warfare.

For several weeks nothing in particular was done, except electing officers, collecting materials, and, in various ways, preparing for a comfortable winter's campaign. It was thought that, when the mountains were covered with snow, the Indians would be compelled to collect in the Valley for shelter and subsistence; and then it would be easy to kill them at a blow. Several small parties were cut off, while in search of food, and it is wonderful how so many human beings found subsistence for months, harassed and surrounded, as they were, by such powerful foes.

But the Newspapers contrived to keep up a kind of sickly interest; for there was no lack of communications from Colonels, or Captains, or Generals, in regard to the marches, counter-marches, and maneuvers of the "Northern" or "Southern Battalion" of the "Army." Occasionally the interest was heightened by accounts under the caption of "Another Battle," which, no doubt, was highly appreciated east of the mountains; but we who heard the verbal statements of some who participated, or who witnessed these affairs, were impressed with the belief that "Another Massacre" would have been a more appropriate heading.

The following are specimens of Battles during the winter. The main body of the Indians had selected for their Head Quarters an angle in the Valley, known as the Meadows, having high, precipitous, and heavily timbered mountains on two sides, and the River in front, between them and their assailants. There was pasturage in this space for the few animals they owned; and as they could be approached only by crossing the River, it was considered too much of a Sebastopol for our Braves to effect an entrance, though canvas boats, and all the appurtenances for the operation, were conveyed to the spot; and great anticipations were entertained of an early termination of the war. But this project proved an entire failure. It was then resolved to keep quiet, and watch until the auspices were more favorable.

On one occasion, several Indians were discovered in three canoes, in the river above the Meadows. A volley was fired, killing all except two, who swam to the opposite side, and immediately shouted defiance, telling the Bostons to come to the Meadows and they would fight them. This affair was published under the flourish of a battle, in which our troops were victorious.

On several occasions parties of warriors found means to get round and waylay a train of pack-mules, on which occurrence, the muleteer and escort generally fled. By the time the Volunteers mustered to the rescue, the cargo was gone, and the Indians not to be found. These cases occurred so often, that the Volunteers became used to defeat, and seemed not to care, or calculate upon anything else; or, at least, they were very careful about risking any thing to prevent it. Battles were to these doughty warriors sheer speculations; and the grand study was how they should be compassed with the least possible risk, and the greatest possible advantage—to *themselves*. They seemed to have little or no sense of moral responsibility, either toward the enemy, or the authorities under whom they served. Patriotism was not only a thing they never saw, but it was what they were wholly incapable of seeing; for no person can cherish this ennobling sentiment in his own breast, at the same time that he is seeking to extinguish it in that of another. They would freely have spent the last dollar in the country, even though the metal it was made of could be transmuted into iron chains, to bind and enslave the Nation. The one purpose that was always kept steadily in view, was greed, and that of the grossest character. The war was likely to be a profitable investment, with good pay, comfortable quarters, and easy work. To hurry matters, under such circumstances, would not be good policy. Like the wary doctor, they did not wish to kill the patient too soon. In short, they took special care of the Goose that laid the Golden Egg.

Efforts in Behalf of Peace

Accordingly, on the morning of the 22d of January, 1856, I rode down to Jacksonville, and found the town in the greatest commotion. News had just arrived that Captain [James] Bruce and company, in pursuing a party of Indians, had dismounted and entered the Timber on foot. The Indians had managed to surround the men, and get possession of their horses; and volunteers were now being mustered to go to the rescue.

This incident was, in the estimation of some, an additional reason why the meeting should be had; but others used it as an argument for no meeting. While these conflicting sentiments were being canvassed in the streets and stores, I engaged the largest room that could be found, and procured the printing of hand-bills, calling for a meeting at the Robinson House, at 2 o'clock, P.M. In posting them round town, such was the opposition, that several were torn down before my face.

The meeting gathered slowly. It was not till after 3 o'clock that many were present; and I had to regret the absence of every one of those who had specially promised to attend. Several speeches were made in favor of war; and then I endeavored to give a brief account of its origin, its management, and its present and probable results; of the advantage of peace, and the ease with which it might be established.

A Reverend Doctor, from New Orleans, argued for continued war, and utter extermination; and another gentleman agreed to make a treaty, but only to massacre all the Indians as soon as they had signed it. My remarks, including several interruptions, occupied nearly two hours; and when the vote was taken, the party who were for war promptly spoke, while some of those who were on the opposite side refused to vote either way. So the meeting broke up, with but one voice raised in behalf of peace.

On leaving the house, a gentleman, who was to me a stranger, addressed me, saying, "You are the only man who dares speak his sentiments openly; if you will furnish me with a copy of your speech in writing, it shall be forwarded to the Indian Department, at Washington."

A few days afterward I met with two men returning from the Camp. They informed me that they had been with the company to relieve Captain Bruce. The Indians had made good their retreat, with the horses. In pursuing them they overtook two women, one of them having an infant. The officers commanded that they should not be hurt. Nevertheless they were clubbed to death; and the child was taken by the heels and had his brains dashed out against a tree. These men declare that they had left the service and would forfeit their claims for the time they had lost, rather than sanction such atrocities. It was afterward ascertained, that the Indians avenged themselves by hanging two white women, whom they held as prisoners.

This is another illustration of the suicidal character of war. Had those women been protected by such peaceful conditions as are founded upon a sense of equal justice, they might now have filled some useful sphere in our midst, with great comfort and joy to their respective families and friends; and if the spontaneous goodness that prompted those men to leave in disgust, were properly exercised, and truly developed in all our private relations and public enactments, and our spears converted into pruning hooks; for then Nations would not rise against Nations, neither would they war any more.

John Beeson met a number of influential reformers in the 1860s. His contacts included Peter Cooper, founder of the Cooper Institute, Lydia Marie Child, author of An Appeal for the Indians, *and Quaker leaders. Beeson became involved with the Universal Peace Society and traveled from Phoenix, Oregon, to Washington, D.C., in 1868 for its annual meeting. Beeson was also interested in hydrotherapy and spiritualism. He died in 1889 and was buried beside his wife, Ann, in a country cemetery near his farm.*

SOURCE
Beeson, John. *A Plea for the Indians; With Facts and Features of the Late War in Oregon.* John Beeson, New York, NY, 1857.

RELATED READING
Beckham, Stephen Dow. *Requiem For a People: The Rogue Indians and the Frontiersmen.* Norman, OK: University of Oklahoma Press, 1971. (Reprinted Oregon State University Press, 1995.)
Beeson, John. *Are We Not Men and Brethren: An Address to the People of the United States, in Behalf of the Indians.* New York, NY: National Indian Aid Office, 1859.
———. *John Beeson's Plea for the Indians: His Lonely Cry in the Wilderness for Indian Rights, Oregon's First Civil Rights Advocate.* Medford, OR: Webb Research Group, 1994.

Encounters with the Northern Paiute, 1860

On the eve of the Civil War the U.S. Army expanded its presence from Fort Dalles into the vast interior of the Pacific Northwest. A primary concern was to establish posts convenient for providing protection to emigrants traveling the Oregon Trail and its alternative routes. Some emigrants followed alleged short-cuts. The Free Emigrant Route headed west from Fort Boise into the Harney Basin, crossed the high desert, and ascended the eastern flank of the Cascades in the upper Deschutes country. The Applegate Trail turned southwest from Fort Hall to traverse the Black Rock Desert of northern Nevada before proceeding into the Klamath Basin and crossing over the southern flank of the Cascade Range into the Rogue River Valley.

Because of potential troubles with Native Americans on these routes, military officials decided to establish a base among the Northern Paiute and Bannock Indians.

The following letters were penned in the field in 1860 by Major Enoch Steen and Captain Andrew J. Smith of the First Dragoons. Except for explorations in the 1820s by Peter Skene Ogden, an employee whose diaries were held confidential in London by the Hudson's Bay Company, Euro-American penetration of the northern Great Basin was poorly documented. John C. Frémont's exploring party had entered the Summer Lake and Klamath lakes region in 1843, but most of the area remained uncharted and largely unknown. Steen and Smith thus filled their letters with observations and sketch maps to try to improve general understanding of the region. Captain Henry D. Wallen had done the same when in 1859 he had passed through the Deschutes, Crooked River, and Harney Basin to explore a wagon trace east to the Great Salt Lake.

Smith's party encountered hostilities on June 23 in a spirited battle with some one hundred and fifty men, probably Northern Paiutes. Smith abandoned his road explorations and soon he and Steen began coordinated action to try to find those who opposed their trespass. In early August the dragoons set out for what Steen called Snow Mountain, a peak subsequently known as Steens Mountain, a vast geological uplift rising dramatically above the Alvord Desert and lying south of the Harney Basin. Steen described the ascent to the summit. The Wasco scouts from the Warm Springs Reservation, serving his company, ruthlessly pursued the unsuspecting Northern Paiutes living in the vicinity of the mountain. The road expedition was transformed into a punitive pursuit of the hard-to-find and even harder-to-catch Indians of the Great Basin. The manuscript letters of Smith and Steen are held in the National Archives.

Letter of June 19, 1860, Capt. A. J. Smith to Capt. A[lfred] Pleasonton.

Camp Exploration 25 Miles East of Lake Harney
    Captain:
    I am happy to inform you of our safe arrival at this point. We have found an excellent wagon road from Buck Creek, crossing the head and passing down the East side of the big meadows, with good grass and water and sufficient wood (and willows & sage) for cooking purposes. I will shorten this route some 20 miles, on my return, as I have ascertained & can cross Cricket [Silvies] River some miles nearer the Lake. It is impracticable to get a Road from this point to the east end of Lake Harney or on the south side of it, on account of an extensive intervening tuly swamp. I will know more about it however before I make my final report. I have an exploring party out in the direction of the Owyhee and will reconnoiter south myself tomorrow. I have seen no place since we left Buck Creek, suitable for a post; the country is destitute of timber (such as would be required for buildings) except small scrubby cedars in few localities. I will examine the country between this & the Owyhee.
    I have selected Separation Camp (See enclosed sketch) two days march from Buck Creek, as the most suitable for the depot of supplies, grass, water & wood in abundance. I have requested Maj. Steen to recommend the same.
    I am Sir Very Respectfully Your Ob[edien]t Servant, A. J. Smith, Capt[ain], 1st Drag[oons]

Letter of June 21, 1860, E[noch] Steen to Capt. A. Pleasonton.

Camp at Smith's Spring, 245 miles from Fort Dalles
    Captain,
    I have the honor to report for the information of the General commanding that I arrive[d] with my command at Lake Harney on the 15th inst[ant] and that I have examined the country in the vicinity of the lake, and returned to this

place, and from the knowledge that I have obtained of it, I think that the most convenient position to establish the Depot of supplyes for Capt. [Andrew] J. Smith's Command would be at my present Encampment (Smith's Spring) on the main road, forty miles this side of the lake and sixteen miles beyond the proposed junction of the Fort Dalles and Eugene City roads.

I send you enclosed a map of the country in the vicinity of Lake Harney and the position of the place recommended for the Depot. I would especially rec-ommend that there would not be *less than one Company with two commissioned officers sent with the supplies*, as the Indians in this country are hostile. On Capt. [Henry] Wallen's road, forty miles N.E. of Lake Harney, in the Blue mountains, the Indians attacked a party of miners from the Willamette Valley, on the 6th inst[ant], wounded one man severely, and stole about seventy horses.

I have not been able to ascertain the number of Indians; some of the miners say that the hills were alive with them, whilst others say they did not see more than twenty or forty at one time. There was in the party of miners sixty-two men well armed, and they had to make a hasty retreat, leaving behind them most of their horses, and provisions.

I did not hear of this attack untill Capt. Smith had left me three days; if he had been with me, I would have combined the two Commands and left a suf-ficient guard with the wagons and provisions, and with the remainder of the troops, I would have followed the Indians into the mountains, but with my Command, I did not have any one to leave with my train if I had followed them with the Company.

You will observe by the map I send enclosed, the position marked "A" where the Indians made the attack and the direction that they run off with the stolen horses. They report the Indians armed with rifles, but the horses that were found dead, were shot with arrows.

From the course that they have taken, they are in the Blue Mountains be-tween the headwaters of the John Days and Crooked rivers. The superinten-dent of Indian Affairs, Mr. [Edward] Geary has not been able to get any Indians to come in; he finds good many deserted lodges; he is of the opinion that they have all fled to the above mentioned place. Mr. Geary will return to the Dalles with the Express. I refer you to him for further information.

I will leave Capt. Smith's road near the headwaters of Buck Creek and travel in a westerly direction to the headwaters of the Des Chutes river, as this will be in a more direct line with his road, which, you will observe by the map does not go directly by Lake Harney.

I am, Sir, very respectfully, Your most obedient Servant, E[noch] Steen, Maj[or] 1st Dragoons, Commanding Wagon Road Expedition from Lake Harney to Eugene City

Letter of June 27, 1860, Capt. A. J. Smith to Capt. A. Pleasonton.

Camp 25 Miles NE of Lake Harney

Captain:

You may be somewhat surprised to learn that my present position is N.E. of Lake Harney only 25 miles. I left Camp Exploration 25 miles East of the lake on the 21st to pursue our course towards the Owyhee River and had arrived on the 23d within twenty miles of the river when we were attacked, on going into camp, by a war party of Indians numbering upwards of 150. More than one half mounted, who came charging up on the pack train yelling hideously, hoping to stampede our animals. The rear guard rushed the train into camp and protected it very handsomely, until the company was deployed on the right and rear when the Indians were mostly congregated. They fought us in this position about an hour and a half when we succeeded in driving them to the hills, about one half mile distant from our camp, where they remained and annoyed us during the remainder of the day, and after dark got down to the windward of our camp and tried to set fire to the grass in order to burn us out; but fortunately our immediate camp was in very green grass. I am happy to state that we defeated the Indians with a loss, on their part; of one killed and many severely wounded, dropped from their horses, and carried off. We got six horses (one a larger sorrel horse that was stolen from Maj. [John F.] Reynolds last summer on Snake river) two guns & accoutrements, quivers &c. It affords me pleasure to have witness to the zeal and gallantry displayed by the officers (Lieuts. Perdon & Wheeler, Jr.) and those of my company as also some of the employees during the short but successful conflict: Dr. Taylor, rifle in hand, was anxious to participate, but I restrained him, thinking his services might soon be required professionally. If I had had a sufficient guard for the train, we could have pursued the Indians and made their defeat more disastrous, no doubt. Mr. [Louis] S[c]holl, and an escort of eight men of my company, were on the Owyhee at the time of the attack, but were sent for and arrived safely in camp in the morning.

A portion of the war party had followed us from this valley and was joined by Indians from the Owyhee, and would undoubtedly have increased their numbers, as we moved on, and annoyed if not rendered our further progress dangerous.

As it as unsafe to send out small exploring parties (as we are compelled to do to examine the country before proceeding) I deemed it prudent to return to Separation Camp on Indian river and await further instructions from the Com[mandin]g Gen[era]l of the Dep[artmen]t. I am inclined to believe that all the Indians, in this region of country are hostile; and as a wagon road cannot be gotten through this season, I would respectfully suggest that the exploring or road making expeditions be ordered to remain in this vicinity and operate against the Indians.

If the Com[mandin]g Gen[era]l would order out immediately some foot troops to establish a camp and protect our trains bringing out sufficient supply of provisions, we (Maj[or] Steen and myself) could make I hope successful campaigns against the Indians.

I have on hand this day this month's supply of provisions.

I am Sir Very Respectfully Your Ob[edien]t Ser[van]t A. J. Smith, Capt[ain] 1st Drag[oons]

Letter of June 29, 1860, Major Enoch Steen to Captain A. Pleasonton.

Camp on Beaver Creek, Long. 120° Lat. 43° 50'

Captain:

I have the honor to report for the information of the General Commanding that I received an express from Capt. Smith this evening about dark, informing me that he had been attacked by a large body of Indians, about fifty miles southeast of Lake Harney, and that he was then on his return to Smith's Spring, forty miles N.W. of Lake Harney.

He informed me that he did not consider his command of sufficient strength to guard his train and follow the Indians.

I will start on my return to Smith's Springs in the morning to meet Capt. Smith and will act in concert with him, prosecuting a campaign against the Indians untill further orders from the headquarters of the Department.

I would respectfully recommend that there would be a command of two mounted Companys sent from Fort Walla Walla towards the Head waters of the John Days river, and to scout the country along the old Emigrant road to Fort Boise, as it is reported that the Indians are in large force in that vicinity.

I would also respectfully recommend that a train of supplys for one month for my Command and Capt. Smith's, be sent to Smith's Springs, and that a guard of at least one company be sent with it.

I am of the opinion that supplys for one month will be sufficient, as we have two months supplys on hand at present, and that we can scout the whole country in the vicinity of Lake Harney in the months of July and August and cause all the Indians to sue for peace by that time or run them out of the country.

The roads not being completed, I could not recommend any place for a military Post, and as there will be no Emigrants to pass by this way untill the roads are finished, it will be useless for troops to remain any longer that to conquer the Indians which can be done in two months. I have been very successful in finding a good road so far, with plenty of good grass, wood, and water.

I send you enclosed a map of the route since we left the Fort Dalles Road; we would have been on the Headwaters of the Des Chutes in two days more.

I am, Sir, Very respectfully Your obedient Servant, E. Steen, Major 1st Dragoons, Comm[andin]g Wagon Road Expedition from Lake Harney to Eugene City

Letter of July 20, 1860, Major Enoch Steen to Captain A. Pleasonton.

Camp Union, O[re]g[o]n

Captain:

In a communication addressed to the Departmental H[ea]dquarters, dated Beaver Creek, Oregon, June 30th 1860, I had the honor to report to the general commanding, the progress made by the troops under my command towards opening a practicable wagon road from Harney Lake to Eugene City, as well as the circumstances which induced me to rejoin Capt. Smith at this place. My express left my camp at Beaver Creek on the 30th day of June and as no return express has yet reached me, I made this report fearing that probably the former express may have been cut off whilst en route to the Dalles. On receiving Capt. Smith's communication, informing me of his affair with the Snake Indians, on the 23d of June and also of his abandonment of his road and return movement. I at once determined to join him at or in the vicinity of Harney Lake.

On the 4th inst[ant] our respective forces were united under my command at a camp on Indian River, about 30 miles North of Harney Lake. Having reason to suppose that the Indians who had attacked Capt. Smith had moved to the north in direction of the headwaters of Crooked and Malheur rivers, on the 6th inst. I left my camp with eight Dragoons of companies "C" and "H," the officers of these companies (except Lieut. Wheeler, who was left in charge of the camp) the topographical and medical officers. The route pursued by me was to the north by the canon of Cricket [Silvies] River, thence East to the headwaters of Malheur river, then south until I struck Capt. Wallen's Wagon Road and later Capt. Smith's which I followed back to my camp on Indian River. The country travelled over by my command is of exceeding roughness, consisting of deep canons, separated by irregular rocky table lands. I was absent from my camp six days and accomplished a distance of one hundred and eighty miles. I made no discovery of Indian signs until the 9th inst. when the trail of a small party which had passed northwards was discovered; on the afternoon of the same day I surprised one Indian man, who endeavoured to escape, but was soon overtaken by a half dozen Dragoons and brought bound to me. Still later in the same day I surprised a small party and took captive one woman and two children and two horses, two men who were with the party escaped under the cover of the thick bushes of the stream on which they were encamped.

The Indians taken are still my prisoners and will be useful in the prosecution of a war against their people. Yesterday I sent the woman to persuade some of her friends to meet me.

Unless an express should reach me within two or three days, giving me the specific instructions of the General commanding, I shall make a scout in the direction of the Snow mountains [Steens Mountain] south of Harney Lake as it is reported the Indians are there in numbers.

In my former report I requested that additional supplies for one month be sent me.

I am Captain very respectfully Your Ob[edien]t Serv[an]t, E. Steen, Major 1st Drag[oon]s Comm[an]d[in]g

Letter of August 3, 1860, Major Enoch Steen to Captain A. Pleasonton.

H[ea]d Q[uarte]rs Expedition Against Snake Indians, Camp on Indian River, Oregon

Captain:

I have the honor to report to the Colonel commanding the arrival of Major Andrew's command on the 2nd Inst. The force now under my command is sufficiently large for the vigorous prosecution of a campaign against the Snake Indians. In the absence of positive information concerning the geography of the country, as well as the camping grounds of any considerable bodies of the

Indians, I have determined from the best information to be obtained to execute with my command the following plans.

Tomorrow I will leave this camp with one hundred Dragoons and sixtyfive Artillery, rations for fifteen days, for the Snow Mountains South of Harney Lake where I have reason to believe the Indians are assembled in force. I will have the smallest passable pack train and will then be able to make rapid marches, and should I meet the enemy to employ my entire force in their chastisement.

Brev[e]t Major Andrews with the remainder of the command in charge of the trains and property of the command will during my absence move to the eastward to a camp in the vicinity of Owyhee River where I will rejoin him. Major [William N.] Grier with his Squadron being on Snake River, my own command being at the Snow Mountain and Major Andrews moving eastward, the Indians if they are in this section of country at all, will be surrounded and I trust will fall into our hands. My future movements will depend upon the results of the plans which I am now about to execute.

The instructions of the Colonel commanding will be shortly obeyed, and I have every hope that the campaign will be terminated speedily and successfully. . . . .

I am very respectfully Your ob[edien]t Serv[an]t, E. Steen, Major, 1st Drag[oon]s Com[mandin]g

Letter of August 18, 1860, Major Enoch Steen to Captain James A. Hardie.

H[ead] Q[uarte]rs Expedition against Snake Indians, Camp at Head of Big Meadows, Or[e]g[on]

Captain:

I have the honor to report for the information of the Colonel commanding the Department, the following details of the operations of the troops under my command, since the date of my last report. On the 4th inst[ant] I left my camp on Indian River, with one hundred Dragoons of Co[mpanie]s "C" and "H," 1st Dragoons, and sixty five men of Co[mpanie]s "A" and "B" 3d Artillery, and all the officers present of these companies, a topographical and medical officer; the command was supplied with twelve days rations, transported by pack mules.

I moved directly for Harney Lake, and reaching it passed to the Eastward so as to strike the Snow Mountains South of it. After leaving Harney Lake some twelve miles, my direction was changed more to the South than I had intended, because of an impassable slough of great dimensions. After two days march from the Lake I finally arrived at a bold mountain stream [Donner and Blitzen River] of about the size of the Umatilla River, upon which I camped. This to which I have given the name of New River, is one of remarkable beauty.

During the four days occupied in reaching this camp, no Indians were seen, nor was anything discovered to indicate their presence in the country. At this camp the Wasco Indians (15 of whom accompanied the command) who were in advance unexpectedly fell upon a single Indian, whom they killed; they reported the discovery of numerous signs of the Snakes on the North slope of the Snow Mountain. I at once determined to follow any tracks and accordingly left camp very early on the morning of the 8th inst. with the Dragoons, leaving the artillery to follow with the packs. I moved directly up the mountain and at noon my Dragoons were in the region of perpetual snow. The Wascos in advance, having surprised a party of two or three Snakes and these having fled to the very summit of the mountain, I followed on and arrived there soon after them.

From the summit looking southward the descent seems impossible; under other circumstances I would not have attempted it, but the Indians had passed down and the pursuers must follow. My command descended by winding along the rocky walls of a cañon upon which with difficulty they could find footing, and in two and a half hours reached the base, having made a descent of six thousand feet; the artillery with the packs arrived at the camp the same day in safety, only one mule having been killed, by falling from the rocks in the descent.

The trail of the Indians was lost in the descent. After having crossed the mountain I made two marches to the South and West. At the last camp in this direction, the Wascos, always in advance, came upon a family, killed one man and took prisoners a woman and two young children. From this camp I sent out scouting parties, but no Indians were met; the Wascos during the day again made some captures of small children and killed one man.

On the 12th inst[ant] I changed my direction to the East, knowing the utter improbability of finding any assemblage of Indians in the section where I was. The march of this day was one of unusual severity, especially upon the Artillery, the distance marched, without finding water, was forty miles. The Dragoons made the march in about fourteen hours, the foot troops occupied a somewhat longer time, but notwithstanding the keen sufferings of individuals, all arrived safe in camp. It now became necessary on account of rations to turn in the direction of the Depot of supplies which I had ordered to a camp on the Big Meadows.

Eastward I passed in the vicinity of the point at which Capt. Smith's command was attacked, and then moved northward and arrived at Major Andrews camp on the 16th inst[ant], having marched 280 miles and having been absent thirteen days.

I have every reason to believe that but very few Indians inhabit the country, through which I have recently scouted and these are secreted in small individual families, in rocks and bushes. I found no fisheries and no grounds for obtaining roots or berries; these could only fall into our hands by the merest accident, bearing to the fact that guides cannot be had who know anything of the country South and West of Harney Lake.

I cannot speak in too high terms of the officers and men of my command. They were always zealous, and the fatigue and suffering of a scout were borne with cheerfulness in prospect of meeting the Snakes in force.

I shall await here a few days to recruit my horses and will send another scout to the East and North in the direction of the Malheur River and Crooked River. In the meantime I will conduct the wagons and supplies to a point on Crooked River w[h]ere my entire force will be united in about twelve days. On my arrival at that place about the 3d of September, I will have but sufficient rations to carry my command back to the Dalles; many of the men of my command are shoeless and their clothing so much torn as not to be a proper protection for their bodies.

I do not know what more can be done against these Indians the present season, and if it meets the approval of the Colonel commanding, will at the conclusion of the scout, which I am now about to make, move my command to the Dalles, where I will arrive about the 20th of September, at which time the rations will have been consumed. I am ignorant of the operations of Major Grier, as no communication has been received from him.

I am, Captain, respectfully, E. Steen, Major, 1st Drag[oon]s, Com[mandin]g

SOURCES

Smith, A. J. Letter of June 19, 1860, to Capt. A. Pleasonton. Box 5, Department of Oregon Letters Received, 1858–61, Part 1, Entry 3574, RG 393, National Archives, Washington, DC.

———. Letter of June 27, 1860, to Capt. A. Pleasonton. Box 5, Department of Oregon Letters Received, 1858–61, Part 1, Entry 3574, RG 393, National Archives, Washington, DC.

Steen, E[noch]. Letter of June 21, 1860, to Capt. A. Pleasonton. Box 5, Department of Oregon Letters Received, 1858–61, Part 1, Entry 3574, RG 393, National Archives, Washington, DC.

———. Letter of June 29, 1860, to Capt. A. Pleasonton. Box 5, Department of Oregon Letters Received, 1858–61, Part 1, Entry 3574, RG 393, National Archives, Washington, DC.

———. Letter of July 20, 1860, to Capt. A. Pleasonton. Box 5, Department of Oregon Letters Received, 1858–61, Part 1, Entry 3574, RG 393, National Archives, Washington, DC.

———. Letter of Aug[ust] 3, 1860, to Capt. A. Pleasonton. Box 5, Department of Oregon Letters Received, 1858–61, Part 1, Entry 3574, RG 393, National Archives, Washington, DC.

———. Letter of August 18, 1860, to Capt. James A. Hardie. Box 5, Department of Oregon Letters Received, 1858–61, Part 1, Entry 3574, RG 393, National Archives, Washington, DC.

RELATED READING

Brimlow, George Francis. *Harney County, Oregon, and Its Range Land.* Portland, OR: Binfords & Mort, Publishers, 1951.

———. *The Bannock Indian War of 1878.* Caldwell, ID: The Caxton Printers, 1938.

Imprisonment at Alcatraz: Chief John of the Rogue Rivers

No single Oregon Indian gained so much attention in the 1850s as the famed warrior, Chief John of the Rogue Rivers. While a bit of uncertainty exists about his identity, this man was probably a Takelman-speaker who, on November 11, 1854, signed the amendment to the Treaty with the Rogue River Tribe of Indians. In 1853 eight Indian leaders had agreed to a treaty of friendship and land cession to the United States. The agreement ceded all of the Rogue River Valley and the surrounding high country from the crest of the Cascades downstream to the mouths of Jump-Off-Joe Creek and the Applegate River. The treaty also provided for the creation of a temporary reservation at Table Rock and for executive authority to create at some future date a permanent reservation.

When the treaty reached Washington, D.C., members of the Senate realized that Joel Palmer, Oregon Superintendent of Indian Affairs, who had negotiated the treaty, lacked official treaty-making powers. To expedite consideration of the treaty, Palmer in 1854 returned to southern Oregon to amend this treaty and one with the Cow Creek Band of Umpqua. Among the signers of the amendment clause to the Rogue River treaty was Te-cum-tom, or "Elk Killer," also identified as Chief John.

War erupted in October 1855, with massacres of Takelman women, children, and aged men by Oregon Volunteers. Te-cum-tom became known as a wily leader, skilled in eluding both the U.S. Army and the Oregon Volunteers. Chief John led his people deep into the canyon of the Rogue River where, on May 28–29, 1856, they engaged in a spirited battle with the First Dragoons at the Big Bend. The U.S. Army suffered twenty-nine killed and wounded before driving the Indians from the hillsides above Foster Creek where the soldiers had established a line of defense. One by one the Indian leaders surrendered and brought their weary, hungry people to Fort Orford. Finally on July 2, Dr. Rodney Glisan noted in his diary: "This morning Captain [E. O. C.] Ord's command arrived, bringing in the famous Old John and his band—the terror of Southern Oregon." Glisan continued: "He is about fifty-five years old—not at all prepossessing in appearance—has a resolute, discontented, and unhappy appearance." John had only thirty-five surviving men in his band but was accompanied by ninety women and ninety children.

John's band was compelled to march north nearly two hundred miles along the rugged Oregon shore from Port Orford to the new Coast Reservation with its agency headquarters at Siletz. The following letters document the way in which Bureau of Indian Affairs officials handled "recalcitrant" chiefs. The BIA agent exercised plenary authority. He had Chief John and one of his three sons slapped into irons. Without a hearing or trial, they were taken by ship to California and imprisoned on Alcatraz Island. As late as 1862, Chief John's two daughters continued to petition the U. S. Army to release him.

Words in Chinook Jargon are followed by English translations.

Metcalfe, R[obert] B. Letter of October 13, 1857, to James W. Nesmith.

Silets Agency
Oct 13th 1857
Dear Sir

About ten days since old John and two of his boys started out with the declaration that their hearts were sick, and that they were not going to stay here and die with sickness that they had rather die by bullets, and were evidently going down below where I had two or three men sowing wheat; to murder them. When they met two Silets indians drew their revolvers and fired upon them killing one of them on the ground and when I called upon Old John to know why he did so; he said that it was none of my business that they would kill who they pleased, and when I asked Cultus Jim (Old John's son) for his revolver John sprang to his feet perfectly wild with rage, drew his revolver half out and told Jim to keep his revolver and fight with it.

I then saw that he was determined on another outbreak, and that nothing would prevent it, but rigid and prompt measures on my part; I therefore sent an express to Capt. [Christopher C.] Augur for a force sufficient to disarm all the Indians on the Reservation when the troops arrived I called upon John for his arms but he refused to give them up. I then requested Lt. [H. H.] Garber to accompany me with his detachment of twenty-five men; with the view of arresting John and Cultus Jim and taking their arms from them, but when we arrived in sight of John's house he and his boys ran to the brush; and we were only able to get two small revolvers, which were given up by those who remained at the house.

We then returned to our quarters disgusted with our success. The following day Cultus Jim came down to a camp near the agency, when Lt. Garber and myself went down to arrest him; he refused to be arrested and after making a desperate resistance drew a concealed revolver ran on the opposite side of his horse from me and fired at me. The ball passed near my head; at which moment Sarg[eant] Clark arrived and he Lt. Garber and myself fired upon him almost at the same instant all three of the balls taking effect killing him on the spot; since that time the excitement has died away and the Indians have given up nearly all of their arms say twenty guns, eight revolvers and seven other pistols; the Indians have promised to give up all of their arms which I think will be done in a few days.

Yours Respectfully, Yr. Obt. Servt R. B. Metcalfe Ind. Agent

Metcalfe, R[obert] B. Letter of April 12, 1858, to Captain C[hristopher] C. Augur, Fort Hoskins, Oregon Territory

Sir:

From Recent hostile declarations of old John and his son Adam I have to request that you arrest them and keep them in confinement until it may be deemed safe to release them; I make this request because I am certain they will kill some good white man the first opportunity and leave the matter to your discretion; after I have made the request, I have then discharged my duty, and if they kill a white man the blame will not attach to me; I will here state what other Indians say in relation to him.

Joe the Klamath chief tole me this morning that John's heard [heart] was bad that he (Joe) had talked to him three days trying to get him to "*Marsh*" [remove] his bad heart, but John finally drove him away after much abuse, threatening to kill him if he talked to him in that way, and asked him when he had become a white man's "*papoose*" &c., he also stated in his talk to Joe that he had deceived me by telling me that his heart was good but that he had only done so because he feared me, that his heart was not good towards the whites and that the "*Salt Chucks*" [Coast Indians] would aid him in making war upon them; John and Adam have each a colt's navy revolver which they carry concealed; "John Lewis" also states that John is determined to kill a white man the first opportunity this he learns from John's daughter with whom he is connected by marriage.

Tyee George also states that John is making every effort in his power to create an outbreak by tribes threats &c. that John and one of his man had tried all night to get the Coast Tribes to join him in making an attack upon the Agency; the same charges are corroborated by more than a dozen Indians; Now you have the facts and have heard them and can take such action in the matter as in

Chief John, probably a leader of the band of Athabaskan-speakers residing on the Applegate River in south-western Oregon, led the fight against volunteer soldiers and the U.S. Army. He remained a defiant chief on the Coast Reservation (Oregon Historical Society OrHi 4,355).

your judgement may seem best, my opinion is that they should be arrested immediately and taken to Vancouver; one or two of his daughters "Kit" and "Fan" to whom he appears much attached might be allowed to accompany him; if you determine to make the arrest it had better be done as you come in, as they can be taken completely by surprise when you can give him to understand that he shall not be hurt and there will be no trouble.

respectfully your obdt. Servt.

R. B. Metcalfe, Ind. Agent

Augur, C[hristopher] C. Letter of April 20, 1858, to Col[onel] T. Morris, Commanding Fort Vancouver, W. T.

Colonel.

On my return home I found a letter from the Indian Agent Mr. Metcalfe—a copy of which is enclosed—detailing the bad conduct of *Old John* and requesting me to have him arrested. I have long entertained the opinion that the indians on this reservation would never be quiet as long as Old John is permitted to remain with them. Although I doubt if he ever succeeded in getting them into open outbreak, still he keeps them in a state of excitement and restless dissatisfaction, and has doubtless made threats against the life of the Agent & some of his employees.

By the last Steamer I reported these facts to the General, and stated my intention to have John & his son arrested and sent to your post, and at the same time recommended that he, with his family be sent to Benicia or the Presidio. I esteem it of the greatest importance that he be sent away from the *vicinity* of the reservation at once, which must be my excuse for troubling you with him & his friends so abruptly. Should no order arrive by next Steamer for his disposition, I shall again urge upon the General to remove him below, as if he remains anywhere in this country he must be strictly confined, where as, if he goes to California there will be no occasion for such severity.

I repeat my conviction that he is a most dangerous indian, not only in reference to the indians on this reservation, but to all in this country, and that he well merits careful attention. The same may be said of his daughters *Fanny* & *Kitty*, who have inherited in an eminent degree their fathers peculiarities.

Very respectfully Colonel, Your obedient Servant

C. C. Augur, Capt. 4th Infy., Army

Rector, W[illiam] H. Letter of September 2, 1862, to W[illia]m P. Dole. p. 255.

In connexion with this agency, I would here speak of a responsibility which I have assumed in releasing from captivity the Indian chief John, who figured so conspicuously in the Rogue River wars of 1853 and 1855.

This chief was a brave and daring leader, and, although of better principles than most of his race, he exerted such a powerful influence over his people that Agent [Robert B.] Metcalf[e] deemed it advisable to cause him and his son Adam to be arrested and placed in confinement. In order that they should be securely confined, they were placed in charge of the military authorities, and by them sent to California, where they have remained prisoners for five years. During my visit to the agency his daughters made a very strong appeal for their release and return to their families. They desired that the remnant of his days might be spent with them. I made application to General [George] Wright, commanding this military department, for their release which was granted. They returned in due time, and were at once sent to Grand Ronde agency. I have seen them but once since their return, but learn from Agent [James B.] Condon that their conduct is unexceptionable, and that they exert a very salutary influence over other Indians in inducing them to remain at home and live like white people. The old man is now far advanced in years, but his son is in the prime of life, and, although he has lost a leg in battling for his life and liberty, he is of great service to the agent. Thus far my act has resulted in good, and I have but little fear that any harm will result from restoring them to liberty.

Patton, J. McF. Letter of October 24, 1862, to Charles E. Mix.

Sir

I have this day transmitted to your address a small package containing a map of Grand Round Agency prepared by James B. Condon Agent in charge. Also the Photograph of "Old John" Chief of the Rogue River Indians, and his son Adam, of whom mention was made in Superintendent [William] Rectors Annual Report. This was taken immediately after their release from prison in California, in May last, and in as much as they are Indians of notoriety in this State, and will occupy a prominent page in its history, I forward them to your Department with the compliments of this office.

Very Respectfully, Your Obt. Servt. J. McF. Patton,
Clerk to Supt. Of Ind Aff

SOURCES

Augur, C. C. Letter of April 20, 1858, to Col[onel] T. Morris. Unregistered Letters and Telegrams Received, Department of the Pacific, 1857–65, Box 1, Entry 3585, Part 1, RG 393, Continental Commands, National Archives, Washington, D.C.

Metcalfe, R[obert] B. Letter of October 13, 1857, to James W. Nesmith. Letter No. 261, Letters Received, Oregon Superintendency of Indian Affairs, Microcopy M–2, Roll 15, RG 75, National Archives, Washington, D.C.

———. Letter of April 12, 1858, to Capt[ain] C. C. Augur. Unregistered Letters and Telegrams Received, Department of the Pacific, 1857–65, Box 1, Entry 3585, Part 1, RG 393, Continental Commands, National Archives, Washington, D.C.

Patton, J. McF. Letter of October 24, 1862, to Charles E. Mix. Letters Received, Oregon Superintendency of Indian Affairs, Microcopy M–234, Roll 613, Fr.545, RG 75, National Archives, Washington, D.C.

Rector, W[illiam] H. Letter of September 2, 1862, to W[illia]m P. Dole.

Annual Report of the Commissioner of Indian Affairs . . . 1862. Washington, D.C.: Government Printing Office, 1863, p. 253–64.

RELATED READING

Glisan, Rodney. *Journal of Army Life.* San Francisco, CA: A. L. Bancroft & Company, 1874.

The Hanging of Klamath Chief George, 1863

Lacking rights of habeas corpus, trial by jury, or protection of persons and prop-erty, Oregon Indians in the mid-nineteenth century were repeatedly subjected to egregious and inhumane treatment. One of the perpetrators was Lieutenant-Colonel Charles S. Drew, a self-styled protector of overland emigrants on the Applegate Trail. Drew was quick to send his views on alleged Indian barbarism to Washington, D. C. As an officer in the Oregon Volunteers, he rose in rank dur-ing the Civil War and commanded troops at Camp Baker on Bear Creek near Phoenix, Oregon. In 1863 he selected the site for Fort Klamath—1,050 acres for the fort and 3,135 acres for a hay reserve—for a military post in the Klamath Basin. No one consulted the Indians about this intrusion into their Wood River Valley.

The following letters document the tragedy that befell Chief George, one of sev-eral contenders for leadership as the control of old Chief Lileks (LaLakes) waned in the 1860s. In the first letter, Indian Agent Amos E. Rogers attested to George's succession to leadership in the spring of 1863. In a second letter Rogers assessed the attitudes and actions of Colonel Drew. Clearly Drew hated equally both Indians and the Bureau of Indian Affairs. These two letters serve as a chilling preface to the letters and newspaper accounts of November 1863, describing what happened when Klamath Indians—not bound by treaty nor confined to a reservation–vis-ited the upper Bear Creek in the Rogue River Valley.

The Klamaths were camping in an area that was known as Dead Indian Country. Several sites in Jackson County used this designation: Dead Indian Creek, Dead Indian Mountain, and Dead Indian Road. By the 1990s the terminol-ogy was deemed insensitive and led to spirited efforts to change the place names. The term "Dead Indian" was prophetically accurate in terms of what happened to Chief George. Drew casually noted: "I directed his removal to Camp Baker where I ordered him executed and he was accordingly hung." Few seemed to note or care what Drew had done. Histories of the Klamath Tribe omit mention of Chief George, would-be successor to Lileks. No one took any action against Drew.

*Skookum John, another leader, was also murdered by Oregon Volunteers when
they tried to arrest him. Details of his death were not reported.*

Letter of April 18, 1863, Amos E. Rogers, Sub Indian Agent for Oregon,
To Whom It May Concern

This may certify that the bearer of this Indian George is now recognized as the
Chief of that part of the Klamath Indians who were formerly under countroll
of La Lake. He George represents to me that some parties in Yreka, Cal[ifornia],
are desirous of locating in the Klamath Lake country, there has been as yet no
treaty concluded with these Indians the U.S. has no title to the land. Persons
locating there must take all the chances.
     Amos E. Rogers, U.S. Sub Indian Agent for Oregon

Letter of August 1, 1863, Amos E. Rogers, Sub Indian Agent for Oregon to
J. W. P[erit] Huntington, Oregon Superintendent of Indian Affairs

Col. [Charles] Drew makes no secret of his hostility and unqualified opposition
to the established and approved policy of the Indian Department; nor does he
of late, seem to omit an occasion of expressing his sentiments. His language is
not unfrequently of the most bitter, harsh, and contemptuous character, concerning the present head of the Indian Bureau at Washington, thence all along
down through the several divisions of this Department. I was at first disposed
to ascribe his severe expressions of bitterness and hostility to some personal
enmity that might be possibly entertained towards myself. In this however I am
now persuaded that I have misjudged.
     You shall hear and judge for yourself.
     On the evening of our arrival at the [Klamath] Lakes Col. Drew said, "When
I get established here, I shall muster the Indians every day for roll call; and
make every one answer to his name! No Indian shall leave here, either, without
a pass from me. I shall plow up a piece of ground next spring, and by G_d, they
have to got to put it in too; if it has to be done at the point of the bayonet. I will
show Uncle Sam that there is a way to get along with Indians, without having a
set of whining Indian sympathizing Agents about to make promises to Indians
never to be fulfilled."
     Here was a pause for a moment. I asked if he expected the Indians to wholly
subsist on what they would raise. He replied that he did not; but said he: "I will
find a way of obtaining such funds as will be necessary to purchase what will be

needed for their subsistence beside what they raise." But said I, "when you ask for this fund will you not come in direct contact with the Indian Department? Will the question not be asked what the Indian Dep[artmen]t is doing in allowing the Military to attend to a branch of business that properly belongs to it?"

Drew said: "this is precisely what I want! I want to come in contact with the Indian Department! I want to get a chance to show it up. If I cannot show the damndest state of things in this Dep[artmen]t that ever existed in any Dep[artmen]t of any Country, then I will ask no pay for my trouble. The Indian Dep[artmen]t is decidedly the damndest humbug from the highest to the lowest, from the head to the very tail that ever existed, or ever could be conceived of. Commissioner Dole, at the Head of the Indian Bureau at Washington, is a *d____d old Indian sympathizer*, whining about after the style of *Old [John] Beeson* of Oregon Indian war notoriety, and from him on down, they have about as much knowledge of the Indian character as my horse has!

"Old Dole is a fair specimen of all the old fogies about Washington, *Lincoln included.* I would just like to get a whack at them. I can show to them and the whole world that the *Ind[ia]n Department is directly and indirectly responsible for the murder of every white man by Indians on this Coast.* The Ind[ia]n Dep[artmen]t is played out so far as I am concerned, and so far as this country is concerned. If it had wanted anything to do with this country, it should have been done here a year ago. It is too late now. The difference between me and the Indian Department is—it, or most of the persons belonging to it—will believe anything an Indian tells them, whereas I won't talk to them at all, nor listen to them. Familiarity breeds contempt, and I would not place any sort of reliance upon what one would say, anyhow. On the other hand I scarcely ever saw an Agent that was not disposed to take an Indians word, as soon as sooner than he would a white mans."

In support of his last position he instanced Dr. [George] Ambrose, Agent here in 1855 & 1856.

What I have repeated above as his words I take from my notes of the trip, written when everything was fresh in my memory. You have his words as they were uttered upon this occasion, save and except some repetitions and gross expressions of profanity which I have chosen to omit.

This is by no means an isolated instance. I had heard him express much the same sentiments upon former occasions. When I learned he was about to take this trip, come three days before his starting, I at once took occasion to see him and proposed to accompany the expedition. He opposed my going, remarking that I could go of course if I insisted, but at the same time thought it better that I should not go. He could see where it would result in harm. I desired him to explain himself.

"Well," said he, "You have got no money to operate with, hence you can have no influence with the Indians. You may promise them something and never fulfill and all this will embarrass me. It is of no manner of use to try to have any influence over these Indians, with no money or means to prove your sincerity. If I were you, I would rest perfectly easy until they give me some means to work with."

I told Col. Drew I was aware that hitherto there had been a want of money, but I now had a small fund to be used for purposes of securing and maintaining the influences he feared would be wanting, and further that I had been assured by the Sup[erintenden]t of Ind[ian] Affairs, if these Indians could be quietly and peacefully removed to their own country and induced to stay there, relieving the settlements of further annoyance on their account, such funds as would be necessary to accomplish this, if within season, could be obtained. My object now in going out with him was to see the Indians and appoint a time to meet them in cousel [council] for the purpose of seeing what could be done, toward the end desired. I was fully aware of the importance of co-operation and harmony between us, and was therefore very willing to consult with him as Commander of the Military Post as to the best means of accomplishing the end sought. I was fully of the belief that the present Sup[erintenden]t of Ind[ia]n Affairs was very desirous of ridding the settlements of further annoyance by reason of these Indians.

The location of this Post [Camp Baker] gave him an opportunity to take a step in that direction. I was certain this opportunity would be improved without delay and the movement would receive all the aid in his power to bestow. Drew replied that "his mind still the same as to the propriety of my going. The Ind[ia]n Dep[artmen]t was a humbug of the largest dimensions." He would not "trust its word for a red cent. It had done more to create disturbance than all other causes combined." He would place no sort of reliance on any branch of this Department. His vehemence had caused quite a crowd to gather around us, which crowd he amused by the expression of his opinion of Commissioner Dole and others much after the manner I have before related.

He professed to have been *aware* that the Sup[erintenden]t had control over a fund, a portion of which could be properly expended for the benefit of these Indians if necessary, yet, although a few minutes before he had taunted me with a lack of money and a corresponding lack of means of maintaining an influence over the Indians. He now said that if he had his way the d____d sons of b____s, should get nothing. He then made precisely the same statement that he subsequently made at the [Klamath] Lakes concerning his design of "compelling them to put in crops &c." It seems to me a self evident conclusion that Col. Drew not only desired but designed to absolutely ignore and destroy all power, authority and influence of the Indian Department.

I have since seen and talked with "George," "Long John," and "Jack," Chiefs of three Bands of Klamaths, who have heretofore been in the habit of coming to the settlements. These all express a disposition of friendship and amity, but at the same time evince no little chagrin at the disposition manifested by Col. Drew to treat them with utter contempt. They complain that Col. Drew has gone into their country, located a Military Post upon their soil, and has never yet sought them to say a single word upon the subject, but on the other hand has refused to see and talk with them when they have sought him, and have avoided them on all occasions. . . .

Petition of November 3, 1863, to the Honorable A. E. Rogers, U. S. Indian
Sub Agent in Oregon

Your petitioners, citizens of Jackson County, Oregon, would respectfully represent that the band of the Klamath Indians known as "George's band," have taken possession of what is known as the Dead Indian Country, in the upper portion of this valley, entered, and are now living in the houses of settlers, killing cattle and stealing horses, and often coming down into the settlements on Bear Creek, and insulting the inhabitants.

On the 27th of October, ultimo, a party of these Indians stopped at the House of James B. Bunyard on Bear Creek. One of them seized him by the collar and another drew a knife swearing that he would kill said Bunyard.

These Indians often pass through the fields of the settlers on Bear Creek, tearing down the fences and leaving the fields open, so that stock enter and do much damage. The high table land known as the Dead Indian Country, where a large portion of this band of Indians intend to pass the winter, has been to a considerable extent taken up by settlers, fenced, and many houses built therein. The houses and fences are being destroyed, the cattle, many of them running in that section, stolen and killed by these Indians, and white men ordered out of it by this band of Indians.

Your petitioners would respectfully ask that this band of Indians, and all other bands of Klamath Indians be removed from that section of country.

All of which is respectfully submitted, and your early action thereon desired. Ashland, November 3d 1863.

Eber Emery	R. B. Hargadine	James Bryant
E. D. Foudry	J. C. Tolman	Hugh Johnston
S. D. Vandyke	Lewis Hiatt	Saml. Colver
Jacob Wagner	J. C. Rasser	J. M. Wagner
W. A. Owen	Chas. R. Klum	J. Sachs
John Hudson	J. M. Smith	Peter Smith
O. Jacobs	M. V. Taylor	T. A. Archer
E. L. Applegate	Harvey B. Oatman	M. Mickelson
S. H. Clanghton	Wm. Condray	John Edsall
John McAllister	Wm. Roberts	Clifton Riley
W. Reams	F. Smith	F. M. Merrill
W. F. Songer	J. Q. Tabor	Giles Wells, Jr.
David Redpath	Marius Walker	Lindsay Applegate
J. L. Riddle	B. Million	W. H. Jaquette
James Thornton	Giles Wells	Wm. Patterson
W. W. Keentner	Morris Hawd	A. V. Gillette
M. Hanley	P. Dunn	H. B. Segbert
E. L. Warner		

Letter of November 9, 1863, Amos E. Rogers, Sub Indian Agent to Lieut. Col. C. S. Drew, Fort Klamath

Sir:

I have the honor to inclose to you herewith copy of a petition signed by Eber Emery, E. D. Foudry and fifty other citizens praying for the removal of Indians from the Dead Indian Country. "George" and "Jack" have established headquarters, it would appear, in the above locality. They have recently evinced a spirit of insolence and defiance in nearly all their communication with the whites. George has told me positively and rather defiantly that he did not intend to go to the Lakes again this winter. Even when told by men that if they would peacibly remain in their own country some assistance would be rendered them by the Dep[artmen]t in the way of subsistence, he replied that he should not return.

My information is that the number of Indians is weekly augmenting in the Dead Indian Country. Citizens are much annoyed by their thefts and insulting and lawless acts. I have therefore to request of you, that, at your earliest possible convenience, you adopt such measures as will answer the prayer of the inclosed petition. I have reason to believe that unless these Indians be speedily removed, a collision between them and the settlers who are being robbed and insulted by them is likely to occur. This, and its consequences, should be avoid if possible.

Please acquaint me of your intended action as early as practicable, so as to enable me to procure such subsistence as will be necessary to supply the Indians while in transit in case they will submit to a peaceful removal. By ascertaining the number of Indians remaining at the Lakes you can judge of the number George has and of the force necessary to detail for their management. I believe George to be disaffected and disposed to give trouble. How many Indians he can control I am unable to say.

Yours Respectfully, Your ob[edien]t Serv[an]t, Amos E. Rogers, U. S. Indian Sub Agent in Oregon

Tye[e] G[e]orge Arrested, *Table Rock Sentinel* (Jacksonville, OR), November 21, 1863

On Thursday evening Town-Marshal Banks arrested George, of the Klamaths, at the instance we understand of Col. [Charles] Drew. Indian Sub Agent Rogers had forwarded a petition from the citizens of the upper portion of the valley, setting forth that George, with part of his faction of the Klamath Indians, had taken possession of the Dead Indian valley; had driven off the settlers, threatened their lives, were destroying their property, etc., and asking that the Indians be removed. On receipt of the petition, the Colonel hastened to this place, and yesterday learning that George was in town, secured his arrest by the Marshal. Yesterday morning the prisoner was taken to Camp Baker by a guard of soldiers, where, we understand, he was to be tried by a court-martial.

George for some time has been aspiring to the war chieftaincy of the Klamaths and undoubtedly has a commanding influence over all as many Indians as any other aspirant in the tribe. La Lake is called by the Indians the Peace or Squaw Tie [tyee or chief], while George numbers among his followers the most insolent and dangerous men of the tribe. He last summer led his party, in connection with the Modocs, in an expedition against the Pitt river Indians, and captured a number of squaws and horses.

There appears to be a general desire in this community that the result of the military examination will be hanging or shooting of George, but we doubt whether sufficient evidence can be found against him to hang him. On "general principles" they might hang him and try him afterwards, and there would be no complaint on the part of our citizens, but we hardly think that responsibility will be taken by the military authorities.

N.B. Parties just returned from Camp Baker inform us that George was hanged about four o'clock. He is said to have confessed to having participated in the murder of the Ledford party (five persons), in the spring of 1859. He also said an Indian known as "Jack," was guilty of the same crime. The cavalry force have returned from Camp Baker to town, with Jack in custody. He will probably share the fate of George. The hideous wailing and moaning of the disconsolate and terror strickened Indians is now being heard all around us. George evinced none of the stoical indifference for which the "noble savage" is so remarkable. He wept like a child.

Letter of November 24, 1863, Col. C. S. Drew to Assistant Adjutant General, U.S. Army, San Francisco, CA.

Sir:

I have to report that on the 14th instant I received by special messenger from Indian Sub Agent Amos E. Rogers, of Jacksonville, an official communication inclosing a copy of a petition from some fifty citizens of Rogue River Valley asking the removal from that vicinity of certain Klamath Lake Indians represented to be committing depredations upon the property of citizens, and in one instance had threatened life itself.

On the 15th I left Fort Klamath for this post [Camp Baker], arriving here on the 16th.

On arriving here I found Lieutenant Underwood who commands here absent, under instructions from me dated 9th inst[ant] to inquire into the matters complained of in the sub Agent's communication, having learned something of the condition of affairs here previous to its reception. Lieut. Underwood returned on the following day, 17th inst[ant], and reported that the allegations set forth in the petition were not wholly true, but that an assault had been made upon Mr. Bunyard as stated with the exception that it was made by one Indian only, though in presence of several more. It appeared true, also, that "George" had taken possession of some vacant premises in the Dead Indian Pra[i]rie and had warned citizens against passing through the grounds he was thus occupying, and that he was excessively insolent to citizens passing in any direction in that vicinity, claiming that he had made arrangements with Sub Agent Rogers to occupy that country. At this time however George and all his band had left that vicinity and gone farther into the mountains, probably through fear that some action would be taken with regard to their conduct.

Lieutenant Underwood however was acting with the greatest precaution, and none of the Indians could see any demonstration whatever concerning them, though a detachment of twelve men detailed from the Horseguard were in readiness for a march at any moment. My own departure from Fort Klamath, and my destination, being known only to the officers there, and my arrival here being unknown to the public, gave additional outward evidence to the Indians that their conduct would not receive any attention from the military, that being the only authority they fear, or for which they appear to have any respect.

Accordingly on the 19th ins[tan]t George and his band returned and en-camped just in the outskirts of Rogue River valley, convenient to secure re-treats to flee to in case of danger, and George himself proceeded to Jacksonville doubtless in quest of Ammunition, as he had been in the habit of obtaining it there from Sandwich Islanders[1] who have squaw wives. Ascertaining his where-abouts I took occasion to see him and to order him to return immediately, with all his band to Klamath Lake. He refused to obey the order, and I immediately procured his confinement in the station house by the City Marshall. On the fol-lowing morning, 20th ins[tan]t, I directed his removal to Camp Baker, where I ordered him executed and he was accordingly hung.

"Jack," the other leader mentioned, was also arrested, but there being no very direct testimony against him, I released him last evening, and today he, and all the other Indians who were in any way under the control of George, have taken up their line of march for the Klamath country, accompanied by a guard.

My action in these premises I believe has been well-timed and productive of good results. That the Indians contemplated mischief there can be no doubt, and the swift and severe punishment inflicted will have a beneficial influence upon all the Indians of this region of country. There are two or three Indians yet at large who should share the fate of George and whom I hope to arrest very soon.

And, while I would be prompt in the punishment of Indian offenses, I would be humane in my policy towards those against whom proofs of wrong-doing are wanting; and on behalf of such I would state that these are now on the way to Fort Klamath over sixty of such Indians, who are destitute of subsis-tence except enough to last them to their destination, and with no facilities to lay in necessary supplies before winter sets in permanently. They return, too, among Indians who have also been improvident, expecting to live during the coming winter on the munificence of the government, having, unfortunately, had much encouragement to believe that a treaty with them would be imme-diately effected. It seems a certainty now that more or less subsistence must be issued to all during the months of December, January, February & March, at least, and perhaps for a part of April. If this should meet the approval of the Department Commander I would suggest that *one-fourth* of a ration of Flour per day be allowed and issued every tenth day to such Indians only as should be actually present at the time of issue, or satisfactorily accounted for. I suggest this mode of issue because it is the only plan that can be adopted to keep the Indians voluntarily away from the settlements, and the cost is comparatively little. I would suggest also that I be permitted to prepare in the spring, say ten acres of ground for vegetables for the Indians, and to see that they cultivate it.

. . . I leave for Fort Klamath tomorrow.

I have the honor to be Very respectfully Your ob[edien]t Serv[an]t

C. S. Drew

The Indians, *Table Rock Sentinel* (Jacksonville, OR), November 28, 1863.

The hanging of Tyee George, of the Klamaths, the arrest and discharge of Jack, a prominent Siwash of the same tribe, and the subsequent removal of all the Indians in the settlements to the Klamath Lake country, have been for the past week the subject of very general comment in our community and we hope to be pardoned for filling a small space in our paper with even so mean a subject as "Indians."

On the eve of going to press, on Friday evening last, persons just arrived from Camp Baker informed us that "George" had confessed to having participated in the Ledford massacre in 1859. This has been contradicted by a number of persons who were present at the execution, and we are therefore led to believe that he made no such confession. He received no trial whatever. Col. Drew having previously determined to hang him . . . . Having no trial, he was convicted of no crime, but the convictions of the people, both civil and military, were strongly against him as a "bad Indian."

Letter of December 7, 1863, Lieutenant Colonel C. S. Drew to Assistant Adjutant General R. C. Drum

Colonel:

I have to report that quiet is again the order here among the Indians. The hanging of "Indian George" and the attempted arrested, and consequent killing of "Skookum John," has had a decidedly beneficial effect.

Very respectfully Your obedient Servant C. S. Drew

SOURCES

Drew, C[harles] S. Letter of November 24 plus enclosures to Assistant Adjutant General [R. C. Drum], Department of the Pacific, Letters Received, 1861–65, Box 23, Part 1, Entry 3584, RG 393, Records of Continental Commands, National Archives, Washington, DC.

Table Rock Sentinel (Jacksonville, OR), November 21, 28, 1863.

RELATED READING

Drew, C[harles] S. *Communication from C. S. Drew Late Adjutant of the Second Regiment of Oregon Mounted Volunteers, Giving an Account of the Origin and Early Prosecution of the Indian War in Oregon.* Washington, DC: Government Printing Office, 1860.

———. *Official Report of the Owyhee Reconnaissance.* Jacksonville, OR: Oregon Sentinel Office, 1865.

Stern, Theodore. *The Klamath Tribe: A People and Their Reservation.* Seattle, WA: University of Washington Press, 1965.

Stone, Buena Cobb. *Fort Klamath: Frontier Post in Oregon, 1863–1890.* Dallas, TX: Royal Publishing Company, 1964.

NOTES

1. More than a hundred Hawaiians and Polynesians worked for the Hudson's Bay Company in the 1830s and the 1840s. A number married Indian women and remained in Oregon following the company's withdrawal to Victoria in 1846.

Treaties with the Tribes of Middle Oregon, 1855–65, and the Klamath, Modocs, and Yahooskin Band of Snakes, 1865

Following the Walla Walla Treaty Council of June 1855, Joel Palmer, Oregon Superintendent of Indian Affairs, traveled to The Dalles to assemble the tribes from the country lying south of the Columbia River to negotiate a treaty of land cession. The territory he sought lay between the John Day River and the crest of the Cascade Mountains. It embraced the watershed of the John Day and Deschutes rivers. Palmer had learned that Governor Stevens, who was also negotiating treaties in the Northwest, included "reserved rights" clauses in his treaties, which Palmer had not done previously. Thus Palmer followed this same plan and in the agreements of land cession, he included reservation not only of lands but the rights of fishing, hunting, gathering, and grazing. These rights were affirmed when Congress ratified the treaty.

In 1865 J. W. Perit Huntington traveled to central Oregon to negotiate new treaties. The spread of Euro-American settlement beyond the mountains and construction of military wagon roads with massive land grants in the region required further resolution of Indian land issues. Huntington, in a much disputed second treaty with the tribes and bands of the Warm Springs Reservation, in 1865 secured their assent to ceding all off-reservation rights. Although the treaty was ratified by the Senate, the tribes insisted it was a fraud. The federal government has generally ignored its provisions.

Also in 1865 Huntington visited the tribes of the Klamath Basin and entered into a formal treaty to create the Klamath Reservation and reserve on-reservation rights. The council drew 1,041 Indians (710 Klamaths, 339 Modocs, and 22 Yahooskins). Huntington noted: "The country ceded by the treaty of 15th October is of vast extent as you can see by the reference to the map—say 15,000 to 20,000 square miles, and presents great diversity of topography, soil and climate. Parts of it are barren mountains and sage plains of no agricultural value, but probably are valuable for grazing purposes, producing a large amount of nutricious grass, but containing little or no land fit for cultivation." He continued, "The valleys of the Klamath Lakes, Rhett Lake, Goose Lake, Lost river and some others have much fertile soil. Some portions are well supplied with excellent timber while in other parts there is very little." The Klamath, Modocs, and Northern Paiute ceded much of their aboriginal homeland in this agreement.

Treaty with the Tribes of Middle Oregon, 1855

Articles of agreement and convention made and concluded at Wasco, near the Dalles of the Columbia River, in Oregon Territory, by Joel Palmer, superintendent of Indian affairs, on the part of the United States, and the following-named chiefs and head-men of the confederated tribes and bands of Indians, residing in Middle Oregon, they being duly authorized thereto by their respective bands, to wit: Symtustus, Locks-quis-sa, Shick-a-me, and Kuck-up, chiefs of the Taih or Upper De Chutes band of Walla-Wallas; Stocket-ly and Iso, chiefs of the Wyam or Lower De Chutes band of Walla-Wallas; Alexis and Talkish, chiefs of the Tenino band of Walla-Wallas; Yise, chief of the Dock-Spus or John Day's River band of Walla-Wallas; Mark, William Chenook, and Cush-Kella, chiefs of the Dalles band of the Wascoes; Tah-simph, chief of the Ki-gal-twal-la band of Wascoes; and Wal-la-chin, chief of the Dog River band of Wascoes.

ARTICLE 1. The above-named confederated bands of Indians cede to the United States all their right, title, and claim to all and every part of the country claimed by them, included in the following boundaries, to wit:

Commencing in the middle of the Columbia River, at the Cascade Falls, and running thence southerly to the summit of the Cascade Mountains; thence along said summit to the forty-fourth parallel of north latitude; thence east on that parallel to the summit of the Blue Mountains, or the western boundary of the Sho-sho-ne or Snake country; thence northerly along that summit to a point due east from the head-waters of Willow Creek; thence west to the head-waters of said creek; thence down said stream to its junction with the Columbia River; and thence down the channel of the Columbia River to the place of beginning. *Provided, however,* that so much of the country described above as is contained in the following boundaries, shall, until otherwise directed by the President of the United States, be set apart as a residence for said Indians, which tract for the purposes contemplated shall be held and regarded as an Indian reservation, to wit:

Commencing in the middle of the channel of the De Chutes River opposite the eastern termination of a range of high lands usually known as the Mutton Mountains; thence westerly to the summit of said range, along the divide to its connection with the Cascade Mountains; thence to the summit of said mountains; thence southerly to Mount Jefferson; thence down the main branch of De Chutes River; heading in this peak, to its junction with De Chutes River; and thence down the middle of the channel of said river to the place of beginning. All of which tract shall be set apart, and, so far as necessary, surveyed and marked out for their exclusive use; nor shall any white person be permitted to reside upon the same without the concurrent permission of the agent and superintendent.

The said bands and tribes agree to remove to and settle upon the same within one year after the ratification of this treaty, without any additional expense to the United States other than is provided for by this treaty; and, until the expiration of the time specified, the said bands shall be permitted to occupy and reside upon the tracts now possessed by them, guaranteeing to all white citizens the right to enter upon and occupy as settlers any lands not included in said reservation, and not actually inclosed by said Indians. *Provided, however,* That prior to the removal of said Indians to said reservation, and before any improvements contemplated by this treaty shall have been commenced, that if the three principal bands, to wit: the Wascopum, Taih, or Upper De Chutes, and the Lower De Chutes bands of Walla-Wallas shall express in council, a desire that some other reservation may be selected for them, that the three bands named may select each three persons of their respective bands, who with the superintendent of Indian affairs or agent, as may by him be directed, shall proceed to examine, and if another location can be selected, better suited to the condition and wants of said Indians, that is unoccupied by the whites, and upon which the board of commissioners thus selected may agree, the same shall be declared a reservation for said Indians, instead of the tract named in this treaty. *Provided, also,* That the exclusive right of taking fish in the streams running through and bordering said reservation is hereby secured to said Indians and at all other usual and accustomed stations, in common with citizens of the United States, and of erecting suitable houses for curing the same; also the privilege of hunting, gathering roots and berries, and pasturing their stock on unclaimed lands, in common with citizens, is secured to them. *And provided, also,* That if any band or bands of Indians, residing in and claiming any portion or portions of the country in this article, shall not accede to the terms of this treaty, then the bands becoming parties hereunto agree to receive such part of the several and other payments herein named as a consideration for the entire country described as aforesaid as shall be in the proportion that their aggregate number may have to the whole number of Indians residing in and claiming the entire country aforesaid, as consideration and payment in full for the tracts in said country claimed by them. *And provided, also,* That where substantial improvements have been made by any members of the bands being parties to this treaty, who are compelled to abandon them in consequence of said treaty, the same shall be valued, under the direction of the President of the United States, and payment made therefor; or, in lieu of said payment, improvements of equal extent and value at their option shall be made for them on the tracts assigned to each respectively.

ARTICLE 2. In consideration of, and payment for, the country hereby ceded, the United States agree to pay the bands and tribes of Indians claiming territory and residing in said country, the several sums of money following, to wit:

Eight thousand dollars per annum for the first five years, commencing on the first day of September, 1856, or as soon thereafter as practicable.

Six thousand dollars per annum for the term of five years next succeeding the first five.

Four thousand dollars per annum for the term of five years next succeeding the second five; and

Two thousand dollars per annum for the term of five years next succeeding the third five.

All of which several sums of money shall be expended for the use and benefit of the confederated bands, under the direction of the President of the United States, who may from time to time, at his discretion determine what proportion thereof shall be expended for such objects as in his judgment will promote their well-being and advance them in civilization; for their moral improvement and education; for building, opening and fencing farms, breaking land, providing after teams, stock, agricultural implements, seeds, &c.; for clothing, provisions, and tools; for medical purposes, providing mechanics and farmers, and for arms and ammunition.

ARTICLE 3. The United States agree to pay said Indians the additional sum of fifty thousand dollars, a portion whereof shall be applied to the payment for such articles as may be advanced them at the time of signing this treaty, and in providing, after the ratification thereof and prior to their removal, such articles as may be deemed by the President essential to their want; for the erection of buildings on the reservation fencing and opening farms; for the purchase of teams, farming implements, clothing and provisions, tools, seeds, and for the payment of employees; and for subsisting the Indians the first year after their removal.

ARTICLE 4. In addition to the considerations specified the United States agree to erect, at suitable points on the reservation, one sawmill and one flouring-mill; suitable hospital buildings; one school-house; one blacksmith-shop with a tin and a gun-smith shop thereto attached; one wagon and plough-maker shop; and for one sawyer, one miller, one superintendent of farming operations, a farmer, a physician, a schoolteacher, a blacksmith, and a wagon and ploughmaker, a dwelling house and the requisite outbuildings for each; and to purchase and keep in repair for the time specified for furnishing employees all necessary mill-fixtures, mechanics' tools, medicines and hospital stores, books and stationery for schools, and furniture for employees.

The United States further engage to secure and pay for the services and subsistence, for the term of fifteen years, of one farmer, one blacksmith, and one wagon and plough maker; and for the term of twenty years, of one physician, one sawyer, one miller, one superintendent of farming operations, and one school teacher.

The United States also engage to erect four dwelling-houses, one for the head chief of the confederated bands, and on each for the Upper and Lower De Chutes bands of Walla-Wallas, and for the Wascopum band of Wascoes, and to fence and plough for each of the said chiefs ten acres of land; also to pay the head chief of the confederated bands a salary of five hundred dollars per annum for twenty years, commencing six months after the three principal bands named in this treaty shall have removed to the reservation, or as soon thereafter as a head chief should be elected: *And provided, also,* That at any time when by the death, resignation, or removal of the chief selected, there shall be a vacancy and a successor appointed or selected, the salary, the dwelling, and improvements shall be possessed by said successor, so long as he shall occupy the position as head chief; so also with reference to the dwellings and improvements provided for by this treaty for the head chiefs of the three principal bands named.

ARTICLE 5. The President may, from time to time, at his discretion, cause the whole, or such portion as he may think proper, of the tract that may now or hereafter be set apart as a permanent home for these Indians, to be surveyed into lots and assigned to such Indians of the confederated bands as may wish to enjoy the privilege, and locate thereon permanently. To a single person over twenty-one years of age, forty acres; to a family of two persons, sixty acres; to a family of three and not exceeding five, eighty acres; to a family of six persons, and not exceeding ten, one hundred and twenty acres; and to each family over ten in number, twenty acres for each additional three members. And the President may provide such rules and regulations as will secure to the family in case of the death of the head thereof the possession and enjoyment of such permanent home and the improvement thereon; and he may, at any time, at his discretion, after such person or family has made location on the land assigned as a permanent home, issue a patent to such person or family for such assigned land, conditioned that the tract shall not be aliened or leased for a longer term than two years and shall be exempt from levy, sale, or forfeiture, which condition shall continue in force until a State constitution embracing such lands within its limits shall have been formed, and the legislature of the State shall remove the restrictions. *Provided, however,* That no State legislature shall remove the restrictions herein provided for without the consent of Congress. *And provided, also,* That if any person or family shall at any time neglect or refuse to occupy or till a portion of the land assigned and on which they have located, or shall roam from place to place indicating a desire to abandon his home, the President may, if the patent shall have been issued, revoke the same, and if not issued, cancel the assignment, and may also withhold from such person, or family, their portion of the annuities, or other money due them, until they shall have returned to such permanent home and resumed the pursuits of industry, and in default of their return the tract may be declared abandoned, and thereafter assigned to some other person or family of Indians residing on said reservation.

ARTICLE 6. The annuities of the Indians shall not be taken to pay the debts of individuals.

ARTICLE 7. The confederated bands acknowledge their dependence on the Government of the United States, and promise to be friendly with all the citizens thereof, and pledge themselves to commit no depredation on the property of said citizens; and should any one or more of the Indians violate this pledge, and the fact be satisfactorily proven before the agent, the property taken shall be returned, or in default thereof, or if injured or destroyed, compensation may be made by the Government out of their annuities; nor will they make war on any other tribe of Indians except in self-defence, but submit all matters of difference between them and other Indians to the Government of the United States, or its agents for decision, and abide thereby; and if any of the said Indians commit any depredations on other Indians, the same rule shall prevail as that prescribed in the case of depredations against citizens; said Indians further engage to submit to and observe all laws, rules, and regulations which may be prescribed by the United States for the government of said Indians.

ARTICLE 8. In order to prevent the evils of temperance among said Indians, it is hereby provided, that if any one of them shall drink liquor to excess, or procure it for others to drink, his or her proportion of the annuities may be withheld from him or her for such time as the President may determine.

ARTICLE 9. The said confederated bands agree that whensoever, in the opinion of the President of the United States, the public interest may require it, that all roads, highways, and railroads shall have the right of way through the reservation herein designated, or which may at any time hereafter to be set apart as a reservation for said Indian.

This treaty shall be obligatory on the contracting parties as soon as the same shall be ratified by the President and Senate of the United States.

In testimony whereof, the said Joel Palmer, on the part of the United States, and the undersigned, chiefs, headmen, and delegates of the said confederated bands, have hereunto set their hands and seals, this twenty-fifth day of June, eighteen hundred fifty-five.

Joel Palmer, Superintendent of Indian Affairs, o. T. [L. S.]

WASCO:
Mark, his x mark.
William Chenook, his x mark.
Cush Kella, his x mark.

LOWER DE CHUTES:
Stock-etley, his x mark.
Iso, his x mark.

UPPER DE CHUTES:
Simtustus, his x mark.
Locksquissa, his x mark.
Shick-ame, his x mark.
Kuck-up, his x mark.

TENINO:
Alexsee, his x mark.
Talekish, his x mark.

DOG RIVER WASCO:
Walachin, his x mark.
Tah Symph, his x mark.
Ash-na-chat, his x mark.
Che-wot-nleth, his x mark.
Te-cho, his x mark.
Sha-qually, his x mark.
Louis, his x mark.
Yise, his x mark.
Stamite, his x mark.

Ta-cho, his x mark.
Penop-teyot, his x mark.
Elosh-kish-kie, his x mark.
Am. Zelic, his x mark.
Ke-chac, his x mark.
Tanes Salmon, his x mark.
Ta-kos, his x mark.
David, his x mark.
Sowal-we, his x mark.
Postie, his x mark.
Yawan-shewit, his x mark.
Own-aps, his x mark.
Kossa, his x mark.
Pa-wash-ti-mane, his x mark.
Ma-we-nit, his x mark.
Tipso, his x mark.
Jim, his x mark.
Peter, his x mark.
Na-yoct, his x mark.
Wal-tacom, his x mark.
Cho-kalth, his x mark.
Pal-sta, his x mark.
Mission John, his x mark.
Le Ka-ya, his x mark.
La-wit-chin, his x mark.
Low-las, his x mark.
Thomson, his x mark.

Charley, his x mark.
Copefornia, his x mark.
Wa-toi-mettla, his x mark.
Ke-la, his x mark.
Pa-ow-ne, his x mark.
Kuck-up, his x mark.
Poyet, his x mark.
Ya-wa-clax, his x mark.
Tam-cha-wit, his x mark.
Tam-mo-yo-cam, his x mark.
Was-ca-can, his x mark.
Talle Kish, his x mark.
Waleme Toach, his x mark.
Site-we-loch, his x mark.
Ma-ni-nect, his x mark.
Pich-kan, his x mark.
Pouh-que, his x mark.
Eye-eya, his x mark.
Kam-kus , his x mark.
Sim-yo, his x mark.
Kas-la-chin, his x mark.
Pio-sho-she, his x mark.
Mop-pa-man, his x mark.
Sho-es, his x mark.
Ta-mo-lits, his x mark.
Ka-lim, his x mark.
Ta-yes, his x mark.
Was-en-was, his x mark.
E-yath Kloppy, his x mark.
Paddy, his x mark.
Sto-quin, his mark.
Charley-man, his x mark.
Ile-cho, his x mark.
Pate-cham , his x mark.
Yan-che-woc, his x mark.
Ya-toch-la-le, his x mark.
Aıpy, his x mark.
Pich, his x mark.

William, his x mark.
Peter, his x mark.
Ischa Ya, his x mark.
George, his x mark.
Jim, his x mark.
Se-ya-las-ka, his x mark.
Ha-lai-kola, his x mark.
Pierro, his x mark.
Ash-lo-wash, his x mark.
Paya-tilch, his x mark.
Sae-pa-waltcha, his x mark.
Shalquilkey, his x mark.
Wa-qual-lol, his x mark.
Sim-kui-kui, his x mark.
Wacha-chiley, his x mark.
Chi-kal-kin, his x mark.
Squa-yash, his x mark.
Sha Ka, his x mark.
Keaui-sene, his x mark.
Che-chis, his x mark.
Sche-noway, his x mark.
Scho-ley, his x mark.
We-ya-thley, his x mark.
Pa-leyathley, his x mark.
Keyath, his x mark.
I-poth-pal, his x mark.
S. Kolps, his x mark.
Walimtalin, his x mark.
Tash Wick, his x mark.
Hawatch-can, his x mark.
Ta-wait-cla, his x mark.
Patoch Snort, his x mark.
Tachins, his x mark.
Comochal, his x mark.
Passayei, his x mark.
Watan-cha, his x mark.
Ta-wash, his x mark.
A-nouth-shot, his x mark.

Hanwake, his x mark.

Pata-la-set, his x mark.

Tash-weict, his x mark.

Wescha-matolla, his x mark.

Chle-mochle-mo, his x mark.

Quae-tus, his x mark.

Skuilts, his x mark.

Panospam, his x mark.

Stolameta, his x mark.

Tamayechotote, his x mark.

Qua-losh-kin, his x mark.

Wiska Ka, his x mark.

Che-lo-tha, his x mark.

Wetone-yath, his x mark.

We-ya-lo-cho-wit, his x mark.

Yoka-nolth, his x mark.

Wacha-ka-polle, his x mark.

Kon-ne, his x mark.

Ash-ka-wish, his x mark.

Pasquai, his x mark.

Wasso-kui, his x mark.

Quaino-sath, his x mark.

Cha-ya-tema, his x mark.

Wa-ya-lo-chol-wit, his x mark.

Flitch Kui Kui, his x mark.

Walcha Kas, his x mark.

Watch-tla, his x mark.

Enias, his x mark.

Signed in presence of —

Wm. C. McKay, secretary of treaty. o. T.

R. R. Thompson, Indian agent.

R. B. Metcalfe, Indian sub-agent.

C. Mespotie.

John Flett, interpreter.

Dominick Jondron, his x mark, interpreter.

Mathew Dofa, his x mark, interpreter.

SOURCE:

Kappler, Charles J. *Indian Affairs Laws and Treaties.* Washington, DC: Government Printing Office, 1904. Vol. II. pp. 714–19.

Treaty with the Tribes of Middle Oregon, 1865

Articles of agreement and convention entered into at the Warm Springs Agency, Oregon, by J. W. Perit Huntington, sup't Indian affairs for Oregon, on behalf of the United States, and the undersigned, chiefs and head-men of the confederated tribes and bands of Middle Oregon, the same being amendatory of and supplemental to the treaty negotiated with the aforesaid tribes on the twenty-fifth day of June, eighteen hundred and fifty-five, and ratified by the Senate of the United States on the eighteenth day of April, eighteen hundred and fifty-nine.

ARTICLE 1. It having become evident from experience that the provision of article 1 of the treaty of the twenty-fifth of June, A. D. eighteen hundred and fifty-five, which permits said confederated tribes to fish, hunt, gather berries and roots, pasture stock, and erect houses on lands outside the reservation, and which have been ceded to the United States, is often abused by the Indians to the extent of continuously residing away from the reservation, and is detrimental to the interests of both Indians and whites; therefore it is hereby stipulated and agreed that all the rights enumerated in the third proviso of the first section of the before-mentioned treaty of the twenty-fifth of June, eighteen hundred and fifty-five—that is to say, the right to take fish, erect houses, hunt game, gather roots and berries, and pasture animals upon lands without the reservation set apart by the treaty aforesaid—are hereby relinquished by the confederated Indian tribes and bands of Middle Oregon, parties to this treaty.

ARTICLE 2. The tribes aforesaid covenant and agree that they will hereafter remain upon said reservation, subject to the laws of the United States, the regulations of the Indian Department, and the control of the officers thereof; and they further stipulate that if any of the members of said tribes do leave, or attempt to leave, said reservation in violation of this treaty, they will assist in pursuing and returning them, when called upon to do so by the superintendent or agent in charge.

ARTICLE 3. In cases which may arise which make it necessary for any Indian to go without the boundaries of said reservation, the superintendent or agent in charge may, in his discretion, give to such Indian a written permit or pass, which shall always be for a short period and the expiration definitely fixed in said paper. Any Indian who, having gone out with a written pass, shall remain beyond the boundaries for a longer period than the time named in said pass, [shall] be deemed to have violated this treaty to the same extent as if he or she had gone without a pass.

ARTICLE 4. An infraction of this treaty shall subject the Indian guilty thereof to a deprivation of his or her share of the annuities, and to such other punishment as the President of the United States may direct.

ARTICLE 5. It is stipulated and agreed on the part of the United States, as a consideration for the relinquishment of the rights herein enumerated, that the sum of three thousand five hundred dollars shall be expended in the purchase of teams, agricultural implements, seeds, and other articles calculated to advance said confederated tribes in agriculture and civilization.

ARTICLE 6. It is further agreed that the United States shall cause to be alloted to each head of a family in said confederated tribes and bands a tract of land sufficient for his or her use, the possession of which shall be guaranteed and secured to said family and the heirs thereof forever.

ARTICLE 7. To the end that the vice of intemperance among said tribes may be checked, it is hereby stipulated that when any members thereof shall be known to drink ardent spirits, or to have the same in possession, the facts shall be immediately reported to the agent or superintendent, with the name of the person or persons from whom the liquor was obtained; and the Indians agree to diligently use, under the direction of the superintendent or agent, all proper means to secure the identification and punishment of the persons unlawfully furnishing liquor as aforesaid.

In testimony whereof, the said J. W. Perit Huntington, superintendent of Indian affairs, on the part of the United States, and the undersigned chiefs and head confederated tribes and bands aforesaid, have hereunto, in the presence of the subscribing witnesses and of each other, affixed our signatures and seals on this fifteenth day of November the year one thousand eight hundred and sixty-five.

J. W. Perit Huntington, [SEAL.]

Sup't Indian Affairs in Oregon, and acting Commissioner on behalf of the United States.

Mark, head chief, his x mark.
Wm. Chinook, his x mark.
Kuck-up, his x mark.
Ponst-am-i-ne, his x mark.
Alex-zan, his x mark.
Tas-simk, his x mark.
John Mission, his x mark.
Lock-squis-squis-sa, his x mark.
Kuck-ups, his x mark.
Hote, his x mark.
I-palt-pel, his x mark.

Sin-ne-wah, his x mark.
Ump-chil-le-poo, his x mark.
Shooley, his x mark.
Tah-koo, his x mark.
Tum-tsche-cus, his x mark.
Tou-wacks, his x mark.
Hul-le-quil-la, his x mark.
Te-ah-ki-ak, his x mark.
Chok-te, his x i-nark.
Kootsh-ta, his x mark.

Done in presence of —
Tallax, his x mark, interpreter.
Donald McKay his, x mark, interpreter.
Charles Lafollett, captain, First Oregon Infantry.
J. W. D. Gillett, school teacher.
Myron Reaves, superintendent farming operations.

SOURCE

Kappler, Charles J. *Indian Affairs Law and Treaties*. Washington, DC: Government Printing Office, 1904. Vol. II. pp. 908–9.

Treaty with the Klamath, Modoc, and Yahuskin Band of Snakes, 1865

Articles of agreement and convention made and concluded at Klamath Lake, Oregon on the fourteenth day of October, A.D. one thousand eight hundred and sixty-four, by J. W. Perit Huntington, superintendent of Indians affairs in Oregon, and William Logan, United States Indian agent for Oregon, on the part of the United States, and the chiefs and head-men of the Klamath and Moadoc tribes, and Yahooskin band of Snake Indians, hereinafter named, to wit, La-Lake, Chil-o-que-nas, Kellogue, Mo-ghen-kas-kit, Blow, Le-lu, Palmer, Jack, Que-as, Poo-sak-sult, Che-mult, No-ak-sum, Mooch-kat-allick, Toon-tuck-tee, Boos-ki-you, Ski-a-tic, Shol-las-loos, Ta-tet-pas, Muk-has, Herman-koos-mam, chiefs and head-men of the Klamaths; Schon-chin, Stat-it-ut, Keint-poos, Check-e-i-ox, chiefs and head-men of the Moadocs, and Kile-to-ak and Sky-te-ock-et, chiefs of the Yahooskin band of Snakes.

ARTICLE 1. The tribes of Indians aforesaid cede to the United States all their right, title, and claim to all the country claimed by them, the same being determined by the following boundaries, to wit: Beginning at the point where the forty fourth parallel of north latitude crosses the summit of the Cascade Mountains; thence following the main dividing-ridge of said mountains in a southerly direction to the ridge which separates the waters of Pitt and McCloud Rivers from the waters on the north; thence along said dividing-ridge in an easterly direction to the southern end of Goose Lake; thence northeasterly to the northern end of Harney Lake; thence due north to the forty-fourth parallel of north latitude; thence west to the place of beginning: *Provided,* That the following-described tract, within the country ceded by this treaty, shall, until otherwise directed by the President of the United States, be set apart as a residence for said Indians, [and] held and regarded as an Indian reservation, to wit: Beginning upon the eastern shore of the middle Klamath Lake, at the Point of Rocks, about twelve miles below the mouth of Williamson's River; thence following up said eastern shore to the mouth of Wood River; thence up Wood River to a point one mile north of the bridge at Fort Klamath; thence due east to the summit of the ridge which divides the upper and middle Klamath Lakes; thence along said ridge to a point due east of the north end of the upper lake;

thence due east, passing the said north end of the upper lake, to the summit of the mountains on the east side of the lake; thence along said mountain to the point where Sprague's River is intersected by the Ish-tish-ea-wax Creek; thence in a southerly direction to the summit of the mountain, the extremity of which forms the Point of Rocks; thence along said mountain to the place of beginning. And, the tribes aforesaid agree and bind themselves that, immediately after the ratification of this treaty, they will remove to said reservation and remain thereon, unless temporary leave of absence be granted to them by the superintendent or agent having charge of the tribes.

It is further stipulated and agreed that no white person shall be permitted to locate or remain upon the reservation, except the Indian superintendent and agent, employes of the Indian department, and officers of the Army of the United States, and that in case persons other than those specified are found upon the reservation, they shall be immediately expelled therefrom; and the exclusive right of taking fish in the streams and lakes, included in said reservation, and of gathering edible roots, seeds, and berries within its limits, is hereby secured to the Indians aforesaid: *Provided, also,* That the right of way for public roads and railroads across said reservation is reserved to citizens of the United States.

ARTICLE 2. In consideration of, and in payment for the country ceded by this treaty, the United States agree to pay the tribes conveying the same the several sums of money hereinafter enumerated, to wit: Eight thousand dollars per annum for a period of five years, commencing on the first day of October, eighteen hundred and sixty-five, or as soon thereafter as this treaty may be ratified; five thousand dollars per annum for the term of five years next succeeding the first period of five years; and three thousand dollars per annum for the term of five next succeeding the second period; all of which several sums shall be applied to the use and benefit of said Indians by the superintendent or agent having charge of the tribes, under the direction of the President of the United States, who shall, from time to time, in his discretion, determine for what objects the same shall be expended, so as to carry out the design of the expenditure, [it] being to promote the well-being of the Indians, advance them in civilization, and especially agriculture, and to secure their moral improvement and education.

ARTICLE 3. The United States agree to pay said Indians the additional sum of thirty-five thousand dollars, a portion whereof shall be used to pay for such articles as may be advanced to them at the time of signing this treaty, and the remainder shall be applied to subsisting the Indians during the first year after their removal to the reservation, the purchase of teams, farming implements, tools, seeds, clothing, and provisions, and for the payment of the necessary employes.

ARTICLE 4. The United States further agree that there shall be erected at suitable points on the reservation, as soon as practicable after the ratification of this treaty, one saw-mill, one flouring-mill, suitable buildings for the use of the blacksmith, carpenter, and wagon and plough maker, the necessary buildings for one manual-labor school, and such hospital buildings as may be necessary, which buildings shall be kept in repair at the expense of the United States for the term of twenty years; and it is further stipulated that the necessary tools and material for the saw-mill, flour-mill, carpenter, blacksmith, and wagon and plough maker's shops, and books and stationery for the manual-labor school, shall be furnished by the United States for the period of twenty years.

ARTICLE 5. The United States further engage to furnish and pay for the services and subsistence, for the term of fifteen years, of one superintendent of farming operations, one farmer, one blacksmith, one sawyer, one carpenter, and one wagon and plough maker, and for the term of twenty years of one physician, one miller, and two schoolteachers.

ARTICLE 6. The United States may, in their discretion, cause a part or the whole of the reservation provided for in Article 1 to be surveyed into tracts and assigned to members of the tribes of Indians, parties to this treaty, or such of them as may appear likely to be benefited by the same, under the following restrictions and limitations, to wit: To each head of a family shall be assigned and granted a tract of not less than forty nor more than one hundred and twenty acres, according to the number of persons in such family; and to each single man above the age of twenty-one years a tract not exceeding forty acres. The Indians to whom these tracts are granted are guaranteed the perpetual possession and use of the tracts thus granted and of the improvements which may be placed thereon; but no Indian shall have the right to alienate or convey any such tract to any person whatsoever, and the same shall be forever exempt from levy, sale, or forfeiture: *Provided,* That the Congress of the United States may hereafter abolish these restrictions and permit the sale of the lands so assigned, if the prosperity of the Indians will be advanced thereby: *And provided further,* If any Indian, to whom an assignment of land has been made, shall refuse to reside upon the tract so assigned for a period of two years, his right to the same shall be deemed forfeited.

ARTICLE 7. The President of the United States is empowered to declare such rules and regulations as will secure to the family, in case of the death of the head thereof, the use and possession of the tract assigned to him, with the improvements thereon.

ARTICLE 8. The annuities of the tribes mentioned in this treaty shall not be held liable or taken to pay the debts of individuals.

ARTICLE 9. The several tribes of Indians, parties to this treaty, acknowledge their dependence upon the Government of the United States, and agree to be friendly with all citizens thereof, and to commit no depredations upon the person or property of said citizens, and to refrain from carrying on any war upon other Indian tribes; and they further agree that they will not communicate with or assist any persons or nation hostile to the United States, and, further, that they will submit to and obey all laws and regulations which the United States may prescribe for their government and conduct.

ARTICLE 10. It is hereby provided that if any member of these tribes shall drink any spirituous liquor, or bring any such liquor upon the reservation, his or her proportion of the benefits of this treaty may be withheld for such time as the President of the United States may direct.

ARTICLE 11. It is agreed between the contracting parties that if the United States, at any future time, may desire to locate other tribes upon the reservation provided for in this treaty, no objection shall be made thereto; but the tribes, parties to this treaty, shall not, by such location of other tribes, forfeit any of their rights or privileges guaranteed to them by this treaty.

ARTICLE 12. This treaty shall bind the contracting parties whenever the same is ratified by the Senate and President of the United States.

In witness of which, the several parties named in the foregoing treaty have hereunto set their hands and seals at the place and date
above written.
J. W. Perit Huntington [SEAL.]
Superintendent Indian Affairs.
William Logan, [SEAL.]
United States Indian Agent.

La-lake, his x mark.	Jack, his x mark.
Chil-o-que-nas, his x mark.	Que-ass, his x mark
Kellogue, his x mark.	Poo-sak-sult, his x mark.
Mo-ghen-kas-kit, his x mark.	Che-mult, his x mark.
Blow, his x mark.	No-ak-sum, his x mark.
Le-lu, his x mark.	Mooch-kat-allick, his x mark.
Palmer, his x mark.	Toon-tuc-tee, his x mark.

Boss-ki-you, his x mark.
Ski-at-tic, his x mark.
Shol-lal-loos, his x mark.
Tat-tet-pas, his x mark.
Muk-has, his x mark.
Herman-kus-mam, his x mark.
Jackson, his x mark.

Schon-chin, his x mark.
Stak-it-ut, his x mark.
Keint-poos, his x mark.
Chuck-e-i-ox, his x mark.
Kile-to-ak, his x mark.
Sky-te-oek-et, his x mark.

Signed in the presence of —
R. P. Earhart, secretary.
Wm. Kelly, captain First Cavalry, Oregon Volunteers.
James Halloran, second lieutenant First Infantry, W. T. Volunteers.
William C. McKay, M. D.
Robert (his x mark) Biddle [Whittle]

SOURCES

Huntington, J. W. P. Letter of December 10, 1864, to William P. Dole. Letters Received, Oregon Superintendency, Microcopy 234, Roll 613, frs. 128–33. RG 75: Records of the Bureau of Indian Affairs, National Archives, Washington, DC.

Kappler, Charles J. *Indian Affairs Laws and Treaties.* Washington, DC: Government Printing Office, 1904. Vol. II. pp. 865–68.

RELATED READING

MacNab, Gordon. *A History of the McQuinn Strip.* Warm Springs, OR: Confederated Tribes of the Warm Springs Indian Reservation, 1972.

Stern, Theodore. *The Klamath Tribe: A People and Their Reservation.* Seattle, WA: University of Washington Press, 1965.

Three

Removals and Reservations

Although confined to a reservation, the families of the Confederated Tribes of Umatilla persisted in constructing traditional lodges. Covered originally with tule mats, these structures were also enclosed with hides and canvas. Lee Moorhouse (1850–1926) photographed this winter scene about 1900 (Northwest Museum of Arts & Culture, Spokane, WA).

THE PRIMARY GOALS of federal Indian policy in Oregon between 1848 and 1877 were to reduce Indian lands, confine native peoples on reservations, and transform them into Euro-Americans. Starting in the late eighteenth century, the United States government had assumed that Indians would assimilate into the mainstream. President Thomas Jefferson perceived Indians as intellectual equals readily amendable to cultural change and integration. He found, in fact, a coincidence of interests: the removal and concentration of Indians on reservations, where they would gain the rudiments of Euro-American civilization would free up land for American citizens. Both would, he thought, benefit from a beneficent government fostering these goals.

Commissioner of Indian Affairs Luke Lea articulated several policies during the formative years of the Oregon Superintendency of Indian Affairs in 1850. He advocated cutting off sale of alcohol to Indians: "The suppression of this traffic has always been considered by the government as one of the most important measures for the civilization of the Indians, and every effort has been made throughout the whole Indian country to keep it beyond their reach." Lea called for peace between tribes. He advocated agrarianism: "Great efforts should also be made among the Indians to induce them to engage in agricultural pursuits, to raise grain, vegetables, and stock of all kinds. It would not be amiss to encourage them, by the promise of small premiums, to be awarded to those who raised the greatest quantity of produce, horses, oxen, cows, hogs, &c."[1]

Lea encouraged Christian missions: "All therefore, who are entrusted with the care of our Indian relations in Oregon, are instructed to give the benevolent and self-sacrificing teachers of the Christian religion whom they find there, equal aid, countenance, and encouragement; and that they merit their good will by uniform kindness and concession to all—leaving them free alike to use such means as are in their power to carry out the good work in which they are respectively engaged."[2] And he promoted "the extension of our laws and regulations over them, being for their own welfare, this class of philanthropists could not more effectually advance their own humane intentions than by inculcating obedience on the part of their wards, at the same time instructing them that they are solely dependent on this, and not on the British government."[3]

A critical phase of federal Indian policy in Oregon—the treaty program—was incompletely implemented. Treaties were integral to dealing formally and fairly with the tribes about their lands and rights. The United States executed hundreds of treaties with tribes between 1778 and 1871 for the purposes of establishing peace and friendship, ceding lands, and laying out mutual responsibilities. The Oregon Indians, however, were resolute in their determination to hold onto at least part of their traditional homeland and retain their fisheries and hunting grounds. While they expressed friendship and peaceful intentions, they were adamant in their opposition to relocating among their enemies or moving to unfamiliar environments. Government officials were equally certain that they knew what was best for the tribes and insisted that they give up their territories and move to new locations.

The initial treaty program failed completely. None of the first five treaties negotiated in the Willamette Valley, those ceding lands on the lower Columbia River, nor those executed on Oregon's southwest coast in 1851, gained ratification. These agreements negotiated by the Willamette Valley Treaty Commission and Superintendent of Indian Affairs Anson Dart had proposed small reservations in the aboriginal homelands rather than removal of the tribes to east of the Cascades. Some of the treaties contained reserved rights. The Senate declined to ratify any of them.

Between 1853 and 1865 the federal government created the following reservations for Oregon tribes. Some reservations were created by treaty; others were set aside by executive order. Some of the treaty reservations, however, were viewed as temporary; the treaties extended discretionary authority to the president to close reservations or to order them split up into individual allotments. The actions to create and diminish the reservations are reported in Charles J. Kappler's *Indian Laws and Treaties* (7 volumes, 1904–ff.).

- Table Rock Reservation. This reservation was created by treaty on September 10, 1853. Located at the northern edge of the Rogue River Valley, it included fertile fields in Sam's Valley and rugged, arid bluffs covered with chaparral along the river. Although the treaty provided for allotment, the reservation was considered temporary and closed with Indian removal in 1855–56 to the Grand Ronde Reservation.
- Cow Creek Reservation. This reservation was created by treaty on September 19, 1853, and was located on Council Creek, a tributary to lower Cow Creek

near Riddle, Oregon, in the south Umpqua Valley. The treaty provided for construction of two houses for chiefs. The government abandoned the reservation when the Cow Creeks fled into the surrounding mountains during the Indian war of 1855–56.

- Umpqua and Calapooia Reservation. This reservation was created by treaty on November 29, 1854, and was located near the confluence of Calapooia Creek and the Umpqua River in the northern part of the Umpqua Valley. The government abandoned the reservation in 1855–56 when its residents were removed to the Grand Ronde Reservation.

- Coast Reservation. Located on the Oregon coast between Cape Lookout in Tillamook County and Tahkenitch Outlet in Douglas County, this reservation was created by executive order on November 9, 1855. It stretched for nearly 125 miles along the shore. It had three administrative units: Alsea Subagency (southern), Siletz Agency (middle), and Grand Ronde Agency (northern). By executive order on December 21, 1865, the central portion of the reservation (including Yaquina River and Yaquina Bay) was opened for settlement; the remaining part, administered at Siletz, became known in time as the Siletz Reservation. On March 3, 1875, Congress opened for settlement the northern part of the reservation between the Salmon River and Cape Lookout (an area administered until then by the Grand Ronde Agency) and the southern part of the reservation between the Alsea and Tahkenitch Outlet south of the Siuslaw River (an area administered as the Alsea Subagency at Yachats).

- Grand Ronde Reservation. James Buchanan created this reservation, located at the head of the South Yamhill River, on June 30, 1857, nearly a year and a half after refugee Indians were colonized at the site.

- Warm Springs Reservation. Located between the Deschutes River and the eastern flank of the Cascades, this reservation was created by treaty on June 25, 1855, for the Warm Springs (Tenino), Wasco, and Wishram. In time a number of Northern Paiute also settled on the reservation. Although located far from the important fisheries on the Columbia River, the reservation afforded access to the Metolius and Deschutes rivers, as well as productive grounds for hunting and root crops.

- Umatilla Reservation. Located in the watershed of the Umatilla River in the Blue Mountains, this reservation was created by treaty on June 9, 1855, for the Cayuse and Umatilla tribes. It was bisected by the Oregon Trail and repeatedly reduced by creation of townsites and railroad rights-of-way.

- Nez Perce Reservation. Located in southeastern Washington, west-central Idaho, and northeastern Oregon, this reservation was created on June 11, 1855, by treaty. The subsequent treaty of June 9, 1863, not signed by Joseph's

Band of Nez Perce, ceded the Oregon part of the reservation in the Wallowa Mountains to the United States. This duplicity became a leading factor in the Nez Perce War of 1877.

• Klamath Reservation. Created by treaty on October 14, 1864, this reservation lay in the northern Klamath Basin and embraced the watersheds of the Williamson and Sprague rivers and portions of upper Klamath Lake. The reservation was reduced by land grants to the Oregon Central Military Wagon Road Company and withdrawals for Crater Lake National Park.

• Malheur Reservation. Ulysses S. Grant created this reservation on September 12, 1872, withdrawing lands from public entry on the North Fork of the Malheur, Silvies River, and east to the South Fork of the Malheur River. Grant enlarged the reservation on May 15, 1875, and reduced it on January 28, 1876. President Rutherford B. Hayes on September 13, 1882, abolished the reservation except for 320 acres, the site of Fort Harney.

Between 1853 and 1855, Superintendent Joel Palmer secured the cession of all land in the Willamette, Umpqua, and Rogue River valleys in treaties ratified by Congress. None of these agreements provided for protection of reserved rights to safeguard the subsistence of the tribes. In August and September 1855, Palmer traveled the coast of Oregon and obtained the signatures of dozens of Indian men to his omnibus coast treaty to cede the country from the Coast Range to the Pacific, from the Columbia River to California. This treaty, though forwarded to Washington, D.C., was never considered by the Senate.[4] The coastal tribes thus found themselves in an exceedingly ambiguous situation. The predicament became more complex as a result of the forced removal to the Coast Reservation of refugee Indians from the Rogue River Indian wars in the southwestern part of the territory.

Removals to the reservations were brutally inhumane. The journal of Agent George Ambrose, penned in January 1856, only hints at the dimension of fear, distress, and suffering of the surviving Rogue River Indians compelled to walk through the snow, rain, and mud from the Table Rock Reservation to the Grand Ronde Reservation. The removals continued for years. The government paid contract Indian hunters such as William Tichenor of Port Orford per capita for the people he rounded up and marched to the Coast Reservation. Some years the officials at the Grand Ronde and Siletz agencies set out with troop escorts to southwestern Oregon to track down Indians who had eluded removal or who had left the reservation and returned to their old homes.

Royal A. Bensell, a soldier assigned to a detail to travel down the coast to Coos

Bay in 1864 to round up Indians who had left the reservation, wrote about the removal. "Amanda who is blind," he noted when passing over Cape Perpetua, "tore her feet horribly over these ragged rocks, leaving blood sufficient to track her by. One of the Boys led her around the dangerous places. I cursed Ind[ian] Agents generally, [Amos] Harvey particularly."[5]

In 1855 Palmer obtained treaty cessions across the Columbia Plateau from the Columbia Gorge to the Snake River. These agreements were the treaties with the Umatilla, Nez Perce, and Warm Springs tribes. Each reserved sizable reservations and each agreement provided for reserved rights of fishing, hunting, grazing, and gathering. In this latter regard these treaties differed dramatically from those west of the mountains.

J. W. Perit Huntington negotiated treaties in 1865 with the Klamath, Modoc, and Northern Paiute. Huntington's treaties provided for "the exclusive right of taking fish in the streams and lakes, included in said reservation, and of gathering edible roots, seeds, and berries within its limits." While these subsistence guarantees were thus confirmed, the Klamath treaty also granted the rights of way for public roads and railroads.[6]

Removals of Oregon Indians took on a new dimension in the 1870s. Because of their involvement in the Modoc War of 1873, the Modocs were removed from the Oregon-California border to the plains of Oklahoma. The Bureau of Indian Affairs imprisoned hundreds of Northern Paiutes from the Great Basin on the Yakama Reservation, leaving the staff of the Malheur Reservation on salary but with no resident Indians. BIA officials sentenced the survivors of Joseph's band of Nez Perce, participants in the Nez Perce War of 1877, to confinement in Oklahoma and, ultimately, to removal to Nespelem on the north-central Columbia Plateau, to the Colville Reservation.

Once confined to reservations, the Indians faced numerous restrictions. For many years U.S. Army troops lived on or adjacent to the reservations. Their roles were to prevent the Indians from leaving and Euro-Americans from trespassing. With little to do except play cards and drink alcohol, the soldiers did not elevate the reservation setting. Their posts included Fort Orford (Port Orford), Fort Lane (Rogue River Valley), Fort Umpqua (mouth of Umpqua River), Fort Hoskins (Kings Valley), Fort Yamhill (South Fork of Yamhill River), Fort Dalles (The Dalles), Fort Klamath (near Upper Klamath Lake), Camp Warner (Warner Valley), and Fort Harney (Harney Basin).

Attitudes toward the residents of the reservations were frequently racist and nasty. In 1871, for example, the *Plaindealer* (Roseburg, OR) reprinted a story from the *Gazette* (Corvallis, OR) about an event at the Coast Reservation:

The Indians like a doctor they have at Yaquina Bay. One noble savage informed a correspondent on the *Gazette*, the other day, that the doctor was a "hyas skookum [powerful] medicine man." He gave a dose of medicine to a klootchman [Indian woman] in the evening, and the aforesaid dusky maiden "kicked the bucket" in the morning.[7]

On the other side of the state, more negative perceptions of Oregon Indians faced the residents of the Umatilla Reservation. Developers of the city of Pendleton and farmers wanting to plant wheat lusted for additional lands. An article in August, 1871, noted:

The Commissioners appointed to negotiate for the purchase of the Umatilla Reservation failed to induce the Indians to sell. It is doubtful if they made much exertion in that direction, on the contrary, Commissioner [Felix] Brunot assured the Indians that they would be permitted to remain there as long as they choose. This is [a] valuable tract of land and it is a shame indeed, that it continues in the hands of those who make but poor use of it."[8]

The following documents confirm that Indians were treated like pawns. The councils—such as that at Yachats in 1875—produced unequivocal confirmation of the views of the tribal leaders, but their convictions and steadfast efforts to retain their homes and lands were ignored.

NOTES

1. Luke Lea. Letter of July 20, 1850, to Anson Dart. *Annual Report of the Commissioner of Indian Affairs . . . 1850*. Washington, D.C.: Office of the Commissioner of Indian Affairs, 1850, p. 119.

2. Ibid.

3. Ibid.

4. The text of this treaty and the signature pages is preserved in the Records of the Oregon Superintendency of Indian Affairs, Microcopy M–2, Roll 28 (pp. 116–127 of the letterbook), RG 75, Records of the Bureau of Indian Affairs, National Archives, Washington, D.C.

5. Royal A. Bensell. *All Quiet on the Yamhill, the Civil War in Oregon: The Journal of Corporal Royal A. Bensell*. Gunter Barth, ed. Eugene, OR.: University of Oregon Books, 1959, p. 150.

6. Charles J. Kappler, ed. *Indian Laws and Treaties*. Vol. 2, *Treaties*. Washington, D.C.: Government Printing Office, 1904, p. 866.

7. "News Clippings," *Plaindealer* (Roseburg, OR.), July 21, 1871.

8. "The Umatilla Reservation," *Plaindealer* (Roseburg, OR.), August 18, 1871.

The Takelmans' Trail of Tears, 1856

Undisturbed for centuries, the Indians of the Rogue River Valley faced a dizzying onslaught of changes and calamities between the 1820s and the 1850s. In less than thirty years the spread of Euro-American settlement, new diseases, ecological disruptions caused by the gold rush, and the results of the failures of federal Indian policy swept through their villages with disastrous consequences. Because they resisted trespass and sought to defend their people, they were labeled "Rogues" or "Rascals." Their own names—Latgawa ["people of the uplands"], Dagelma ["people along the river"], and Shasta—were largely lost in the rush of events. To the victors who drove them from their lands, they were "savages" and "Rogues."

Forced removal to the Table Rock Reservation in the waning months of 1855 concentrated the sick and the healthy refugees in unfavorable circumstances. Many Indians were reluctant to leave their villages and relocate on the reservation. An attack of October 1855 by the "Exterminators" from the mining camps at Jacksonville precipitated the Rogue River Indian War of 1855–56 and the flight of many of the able-bodied Indians west into the canyon of the Rogue River.

As the war slowed with the onset of winter snows and bitter cold, Indian Agent George Ambrose collected the Indians who had remained on the reservation and others scattered throughout the valley and planned their removal. The 1853 treaties had provided only that the Table Rock Reservation would serve temporarily as a holding place for the Indians. In accord with the national policy of removal and relocation, Ambrose set in place Superintendent Joel Palmer's larger scheme to colonize all of the Indians of western Oregon on the Grand Ronde and Coast reservations.

Born in Pickaway County, Ohio, in 1823, George H. Ambrose had emigrated with his wife, Ellen Frances, overland to Oregon in 1850. Sensing the opportunities of the Rogue River region, they filed upon a Donation Land Claim and settled in 1852 in Jackson County. On the removal of S. H. Culver as agent because of charges as to his use of agency assets, Ambrose took over administration of the Rogue Valley Indian Agency. Ambrose believed all was under control and declared so in the fall of 1853 in a series of letters signed "A Miner" in the Oregon Statesman. *His optimism was dashed by the massacre of twenty-three Indian women, men, and children at the mouth of Butte Creek on October 8 by volunteers led by James A. Lupton.*

Ambrose in February 1856 directed the removal of the surviving Indians of the Rogue River Valley. The Indian refugees departed the Table Rock Reservation to take the trail west via the Rogue River and then north to the Umpqua and Willamette valleys. Ambrose's diary, a chronicle of the journey northward via the Applegate Trail, is terse and, at times, callous in its lack of feeling for the suffering and dislocation of fellow human beings. Ambrose readily admitted in his account that the wagons to haul the aged and ill were inadequate for the task. His diary further noted—without comment—the deaths of eight people and the births of eight children during the journey.

The snow, mud, shortages of food, and constant fear experienced by the refugees received scant notice by Ambrose. Pursued for days by Timeleon Love, a self-styled executioner of Indians, the agent was largely ineffective in staving off Love's designs. The Indians, clearly, feared that Ambrose was perhaps leading them to slaughter. Love's dogged pursuit of their party and the inadequate military escort surely gave great cause for alarm and anxiety.

[February] 23d. Saturday, the weather still continues pleasant. It was found necessary to have more teams than at first contemplated. I accordingly proceeded to Jacksonville for that purpose, and also to provide some articles, such as clothing and blankets to add to the comfort of the Indians, although the weather is sett down as pleasant. It certainly would be regarded as such, especially at this season of the year, however the nights are quite frosty and the mornings cool, sufficiently so, to render it necessary that they should be provided with Tents, Blankets, shoes & such necessaries as would tend to promote their comfort while on their journey which being procured the day was spent in distributing the articles among them. Also two additional teams were secured to convey the sick, aged and infirm. Our teams now number eight which I fear will not be sufficient. Thirty four Indians are disabled from traveling by reason of Sickness aside from the aged & infirm, who will as a matter of course have to be hauled.

[February] 24th Sunday, remained in camp a fine and beautiful day too, our first idle day spent in camp.

[February] 25th Monday, a heavy frost last night, on consequence of some Indian horses straying off during the night we were unable to get our early start. About Eleven oclock we all got under way. Our rout[e] lay immediately down the [Rogue] River on the South bank of said stream, a level & good road. We traveled today a distance of eight miles, encamped on a small stream [Foots Creek] near its outlett in Rogue River.

[February] 26th Tuesday frosty and cool. All things being arranged we took up our line of March which shall lay immediately down Rogue River. In about five miles we arrived at Jewett Ferry which occupied several hours in crossing which being done we encamped for the night, it being the only camp we could reach before nightfall.

[February] 27th Wednesday. The weather continues cool & frosty. Our rout[e] still lay down [the north bank of] Rogue River, over rough rocky ground. We marched today a distance of ten miles and camped at Patterson's old Ranch, good water but not much grass.

At this point the refugee Indians turned north on the Applegate Trail in the vicinity of present Grants Pass to ascend the slopes of Sexton Mountain.

[February] 28th Thursday, frosty & cool again this morning. While about preparing to leave camp some person killed an Indian who had wandered off some distance from camp in search of his horse which had strayed off during the night, which caused some considerable excitement among the Indians as it went to prove the statement previously made by some evil disposed persons, to wit: that they would be killed by the way. We learned this morning that a party of evil disposed persons have gone in advance of us, as is supposed to annoy us, or kill some friendly Indians. A messenger was immediately dispatched to Capt. [Andrew J.] Smith at Fort Lane for an additional force to escort us to or thro[ugh] the Canyon if it should be found necessary. We also learned that an individual by the name of Timeleon Love was the person who killed the Indian this morning and that he composes of the party that had just passed. We drove today a distance of eleven miles and encamped on the west bank of Jump Off Jo[e] Creek where we will most probably remain till the arrival of Capt. Smith.

[February] 29th Friday, we remained in camp all day, quite a pleasant day. Capt. Smith arrived about two oclock. Today we had another Indian to die the first by disease on the road, although many are very sick, however there are no new cases of sickness occurring.

March 1st. Saturday, quite a pleasant spring like morning. Everything being in readiness by times we took up our line of march over a rough hilly mountainous country, and the roads were truly in a horrible condition. I omitted to mention that on Thursday last we took a Northward direction and left the Rogue River to the South of us which brought us among some rough hills, between the Umpqua and Rogue River. After passing the Grave creek Hills we learned that Mr. Love and some others were awaiting us at the house, intending to kill an Indian. Upon going to the house I found it to be a fact, talked with the gentlemen, told them the consequences, went back & requested Capt. Smith to arrest Mr. Love and turn him over to the civil authorities. We passed the house however without any difficulty and encamped on a small stream [Coyote Creek] two miles North of Grave Creek. We drove today a distance of eight miles. We are now in the midst of an hostile Indian Country & not entirely free from danger.

[March] 2d. Sunday, clear & frosty. Upon consultation it was deemed best to move forward, as we went in an enemys country & neither forage nor grass could be had for our animals. We found the roads horrible as we traveled on, after traveling hard all day we made a distance of twelve miles & encamped for the night on the West bank of Cow Creek one mile above the crossing.

[March] 3d Monday, the mornings still continue quite cool & frosty, our rout[e] lay almost directly North over somewhat better ground than for two days previous. Our cattle was jaded considerable by our continuous marches, without forage or grass, neither of which could be procured. We drove a distance of seven miles & encamped just within the mouth of the canyon.

The refugees now faced the difficult descent of Canyon Creek, a dozen miles of boulders, steep sidehills, and repeated fords. The route, in spite of a decade of use by overland emigrants, yet tested travelers.

[March] 4th Tuesday, the weather still continues fine for the season, during the night our cattle deserted us passing thru the canyon & crossing South Umpqua a distance of twelve miles. Some few of them took the other end of the road, finding it impossible to collect the cattle in time to move. I took the Indians in advance & went through the canyon before night in order to obtain supplies [in Canyonville] of which we were getting quite short. In passing through I found some heavy obstructions the high waters during the fore part of the winter had thrown in large drift logs & a slide from the mountain had filled up the channel of the creek, all of which required to be removed before wagons could pass which was accordingly done by Lieut. [Charles N.] Underwood who sent a detachment in advance for that purpose, the persons who were sent in search of the missing cattle, returned with all but four head.

[March] 5th Wednesday, the Indians remained in camp today at the mouth of Canyon creek awaiting the arrival of the wagons about three or four oclock in the evening they made their appearance. The cattle very much jaded & tired as no forage could be had. I secured the best pasture I could find & turned them in that. An Indian girl died this evening. We were now a distance of eleven miles from our camp of the evening of the third being occupied two days in making it. Mr. Love who still continues to follow us was arrested & put under guard.

[March] 6th Thursday, this morning the cattle were collected together preparatory to making a start, and of the cattle still missing I sent a man back through the canyon in search of those that went in that direction. Towards noon three were discovered in the hills on the North side of the South Umpqua & brought up to camp this evening. Good road this morning until we reached South Umpqua, which stream we ascertained we could ford with the wagons. The foot passengers were all ferried whilst the teams were crossing & ready to resume their march. Here we ascended a considerable hill & passing thru some oak knowles come to a very narrow pass around the spur of a mountain which projected down to the waters edge, and around which a road had been dug out of the rock wide enough for wagons to pass, emerging from here we came out in full view of an open prairie, found the road good. We traveled today a distance of eight miles, & camped on the North bank of South Umpqua near [William] Weavers.

[March] 7th Friday, the weather still continued cool & frosty of nights and pleasant thru the day. Our road today hilly & in places quite rocky. An Indian woman died this morning & the number of sick increasing. It was found necessary to hire or buy another team. I soon procured one & continued our march. We drove today a distance of ten miles & encamped in Round Prairie on the South Umpqua yet.

[March] 8th Saturday, From camp this morning we had a good road for about two miles. Here we commenced ascending a mountain [Roberts Mountain] on the summit of which a wagon upset & broke out a tongue which caused considerable delay. After fixing a temporary arrangement we were enabled to go down the mountain a distance of four miles and encamped on Roberts creek. About two oclock in the afternoon in order to repair our wagon before proceeding further which was accordingly done before night. Traveled today a distance of Eight miles.

[March] Sunday 9th Quite a pleasant day, but owing to our proximity to the hostile Indians, it was deemed advisable to continue our march, which was accordingly done. Mr. Cain who had been sent in search of the missing cattle returned. He stated that he had found the cattle in the evening of the sixth and corrected them on the south side of the canyon, that during the night he believes they were stolen by the Indians, as hostile Indians were seen in that vicinity, & appearances went to show that they had taken them. Our road still continues down the South Umpqua River over a broken uneven country. The roads growing worse as we went North. We traveled today a distance of Eight miles & encamped on the bank of a little muddy branch about two miles north of Roseburg.

[March] 10th Monday, a very fine morning indeed, we got an early start this morning found the roads very bad. In about two miles we arrived at Winchester Situated on the south bank of the Umpqua. Here we had to ferry the river, which occupied us about three hours. We then ascended a considerable hill and traveled over a rough prairie Country, very muddy roads. We found a very pleasant camp about four miles North of Winchester on Camas Swail Creek, a distance of Seven miles. This morning a write of Habais [habeas] Corpus was served on Lieut. Underwood to show cause why he detained & held in custody unlawfully the person of Timeleon Love, to which he made a return that he held him by the authority of a legal Indian Agent & according to law & that said Love was held only to be turned over to the civil authorities according to law. Lieut. [William Babcock] Hazen was left at Winchester in charge of the guard & to turn the prisoner over to the proper officers of the law.

[March] 11th This morning the teams were got up quite early and preparations were made for starting. I then proceeded to Judge [Matthew P.] Deady's and caused a writ to be issued for the arrest of Timeleon Love for the murder of a friendly Indian on the 28th day of February last. Before the service of the warrant Mr. Love had effected his escape. We found the roads in a horrible condition and grass quite scarce. The teams drove but three miles today & encamped for the purpose of attending the trial.

[March] 12th Wednesday, cloudy & threatening rain, we had some trouble in finding our cattle. We however succeeded in getting them together about ten oclock. After traveling through a canyon about one and a half miles we arrived at Calapooia Creek. Our rout[e] lay directly up the creek for two & a half miles over hilly but prairie Country when we crossed the stream on a bridge at [Dorsey] Bakers mill. For the remainder of the day our rout[e] lay northward & over some steep hills. About four miles from the mills we struck camp at what is called oakland. Two deaths occur[r]ed today since we camped—one man & one woman.

[March] 13th Thursday, this morning we had quite a shower of rain rendering it quite unpleasant traveling. After burying the dead we took up our line of march over a rough hilly & uneven country. Our cattle traveled brisk today. About two oclock we struck camp on the bank of a small stream by the name of Elk Creek near Jesse Applegates [at Yoncalla]. The day was quite cool with frequent showers rendering it unpleasant traveling. We however traveled about twelve miles.

[March] 14th Friday, cloudy & show[e]ry. By keeping our cattle in pasture we were enabled to get an early start. Our rout[e] lay down Elk creek thru a rough canyon which we found quite muddy. We crossed Elk & Pass creek & several other streams. After crossing Pass Creek our road lay immediately up the creek & bounded by high mountains on either side. We drove eight miles today & camped at the foot of the Calapooia Mountains.

Ambrose took the Indian refugees northward via the Trappers' Trail, the old overland route between Oregon and California. The travelers entered the upper Siuslaw watershed near Lorane, Oregon.

[March] 15th Saturday, Cloudy. This morning our cattle were missing and upon search we ascertained they had crossed the Mountain pursuit was immediately made & they were found about ten miles from camp [on Pass Creek]. They were bro[ugh]t back and we were ready to start by two oclock. From camp we commenced our ascent up the mountain at first quite gradual. After ascending some distance we arrived at the Summit. We then followed the ridge of the mountain some distance before we commenced the descent. The road was quite dry over the mountain and till we were near the base, when we found some very heavy mud. The last team arrived in camp after traveling a distance of eight miles. One woman died today.

[March] 16th Sunday, Cloudy with occasional sunshine. Remained in camp all day to rest. Nothing occurred worthy of relation.

[March] 17th Monday. This morning we took up our line of march in northward direction. the roads were quite hilly and places very muddy. This morning while crossing a small stream a teamster broke a wagon tongue which delayed us an hour to repair after which we proceeded without any further difficulty for the remainder of the day. We encamped tonight on the west bank of Rock Creek, a distance of thirteen miles form when we started. Arrived in camp by four oclock.

[March] 18th Tuesday. Cloudy & threatening rain. During the night an Indian died which detained us a short time to bury. However by nine oclock we were in readiness to start. We traveled over a level flat country in places quite muddy. The greatest difficulty we experience is in obtaining grass for our cattle, which we find to be exceedingly scarce. We drove today a distance of twelve miles, camped in an oak grove near the claim of Mr. Smith.

[March] 19th Wednesday, cloudy & threatening rain, quite show[e]ry thru the day. We continued our march down Long Tom [River] & passed over some very muddy roads. We traveled today a distance of fourteen miles & encamped on the bank of Long Tom at Starrs Point [Monroe, OR].

[March] 20th The weather still continues cloudy and threatening rain. We secured a good pasture last night for our cattle & this morning quite early were underway. Our rout[e] lay immediately down Long Tom over a level Prairie Country. In consequence of the recent rains our wagons drag[g]ed along heavily all day. We drove a distance of fifteen miles and encamped on the bank of Marys River, at the Ferry [at Corvallis, OR.], a very hard days drive but no camp could be found short of this.

[March] 21st Friday, clear & pleasant. This morning we were two or three hours in ferrying the river, for two or three miles we found the roads very muddy. About three miles North from Corvallis our road improved very much, becoming rolling & dry. We traveled today a distance of twelve miles and encamped near the claim of Mr. Rude.

[March] 22d. Saturday, cloudy weather again. This morning for several miles our road was in excellent condition. We then found some very bad road and Sloughy Prairie to cross over after which we arrived at the South Luckymute, which we crossed on a bridge. Still continuing our course Northward in a few miles we arrived at Little Luckymute which we also crossed on a bridge & passed upon the North bank of the stream a short distance and encamped near a little oak grove. Traveled twelve miles.

[March] 23d Sunday, remained in camp all day quite a pleasant weather.

[March] 24th Monday got an early start this morning and had an excellent road. We drove a distance of fifteen miles & encamped near Mr. [James M.] Frederick's.

[March] 25th Tuesday, clear & pleasant. We got an early start this morning and after driving hard all day reached the [Grand Ronde] reservation about four o'clock in the evening after driving a distance of sixteen miles. So ends my journey & journal. After a period of thirty three days in which time we traveled a distance of two hundred & Sixty three miles. Started with three hundred and twenty-five Indians. Eight deaths and eight births, leaving the number the same as when started (Ambrose 1856:10).

The Ambrose diary hints at the dimensions of suffering and tragedy endured by the Indians of southwestern Oregon in the 1856 removals to the new reservations. Similar forced marches northward befell the natives of the Umpqua and Willamette valleys as well as several bands brought along the coastal trail from Port Orford to the Siletz Agency on the Coast Reservation during the summer. "It almost makes me shed tears to listen to them as they totter along," observed Lt. E. O. C. Ord who witnessed one of these removals. The Ambrose diary documented the closing chapter of millennia of Indian tenure in the Rogue River Valley. Left behind were the bones of parents, grandparents, and ancestors, ages-old villages and fisheries, and a way of life well-tuned to the rhythms of a beautiful land.

SOURCE

Ambrose, George H. Journal of the Removal of the Rogue River Tribe of Indians Commencing on the 22nd Day February, [1856]. Letters Received, Jan. 1–Dec. 31, 1856, Microcopy M-2, Roll 14, Oregon Superintendency of Indian Affairs, National Archives, Washington, DC. [Printed as "Trail of Tears: 1856 Diary of Indian Agent George Ambrose," Stephen Dow Beckham, ed. *Southern Oregon Heritage* 2(1)[Summer, 1996]:16–21.

RELATED READING

Beckham, Stephen Dow. *Requiem For a People: The Rogue Indians and the Frontiersmen.* University of Oklahoma Press, Norman, OK, 1971. (Reprinted: Oregon State University Press, Corvallis, OR, 1996.)

"My People Are All Dying," 1857

J. Ross Browne, special agent for the Department of the Interior, inspected West Coast reservations in 1857 and, during his travels, held councils at Grand Ronde and the Coast Reservation. Browne found a desperate situation at Grand Ronde. The doctor reported 168 Indians sick and thirty in the hospital. After his inspection, Browne estimated five times that number were ill and only three were in the hospital. Although he reported 2,320 acres under cultivation, the soil was barren, cold, and largely unfertile clay. About forty Indian men, hired at $30 per month, worked the farm. "They say, very justly," noted Browne, "that whilst they are willing to work for themselves, they do not want to raise crops to feed the lazy Indians of other tribes, who would rather starve than work."

Browne reported on the impossible situation. The surviving refugees could not possibly return to their old homes. Their village sites had been taken by settlers and miners. The newcomers had killed off the game and viewed the Indians with hostility. The reservation was ill-suited for agriculture and afforded only rudimentary shelter, clothing, and subsistence. The reservations were death camps for the displaced and dispirited natives of western Oregon.

Grand Ronde Council, September, 1857

In the following speech, Chief Sam (identified in the treaties as To-qua-he-ar in 1853 and as Ko-ko-ha-way in 1854) confronted the failed promises of his tribe's ratified treaty. In October 1855, his people had been murdered and driven from the Table Rock Reservation in the Rogue River Valley. They were rounded up and held at Fort Lane until January 1856, when their agent removed them overland to the Grand Ronde Reservation, where they died wholesale of exposure, starvation, and new diseases. Chief Sam pleaded with Browne for better treatment.

Before we came to the [Grand Ronde] Reservation, myself and my people were promised cattle, horses, clothing, &c. We were to have coffee and white sugar.

We were to have, each, a piece of land to cultivate. What we raised by our own labor was to be ours, to do as we pleased with.

Now we have not had any of these things. The Government—Uncle Sam—has not complied with these promises. We have waited and waited because the Agents told us to be patient, that it would be all right bye-and-bye. We are tired of this. We believe Uncle Sam intends to cheat us. Sometimes we are told that there is one Great Chief and sometimes another. One Superintendent tells us another thing, and another Great Chief removes him. Who are we to believe? Who is your Great Chief, and who is to tell us the truth?

We don't understand the way you act. With us, we are born chiefs; once a chief, we are a chief for life. But you are only common men, and we never know how long you will hold your authority, or how soon the Great Chief may degrade you, or how soon he may be turned out, himself. We want to know the true Head, that we may state our conditions to him. Let him come here, himself, and see us. So many lies have been told him that we think he never hears the truth, or he would not compel us to suffer as we do.

Captain [Andrew J.] Smith, U. S. A., [Joel] Palmer, [R. B.] Metcalfe, and others promised us that as soon as the war was over we would be permitted to return to our country. Now the war is over. Why are we kept here still? This is a bad country. It is cold and sickly. There is no game on the hills. My people are all dying. There will soon be none left. The graves of my people cover the valleys. We are told that if we go back, we will be killed. Let us go, then, for we might as well be killed as die here.

The Table Rock Reservation was made under the Treaty of September 10, 1853. We made it with Generals [Joseph] Lane and [Joel] Palmer. When the last war broke out we were driven away from there. We never sold Uncle Sam that land. General Lane is now here. He knows what was told us; that we would have to leave it for a while. But we never sold it. If Uncle Sam intends to keep it from us, then let him pay us for it.

Siletz Council, 1857

Browne crossed through the Coast Range to the Siletz Agency on the Coast Reservation, where he learned that a number of chiefs had requested Agent Robert B. Metcalfe to permit them to describe their situation and needs to him. On September 21 a large crowd assembled at the Siletz warehouse. The following is the record of the "Wa-wa, or Talk, with the principal Chiefs and headmen of the Tribes on the Siletz Reservation." The speakers included "Joshua," possibly

Ene-wah-we-sit, identified in July 1854 as chief of the "Joshua" or Ja-shute Band from the lower Rogue River; "John," a well-known tribal leader from the Applegate River and a signatory to the treaty of September 10, 1853; and "Jim," chief of the Tututni or Tootootenays, a leader of the band living in the Rogue River canyon below the mouth of the Illinois River.

The Interpreter was directed to communicate to them as follows:

In consequence of many conflicting statements which had reached the President in Washington relative to the Indian tribes in Oregon, and their conduct both before and since the war, it was very difficult for him to determine what were the facts, and as his heart was good towards them, it pained him to learn that after all he had done for their benefit they still appeared to be dissatisfied. Now although he had great confidence in the Agents whom he appointed to live with them and whom he said to take care of them and teach them how to work like white people in order that they might no longer suffer for the want of food and clothing, yet as many people wrote to him that they were not contented and wanted to go to war again, he had thought it best to send an Agent to talk with them and take down what they said in writing, in order that he might hear, as with his own ears, how they were disposed towards him, and why they were dissatisfied. The President was powerful and had nothing to fear from them. His heart was good towards them and he wanted them to be satisfied, and be at peace with him and all his people. If the Agents did not treat them well, he desired to know it from their own mouths; but until he was satisfied that such was the case, they must obey the Agents in all things and look to them as their friends and teachers.

JOSHUA: It is very good in the President to do this. We are glad to see a messenger from him come among us, that we may state our wants, and have our talk sent to him direct. I want to say for my people that we have not been dealt with in good faith. When we made the Treaty [of September, 1855], Gen[era]l [Joel] Palmer told us we were to have a horse apiece; that we were to have nets to fish with; cooking utensils, sugar, coffee, &c., when we came on the reservation that we were to have a mill to grind our wheat, and make timber to build our houses; that we were to have everything we wanted for ten years; that we would have a white Doctor and plenty of medicines and none of us would die. That all these things were to be given to us in payment for our lands; that we would not have to work for them, but had a right to them under the Treaty.

The Agents treat us well, except George [?] at the Yaquina. I do not like him. He troubles our women. He beats them. This is all I have to say.

John [Charles] Bradford (ca. 1842–?), Coast Reservation, Siletz, held large obsidian blades and wore a headdress decorated with a row of bright red feathers from the pileated woodpecker, traditional symbols of wealth at an outdoor fish-processing camp (Oregon Historical Society Folder 556–J)

JOHN: It is well that you should understand what little I have to say. I never saw you before, but expect you come here for a good purpose. It is good in the President to send to know what our hearts are. For my own part, my heart is sick. Many of my people have died, since they came here; many are still dying. There will soon be none left of us. Here the mountains are covered with great forests. It is hard to get through them. We have no game; we are sick at heart; we are sad when we look at the graves of our families.

A long time ago we made a treaty with Palmer. There was a piece of land at Table Rock that was ours. He said it should remain ours, but that for the sake of peace as the white settlers were bad, we should leave it for a while. When we signed the paper that was our understanding. We now want to go back to that country.

I am glad I can now send my talk to the President. During the war my heart was bad. Last winter when the rain came and we were all starving, it was still bad. Now it is good. I will consent to live here one year more. After that I must go home. My people are dying off. I am unable to go to war but I want to go home to my country.

GEORGE: I also want to tell you what my heart is. What the white chiefs have said to me I have not forgotten. When Palmer was buying our lands, we sold him all our country except two small tracts, one on Evans Creek and one on Table Rock. That portion was reserved for our own use. We did not sell it; and such was the understanding when we signed the Treaty.

I would ask am I and my people the only ones who have fought against the whites that we should be removed so far from our native country? It is not so great a hardship to those who have always lived near here. But to us it is a great evil. If we could be even on the borders of our native land, where we could sometimes see it, we would be satisfied. I have kept silent until now. The time has come when I can talk out. I want the President to know how we feel about it. I am carried farther away from my country than anybody else. My heart is not bad. It is sick. Palmer told us when he bought our country we could live at Table Rock and Evans Creek for five years. There we would have to come to the reservation. I told Palmer we would never consent to sell him those lands. We wanted them to live upon. We could always fish and hunt there. We only wanted the mountains, which were of no use to the whites.

I am told the President is our Great Father. Why then should he compel us to suffer here. Does he not know that it is against our will? If he cannot fulfill the promises made to us through his agents, why does he not let us go back to our homes. Does he like to see his children unhappy? We are told that if we go back, the white people will kill us all—that their hearts are bad towards us. But, the President is powerful. Let him send a paper to the whites and tell them not to trouble us. If he is powerful they will obey him. We are sad now. We pine for our native country. Let us go back to our homes, and our hearts will be bright again like the sun.

Before I end my talk, I would ask what has become of our guns. Palmer took them from us in pretence that he would return them as soon as we reached the reservation. We have never seen them since. Has he stolen them?

JOHN: I have a word more to say and then I am done. My heart is for peace. When there was war we fought like brave men. But there were many of us then. Now there are few. I saw after we had fought for our country that it was no use, that we could not stand it long. I was the first to make peace. My people were dwindling away before the white man. All the tribes that were united with us were fighting in different parts of the country. But they were badly provided with arms. The whites were numerous and rich. They had muskets and am-munition. My son-in-law went to the Dall[e]s to live with the Yakimas and Clickitats. I made peace, and sent word to him to tell them I had made peace and it was no use to fight any more. For this, I think we deserve well of the President. He ought to let us go home, and not compel us to remain here where we are all dying.

JIM, Chief of the Too-too-tenays: My talk shall be short. I think we have been here long enough. We came from the mouth of Rogue River. There we had plenty of fish. It is a good country. We want to go back to our old fishing and hunting grounds. What George has said is our heart. We have long been wishing to see this Tyee, sent here by the President. We want to tell the truth. We want the President to know our condition. This Tyee is writing our names on paper. We hope that paper will be sent back to us. We are afraid to have our names on it. If it should be lost we will all die.

The talk having thus ended, I desired the interpreter to communicate to the Indians as follows: I had listened to what they had to say with great atten-tion, and taken it all down in writing. Every word of it would be transmitted to the President at Washington. He would read it all as if he heard it with his own ears. It was true they had many causes of complaint, but this was owing to circumstances over which the President had no control. The people on the other side of the great deserts, where he lived, were very numerous. They came many of them from far off countries across the sea and every year they became so numerous that the country became too small for them. Then they came over here to seek a place to live in. Here they found many tribes of Indians, and at first they were peaceable because there were not many of them. Soon, however, as they kept coming and became more numerous, they had to cultivate the lands to live by; and they got into trouble with the Indians. Now, the President being unable to stop all these white people from over-running their country, asked the Grand Council to pay them for their lands and furnish them with a place to live on, where they could be kept apart from the whites and protected against the hostilities of bad men. Why should they now desire to go back? They were fed and clothed; they had plenty of beans and flour; good blankets and shelter from the rain. Soon they would have fields of their own, but they must work. All white people had to work. The shirts and blankets they wore were made by white men's labor. Were they better than white men that they would live without working? If they went back, they would all be killed. Their country was all settled up, and the game was nearly gone. In a few years there would be neither deer nor elk upon the hills. They ought to be paid for their lands. If Gen. Palmer deemed them about Table Rock and Evans Creek it was wrong. But it would all be fairly represented to the President. In the meantime, however, they must remain quietly on the reservation. If they undertook to go back to their homes, they would be shot down and then the President's heart would be sad because he could no longer protect them.

SOURCES

Browne, J. Ross. Letter of November 17, 1857 to J. W. Denver. Microcopy M-234, Roll 610, frs. 137–145, RG 75, Records of the Bureau of Indian Affairs, National Archives, Washington, DC.

House of Representatives. *House Executive Document No. 39*, 35th Congress, 1st Session, pp. 27–38.

RELATED READING

Dillon, Richard H. *J. Ross Browne: Confidential Agent in Old California.* Norman, OK: University of Oklahoma Press, 1965.

Douthit, Nathan. Joseph Lane and the Rogue River Indians: Personal Relations Across a Cultural Divide. *Oregon Historical Quarterly*, 95(4)(Winter 1994–95):472–506.

Schwartz, E. A. *The Rogue River Indian War and Its Aftermath, 1850–1980.* Norman, OK: University of Oklahoma Press, 1997.

"We Do Not Want to Be Slaves": Lament of the Siletz Chiefs, 1862

In June 1862, William Rector, Oregon Superintendent of Indian Affairs, visited the Coast Reservation. He recorded the comments of the chiefs about conditions with their people and forwarded his report to the Commissioner of Indian Affairs in Washington, D.C. "They will expect a reply from you in relation to their treaty," he noted. "I hope you will write something to them. It would be gratifying and give me much assistance in restoring their shaken confidence in the government."

The situation at Siletz was dire because of the failure of the U.S. Senate to ratify the Oregon Coast treaty of 1855. More than twelve hundred Indians under the jurisdiction of the Coast Reservation were without annuities, yet their lands from the Umpqua River to California and Cape Lookout to the Columbia River had been appropriated by settlers. In southern Oregon gold miners had dispossessed the Sixes, Quatomah, Tututni, Chetco, and other bands of their lands along the rivers and shore in a quest for black sand gold. Next came farmers seeking pastures for sheep, cattle, and horses. The presence of these newcomers in the coastal zone was in violation of the Organic Act of 1848 creating the Oregon Territory but in accord with the Donation Land Act of 1850. The situation was perplexing and troubling to the native people.

The chiefs spoke with Rector on May 24th, 1862.

Sixes George addressed the Superintendent as follows.

We look upon you as our leader and friend. We are glad to see you, and talk with you. I do not wish to offend you, but I must talk straight (Truth). [Joel] Palmer was the first "Ty-ee" (Supt. Ind. Affairs) I ever saw. He gave me good advice and I have obeyed it. Our country was on the Sixes River. We were in three tribes, and each tribe had their own chief. Our country bordered on the Coquille River. We made a treaty with Palmer, and sold our country to the white people and came here. Since then we are told that the President had to approve the Treaty, and that he has not done so yet.

If the President does not approve our Treaty, then we have not sold our country, and wish to go back to it again. Your people have got the gold of our country. Will they pay us for it? We have never been at war with the whites, and never killed anybody. The Indians that have killed the whites, have had their treaty ratified and ours is not.

I think our people have improved some, and would become like white people if they had any help. Palmer told me that I would be a white man in ten years. I have been here five years and am not a white man yet. I don't know but I will soon be a horse as I am eating oats.

Do you know of any country where white people eat oats like horses? Our people have had to eat frozen potatoes, that are rotten, and the carcasses of dead horses. They are dying very fast, and my heart is sick. I think rotten potatoes are not good for any people. I can eat oats but don't like them.

My people complain of hunger and want to go back to the Sixes River again. I would rather have our Treaty ratified and have the things we bargained for and stay on the reservation. Do you think you are paying us for our Country by giving us one blanket to every four or five Indians, and given us such things as oats and rotten potatoes to eat?

If I was allowed a gun I could kill some elk. I never did kill any white man. You should not be afraid of me. When we started to come here our guns were taken from us, and we have not seen them since. They promised to give them back when we got to the Reservation. I don't know that I will ever see you again. And I talk plain, as I would if the President was here. I have never [said] this to the Agent, because I knew he had nothing to do with the treaty. I have told the truth & am not ashamed.

OLD BILL OF THE ROGUE RIVERS

I have not much to say to you now and will talk after a while. I will say a few things and talk straight (Truth). I will say that the Indians here are used like slaves, and have been ever since [Robert B.] Metcalf[e] left. We have but little to eat, and sometimes nothing at all. Potatoes that are rotten are not good for any people to eat. Many of our people have no clothes. We have suffered much and many have died. If you will let us go back to our country, we can do better. Metcalf[e] gave us Beef and flour, when we first came here, and we want it now, or if you cannot give it to us let us go home and provide for ourselves. We were promised by Major [Robert C.] Buchanan that we should return after four years, and we want to go now or have better treatment.

This is my mind.

WILLIAM, CHIEF OF THE CHETCOES

I say what Old Bill has said. He is old and talks straight (Truth). We are treated like slaves, and not as we were promised. We want to go home, or have what was promised. The goods you [sent] to us in the little ship was not given to us. I don't know what became of them. We got one cup full of flour for one days work. We are slaves. Nine of my people have died last winter from hunger and cold. I do not like the Agent to abuse my people. We are willing to stay here and believe we can make our own living if we are furnished with things to work with. We should have one wagon, and two yoke of cattle for each tribe. Our women are packed like mules. They have all the potatoes and pack all the wood. They packed most of the things the ship brought from the Depot [on Yaquina Bay] to the Agency (a distance of Six Miles) and got one cup of flour for a days work.

We do not want to be slaves. We want to work for ourselves.

This is my mind.

ER CHES-SA, CHIEF OF THE SIXES

I want you to write my words and send them to the President. I don't want to offend you, but I want to talk straight to you. It may be the last chance that I will ever have. If the President was here, I would talk to him as I do to you. I am an old man and not ashamed to talk. Mr. [Edward] Geary promised to write to the President, but that is the last I have heard about it.

I don't want to be an Indian any longer. We were told that we would soon be like white men, if we came to the Reservation. My people have lost all confidence in the white men, but I have not. I want you to give us all the help you can. I fear when I die my people will scatter like birds. I have no confidence in Mr. [Benjamin] Biddle. I want another agent, that will give us what you send here for us, and not sell it, and abuse us. I know that you sent the ship here with flour and clothes for the Indians. I know that some of my people have died from hunger and cold. Do you think one blanket is enough for four or five Indians, and that one shirt or pantaloons will last all year. If you want us to live like white men, you must help us, as we want all the help we can get. We want carts to haul our potatoes and wood in. Our women pack everything now. Is that the way white people do?

I want a gun. If I had a gun I could kill some Elk. I want my people to be permitted to go outside to work for clothes. I want something done with the mills. I have never received any good from them. My people want camp kettles, and other things to cook in. We want to live like white people, and we look to you for help.

I hope Mr. [George] Meginson (this is the Farmer) will not leave us. We could not live without him.

This is my mind. I am done.

JOE LANE CHIEF TOO TOO TE NAYS

I have not much to say. I agree with all that has been said. I will ask you for some things to cook with, camp kettles and frying pans. I fear that we will suffer next winter, because there is no grain growing on the farms, none sowed last fall and but little oats this spring. I want permission to go out with some of my people, and work for clothes.

I am done.

Catfish speaks.

I don't know how it is that I am not payed for making fence around the Agents house. I think I should be payed for work that I have no use for. I know some of my people have died for want of food. I did believe the Doctors killed them (Indian Doctors who work by charm). I killed a Doctor and sorry for it now, and will not kill any more.

Rector closed the minutes by noting that several other men spoke but that their sentiments echoed those he had recorded. "I have not deemed it necessary to transmit them," he noted. In spite of the lament of the chiefs of the tribes held on the Coast Reservation, little changed. The 1855 treaty remained tabled and, in 1871, Congress suspended the treaty process. There was thus no prospect for them gaining annuity goods. The legislature prohibited the sale of guns and ammunition to them. The agent and the Army confined them to the reservation.

SOURCE

Rector, William H. Letter of June 10, 1862, to William P. Dole. Letters Received from the Oregon Superintendency, Microcopy —234, Roll 613, Frames 397–404. RG 75: Records of the Bureau of Indian Affairs, National Archives, Washington, D.C.

RELATED READING

Schwartz, E. A. *The Rogue River Indian War and Its Aftermath, 1850–1980*. Norman, OK: University of Oklahoma Press, 1997.

The Great White Father Gave and He Took, 1871

On March 14, 1871, President Ulysses S. Grant, acting upon the recommendation of Alfred Meacham, Oregon Superintendent of Indian Affairs, and H. R. Clum, Acting Commissioner of Indian Affairs, set aside the Malheur Indian Reservation in the Harney Basin. A region fed by the Silvies and Malheur rivers, the reservation contained tens of thousands of acres of lush meadows and lay adjacent to one of the greatest concentrations of ducks, geese, pelicans, cranes, and other birds in North America. The lands, between the forty-second and forty-fourth parallels of north latitude, were on the great flyway for migratory birds. Antelope and mule deer grazed on the bunchgrasses amid the rolling sea of sagebrush and thickets of pine and juniper.

Grant's order, more sharply defined on September 12, 1872, withdrew the reservation from public entry, except for the checkerboard claims of the wagon road companies. The reserved lands lay between the Malheur and Silvies rivers and extended from Strawberry Butte to Malheur Lake. Except for the Walpapi and Yahuskin bands who were included in the Klamath Treaty of 1864, the Northern Paiutes of southeastern Oregon had remained without reserved lands until this executive order. On May 15, 1875, President Grant enlarged the Malheur Reservation to 1,778,580 acres. The pressure of cattlemen, however, accelerated dramatically and on January 28, 1876, Grant "restored to the public domain" most of the reservation and dashed the hopes of the Northern Paiute. In 1883 and 1889 presidents Chester A. Arthur and Grover Cleveland further reduced the Malheur and old Camp Harney reservations. These actions left the Northern Paiutes virtually landless in their own homeland.

Chief Winnemucca, headman of one of more than twenty bands of Northern Paiute in Oregon, Nevada, California, and Idaho, challenged federal officials about their actions. The chief, his daughter, Sarah, his son, Natchez, and a cousin, Captain Jim, traveled to Washington, D.C. In January 1880, Natchez addressed the following to Secretary of Interior Carl Schurz. Natchez, in particular, questioned the imprisonment of hundreds of Northern Paiute on the distant Yakima Reservation in Washington Territory.

You, Great Father of the Mighty Nation, my people have all heard of you. We think you are the mightiest Father that lives, and to hear your own people talk, there is nothing you can't do if you wish to; and, therefore, we one and all, pray of you to give us back what is of no value to you or your people. Oh, good Father, it is not your gold, nor your silver, horses, cattle, lands, mountains we ask for. We beg you to give us back our people, who are dying off like so many cattle, or beasts, at the Yakima Reservation.

Oh, good Father, have you wife or child? Do you love them? If you love them think how you would feel if they were taken away from you, where you could not go to see them, nor they come to you. For what are they to be kept there?

When the Bannocks came to our people with their guns, my father and I said to them everything that we could, telling them not to fight. We had a talk three days, and only one man got up and said he would go with them. That was Oytes, with about twenty-five or thirty men. Oytes is a Harney Lake Piute.

We Piutes never had much of anything. The Bannocks took everything we had from us. They were going to kill me, with three white men, who were living near by. I feared I could not get away, but thanks to Him who lives above us, I did get away with the three white men. They followed us about twenty miles as fast as their horses could run. My horse fell down and died. I cried out to Jack Scott, and he let me jump up behind him, but he left me and rode on. I ran a little way till I came to a creek, up which I ran, and in that manner I got away.

So you see, good Father, we have always been good friends to your people. If you will return our people whom you sent away to Yakima Reservation, let them come to the Malheur Reservation, and make the bad ones stay where they are. In time I and my people will go there too, to make us homes; and, also, send away Mr. [William] Rinehard, whom we hate.

Sarah Winemucca (1844?–91), later recalled in her autobiography the following:

This is what my brother said to Secretary Schurz, and I am surprised to see that in their own Report they say, "In the winter of 1878–79 a self-constituted delegation, consisting of the Chief Winnemucca and others of his band visited this city, and while here made an agreement, etc., to remove to Malheur, and receive allotments of one hundred and sixty acres to each head of a family, and each adult male; they were to cultivate the lands so allotted, and as soon as the law would enable it, patents therefore in fee-simple were to be issued to each allottee," etc.

I say we did not come on of ourselves; we were sent for, and neither my father or brother made any agreement to go to Malheur until those who belonged there could come back from Yakima, and till Reinhard should be sent away.

I said one day I was going to lecture, as the people wanted me to, and try to get a little money to buy something for my father. Mr. Hayworth told what I said, and we were all sent for to go to the office of the Interior. We went in and sat down. Secretary Schurz said to me,

"Sarah, so you are bound to lecture."

I said, "People want me to."

"I don't think it will be right for you to lecture here after the government has sent for you, and your father and brother, and paid your way here. The government is going to do right by your people now. Don't lecture now; go home and get your people on the reservation—get them located properly; and then, if you want to come back, write to us, and tell us you want to come back and lecture, and we will pay your way here and back again."

He told me they would grant all I asked of them for my people, which they did; yes, in their minds, I mean in writing, promises which, like the wind, were heard no more. They asked where I was going to stop after I got home. "We want to know, so that we can send you some canvas for tents for your people. You can issue it to them. Can you not?"

I said, "Yes, if it comes."

"We will send enough to make your people one hundred tents. You can issue it, and give the names of each head of the families, and send them back here."

I said, "I shall be at Lovelock's in Nevada." "We will send it as soon as you get home . . . ."

On Saturday we were taken to the White House to see the President. We were shown all over the place before we saw him. A great many ladies were there to see us. At last he walked in and shook hands with us, then he said,

"Did you get all you want for your people?"

I said, "Yes, sir, as far as I know."

"That is well," he said, and went out again. That is all we saw of him. That was President [Rutherford B.] Hayes.

The arguments of the Northern Paiutes appeared successful. Secretary Schurz on July 20, 1880, released the Paiute prisoners from the Yakima Reservation, compelling them, however, to return home at their own expense. Natchez expressed the appreciation about the outcome of the mission to Washington, DC:

You give my people homes and lands where they can live. I don't know: maybe you will hear that Natchez Winnemucca is on the warpath, murdering whites. When you hear that, then come in person, or send someone to have me brought right here, and I will not flinch or tremble when you put the rope around my neck to hang me. Instead of that, in twenty years, or many years, it may be when we are old, or when we are gone and young men are in our places, some of my people will be helped by this, so that by getting an education they will hold high position like yourself. I want to think you again for my people.

Tragically, the Northern Paiutes were destined to decades of wandering. In 1897, they secured 115 public domain allotments in the eastern part of the Harney Basin, but not until 1935 did the federal government establish the Burns Indian Colony on 760.32 acres near Burns, Oregon. Congress finally confirmed the reservation on October 13, 1972.

SOURCE

Hopkins, Sarah Winnemucca. *Life Among the Paiutes: Their Wrongs and Claims.* New York, NY: G. P. Putnam, 1883, pp. 219–22.

RELATED READING

Canfield, Gae. *Sarah Winnemucca of the Northern Paiutes.* Norman, OK: University of Oklahoma Press, 1981.

Forbes, Jack D. *Nevada Indians Speak.* Reno, NV: University of Nevada Press, 1967.

Fowler, Catherine S., and Sven Liljeblad. Northern Paiute. *Handbook of North American Indians, Vol. 11, Great Basin.* Washington, DC: Smithsonian Institution, 1986, pp. 435–65.

Wheeler-Voegelin, Erminie. The Northern Paiute of Central Oregon: A Chapter in Treaty-Making, *Ethnohistory* 2(2):95–132, (3):241–72, 3(1):1–10.

Zanjani, Sally. *Sarah Winnemucca.* Lincoln, NE: University of Nebraska Press, 2001.

"I Did Not Want to Kill Them": Proceedings of a Military Commission, 1873

For a few months in 1873 the Modoc tribe became part of the national daily news. Signatories to the treaty with the Klamath and Yahuskin Band of Snakes [Northern Paiute] in 1865 with the United States, the Modocs agreed to cede their homeland in the vicinity of Tule Lake, Lower Klamath Lake, and Clear Lake to settle at Yainax Agency on the Klamath Reservation. Having relocated, the tribe faced compulsory farming, suppression of traditional religion and shamanism, and the ardent missionary work of Indian Agent Leroy S. Dyar. While some Indians accommodated and accepted reservation life, Captain Jack's Modoc band did not. These people went home.

The pursuit of the Modocs and the demand that they return to the Klamath Reservation sparked the Modoc War. The U.S. Army, Indian scouts from the Warm Springs and Klamath reservations, and a contingent of journalists surrounded Captain Jack's band in its stronghold, a labyrinth of lava tubes near the shores of Tule Lake. On April 11, 1873, an unarmed Peace Commission met with the Modocs. During the deliberations, the Indians attacked. They killed General E. R. S. Canby and Rev. Eleasar Thomas and seriously wounded Alfred Meacham, former Oregon Superintendent of Indian Affairs.

For several more weeks the Modoc War held the nation's attention. Three companies of Oregon militia, not requested by the Army, showed up to fight. A war of attrition followed and was reported by daily telegraphic coverage. More and more Modocs either surrendered or deserted until finally, in June, the war ended. Since the Modocs were not citizens of the United States, another contest erupted about how to treat the survivors. Oregon Governor Lafayette Grover intended to take the alleged Modoc murderers for trial and execution in Jackson County. The U.S. Army considered shooting the tribal leaders, hanging those responsible for the killings of the Peace Commissioners, incarcerating the remaining Modoc men at Alcatraz, and distributing the surviving women and children among other tribes. But the Attorney-General ruled that "common law of war" necessitated a trial for the violating of an implied truce.

The following selection is from the "Proceedings of a Military Commission"
held July 1–9, 1873, at Fort Klamath. On trial for "murder, in violation of the laws
of war" were Captain Jack, Schonchis, Boston Charley, Black Jim, Barncho, and
Sloluck. None of those charged had any prior knowledge of the "laws of war," but
that seemed to matter little as the proceeding moved forward. Lt.-Col. Washington
L. Elliott presided; Maj. H. P. Curtis served as judge-advocate.

Following reading of charges and questioning of several prosecution witnesses,
Elliott permitted the accused Indians to pose questions. Captain Jack summoned
Scar-Faced Charley, Dave, and One-Eyed Mose. Each testified.

KIENTPOOS (Captain Jack): I will talk about Judge [Alexander M.] Roseborough
first; he always told me to be a good man; he said, "I know the white man's
heart, but not the Indian's heart so well." Roseborough never gave me any advice but good advice. I have known a great many white people; I have known
there was a great many of them had good hearts; I don't know all of the Indian
chiefs around, and I don't know what their hearts were. Judge Roseborough
told me to be a good man, and do the right thing by my fellow-man. I considered myself as a white man; I didn't want to have an Indian heart any longer;
I took passes from good white men who gave me good advice. I knew all the
people that were living about the country, and they all knew I was an honest
man, and that I always acted right, nor did anything wrong.

You men here don't know what I have been heretofore; I never accused any
white man of being mean and bad; I always thought them my friends, and
when I went to any one and asked him for a pass, he would always give it to me;
all gave me passes, and told those people who had to pass through my country
that I was a good Indian, and had never disturbed anybody. No white man can
say that l ever objected to their coming to live in my country; I always told them
to come and live there, and that I was willing to give them homes there. I would
like to see the man that ever knew me to do anything wrong heretofore; I have
always dealt upright and honest with every man; nobody ever called me mean,
except the Klamath Indians; I never knew any other chief who spoke in favor
of the white men as I have done, and I have always taken their part, and spoken
in favor of them; I was always advised by good men in Yreka, and about there,
to watch over white men when traveling through my country, and I have taken
their advice and always done it. I would like to see the man who started this
fuss, and caused me to be in the trouble I am in now.

They scared me when they came to where I was living on Lost River, and
started this fight. I cannot understand why they were mad with me. I have

always told the white man heretofore to come and settle in my country; that it was his country and Captain Jack's country. That they could come and live there with me and that I was not mad with them. I have never received anything from anybody, only what I bought and paid for myself. I have always lived like a white man, and wanted to live so. I always tried to live peaceably and never asked any man for anything. I have always lived on what I could kill and shoot with my gun, and catch in my trap. [Frank] Riddle knows that I have always lived like a man, and have never gone begging; that what I have got, I have always got with my own hands, honestly. I should have taken his advice. He has always given me good advice, and told me to live like a white man; and I have always tried to do it, and did do it until this war started. I hardly know how to talk here. I don't know how white people talk in such a place as this; but I will do the best I can.

THE JUDGE-ADVOCATE [Washington Elliott]: Talk exactly as if you were at home, in a council.

CAPTAIN JACK: I have always told white men when they came to my country, that if they wanted a home to live there they could have it; and I never asked them for any pay for living there as my people lived. I liked to have them come there and live. I liked to be with white people. I didn't know anything about the war—when it was going to commence. Major [James] Jackson came down there and commenced on me while I was in bed asleep. When [Alfred] Meacham came to talk to me, he always came and talked good to me. He never talked about shooting, or anything of that kind. It was my understanding that Ivon Applegate was to come and have a talk with me, and not to bring soldiers, but to come alone. I was ready to have a talk with any man that would come to talk peace with me. The way I wanted that council with Applegate to come off, was, I wanted Henry Miller to be there and hear it. He always talked good to me and gave me good advice. Miller told me he wanted to talk with me, and wanted to be there when Applegate met me, and wanted to talk for me and with me. Dennis Crawley told me he wanted to be there to talk with me when Applegate came. He told me I was a good man, and he wanted to see me get my rights.

It scared me when Major Jackson came and got there just at daylight, and made me jump out of my bed without a shirt or anything else on. I didn't know what it meant, his coming at that time of day. When Major Jackson and his men came up to my camp, they surrounded it, and I hollored to Major Jackson for them not to shoot, that I would talk. I told Bogus Charley to go and talk, until I could get my clothes on. He went and told them that he wanted to talk;

that he didn't want them to shoot. Then they all got down off their horses, and I thought then we were going to have a talk; and I went into another tent. I thought then, why were they mad with me; what had they found out about me, that they came here to fight me. I went into my tent then and sat down and, they commenced shooting. My people were not all there; there were but a few of us there.

Major Jackson shot my men while they were standing round. I ran off; I did not fight any. I threw my people away that they had shot and wounded. I did not stop to get them. I ran off, and did not want to fight. They shot some of my women, and they shot my men. I did not stop to inquire anything about it, but left and went away. I went then into the lava-beds. I had very few people, and did not want to fight. I thought I had but few people, and it was not of any use for me to fight, and so I went to the lava-beds. While l was on my way to the cave, there was a white man came to my camp. I told him the soldiers had pitched onto me, and fired into me while I was asleep, but I would not hurt him—for him to go back to town, home. I went into the lava-beds and staid there. I didn't go to any place, I did not want to fight, and I did not think about fighting any more.

I didn't see any white men for a long time. I didn't want to kill anybody. I went to my cave and there I staid. John Fairchild came to my house, and asked me if I wanted to fight, and I said no, I had quit fighting, that I did not want to fight any more—him nor anybody. The Hot Creek Indians then started for the reservation and got as far as Bob Whittle's, on Klamath River, and there the Linkville men scared them and they ran back. They were going to kill them. Then the Hot Creeks came to my camp and told me the whites were going to kill them all. They got scared by what the white men had told them, that they were going to kill them all.

There were some of the Indians I left at Fairchild's; they were talking about bringing them by the way of Lost River. They ran off too. When they all got to my place I told some of them to go back to Fairchild's. The Hot Creek Indians came from the other side and came to my place. Hooker Jim came from this side, the east side of Lost River or Tule Lake, and they came around the lower end of Tule Lake and came to my place. I didn't know anything of any settlers being killed until Hooker Jim came with his band and told me. I didn't think that they would kill the whites when they went around that way. I did not believe it. I did not want them to stay with me. None of my people had killed any of the whites, and I had never told Hooker Jim and his party to murder any settlers; and I did not want them to stay with me. I don't know who told them to kill the settlers. I always advised them *not* to kill white people. I told Hooker that I never had killed any white person, and never had advised him to kill them; that he killed them of his own accord, not from my advice. I thought all of the white men liked me that was living in my country. I always thought they did. They always treated me well.

(To Hooker Jim:) What did you kill those people for? I never wanted you to kill my friends. You have done it on your own responsibility.

Then I thought that, after hearing that those white people had been killed, that the whites would all be mad at me. And it troubled me and made me feel bad. I told them it was bad, and they ought not to have done it. I knew that the white people would be mad at me just on account of this Hooker Jim killing so many white people when he had no business to do it. After l had left Lost River, I had quit then, and l had not fought any, and did not intend to fight anymore. Fairchilds told me that that was bad; that they had killed the settlers; that it was wrong; and if they did not quit fighting there, the chances were the soldiers would all come on us again and kill us all, if we did not make peace then. I told Fairchilds that l did not want to fight any more; that I was willing to quit if the soldiers would quit. Fairchilds then never came to my house any more for a long time after the Indians that were stopping with him had run off. He was afraid to come then any more. It was a long time that I heard nothing from him. Nobody came to my place, and I could not get any news. After a great while Fairchild came again with a squaw, and told me I had better make peace, for the white people were all mad at us. For a good while then there was nothing going on, and again the soldiers came there. When the soldiers came they came fighting and fought all day. The first day the soldiers got there they fought a little; the next day all day. The soldiers came and they fought a part of two days and then went away again.

Link River John came and told me not to be mad at them. I told them that I never had killed anybody and never wanted to. When Fairchilds came in to see me I told him I was not mad at anybody, and did not want to fight, and did not want any more war. I told Fairchilds l did not know what they were mad with me about; that I was willing to quit fighting; willing for both sides to quit it and live again in peace. I told him that I did not want the Lost River country any more; that as there had been trouble about that, I wanted to go to some place else and live, and did not want to live there any more. I told them there had been blood spilt there on Lost River, and that I did not want to live there; that I would hunt some other place and live; and that I was willing to quit fighting if they would let me alone. I do not deny Fairchilds, or anybody else, that

I wanted to talk good talk. I always wanted to talk good talk. I wanted to quit fighting. My people were all afraid to leave the cave. They had been told that they were going to be killed, and they were afraid to leave there; and my women were afraid to leave there. While the peace talk was going on there was a squaw came from Fairchilds and Dorris's, and told us that the peace commissioners were going to murder us. That they were trying to get us out to murder us. A man by the name of Nate Beswick told us so. There was an old Indian man came in the night and told us again.

INTERPRETER: That is one of those murdered in the wagon while prisoners by the settlers.

CAPTAIN JACK: This old Indian man told me that Nate Beswick told him that that day Meacham, General Canby, Dr. Thomas, and Dyer were going to murder us if we came at the council. All of my people heard this old man tell us so. And then there was another squaw came from Fairchilds and told me that Meacham and the peace commissioners had a pile of wood ready built up, and were going to burn me on this pile of wood; that when they brought us into Dorris's they were going to burn me there. All of the squaws about Fairchilds and Dorris's told me the same thing. After hearing all this news I was afraid to go, and that is the reason I did come in to make peace.

Riddle and his woman [Tobey, or Winema] always told me the truth, and advised me to do good, but I have never taken their advice. If I had listened to them instead of to the squaws, that were lying all of the time, I would not have been in the fix that I am in now.

The reason that I did not come when the wagons came after me was, this squaw had come the night before and told me they were going to burn me, and I was afraid to come. I can see now that the squaws at Fairchild's and Dorris's were lying to me all the time; and Bob Whittles's wife lied to me. If I had listened to Riddle I would have been a heap better off. Bob Whittles's [wife] came to see me and she told me that I was not her people, and she did not want to talk anything good to me. She always gave me bad advice. She told me that if she did not come back again right straight, that I might know the soldiers would be on to me.

I have told you about the advice that I heard and the main cause of never coming in and making peace. I was afraid to come. I don't consider myself, when you came to have a talk with me, the chief then. When you and the reporters came in the cave with you, I didn't know what to say; I didn't know anything about fighting then, and didn't want to fight. Your chief makes his men mind him and listen to him, and they do listen to what he tells them, and they believe him; but my people won't. My men would not listen to me. They wanted to fight. I told them not to fight. I wanted to talk and make peace and live right; but my men would not listen to me. The men that were in the cave with me never listened to what I said; and they cannot one of them say, and tell the truth, that I ever advised them to fight. I have always told my people to keep out of trouble; that when I met in council I wanted to meet in peace and in a friendly way. I told them when they would not listen to me, that if they wanted to fight, and would fight, they would have to fight; but they would not do so from anything that I told them; that it was against my will to fight.

By my being the chief of the Modoc tribe, I think that the white people all think that I raised the fight and kept it going. I have told my people that I thought the white people would think that about me; and I didn't want to have anything to do with it; that if they wanted to fight they would have to go on their own hook.

Hooker Jim was one that agitated the fighting: that wanted to fight all of the time. I sat over to one side with my few men and did not say anything about fighting. Now I have to bear the blame for him and the rest of them.

Schonchis was with Hooker Jim; he was on Hooker Jim's side. I was by myself with my few men that I had, and did not have anything to say. They were all mad at me. Then I would think that the white people would think that I was the cause of all this fuss; and then I would think again that they surely could not think so, when they knew that these other men had committed these murders. I would talk to them, but they would not listen to me. I told them that I liked my wife and my children, and I did not want any trouble, but wanted to live in peace; but they would not listen to what I would say. I had not done anything. I had not shot anybody. I never commenced the fight.

Hooker Jim is the one that always wanted to fight, and commenced killing and murdering. When I would get to talking they would tell me to hush! that I didn't know anything; that I was nothing more than an old squaw. I and Hooker Jim had a fuss, and I told him that I had not done anything mean; that he had been murdering the settlers. And I got my revolver, and if I could have seen him through the canvas I would have killed him. I thought that I would kill him; and I wanted to kill him, for he is the one that murdered the settlers on Tule Lake. I thought that the white people were mad because I was living on Lost River, and that they wanted that land there; that is what I thought when the fight commenced. I then had a fuss with another Indian because I got mad at Hooker Jim—an Indian called George. George and I had a quarrel, and he told me I was nothing but an old squaw; that I never had killed anybody; that he had killed white people and had killed lots of soldiers — him and Hooker Jim. Hooker Jim said, "You are like an old squaw; you have never done any fighting yet; we have done the fighting, and you are our chief. You are not fit to be a chief."

I told him that I was not ashamed of it; that I knew I had not killed anybody, and I did not want to kill anybody, and I would have felt sorry if I had killed any white people. They told me that I was laying around in camp and did not do anything, but lay there like a log, and they were traveling around and killing people and stealing things. That they, Hooker and George, were not afraid to travel. They said "What do you want with a gun? You don't shoot anything with it. You don't go any place to do anything. You are sitting around on the rocks." I told them that I knew and was not ashamed to be called an old squaw; that I thought I done my duty by telling them to keep the peace; but they would not listen to me. I told them that they run around and committed these murders against my will.

Scar-faced Charley told me that he would go with Hooker and them; that he could fight with them; that I was nothing but an old squaw. I told them then if that was what they were going to do, why they could go on their own responsibility; that I did not want to go with them; that I did not want to live with them. Scar-faced Charley will tell everything that he knows. He don't want to keep anything back; neither do I want to keep anything back.

Captain Jack then requested to be allowed to suspend further remarks, and to continue to-morrow, which request was granted.

Captain Jack, prisoner, continued his remarks to the commission as follows:

The four scouts have told you they didn't know anything about the murder of General Canby; and they advocated the murder of General Canby with me. The Indians that told that the talk took place in my house about the murder of General Canby, lie. It was their own house it took place in. I don't want to keep anything back. I do not want to tell a lie about it. I would like to know why they told that they did not want to fight; or didn't say anything in regard to fighting. They all talked to me and were all in with it, because we didn't want to move off to any country that we didn't know anything about. I would like to know why Hooker Jim could not tell who he wanted to kill when he went out there. He says he went there to kill a man; but he would not tell the man he wanted to kill. Meacham was the man he wanted to kill. Them four scouts knew all about it; and they were in our councils when we were holding councils, and they all wanted to kill the peace commissioners; they all advised me to do it. I thought that it would all be laid on to me, and, I wondered to myself if there could be any other man that it could be laid upon.

Another thing that made me afraid to meet the commissioners, the Indians lied to me and told me that Dr. Thomas and the other peace commissioners had pistols with them, and wanted to kill us. I told them that I didn't see any pistols with anybody, and they surely must have lied. I told them that I did not want to have any trouble with the peace commissioners; that I did not want to kill them. Hooker Jim, he said that he wanted to kill Meacham, and we must do it. That is all I have got to say.

The Modocs were tried under rules of war which they did not know and by a military commission of a country in which they were denied citizenship. The judge-advocate closed by reminding the commissioners that the Modocs were bound by treaty to remain at the Yainax Agency and that twice Alfred Meacham had had to compel them to return to the Klamath Reservation. He argued that Capt. James Jackson and his troops were acting under correct orders when they pursued Jack's band. He refuted Jack's charge's that Captain Jackson had acted in an unmilitary manner. On July 9 the Military Commission found all six prisoners guilty and sentenced each to hang. On August 22 President Grant ordered the executions.

The Universal Peace Union, founded in 1866, requested Grant to exercise clemency. Alfred Love, president, and Lucretia Mott, vice-president, argued that there were no executions of Confederates after the Civil War. The American Indian Aid Association denounced the trial. Elisha Steele, sheriff of Siskiyou County, California, and a man highly knowledgeable about the Modocs, petitioned for clemency. H. P. Curtis, judge-advocate, subsequently argued that Sloluck and Barncho were "merely tools in the hands of other and abler men" and should not die. As the public outcry grew, President Grant modified the sentences—four were to hang and Sloluck and Barncho were to receive life imprisonment at Alcatraz.

In September the Fort Klamath carpenter constructed the gallows, a scaffold thirty feet long, to hold six prisoners. Nearby the workmen opened six graves. On October 3 soldiers brought the men, held in shackles, by wagon to the gallows. Only then did the two younger men discover they were not to die. The night following the execution, someone opened Captain's Jack's grave, stole the body, and rushed it to Yreka for embalming. Eventually his remains, reduced to a skeleton, were displayed in the museum of the Surgeon-General's Office in Washington, DC.

SOURCE
Elliott, Lt.-Col. W. L. and Maj. H. P. Curtis. Proceedings of a Military Commission Convened at Fort Klamath, Oregon, for the Trial of Modoc Prisoners, July, 1873. *House Executive Document No. 122*, 43 Congress, 1 Session. Government Printing Office, Washington, DC., 1873.

RELATED READING

Foster, Doug. Imperfect Justice: The Modoc War Crimes Trial of 1873. *Oregon Historical Quarterly*, 100(3)(Fall 1999):246–87.

Helfrich, Devere. Fort Klamath Cemetery and the Modoc Graves, *Klamath Echoes*, 1968, pp. 8–9.

Murray, Keith. *The Modocs and Their War*. Norman, OK: University of Oklahoma Press, 1959.

Payne, Doris Palmer. *Captain Jack, Modoc Renegade*. Portland, OR: Binford & Mort, Publishers, 1938.

Quinn, Arthur. *Hell With the Fire Out: A History of the Modoc War*. Winchester, England: Faber and Faber, 1998.

Riddle, Jeff C. *The Indian History of the Modoc War and the Causes That Led to It*. San Francisco, CA: Marnell & Company, 1914.

Council Held With the Indians of Alsea Sub-Agency, Yachats, Oregon, 1875

"Why do the whites have sick hearts for our land," lamented an Alsea chief in the Yachats council. The growth of settlement in western Oregon, interest in logging and lumbering, and hunger for Indian lands led to intense lobbying of the federal government to reduce the Coast Indian Reservation. Originally reaching for 125 miles along the coast from Cape Lookout in the north to near the mouth of the Umpqua River in the south, the reservation contained small harbors at Siletz Bay, Yaquina Bay, Alsea River, and the Siuslaw estuary. The reservation had three administrative units: a southern component under the Alsea Sub-agency at Yachats; a central unit under the Siletz Agency at Siletz; and a northern unit lying between Devil's Lake and Cape Lookout under the Grand Ronde Agency.

In 1865 President Andrew Johnson caved to pressure and opened the central section of the reservation—the watershed of the Yaquina River—to Euro-American settlement. His executive order also withdrew parts of the lands in the Alsea Sub-agency and Siletz Agency. Settlers moved in to establish Yaquina City, Toledo, and Newport on what had been the Indian reservation.

The land hunger mounted. Settlers coveted the lush meadows along the Nestucca River and anticipated homesteading the watersheds of Neskowin Creek and the Salmon River. The Siuslaw country in the southern part of the Coast Reservation attracted the interest of lumbermen, cannery owners, shipbuilders, and settlers. On March 3, 1875, Congress passed a law to open the part of the reservation lying between the Salmon River and Cape Lookout in Tillamook County and the portion south of the Alsea River in Lincoln and Lane counties. Congress required the Bureau of Indian Affairs to secure the consent of the Indians of the Alsea Sub-agency as a condition. More than five hundred Alsea, Coos, Lower Umpqua, and Siuslaw Indians resided in the southern area affected by this statute.

The Coos and Lower Umpqua had been removed in 1856 and held prisoners for three years at Fort Umpqua on the windswept sandspit at the mouth of the Umpqua River; in 1859 they were marched by the U.S. Army north over Heceta Head to Yachats. From 1859 to 1875 these refugee Coos and Lower Umpqua, residing among the Alsea, had attempted to clear thickets of spruce, thimbleberry, alder, and willow along the ocean north of the Yachats River. The Indian agents ordered them to try to raise wheat, corn, and potatoes in the swampy bogs near the sea. More than fifty percent of the Indians perished during those years. On June 17, 1875, J. H. Fairchild, agent from Siletz, and George P. Litchfield, agent of the Alsea Sub-agency, assembled the Alsea, Coos, Lower Umpqua, and Siuslaw to secure their consent to the Act of Congress. The voices recorded that day confirmed the sentiments of the native peoples.

GEORGE LITCHFIELD: My friends I have come today in consequence of orders from the Commissioner of Indian Affairs, who has directed Mr. Fairchild the Agent at Siletz to come and in company with myself make you certain propositions. These propositions we now come to make. The Commissioner thinks it would be better for you to remove to Siletz, where you can have certain advantages you cannot have here. You can there have help to cultivate farms that will be given you, and will also have the advantages of a mill they expect to build this summer. I have been with you now about two years and you know I never promised anything unless I knew I was going to be able to fulfill that promise. I will not now talk much but will let Mr. Fairchild talk to you as he can better inform you of the advantages he will be prepared to offer you there. I will now introduce to you Mr. Fairchild the agent at Siletz.

J. H. FAIRCHILD: My friends, I have not come here on my own business today. I have heard good accounts of you, from your agent and others, and have long wished to see you. I have heard that you were among the best Indians on the coast and I am glad to meet you now. But today I have come to say to you what your Great Father who is my chief told me to say. You know that the whites have long desired your country and I have been told they have troubled you very much on this account. They have also wanted the land at Siletz and my Indians have long had sick hearts fearing they would have to remove from their country. These white people said the Alsea Indians are only a few yet they occupy very much land. They cannot cultivate this land; it is much more than they need. They also said: The Siletz Indians are not more than one thousand in number, yet they have all the land from Cape Foulweather to near the Tillamook. Why should the Indians hold so much land when there are so many white people who cannot get farms?

I am now telling you what these people said. Well they said all these things to Congress. The Congress is the Great Council of the Whites. Congress makes the laws. Everybody must obey the laws of Congress. The President, great and powerful as he is, your agent Mr. Litchfield, myself, and all the whites, and all Indians must obey the laws of Congress. Well these people made all these complaints, year after year, to Congress and last winter Congress made a law on the subject. Congress said, "Yes it is true the Alsea and Siletz Indians occupy much more land than they can cultivate. It is true there are many whites who want farms and would like a part of these Reservations. We have been for years paying thousands of dollars for blankets, food &c. for these Indians. Now we will make the Siletz Reservation extend from Cape Foulweather to the mouth of Salmon River and from the Ocean to the Coast range of Mountains. There will be enough good land for all the Siletz and all the Alsea Indians. We will give them all that country and no one shall trouble them any more and we will give each head of family and each single man a farm, for his own property, of as much land as he can cultivate, and will help them to teams, ploughs, harrows, and agricultural implements to till the soil, and we will make all the rest of Siletz and Alsea Reservations public land open to settlement by the whites." They also said "we will not drive these Indians. We will send men to talk strai[gh]t and true to them, and before we move them [we] will get their consent."

Now my friends I have come to see and talk with you in consequence of this law. The Com[missione]r of Ind[ian] Affairs wrote to me, Mr. Litchfield is Agent of the Alseas. You are Agent at Siletz. This law affects both your people. Do you go to Alsea and with Mr. Litchfield have a talk with these people. Tell them these things and tell them what you are prepared to do for them at Siletz. Tell them the Government desires them to go and that all the money appropriated for them will be expended at Siletz for their benefit.

My friends I presume you have heard of this law from white people. I have been told that you have heard that I would offer you a large sum of money to move to Siletz. From Mr. Litchfield you have heard the truth. Whether other white men have told you the truth I do not know. We have not come to offer you money, but to say to you that if you will come to Siletz, I will give each man of you a good farm which will always be his own property. You see white people anxious to secure farms. Why is this? Because the whites know the value of land. They know that if a man gets a piece of land as his own property, and works and improves it, he will soon become well off. Each man of you can get a piece of land for a farm if you come there.

Further the Government will help you to teams, harness, ploughs, harrows, cows, and other stock, and there is no reason why you should not soon be comfortably well off. If the whites come and settle around you here what chance will you have? Now I have told you what I was instructed to tell you and that is

Doloose ("Chief Jackson") of the Coos died in January 1907 at Coos Bay. His daughter,
Lottie Evanoff (left), served as linguistic informant for the Smithsonian Institution.
Also pictured are his second wife (with shell necklaces), another daughter, and a large
container of basketry materials (Beckham).

all I have to say, except, that if you come to Siletz you can do well. Many of our
Indians are well-off. There is no reason why you should not do as well.

I have seen many Indians who always lived among the whites. They are poor.
I have seen on many Reservations Indians well off. Why is this difference? I will
tell you. The Government helps the Indians who come to Reservations but does
not help those who live among the whites. This is a matter of great importance
to you, and I hope you will carefully consider your words and come to such
conclusions that you will not afterwards be sorry. You have a good Agent and
some good country. If you decide to remain I cannot tell what the result will
be. If you come to Siletz I think I can promise you good treatment, each one a
good farm, and help to cultivate the land. Also schools for your children.

There is another thing I may mention. At Siletz we have an organized church
of God. Your Agent has had no opportunity of organizing one here, but there we
have one, and you and your children can learn how you may be enabled to live
right in this life, and have eternal Life in the world to come. The Government

has also promised this season to build a saw and grist mill at Siletz, and you would have the benefit of that also. That is all I will say now.

GEORGE LITCHFIELD: I will talk a little more. The Commissioner sent me a letter in which he instructed me to say to you that he thought it would be well for you to move this summer. He also suggested that Pres. Grant was probably more favorably disposed towards the Indians than a future President might be on which account he thought it would be better for you to move now. Should you move you would doubtless have many advantages. You would have an interest in the mills they expect to build there this summer and would doubtless do well. Now we have only to hear what you have to say.

WATSON, Chief of Alsea: This thing I will talk right. Longtime ago the Great Chief made two Indian Countries. He made the Yaquina (or Siletz) Reservation and the Alsea Reservation. About this thing you have told us I will talk strai[gh]t. I do not wish to leave my country. I want to live and die there.

ALBERT, Chief of Alsea: I very much want to tell this man my heart. This is my heart. I very much want to remain in my country. I want all these old people to speak today. If the Chief in Washington says work your land well, that is right to me. If we live on our land it will be well. It is our Country and we want it. When we die we want it to go to our children and for them to give it to their children. We live on our own land. It was the land of our fathers and we want our children to live there. (The Alseas are living their old country.) We have houses which we built ourselves, have little farms and places, and we do not want to give them up even if our land is not all fenced.

WILLIAM, another Alsea Chief: This thing I want to say to you two men. This is our own land. Our children live there. If we die our children will get it. We want to tell the Chief in Washington our mind through these two men. If an Agent comes to us he looks after us. He wants to look closely to us and see that we live on our land and do right. We have houses. There are two mills up the Alsea River. We brought our lumber there. We saw logs and take to the mills and then get lumber for our houses. All our stock we keep on our own land. Never have we done wrong to the whites. Never have we killed a white man. Why do the whites have sick hearts for our land. They have long wanted to drive us off. We have remained quiet. We are afraid of the whites. We are now comfortably fixed.

JOHN, Head Man of Alsea: I want you to know my mind. Two of our old chiefs Albert and Watson were afraid to speak. They said they did not want to leave. They said we bought the lumber for our houses ourselves. No Agent bought it for us. I want to say the same thing. I am not afraid to live at Alsea. That is my country. I have nothing to fear if the whites come here. We have no horses, sheep or cattle for them to get. We have nothing to fear if they do come. I do not want to leave. I want to stay. I do not want to be moved like the Coos and Umpquas. Long ago Gen. [Joel] Palmer came to their country. He said to those people, "Suppose you leave your country, before long you will become like the whites."

Some time ago I went to Siletz and saw Mr. Fairchild. (Reported to Commissioner in letter of Jan[uary] 28th 1874.) I said I did not want to be like the Coos and Umpquas. They live here now. Many years they have been dying off. Their women have suffered from exposure gathering mussels on the rocks. Palmer did not tell them they must live on mussels when they were brought here. They were told they would get sugar coffee and flour. For that reason I do not want to take any more of the white man's promises. I am afraid to go to another country. I have no money. Where would I get flour at Siletz. I saw at Siletz those who had money had provisions. You know sometime since I said I could not improve without help. I have seen many Coos and Umpqua Chiefs at Alsea without food. I never saw them get much from the Agent. I want to die where I live. By and by when I die I want my children to get my house. I have a strong heart to live in my house, which I built myself, of lumber that I bought without help from the Agent. All our people got their houses the same way. That is all.

DOCTOR JOHN (leading man of the Alsea): I live in my house. I have two little places. One is where I catch fish. These are mine. I want to keep them. It is my house. No white man gave it to me. I built it myself. That is all.

ALSEA JACK: You know me. I am a poor man. I know the hearts of the whites. I am strai[gh]t with all. People say I am bad. That is not so. I live on my land. I have a sick heart. Once in a while a bad white man does wrong to us. Not all the whites are so. I want to keep my land. All have said they want their land. That is my heart. If all are of my mind no one will get our land. I raise my own potatoes. I have worked my land and intend to improve it more and build me a new house. Every summer I want to clear more land. I want all my people to do as I do, work. If they do they will not be hungry. I don't want to be like the old people who have nothing planted. The whites have made us like themselves. That is why we work our land. By and by all will do so. They all make fences and houses. Now we want to stay where we are. We want to fix everything right around us. That is all.

SIUSLAW JOHN, Chief of the Siuslaw: I do not know you Mr. Fairchild. I know you Mr. Litchfield. I will give you my mind. You understand our language. I will not talk much. Ever since you have been here I have talked to you.

I have always wanted you to send my words to Washington. I do not want to hear any more about this thing. A long time I have heard it. I thought it was all settled long time ago. As long as I live on my land I am not sorry if I have nothing. My people have all the same mind as I have on this point. I don't want you to help the Chief in Washington get our land. I understand the Washington Chief wants to send us money. What for?

I know the mind of my people. They do not want money. It is long since we had money and we no longer care for it. I have only a little place and no money. Yet my heart is not sick. The Great Chief sends money to the Indians but does not understand their hearts. At first, the whites promised many things. The people will never do again as they once did, sell their land. If I was to talk many days, I should say the same thing. It was not my wish to come here at first, but the Great Chief desired it. This thing I will not give up. Gen. Palmer gave us this country and I will never give it up. That is all.

Siuslaw Dick, head man: I do not want to talk long. Long time this has been my country. My heart has been heavy on that account. It was never my wish to give up my country. This is the first time I ever saw Mr. Fairchild. It is not my mind to leave my country. I have a strong heart to stay there. I will never move a step from my country. It is like they were trying to haul me to Siletz by telling me of fine things they will give me there. I shall always be of the same mind. I will not receive a dollar of their money. If they should say there was plenty of money at Siletz, I would not go. I will not go under any circumstances.

In my country I want to die. I will not change my mind. I will not go to another country to die. Before I ever saw a white man I raised produce on my land. I wish the whites would let us alone. That is all my heart. We are very poor now. Let us alone. It will be better to stop talking about our country.

Siuslaw George, head man: I do not want to put myself ahead of the old people here, but I will talk a little. What makes the whites think our people are no better than dogs. Let them talk as much as they please. How can the whites believe in a just God and try and drive the Indians off their land. It would be well if they would make our Country better by helping us here. Long ago when I was a boy I heard of this driving Indians. That is the way they did and now the Indians are nearly gone. My father died on my land. Well for us to die there. If our children grow up it will be good for them to take our country and be buried there. There are but few of us and we do not want to go to another country to die.

Joe Scott, Chief of [Lower] Umpqua: This day it is as if we were all on the same road. I have long had a sick heart on account of Mr. Fairchild coming today. Long the Great Chief has not understood our minds. Today I am in good heart because I see my words written down. I don't want to do as Mr. Fairchild advised.

Perhaps the Great Chief will make us poor but we don't want to do this thing. We don't want it even talked about. This was not always my country. I am a driven man. I will not give up my land on that account. This is my country now and no one has any right here. It is true we are nearly all gone. When we first came here I understood the Great Chief to make us certain promises. We made a treaty. We never received the things promised. The Great Chief may say now, "I will give you many good things," but I don't want to hear such talk. I have heard too many promises now. Long the Great Chief has said, "I will give you many good things and you will grow upwards," but we have never got these and are sick of hearing such talk. We have had different agents here but it seems as if we had only now got an agency.

If Litchfield remains with us we will continue to improve, as we now do. We did not ask for things long ago, but the Great Chief promised them. Agent after agent has made promises, but till Litchfield came we got nothing.

SOPENNY, head man [of Lower] Umpqua: I want to talk one way always. My mind is the same now that it was when Inspector Kemble was here. If I was in my old country, the Umpqua, I should say the same. The Great Chief gave us this land. I have long lived here and have improved my land. Once I lived in another country which the whites got. It is all right now. No whites live here and I am satisfied. I am growing old here. Why do these people all have heavy hearts? Because they fear being driven away. They have long feared this. All these young men when they grow up will talk the same. We will not give up our land. I know the whites have much money, but I want none of it though I am poor. Many have died here every winter. All the agents say, "this is your land." My father lived always at Siuslaw. We don't want anybody to say any more "you will grow up at Siletz." I[n] our old country we left good houses which made my heart heavy. They said we would grow up if we came here.

UMPQUA TOM, leading man: I have but little to say. I say as the others have said, the same as my Chief Scott has said. I am not afraid to live here. The Great Chief knows this is our land. He knows it. It is a great thing for us, about our land. This is a good country for us. I was young when we came. Now this is our home. They may try to drive us off many years but we will never give it up. They got our father's land. The Great Chief got the better of us long ago. We don't want to hear a thing about this. The Great Chief got the better of us long ago with the same promises we hear today. This is our land and we are doing well here.

Coos Jeff [Harney], head man of the Coos: I am glad to see Mr. Fairchild in my country today. I have long heard of this thing. It is like we were not living right. We are in trouble. I was ashamed when one man said "he did not want to be driven like the Coos." Yes it is like the whites had made us poor by driving us from our old country. I have a heavy heart on account of the treaty we made [in September, 1855] with Gen. [Joel] Palmer (unratified).

We came a long distance from that country. It was not a small country we gave the whites. It was a large country. You see me Mr. Fairchild today. You do not see me have much property. When we sold our land we never received any pay. You do not see me with team or wagon. I do not owe anybody anything, but the Great Chief owes me a great deal for the country we sold. We have left two countries now. I think on that account the Great Chief will not insist on our leaving this country. We have not received much help, yet we do very well.

Pumley, Coos Indian: I am almost an old man now. Long ago our chief had a good heart to the whites. Long ago the Great Chief traded for our old country and gave us this country from the Yaquina to the Siuslaw. We have long lived here, though it seems as if we had only just now got an agent. We are determined not to give up our country. We came here from a distance and strongly desire to keep our country. The Great Chief owes us a great deal now. The agent form Siletz has come to see us now. No one came to see us and find out how much the Great Chief owes us. How long will it be before we get it. We are nearly all dead now and it is a great thing for us. They told us first, "you will all get wagons, the Umpqua, the Coos, the Alseas." So they told us.

We are all determined we will never give up this land. We are firmly determined to keep it. All of us, men, women, and children are decided on that point. I know all their minds.

George Cameron, Coos Indian: My heart is full of this matter. It is like bad whites had taken us from our old country and brought us here. I do not want it that way now. How long will it be before we become like the whites. Long since the Great Chief gave us this country. Long ago Gen. [Joel] Palmer made a treaty with us which was never carried out. The whites do not lie to each other. If they owe each other, they pay. Why did they not pay us as they agreed when we made the treaty. I do not want them to make any more promises of what they will do if we will leave our country. Our Chief who helped make the treaty died and got nothing from Washington. I do not want to give up my country like that any more. I am doing well here, and mean to stay. It will be well if the Great Chief will hear what we say.

[Jim] Buchanan, Coos: I have heard for a long time that Mr. Fairchild was coming here to talk to us. I think the Coos are as good as any Indians. The first time our fathers saw the whites they regarded them as friends. I was a boy then. They drove us here. We gave a large and valuable country to the whites. There is coal there. We have never received a dollar for our land. We are doing well and it is best for us to remain here now. We have made this a good country ourselves. If the Gov[ernmen]t would help us a little here it would be well. We have long been told there was money coming for us, but we have never seen a cent. We have no teams. You will not see many teams here. If you could send a good paper to Washington our hearts will be glad. We would be glad if we could increase in numbers here.

ROBERT BURNS, Coos: If I was a big man I would not be ashamed to speak. I wish to say one thing to you two agents. I want you to have good hearts toward the Coos Indians. If you will help us in this matter with the Great Chief we shall be glad. You are paid to look out for Indians, and now we want you to look out for our interests. Long ago the whites told us they wanted us to grow and improve, and they would help us to become like themselves. If a good agent is here we improve. One thing. They try to help the Indians and keep moving them. That is wrong. If one should put down $500,000.00 we would not take it for our country. If the whites get land they improve it and desire to keep it. So it is with us. We have improved this land and like it. True we can not read and write. When we speak, our words do not go strai[gh]t to Washington. That is one thing that has kept us down and another is that when our words do get there the answer does not come srai[gh]t to us. If the Great Chief understands our minds it is well. We do not want to be hauled. We want to stay here. If we get a good agent it seems as if the Great Chief wanted to remove him. That is also a reason why we do not improve faster.

COOS TOM, leading man: I want to talk a little because a good man has come today. I don't want to be moved from here. We gave up a good country when we came here. I think the Great Chief understands that the Coos people are good. We will never give up this country. We want to live and die here. When we send word to Washington it seems as if it never reached there. We don't want the whites to feel bad if we live here and improve and come up. We have no thoughts of leaving this country. Our people are few and we don't want the whites to feel bad if we grow up and are helped a little. My heart is sad to think the Great Chief keeps ta[l]king about our giving up our land. I think we will improve this summer under our good agent and we want to be let alone.

JACK RODGERS, Chief of Coos Indians: I did not at first understand what Mr. Fairchild said. (He was sick and not present at the beginning of the council.) My people told me though I knew before they were talking about this country. My people do not want to leave here neither do I. I think if my people do right they will improve and become like the whites. When the whites first saw us they gave us a few things. Afterwards they said, "Let [us] have your land." They talked one year and we then gave it up. Then we went to the Umpqua. Today I am not like them. I am not hungry for blankets, shirts, &c. This country looks good to me now. I would like to have the Washington Chief help us to become like the whites.

I have been absent at Coos Bay and return to find a good school in operation, and my people's children learning like the whites. Today I do not want you to push us on a bad road. If my people are hungry there are plenty of fish close at hand. It is a good country for fish and game. My people are very much afraid of the idea of moving. It seems as if since we left our old country we had no friends. Today we want our agent to write a strong paper to Washington and help us. Several have said today that we did not want any money. How can they get along unless they are helped?

My people the Coos and Umpquas are very much like the whites now. We only have a few houses. The Great Chief did not give them to us. We are like the whites in this. We do not wish to give up our Country. The whites live at Yaquina and Umpqua 25 miles distant. I think that is right. I think when we gave up the country between Yaquina and Alsea it was enough. Don't drive or haul us. It will be useless for anymore agents to come and talk with us on this matter. We never will give up our country. We have a great variety of food which is produced here and that is the reason we do not wish to leave. Neither whites nor Indians made this country. God made it. We do not want to give it up.

MR. FAIRCHILD: My friends I have heard all you have said. I have heard many men who all speak one way. I will faithfully send a copy of your words to the Great Chief in Washington. What the result will be, I am unable to say. I am glad you have a good agent in whom you have confidence and that you are improving. It is possible that Congress and the President have been misinformed respecting your wishes. I feel sure you will do what your agent tells you, and he will advise you right.

One thing I wish to say. You seem to think the Great Chief does not pay attention to your wishes. Remember he has many Indians to look after and can spare but little time for each tribe.

MR. LITCHFIELD: I will say a few words more. Do not trouble yourselves about this matter. Do not get angry, and I want you to be careful and not give any of the whites cause for offense. If they talk bad, don't get angry, keep your temper, and by all means do nothing to offend them. I want you to take my word on this matter. Perhaps white people will come here to look at this land; treat them well. Do not be angry with them, do not be insolent or talk bad to them. Keep careful watch over your tongues, your hearts and your hands. This thing will all turn out for the best for you. The council will now close.

Congress did not rescind the act of March 3, 1875. In spite of the failure to secure the assent of any of the tribes and the record of the vehement objection of the leaders to the closing of the Alsea Sub-agency, the Bureau of Indian Affairs terminated its operations and withdrew trust responsibility over the southern portion of the Coast Reservation during the summer of 1875. Settlers poured in. Many of the Alsea moved to the reduced Siletz Reservation. The Coos and Lower Umpqua drifted south along the coast. Some settled among the Siuslaw, particularly on the North Fork east of Florence. Many more returned to the Umpqua estuary and Coos Bay, landless in their traditional homelands.

To this day the Coos, Lower Umpqua, and Siuslaw tribes have received no settlement from the United States for the taking of 1.7 million acres of their aboriginal lands under the unratified treaty of 1855. The tribes received in trust a 6.1–acre reservation in Coos Bay, Oregon, a gift to the United States in 1940 from Louis J. Simpson and William Robertson. The Bureau of Indian Affairs erected a tribal hall on the property in 1941. The tribes retain cemeteries at the Cape Arago Lighthouse, the Empire Pioneer Cemetery, Lakeside Cemetery, and one on the North Fork of the Siuslaw River. In 2005 the United States transferred to the tribes the U.S. Navy Facility at Coos Head, a tract on the cliffs at the entrance to Coos Bay.

The Alsea integrated into the population of the Siletz Reservation and, in litigation before the Court of Claims, secured a judgment in 1945 for the taking of their lands without ratified treaty.

SOURCE

Fairchild, J. H. Minutes of Council held June 17th, 1875 with the tribes on the Alsea Reservation. Letters Received by the Office of Indian Affairs, 1824–80, Oregon, 1875. RG 75, National Archives, Washington, DC.

RELATED READING

Beckham, Stephen Dow. *The Indians of Western Oregon: This Land Was Theirs.* Coos Bay, OR: Arago Books, 1977.

Schwartz, E. A. "Sick Hearts: Indian Removal on the Oregon Coast, 1875–1881," *Oregon Historical Quarterly* 92(Fall, 1991):228–64.

Van de Velde, Paul, and Henriette R. "Charles I. Litchfield," *South Lincoln County and Its Early Settlers*, Lincoln County Historical Society Publication No. 4–A, n.d.

"Some Men Say They Are Our Friends," 1875

The experiences of Alfred Meacham as Oregon Superintendent of Indian Affairs and as a member of the Peace Commission to the Modocs in 1873 transformed his life. He nearly died from his wounds in the attack on the Peace Commission but redoubled his energies to fight for Native Americans. In 1875 Meacham departed from Salem, Oregon, with his lecture company, a contingent of four of the state's Indian leaders. His goal was to enable these speakers to inform the citizens of the United States about the injustices and mistreatment of American Indians. The Indian delegation was the first from Oregon to meet with President Ulysses S. Grant and Commissioner of Indian Affairs, Edwin P. Smith.

The Native Americans in the lecture company were Toby (Wi-ne-ma) Riddle, George Harney (Ol-ha-the), Dave Hill (Wal-aiks-ski-dat), and Tecumpsha (Yum-nis-Poe-tis). Oliver C. Applegate, a scout during the Modoc War, Frank Riddle, a Kentuckian who had married the Modoc Wi-ne-ma (also known as Toby or Tobey), and their son, Charka, traveled with the contingent. Toby and Frank Riddle had served as interpreters for the U. S. Army during the Modoc War and the military tribunal trying the vanquished Indian leaders. Harney was the son of Chief John, a famed chief and military leader during the Rogue River Indian Wars of the 1850s; Harney himself was a leader on the Coast Reservation and resided at Siletz.

David Hill and Tecumpsha—as they were known to Meacham and the public—were close friends and members of the Klamath tribe. Wal-aiks-ski-dat, "the left-handed chief who lives between two rivers," had converted to Methodism through the missionary work of Indian Agent L. S. Dyar. He took the name David Hill. Yum-nis Poe-tis, "the chief without beauty," was a traditional shaman but had also accepted Christianity and taken the name Tecumpsha, or Tecumseh. As spokesmen for their tribe, these men, Meacham reflected, "had only my promise to take care of them, and to give them an opportunity to see, and hear, and talk for their races. This was the inducement, this alone, and this was sufficient."

The Meacham Indian Lecture Company traveled first to Sacramento, then east by rail to St. Joseph, Missouri. There Scar-Face Charley, Steamboat Frank, and

Shacknasty Jim—Modocs exiled to the Indian Territory in Oklahoma—joined the group for the East Coast circuit in the spring of 1875.

The speech of David Hill vividly spoke to the predicament of Native Americans. Hill gave these remarks in Independence Hall, Philadelphia, on March 24, 1875.

I feel like a very small man in this place. Among my own people I am not a small man. This seems like a sacred place where men ought to think, and not talk. My heart is wandering away to the Great Spirit, and I am asking Him why my people did not hear about the new law that was made here. They were very poor, and had not many horses, perhaps that was the reason why he did not tell them.

My people have lately heard that there was a new law, and they sent me to see about it. If it is a good law, my people want a part of it. I think it must be good, because I see with my own eyes what the white man can do with this law. I am glad in my heart that I have seen the place where this new law started. Maybe I can take some of it back to my people. When I look at the great men who made the new law, they seem to be a long way off from me, and I think I cannot catch up with them.

The white man lives upon the top of a high mountain. He can see many things which I cannot. When I look inside of myself, I wonder what makes the difference. I know that my skin is red, but my heart is just like the white man's heart. When I think these things over, I feel like as if I was lost in a dark mountain, and did not know the way out. There are some things I do not understand. I know that the Negro was a slave, and that the white men had a big war about it. I know that he is all the same as a white man now. I see some men that are not like the white men. They were born on some other land. They are Irishmen, Englishmen, Spaniards, Portuguese, and some Chinamen too; all these men are just the same as the white men. They go where they wish to, and nobody says "No." They vote and build houses. Why is all this? An Indian cannot go anywhere without his agent gives him a paper. He is just the same as a slave. He is not free. He seems to be a stranger everywhere. Men look at me as though I was a mountain lion. They seem to think that I am a wild man. I am not wild. *I am a man. Why* do you treat my people as if they were all crazy, and had no sense? My people are no fools. You know more than we do about these things, and some things you do not. I hear your spirit-man pray. He does not say anything about the Indian to the Great Spirit. I was in the great law house at Washington, (referring to the Capitol.) I saw Negroes there. I saw every kind of people there, but Indians.

Wal-aiks-ski-dat (David Hill), a Klamath delegate to Washington, D.C., spoke on March 24, 1875, at Independence Hall, Philadelphia. He was a member of the Meacham Indian Lecture Company (National Archives, 56-ID-13).

I think the laws that are made are not straight, they are crooked. They leave the Indian out. He has no one to talk for him. Do you think this is what the men up there meant? Did they intend that everybody should have a chance to talk except the Indian? They look like good men (pointing to the faces of the signers of the Declaration on the wall.) Perhaps they see me now. I am not ashamed to look them in the eye. Some men say that are our friends. If they are our friends, why do they not ask us about what we want? They send men to the reservations and do not ask us if we want them. I went to see the President. He looks just like any other man. I was not afraid of him. I intended to tell him what my people wanted, but his ear was too small, he could not hear me. I brought all the things in my heart away.

Then I went to see the Commissioner. He had large ears. He *seemed* to listen to what I had to tell him, but I looked him in the eye. He did not put the things I told him in his heart. My heart got sick, because I had came a long way with Colonel Meacham to see these men, but they would not take the words I gave them. I saw a colored man talking to the Commissioner, and he listened to all the colored man said. I have got my heart full of the things I have seen. Some things make me feel *sick*. When I came here I thought I had a part in all I saw. Now I do not think so. Some things have been told me that are true, and some are not true. It is not true that an Indian can be a white man. Yes he can be like a white man, but the *white man won't let him. He stands on the Indians's head.* He will not let him *get up.* When the Indian tries to stand by the side of the white man, he pushes him away. He does not push the Negro away, not the Spaniard.

I ask Colonel Meacham why is this? He told me it was because the Indian could not vote. I can vote if the white man will let me. Some white men say an Indian is wild and don't know how to vote. I would not vote for whisky. I would not vote for a gambler. I know a good man when I see his eyes and hear him talk. I want the white man to get off my head. I want an even start, and if I cannot keep up with him, I must go behind him. But some of the Indian can keep up. I hear about your "big Sunday" that is coming next summer, (referring to the centennial celebration). I know about that too. When that "big Sunday," comes, I want to hear your great chiefs talk. I want them to change the law so that an Indian can have a chance to travel on the same road with the white man and the Negro. I want my children to have a part in this country. They are in school now, and they can read books. I hope you men who have talked so straight to us will have the law changed, so that all may have an even chance to own houses, and build great bridges, and make laws. All I have said comes from my heart, and the Great Spirit has heard me talk. He knows that my heart is good, and my tongue is straight. I want your spirit-men (meaning ministers of the church,) to talk to the Great Spirit for my people. I want all good white men to stand by me when *I try to be a man. I want the soldiers taken away from my country, and the whisky men kept away, and then if we have good agents, we will get along well enough.* Maybe some time my people will sing with your people, and we shall all be like one people. You have heard my people speak, when I have talked. You have seen their hearts. I have spoken.

Hill's reference to the "new law" was most likely to the transfer of land grants in the 1870s to the Oregon Central Military Wagon Road Company by the State of Oregon. In 1864 Congress authorized the subsidy of up to six square miles of land for every mile of road built. A company based in Springfield, Oregon, secured the right to construct the road from the head of the Willamette Valley to Boise, Idaho. When the surveyors crossed the Cascade Range at Summit Lake, however, they turned south through the well-watered meadows of the Klamath Reservation to carve out 93,150 acres. Their meandering route bisected the Klamath lands and took much of the most productive acreage reserved by the 1864 treaty.

David Hill, whose speech confirmed considerable disillusionment, disappeared during the lecture tour. Eventually he "rode the rails" across the continent to the reservation and subsequently served in the Indian Police Force. Hill was murdered in 1889 at the Lost River Fishery. Tecumpsha died in 1876 "under ambiguous circumstances."

SOURCE

Meacham, Alfred. *Wi-ne-ma (The Woman-Chief) and Her People*. Hartford, CT: American Publishing Company, 1876, pp. 103–7.

RELATED READING

Stern, Theodore. *The Klamath Tribe: A People and Their Reservation*. Seattle, WA: University of Washington Press, 1965.

Sarah Winnemucca: "A Notorious Liar and Malicious Schemer," 1880

The accusations flew in all directions in 1880 when Sarah Winnemucca took to a national lecture circuit and began writing newspaper columns. Her mission was to denounce the imprisonment of Northern Paiutes and the tenure of William V. Rinehart as Indian Agent on the Malheur Reservation. Winnemucca dared to challenge the actions both of the Bureau of Indian Affairs and of Rinehart, formerly an officer with the Oregon Volunteers. Her success as a lecturer and the wave of support which rose for her causes caused consternation in the "Indian ring" and with Rinehart in particular. Winnemucca and her father traveled to Washington, D.C., and during the winter of 1879–80 visited with Secretary of Interior Carl Schurz to press for the release of five hundred Northern Paiute held on the Yakima Reservation in Washington Territory.

The following documents confirm how Rinehart sought to destroy Sarah Winnemucca. They are a classic example of ad hominem attack. The focus was on the alleged moral failings of Winnemucca, not on the charges that she levelled against the BIA or Agent Rinehart. On January 15, 1880, Rinehart wrote to the Commissioner of Indian Affairs, enclosing three affidavits that he had solicited charging her with prostitution, drunkenness, and dishonesty. To Rinehart's dismay, two months later he received notice of Winnemucca's appointment as his interpreter. Rinehart fired back to Washington a newspaper article and a petition signed by nine residents of Canyon City further attacking Winnemucca.

Sarah Winnemucca tried to get in the last word. Her Life Among the Piutes *(1883) contained an eighteen-page appendix of testimonials to her character. Major-Generals Oliver O. Howard and Irvin McDowell, Lieutenant-Colonel James W. Forsyth, Adjutant-General C. E. S. Wood, and others attested to her veracity and conduct. Winnemucca became one of the best-known Native American women of the nineteenth-century American West. Her nemesis, W. V. Rinehart, has gained little more than a footnote in history.*

Letter of January 15, 1880, from W. V. Rinehart, Malheur Agent at
Camp Harney to E. A. Hayt, Commissioner of Indian Affairs.

I send inclosed affidavits tending to establish the true character of Sarah
Winnemucca, former interpreter at this Agency. This is deemed necessary in
order to meet the false charges made by her recently in her public lectures at
San Francisco and extensively noticed in the public press of the country. Her
character for veracity and virtue has been alluded to by me in former reports,
but it has not been deemed necessary to resort to actual proof of her true
standing in this community until the present, when it seems likely that the
Dep[ar]t[ment may be called upon to consider hers in connection with my
own character.

It is reported that she is now on the way to Washington with the purpose of
interviewing your office, with a view of securing my removal for causes to be
assigned by her.

Comment upon these affidavits is deemed unnecessary, further than to say
I believe them to be true; and, so notorious is her ill-fame, that I feel assured
I could obtain the evidence of scores of the best men in this country, as to her
general bad character.

Affidavit of William Currey, January 13, 1880

State of Oregon, County of Grant
    I, William Currey, being first duly sworn according to law, depose and say
that I am a citizen of the United States over twenty-one years old and a resident
of Harney Valley County and State aforesaid; that I am by occupation a stock
raiser and have been for the last seven years; that I am acquainted with Sarah
Winnemucca, former interpreter at Malheur Agency and have known her for
the last four years; that I served in the capacity of courier for the army during
the recent Indian outbreak of the Bannock and Piute Indians and had extensive
opportunities to learn the general reputation of this Indian woman among
the citizens of Eastern Oregon and also in the army; that I think I know her
reputation for truth and veracity & that she is generally regarded, where she is
known, as untruthful and not entitled to be believed; that, in addition to her
conspicuous untruthfulness, she is generally regarded by those who know her,
as a common prostitute and thoroughly addicted to the habits of drunkenness
and gambling.
    William Currey

Subscribed and sworn to before me on this 13th day of January 1880, at Camp Harney, Oregon. W. V. Rinehart, U. S. Indian Agent

Affidavit of Thomas O'Keefe, January 13, 1880

State of Oregon, County of Grant

I, Thomas O'Keefe being first duly sworn according to law, depose and say; that I am a discharged Soldier from the United States Army, and at present a resident of Fort Harney, County of Grant and State of Oregon; that I have been personally acquainted with Sarah Winnemucca, former interpreter, at Malheur Agency, Oregon, for the last six years; that in consideration of a bottle of whiskey and $5 I had illicit intercourse with the said Sarah Winnemucca; that between November 1st and December 20th 1878 the said Sarah Winnemucca sent me notes to meet her for the purpose of having intercourse with her; that in consideration of whiskey furnished her I had intercourse with the said Sarah Winnemucca between the dates specified; that she lived in open prostitution with John Gum, an enlisted man of Co. "K" 1st Cavalry; that her reputation for veracity among citizens and soldiers is bad, the general impression being that she could be bought for a bottle of whiskey.

Thomas O'Keefe

Subscribed and sworn to before me at Camp Harney, Oregon, this 13th day of January AD 1880. W. V. Rinehart, U.S. Indian Agent

Affidavit of W. W. Johnson, January 13, 1880

State of Oregon, County of Grant

I, W. W. Johnson, being first duly sworn according to law, depose and say that I am a citizen of the United States over twenty-one years old and a resident of Camp Harney, County and State aforesaid; that I am personally acquainted with Sarah Winnemucca, former interpreter at Malheur Agency, Oregon; that I k[n]ew her while she was serving in said capacity; that I was employed at the same time as Blacksmith at said Indian Agency; that I served as Blacksmith for Col. Bernard's command in the field during the recent hostile outbreak of the Bannock and Piute Indians where she served as interpreter; that I am well acquainted with the general reputation of said Sarah Winnemucca in this region, among citizens and soldiers; that wherever known she is generally regarded as untruthful and not entitled to be believed and further that she is known to be addicted to the vices of drunkenness, gambling and common prostitution.

W. W. Johnson

Subscribed and sworn to before me at Camp Harney, Oregon, this 13th day of January, A.D. 1880. W. V. Rinehart, U.S. Indian Agent

Letter of March 20, 1880, from W. V. Rinehart to the Commissioner of Indian Affairs

Sir:

I have the honor to acknowledge receipt of your letter (A) of date Jan[uar]y 26, 1880, appointing Sarah Winnemucca as interpreter at this Agency, at an annual compensation of $470, from said date; and directing that, upon her arrival at this Agency, her name be submitted upon the usual descriptive statement for the action of your office.

She has not yet arrived at this Agency; and before submitting her name to your office as a proper person to fill the important position of Interpreter, I deem it my duty to advise your office of her notoriety as an untruthful, drunken prostitute, by directing your attention to the affidavits accompanying my letter of Jan[uar]y 14, '80, to the inclosed editorial remarks copied by the *Bedrock Democrat* of Baker City Oregon, and also inclosed copy of a Statement Signed by nine of the leading citizens of Canyon City.

The earlier history of her connection with this agency may be learned, in part, by referring to my report (with inclosures) dated December 23, 1876. It was public[ly] known then, as now, that her last occupation before coming to this Agency as interpreter for Agent [Samuel] Parrish, was in a public house of ill-fame at the town of Winnemucca, Nevada.

Among the "other sufficient causes" alluded to in my report to Gen[era]l Howard's Headquarters, for which she was discharged from the position of Interpreter, was that one of my white employees saw her in bed with an Indian man in the mess-house. In view of such facts, and knowing as I do that this is only part of her infamous history, I am induced to venture the opinion that she is not a proper person to serve in any capacity at this or any other Indian agency.

Very respectfully, W. V. Rinehart, U.S. Indian Agent

Letter of January 14, 1880, Citizens of Canyon City to T. H. Brents

Dear Sir:

We, the undersigned citizens of Grant County, Oregon, having for many years been acquainted with Major W. V. Rinehart, take this method of presenting, through your kindness, to the Honorable Commissioner of Indian Affairs the following favorable facts:

1st That Major W. V. Rinehart, present U.S. Indian Agent at Malheur Indian Agency in Oregon, was a resident of this county for many years prior to his appointment to his present position. That he always maintained, and yet maintains the confidence of this community for honesty, integrity and reliable business qualities.

2nd That we have seen with amazement the charges brought against him by an Indian woman calling herself Sarah Winnemucca; not that anything this woman can say or do amazes us, but that an intelligent public and high officials should give any credence to the statements of such a person is startling to us.

3rd Our long residence in close proximity to the Malheur Indian Agency has rendered us familiar with the character and habits of this woman; and we unhesitatingly say that it is provable by good and legal testimony that Sarah Winnemucca is, and for years has been a common prostitute, addicted to drunkenness. That it is well understood that by reason of her known and notorious lewd and lascivious habits she was some time ago discharged by Major Rinehart from Government employ. That her influence with the Indians has always been to render them licentious, contumacious and profligate. That this woman has been several times married, but that by reason of her adulterous and drunken habits, neither squawmen nor Indians would long live with her. That in addition to her character of Harlot and drunkard, she merits and possesses that of a notorious liar and malicious schemer.

Wherefore, as citizens, we ask that, if any notice be taken of her statements, those accused by her have a full and fair opportunity to be heard concerning them; and as a personal favor to each of us, we ask that you present this to the Hon. Commissioner of Indian Affairs and to the Hon. Secretary of the Interior.

Very respectfully, Your Ob[edien]t Servants

John Muldrick, Phil Metschan, William Hall, Edwin Hall, J. W. Church, J. H. Wood, F. C. Sels, D. G. Overholt, and Wm. Luce

Newspaper clipping from the *Bedrock Democrat* (Baker City, OR) attached to the petition

A DRUNKEN PRINCESS

The Esmerelda (Nev.) *Herald* says the Piute Princess, Sallie Winnemucca, has recently been making the atmosphere of Elko county decidedly torrid. A short time since she returned from Washington, and, on setting foot on her native heath, proceeded to get "biling" drunk. An item appearing to that effect in the *Silver State*, the Princess challenged the editor to mortal combat with scalping knives, and for sending such challenge she was arrested and held in durance vile. This same Sallie Winnemucca has lately been receiving a great deal of notice at the hands of the press, even many of the Pacific slope journals landing the squaw in a Fennimore Cooper style. Time does not improve the Princess much. She has been a prostitute and drunkard ever since the age of seventeen, and, although that Good General, Freedman's Bureau [Oliver O.] Howard, tried two years ago to induct some Christianity into her while she was with his command in the Bannack war, it seems to have been a failure, and Sallie is still the dirty, broken wanton she always was.

SOURCE

Bureau of Indian Affairs. Sarah Winnemucca, Item 268, Special Files of the Office of Indian Affairs, 1807–1904, Microcopy M-574, Roll 74, RG 75, National Archives, Washington, DC.

RELATED READING

Canfield, Gae. *Sarah Winnemucca of the Northern Paiutes.* Norman, OK: University of Oklahoma Press, 1981.

Fowler, Catherine S., and Sven Liljeblad. Northern Paiute. *Handbook of North American Indians, Vol. 11, Great Basin.* Washington, DC: Smithsonian Institution, 1986, pp. 435–65.

Scherer, Joanna Cohan. The Public Faces of Sarah Winnemucca, *Cultural Anthropology* 3(2[May, 1988]):178–204.

Scordato, Ellen. *Sarah Winnemucca: Northern Paiute Writer and Diplomat.* New York, NY: Chelsea House, 1992.

Senier, Siobhan. *Voices of American Indian Assimilation and Resistance: Helen Hunt Jackson, Sarah Winnemucca, and Victoria Howard.* Norman, OK: University of Oklahoma Press, 2001.

Zanjani, Sally. *Sarah Winnemucca.* Lincoln, NE: University of Nebraska Press, 2001.

The Indian History of the Modoc War, 1914

Jeff C. Riddle (1863–1941) was the son of Wi-ne-ma and Frank Riddle. His father was a southern white man who named him for Jefferson C. Davis, president of the Confederacy. His mother, Wi-ne-ma (Nan-ook-too-wa, Tobey, or Toby), was a Modoc woman who served as an interpreter during her tribe's war with the U.S. Army and as a lecturer with Alfred Meacham's touring Indian company in the 1870s.

"I want to say here," wrote Riddle, "that my education is limited as all the school I had was only six weeks, so what little education I have I learnt myself. I know that some people will find fault with my history, but I have given nothing but plain facts and nothing but the truth." This was Riddle's disclaimer to a remarkable book, The Indian History of the Modoc War and the Causes That Led to It *(1914). Written as a rejoinder to the "blood and thunder" narrative of William R. Drannan's* Thirty-One Years on the Plains and in the Mountains *(1900), Riddle's history was the first book by an Indian writer to assess an Indian war in Oregon. "In my work," he noted, "I aim to give both sides of the troubles of the Modoc Indians and the whites." "The Indian side," he asserted, "has never been given to the public yet."*

The following selection is Chapter 5 from Riddle's book. He described in this narrative the decision to force the removal of the Modocs from their homeland near Tule Lake, California, to the Yainax Agency on the Klamath Reservation in Oregon. Riddle wrote with candor about the atrocities that preceded the armed resistance of the Modocs to the U.S. Army.

November 28th, 1872, the agent at Klamath agency sits in his office reading a telegram from the Secretary of War at Washington, D. C. The message read like this: "Major [James] Jackson, Fort Klamath, Oregon: Go to Lost River and move Capt. Jack and band of Modoc Indians onto the Klamath Indian reservation, Oregon; peaceable if you can, but forcible if you must."

Tobey Riddle rode towards Lost River from Yreka, California. She pats her bay mare on the neck, saying, "This has been a hard trip for you today. I will soon get there, Snippy, but we cannot stay long at Capt. Jack's camp. We must go on tonight towards Yainax." Tonight the noble animal strains its every nerve. She goes away in a fast trot, then at a gallop, then off like the wind. At last she reaches the top of the small ridge. She stops her faithful mare, looks long at the white specks of canvas at Jack's camp, and says to herself, "I guess my people are safe yet!" In a few minutes Tobey is among her people. They gathered around her. She tells in these words, "I am glad to see all of you. I left my home this morning about fifty-eight miles. I cannot stay overnight here. I must go on to my father and brother." Jack replies, "Cousin, you look tired and anxious; what is the matter? Your folks are just over the hill at Nuh-sult-gar-ka. Your brother, Charley, is better. Did you hear of him being sick?" Tobey shook her head. She was crying. After she overcame her grief, she said, "The soldiers will be here tomorrow. I rode hard in order to reach you people. What I want to tell you is this: "Do not resist the soldiers. Do not offer fight; if you listen to the officers, you people will not get hurt. Go back to the agency. You all know John Schonchin's brother and my brother, Charley. All their people are living at Yainax, and no one bothers them. They are Modocs. Go to Yainax, where the other Modocs are. You will be safe if you take my advice, but if you fight the soldiers, all of you will be killed. You cannot whip the white people. There is too many of them. You people could never kill all the soldiers the government could send here." Capt. Jack: "I do not want to fight, and I do not expect to fight without the soldiers force me to fight; if I am forced to take up arms gainst the soldiers, I will die game."

While Jack was still talking, Tobey Riddle mounted her trusty animal. She reined her animal around and said, "Farewell, my people, we may never meet in this world again, but if you people just take my advice, you will all die natural deaths, one by one, near your native country." She tapped her trusty animal on the neck. The mare started in a gallop on the trail headed for Nuh-sult-gar-ka, where now stands the town of Bonanza, Oregon. Tobey arrived at her destination long after sun down, told her folks that the soldiers would be after the Modocs, over on Lost River tomorrow. Some of the Indians packed up that same night and made their way towards Yainax, Oregon. The ride Tobey Riddle made was on the 17th [28th] day of November, 1872. The distance this woman rode on that short November day was about seventy-five miles.

As soon as Tobey left Capt. Jack's village on Lost River, Oregon, near the Natural Bridge, Scar-Face Charley, Shaknasty Jim, Bogus Charley, Steamboat Frank, Hooker Jim, Skukum Horse, Curley Headed Jack and others got their ponies and started around the north side of Tule Lake to see the settlers. They told the white settlers; namely, Boddys, Brotheringtons, Overtons, Miller,

Modocs on the lecture circuit: Shacknasty Jim, Steamboat Frank, Tobey (Winema) Riddle, and Scar-faced Charley (standing), Frank Riddle and Jeff Riddle, subsequently author of *The Indian History of the Modoc War* (seated) (Denver Public Library, Western History Collection, X-32143).

Bibus, Browns and all the others that the soldiers would be at their village the following day. If the soldiers did not treat them right, they were going to fight. "We came here to see you men. All we ask of you men is to stay at your homes. Take no hand against us. We promise that not one of you will be hurt. Just stay at your homes. Let the soldiers lick us." The settlers all promised to stay at their homes. The Indians went back to their villages, well satisfied with their mission. After sundown a company of soldiers, cavalrymen, commanded by Major Jackson, was dismounting near a ford on Lost River, four miles from the Indian village up the river. The ford is now called Stukel Ford. The commander told his brave soldiers: "We will wait here till near the morning hour; then we will go down and pay the reds a visit." Eight or nine miles southeast of the company of soldiers, fifteen or twenty settlers had collected together in one of the settler's homes, and were talking about the war. They were preparing for war against the Modocs.

Kind reader, these men are the same men that had promised Scar-Face Charley and his men that same evening, that in case the Modocs got into a fight with the troops, they would stay home and do as the Indians had requested them to do. Capt. Jack and John Schonchin stayed up till a late hour that night, trying to reach some conclusion for the following day. They decided one and all to not offer battle, unless the soldiers forced them to fight. All of the Indians went to their lodges and were soon sleeping, not thinking in the least that they would be routed by daylight. There was not one of them but what thought the soldiers would come to their villages in day time. They soon afterwards found out that was not the case.

Long before the dawn of day on the morning of November 29, 1872, the soldiers were on their way down Lost River, headed for the Modoc village on the south bank of Lost River. The captain called a halt about one mile from the village, told the boys it was too dark to [do] good shooting yet. "We will go on when it gets lighter," he says. If one could have penetrated the darkness, he could have seen fifteen or twenty men, less than a mile from Curley Headed Doctor's lodge, and four or five other lodges on the north bank of Lost River, straight across from Jack's lodge. This body of men are the settlers. These men were very anxious to secure a few Modoc scalps at the risk of their own lives.

The Indian dogs had been barking nearly all night. The old squaws had been very uneasy on account of the barking of the dogs. One or two of the old women did not go to sleep all night. Just at daybreak, one old woman went out and started up the river. She was on the south side. She had not gone but a short distance when she discovered the soldiers advancing. She turned, got back in the village and gave the alarm. Every Indian was up and dressing in no time to speak of. One of the braves jumped in a canoe and paddled across the river and told the Indians on the north side that the soldiers were right at their village. One of the Indians on the north side of the river went out to see about his pony he had picketed. He run onto the settlers. The men told the Indian they had come there to watch the battle, if any should take place. The Indian let on as if he believed what they was telling him. At the same time he told the writer, afterwards at Yainax, he was expecting every moment to be struck down. The Indian's name was Little Tail, now deceased.

The soldiers rode right up to Capt. Jack's lodge and stopped. Then they advanced a few steps on foot and halted. By that time the braves were all around through the village. Major Jackson demanded Capt. Jack. Scar-Face Charley told the major he would go and get him. Jack appeared in a few minutes. A few of his men were with him. Every Indian had his gun with him. Jackson told Capt. Jack that the Great Father had sent him to go and get him, Jack and all his people and put them on the Klamath reservation. Jack replied, saying, "I will go; I will take all my people with me, but I do not place any confidence in anything you white people tell me. You see you come here to my camp when it is dark. You scare me and all my people when you do that. I won't run from you. Come up to me like men, when you want to see or talk with me."

The major assured Jack he did not want any trouble. He says: "Jack, get all your men up here in front of my men." Jack called his men together. They did it, eyeing the soldiers closely. Some of the old men were saying, "Maybe this man wants to repeat what Ben Wright did to us Modocs years ago." When all the Modocs got in front of Jackson and his soldiers, Jackson says to Capt. Jack: "Now, Jack, lay down your gun here," pointing to a bunch of sage-brush. Jack hesitated. At last Jack says: "What for?" Jackson told him, "You are the chief. You lay your gun down, all your men does the same. You do that, we will not have any trouble." "Why do you want to disarm me and my men for? I never have fought white people yet, and I do not want to. Some of my old men are scared of what you ask me to do." Jackson said: "It is good, Jack, that you do not want to fight whites. If you believe what you say, Jack, and you will give up your gun, I won't let anyone hurt you."

Jack looked at his own men and ordered them to lay down their guns. Every Indian stepped up smiling, and laid down his trusty muzzle-loading rifle. Scar-Face Charley laid his gun down on top of the pile of guns the Indians had stacked, but he kept his old revolver strapped on. Jackson ordered him to take his pistol off and hand it over. Scar-Face said: "You got my gun. This pistol all lite. Me no shoot him you." Jackson ordered his lieutenant, Boutelle, to disarm Scar-Face, whereupon Lieutenant Boutelle stepped forward and said: "Here, Injun, give that pistol here, d——m you, quick." Scar-Face Charley laughed and said: "Me no dog. Me man. Me no fraid you. You talk to me I just like dog. Me no dog. Talk me good. I listen you." Boutelle drew his revolver, saying, "You son —— b——, I will show you now to talk back to me." Scar-Face said, "Me no dog. You no shoot me. Me keep pistol. You no get him, my pistol." Boutelle leveled his revolver at Scar-Face's breast. Scar-Face drew his pistol. At the same instant, both pistols made but one report. The Indian's bullet went through Boutelle's coat sleeve. Scar-Face jumped and got his gun. Every Indian then followed suit. The soldiers opened fire on the Indians. Not more than thirty feet from them, the Indians piled on one another, trying to get their guns. After the Indians got their guns they gave battle. The soldiers retreated after a few minutes of firing, leaving one dead and seven severely wounded on the field. The Modocs lost one warrior killed and about half a dozen wounded. The Modoc warrior killed was known as Watchman; his Indian name was Wish-in-push.*

When the Indians saw that their comrades on the south bank was into it, they jumped in their dugouts to go across and assist in the fight. When they were about in the middle of the river, the settlers on the north bank fired on them. George Faluke fired the first shot, saying: "Up at them, boys!" The Indians returned the fire from their dugouts. They turned around and paddled back to the north side. By the time the Indians got on the bank the settlers were way back in the thick, tall sage-brush, shooting all the time with but little effect, only killing one old squaw on the north side, killed one little baby, shot out of its mother's arms while she was running to get in the thick tules. One man had his arm broken. His name was Duffey. On the white side three men were killed. On the south side one able-bodied warrior was killed; one girl about fifteen years old killed; two small children killed; one old woman, helpless, very old, burned up; Skukum Horse shot below the right nipple, making a bad wound.

After the Indians repulsed the soldiers, the women took to their dugouts, many going along the river through the tules, towards the lake on foot. Some of them hid right close to their camp so they could leave under cover of darkness the folowing night. The warriors got together, some on both sides of the river. The older men started right for the Lava Beds, and quite a few of the women and children in their dugouts or canoes. The Indians on the north bank of Lost River collected together and decided to kill the settlers. The settlers had all gone home. About ten o'clock a.m. Hooker Jim led the Indians on to the settlers' homes. By sundown Hooker Jim and his men had killed eighteen settlers, but they never touched a white woman or a child. Bogus Charley told Mrs. Boddy that she need not be afraid of him. He said this just as Mrs. Boddy used to tell it. "Don't be afraid, Mrs. Boddy, we won't hurt you. We're not soldiers. We men never fight white women; never fight white girl, or baby. Will kill you women's men, you bet. Soldier kill our women, gal, baby, too. We no do that. All I want is something to eat. You give, I go. Maybe I see white man; I like kill him. No like kill white woman." She said she gave him flour, sugar, and coffee. He thanked her and went on his mission of killing.

Kind reader, would these settlers have been killed if they had stayed at their homes as they were requested to do by the Indians? No, sir. The settlers would never have been bothered, not a bit more than their wives were. The Modocs never harmed one child or woman since Capt. Jack became a chief. Major Jackson's soldiers shot down women and children in Jack's village. Mind, kind reader, these men that shot the squaws and children were white men, government soldiers, supposed to be civilized. Jack, a born savage, would not allow his men to do such a coward's work, as he called it.

When the soldiers saw that the Indians had all left their village along in the afternoon, they went back to see after their dead. The soldier boys found a very old squaw. She was so old she could not walk, was blind, could not see. The soldiers took tule matts and heaped them up on the old squaw till they got a big pile heaped on her, say like a load of straw. One of the boys lit a match and set the pile of tule matts on fire that they had heaped on that poor old help-less blind squaw and burned her up alive. After the matts burned up, the body of the old squaw was laying drawn up burned to a crisp. One of the officers saw her. He said: "Boys, kick some sand over that old thing. It looks too bad!" Mind you, gentle reader, this happened right under the eyes of the officers of this United States government that was in command that twenty-ninth day of November, 1872.

I can write many and many such doings on the white's side. It was not the Indians altogether that did the dark deeds that happened in early days in the West. The people at large never got the Indian side of any of the Indian wars with the white people of the United States, although some tribes did some aw-ful bad deeds. On the other hand, the white people did the same. The Modoc Indians never killed white women or children after Capt. Jack became chief of the Modocs. Jack would never allow such doings.

SOURCE:

Riddle, Jeff C. *The Indian History of the Modoc War.* San Francisco, CA: Marnell & Company, 1914, pp. 39–49.

RELATED READING:

Gridley, Marion E. Winema: The Peacemaker. *American Indian Women.* New York: Hawthorn Books, 1974, pp. 61–65.

McLeod, Kenneth, Jr. A Heroine Rests, *Klamath Echoes,* 1964, p. 44.

Meacham, Alfred. *Wi-ne-ma (The Woman-Chief) and Her People.* Hartford, CT: American Publishing Company, 1876, pp. 103–7.

Murray, Keith. *The Modocs and Their War.* Norman, OK: University of Oklahoma Press, 1959.

Payne, Doris Palmer. *Captain Jack, Modoc Renegade.* Portland, OR: Binford & Mort, Publishers, 1938.

Sherrow, Victoria. Winema: Brave Mediator in the Modoc War. *Political Leaders and Peacemakers.* New York: Facts on File, 1994, pp. 88–97.

Sonneborn, Liz. Winema (Nan-ook-too-wa, Kaitchkwa, Windema, Tobey Riddle) (1836–1932): Modoc Peacemaker and Interpreter. *A to Z of Native American Women.* New York: Facts on File, Inc., 1998, pp. 194–97.

NOTE

*This is Major F. A. Boutelle's version of the affair with Scarface Charley, as written by him for Cyrus Townsend Brady's book entitled, "Northwest Fights and Fighters," from pages 266 and 267.

Major Jackson finally rode over to me and said, "Mr. Boutelle, what do you think of the situation?" "There is going to be a fight," I replied, "and the sooner you open it the better, before there are any more complete preparations." He then ordered me to take some men and arrest Scarface Charley and his followers. I had taken the situation in pretty thoroughly in my mind and knew that an attempt to arrest meant the killing of more men than could be spared, if any of the survivors were to escape. I was standing in front of the troop. I called out to the men, "Shoot over those Indians," and raised my pistol and fired at Scarface Charley. Great minds appear to have thought alike. At the same instant, Charley raised his rifle and fired at me. We both missed, his shot passing through my clothing over my elbow. It cut two holes through my blouse, one long slit in a cardigan jacket, and missed my inner shirts. My pistol bullet passed through a red handkerchief Charley had tied around his head, so he afterwards told me. There was some discussion after the close of the war, as to who fired the first shot. I use a pistol in my left hand. The track of Scarface Charley's bullet showed my arm was bent in the act of firing, when he fired. We talked the matter over, but neither could tell which fired first. The fight at once became general. Shots came from everywhere, from the mouth of the tepees, from the sage brush on our left, from the river bank and from the bunch of braves in which Scarface Charley was at work. As soon as I had time to see that I had missed, I suppose I fired another shot at Charley, at which he dropped and crawled off in the brush. Just then an Indian dropped on his knees in the opening of a tepee a few yards from our right front, and let slip an arrow at me. This I dodged and the subsequent proceedings interested him no more.

Four

Walking the "White Man's Road"

Isty-ile-she, wife of Kheallah (Dick Johnson), endured the murder of her husband
by settlers in 1858 at Yoncalla. She died at the Grand Ronde Reservation in the spring
of 1909, three years after her portrait was taken by Jacob Calvin Cooper (1845–1937)
(Oregon Historical Society Folder 556–I).

In the 1850s the Bureau of Indian Affairs embarked on a century of programs to "civilize" Native Americans. Commissioner George W. Manypenny (1808–92) articulated a philosophy to shape the federal policy by transforming Indians from semi-autonomous members of tribes into "wards" of the federal government. He argued that this action would protect Indians from unscrupulous agents and land-hungry settlers. Manypenny thus endorsed allotment of lands in trust to individual Indians, hoping to foster agricultural self-sufficiency, and accelerate the cession of lands by treaties to the federal government. His book, *Our Indian Wards* (1880), summarized his views.

In the nineteenth century the federal government embraced a narrow definition of "civilization" for Native Americans. It was largely premised on their conversion to an agrarian life way. Whether fishers, hunters, or gatherers, Indians were to grasp the plow, hoe, and shovel and farm their way into a new existence. Even though some reservations had abundant fisheries and traditional resources, the agents sought to convert the Indians to new subsistence patterns. They demanded that they clear forests to create fields, till and plant, weed and hoe, and harvest crops. Invasions of bracken fern, grasshoppers, smut, and hungry deer, or repeated freezes because of elevation did not deter the government commitment.

Repeatedly crops failed. The Klamath and Malheur reservations at nearly a mile high were particularly problematic for farming. The Warm Springs Reservation was remarkably arid and ridden with rocks cast from the volcanic peaks to the west. The Coast Reservation was a temperate rain forest, totally unsuitable for raising wheat, corn, oats, and other crops that were part of the Bureau of Indian Affairs program. The Grand Ronde Reservation lay in a setting of thick clay soil and was subjected to cool ocean breezes sweeping across the low pass at the head of the Salmon River. Hot summers and insect invasions took a toll on the crops on the Umatilla Reservation.

Reservation realities included dishonest agents who plundered the annuities due under the treaties. The Indians had little or no recourse. Most were illiterate and, if they knew how to read and write, they lacked the know-how to communicate their concerns to officials in Washington, D.C., who might or might not respond. And while the military posts established in the mid-1850s adjacent to or on each reservation helped reduce trespass onto the Indian lands, the soldiers contributed to immorality and the flow of alcohol into the tribal communities. Fort Umpqua, Fort Hoskins, Fort Yamhill, and Siletz Blockhouse were connected to the Coast and Grand Ronde Reservations. Fort Dalles, Fort Klamath, and Fort Harney served the Warm Springs, Klamath, and Malheur reservations. Fort Walla Walla was located near to the Umatilla and Nez Perce reservations.

Other reservation realities were inefficient and often inoperable sawmills and grist mills. The natives were expected to move from mat and plank slab lodges into frame houses, but they seldom had sufficient lumber or other materials to erect the new dwellings. The grist mills that were to grind their wheat and corn into flour and meal were plagued with engineering problems. Dams washed out. Millers headed off to more profitable employment. The appropriations often proved insufficient to replace equipment and keep the operations underway.

During the administration of President Ulysses S. Grant, 1868–76, the government ran two contradictory Indian policies. Both affected the Indians of Oregon. The "Force Policy" was largely mounted by the U.S. Army. Its goal was the military subjugation of Indians and their confinement under guard on reservations. The Modoc War of 1873, the Nez Perce War of 1877, and the Bannock War of 1878 were three instances where the "Force Policy" had major implications for Oregon tribes.

The "Peace Policy" was instituted by humanitarians who sought to clean up the BIA, drive forward the "civilization" programs, and bring greater economy and efficiency to dealing with tribes. To accomplish these goals the federal government turned over the reservations to various denominations. The Methodists were given control of the Klamath, Warm Springs, and Siletz reservations; the Catholics got Grand Ronde and Umatilla; and the Congregationalists got Malheur. While this policy and its program results may have appeared good in theory, they blurred the separation between church and state and led to a new round of coercion of tribes in matters of religion. It also meant that each denomination expected to control all purchases and employment at the agencies.

"To the victors belongs the spoils," lamented the disillusioned Agent Edmund Swan, who disputed the management by the Methodists of the Siletz Reservation. In 1880 Swan wrote to Secretary of Interior Carl Schurz:

> As you are doubtless aware, the Methodist Episcopal Church have charge of this mission, and they seem willing that the Agent whom they have recommended here, be allowed to manage affairs as he deems best; business as well as Christian work, but just here the Oregon Conference steps in and presumes to not only dictate what the Agent shall do, but whom he shall employ; and of whom he shall purchase; and even what he shall pay. For instance he must employ Methodists because they are Methodists, regardless of their efficiency. The purchases must be made of Methodists exclusively without regard to cost.[1]

In the era of learning to "walk the white man's road," some Indian leaders took their case to the public. Alfred Meacham (1826–82), Oregon's remarkable Superintendent of Indian Affairs in the years 1869–72, became their champion. "On every reservation and in every tribe and band," he wrote, "there may be found strong men born to lead, and whenever they once feel within them the possibility of manhood, they will take hold with zeal and determination that perpetuates so long as they have confidence as the representatives of the Government."[2] Although he was fired because of political pressure against his views that Indians should have the say about their annuities and should determine their own futures, he put together a lecture company that enabled a number of tribal speakers to address audiences across the United States about the problems confronting their people. His advocacy was shaped by the realities of reservation and tribal life he had witnessed in Oregon.

Oregon Indians tried to chart a course in the midst of the mounting pressure to bow to "civilization" programs. Many acquiesced and permitted their children to attend reservation day schools and boarding schools. From their establishment, each reservation had a day school even though they operated often only during the summer months and drew fewer than twenty or thirty students. By the 1870s, however, the boarding school gained strong federal support as the means best to transform young people into members of the majority culture. The Bureau of Indian Affairs established boarding schools on each Oregon reservation following the Civil War.[3]

Reservation Schools

Reservation	Date	Capacity
Siletz	October, 1873	80
Grande Ronde	April, 1874	80
Klamath: Agency	February, 1874	110
Warm Springs: Sinemasho	August, 1882	75
Klamath: Yainax	November, 1882	100
Umatilla	January, 1883	75
Warm Springs: Agency	June, 1884	60

In 1879 Lieutenant Melville C. Wilkinson, U.S. Army, went on special detail to establish an Indian manual-labor training school on the campus of Pacific University in Forest Grove, Oregon. The college's trustees set aside four acres and the federal government appropriated $5,000 to construct three "rough frame buildings": dormitories for boys and girls and a structure for instruction. Wilkinson opened the school on February 25, 1880. The educational program included sewing, cooking, and cleaning for girls, and shoemaking, blacksmithing, carpentry, and farming for boys.[4] H. J. Minthorn became the second superintendent in 1883 and reported an enrollment of about one hundred students. But the site had problems including lack of federal ownership of the land and no nearby property for the farming program.[5]

Finally, in 1885, officials of the Bureau of Indian Affairs decided to accept offers of donated land located on the Oregon & California Railroad four miles from Salem. The deed of April 21, 1885, conveyed to the United States 177.32 acres. The Oregon legislature passed a concurrent resolution endorsing the project and the permanent location of the school—named "Chemawa" by Superintendent J. M. Haworth and also, for a time, known as the Harrison Institute. Further land acquisitions increased the school site to 262.24 acres. These new properties were purchased from the income earned by Indian children picking hops.[6]

Harsh, arrogant attitudes persisted toward Oregon's native peoples. On April 14, 1886, *The Oregonian* published the editorial "Treatment of the Indian." The comments were a mirror to the times:

The stern salutation of the Anglo-Saxon to all other races has been 'Root Hog or Die;' and in New England the Indian hog has generally gone into the Puritan pork barrel. In New England, in India, in Egypt, in Africa, in Ireland, at the South or on our Indian frontier the Anglo-Saxon holds and enforces his belief that power and property belong to those who are bold enough to capture and strong enough to keep them.

The American who arraigns England for her usage of Ireland knows perfectly well that England's title to Ireland is just as valid as our own title to the lands we have won from the Indian. It is the title of conquest. The Indian has the same sentimental grievance against the descendants of the Puritan that the Irishman has against the successor of Henry the Second, Queen Elizabeth, and Cromwell. The birthright of barbarians to their soil is largely a fiction. A nation keeps its land and freedom until it loses them by folly, by disunion, by the superior strength and craft of another race that swings a keener sword in a stronger or more skillful hand.

The law of nature is with man as with animals; it is the survival of the strongest. It is no moral indictment of title to say that it was won at the point of the bayonet. The sword of the Puritan was the first ploughshare of New England civilization. The savage man has no more inalienable title to his soil than a tiger to his lair; the human wild beasts must go with the tigers, when civilization with its sword slashes its way through forest and jungle. Civilization cannot starve nor halt in its march to consider the sentimental birthright of barbarians to perpetuate the black night of superstitious ignorance and degradation, which is their freedom so-called.[7]

In 1887 Congress passed the General Allotment Act. The law was premised on the transformation of Native Americans from dependency to citizenship. Once tribal leaders agreed to allotment of reservation lands, the tribal estate was to be divided into individual parcels, the deed held in trust by the United States for a minimum of twenty-five years. At the expiration of that date, a competency determination would confer citizenship on the individual. Indian agents evaluated competency by such factors as choice of clothing, condition of housing, success in farming, and mastery of English. Failure to gain competency meant continued wardship and non-citizen status. The government would issue a fee-patent, or deed, and the Indian citizen could then begin paying taxes on the property. Allotment thus was an overt assault on tribalism, for it divided the communally held property into a checkerboard of individual parcels that soon were held in a variety of categories: individual trust land, individual fee land, tribal trust land, and non-Indian land acquired through purchase or foreclosure for non-payment of taxes.

Commissioner T. J. Morgan articulated the federal agenda in his annual report of 1892:

Citizenship, accompanied by allotment of lands, necessarily looks toward the entire destruction of the tribal relation; the Indians are to be individualized and dealt with one by one and not en masse; they are to stand upon their own personal rights and be freed absolutely from the trammels of the tribe and the limitations of chieftaincy.

Morgan continued:

Citizenship is simply opportunity. To confer upon an educated Indian, ignorant of the English language and unaccustomed to American ways, the full privileges of liberty does not necessarily carry with it any advantage to him. It does not change his nature; confers upon him no new faculties; does not increase his intelligence; does not necessarily awaken any new desires, and may be practically a mockery.[8]

Some tribal leaders dared to challenge allotment. Bureau of Indian Affairs officials moved from reservation to reservation to hold conferences to secure through argument the consent of the tribes to the division of their lands. At the allotment council at Siletz in May 1891, a number of leaders argued against the new government program. Charlie Depoe, a police judge, said:

We agreed to give up our homes and native country and come to the Siletz reservation. The reservation then extended along the coast a distance of 100 miles, and to the summit of the Coast range of mountains. This was to be the future home of my people and their children forever. The government was to help us until we were able to take care of ourselves. Upon this reservation my people have lived for thirty-six years, until nearly all of our once strong tribes have died. Only a few remain. Without our consent or knowledge the whites have taken from us the Yaquina bay country with its fine fisheries, and opened it up for white settlement, and we have never received a cent for it. This land is now worth thousands of dollars to the whites.

On the North Alsea a large strip of our country was taken without our consent and opened to white settlement, and now it is proposed to still reduce our portion of land to eighty acres to each head of the family, instead of the 160 acres that the government promised us. This confuses me. I don't know which way to go. I am blind. I am getting old and must soon die, but from the bottom of my heart I will never accept eighty acres when I was promised 160. I am justly entitled to that much, and then I will be satisfied.[9]

Charlie Depoe's protest was ignored. Allotment proceeded at Siletz in 1892. Individual holdings tallied about forty-three thousand acres; tribal lands were approximately three thousand acres. The remaining lands—191,798 acres—were declared "surplus" and were opened to homesteaders and timber companies. The tribe received a token payment of $142,600 for this property. Depoe's allotment was a rocky section of the coastline with a small harbor; today it is known as Depoe Bay.

The following selections illustrate the challenges of coping with the "Force Policy," the "Peace Policy," allotment, eroding treaty rights, forced acculturation of children, looting of old villages and cemeteries for artifacts, and treatment of native people in textbooks.

NOTES

1. E. A. Swan, Letter of September 11, 1880, to Carl Shurz. Department of Interior Appointment Papers, Oregon, 1849–1907, Microcopy 814, Roll 9, National Archives, Washington, D.C.

2. Commissioner of Indian Affairs, *Annual Report of the Commissioner of Indian Affairs . . . 1870* (Washington, D.C.: Government Printing Office, 1870), p. 513.

3. Commissioner of Indian Affairs, *Annual Report of the Commissioner of Indian Affairs . . . 1892*, p. 52.

4. Ibid., pp. 891–894; Cary C. Collins, The Broken Crucible of Assimilation: Forest Grove Indian School and the Origins of Off-Reservation Boarding School Education in the West. *Oregon Historical Quarterly*, 101(4)(Winter, 2000), pp. 468–77.

5. Commissioner of Indian Affairs, *Annual Report of the Commissioner of Indian Affairs . . . 1892*, pp. 891–94.

6. Ibid.; SuAnn M. Reddick. The Evolution of Chemawa Indian School: From Red River to Salem, 1825–1885. *Oregon Historical Quarterly*, 101(4)(Winter, 2000), pp. 456–63.

7. "Treatment of the Indian," *The Oregonian* (Portland, OR), April 14, 1886.

8. Ibid., pp. 6–7.

9. "The Passing of the Red Man: An Aged Siletz Chief Declaims Against the White Man's Injustice," *The Oregonian* (Portland, OR), May 5, 1891.

"Natural Oratory": Allen David, Klamath Chief, 1869

The advent of Bureau of Indian Affairs administration on the Klamath Reservation led to the deposing in 1868 of aged Chief Lileks. Firm in his opposition to the ending of Indian slavery in the region and waning in physical powers, Lileks yielded leadership in an election that pitted Allen David against Henry Blow. Both were younger men of executive abilities and knowledgeable about the ways of the Euro-Americans. Their candidacy heralded a significant shift from traditional succession in leadership to a reservation political organization.

Allen David, a treaty signatory identified as Boos-ki-you in 1865, was described as "a tall, handsome, and popular young brave from the upper country." His support came from both Klamath and Paiute. David served as chief until 1876, when he found the personal financial burdens of office too great to continue. He was succeeded by Henry Blow. In 1869 Alfred Meacham, Oregon Superintendent of Indian Affairs, visited the Klamath Reservation and met with its leaders. "The Klamath chief, Allen David, arose to reply amid surroundings characteristic of Indian life,—a perfect solemn silence broken only by his voice," he wrote. "I then heard the notes of natural oratory, coming in wild, but well-measured words, and recognized for the first time fully that nature does sometimes produce noble men without the line of civilized life."

Dr. Donald McKay recorded David's speech to the superintendent. David spoke forthrightly about the needs of his people, the sexual predators among the white men, and the difficult road he felt the Indians of the Klamath Reservation would have to follow. Chief Allen David died in August 1906, and was buried on the Klamath Reservation.

Said Allen David, I see you. All my people see you. I saw you at Sprange [Sprague] river. I watched your mouth. I have seen but one tongue. I have looked with your eyes. I have seen your heart. You have given me another heart. All my people will have white hearts. When I was a little boy I lived here. I have always lived here. A long time ago a white man told me I could be like him. I said my skin is red, it cannot change; it must be my heart, my brain, that is to be like a white man. You think we are low people. May be we are in your eyes. —Who made us so? We do not know much; we can learn. Some of the officers at the fort (referring to Fort Klamath, six miles from the agency) have been good men some of them have been bad men. Do you think a good white man will take an Indian wife? A white man that will take an Indian wife is worse blood than Indian. These things make our hearts sad. We want you to stop it . . . . Your ears are larger. Your heart is larger. You see us. Do not let your heart get sick.

Take a white man into the woods, away from a store; set him down, with nothing in his hands, in the woods, and without a store to get tools from; and what could he do?

When you lay down before us the axes, the saws, the iron wedges and nails you have promised us, and we do not take them up, then you can say we are "callous" lazy people. You say your chief is like me. That he is an Indian I am glad. What can I say that is worth writing down? Mr. [Eli] Parker does not know me. When you do all Mr. [J. W. Perit] Huntington promised in the treaty, 1864, we can go to work like white men. Our hearts are tired waiting for the saw-mill. When it is built, then we can have houses like white men. We want the flour-mill; then we will not live on fish and roots. We will help to make the mills. We made the fences on the big farms. We did not get tired . . . .

Give us strong law; we will do what your law says. We want strong law we want to be like white men. You say that Mr. Parker does not want bad men among our people. Is B. a good man? he took Frank's wife is that good? We do not want such men. Is—— a good man? he took Celia from her husband is that right? Applegate gave us good laws he is a good man. Applegate told us not to gamble. Capt.—— won thirty-seven horses from us. He says there is no law about gambling. Applegate said there was. Which is right? . . . .

Mr. Meacham said, You need not be afraid to talk Keep nothing back. Your people are under a cloud. I see by their eyes that their hearts are sick; they look sorrowful. Open your hearts and I will hear you; tell me all, that I may know what to do to make them glad.

Allen David said, I will keep nothing back. I have eyes I can see that white men have white hands. Some white men take our women they have children they are not Indian they are not white they are shame children. Some white men take care of their children. It makes my heart sick. I do not want these things. Indian and Indian we do not want any more shame children. A white man that would take an Indian squaw is no better than we are.

Our women go to the fort they make us feel sick they get goods sometimes greenbacks. We do not want them to go there we want the store here at the agency; then our women will not go to the fort . . . . Last Sunday some soldiers went to Pompey (Indians) they talked bad to the women. We do not want soldiers among our women. Can you stop this? Our women make us ashamed. We may have done wrong give us strong law. . . .

You say we are looking into a camp-fire; that we can find moonlight. You say there is a road that goes toward sunrise. Show me that stone road. I am now on the stone road. I will follow you to the top of the mountain. You tell me come on. I can see you now. My feet are on the road. I will not leave it. I tell my people follow me, and I will stay in the stone road.

SOURCE

Meacham, Alfred B. *Wigwam and War-Path; Or the Royal Chief in Chains.* Boston, MA: John P. Dale and Company, 1875, pp. 256–58.

RELATED READING

Applegate, Lindsay. Letter of January 30, 1869, to Alfred B. Meacham. *Annual Report of the Commissioner of Indian Affairs . . .1869.* Washington, DC: Government Printing Office, 1870, pp. 176–77.

Stern, Theodore. *The Klamath Tribe: A People and Their Reservation.* Seattle, WA: University of Washington Press, 1965.

"It Was the Indians' Money": Problems at Grand Ronde, 1869

Alfred Meacham did not mince words. He spoke and wrote forthrightly about conditions of Native Americans in his service as Oregon Superintendent of Indian Affairs, 1869–72, as a Peace Commissioner in the Modoc War, 1873, and as editor of the Council Fire, *the journal of the Indian Rights Association. A proponent of Grant's "Peace Policy" and an avowed champion of the ability of Indians to move within a single generation from their aboriginal condition to integration into American society, Meacham won few friends in the Euro-American community. His advocacy for Indian rights cut short his tenure as Oregon Superintendent but only redoubled his determination to speak and write for the causes of native peoples.*

In the following selection Meacham described his visit in 1869 to the Grand Ronde Reservation, a tract at the head of the South Fork of the Yamhill River to the west of the Willamette Valley. Set apart by executive order in 1857, the reservation held the surviving Indians of the Umpqua and Willamette valleys, some bands from the Rogue River Valley, and a few children from the bands along the northern Oregon coast who were brought to the reservation schools. From 1856 to 1865 Fort Yamhill, a U.S. Army post, held a garrison of soldiers whose role was to keep Indians on the reservation and trespassers off.

Meacham discussed conditions on the reservation and reported on a general council with the tribes. Native speakers included Jo Hutchins of the Santiams; Louis Neposa [Napassant] (1813–88) and Solomon Riggs, treaty chiefs of the Umpqua; and Wapato Dave of the Tualatins, who once resided at Wappato Lake near Forest Grove. Meacham then wrote forcefully about the ownership of the resources of the reservation. "The Indians of Grand Round own the mills. The funds invested in their erection did not belong to the agent or Government. It was the Indians' money, and was so expended at their knowledge and request," he concluded. Meacham's voice and view were largely ignored. The reservation assets remained at the discretion of the agents, not the tribes whose treaty annuities passed through their hands.

I made my first official visit to this agency in the latter part of September, 1869. Captain Charles La Follette was then acting agent.

The road from Salem was over a beautiful country, settled by white men, who had transformed this once wild region into a paradise. The first view of the agency proper was from a high ridge several miles distant. On the right and left were clustered the houses of the several tribes, each one having been assigned a location. Their houses were built of logs or boards, and rudely put together. Every board had cost these poor people an acre of land; every log counted for so much money given in compensation for their birthrights to the soil of the matchless valley of the Willamette.

As we stood on the dividing ridge separating this agency from the great valley I have mentioned, looking toward the west, we beheld, nearest on the left, old Fort Yamhill, with its snowy cottages, built for the accommodation of the officers of the army in the days when gallant [Philip] Sheridan was a lieutenant, and walked its parade-grounds with a simple sword dangling by his side and bars on his shoulders, holding beneath his military cap a brain power waiting for the sound of clanking chains and thundering cannon to call him hence to deeds of valor that should compel the laurel wreath of fame to seek his brow, little thinking then, while guarding savages, that away off in the future, his charger would impatiently call him from repose, and bear him into the face of a victorious enemy with so much gallantry that he would turn an apparent defeat into a glorious victory.

Immediately on our right were the huts of the people for whose especial intimidation the costly palaces and beautiful cottages had been built. The huts or houses were built on the hillsides sloping toward the valley. They presented the appearance of a small, dilapidated town that had been 'cut off' by a railroad; but they were peopled with Indians who were trying to imitate their masters . . . .

To resume, Grand Round valley, the name of which suggests its size and shape, lay stretched out before us, a beautiful picture from Nature's gallery, embellished by the touches that Uncle Sam's greenbacks had given to this agency in building churches, halls, and Indian houses, together with a large farm for general use, and small ones for individuals.

At every change of Government officers, Reservation Indians show the liveliest interest, and have great curiosity to see the new man. My arrival was known to all the people very soon. The Indians of this agency were more advanced in civilization than those of any other in Oregon. They had been located by the Government, fifteen years previously. Many of them were prisoners of war, in chains and under guard, and bad been subjugated, through sheer exhaustion; others were under treaty. Their very poverty and the scanty subsistence the

Government gave, was to them a blessing. Permitted to labor for persons who lived "outside," passes were given each for a specified time. Thus their employers became each a civilizer.

At the time of my first official visit, they had abandoned Indian costume, and were dressed in the usual garb of white men; many of them had learned to talk our language. At my request, messengers were sent out, and the people were invited to come in at an early hour the following day. Before the time appointed they began to arrive. A few were on foot, the remainder in wagons, or on horseback; the younger men and women coming in pairs, after the fashion of white people around them, all arrayed in best attire, for it was a gala day to them. I noticed that in some instances the women were riding side-saddles, instead of the old Indian way, astride.

The children were not left at home, neither were they bound in thongs to boards, or swinging in pappoose baskets; but some, at least, were carried on the pummel of the father's saddle. They were clothed like other children. Strange and encouraging spectacle, to witness Indian men, who were born savages, conforming to usages of civil life. When once an Indian abandons the habits and customs of his fathers, and has tasted the air which his more enlightened brother breathes, he never goes back so long as he associates with good men.

These people, in less than twenty years, under the management of the several agents, had been transformed, from "Darwin's" wild beasts, almost to civilized manhood, notwithstanding the croaking of soulless men who constantly accuse United States agents of all kinds of misdemeanors and crimes.

When they were first located, they numbered about twenty-one hundred souls. At the time of which I write, they had dwindled away to about half that number.

When the hour for the talk arrived the people filled the council house, and crowded the doors and windows, so that we found it necessary to adjourn to the open air for room and comfort. The agent, La Follette, went through the form of introducing me to his people, calling each one by name.

This ceremony is always conducted with solemnity; each Indian, as he extends the hand, gazing steadfastly into the eye of the person introduced. They seem to read character rapidly, and with correctness equal to, and sometimes excelling, more enlightened people.

First, a short speech by Agent La Follette, followed by the "Salem tyee,"— superintendent. I said that "I was pleased to find them so far advanced in civilization; that I was now the 'Salem tyee.' You are my children. I came to show you my heart, to see your hearts, to talk with you about your affairs."

Jo Hutchins—chief of Santiams—was first to speak. He said: "You see our people are not rich; they are poor. We are glad to shake hands with you and show our hearts. You look like a good man, but I will not give you my heart until I know you better." Louis Neposa said: "I have been here fifteen years. I have seen all the country from here to the Rocky Mountains. I had a home on Rogue river; I had a house and barn; I gave them up to come here. That house on that hill is mine"; pointing towards the house in question.

Indian speeches are remarkable for pertinency and for forcible expression, many of them abounding in flights of imagination and bursts of oratory. Much of the original beauty is lost in the translation, as few of them speak in the English language when delivering a speech. Interpreters are often illiterate men, and cannot render the subject-matter with the full force and beauty of the original, much less imitate the gesture and voice.

During my residence in the far West, and especially while in Government employ, I have taken notes, and in many instances, kept verbatim reports, the work being done by clerks of the several agencies. I have selected, from several hundred pages, a few speeches, made by these people, for use in making up my book. It will be observed that the sentences are short, and repetitions sometimes occur. In fact, these orators of nature follow nature, and repeat themselves, as our greatest orators do, and their skill in the art of repetition is something marvelous. This is peculiar to all Indian councils, though not always recorded. The following are word for word, especially Wapto Dave and Jo Hutchins' speeches:—

Black Tom said: I am a wild Injun. I don't know much. I have not much sense. I cannot talk well. I feel like a man going through the bushes, when he is going to fight; like he was thinking some man was behind a bush, going to shoot him. I have been fooled many times. I don't know much. Some tyees talk well when they first come. I have seen their children wearing shirts like those they gave me; may be it was all right. I don't know much.

Solomon Riggs—chief of the Umpynas—said: I am not a wild man. I have sense. I know some things. I have learned to work. I was born wild, but I am not wild now. I live in a house. I have a wagon and horses that I worked for. They are mine. The Government did not give them to me. That woman is my wife, and that is my baby. He will have some sense. I show you my heart. I want you to give me your heart. I don't want to be a wild Injun. See speech of Solomon Riggs in Salem Council.

All the "head men" made short speeches, after which we came to business talk.

Superintendent Meacham said: I see before me the remnants of a great people. Your fathers are buried in a far country. I will show you my heart now. You are not wild men. You are not savages. You are men and women. You have sense and hearts to feel. I did not come here to dig up anything that is buried. I have nothing to say about the men who have gone before me. That is past. We drop that. We cannot dig it up now. We have enough to think about. I do not promise what I will do, except I will do right as I see what is right. I may make some mistakes. I want to talk with you about your agent. I think he will do right. He is a good man. I will help him. He will help me. You will help us. You are not fools. You are men. You have a right to be heard. You shall be heard. We are paid to take care of you. Our time belongs to the Indians in Oregon. The Government has bought our sense; that belongs to you. The money in our hands is not ours, it is yours. We cannot pay you the money. The law says we must not; still it is yours. You have been here long enough to have sense. You know what you want. You can tell us. We will hear you.

If you want what is right we will get it for you. You need not be afraid to speak out. The time has come when a man is judged by his sense, not his skin. In a few years more the treaty will be dead. Then you must be ready to take care of yourselves. You need not fear to speak. Nobody will stop your mouth. We are ready now to hear you talk. We have shown our heart. Now talk like men. I have spoken.

A silence of some moments followed. The chiefs and head men seemed taken by surprise. They could not comprehend or believe that the declarations made were real; that they were to be allowed to give an opinion in matters pertaining to their own interests. I would not convey the idea that my predecessors had been bad men. They were not; but they had, some of them, and perhaps all of them, looked on these Indians as wards, or orphan children. They had not recognized the fact that these people had come up, from a low, degraded condition of captive savages, to a status of intelligence that entitled them to consideration. The people themselves had not dared to demand a hearing. They were subjugated, and felt it too; but I know in their hearts they often longed for the boon that was offered to them.

It is due to the citizens who occupy the country adjoining this agency, in whose employ the Indians had spent much time in labor on farm, wood-yards, and various other kinds of business, that they had, by easy lessons, and, with commendable patience, taught these down-trodden people that they had a right to look up. "Honor to whom honor is due."

Wapto Dave, a chief of a small band of Waptos, was the first to speak. He delivered his speech in my own language: The boys all wait for me to speak first; because me understand some things. We hear you talk. We don't know whether you mean it. Maybe you are smart. We have been fooled a heap. We don't want no lies. We don't talk lies. S'pose you talk straight. All right. Me tell you some things. All our people very poor; they got no good houses; no good mills. No wagons; got no harness; no ploughs. They get some, they work heap. They buy them. Government no give em. We want these things. Maybe you don't like my talk. I am done.

Jo Hutchins—Chief of Santiams—said: I am watching your eye. l am watching your tongue. l am thinking all the time. Perhaps you are making fools of us. We don't want to be made fools. I have heard tyees talk like you do now. They go back home and send us something a white man don't want. We are not dogs. We have hearts. We may be blind. We do not see the things the treaty promised. Maybe they got lost on the way. The President is a long way off. He can't bear us. Our words get lost in the wind before they get there. Maybe his ear is small. Maybe your ears are small. They look big. Our ears are large. We hear everything. Some things we don't like. We have been a long time in the mud. Sometimes we sink down. Some white men help us up. Some white men stand on our heads. We want a school-house built on the ground of the Santiam people. Then our children can have some sense. We want an Indian to work in the blacksmith shop. We don't like half-breeds. They are not Injuns. They are not white men. Their hearts are divided. We want some harness. We want some ploughs. We want a sawmill. What is a mill good for that has no dam? That old mill is not good; it won't saw boards. We want a church. Some of these people are Catholics. Some of them are like Mr. Par[r]ish, a Methodist. Some got no religion. Maybe they don't need religion. Some people think Indians got no sense. We don't want any blankets. We have had a heap of blankets. Some of them have been like sail-cloth muslin. The old people have got no sense; they want blankets. The treaty said we, every man, have his land. He have a paper for his land. We don't see the paper. We see the land. We want it divided. When we have land all in one place, some Injun put his horses in the field; another Injun turn them out. Then they go to law. One man says another man got the best ground. They go to law about that. We want the land marked out. Every man builds his own house. We want some apples. Mark out the land, then we plant some trees, by-and-by we have some apples.

Maybe you don't like my talk. I talk straight. I am not a coward. I am chief of the Santiams. You hear me now. We see your eyes; look straight. Maybe you are a good man. We will find out. Sochala-tyee,—God sees you. He sees us. All these people hear me talk. Some of them are scared. I am not afraid. Alta-kup-et, —I am done.

Here was a man talking to the point. He dodged nothing. He spoke the hearts of the people. They supported him with frequent applause. Other speeches were made, all touching practical points. The abstract of issues following that council exhibit the distribution of hardware, axes, saws, hatchets, mats, iron wedges; also, harness, ploughs, hoes, scythes, and various farming implements. The reasonable and numerous points involved many questions of importance, which were submitted to the Hon. Commissioner of Indian Affairs, Washington city.

Without waiting for red tape, we proceeded to erect a new saw-mill. The Indians performed much of the necessary labor. With one white man to direct them, they prepared all the timber, built a dam, and cut a race, several hundred yards in length, and within ninety days from "breaking ground" the new saw-mill was making lumber.

The Indians formed into working parties and delivered logs as fast as the mill could saw them. Mr. Manrow, a practical sawyer, was placed in charge of the mill, and, with Indian help only, he manufactured four to eight thousand feet of lumber per day. He subsequently remarked that "they were as good help as he wanted."

The understanding before commencing work on the mill was to the effect that it was to belong to the Indians on Grand Round Agency, when completed. Those who furnished logs were to own the lumber after sale of sufficient quantity to pay the "sawyer," the whole to be under control of the acting agent.

Misunderstandings seem to have arisen between the agent and Indians, growing out of the sale of lumber manufactured by the mill. The only misunderstanding that could have arisen, was that wherein the Indians claim that "the Government would pay the expense of running it,"—the saw-mill—and they—the Indians—should have the lumber to dispose of as they thought best, claiming the right to sell it to the whites outside of the Reservation."

It was so agreed and understood as above stated, that the Government agent was to manage the business, pay the sawyer, and meet such other expenses as might *accrue, out of the sale of lumber,* and the *remainder to belong to parties furnishing logs,* with the privilege of selling to persons wherever a market could be found. If any other plan has been adopted, it is in violation of the agreement made with the Indians at the council that considered the question of building the mills. A full report of that council was forwarded to the Commissioner at Washington, was filed in the office of Superintendent of Indian Affairs, Salem, Oregon, and was, or should have been, recorded on the books at Grand Round Agency.

The *Indians* of Grand Round *own* the *mills*. The funds invested in their erection did not belong to agent or Government. It was the Indians' money, and was so expanded by their knowledge and request. The sweat of these people was dropped in the long race, cut for the mills. Every stick of timber in them was prepared, partly at least, by Indian labor. They had accepted this little valley at the bidding of a powerful Government, who had promised them mills (see treaty of 1855), and had constructed inferior machinery, at enormous expense, that had never been worth one-half the greenbacks they had cost.

These people have advanced more rapidly in civilization than any other Indian people on "the coast." They had learned a great amount of useful knowledge while working for the white men, to make a living for their families, when the Government had failed to furnish subsistence for them. They were now ready to take care of their interests, when men paid to instruct them had performed their duty.

If these Indians are ever to manage for themselves, why not begin with easy lessons, while they have, or are supposed to have, an agent, whose duty it was to stand between them and the stronger race with whom they are to mingle and associate?

I repeat that these Indian men own the mills, and are entitled to the proceeds, and that it is, and was, an agent's duty to transact such parts of the business as the Indians could not themselves. What if it did require labor and care to prevent confusion? The agent was paid for his time, his business talent, and, if he was unwilling or incompetent, he was not in a proper position.

The agent says, "I have allowed them one-half the lumber made, when they wished to use it for building purposes, retaining the other half for the department, until such time as it can be used in improvement, or otherwise disposed of for their common benefit." If the department required lumber, let the Indians be the *merchants,* and receive the pay. To dispose of it for their benefit was to compel those who were willing to labor to support those who were not.

SOURCE

Meacham, Alfred B. *Wigwam and War-Path; Or the Royal Chief in Chains.* Boston, MA: John P. Dale and Company, 1875, pp. 101–2, 109–22.

RELATED READING

Edward S. Phinney. Alfred B. Meacham: Promotor of Indian Reform. Ph.D. Dissertation, University of Oregon, Eugene, OR., 1963.

"An Educated Paiute Woman," 1870

Sarah Winnemucca (1844–91) was notable among the Native American women of the nineteenth century. Born in the Humboldt Sink region near the Oregon-Nevada border, she was the daughter of the leader of a Northern Paiute band, Winnemucca, and the granddaughter of Truckee, also a chief. Her family traveled widely in its seasonal round. Sarah, as a young woman, learned English. In 1864 she was on stage in Virginia City, Nevada, and in October of that year appeared with her father, sister, and eight other tribal members in San Francisco as part of an all-Indian show. The Northern Paiutes presented "a series of Tableaux Vivants, illustrative of Indian life" and were supported by a lecture and music. During the Bannock War of 1878 she served as interpreter, courier, and scout for General Oliver O. Howard.

Extremely conscious of her persona, Sarah Winnemucca groomed her public to perceive her as an "Indian princess." She traveled to Washington, D.C., in 1880 as part of a Paiute delegation. Following her marriage in 1881 to Lieutenant Lewis H. Hopkins, her third white husband, she planned another eastern trip, this time to lecture to crowds about the mistreatment of the Paiutes on the Malheur Reservation in Oregon and their imprisonment on the Yakima Reservation in Washington. The Boston Evening Transcript *described her appearance: "She enjoyed creating a dramatic impression, dressed in fringed buckskin and beads, with armlets and bracelets adorning her arms and wrists. She even included the affection of a gold crown on her head and a wampum bag of velvet, decorated with an embroidered cupid, hanging from her wrist." During her 1883–84 eastern circuit, Sarah Winnemucca delivered more than three hundred lectures.*

In 1881 Indian reformer Helen Hunt Jackson wrote the memorable volume, A Century of Dishonor: A Sketch of the United States Government's Dealings with Some of the Indian Tribes. *Jackson included in the appendix the following "Letter from Sarah Winnemucca, An Educated Pah-ute Woman." In this letter of 1870 Sarah championed the role of her father, Winnemucca, as "head chief of the whole tribe." Her claim was not true. While her father and grandfather were important band leaders, the Northern Paiute did not possess an overarching tribal political structure. She posed for Major Douglas a series of probing questions.*

To Major H. Douglas, U. S. Army:

Sir: I learn from the commanding officer at this post that you desire full information in regard to the Indians around this place, with a view, if possible, of bettering their condition by sending them on the Truckee River Reservation. All the Indians from here to Carson City belong to the Pah-Ute tribe. My father, whose name is Winnemucca, is the head chief of the whole tribe; but he is now getting too old, and has not energy enough to command, nor to impress on their minds the necessity of their being sent on the reservation. In fact, I think he is entirely opposed to it. He, myself, and most of the Humboldt and Queen's River Indians were on the Truckee Reservation at one time; but if we had stayed there it would be only to starve. I think that if they had received what they were entitled to from the agents, they would never have left them.

So far as their knowledge of agriculture extends, they are quite ignorant, as they have never had the opportunity of learning; but I think, if proper pains were taken, that they would willingly make the effort to maintain themselves by their own labor, providing they could be made to believe that the products were their own, for their own use and comfort. It is needless for me to enter into details as to how we were treated on the reservation while there. It is enough to say that we were confined to the reserve, and had to live on what fish we might be able to catch in the river. If this is the kind of civilization awaiting us on the reserves, God grant that we may never be compelled to go on one, as it is much preferable to live in the mountains and drag out an existence in our native manner. So far as living is concerned, the Indians at all military posts get enough to eat and considerable cast-off clothing.

But how long is this to continue? What is the object of the Government in regard to Indians? Is it enough that we are at peace? Remove all the Indians from their military posts and place them on reservations such as the Truckee and Walker River Reservations (as they were conducted), and it will require a greater military force stationed round to keep them within the limits than it now does to keep them in subjection. On the other hand, if the Indians have any guarantee that they can secure a permanent home on their own native soil, and that our white neighbors can be kept from encroaching on our rights, after having a reasonable share of ground allotted to us as our own, and giving us the required advantages of learning, I warrant that the savage (as he is called to-day) will be a thrifty and law-abiding member of the community fifteen or twenty years hence.

Sarah Winnemucca (1844–91) developed several non-Indian style costumes for her public lectures. In this portrait taken in Baltimore about 1883–84 she wore a crown-like tiara and carried a beaded bag, objects not used by the Northern Paiute (Denver Public Library, Western History Collection).

Sir, if at any future time you should require information regarding the Indians here, I will be happy to furnish the same if I can.

Sarah Winnemucca.

Camp McDermitt, Nevada, April 4th, 1870.

Within two years of the appearance of Jackson's A Century of Dishonor, *Sarah Winnemucca published* Life Among the Paiutes: Their Wrongs and Claims *(1883). In this first autobiography written by a Native American woman, Sarah Winnemucca drew heavily from the lectures she gave to eastern audiences. Mary (Peabody) Mann, wife of educator Horace Mann, served as editor; her sister, Elizabeth Palmer Peabody, helped raise funds to pay for the printing. Mann noted: "It is the first outbreak of the American Indian in human literature, and has a single aim—to tell the truth as it lies in the heart and mind of a true patriot." The following selection described the opening of the school on the Malheur Reservation and the termination of services of Indian Agent Samuel Parrish, a man much admired by the Northern Paiutes for his fair dealing. Winnemucca vented considerable anger at William V. Rinehart, successor agent at Malheur, but did not alter the course of federal policy toward her people.*

At last our school-house was done, and my people were told that it was ready, and for the little children to come to school. It was the first day of May, 1876, Mrs. Parrish was to be teacher, and I was to help her, and get the same pay for teaching the children English. I had given up my position as interpreter to my cousin Jarry, because he was almost blind. I asked Mr. [Samuel] Parrish to give it to him, because he had a wife and daughter, and no way of making a living for them. So Mr. Parrish sent for him to come and take my place.

On the first of May Mrs. Parrish and I opened the school. She had her organ at the school-house, and played and sang songs, which my people liked very much. The school-house was full, and the windows were thrown open, so that the women could hear too. All the white people were there to sing for them. I was told to tell the children to sing. All of them started to sing as well as they could. Oh, how happy we were! We had three hundred and five boys, twenty-three young men, sixty-nine girls, and nineteen young women. They learned very fast, and were glad to come to school. Oh, I cannot tell or express how happy we were! Mrs. Parrish, the dear, lovely lady, was very kind to the children. We all called her our white lily mother.

We had not been teaching but about three weeks when very bad news came. Our white father, Parrish, told me to tell all the people to come to the school-house. They all came with sad faces, because I had already told them that our white father was going away to leave us. Then he told us that he had received a letter from our Big Father in Washington, saying another man was to come in his place,—a better man than he. "I am sorry to leave you," he said, "because I know I can make a good home for you. The man who is coming here to take care of you all is a good man. He can teach you better things than I, and maybe he will do more than I can. You must do just as he wants you to do. Go right along just as you have done while I was with you. You all know who he is. He used to live in Canyon City, and have a store there." My people began to say to one another, "We know him, then." The mail-carrier said, " I know him, for I know he had a store there." Egan, the sub-chief, said,—

"Our Father says he is going away. Now I have been thinking that some of you may have said something against our father. You might have done it without thinking that something would come of it. You all know that white men make a mountain of little things, and some of them may have heard something and told it on him." They all said, "We have had nothing to say against our father. Why should we do so when he has been so good to us?" Oytes got up and said, "We will not let our father go; we will fight for him. Why should we let him go? We have not sent for another father to come here. He has been doing everything for us, and we have made no complaints against him. We will all stand by him. He has taught us how to work, and that's what we want, and the white lily is teaching our children how to talk with the paper, which I like very much. I want some of the young men to go and tell our father Winnemucca to come here as soon as he can. I know he will think as I do. I say once more, we will not let him go."

I told our agent everything that was said by my people. Then he told me to say to them that it was not because he had done anything that was not right, that he must go away. It was because they said he was not a Christian and all the reservations were to be under the Christian men's care. "Before I go," he said, "I am going to plant for you, and help you all I can. I will give Egan and Oytes land for peas; Oytes, just on the other side of the river for him and his men, and Egan at the Warm Spring, which is just half a mile away on the east, and to Jarry Lang, and Sarah Winnemucca, and others, on this side of the river. Come right along, just as before, and we will plant whatever you want for the winter. Your new father will not be here until the first of July." He asked each one of us what we wanted planted. Egan said, " I want potatoes and a little wheat." Oytes said the same. My cousins asked me what I wanted. I said, "We have horses enough to need oats and barley." Mr. Parrish said, "Just as you like." I said, "I will have wheat, and you oats, and we will have all kinds of vegetables." Then our white father said to Egan, "There are eight ploughs. Some of your men can help to plough, and we will get everything in." He also told Egan that he could not keep Jarry any longer as interpreter. My cousin was married to Egan's niece, and Mr. Parrish gave me back my place as interpreter. All my people went to work just as before. In a very short time everything was put in.

During that time, Gen. O. O. Howard and his daughter and Captain Sleighton came to visit us. We were all very glad to see him. He came to see if my people would allow him to build a military post at a place called Otis Valley, ten miles from the agency. He wanted to move Camp Harney to that place. The subchief, Egan, said to him, "I like all the soldiers very much. We must see first what our brother Winnemucca says. We have sent for him, and we look for him every day. When he comes he can tell you whether you can build there or not." General Howard said, "All right, you can tell Mr. Parrish, and he will write to me. I am very glad you are getting along so nicely here. I like to see all the Indians get along in this way. Go on just as you are doing; you will soon be like the white people."

Egan got up and said to him, "You are our Big Soldier Father. We would like to have you come and see us, and see that no bad men come and take away our land. You will tell your soldiers to keep them off the reservation." He promised he would see to it, and he staid all night. The school stopped at this time. Our names were put each on our grain-field or garden. My father came and told him all, and we went to see the agent. My father took his hands in his, and said, "My good father, you shall not leave me and my people. Say you will not go."

He answered: "It is not for me to say. I would like to stay, but your Big Father in Washington says that I must go, and that a better man is coming here. You will like him, I know."

Father said: "I do not want any one but you. I am going to see the soldier-father to-morrow. I know they will keep you here for me, or I think they can if they wish to."

Mr. Parrish said, "They can do nothing against the government."

My father sat a long time without saying a word.

At last Mr. Parrish said:—

"Come with me, Winnemucca, I want to give you some things. Come with me." So we went to our store-house. After we got there father stood in one corner of the room, like one that was lost.

Mr. Parrish said, "What kind of clothes do you want?"

Father said, "I don't want anything if you are not going to stay with me. I don't want anything from you, because it will make me feel so badly after you are gone."

It is the way we Indians do. We never keep anything belonging to our dearest friends, because it makes us feel so badly, and when any of our family die, everything belonging to them is buried, and their horses are killed. When my poor mother was yet living every time we went near the place where my poor grandfather was buried she would weep. I told father the way white people did if they were to part for a long time was to give each other something to remember each other by, and they would also keep another's picture, if he was dead. "Father," I said, "you had better take what he gives you, for he will feel badly if you don't." So father took everything he gave him. . . .

SOURCES

Jackson, Helen. Appendix VII, Letter from Sarah Winemucca. *A Century of Dishonor: A Sketch of the United States Government's Dealings with Soime of the Indian Tribes.* New York: Harper and Brothers, 1881. Reprinted: Norman, Oklahoma: University of Oklahoma Press, 1995.

Hopkins, Sarah Winnemucca. *Life Among the Paiutes: Their Wrongs and Claims.* New York, NY: G. P. Putnam, 1883.

RELATED READINGS

Brimlow, George Francis. The Life of Sarah Winnemucca: The Formative Years, *Oregon Historical Quarterly* 53 (1952):103–44.

Canfield, G. W. *Sarah Winnemucca of the Northern Paiutes.* Norman, OK: University of Oklahoma Press, 1983.

Fowler, Catherine S. Sarah Winnemucca, Northern Paiute, ca. 1844–1891, *American Indian Intellectuals.* Margot Liberty, ed. Proceedings of the American Ethnological Society. St. Paul, MN: West Publishing Company, 1976.

Gehm, Catherine. *Sarah Winnemucca: Most Extraordinary Woman of the Paiute Nation.* Phoenix, AZ: O'Sullivan Woodside, 1975.

Minor, Rick, and Stephen Dow Beckham. History and Archaeology of the Malheur Agency/Agency Ranch Site, Malheur County, Oregon. Heritage Research Associates Report No. 273 submitted to USDI Bureau of Reclamation, Snake River Area Office, Boise, ID., 2003.

Rosenberg, Ruth. Sarah Winnemucca, 1844–17 October 1891. *Native American Writers of the United States.* Kenneth M. Roemer, ed. Detroit, MI: Gale Research, 1997, pp. 316–21.

Scherer, Joanna Cohan. The Public Faces of Sarah Winnemucca, *Cultural Anthropology* 3(2[May, 1988]):178–204.

Scordate, Ellen. *Sarah Winnemucca: Northern Paiute Writer and Diplomat.* New York, NY: Chelsea House, 1992.

Zanjani, Sally. *Sarah Winnemucca.* Lincoln, NE: University of Nebraska Press, 2001.

"Many Things Were Promised," 1871

Several Pacific Northwest treaties contained the provisions of the Treaty with the Omaha of 1854. This treaty, used as blueprint for negotiations, gave the President discretion to order survey and assignment of reservation lands as lots assigned to individual Indians willing to participate in such a program. The treaty with the Kalapuya and other tribes and bands of the Willamette Valley of January 22, 1855, contained the allotment provision in Article Four.

On September 14, 1871, the Bureau of Indian Affairs scheduled a council on the Grand Ronde Reservation to press the agenda of dividing the tribal land ownership into individual allotments. Felix R. Brunot (1820–98), a member of the Board of Indian Commissioners, and his clerk, T. K. Cree, from Washington, D.C., joined Alfred B. Meacham (1806–82), Oregon Superintendent of Indian Affairs, and Rev. Josiah L. Parrish (1806–95) of Salem in the conversation with reservation leaders. Meacham represented the transition to the "Peace Policy" initiative of the Grant administration in dealing directly with tribes. Parrish had joined the Methodist Mission in Oregon in 1840, served at the Clatsop Plains station, and worked as the first Indian agent at Port Orford in 1851–52.

The council included discussions with several leading figures of the Grand Ronde tribes. Peter Kinai (Cornoyer) (ca. 1833–ca. 1880) was a Tualatin. In 1877 he served as a linguistic and cultural informant for Albert Gatschet, who used the data in "The Kalapuya People," Journal of American Folklore *(1899). Melville Jacobs drew upon these notes for* Kalapuya Texts *(1945). Billy Williamson was probably a Kalapuya from Marys River. Solomon Riggs (ca. 1830–?) was an Umpqua Indian. Riggs and his wife, Jane, had eleven children. Louis Nip-pe-suck (Napassant) (1813–88), adopted by the Umpqua, signed their treaty in 1854 and was considered a chief. His first wife was Nez Perce; his second was Klickatat. Records of Nip-pe-suck's children appear in the St. Paul, St. Louis, and Grand Ronde Catholic registers. Henry Kilke [Yelkes] was a Molalla. The native representatives thus reflected the diverse bands and tribes removed to the Grand Ronde Reservation.*

Thomas K. Cree recorded the minutes of the council. The tribal leaders made clear their needs, frustrations, and hopes.

This reservation is situated near the celebrated Willamette Valley, is a fair piece of land, and in a good state of cultivation. There is not a wigwam on the reservation. Every Indian lives in a comfortable house. All, men and women, dress as whites, and are generally dressed with neatness and care. Many speak English, and almost all are engaged in farming. They are just about completing a mill-race, all the labor on which was done by the Indians, without any pay, and all the expense incurred was with their consent deducted from their annuity money. The funds for the employment of most of the employees had been exhausted, and the Indians evinced a great anxiety that an opportunity should be given them to acquire a knowledge of the trades.

A council was held at the agency buildings with the Indians of this reservation at 2 p.m. to-day. There were in attendance Hon. Felix R. Brunot and his clerk, T. K. Cree; Hon. A. B. Meacham, superintendent of Indians affairs for Oregon; Rev. Mr. [Josiah L.] Parrish, of Salem, and most of the Indians on the reservation.

Mr. Meacham opened the council by saying: We begin a new kind of talking to Indians to-day. Mr. Brunot comes from Washington. He is a good man and believes God sees and hears him, and he always asks God to bless him when he talks.

MR. BRUNOT: When the white men have a council they always pray before beginning it. The Indians must be taught the same, or they will not know that it is right. He then asked Rev. Mr. Parrish to lead in prayer.

MR. BRUNOT: Mr. Meacham has told you I came from Washington. I will tell you why I came. The President is interested in all classes of all his people, and wants to know how all of them are getting along. He hears many things about you, and he sent me to hear what you have to say, and to carry your words back to him. I am glad to find here, not Indians with paint and blankets, but men like white men, living in houses, with fields of grain about them, and working like white men. If I had not heard to the contrary from others I would think that in everything you were like white men. Some things I hear make me sorry. Among some of the Indians there is much whiskey-drinking. When I see that I know they are poor and miserable, and their children must either starve or beg. Some places the Indians are gamblers. Where whites or Indians are gamblers they can never amount to anything.

There is one thing I want you to take into your hearts. The white man thinks unless land is cultivated it is a waste of the soil. They think if the Indians don't cultivate it the whites ought to have the land. The way to get rid of them is to cultivate it yourselves. Mr. Meacham is arranging to give each man his own place. You are getting the saw-mill so that you will have plenty of lumber to build houses, and I hope every one of you will get a good house before the treaty runs out. When I go to Washington I will tell the white people what kind of Indians I saw. I will tell them of your fields and houses, and of your roads, that are better than the white man's roads. I will tell that I saw Indians running a threshing-machine, and I will tell them that in three years from now the Indians will have given up the habits that are keeping them back. They will send their children to school. That you have learned that temaminus [spirit power] is bad, and that you are going to quit it. That you are going to do steady work as the white man does. That you will quit gambling and drinking. That you will take the white man's laws instead of the Indian laws, and the you can vote, and some day some of your children will be sent to Washington to make laws.

You have had many agents here. I don't know any of them. Some may have been bad, but it is not the President's fault. He means to send good men, and I think you will have a good man. I do not know who it will be, but whoever it is I want you to try him and do your part. You must listen to his advice. I might talk till the sun goes down and tell you something good, but I want to hear your words and carry them to Washington.

MR. MEACHAM: You have heard me often. You know my heart. I told Mr. Brunot you were not Indians, but men. I want you to talk like men.

PETER CONNOYER: I have not much to say. For four or five years I have wanted my lands surveyed. It is now being done, and I want to settle down on it and live and die on it. Our saw-mill is almost done. Now we want a grist-mill. We need it, and we ought to have perhaps $10,000 to build it. I want Mr. Brunot to know when he sees us dressed up that we bought the clothes ourselves. We get no blankets. We ought to have some, for the Indians who are poor. We need harness and we need teams. It takes money to but them. I hope my people will all take lands. They get from forty to one hundred acres each family. The treaty was to give each man twenty-five acres. We need cradles, scythes, and forks, and it will take money to but all these. It will take $30,000 to buy all of them.

Gambling—I don't know what the Indians will say about it. I don't gamble myself, and don't believe in it. About religion—I am a Catholic; so are all my family. All the children are Catholics. We want the sisters to come and teach the girls. The boys, I don't care whether the Catholics or Protestants have them. The priest [Adrian Croquet] lives here. He does not get any pay. He teaches us to pray night and morning. We must teach the little girls. I am getting old, but I am easily led astray; I may go to a race, bet a little, but I don't want my children to learn it. It is bad. I ought not to do it myself. We get off the side of the road, where no good men see us, and we gamble, but when a good man comes along we are ashamed of it. So it is with the white man when he does what he knows is wrong. We go to a temanimus doctor, and do many things that we ought not, but we do not teach our children things. Our lands we want to get as soon as possible. We need a carpenter, blacksmith, and miller, so that our children can learn. (Peter spoke in English, though a full-blooded Indian.)

JOE HUTCHINGS: (Speaks English fluently, but talked in Chinook.) I am glad to see Mr. Brunot. We are not wild Indians; we are like white people. The treaty is gone.[2] I think I am a good man. Meacham is a good man. He told us Mr. Brunot would come. I have my land. In a short time I will be like a white man. My children will be like white men. The Indians made a treaty before they came here. Then there were no half-breeds among us. When I was wild like an Indian they said they would make a good white man of me, and I made up my mind to be like a white man. Five years ago many were Indians; now they are white men. They promised to show me how to plow, but the agents came and did not teach me.

When Meacham came we looked for him to do right. Mr. Meacham prom-ised a school-house for our children to go to school. I have seen the agents here for sixteen years, they have taught us nothing. You see our houses; we worked outside [off the reservation] and made money and bought them. When the treaty was made many things were promised us. We never got any of them. That is wrong. The superintendent here now knows what is needed. I won't ask for a horse or cow, or anything; he knows what is needed. Suppose one town had only one set of harness, how would they get along? Our people go outside and get horses, and they get harness, and plow with them. There were oxen and cows here, but I don't know what has become of them. You see these chiefs, (Indians;) they know all about there things.

If we did not work we would be very poor. Mr. Meacham said there was no money for a saw-mill or a flour-mill, so we agreed to help the work, and have done so.

I think I am a good Indian. I am a chief. Mr. Brunot said good words to us. We ought to work. We need the grist-mill now. When we first made the treaty it was not said whether a priest would teach us or somebody else. I know what was promised us. I was promised eighty acres of land, others less. If we had had a good agent we would have been better off. The agents wanted only the money; they did not want to help the Indian. The blankets and shoes and goods for Indians—the house was full of them. I did not know who got them; perhaps a rat tyee (rat chief) got them; but I am an Indian, and think it all right. Outside belongs to the whites. Indians sold it, but I never saw the money. If I had it I would buy plows and wagons. Some of my people are in the penitentiary. I don't know why there were put in. I want to know what they did to put them there.

BILLY WILLIAMSON: I think it is good for Mr. Brunot to come. This summer we see things as we never did before. Since Mr. Meacham came this summer our eyes have been opened. Our saw-mill is almost done, and we expect to have a grist-mill soon. Mr. Brunot comes from Washington, and I want to know whether what I said before, and that now, was put on paper—did my words go to Washington? Then the Indians were all separated; now they are all here. If you go to see their homes you will find many things they made themselves. They learned it from the whites outside. The men on the reservation did not learn us. When the treaty was made we were very poor. For fifteen years we have been talking about what was needed. Do they know it at Washington? Some white men say we will only get twenty acres. Where I came from I had not only twenty acres, but a hundred. Everybody knows we are poor. I had a cow and a yoke of oxen long ago; that is all I have now.

I don't want to lie to God. I don't think I am a very good man. I may tell a lie; I am an Indian. I speak the truth. I don't drink. I don't do as Indians did in old times. I have quit that. We can't do everything in a day. If we get our land we need cows and horses and plows and wagons. Then we won't go outside; we will stay here. There are a few half-breeds here. I think nothing about that; they have families here. I want to know if money was sent here for us. Now we are like white men. You know about God; so do these Indians. I speak no bad words. White men and Indians are all alike. Some Indians here have been shot and whipped by white men for nothing. White men gave them whisky and got them drunk, and now they get them into the penitentiary.

SOLOMON RIGGS: I am glad to see Mr. Brunot here. I want him to take my words to the President. I am going to speak true. It has been promised that our land should be surveyed; I am glad to see it is done. We are promised a saw-mill; I see it too; I am glad of it; I want lumber. When I get my land it is mine, and while I live I will stay on it. Three or four years ago I was like as if I had been asleep; now I am awake.

Agents five or six years ago never said to raise anything. When Mr. Meacham came he said we must raise grain as the whites do, and all of the Indians have done so. Now we want a grist-mill. There are plenty of old people about me; they are poor; I am young and can take my wheat outside. Many old people ask me to talk about the mill for them. Some agents here have made us poor. We can't help the old people. We need plows and harness, and when we have them we will be like white people, and will make our living the same way. You have promised to take care of the Indians as a man does of his children. Now we can take care of ourselves. I will be very glad to have a school. We want our children to go to it; that is where they learn sense. Mr. Brunot's father sent him to school, and now he is a man; so we want to send our children to school, and they will learn.

JOE HUTCHINGS: (a fine-looking, well-dressed man, wore a white shirt, buck gauntlets, and spoke English well; a very intelligent, sensible man). The people have hid in their hearts the truth about the half-breeds. They have been employed about the mills and shops. We want our children to learn and be employed instead of the half-breeds and whites. We don't want the half-breeds to interfere with us. They are getting the good things instead of the Indian; they are getting cows and horses. I don't know where they came from or who gave them to them. We want a white man in the mill, and we want our Indian boys taken there, and kept there until they learn, and they will be able after a while to run it themselves. As at the mills, so at the blacksmith-shop. A white man works at the wagon-shop, and a young Indian works with him. They will learn and soon they can make wagons themselves. The Indians will soon learn themselves and can do without the white man.

SAMSON: (an old Indian who spoke in English.) How long will it be before the Indians learn it? They are jealous of the half-breeds. The boys will go and stay a while and then run away. It is too late now; the half-breeds stay and learn the trades, and are now employed.

JOE HUTCHINGS: If a white man and an Indian were put in the mill, the Indian will soon learn and the white man can be done away with, and the Indian will run the mill. If the Indians work in the mill like the white men, they ought to be paid like white men. Mr. Meacham says by and by the Indian will learn; they will never learn; we want those employed now. The white man said long ago the Indians ought to learn. I know the Indians have not learned. But now we have waked up and want to begin. If Mr. Meacham says these things will be done to-morrow, always to-morrow, they will never be done. I want it done to-day. Mr. Meacham says we have no money, but a blacksmith ought to be put in the shop, and the Indian taught, and so in all of the shops. If the old men had been taught in the schools, they would have known these things. Now we want our boys taught. You employ the doctor; I am glad of it; if you did not, and we got sick, we would die; but the doctor comes and we get strong and able to work.

JACOB-ADAM-CHOTT: I am glad to see Mr. Brunot. Our mills got bad and we said so to Meacham, and he told us we would have a mill, but we must work. We did work and soon it will be done, and we will get lumber; and we will have a flour-mill, he said, and now we need it. We need a blacksmith; a white man to teach the Indian, and the white man can quit helping us. Our boys will get like white men. And we want a school-house. We are to-day as if we knew nothing. I am like my father, I cant read and write. Men say I am a white man, but I am only a little like a white man. Some time ago we said we were poor; we want to know if the President sent money here. I never saw any. Did the President send these culter (bad) blankets, worth about three dollars? And this culter (bad) calico? I don't want such poor things.

I see how many acres a white man has. I don't want to sell my land to the whites. I want money for my land. I want a good coat and pants, a good house. In a year I want to have money in my hands. I don't want these worthless things. White men would say they were cheated out of their lands, if you did so by them. If you send good blankets, plows, wagons, I would take that. We all want wagons and horses. The Government never gave us any of them. We went out and worked for them. Agents have never done right by us. They took our money away from us. The past year I saw nothing. Now I want to get something. You owe it to us. Long ago we did not wear pants. You want to see us like whites, so you must give us these things.

JOHN COUCHEY: What did the chief come for? I now know he came to see the people. I now want to talk to the chief. We want the things given to us that were promised long ago. We are no more in want of a saw-mill, we have it. Long ago we were promised things, they did not come; but now we are set upon a grist-mill. We want the mill so that our people can get bread. The chief said long ago we should have lands, and now we will get them. And we want word carried to the President that our hearts are glad for this. Besides the land, we need horses, plows, and harness. Long ago we gave our land to the whites, and now they own the land. Your talk is good, and what we say is from our hearts. I have never received a wagon, or plow, or harness. Some of the others have; that is why I tell of them. Our land outside we never received anything for. So all the old people talk. All the land which has been bought has been bought with a small amount; say land was as large as all the lands about here; it is as if I had given them away for nothing. In the past I have asked for the things that were promised, but they never came. You talk differently to-day from what the white chief talked before.

Tom Shasta: Some time ago (Miepay) you came and talked to us, and told us good things. Now, Mr. Brunot has come a long way; it is good. The Indian wants to be good, and he likes the whites. Long ago I had no coat, pants, or hat. Papers came from the States and said we will be like the whites. Now I am getting old. I understand what you say. You are getting tired talking to the Indians. We want them all to be good. On most of the reservations the Indians are not like the whites. The whites are all over the country. They make money, and plenty of it, everywhere. The Indians get poorer every day. If you want us to be like whites, give us what we need. We have received many things, but not what we need. All we got is gone, and we don't know anything. We have learned a little.

All are good, and we know what we need. We understand better what you want of us. You see all have hats. Our women are dressed like the whites, and they all want things like whites. In the shops there are no Indians who understand how to make wagons. No Indians can run the mill. We want a white blacksmith and a miller. We can't be like white men without somebody to learn us. After a while we want a school; but these things we must have now. The Indians never asked for them before; the whites said for them to have them, and now we want them. Our lands are surveyed. You must take care of [them] like you would of children. When you get a school the children will learn to read. You must tell the Indian what is true. You would be ashamed if the Indians could write the truth to Washington themselves. When the money and things arrive here they go into the warehouse and the Indian never sees them. So with all the agents. They never give us what is sent for us. If the agent tells us what is good we will keep it in our hearts. Plenty of supply has come here; we don't know how much.

Tom Curl: All these chiefs have not fathers. If a man is good or bad, so he will talk. A long time ago I understood what was told me. When the treaty was made we understood it. Then I was young; now I am old. It would take ten days to tell all I know. If you would get these Indians all right you must stay and see to them. Some of the Indians are good; some are bad. I have not seen what was promised us. At one time we got shoes, hats, tobacco, and everything, and we expected they would always come. We were promised food for the poor, and we thought it would be so. All that was told us then I throw away. You see us here. It looks all right; but you should go to the poor men's houses, and see what they need. All do not work. Some are poor, sick, and old.

I am glad you came. You ought to stay always. All that was promised us in the papers you might as well destroy. Some new folks ought to come and get new papers, and we would believe them. The first thing ought to have been the grist-mill; the saw-mill last. We need the mills to keep the poor from getting hungry and sick. Everybody has not money to buy food. When the mill is done we ought to have wheat put into it and ground, and given to the poor until they die, and then they quit wanting it. The old folks don't care about the school; only the children need it. The old folks need only food to keep them from dying.

We need a blacksmith, carpenter, and miller, and then we will be like the whites. There is too much work for one blacksmith. We ought to have three or four in different places. It is nothing to me. I may die to-day or to-morrow. I am talking for others. Every man ought to have a plow and harness like the whites. If a wagon comes to the shop here it has to wait two or three days before it is fixed. If a white man has a wagon broken he takes it and has it fixed at once. One mill and one saw-mill is enough. Those that don't know how to plow should go to work and learn. Some get a bushel and a half to sow; some get two bushels; others three bushels. That is why the Indians go away. When they want oxen to plow they can't get them. When they want potatoes to plant they can't get them. The chiefs get them. They are not the only ones who sold their lands. The bad men have fathers, and all like to get something as well as the chiefs.

We ought all to be treated alike. If a bad man comes, let him have things. If a good man sees a bad man packing off things he thinks that bad. I never got anything for my lands. The whites get rich on our lands that we sold. When the whites came to this country they had no shoes. They ate cammas just as we did; and now these same men treat the Indians like dogs and rats. If we had not whites in this country we would live as we did them. Their hogs and cattle eat the Indians' food.

We want to get good blankets, not paper blankets. I do not know what our boots are made of. If we hit anything they break in pieces. We did not want sugar and coffee and such things. When I got big I saw whisky. They told me to smell it. It made me sick. They told me to drink it; that it was good. I drank it. I know whites and Indians both drink it; it kills them. I think you ought to quit making whisky, and wine, and beer. The whites say, "Why do you drink whisky?" We don't make it; the whites make it, and give it to us, and they say they will put us in jail for drinking it. Whenever they have war, whisky is sent, and they drink it, and it makes them brave. When they are cold the white man says it makes them warm. When I have a bottle of whisky, and a man says he is cold, I give him a drink. Everybody knows the Indian don't make it. If I had a handfull of money, and went outside, the white man would take the whole of it, and go and get a bottle of whisky for four bits and give it to me. White men taught me to drink.

HENRY KILKE [Yelkes]: (Molally.) Long ago the chief said we would buy your lands. The calico and other things, they said, we give you. We want to know about our lands. I have a wagon; I bought it. My house I got the same way. My clothes I bought; the Government never gave me any of them. I got harness, and oxen, and a plow, some time ago. I guess that was all I got for my lands. Now we want to know what we will get for our lands. We need a grist-mill, harness and horses, and plows and wagons, and that is all we want.

LOUIS NIP-PE-SUCK: We are glad to see you here from Washington. If we had a superintendent like Meacham we would have done much better. We are always glad to see him come. We know his heart. We wish Mr. Brunot could go around and see the houses; I don't say to stay a couple of months, but to stop a day or two. You see all these Indians are not wild. They have clothes like whites. Some time ago some of the Indians had flat heads. The whites said it was bad, and they quit. The superintendent before got here at night and left in the morning; never said anything to us. We understand what Mr. Meacham tells us. You hear what has been said. You may take these words, or may be not. We sent our words east before, but they never went.

Mr. Meacham promised us a mill. We have it. He said our lands should be surveyed, and it has been done. We need a grist-mill. Everybody has not a team to go away off to mill. You say we do not plow deep. We have not enough horses to plow deep. Some men have good horses, plow deep and get good crops. You may think what we say is not true, but I think it is true. If we had had a good superintendent we would be all right. Some of our people are poor. That is why we talk about plows and wagons. Strong men can work and get them, but all cannot.

Since I have been here I think I have not done anything wrong. Everybody knows I am a chief. I think I am a good man and speak the truth. I have helped the Indians. I have asked the agent to help them. What have I done wrong? They have just gotten their eyes open. Long ago I told them to put a boy in the blacksmith-shop, and carpenter and tin-shop. None of them wanted to learn. One went into the tin-shop and learned; then he learned blacksmithing; then to be a carpenter. Joe also learned to be a blacksmith; now he is a carpenter. Now they cannot afford to have so much work done.

Now the land is surveyed, who had it done? I talked to the agent and had it done. Some of the Indians say it was bad. I wanted to give each a home to stay on. If it was not surveyed outside somebody would jump the claim. So they would here. I think I helped the Government and helped the Indians. The horse Crawford gave me; it is nothing; it was lame; I don't care for it. [Joel] Palmer, who was superintendent, was a good man. I had a good farm outside, at Umpqua. I have sixty head of cattle. I lost them all helping the Indians. I did not want to come here.

MR. BRUNOT: Some of you men want six blacksmith-shops and three wagon-maker shops; some want a great many plows, clothes, and other things. If I had all the plows in the country, and all the blacksmith-shops in the country, I do not think I would give you so many, and this is the reason: If I wanted an Indian to be as the best white man in the country, would I set him on the fence, and bring him good, and clothes, and a bed? If I did that, he would never be able to do anything for himself. I want you to get things as white men do. You must work and get them yourselves. I do not promise you anything.

My heart is for you to get everything you ought to have from Washington, but I don't promise you anything, for I am not the President. I will carry your words to him, and tell him you are trying to do right. The treaty is almost over. I hope you will get all that is coming to you, but you must make the most of it. It is not yet too late to learn something. If you have no place here to teach them, Mr. Meacham can fix it so that your boys can go to town and learn. Some one said they only got a little wheat to sow. How does the white man do? He saves as much of his crop as he needs for seed. I will take your words to the President, and he will be glad to hear that you are men.

MR. MEACHAM: I am proud of you; you are not savages, but men. Sometimes the Government is slow, but it will do right in the end. The land is surveyed; every man shall get his land. All will be right. The saw-mill is almost done. You have made it yourselves. No white man owns any of it; it is yours. I asked you if you wanted a mill; you said yes; and so the money sent for blankets and calicoes goes to pay for your mill. Mr. Rhinehart says in ten days the saw-mill will be done. Now, if you take the stones of the flour-mill, build a little house beside the saw-mill, and move the grist-mill stones into it, use the same wheel, it will take but little money and little time. But it will take more money from your blankets and calico. I want to know what you want.

Mr. Brunot then spoke to them on polygamy, care for the old people, and other subjects tending to their welfare; after which Rev. Mr. Parrish talked to them in Chinook, contrasting their present social condition and appearance with the time when he first came among them; when they wore no clothes and ate grasshoppers, and pounded sunflower seeds.

All the Indians then shook hands with and bade good-bye to Mr. Brunot and the gentlemen who accompanied him.

The Grand Ronde council of 1871 documented the impoverished condition of the Indians who but four decades before had held the fertile Willamette and Umpqua valleys. The hopes of their leaders for farming equipment, a sawmill and lumber to erect homes and barns, and a school with teachers remained unfulfilled. The 1855 treaty included $50,000 for these services. The delivery had been incomplete and unsatisfactory. The leaders also affirmed their willingness to adapt to American culture. "You want to see us like whites," said Jacob-Adam-Chott, "so you must give us these things."

The program envisioned by Alfred Meacham led to surveys of the northern part of the Coast Reservation from Devil's Lake to the Nestucca in anticipation of grants of individual allotments to Indians of the Grand Ronde Reservation. Meacham's active role in attempting to reform Indian affairs, however, led to his dismissal in 1871 and the abandonment of allotment at Grand Ronde until early in the twentieth century. When that process was finally carried out, on June 27, 1901, the Indians of the Grand Ronde Reservation relinquished 25,791 unallotted acres for $28,500 in per capita payments and 440 acres held for administrative purposes. The goals of the council chaired by Brunot in 1871 were finally achieved. Tragically, however, succeeding generations born after 1901 had no lands from which to select allotments. The alleged "surplus lands" had passed to the public domain and Euro-American settlers.

SOURCE

Minutes of a Council with Grande Ronde Indians at Their Reservation, Oregon, by Commissioner Felix R. Brunot. *Report of the Commissioner of Indian Affairs . . . 1871*. Washington, DC: Government Printing Office, 1872, pp. 148–53.

RELATED READING

Beckham, Stephen Dow. *The Indians of Western Oregon: This Land Was Theirs*. Coos Bay, OR: Arago Books.

NOTES

1. Readers will note that the text following refers throughout to the Grande Ronde, a mis-spelling. The Grande Ronde Valley is in northeastern Oregon, the Grand Ronde Reservation is in coastal Oregon.

2. The annuity provisions of the treaty of 1855 ran for twenty years. Tribal members had become keenly aware of the problems they faced with the termination of payments under their treaty.

"I Will Speak With a Straight Tongue"

Few Native Americans rank as high in name recognition as Chief Joseph. Appropriately identified by Alvin M. Josephy, Jr., as one of the "patriot chiefs," Joseph was a charismatic figure who gained national attention in the 1870s when he and his people resisted forced removal to the Nez Perce Reservation in Idaho. Knowing that the Nez Perce treaty of 1855 had reserved his band's homeland in northeastern Oregon, Joseph contested the second treaty of June 9, 1863, which he did not sign, whereby the Nez Perce in Idaho ceded the Wallowa Valley in Oregon.

Born in a cave near Joseph Creek in 1840, Joseph was named Hin-mah-too-yah-lat-kekt. His father, Tu-eka-kas, visited the missionaries Henry and Eliza Spalding at Lapwai, Idaho, in 1838 and was given the name Joseph. A year later Spalding baptized him into the Presbyterian Church. Old Joseph in 1855 signed the Nez Perce treaty negotiated by Isaac I. Stevens and Joel Palmer. Chief Joseph denied in 1879 that his father had signed this treaty. The treaty in the National Archives, however, a document never seen by the son, carried as the third signer, "Joseph, his x mark." As settlement, disease, and warfare spread, Old Joseph severed his affiliation with Christianity. He died in 1871 in the Wallowa Valley.

Following ratification of the second Nez Perce treaty in 1867, pressure mounted to drive Joseph's band from northeastern Oregon to the much-reduced reservation in Idaho. Settlers began their invasion in 1872 but, momentarily, President Grant listened to the pleas of the Indians and by executive order created the Wallowa Valley Reservation. Two years later Grant rescinded his order and threw the valley open to homesteading and cash entry. Tensions mounted. In 1876 General Oliver Otis Howard received orders to compel the removal. Howard gave Joseph's band thirty days to move from the valley to the flood-swollen crossing of the Snake River.

Joseph commenced the removal but hostilities broke out and raged from June to October. During that period Joseph led men, women, and children on an epochal journey via the Lolo Trail to Yellowstone National Park and almost into Canada before they were captured by the U.S. Army. A fascinated nation read telegraphed accounts of the remarkable staying action, military prowess, and skill of the Nez Perce in eluding their pursuers. The Nez Perce War seemed wrong to many. Joseph and his followers were sent to Kansas and finally to the Quapaw Reservation in Indian Territory (Oklahoma).

The following remarks appeared in 1879, shortly after Joseph and Yellow Bull visited Washington, D.C., to plead with Congress and President Rutherford B. Hayes that they be allowed to return to their homes. "It is still our land," Joseph insisted. "It may never again be our home, but my father sleeps there, and I love it as I love my mother."

My friends, I have been asked to show you my heart. I am glad to have a chance to do so. I want the white people to understand my people. Some of you think an Indian is like a wild animal. This is a great mistake. I will tell you all about our people, and then you can judge whether an Indian is a man or not. I believe much trouble and blood would be saved if we opened out hearts more. I will tell you in my way how the Indian sees things. The white man has more words to tell you how they look to him, but it does not require many words to speak the truth. What I have to say will come from my heart, and I will speak with a straight tongue. An-cum-kin-I-ma-me-hut (the Great Spirit) is looking at me, and will hear me.

My name is In-mut-too-yah-lat-lat. (Thunder traveling over the Mountains). I am chief of the Wal-lam-wat-kin band of Chutepa-lu or Nez Perces (nose-pierced Indians). I was born in eastern Oregon, thirty-eight winters ago. My father was chief before me. When a young man, he was called Joseph by Mr. Spaulding, a missionary. He died a few years ago. There was no stain on his hands of the blood of a white man. He left a good name on the earth. He advised me well for my people.

Our fathers gave us many laws, which they had learned from their fathers. These laws were good. They told us to treat all men as they treated us; that we should never be the first to break a bargain; that it was a disgrace to tell a lie; that we should speak only the truth; that it was a shame for one man to take from another his wife, or his property without paying for it. We were taught to believe that the Great Spirit sees and hears everything, and that he never forgets; that hereafter he will give every man a spirit-home according to his deserts; if he has been a good man, he will have a good home; if he has been a bad man, he will have a bad home. This I believe, and all my people believe the same.

We did not know there were other people besides the Indian until about one hundred winters ago, when some men with white faces came to our country. They brought many things with them to trade for furs and skins. They brought tobacco, which was new to us. They brought guns with flint stones on them, which frightened our women and children. Our people could not talk with these white-faced men, but they used signs which all people understand. These men were Frenchmen and they called our people "Nez Perces," because they wore rings in their noses for ornaments. Although very few of our people wear them now, we are still called by the same name. These French trappers said a great many things to our fathers, which have been planted in our hearts. Some were good for us, but some were bad. Our people were divided in opinion about these men. Some thought they taught more bad than good. An Indian respects a brave man, but he despises a coward. He loves a straight tongue, but he hates a forked tongue. The French trappers told us some truths and some lies.

The first white men of your people who came to our country were named Lewis and Clark. They also brought many things that our people had never seen. They talked straight, and out people gave them a great feast, as a proof that their hearts were friendly. These men were very kind. They made presents to our chiefs and our people made presents to them. We had a great many horses, of which we gave them what they needed, and they gave us guns and tobacco in return. All the Nez Perces made friends with Lewis and Clark, and agreed to let them pass through their country and never to make war on white men. This promise the Nez Perces have never broken. No white man can accuse them of bad faith, and speak with a straight tongue. It has always been the pride of the Nez Perces that they were the friends of the white men. When my father was a young man there came to our country a white man (Rev. Mr. Spaulding) who talked spirit law. He won the affections of our people because he spoke good things to them. At first he did not say anything about white men wanting to settle on our lands. Nothing was said about that until about twenty winters ago, when a number of white people came into our country and built houses and made farms. At first our people made no complaint. They thought there was room enough for all to live in peace, and they were learning many things from the white men that seemed to be good. But we soon found that the white men were growing rich very fast, and were greedy to possess everything the Indian had. My father was the first to see through the schemes of the white men, and he warned his tribe to be careful about trading with them. He had suspicion of men who seemed so anxious to make money. I was a boy then, but I remember well my father's caution. He had sharper eyes than the rest of our people.

Next there came a white officer (Governor Stevens), who invited all the Nez Perces to a treaty council. After the council was opened he made known his heart. He said there were a great many white people in the country, and many more would come; that he wanted the land marked out so that the Indians and white men could be separated. If they were to live in peace it was necessary, he said, that the Indians should have a country set apart for them, and in that country they must stay. My father, who represented his band, refused to have anything to do with the council, because he wished to be a free man. He claimed that no man owned any part of the earth, and a man could not sell what he did not own.

Mr. Spaulding took hold of my father's arm and said, "Come and sign the treaty." My father pushed his arm away, and said: "Why do you ask me to sign away my country? It is your business to talk to us about spirit matters, and not to talk to us about parting with our land." Governor Stevens urged my father to sign his treaty, but he refused. "I will not sign your paper," he said; "you go where you please, so do I; you are not a child. I am no child; I can think for myself. No man can think for me. I have no other home than this. I will not give it up to any man. My people would have no home. Take away your paper. I will not touch it with my hand."

My father left the council. Some of the chiefs of the other bands of the Nez Perces signed the treaty, and then Governor Stevens gave them presents of blankets. My father cautioned his people to take no presents, for "after a while," he said, "they will claim that you have accepted pay for your country." Since that time four bands of the Nez Perces have received annuities from the United States. My father was invited to many councils, and they tried hard to make him sign the treaty; but he was firm as the rock, and would not sign away his home. His refusal caused a difference among the Nez Perces.

Eight years later (1863) was the next treaty council. A chief called Lawyer, because he was a great talker, took the lead in this council, and sold nearly all the Nez Perces country. My father was not there. He said to me: "When you go into council with the white man, always remember your country. Do not give it away. The white man will cheat you out of your home. I have taken no pay from the United States. I have never sold our land." In this treaty Lawyer acted without authority from our band. He had no right to sell the Wallowa (*winding water*) country. That had always belonged to my father's own people, and the other bands had never disputed our right to it. No other Indians ever claimed Wallowa.

In order to have all people understand how much land we owned, my father planted poles around it and said:

Inside is the home of my people—the white man may take the land outside. Inside this boundary all our people were born. It circles around the graves of our fathers, and we will never give up these graves to any man.

The United States claimed they had bought all the Nez Perces country outside of Lapwai Reservation, from Lawyer and other chiefs, but we continued to live on this land in peace until eight years ago, when white men began to come inside the bounds my father had set. We warned them against this great wrong, but they would not leave our land, and some bad blood was raised. The white men represented that we were going upon the war-path. They reported many things that were false.

The United States Government again asked for a treaty council. My father had become blind and feeble. He could no longer speak for his people. It was then that I took my father's place as chief. In this council I made my first speech to white men. I said to the agent who held the council:

I did not want to come to this council, but I came hoping that we could save blood. The white man has no right to come here and take our country. We have never accepted any presents from the Government. Neither Lawyer nor any other chief had authority to sell this land. It has always belonged to my people. It came unclouded to them from our fathers, and we will defend this land as long as a drop of Indian blood warms the hearts of our men.

The agent said he had orders, from the Great White Chief at Washington, for us to go upon the Lapwai Reservation, and that if we obeyed he would help us in many ways. "You *must* move to the agency," he said. I answered him: "I will not. I do not need your help; we have plenty, and we are contented and happy if the white man will let us alone. The reservation is too small for so many people with all their stock. You can keep your presents; we can go to your towns and pay for all we need; we have plenty of horses and cattle to sell, and we won't have any help from you; we are free now; we can go where we please. Our fathers were born here. Here they lived, here they died, here are their graves. We will never leave them." The agent went away, and we had peace for a little while.

Soon after this my father sent for me. I saw he was dying. I took his hand in mine. He said: "My son, my body is returning to my mother earth, and my spirit is going very soon to see the Great Spirit Chief. When I am gone, think of your country. You are the chief of these people. They look to you to guide them. Always remember that your father never sold his country. You must stop your ears whenever you are asked to sign a treaty selling your home. A few years more, and white men will be all around you. They have their eyes on this land. My son, never forget my dying words. This country holds your father's body. Never sell the bones of your father and your mother." I pressed my father's hand and told him I would protect his grave with my life. My father smiled and passed away to the spirit-land.

I buried him in that beautiful valley of winding waters. I love that land more than all the rest of the world. A man who would not love his father's grave is worse than a wild animal.

For a short time we lived quietly. But this could not last. White men had found gold in the mountains around the land of winding water. They stole a great many horses form us, and we could not get then back because we were Indians. The white men told lies for each other. They drove off a great many of our cattle. Some white men branded our young cattle so they could claim them. We had no friend who would plead our cause before the law councils. It seemed to me that some of the white men in Wallowa were doing these things on purpose to get up a war. They knew that we were nor strong enough to fight them. I labored hard to avoid trouble and bloodshed. We gave up some of our country to the white men, thinking that then we could have peace. We were mistaken. The white man would not let us alone. We could have avenged our wrongs many times, but we did not. Whenever the Government has asked us to help them against other Indians, we have never refused. When the white men were few and we were strong we could have killed them all off, but the Nez Perces wished to live at peace.

If we have not done so, we have not been to blame. I believe that the old treaty has never been correctly reported. If we ever owned the land we own it still, for we never sold it. In the treaty councils the commissioners have claimed that our country had been sold to the Government. Suppose a white man should come to me and say," Joseph, I like your horses, and I want to buy them." I say to him, " No, my horses suit me, I will not sell them." Then he goes to my neighbor, and says to him: "Joseph has some good horses. I want to buy them, but he refuses to sell." My neighbor answers, "Pay me the money, and I will sell you Joseph's horses." The white man returns to me, and says, "Joseph, I have bought your horses, and you must let me have them." If we sold our lands to the Government, this is the way they were bought.

On account of the treaty made by the other bands of the Nez Perces, the white men claimed my lands. We were troubled greatly by white men crowding over the line. Some of these were good men, and we lived on peaceful terms with them, but they were not all good.

Nearly every year the agent came over from Lapwai and ordered us on to the reservation. We always replied that we were satisfied to live in Wallowa. We were careful to refuse the presents or annuities which he offered.

Through all the years since the white men came to Wallowa we have been threatened and taunted by them and the treaty Nez Perces. They have given us no rest. We have had a few good friends among white men, and they have always advised my people to bear these taunts without fighting. Our young men were quick-tempered, and I have had great trouble in keeping them from doing rash things. I have carried a heavy load on my back ever since I was a boy. I learned then that we were but few, while the white men were many, and that we could not hold our won with them. We were like deer. They were like grizzly bears. We had a small country. Their country was large. We were contented to let things remain as the Great Spirit Chief made them. They were not; and would change the rivers and mountains if they did not suit them.

Year after year we have been threatened, but no war was made upon my people until General Howard came to our country two years ago and told us that he was the white war-chief of all that country. He said: "I have a great many soldiers at my back. I am going to bring them up here, and then I will talk to you again. I will not let white men laugh at me the next time I come. The country belongs to the Government, and I intend to make you go upon the reservation."

I remonstrated with him against bringing more soldiers to the Nez Perces country. He had one house full of troops all the time at Fort Lapwai.

The next spring the agent at Umatilla agency sent an Indian runner to tell me to meet General Howard at Walla Walla. I could not go myself, but I sent my brother and five other head men to meet him, and they had a long talk.

General Howard said: "You have talked straight, and it is all right. You can stay in Wallowa." He insisted that my brother and his company should go with him to Fort Lapwai. When the party arrived there General Howard sent out runners and called all the Indians in to a grand council. I said to General Howard, "We are ready to listen." He answered that he would not talk then, but would hold a council next day, when he would talk plainly. I said to General Howard: "I am ready to talk to-day. I have been in a great many councils, but I am not wiser. We are all spring from a woman, although we are unlike in many things. We can not be made over again. You are as you were made, and as you were made you can remain. We are just as we were made by the Great Spirit, and you can not change us; then why should children of one mother and one father quarrel—why should one try to cheat the other? I do not believe that the Great Spirit Chief gave one kind of men the right to tell another kind of men what the must do."

General Howard replied: "You deny my authority, do you? You want to dictate to me, do you?"

Then one of my chiefs—Too-hool-hool-suit—rose in the council and said to General Howard: "The Great Spirit Chief made the world as it is, and as he wanted it, and he made a part of it for us to live upon. I do not see where you get authority to say that we shall not live where he placed us."

General Howard lost his temper and said: "Shut up! I don't want to hear any more of such talk. The law says you shall go upon the reservation to live, and I want you to do so, but you persist in disobeying the law" (meaning the treaty). "If you do not move, I will take the matter into my own hand, and make you suffer for your disobedience."

Too-hool-hool-suit answered: "Who are you, that you ask us to talk, and then tell me I sha'n't talk? Are you the Great Spirit? Did you make the world? Did you make the sun? Did you make the rivers to run for us to drink? Did you make the grass to grow? Did you make all these things, that you talk to us as thought we were boys? If you did, then you have the right to talk as you do."

General Howard replied, "You are an impudent fellow, and I will put you in the guard-house," and then ordered a soldier to arrest him.

Too-hool-hool-suit made no resistance. He asked General Howard: "Is that your order? I don't care. I have expressed my heart to you. I have nothing to take back. I have spoken for my country. You can arrest me, but you can not change me or make me take back what I have said."

The soldiers came forward and seized my friend and took him to the guard-house. My men whispered among themselves whether they should let this thing be done. I counseled them to submit. I knew if we resisted that all the white men present, including General Howard would be killed in a moment, and we would be blamed. If I had said nothing, General Howard would never have given an unjust order against me men. I saw the danger, and, while they dragged Too-hool-hool-suit to prison, I arose and said: "*I am going to talk now. I don't care whether you arrest me or not.*" I turned to my people and said: "The arrest of Too-hool-hool-suit was wrong, but we will not resent the insult. We were invited to this council to express our hearts, and we have done so." Too-hool-hool-suit was prisoner for five days before he was released.

The council broke up for that day. On the next morning General Howard came to my lodge, and incited me to go with him and White-Bird and Looking-Glass, to look for land for my people. As we rode along we came to some good land that was already occupied by Indians and white people. General Howard, pointing to this land, said: "If you will come on the reservation, I will give you these lands and move these people off."

I replied: "No. It would be wrong to disturb these people. I have no right to take their homes. I have never taken what did not belong to me. I will not now."

We rode all day upon the reservation, and found no good land unoccupied. I have been informed by men who do not lie that General Howard sent a letter that night, telling the soldiers at Walla Walla to go to Wallowa Valley, and drive us out upon our return home.

In the council, next day, General Howard informed me, in a haughty spirit, that he would give my people *thirty days* to go back home, collect all their stock, and move on to the reservation, saying, "If you are not here in that time, I shall consider that you want to fight, and will send my soldiers to drive you on."

I said: "War can be avoided, and it ought to be avoided. I want no war. My people have always been the friends of the white man. Why are you in such a hurry? I can not get ready to move in thirty days. Our stock is scattered, and Snake River is very high. Let us wait until fall, then the river will be low. We want time to hunt up our stock and gather supplies for winter."

General Howard replied, "If you let the time run over one day, the soldiers will be there to drive you on the reservation, and all your cattle and horses outside of the reservation at that time will fall into the hands of the white men."

I knew I had never sold my country, and that I had no land in Lapwai; but I did not want bloodshed. I did not want my people killed. I did not want anybody killed. Some of my people had been murdered by white men, and the white murderers were never punished for it. I told General Howard about this, and again said I never wanted war. I wanted the people who lived upon the lands I was to occupy at Lapwai to have time to gather their harvest.

I said in my heart that, rather than have war, I would give up my country. I would give up my father's grave. I would give up everything rather than have the blood of white men upon the hands of my people.

General Howard refused to allow me more than thirty days to move my people and their stock. I am sure that he began to prepare for war at once.

When I returned to Wallowa I found my people very much excited upon discovering that the soldiers were already in the Wallowa Valley. We held a council, and decided to move immediately, to avoid bloodshed.

Too-hool-hool-suit, who felt outraged by his imprisonment, talked for war, and made many of my young men willing to fight rather than be driven like dogs from the land where they were born. He declared that blood alone would wash out the disgrace General Howard had put upon him. It required a strong heart to stand up against such talk, but I urged my people to be quiet, and not to begin a war.

We gathered all the stock we could find, and made an attempt to move. We left many of our horses and cattle in Wallowa, and we lost several hundred in crossing the [Snake] river. All of my people succeeded in getting across in safety. Many of the Nez Perces came together in Rocky Canon to hold a grand council. I went with all my people. This council lasted ten days. There was a great deal of war-talk, and a great deal of excitement. There was one young brave present whose father had been killed by a white man five years before. This man's blood was bad against the white men, and he left the council calling for revenge.

Joseph then related the epochal events of the exodus of his people during the war of 1877. "I would have given my own life if I could have undone the killing of white men by my people," he said. "I blame my young men and I blame the white men." Joseph laid primary blame for the war on General Howard: "If General Howard had given me plenty of time to gather up my stock, and treated Too-hool-hool-suit as a man should be treated, there would have been no war."

In 1889 the allotment process commenced on the greatly reduced Nez Perce Reservation on the Clearwater River in Idaho. Joseph refused to take an individual tract and argued that his own lands were in the Wallowa Valley of Oregon. In 1897 Joseph traveled to Washington, D.C., to complain about encroachments of miners on the Colville Reservation, to renew his claim to the Wallowa Valley, and to participate in New York City in the dedication of President Grant's tomb. Finally in 1899 Joseph, for the first time since the war of 1877, visited the Wallowa Valley. Looters had desecrated his father's grave and stolen the skull.

Local settlers at a public meeting told him that none would consent to sell land for a Nez Perce Reservation in the valley. Following a second visit to Washington, D.C., where he again pressed for the right to land in Oregon, Joseph returned to the Pacific Northwest and on November 11, 1903, addressed the students of the University of Washington:

My Young Friends:

I am pleased to meet you all and glad to see so many present. It always gives me pleasure to meet my white friends. I seem to have so many more now, than during my younger life. I am an Indian but the same blood that courses through my veins flows through yours. I was born and reared [to lead] the free, open and unrestricted life of a brave and haughty warrior. When I reached manhood I found that conditions were rapidly changing and without going into details, fought for my people, my land and my home. I fought for the inheritance left me by my forefathers and given me by [the Creator]. I was vanquished, conquered and subjugated, and have keenly felt the humiliation of defeat. But I have come to fully realize the kindness and generosity of the whites. I now see that they are my friends.

In my declining years, I long to return to my old home in Wallowa Valley, where most of my relatives and friends are sleeping their last sleep. I have repeatedly petitioned the Great Father in Washington to transfer my self and small band to our old home, that we may die in the Country, having so many tender memories. I have made frequent visits to Washington and have met many persons high in official life. They have all promised to render their assistance, but it has been, wait, wait, wait. On my last visit to the Capital City, I had the honor and pleasure of meeting President Roosevelt who treated me with much consideration. He assured me that a committee would be sent out to investigate my condition and surroundings. This committee was to be at my home last July but they have not yet come. This is but one instance of the duplicity shown me by the Government. I hope you will all help me and render me what assistance you can in securing long delayed justice. To return to Wallowa Valley, is a wish I cherish very dearly. That is all.

In the spring of 1904 Joseph attended the graduation at Carlisle Indian Industrial School in Pennsylvania and was seated with General Oliver O. Howard. He visited the St. Louis Exposition and returned to Nespelem, Washington, for July Fourth celebrations. Joseph died at Nespelem on September 21. In 1997 the Nature Conservancy purchased 10,000 acres in the Wallowa Valley and deeded it to the Nez Perce Tribe of Idaho. Joseph's band, not direct beneficiaries of this highly symbolic act, are members of the Confederated Tribes of the Colville Reservation where many live in north-central Washington.

SOURCES

Chief Joseph. "An Indian's Views of Indian Affairs," Introduction by William H. Hare, *The North American Review*, 1879, pp. 415–33.

Meany, Edmund. Papers, Chief Joseph File, Box 61, Archives, University of Washington, Seattle, WA.

RELATED READING

Beal, Merrill D. *I Will Fight No More Forever*. Seattle, WA: University of Washington Press, 1963.

Josephy, Alvin M., Jr. *The Nez Perce Indians and the Opening of the Northwest*. New Haven, CT: Yale University Press, 1971.

Gidley, M. *Kopet: A Documentary Narrative of Chief Joseph's Last Years*. Seattle, WA: University of Washington Press, 1981.

Howard, Helen Addison and Dan L. McGrath. *War Chief Joseph*. Lincoln, NE: University of Nebraska Press, 1941.

McWhorter, L. V. *Hear Me, My Chiefs*. Caldwell, ID: Caxton Press, 1952.

Ray, Verne Frederick. *Ethnohistory of the Joseph Band of Nez Perce Indians, 1805–1905*. Indian Claims Commission Docket No. 186. New York City, NY: Garland Publishing Company, 1974.

Treaty Rights: Umatilla Reservation, 1874

In Article 1 of their treaty of June 9, 1855, the Walla Walla, Cayuse, and Umatilla tribes reserved the "privilege of hunting, gathering roots and berries and pasturing their livestock on unclaimed lands in common with the citizens" throughout the millions of acres they ceded to the United States. Ratified by Congress on March 8, 1859, this agreement predated Euro-American settlement in northeastern Oregon. The treaty clause sought to create the means for the survival of these Plateau people who were consummate breeders and users of horses. Their vast herds enabled them to travel annually eastward into the northern Rockies and sometimes to the plains beyond to hunt for buffalo and to barter with the Blackfeet and Crow. Their herds attracted the attention of the Hudson's Bay Company, which established its "horse farm" along the Walla Walla River and there outfitted its brigades to trap and trade in the Snake River watershed and the northern Great Basin.

"Umatilla is known to be a great country for horses," observed Alfred Meacham. "I doubt if anywhere on this continent there can be found horses of greater speed or powers of endurance." Founder of a stagehouse atop the Blue Mountains on the wagon road between Umatilla Landing and the Grande Ronde Valley, Meacham had come to know the Confederated Tribes of the Umatilla Reservation as friends and neighbors. In 1874 he penned a vivid description of the importance of the horse to the Indians of that region. As an Indian rights advocate, Meacham stressed the treaty rights of grazing and hunting but noted "this right is scarcely acknowledged by the settlers of the places they visit, under the treaty."

The Umatilla Indians rear horses by the thousands, never feeding or stabling, but always herding them, when the owner has enough to justify the expense of hiring an Indian herder. The horses run in bands of fifty to one hundred, and, seldom mix to any considerable extent. If, however, there should be several bands corralled together, the master-horse of each band soon separates them. When turned out on the plains they are very exacting, and many a battle is fought by these long-maned captains, in defence, or to prevent the capture, by the others, of some one of their own.

Cayuse horses are small, from twelve to fifteen hands high; are of every shade of color, and many of them white or spotted, bald-faced, white-legged and glass-eyed. They are spirited, though easily broken to the saddle or harness. As saddle-horses they are far superior to the common American horse, and for speed and power of endurance they have no equals.

The Indians are accurate judges of the value of their animals and have strong attachments for them; seldom disposing of a favorite except in case of real necessity.

The small scurvy ponies are sold in large numbers, for prices ranging from five to twenty dollars each. A medium-sized saddle-horse sells for about forty dollars; a first-rate horse, one hundred dollars; and if a well-tried animal that can make one hundred miles one day, and repeat it the next, one hundred and fifty dollars.

The small, low-priced ponies are capable of carrying a common man all day long, without spur or whip. They are bought by white men for children's use, and for ladies' palfreys. They are docile, tractable, and fond of being petted. I know a small white pony, with long mane, and not more than forty inches in height, that was taught many tricks,—going through the hotel dining-room, kitchen, and parlor; sometimes following his little mistress upstairs; lying down and playing dead horse, kneeling for prayers, asking for sugar, by signs; in fact, a fine pet. And yet the little fellow would canter off mile after mile with his mistress.

Major [W. H.] Barnhart, of Umatilla, owned a small Cayuse, about thirteen hands high, that would gallop to the Columbia river, thirty-one miles, in two hours, with a man on his back, and come back again at the same gait.

I once made an investment of five dollars in an unbroken pony, paid an Indian one dollar to ride her a few minutes, took her home and gave her to a little daughter, who named her "Cinderella." After a few days' petting, she often mounted and rode her fearlessly.

This one was a bright bay, with a small star in the forehead, with long mane extending below the neck, a foretop reaching down to its nose.

The Indians teach their horses, by kindness, to be very gentle. Often on the visits which they make to old homes, a little pic-i-ni-ne (child) is securely fastened to the Indian saddle, and the horse is turned loose with the band.

On all their journeys they drive bands of ponies, presenting a grotesque scene: horses of all ages, sizes, and colors; some of them loaded with camp equipage, including cooking arrangements, tin pans, kettles, baskets; also bedding of blankets, skins of animals; always the rush matting to cover the poles of the lodge, and going pell-mell, trotting or galloping. The women are chief managers, packing and driving the horses.

Ed Chapman (ca. 1873/75–1931), a Cayuse, anticipated entering the sweat lodge,
a ritual return to the womb of "Mother Earth." The prayers, singing, and sweating in the
lodge help restore health and focus spiritual energy. The photograph was
taken about 1900 by T. Lee Moorhouse (1850–1926) (University of Oregon,
Moorhouse 4,285).

An Indian woman's outfit for horseback riding is a saddle with two pommels, one in front, the other in the rear, and about eight inches high. The saddles are elaborately mounted with covers of dressed elkskins, trimmed profusely with beads, while the lower portion is cut into a fringe, sometimes long enough to reach the ground.

These people seldom use a bridle, but, instead, a small rope, made of horse-hair, in the making of which they display great taste. It is fastened with a double loop, around the horse's lower jaw. They carry, as an ornament, a whip, differing from ladies riding-whips in this, that the Indian woman's whip is made of a stick twelve inches long, with a string attached to the *small* end, to secure it to the wrist. The other, or larger end, is bored to a depth of a few inches, and in the hole is inserted two thongs of dressed elk-skin, or leather, two inches wide and twenty in length.

The Indian woman is last to leave camp in the morning, and has, perhaps, other reasons, than her duties as drudge, to detain her; for she is a woman, and depends somewhat on her personal appearance especially if she is unmarried. If, however, she is married, she don't care much more about her appearance than other married women, unless, indeed, she may have hopes of being a widow some day. Then she don't do more than other folks we often see, who wish to become widows, said wish being expressed by feathers, and paint on the face and hair.

However, these Umatilla Indian maidens, who have not abandoned the savage habits of their people, are proud and dressy, and they carry with them, as do the young men, looking-glasses, and pomatums, the latter made of deer's tallow or bear's grease.

They also, I mean young people especially, carry red paints. Take, for illustration, a young Indian maiden of Chief Homli's band, when on the annual visit to Grand Round valley.

Before leaving camp she besmears her hair with tallow and red paint, and her cheeks with the latter. Her frock, made loose, without corset or stays is richly embroidered with gay-colored ribbons and beads, and rings of huge size, with bracelets on her wrists and arms.

Then suppose you see her mount a gayly caparisoned horse, from the right-hand side, climbing up with one foot over the high saddle, sitting astride, and, without requiring a young gent to hold the horse, place her beaded-moccasined feet in the stirrups, and, drawing up the parti-colored hair rope, dash off at what some folks would call breakneck speed, to join the caravan.

No young man had ever caught up her horse from the prairie, much less saddled it. But, on the other hand, she has probably brought up and saddled for her father, brother, or friend, a horse and prepared it for the master's use.

The young men who are peers of this girl do not wait to see her mounted and then bear her company. Half an hour before, they had thrown themselves on prancing steeds, and with painted cheeks, hair flowing, embellished with feathers, and necklaces of bears' claws, and brass rings, and most prominent of all, a looking-glass, suspended by a string around the neck.

The women manage the train and unpack the horses, make the lodge in which to camp, while their masters ride along carelessly, and stop to talk with travellers whom they meet; or it may be dismount at some way-side house and wait until it is time to start for the camp, where the lodge is built for the night.

There are, however, Indian men who are servants, and these assist the women.

When the site of the camp is reached, our young squaw dismounts, and, throwing off her fine clothes, goes to work in earnest, preparing the evening meal, while the gay young men, and the old ones, too, lounge and smoke unconcerned.

Remember, I am speaking now of Homli's band of the Walla-Wallas. There are Christianized Indians on Umatilla Reservation, that have left behind them their primitive habits,—men of intelligence, whose credit is good for any reasonable amount in business transactions, and who occupy houses like civilized people. But the major portion are still wrapped in blankets, and thoroughly attached to the old customs and habits of their ancestors. They have a magnificent country, and are surrounded by enterprising white men, who would make this land of the Umatilla the most beautiful on the Pacific coast.

It may be many years before these people will consent to remove. In one sense it does seem to be a wrong, that so many prosperous homes as this should afford, must be unoccupied.

In another sense it is right, at least in that those who live upon it now are the lawful owners, and therefore have a right to raise horses on land that is worth five, ten, and twenty dollars per acre, if they choose. So long as they adhere to their old ways, no improvements may be expected. They will continue to raise horses and cattle, to drink whiskey and gamble, becoming more and more demoralized year by year; and in the mean time vicious white men will impose on them, often provoking quarrels, until some political change is made in the affairs of the Government, and the present humane policy toward them will be abandoned, and then their land will become the spoils of the white man. It were better for these people that they had a home somewhere out of the line of travel and commerce; or, at least, those who continually reject civilization. It is not to the disadvantage of those whose hearts are changed that they should remain. While the Government protects them they will enjoy the advantage of intercourse with business men. With those, however, who do not evince a willingness to become civilized, it is only a question of time, when they will waste away, and finally lose the grand patrimony they now possess.

I do not mean that it will ever be taken by force of arms, for the sentiments of justice and right are too deeply seated in the hearts and lives of the people of the frontier to permit any unjustifiable act of this kind to be committed; but designing men will, as they have ever done, involve good citizens in difficulties with Indians, who, so long as they cling to their superstitious religion, will retaliate, shouting "blood for blood"; and then the cry of extermination will be extorted from good men, who do not and cannot understand or recognize this unjust mode of redress.

Under the treaty with these Indians, they are to enjoy the privilege of hunting and grazing on the public domain in common with citizens; but this right is scarcely acknowledged by the settlers of places they visit, under the treaty.

SOURCE

Meacham, Alfred. *Wigwam and War-Path; Or the Royal Chief in Chains.* Boston, MA: John P. Dale and Company, 1875, pp. 200–206.

Silent Testimony: Middens of the Southwestern Oregon Coast, 1873

For centuries the native places of southwestern Oregon had pulsed with life. They bore wondrous names: Sacl-req-tun, "Village On the Dark Side of the Canyon Where the Sun Never Shines," Na-ta-xi-li-i-tunne, "People By a Small Mountain On Which Is Grass," Sun-Sun-nes-tunne, "People at the Small Beach," and Dul-dul-ca-wai-a-me, "Village Where There Are Plenty of the Insects Called Dul-Dul [Dragonfly]."

Disruptive warfare and removals of the Indians of southwestern Oregon from both the coast and interior valleys to the Coast and Grand Ronde reservations in 1856 left hundreds of abandoned villages, fishing sites, quarries, spirit-quest locations, and burial grounds. No more did these places echo with human voices. Never again did a hand bring a bone needle against the tule fibers to sew matting. No longer did chips of wood fly as a craftsman carved a handsome dugout canoe. Never again did a young person stack stones and sing, dance, and pray at a vigil site to await the inspiration of a guardian spirit. These places and practices slipped from use and memory of succeeding generations.

In the 1870s Alexander W. Chase, an employee of the U.S. Coast Survey, mounted a reconnaissance of the headlands and shoreline of Curry County. He mapped and recorded elevations, identified off-shore rocks, and noted geographical features. At sea the crews sounded the depths and recorded the data on navigational charts. "The Indian tribes that once inhabited the coast line of the northern portions of California and the southern of Oregon have almost entirely disappeared," he noted. "The particular section of coast referred to was depopulated after the great war of 1856, called the Rogue River war." Chase found scattered across the headlands the stone and bone tools of these vanished people. His fascination with the artifacts and evidence of human enterprise led to his 1873 article, "Indian Mounds and Relics on the Coast of Oregon," the first archaeological account and artifact typology for the region.

In 1874 Paul Schumacher published an account of his archaeological investigations at Chit [Chetco], Nat-e-net [Lone Ranch], Hustenate [Hustenaden Creek],

and Chêtl-ê-shin [Crook's Point] in southern Curry County. He enumerated 291
items, which he presented to the Smithsonian Institution. In 1875 Schumacher re-
turned to Curry County to secure artifacts for the Smithsonian displays of Native
American material culture at the Centennial Exposition in Philadelphia. The fol-
lowing report covered Schumacher's travels and excavations from September 27 to
November 4, 1873, between Port Orford and the Chetco River. Schumacher used
the Danish term "kjökkenmödding" (kitchen midden) to refer to the deposits of
shell, fire-cracked rock, carbon, and other materials in the deserted village sites of
southwestern Oregon.

With two hired men and a camp outfit, I left San Francisco toward the end of
September, 1873, on board of the United States revenue-cutter *Richard Rush*,
Captain Baker, having received permission to take passage on one of her north-
ern cruises. We made landing at Port Orford, in Oregon, September 27, and the
following day pitched our first camp near the fresh-water lagoon [Garrison
Lake], a little to the north of the point.

From here I dispatched one of the men 45 miles down the coast to Pistol
River to bring pack-animals, for which arrangement had already been made;
I also engaged, in addition to the help already employed, two Oregonians in
my party, whom I knew to be good packers and able hands for an expedition
full of hardships, exposure to the elements, and hard labor all of which I justly
anticipated.

Before the arrival of men and animals, I, with one man left, investigated
the neighborhood of the lagoon, so advantageously adapted the location of
aboriginal settlements. Near the mouth of the lagoon, we discovered the site
of a small settlement, the location of the huts being still indicated by several
circular depressions, with an embankment around it of 1 or 2 feet above the
average level of the somewhat elevated position, which, toward the sea abruptly
terminates in a bluff of nearly 50 feet. Across the river, dunes border the ocean
for about a mile to the northward. Looking in that direction, we gain a good
view, although a part of the lake, or lagoon is hidden by the heavy timber on
the right, while to the southward the steep ascent of the high rocky point immediately obstructs any view in that direction; leaving a grassy, steep cañon to
the eastward, with a small running stream of good water, which passes at the
foot of the settlement. About half-way from this station to the lake, and on the
county trail, we find another small deserted *rancheria*.

The shells, which are at the first more mixed with sand and overgrown with
grass, are here quite bare on the surface, which adds a fresher appearance. I

looked for graves, employing the methods suggested in my southern tour, but all failed; and as even the house-sites yielded no skeletons I was inclined to believe that no graves exist here, where, by the signs, dwellings had existed only for a short time. At the mouth of the creek which supplies the small scattered town of Port Orford with water, is seen a moderately large shell-mound, partially washed away by the waters of the creek and the ocean as well, while back of the bluff, where the ground gently descends, several buildings and a garden cover the site of the deserted Indian town, thus making an exploration of the place impracticable.

During our reconnaissance, the Indians still dwelling in several places northward from here, and many others, well armed with rifles, who were passing on hunting excursions, watched our proceedings rather suspiciously, but made themselves welcome in our camp, and enjoyed our somewhat aboriginal dinners with much gusto. The meeting with Indians is not pleasant to an explorer of their forefathers' deserted hearths, as their friendly feeling is easily disturbed, and their superstitions alarmed by researches among the remains and graves of their ancestors; for this reason we did not visit Elk River, Sixes River, and other localities north of Port Orford, where Indians still live.

Our animals had in the mean time arrived, and after experiencing the first rain of the winter season, we started, on October 6, upon our way to Rogue River.

About 10 miles south of Port Orford, in the neighborhood of the rocks called "Three Sisters," on the bank of a creek, and close to the abrupt shore, we find the kjökkenmöddings of a former people located on a small flat—now covered with an orchard—bordered by the creek, and toward the sea by the ascending shore, the close proximity of which is only revealed by the roaring of the ocean, while an open view is had back in the valley. This station, I think, was the northernmost *rancheria* of the *Yu-kwâ-chi,* while another, one is found at Mussel Creek, about 5 miles farther south, and the largest of all at Yukwa Creek (which stream is now usually termed Euchre Creek, being a more familiar expression to the Oregonians of the present day). All these places are now under cultivation and partially occupied by building, whereby the signs, save the kitchen-refuse of the former inhabitants, became obliterated and covered. From Yukwa Creek, the trail trends back from the coast, and we could not observe the smaller settlements said to exist between here and Rogue River. A thick fog was also a strong impediment to our observations during the entire trip from Port Orford to Rogue River.

Arriving at Rogue River, we went into camp below the ferry, located at the place where the main *rancheria* of the *Tu-û-to-ni* once existed, about five miles from the mouth, and on the right or north bank of the river. Over the main *rancheria*, marked by a thick layer of kjökkenmöddings, we find the usual obstruction, an orchard; while across the rivulet (the efflux of a spring issuing but little over 150 yards across farther up on the rocky rise), the house-sites remained well defined; which we also notice 150 yards farther up the river, in an indentation of the steep shore, and still in another similar nook at a distance of 100 yards farther on.

These places were still inhabited at the time of the Rogue River war in 1856, when here, on the left bank of the river, just across from the main *rancheria*, peace was accepted by the leader of the United States Army, and the Indians were accordingly removed to reservations. The present owner of the land and ferry [William H. Bagnell], a "squaw-man," liberally gave us permission to dig in his orchard, where all signs of former houses were obliterated by the plow and obstructed by high weeds and trees.

Although we made a careful search for graves, the many test-holes we dug revealed only sites of houses; the kitchen-refuse consisting of all kinds of shells (see Smithsonian Report of 1873) and a great many bones of elk and of deer, averaged about 8 feet in depth at the main station, while none were found across the rivulet on the rocky ascending bottom, where it is likely the rains had washed them into the river, and very few, not enough even to form a layer, at the two upper town-sites. The houses we excavated were square; that is to say, the subterranean part reached to a depth of about 4 feet below the surface, and measuring variously from 6 to 10 feet square. The casing of the excavation consisted of boards arranged horizontally, contrary to the vertical position in the houses of the present Klamath Indians, and was kept in its place by posts along the front.

The general impression which the traces of an old aboriginal town-site makes is that of a group of huge molehills inverted or sunk to a small rim at its base. Although the excavation was found to be square, the remaining concavities, always shallow, and hardly ever more than 3 feet deep, were circular, which is attributed to the circular embankment that still surrounds it and to the natural action of the elements in filling up a depression in loose ground. No doubt, the superstructure of the hut was of a circular shape, corresponding to the remaining embankment, and was probably placed in such a manner as to meet conically, and was covered with earth, &c.

The fireplace we find on one side of the floor in a small excavation, and the smoke escaped through a draft-passage, as shown in section sketch (B) and the plan (C). We find among these house-sites a few well-preserved ones, exceptionally with square embankments (compare the sites of the first branch settlement), but they are no doubt of recent date, and a modification between an aboriginal hut and a white man's shanty [sweat lodge], such as we had occasion to witness among the present Klamaths at the mouth of the Klamath River, one of which I show in sketch (D), as also an inner view (E), a plan (F), and a section (G).

The inner view shows the depression, which is in this case pentagonal, incased by boards placed horizontally, with a fireplace in the center. The excavation is reached by a notched board, after entering the house through a circular door near the ground. The remains of the square structures of the Tu-tu-to-ni show, as at the Klamath, the marks of an ax, while the wooden parts of the older circular ones are charred at the ends and split with elkhorn wedges, of which we find so many among the *débris*.

In one of the ruins we excavated on the main *rancheria* was found a boat-shaped vessel, or disc, about nine inches in length, made, like those of our collection obtained on the islands of Santa Barbara Channel, of magnesian mica, showing also strong marks of having been exposed to fire, seemingly for the purpose of cooking food in it; furthermore, a beautiful ladle of stone, a nicely finished wedge of slate as used for repairing canoes; and among the kjök-kenmöddings we dug over, arrowheads and knives of stone, and many bone-carvings, were uncovered.

I cannot account for our utter failure in finding any skeletons in the main *rancheria* (the ground being well adapted for graves), either in a regular cemetery or buried in houses, as we gave our attention to both modes of interment. A cemetery probably existed in front of the *rancheria*, near the brink, where the kjökkenmöddings steeply descend to the edge of the river, which had, since the depopulation of the *rancheria*, risen very high, and nearly reached the top of the kitchenmiddings, according to the mark set by the present owner of the place, and washed away a large part of the refuse.

About two miles up the river from the main settlement, another *rancheria* existed, in a nice spot, sheltered by a ridge, and bordered on one side by a small stream [Indian Creek] at the foot of a steep-rising, while in front the beautiful Rogue River displays its picturesque scenes. The kjökkenmöddings average here a depth of two feet only. While searching for the burying-ground, we sunk many test-holes all over the place, and finally came upon a grave. It was dug three feet into the sandy soil; the sides of the lower part were lined with boards; the skeleton, doubled up in the usual manner, was resting on its back, facing the east, and was covered by a board secured by several stones, and the hole filled even with the surface of the surrounding ground. Nothing was found with the skeleton.

Rogue River was alive with trout and thickly stocked with salmon at the time of our visit; hundreds of them could be seen splashing at short intervals on the surface of the water, or resting motionless in the deep eddies near rocks and bluffs. In front of the lower or main settlement are several rocks above water, of which the farthest one out was the principal fishery of the Tu-tu-to-ni, and gave rise, it is said, to many disputes and quarrels. The rock is but eight feet above the surface of the river at common height, which elevation is well adapted for the spearing of fish by torch-light; the torch was placed in a crevice near the water-mark of the rock's face to attract the fish from out the deep holes near enough to the surface to be in easy reach of the expert spearsman. As the adjoining country of the Rogue River is also an excellent hunting ground, of course the favorable places along its banks had been settled by Indians. This is demonstrated by several deserted camps, formerly inhabited by the *Me-ka-nê-ten,* before the mouth of the Illinois River is reached, where the main tribe of the *Shis-ta-kûs-ta* dwelt. On both banks of the mouth of the Rogue River were the *Yû-sut* stationed. That place is now obliterated by buildings and improvements.

While at Rogue River, the weather had become threatening, and rain set in on the morning of October 17 while we were finishing our preparations to move down to Pistol River. It was tedious, disagreeable work that day: the miserable trails had become slippery, and in consequence almost impassable even for our mules, which showed much opposition to carry a heavy load, made more so by a soaking rain. But all went on as well as could be expected under such disadvantageous circumstances, thanks to our experienced packers, until dark night set in, when we neared the roaring ocean, where the trail, almost at our destination, trends down a steep bluff, and passes at its base over bowlders; there our animals became terrified by a loose pack to such a degree that nothing could check them, and they darted off in a fall stampede, scattering the packs along the beach. This caused us considerable trouble during the rainy night in searching for and removing the stuff out of the reach of high tide.

The next day we established our camp, and began excavations at the main *rancheria* of the *Chêtl-ê-shin* on the elevated ground at the last bend near the mouth and north of the stream called Pistol River.

The tribe of the Chêtl-ê-shin once occupied the country between Cape Sebastian in the north and Mack's Arch in the south, a very prominent arch-rock lying about a mile to the southwest of Crook's Point, and nearly as far from the shore—in all about eight miles in a straight line southward of Cape Sebastian. Almost opposite of Mack's Arch, from which the tribe received its name *(Chêtl-ê-shin,* meaning, *big rock,* as I was informed by a Chetko Indian), are found the extensive remains of their southernmost village. The next im-

portant one going north is at Crook's Point, a minor one at the eddy of the
Pistol River, whence the stream runs parallel with the ocean beach for about
a half mile to its outlet, where the main settlement is located. To the north of
Cape Sebastian was the hunting-ground of the Ya-sut, having had their main
station on both banks at the mouth of Rogue River, as already mentioned.
South of Mack's Arch, the range commences which was formerly claimed by
the *Khust-e-nête.*

There are still visible at the main station of the Chêtl-ê-shin about fifty depressions of former houses, some of them obliterated by others of a subsequent
occupation, and others again filled in by the Indians as if on purpose, and not
by the action of time. After considerable work was done in searching for a
cemetery, but without the desired result, we again resorted to the house-sites,
and especially to those filled up by human hands, which was proven to be a
fact by finding human skeletons interred at the bottom of the excavation. The
corpses were found without exception in the subterranean part of the ruined
houses, which were here like those at Rogue River in size and wooden linings,
but without the draft-passages for the smoke to escape. Doubled up, the skeletons were resting near the wall of the excavation, and faced the fireplace, as
indicated in sketches (H and I), which part was the most deeply covered with
earth, whereby the remaining surface indentation of such a house-site was easily discernible by an enlarged embankment, in contrast to those which were not
shaped through a burial, but had adopted the form of an inverted mole-hill by
the natural action of filling-up, caused by time and the elements.

In one instance, two skeletons were found buried in one house, where a re-
opening seemed to be evident by the flattened and unusually enlarged covering
earthwork. Such a singular indentation in which a burial was made will be better understood by comparing the section diagram (H) with that of a common
formation (B), in which latter no burial had occurred. The earth covering the
skeletons was strongly mixed with charcoal, pieces of charred wood, fragments
of animal bones, and shells blackened and partially consumed by fire. On the
floor on which the skeletons rested was found a layer of ashes of several inches
in thickness. But the fire had not affected the skeletons, as in no instance was
any such damage observed, and even the remains of matting, furs, and other
similar perishable material were not injured by it. It seems, therefore, evident
that the hut was demolished by fire, after the owner had expired, and was buried in the ruins, covered with rubbish and earth surrounding his house. Except
some glass beads found with a female skull, and three roughly-cast copper
buttons with that of a male, nothing was unearthed that had apparently been
deposited with the dead. Of course, in the mass of *débris* we worked over, divers

articles were found but not in such a position as to indicate an intended deposit of property of the dead in accordance with a religious or superstitious rite.

We find another large shell-mound located on loose sand about four hundred yards northward from the main settlement, where all the characteristic indications of a permanent settlement are noticed, excepting the house-sites, which likely had become filled up and obliterated by the sand drifts to which this place is exposed, as well as by the heavy rains during the winter. A stream of water passes the base of the dune, but disappears in the sandy beach. Back of the shell-mound, the ground rises gradually for a distance before it reaches the foot of a steep ridge extending back from the shore, and defining the lower boundary of an almost impenetrable country by its rough topography, its forests, and dense growth of underwood, the safe home of all kinds of game, panther, and bear. A few hundred yards up the coast from the shell-mound, near the bluff, we find indications of several house-sites, and much decayed shells and animal bones, mixed with sandy soil, producing that peculiar ash-like appearance. Neither at this place nor at the shell-mound did we discover any skeletons; and only a small addition to our collection was obtained in surface findings. In the right bank of the Pistol River on the elevated bluff running parallel with the ocean beach, several small shell-mounds were met with; as also on the bare dunes across the river, &c.; but of these I have spoken in the Smithsonian Report of 1873.

At Pistol River, we were detained for several days by heavy rain, during which time I made a trip ten miles (by the trail) down the coast, to a place known as Hustenate, where the old *rancheria* of the *Khust-enête* is located. Here the well-defined cemetery was readily found. Mack's Arch is the northern boundary of the Khust-e-nête, and Whale's Head, a prominent landmark on the ocean shore, about eight miles southward, is the southern boundary, whence the territory formerly occupied by the Chetkos extends southward. The next day we moved a light camp to Hustenate over a very rough trail, and reached that place in a heavy fall of rain of a winter storm just setting in. During the night, our tent was blown down, and shelter had to be sought for in a small shanty open to rain and wind. The location of the *rancheria* is sheltered toward the south by a rise and outreaching bluffs, while back of it, and to the northward, the ground rises rapidly, leaving a steep opening, from which issues a creek of considerable volume, which was much swollen by the rains at the time of our visit.

The ground on which the *rancheria* is located has been disturbed by many slides, some of which evidently occurred since the place was abandoned by the Indians. Decayed shells and bones, mixed with sand brought up from the beach, a mass of vegetable mold and rubbish, and all sizes of beach-stone, constitute the compost of the surface-layer to a depth of two to five feet, below which dark humus is found, over a soft slaty formation of a grayish color, which is coal-bearing. The house-sites are, as usual, irregularly located over a space of a hundred yards in length and something less in width.

Considering the condition on the ground upon which we find the aboriginal settlements on the Oregonian coast visited by our expedition, the opinion I have expressed in my previous report of such settlements on the southern coast of California holds good for this locality also: that all such stations had been established either on sandy ground, or that the nature of the ground had been artificially changed by layers of sand carried thither when it was rocky or hard. Sandy soil was necessary to the rude and imperfect tools for the erection of houses, which were partially dug in the ground, and surrounded by embankments. It was also a requirement for cleanliness, and healthful through its absorption of moisture in rainy seasons. About fifteen feet from the creek as well as from the shore, and but fifteen to twenty feet above the sea are two rows of graves dug in dark, coarse soil, bare of shells and sand, each grave being distinct one from another.

On digging, the graves were found to be very shallow, the skeletons being interred but one and a half to two feet below the surface. The sides of the excavations were lined with split redwood boards, about four feet in length and a foot in width, placed edgewise, and reaching to the floor of the grave, which was covered with beach-sand to the thickness of about one inch; the width was not over two feet, and both ends of the excavation were open, that is say, without lining. The corpses were found doubled up in the usual manner, lying on their backs, or sideways, and facing the *rancheria* in a southeastward direction, although some were found just in an opposite way. Immediately above the body was placed a board resting on the lining, to which it was secured by cobble-stones of various sizes, some weighing as much as fifty pounds. The grave was then filled up with earth, and covered with another wide board to an even level with the surface, and probably, if we trust the remains of a few redwood stakes in close proximity to the grave, was also fenced in.

I entertain no doubt that the worldly goods of those buried here, of which we did not find anything in the graves (excepting a few money-shells and glass beads), were placed on the top-board of the grave, a custom made evident by the of the present Klamath Indians. I lay before the reader a grave of the last-named tribe (Sketch K, and give also a plan (L), with some tools placed on the top-board, as copied in their *rancheria* at the mouth of the Klamath River, which might be well accepted as the restoration of a Khust-e-nête grave, of which but the surface board remained, while time and elements annihilated a

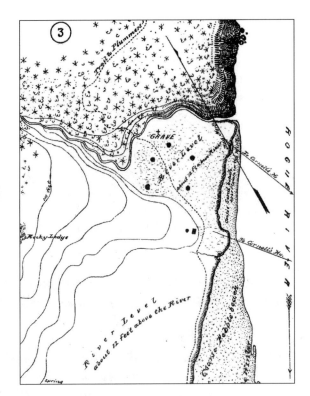

In the course of his archaeological investigations in Curry County, Paul Schumacher created a number of detailed maps illustrating former village sites, burial locations, and fisheries. This map was from the lower Rogue River reconnaissance.

part of the articles deposited over the grave, and casual visitors destroyed and carried away the rest. With babies' skeletons, and a young woman's corpse, we found some much-decayed money-shells (*Dentalium entalis*), which served to ornament the living, and were probably intended as a means for the frail little ones to pay the ferryman of the Indian Styx. A few glass beads were also found with skeletons of grown females. The shape of the skulls is remarkable for the artificial deformity, the forehead receding and the occiput protruding disproportionately.

We moved back to Pistol River in stormy weather, which increased during the following day to one of those heavy Oregon winter storms that define epochs in the chronology of the country people. Pistol River swelled rapidly, and overflowed most of the valley near its mouth. Large tracts of the river-bank were washed away, and countless trees, among them gigantic spruces were seen floating in rapid drifts to sea or ramming in at some bend of the river, soon forming floating islands. The stream being impassable even with a boat, it took five days before we ventured to cross with the pack-train on our way to Chetko; which place, 30 miles distant by trail, we reached after two days, as the trails were bad and much obstructed by fallen timber.

At the mouth of Chetko River we opened eleven graves, and found the dead buried in the same manner as noticed at Khustenête; only that each grave was, in addition, marked with a small heap of beach-worn rocks, whereby its location was easily recognized. Nothing was found buried with the dead, though several articles were discovered among the rubbish. The graves were located about 20 yards northwestward of those described in the Smithsonian Report of 1873.

From Chetko we moved, on the 4th of November, our camp-equipage and collection down to Crescent City for shipment with the first schooner. The steamboat connection between this place and San Francisco had already ceased for the winter, and we were compelled, as no schooner was at anchor and none soon expected, to go overland to Humboldt and thence by steamer to San Francisco.

Schumacher's archaeological investigations were little more than grave robbing. His admitted nervousness about encountering surviving native peoples confirmed the illicit nature of his supposed investigations. Yet Schumacher rose above the looter to pen an account of his explorations, to submit drawings of the sites and features he observed, and to turn his collection over to the Smithsonian Institution, where they are still housed. Chase and Schumacher were the first Euro-Americans to express interest in the prehistory of western Oregon. They had a genuine fascination with the technology and life ways of the largely vanished native people.

SOURCE

Schumacher, Paul. Researches in the Kjökkenmöddings and Graves of a Former Population of the Coasts of Oregon. *U. S. Geological and Geographical Survey of the Territories, Bulletin 3*(1)(1877):27–35.

RELATED READING

Chase, H. A. Indian Mounds of the Coast of Oregon, *American Journal of Science*, (1873):26–32.

Lyman, R. Lee. Alexander W. Chase and the Nineteenth-Century Archaeology and Ethnography of the Southern Oregon and Northern California Coast, *Northwest Anthropological Research Notes* 25(2)[1991]:155–255.

Schumacher, Paul. Remarks on the Kjökken-möddings on the Northwest Coast of America, *Annual Report of the Board of Regents of Smithsonian Institution for 1873* (1874), pp. 354–62.

———. Aboriginal Settlements of the Pacific Coast, *Popular Science Monthly*, 10(1877):353–56.

Textbook Treatment, 1925

"The Indians of the Oregon country represented various stages of savage and barbarian culture, but it cannot be said that any of them possessed even the rude beginnings of civilization." These words introduced generations of sixth-grade students to the natives of Oregon. In 1921 the Oregon Superintendent of Public Instruction, responding to the Oregon Historical Society, Oregon Pioneer Association, Sons and Daughters of the Oregon Pioneers, and the Oregon State Teachers' Association, required the study of state history in the elementary schools. Lacking curriculum materials, teachers initially had to create their own courses of study. Some invited aged pioneers and local Native Americans to visit their classes to help teach history. Others explored the Oregon Historical Quarterly and the Oregon Pioneer Association Transactions for information.

In 1925, Row, Peterson and Company of Chicago, published a History of Oregon; the "Old Oregon Trail" medallion designed by Avard Fairbanks appeared on the textbook's cover. The book coincided with a rising interest in the saga of overland emigration and efforts of the Old Oregon Trail Association to mark the route and commemorate the deeds of the pioneers. Congress embraced this enthusiasm when it authorized the special coinage—over a four-year period—of an Oregon Trail commemorative fifty-cent silver coin.

The authors of A History of Oregon envisioned their history as providing an acquaintance "with the careers of those men and women who have helped to make the state" and an understanding of the "influences which have shaped our state life and institutions." Robert Carleton Clark, born in 1877 in Texas, earned a Ph.D. in history in 1905 at the University of Wisconsin and in 1907 joined the Department of History, University of Oregon, where he served as chair until his death on December 4, 1939. His interest in western history led to his also writing A History of the Willamette Valley (1927), a large volume to which were appended two volumes of biographies. Robert Horace Down (1883–1942), lawyer and history teacher at Franklin High School in Portland, and George Verne Blue, a professor of history at the University of Hawaii, served with Clark as co-authors of the elementary textbook.

Nearly 300 of the 349 pages in A History of Oregon *dealt with the state's history prior to 1870. The second chapter, "The Indians of Oregon," introduced students to the culture and history of the state's native population. The text stressed the themes of the Indians' lack of civilization (since civilization was premised on a "settled agriculture"), rudeness of life ways, penchant for warfare, drudgery of the women, and the inevitable vanishing of the Indian race. A Darwinian maxim shaped the approach. "He could not survive in competition with the dominant race," concluded the authors.*

THE INDIANS OF OREGON. The Indians were the first historic people to dwell in the Oregon Country. We do not know how long ago they first came into possession of the land. Neither can it be said with certainty whence or how they came, or to what race they originally belonged. It is believed, however, that they arrived in America from some part of Asia. They could have made the journey by following the coast of Siberia, crossing Bering Strait, and coming southward from Alaska along the western coast of the American continent. In historic times boats carried by winds and ocean currents have drifted eastward from Asia far across the Pacific Ocean to the coasts of California and Oregon. It may be that in this manner America was first peopled by the red men.

At the time of the coming of the white men, the American Indians, in various localities and in various tribes, represented every stage of human development and culture from the lowest savagery up through barbarism into the beginnings of civilization. The most advanced tribes to be found were the Incas of Peru, the Mayas of Central America, and the Aztecs of Mexico. Those tribes were emerging from barbarism into civilization. They alone of all American Indians had a written language, always a characteristic of civilized peoples. Among the more advanced barbarians were the Iroquois of New York, who outstripped all other Indian tribes of North America in the science of government. Their strong confederacy—The Five Nations—played an important part in the early history of the European colonies along the northern Atlantic coast.

THE OREGON INDIANS WERE TRUE SAVAGES. The Indians of the Oregon country represented various stages of savage and barbarian culture, but it cannot be said that any of them possessed even the rude beginnings of civilization. They had neither a written language nor a settled agriculture. It can hardly be said that they tilled the soil at all. Some tribes, which migrated with the seasons, were wanderers over the face of the earth. They ate wild fruits and berries, they even subsisted upon insects. They were always poor, always hungry and miserable. They had bows and arrows, and they knew how to fish and hunt, but beyond that stage they had not progressed. Those were truly savage men.

For the most part the Oregon Indians were both savage and barbarian. When the first white men came the natives possessed only bows and arrows for weapons. They lived principally by fishing and by the chase. Nevertheless they had learned to do many things which indicate a higher stage of culture. The Haidas of Queen Charlotte Islands and Alaska understood something about architecture and did very good wood carving. Many tribes possessed domestic animals, among which were the dog and the horse. They made rude tools and utensils, among them canoes and looms for weaving. Some made pottery, stone implements, and other utensils which helped to make living easier. Finally, they had begun to carve rude pictures and primitive inscriptions upon the rocks, on canoes, and on their houses and monuments. This indicates the first emergence from barbarism.

THE WILLAMETTE VALLEY INDIANS. At one time the Willamette Valley also held a large Indian population. Lewis and Clark, who in 1806 penetrated this region to the present site of Oregon City, heard from the Indians who lived in the territory about the falls of the Willamette River, that the tribe of the Calapooias occupied forty villages. In the valley as a whole, Samuel Parker[1] in 1841 saw seventeen tribes or villages with a population of about eighty-eight hundred. By the Treaties of Dayton of 1855, all the tribes in the Willamette Valley agreed to sell their hunting grounds to the settlers and go upon reservations. Two years later, at the time of their removal, they numbered six hundred sixty-six, divided into many small bands. By the year 1880 the Calapooias at the Siletz and Grand Ronde reservations numbered only three hundred fifty-one persons; ten years later those had dwindled to one hundred sixty-four. In 1905 only one hundred thirty remained. In 1909 only five Santiams were alive, and but one hundred three Oregon Shoshones.

DISAPPEARANCE OF THE OTHER TRIBES. The Shastas and other Rogue River tribes, which totaled about two thousand at the time they were sent to the Siletz and Grande Ronde reservations, have likewise perished. The Nestuccas and the Nehalems are extinct—cut down by the ravages of war, by the white man's diseases, and by dissipation. The freedom-loving Cayuse, who knew how to fight and die, but not how to live with the white man as a master, has vanished from his grassy plains, which are today filled with populous cities. Iron trains now thunder among the hills, where, not long ago, the red man pitched his tepee in the woods.

GOVERNMENT OF THE INDIAN TRIBES. The Indian tribes of our state had numerous primitive political, social, and religious institutions. The prevailing form of government was the tribal village. It had neither mayor, aldermen, nor court. The village chief, or headman, was sometimes a hereditary ruler, and

Hop-picking and other agricultural harvests depended extensively on the labor of the Indians from the Coast, Grand Ronde, and Warm Springs reservations. Agents gave passes to individuals and families to work each year to earn income (Oregon Historical Society, Folder 560).

sometimes he was appointed or elected by his fellows. If the son of the chief were unfit to rule, he was deposed; authority was then given to one who was esteemed worthy in the eyes of the community.

Villages were organized for war, and war was a regular institution among all the tribes. The authority of the chief, local only in time of peace, was considerably increased when a village or a group of villages went to war with another tribe or with the whites.

In all his pageants, war and the trappings of war occupied the center of the Indian's interest. The chief who went on a visit to a neighboring village, or who received a passing visitor, white or red, did so in the full regalia of war, attended by all his men-at-arms. So completely did war occupy the time and attention of some tribes that even villages of the same tribe frequently assailed one another. One village warred upon another of the same tribe without violation of national unity or tribal sentiment. This was true especially among the Tututni.

THE EVIL CONSEQUENCES OF WAR. War, too, retarded the cultural progress of the Indian tribes because war is always disturbing and destructive. It is recorded by those who know that the tribal wars among the Indians of the Oregon Country were very tame affairs in which little blood was shed. It may be that the effects of such conflicts have been exaggerated in narratives composed by writers of more recent times.

WOMAN'S PLACE IN INDIAN LIFE. Woman had little or no part in the control of Indian affairs. Both before and after marriage she was a drudge, often little better than a slave. All labor in the home fell upon her, since the men were often away, hunting, fishing, or on the warpath. The women attended to the preparation of skins for clothing, made mats and other utensils, and supervised the gathering of food. When the tribe was on the march the women had the care of the camp. Often they accompanied the men to war, and instances are known in which they even took part in battle.

Among the Shoshones of eastern Oregon, Indian husbands were the absolute proprietors not only of their wives but of their daughters as well. They disposed of their women by barter or otherwise. It is said that some mothers even killed female infants to save the offspring from later miseries like those which they themselves suffered.

MARRIAGE CUSTOMS OF THE INDIANS. The Calapooias practiced wife purchase. Among them, however, women were not differently treated on that account. At that, the practice of wife purchase does not mark the Calapooias as particularly low in the scale of human progress, for some modern nations, which possess the institutions of civilization, practice wife purchase even today. Indeed it is rather common in many Asiatic countries.

A more deplorable custom which seriously affected the position of women among the Indian tribes was that observed among the Tututni of southern Oregon. This was the practice of polygyny, or the marriage of several women to one man. While this custom is in itself abhorrent to us, its worst feature was the Tututni practice of burying alive a man's wives in the grave with the deceased at the time of his death. Fortunately, however, polygyny was not practiced to any great extent even among the Indians of this region.

THE WORK OF INDIAN WOMEN. Indian art found its expression largely in the work of women. Klamath and Modoc women were noted basket weavers and their wares often found their way to the shores of the distant Pacific. On the Northwest Coast the women of some tribes made robes and blankets out of dog's hair.

The Haida Indians, of Queen Charlotte Islands, traced their descent back to two women. Those were honored as the founders of the two clans which formed the tribe, the Eagle Clan and the Raven Clan. Theoretically each clan was descended from one woman. Haida women were noted wood carvers and painters, and they were the most efficient canoe and house builders on the Northwest Coast. Their canoes, which were very large, were sometimes hollowed out of single logs of cedar. The houses were constructed of large cedar beams and planks, which in ancient times were worked out with stone axes and hatchets.

SLAVERY AMONG THE INDIANS. Slavery was thoroughly interwoven with the social system of the coast Indians, and, to a lesser extent, with that of the Indian dwellers in the Willamette Valley. Those peoples, who lived upon salmon and thus had a never-failing food supply, possessed fixed homes. The tribes in eastern Oregon and along the upper Columbia River, on the contrary, because of their nomadic habits and roving dispositions, did not own slaves. Some eastern tribes, like the Klamaths and Modocs, were not, however, averse to enriching themselves by selling slaves to the Chinooks and the other coast tribes. W. F. Tolmie, who was with the Hudson's Bay Company, observed the prevalence of slaveholding and the traffic in slaves throughout the region from south to north. There was, however, one notable exception. The Cowlitz tribes, on the north bank of the Columbia River, procured their slaves from the tribes about Puget Sound. The Klamaths and Modocs secured theirs by raiding the villages of the Pitt River Indians. Slavery existed long before the settlements of the white men were made. Alexander Ross saw a considerable traffic in slaves about the mouth of the Columbia River in 1811, and [John] Jewitt, at Nootka Sound, saw nearly fifty male and female slaves in Maquina's household at one time. The Klamath word for slave was *lugsh*, which means "to carry a load." This indicates that among those Indians slaves were used for carrying burdens and for other menial tasks. The Indians treated their slaves well because they were valuable.

THE EDUCATION OF INDIAN CHILDREN. Indian boys and girls did not go to schools such as we have today. Nevertheless their education, such as it was, was well taken care of. It was unnecessary for them to learn to read or write; the spoken language only was used. Instruction of a certain kind was necessary, and this was learned in the family, or about the camp fire, or at tribal ceremonies. Such learning consisted of tribal lore, or *folklore*, as we term it. Chiefs, prophets, soothsayers, storytellers, magicians, and medicine men transmitted the traditions and legends of the people from generation to generation by word of mouth. The Oregon Indians, like nearly all other primitive peoples, had secret rites into which the men of the tribes, and sometimes the women, too, were initiated under certain circumstances. How to hunt, to fish, to follow the deer and elk, how to make canoes and arrows, how to weave mats and baskets—those were the things which the boys and girls had to learn in those days long ago. Only by learning them were they enabled to live, to survive, amid hostile and unfavorable surroundings.

"Before" and "After" portraits of Indian students in July, 1881, at the Forest Grove Indian Industrial and Training School transformed by haircuts, "civilized" clothing, military drill and an "English only" curriculum. L. G. Davidson took the photograph (Beckham).

INDIAN RELIGIOUS AND BURIAL CEREMONIES. The religion of the Indians of prehistoric Oregon was as primitive as their mode of living and their art. To a great extent their religion was expressed in their art. The totems of the far Northwest and of Alaska, as well as the rude stone carvings of strange birds and other creatures which are found along the Columbia River, were attempts to express the Indian's hopes, fears, and beliefs.

He also expressed his beliefs in the ceremony of burial. When an Indian died his relatives spoke in whispers. The deceased was wrapped in his blanket, and his personal ornaments and valuables were laid with him in the place of interment, which was invariably a secluded spot near a river, on an elevated site, or in a tree. The Chinooks buried many of their dead in canoes. Alexander Ross saw more than a hundred such burial canoes at one burial place of the Chinook tribe.

The Calapooias buried in graves similar to those we use. This people also raised many burial mounds in the Willamette Valley. During the first few days after burial the relatives went to the grave at sunrise and at sunset to sing songs of mourning and praise. The Haidas believed in reincarnation, that is, that the spirits of the departed come back in the bodies of other people or in the bodies of animals. It was the ambition of every Chinook to acquire a guardian spirit which should accompany him everywhere and warn him of approaching danger.

Various tribes worshipped the coyote as the embodiment of wisdom and cunning. The Klamaths believed that the world was created by Kemush. The legend of the Thunder Bird may be traceable to the California condor, a gigantic vulture which may have ranged farther north in prehistoric times, but which is now nearly extinct, as it is found only seldom even in the high sierras. The Indians believed that the Thunder Bird was the messenger of the gods, of which there were many. They believed there were spirits or gods in everything—the bear, the eagle, the coyote, the sun, the moon, and the stars. They believed that every lake and every stream was haunted—some by happy or good spirits, others by unhappy or bad spirits. Those latter were often heard wailing in the night. If they caught an Indian they took his soul away. He then died unless the charmers or medicine men could get it to return.

THE INDIANS LOSE THE OREGON COUNTRY. The red man once lived undisturbed in Oregon; his villages filled every valley. Now, however, his thousands of warriors and hunters, his dark-eyed maidens and careless children are no more. Why did he lose this beautiful and generous land? Many explanations might be given. Epidemics, war, whisky, dissipation, and tuberculosis wasted his strength and his numbers. Settlers eagerly seeking his land came in ever-increasing trains. Against his will reservations enclosed him. On those he lived and died, always expressing a strong desire to return to his native land, always filled with superstitious awe at having his body buried in a foreign soil. Many who failed in a desperate attempt to regain their former freedom died from a depression of spirit. Today only a remnant remains. These are the wards of the Nation, carefully watched over, their wants provided for. Those of the new generation, born on the reservations, have become reconciled to the new plan of life. If they can do what their ancestors could not achieve, they may survive. For, after all is said, the Indian vanished because he could not learn the ways of the white man. He could not survive in competition with the dominant race.

Clark, Down, and Blue's A History of Oregon *was used in Oregon schools for more than thirty years. While interesting only as a period piece, the book is yet consulted. By the authors' own admission, their second chapter was deficient. "There is no adequate treatment of the history of the Indian tribes of the Oregon Country," they wrote. The bias and racism which resounded through their narrative, however, was theirs. They claimed that the contents of their essay were "taken largely from Bulletins of the United States Bureau of Ethnology and other official sources." The BAE bulletins did not contain these perspectives. The other "official sources" were left unidentified. Two of the five books cited, Frederick H. Balch's* Bridge of the Gods, *and Jacob C. Cooper's* The Yamhills, *were fiction.*

George Himes, curator of the Oregon Historical Society, crafted a memo of twenty pages of errors he found in the 1925 edition. The above selection, drawn from Chapter 2, is from the revised 1926 edition. In spite of the corrections, Multnomah County educators declined to adopt this text—the only teachers to take this position in Oregon.

SOURCE

Clark, Robert Carlton, Robert Horace Down, and George Verne Blue. *A History of Oregon.* Chicago, IL: Row, Peterson and Company, 1926. Chap. 2: 16–18, 21–23, 25–30, 32–36.

NOTE

1. Parker, a missionary, visited the Willamette Valley in 1835.

Five

Prospects of a New Deal

Chief Tommy Thompson (1863?–1959), his wife Flora, and her granddaughter Linda M. George posed in their formal clothing in the late 1940s at Celilo Falls. Thompson served for decades as the village chief and arbiter of fishing disputes (Oregon Historical Society 68,514)

THE FIRST THREE DECADES of the twentieth century were bleak and depressing for many Native Americans. Oregon tribes suffered accelerating loss of lands, frustration at the impossibility of overcoming the congressional prohibition against Indian litigation, serious concerns about education and health, an inexorable downward decline in population, and the passing of elders whose lives, language, and culture were grounded in traditional life ways. Although their neighbors were not overtly hostile, some treated them as the "vanishing Indian." Indians living both on and off reservations were marginalized. They lived at the fringes of American society. Few solicited their views or sought their inclusion.

Oregon Indians were romanticized in sentimental art (such as the plaster-of-Paris sculptures at the Lewis & Clark Centennial, 1905, or cameo portraits in the Vista House, 1918), Hiawatha-type poems (such as *The Legend of the Coos*, 1906), and in exotic novels (such as Frederick Homer Balch's *Bridge of the Gods*, 1890, or Jacob Calvin Cooper's *The Yamhills: An Indian Romance*, 1904, and its follow-up, *Red Pioneers: Romance of Early Indian Life in the West*, 1928). They were invited to participate in parades, pageants, and round-ups, but were expected to don inappropriate Plains-style feathered headdresses and, at times, to dance. Oregon authors—Eva Emery Dye (*The Conquest*, 1902) and Amy Jane Maguire (*The Girl Who Led Them*, 1905)—elevated Sacagawea into the guide of the Lewis and Clark Expedition. This young Shoshone woman who had never before crossed the Rocky Mountains became the suffragists' heroine guiding a military expedition through to the Pacific. They transformed Sacagawea into a symbol for their political objectives. Her statue with her index finger pointed west was funded largely by Oregon women and appeared to confirm her arrival as a woman with a usable past.

The Improved Order of Redmen, a fraternal lodge with a women's auxiliary known as the Degree of Pocahontus, promoted citizenship and preservation of the "beautiful legends and traditions of a once-vanishing race." The Order of the

Arrow, a Boy Scout honor society founded in 1915, affected Indian ceremonies replete with chiefly figures and secret rituals around a campfire. Civic organizations sometimes included Indian tableaux where non-Indians, often costumed in bizarre, feathered outfits, read or recited lines of supposed native oratory. While these organizations and events were usually respectful of Native American traditions and eloquence, the use and presumption of Indian lore were indicative of attitudes and actions that Indians, a doomed race and no longer an existential threat, might be appropriated.

The General Allotment Act of 1887 set the stage for large-scale assaults on the remaining native land base in Oregon. Illustrative of its impacts was the situation at the Siletz Reservation, the last unit of the once nearly million-acre Coast Reservation on the Oregon seaboard. Tribal members agreed in a council in 1892 to allotment. The decision led to survey and granting of 44,000 acres to tribal members, 3,000 acres as tribal land reserves, and the declaration that the remaining 178,000 acres were "surplus lands." Prized for its stands of virgin timber, the former reservation attracted the Oregon "Land Fraud Ring" and others to scramble for its assets. S. A. D. Puter, author of *Looters of the Public Domain* (1908), described the plundering of the Siletz Reservation as "an area equivalent to about 1,300 homesteads of 160 acres each, or practically 200,000 acres in round numbers, and is worth today at a conservative estimate, more than $8,000,000!"[1]

In time allotment also came to the Grand Ronde, Warm Springs, Klamath, and Umatilla reservations. The law was inherently unfair. Not all reservation land was of equal value, but the statute did not differentiate in the acreage as a function of its utility or monetary value. Some Indians got good allotments; some received poor ones. Some Indians obtained land with water and grazing prospects; others received isolated, forested parcels with no immediate opportunity for monetary return. Some gained land already improved by years of labor; others got lands absent any amenities.

Allotment unleashed the nightmare of checkerboard ownerships. The law divided reservations so that in fairly short order they had individual trust lands, fee lands (those patented to an Indian owner and subject to taxation), tribal lands, and non-Indian lands (those subjected to tax foreclosure or sold to people not members of the tribe). These complex ownerships rendered difficult all matters of securing rights-of-way for roads, erecting drift fences to manage livestock, fire protection, reforestation, and, in subsequent years, land-use planning.

Allotment created the unreal world of heirships. When an allottee died, his or her lands passed in fractional shares to surviving children, or grandchildren, or brothers and sisters, or nieces and nephews. When those individuals died, the land was again divided. By the 1930s the morass of allotment issues plagued the BIA, tribes, and individuals. It became a subject of divisiveness in the hearings on the Indian Reorganization Act (1934). Indians who retained their allotments were loathe to support a law that proposed the return of their lands to the tribe to reconstitute the former reservation. The General Allotment Act of 1887—premised on the assumption that land ownership would accelerate Indian assimilation—had become the nightmare that refused to go away.

The Indian Reorganization Act attempted to affirm tribalism and correct a host of problems for Native Americans. It was voluntary. To come under I.R.A., a tribe had to vote affirmatively to accept the law. If the vote were favorable, a tribe then could participate in the benefits and reequirements of the statute. It had to draft a written constitution and bylaws and submit its governing documents to the Interior Department for approval. This was a step a number of tribes declined to take. If it gained approval under the I.R.A., a tribe could charter corporations, borrow money from a revolving loan fund, and submit proposals for purchase of new reservation lands. I.R.A. implemented preference hiring for Native Americans by the Bureau of Indian Affairs. It also stopped religious coercion in B.I.A. schools.

Of great importance, I.R.A. stopped the allotment process and curtailed any further sale of allegedly surplus tribal lands on reservations. It extended trust over all allotments indefinitely. I.R.A., however, did not stop the nightmare of fractional heirships. The passing of each generation further and further divided ownerships of trust properties. If an allotment produced income from sale of timber, a grazing or farming lease, withdrawal of rock or gravel, or other resources, the Bureau of Indian Affairs collected the proceeds and, in theory, distributed them fractionally to all heirs. The problems were immense. The BIA slipped behind in probating Indian estates. Funds accumulated. The BIA lost track of heirs, especially those who left the reservation, enlisted in the military, or did not leave address information with agency officials or family. The trust funds debacle began with allotment and remains unresolved in the early twenty-first century.

The early twentieth century posed numerous other challenges for Oregon Indians. Although not enforced, the state's miscegenation statute remained law until 1955. Marriage between Indians and non-Indians was punishable by fines and imprisonment. Not until June 2, 1924, did President Calvin Coolidge sign the Indian Citizenship Act that, at last, extended citizenship to all Indians.[2] In spite of this law, Indians still had difficulty registering to vote or having the right to purchase beer and other alcohol. Oregon's expedient was to issue a "competency" card to Indians who, it believed, were able to drink moderately.

Of extreme frustration to tribes was their inability to gain standing in federal court to litigate about the taking of aboriginal lands without payment or with insufficient payment, or the mismanagement of reservation resources in violation of federal trust responsibility. Congress invoked sovereign immunity in 1868. In succeeding years only the Nehalem, Clatsop, and Cathlamet in Oregon were successful in securing permission to sue (in 1899). By 1918 George Bundy Wasson, a graduate of Chemawa and Carlisle schools, was actively working for several Oregon tribes to gain congressional assent to litigation. Wasson's labors were vexing. For example, five times the Cow Creek Band of Umpqua, through his efforts, got bills introduced in Congress. The fifth time their bill passed the House and the Senate, but was vetoed on April 25, 1932, by President Herbert Hoover, who stated that the United States could not afford this litigation in the midst of the Great Depression.

Indian parents also had concerns. Their children were first enrolled in reservation schools. The curriculum was entirely the dictate of the majority culture and taught in the English language. The presumption in both day schools and off-reservation boarding schools was that Indian children were destined for manual-labor jobs. Boys received training in blacksmithing, shoe repair, carpentry, tailoring, and farming. Girls were taught cooking, sewing, laundry work, gardening, and related domestic chores. The brightest catapulted from reservation or local schools to Chemawa School at Salem, Greenville School near Redding, California, Riverside School near San Bernardino, or Cushman School at Tacoma. The BIA sent other students to Haskell Institute in Lawrence, Kansas, or to Carlisle Indian School at Carlisle Barracks, Carlisle, Pennsylvania.

Parents missed their children. Sometimes they were gone for months; usually they were absent for years. The BIA also operated the "Outing System." When young people had completed studies at off-reservation boarding schools, they were compelled to enter two years of apprenticeship to a Euro-American family. This assignment was an unpaid, indentured role as a servant or laborer in a lonely, often exploitive environment. When children returned home, they were often distant or alienated from family, reservation, and tribe.

The Bureau of Indian Affairs premised the boarding school of the late nineteenth and early twentieth centuries on training a new generation of tribal leaders; the legacy proved mixed. Rather than nurturing new leaders, the schools often produced other results. The young people who endured years of isolation and acculturation at these institutions met and married like individuals. They did not return to the reservation or the tribe, but, instead, entered mainstream American culture. Others returned, but they found conditions at home and on the reservation so alien to what they had come to know that they, too, severed tribal relations.

John Collier was named Commissioner of Indian Affairs in 1933. He and his principal legal advisers—Nathan Margold and Felix Cohen—hoped to reverse the impacts of allotment, acculturation, and dependency. They initiated several actions in 1933 when they took over the Bureau of Indian Affairs. Cohen began the monumental task of compiling the *Handbook of Federal Indian Law* (1942). This massive compendium summarized preceding periods of federal Indian policy, statutory authority, and judicial decisions. Cohen's volume became an invaluable tool for tribal members, lawyers, and politicians as they tried to sort through the complex legacies of one hundred sixty years of federal actions toward Native Americans.

Collier and his staff worked closely with congressmen Burton K. Wheeler and Edgar Howard to develop the Indian Reorganization Act. This law attempted, in its draft, to capture the reforms that critics of federal Indian policy had advocated for years. The IRA, however, was the product of politics, not idealism. Some of its key provisions, such as a Indian court system envisioned by Collier, were excised from the bill. Nevertheless, the legislation moved forward and proved, in its time, pivotal. [3]

To promote the IRA, Collier and his staff set out across the country to explain the proposed law. Unfortunately, Collier's "road show" did not circulate the draft legislation. Native Americans were told of the proposed statute's intent, but they were not permitted to read it. The ambiguities it suggested but did not document were alarming to many. Aged tribal leaders, having little faith in the federal government, were dubious. Owners of allotments were alarmed at the prospect of the loss of their lands through reconstitution of tribal reservations. Some leaders began to understand that approval of governing documents by the Secretary of Interior might singularly undermine tribal authority.

While the New Deal marked a dramatic new direction in federal Indian policy, it also instituted other programs that, in the longer term, had great consequences on Indians in Oregon. Construction commenced in 1935 on Grand Coulee Dam. When this massive structure spanned the Columbia, it closed off all of its upper tributaries to anadromous fish. As initially designed, Bonneville Dam in the western Columbia Gorge also had no fish ladders. At the eleventh hour the Corps of Engineers bowed to pressure to construct ladders for fish passage on Bradford Island. These massive federal projects were portents to change that were to affect treaty rights, subsistence, and tribal economies.

The New Deal did generate some direct benefits for tribes. The Indian Civilian Conservation Corps (CCC-ID) mounted numerous reservation projects. These included tribal halls and clinics for the Confederated Tribes of Siletz, Confederated Tribes of Grand Ronde, and Confederated Tribes of Coos, Lower Umpqua and Siuslaw. On reservations east of the Cascades, native young men erected corrals and fences, eradicated noxious weeds, constructed reservoirs, built roads and trails, and strung telephone wires to improve communications.

The following selections are drawn from the early twentieth century. They reflect the efforts of Oregon Indians to try to obtain jurisdictional acts for land claims, to serve in the military, and to cope with the adjudication of treaty-protected fishing, gathering, and hunting rights across the Columbia Plateau. Most particularly, they lift up the native perspective on the Indian Reorganization Act and the challenges of trying to grasp a major shift in federal Indian policy and its ramifications for tribes and individuals.

NOTES

1. S. A. D. Puter, *Looters of the Public Domain.* Portland, OR: The Portland Printing House, Publishers, 1908, p. 469.

2 Michael T. Smith, The History of Indian Citizenship, *Great Plains Journal,* 10 (Fall, 1970):25–35.

3 Lawrence C. Kelly, The Indian Reorganization Act: The Dream and the Reality, *Pacific Historical Review,* 44(August, 1975):291–312.

The Indian New Deal: Chemawa Hearings, 1934

Conditions among Indian communities in the 1920s were deplorable. In 1928 the Meriam Report, a nationwide, fact-finding investigation funded by John D. Rockefeller, Jr., confirmed widespread poverty, unemployment, early death, emotional distress, and accelerating loss of lands by both tribes and individual Indians. The authors of the report called for reorganization of the Bureau of Indian Affairs and strengthening of the Indian Health Service. The report found the BIA boarding-school system "grossly inadequate," with conditions of overcrowding, inadequate food, harsh discipline, and poorly paid teachers.

In the 1920s John Collier had leveled repeated attacks on federal Indian policy. A social worker who found validity in Native American life ways in the Southwest, Collier in 1923 founded the American Indian Defense Association. In 1933 President Franklin D. Roosevelt named Collier, one of the sharpest critics of federal Indian policy, as Commissioner of Indian Affairs. Collier and his colleagues moved immediately to attempt to institute an Indian New Deal. The Indian Reorganization Act (1934), also known as the Wheeler-Howard Act, was the centerpiece in their program. The IRA was premised upon tribal consent—no tribe would be forced to accept the provisions of the new law.

In March 1934, more than five hundred tribal delegates converged on Chemawa Indian School for the Pacific Northwest field hearing on the Indian Reorganization Act. The speakers explained its provisions: an end to allotment, indefinite extension of the trust status of lands, a revolving loan fund, technical assistance to tribes, Indian preference hiring in the BIA, and encouragement to adopt formal constitutions and by-laws. To many of the elders and chiefs, the IRA was just another "do-good" effort aimed at the poor Indians. Younger delegates, however, expressed considerable interest in the provisions and saw the law as a new means for tribes to move into modern America.

The following newspaper articles covered the Chemawa conference. George Palmer Putnam, crusading editor and publisher of the Capital Journal *(Salem, OR.) argued vigorously on behalf of the IRA. "The new deal cannot undo the* wrongs of the past," he observed, "but it can assure justice in the future, and should be welcomed by all fair minded people."

March 6, 1934, *Capital Journal*
SELF GOVERNMENT TOPIC FOR INDIAN CONFERENCE HERE

Delegates From 75 Northwest Tribes To Meet At Chemawa Thursday and Friday for Conference With Federal Officials on Provisions of Howard-Wheeler Bill

Spokesmen from at least 75 Indian tribes in the northwest are expected here Thursday and Friday to attend a conference between U.S. Indian bureau officials and the Indian council of the northwest relative to the self government proposal now being considered by congress.

The council is composed of 150 members and is headed by Don McDowell of Blanchard, Wash., president of the northwest federation of American Indians. There are 14 districts under the jurisdiction of the council, including all northwest tribes, as far east as Montana and taking in northern California. Sessions will be held at the Salem Indian school at Chemawa.

Proposed legislation would give to Indians under federal tutelage the freedom to organize for local self government and economic enterprise and to provide training in administrative and economic affairs, according to Superintendent [W. Carson] Ryan of the Indian school. The measure would also seek to conserve and develop Indian lands and to promote a more effective administration of Indian tribes and communities. A federal court of Indian affairs would also be established.

Commissioner Collier, headed to the coast from similar conferences held in the Dakotas, is seeking to persuade the Indians that the legislation, known as the Howard-Wheeler bill, would bring about a general improvement in conditions. He is explaining that the proposed new plan, while bringing about an almost complete reversal of government policies toward Indians, the proposed change will not jeopardize the security of the Indian as a federal ward even though eventual self government is contemplated.

March 8, 1934, *Capital Journal*
INDIAN TRIBES OF NORTHWEST IN CONFERENCE

Assemble at Chemawa To Discuss New Self Government Plan

Assistant Commissioner Zimmerman Explains Proposed Program

Tribal chieftains, counselors and delegates from the major tribes of the northwest gathered at the Salem Indian school at Chemawa here today for a two-day discussion of the proposed Wheeler-Howard bill in congress looking towards self government for the Indian and to hear of its advantages from William Zimmerman, Jr., assistant Indian commissioner, who heads a group of specialists on Indian affairs from Washington, D.C. More than 500 were in attendance at the opening morning session with more expected during the day and Friday. All are being housed and fed at the school, presenting a problem for Superintendent Ryan as the school commissary and contents were destroyed by fire last Saturday.

During the past two generations, the Indians of the United States have steadily been losing their property and as the wealth of the nation increased, that of the Indian has been melting away, Commissioner Zimmerman told the delegates in presenting the fundamental conditions of the Indian as understood by the government.

"The Indian of the United States has been living under conditions that puts him at the mercy of the Indian bureau and the guardianship of the government, intended to make the Indian prosperous and free has been having the opposite effect," he said. "If this guardianship is to continue to do some of the things it has done in the past and has been doing, it had better be thrown aside. It is the purpose of the proposed bill to cure the evils that have arisen and not to abolish the guardianship but to reform it and do good instead of bad things. The guardianship should not end."

Stenographic reports are being made, with translation made at the time of the remarks by younger to older Indians, many of whom cannot understand the English language. A speaker voices a sentence. There is a murmur through the auditorium as his remarks are translated into tribal tongues, and then another sentence.

Specialists in various sections of the bill will take up the bill, detail by detail, with sectional meetings during the afternoon and evening. Conferences will be held by the leaders of the delegations and through spokesmen, Friday morning will give their comments. In the afternoon there will be a discussion of objections or criticisms to the proposed plan with a final expression to be given Friday evening. No formal vote will be taken here as the main purpose of the meeting is to obtain the reaction of the Indian to the proposed change.

The official party, in addition to Commissioner Zimmerman, includes Robert Marshall, of the forest division of the Indian bureau; Ward Sheppard, land specialist; Melvin Siegel, an attorney for the department of the interior and Walter Woehkle, special assistant to Commissioner Collier, who left the party in the Dakotas to attend a similar conference in New Mexico. Traveling with the group from the series of plains meetings is Dr. Henry Roe Cloud, a graduate of Harvard university and superintendent of the Haskell Indian school. He is a full-blooded member of the Winnebagos. The party will meet with other groups including the Navajos, Pueblos, in southern California, Phoenix, Oklahoma and in Minnesota and Wisconsin.

The meeting here is the largest gathering of Indians in modern times. A number of the older men, including a group of Yakimas, are in full Indian dress while the tall hats, bright neckpieces and moccasins are conspicuous. While a great many wear their hair in long braids, the major portion appear in business suits, many of whom are college and high school graduates.

Some ideas of the complexity of the gathering is to be conceived from the statement of Superintendent Ryan in regard to the Siletz reservation near the coast. Of some 300 Indians on the reservation there are 25 tribes. Approximately 75 tribes are represented at the meeting.

March 9, 1934, *Capital Journal* (Salem, OR.)
INDIANS TALK PRO AND CON OF NEW DEAL
Younger Tribesmen Favor Program and Older Chiefs Oppose
Favorable Sentiment Grows, 14 Main Points Change in Policy
Chiefs and other veterans of the Indian councils whose commands in earlier days were law, today appeared to be giving way to the younger braves and logical arguments of their white officers in favor of the general principle of the Wheeler-Howard bill of Indian rights, which would revolutionize the control of the First American under federal jurisdiction.

Last night the redskins threw the white man's program for entertainment to the four winds and held tribal pow wows to make their own "medicine." It was at these sessions where earlier sentiment against a change in Indian life began and many expressions of favor for the main features of the Indian bill were voiced.

The Indians today also had their inning on the floor of the convention. While yesterday the tribesmen and their women listened mostly to William Zimmerman, assistant commissioner of Indian affairs, and his staff from the national capital, both in English and then interpreted in Indian tongue, today the delegates were asked to voice their criticisms and suggestions to the proposal before congress.

Chiefs of the tribes as a rule held strongly to the negative argument, while many sons and direct descendants of former famous chieftains led the arguments for a change, which they declared would give them more voice and more activity in operations of their own affairs.

As finally outlined to the Indians at the pow wows last night, the new act, sweeping in nature and the most far-reaching measure of legislation in the history of federal control, was featured by 14 main points of change:

Stopping the rapid draining of Indian lands and other natural resources into white ownership.

Curbing the hitherto almost autocratic powers of the office of Indian affairs over the persons, property, and institutions of Indians, by substitution of a cooperative and advisory relationship.

Establishing an elementary form of self government.

Striking a double blow at dissipation of the Indian estate and progressive pauperization of the Indians and the suppression of Indian tribal and social and religious institutions.

Repeal of the allotment law of 1887 through which the Indians have lost two-thirds of their lands to the whites.

Prevent any further alienation of Indian lands outside Indian ownership.

To put allotted lands back into community ownership, even if condemnation necessary, and carefully safeguarding the vested rights of Indian allottees and heirs.

Taking over by state or local communities, the cost to be reimbursed by the federal government, many functions of health, education and other Indian services.

The Indian community may appoint a qualified Indian to any vacancy in the Indian service is such candidate is found to possess the necessary qualifications, and lowering of civil service requirements.

Program of educating Indians as administrators, judges, public health officials, foresters, grazing experts, engineers, nurses, accountants and experts in other fields.

Compulsory transfer of unsatisfactory local officials of the Indian service on charges brought by the Indian community.

Creation of a United States court of Indian affairs.

Appointment of ten special federal attorneys to assist and advise Indian communities, and

To save vast sums of public money by setting the Indians at least on the road to self-support.

March 10, 1934, *Capital Journal*

PROTECTING THE INDIANS [Editorial by George Palmer Putnam]

Indian tribal delegates from all over the northwest at Chemawa have been listening to an explanation of the proposed new deal for Indians as suggested by Commissioner Collier to prevent their continued exploitation. The sentiment of the elder chieftains, conservative as age always is, is against the change, that of the younger element favorable to it. The decision will be left to a plebescite of the Indians.

Broken faith shown by whites in treaties of the past, have made the elder tribesmen suspicious of any proposed reform, lest they be gyped again. The younger men vision a better opportunity for equality with the whites.

If the bill were adopted, tribes would be unified into communities. Indian land in scattered parts, would be joined in a combined and cooperative project. Self-government, to a much greater degree than they now have, would be given them. The preservation of tribal, social and religious institutions would be insured. Instead of being exploited, oppressed and virtually robbed of most of their possessions as in the past, they would receive official protection.

The treatment of Indians has been one of the shameful scandals of history. What has been going on is summarized in a recent issue of *Colliers Weekly*.

> There has been a steady misapplication of funds, breach of trust, confiscation of land, neglect and actual cruelty. A cool billion of the Indian's current cash has been made magically to disappear from right before his eyes, while at the same time his land holdings have shrunk miraculously from 133 millions to less than 47 million acres.
>
> Only recently the poor Navajos have had to sit idly by and see an official of the government sell to his friends for a paltry $1,000 an oil structure which those friends immediately disposed of for several millions.
>
> The Mescalera Apaches, 696 in number, have been systematically robbed. In 1930 the Indian bureau spent in merely administering the business affairs of this small tribe, the amazing sum of $306 for every man, woman and child.
>
> The Montana Blackfeet 15 years ago agreed to let the commissioner go ahead with an irrigation project. Up to date $221 per acre has been expended on it, or 55 times as much as the Indians were told it would cost. The Indian bureau, year after year, has been able to use this irrigation project as an excuse for squandering Indian money.

The new deal cannot undo the wrongs of the past but it can assure justice in the future, and should be welcomed by all fair minded people.

SOURCE

Capital Journal (Salem, OR), March 6, 8, 9, 10, 1934.

RELATED READING

Bureau of Indian Affairs. Minutes of the Northwest Indian Congress, March 8–9, 1934, Records of the Indian Organization Division, Records Concerning the Wheeler-Howard Act, 1933–37, Entry 1011, Box 3, RG 75, National Archives, Washington, D.C.

Kelly, Lawrence C. The Indian Reorganization Act: The Dream and the Reality, *Pacific Historical Review*, 44 (August, 1975):291–312.

———-. United States Indian Policies, 1900–1980, *Handbook of North American Indians, Vol. 4, History of Indian-White Relations*, pp. 66–80. Washington, DC: Smithsonian Institution, 1988.

Philip, Kenneth R. John Collier's Crusade for Indian Reform, 1920–1954. Tucson, AZ: University of Arizona Press, 1977.

Zimmerman, William. The Role of the Bureau of Indian Affairs Since 1933, *Annals of the American Academy of Political and Social Science* 102 (May, 1957):31–40.

———-. Tribal Self-Government and the Indian Reorganization Act of 1934, *Michigan Law Review* 70 (April 1972):955–86.

Voices From Siletz: Wrestling With the Future, 1934

On February 10, 1934, the leaders of the Siletz Confederated Tribes met in general session to discuss the Indian Reorganization Act. Over several preceding days, the tribal members had weighed the new law and ultimately adopted twelve stipulations before it would accept the IRA. Central to their concerns were the rights of individual allottees to retain their lands and pass them on to their heirs, not to have the property escheat at their deaths to community property. The Siletz also requested $116,250 to help establish self-government, a resident doctor and hospital building, and $150,000 to acquire property for landless members. A number of tribal members were worried that adopting the IRA would interfere with the tribe's efforts to secure a land claims jurisdictional act.

Charles E. Larson, a Chinook Indian and representative of the Bureau of Indian Affairs, opened the meeting and during its course responded to questions. A number of tribal leaders entered the discussion, repeatedly raising concern about the rights of heirs to inherit property but also expressing doubts about the challenges of self-governance. Clearly consideration of the IRA was a watershed experience where soul-searching and weighing of what steps to take were foremost in the minds of those who participated. Reorganization pushed American Indians to the edge of a new world; not all were prepared to step into it.

The following are verbatim minutes recorded on the afternoon of February 10. When the final vote came, thirty-seven endorsed the IRA and sixty-three voted against. The Siletz tribes did not organize under the provisions of the Indian Reorganization Act.

COQUELLE THOMPSON: I've noticed in these meetings, we find people who jump up and say: "We can't do that." But have you really tried? Be frank with yourself. Have you? In your own home where your minor governing problems come up, have you ever tried? That is where it begins. I discussed this idea of self-government once with Mr. Service but I didn't draw it up. You know that we will all have to have a leader eventually and you will be represented by that leader and the words you speak will go through this leader and he in turn will try to the best of his ability to grant what you ask, as your representative. You are familiar with the workings of the State government and the Federal Government and even our city government. You have a voice in it in that you vote. The same will apply here on this little self-government reservation, if we adopt it.

It will do no good at this time to go into detail about this. It is for you to understand that you will be governed by laws the same as the whites are on the outside. In time, when we are ready to be turned loose to walk for ourselves and speak for ourselves, we will be familiar with the laws on the outside and we can carry on. I know you are asking: "Will there be any such day when we will be turned loose?" We do not know but suppose there is, will we be capable of taking care of ourselves? That is the light I cast upon the subject that was assigned to me.

Mr. [Charles] Larsen: You have now heard discussions on the various subjects that have been assigned to the councilmen. There are no doubt many of you ready to get up now and give your opinions. We want your opinions on this problem now. Don't wait until you leave the hall and say: "I could have told then something." Say it now. What the Commissioner wants us to do is to look into the future; have some hope in the future. He has tried his best to make conditions so that we can live peaceably.

Arthur Bell: I think the councilmen brought up a few problems that are to be put before the people.

Mr. Larsen: If you vote in favor of this Indian self-government, you want to know that you will have something that will not be taken away from you. We have heard expressions throughout the meetings that the government has put over so many things on the Indian. We can't blame you but I am asking you to express your opinions so that when the Commissioner reads your statements, he will know just what you think about it. Before Mr. [Elmer] Logan reads his report, I think we should have an interpreter to interpret in Indian the statement as read by the secretary. (Mr. Archie Johnson is chosen as interpreter). (Mr. Logan reads report, after which the councilmen withdrew to complete their report).

Abe Logan: I am in favor of the treaty. We ought to put in a claim for our treaty. We want our money that we have been promised before this time to our grandfathers. That's my favor. I would rather be just the same as it is now and I will be very well satisfied if the treaty is settled with us just because that is a true bill and got more money in it. They will talk about giving us fifteen or twenty hundred dollars but that is just like fifteen cents to a big family. That's why I believe we got to put in this claim about the treaty. I know how my people suffered for the land where they were born and raised. I am not going to make up my mind to join this self-government. If my children are willing to join they can join. I am going to stay with my treaty money. If I ever get it, I will be glad to get it.

MR. LARSEN: I am glad to hear Mr. Logan express his opinion—just what he thinks. That is what the Commissioner wants to know, just how you feel about it. I have been presenting the one side of the question so you will got some idea of what is trying to be done. We will present the last of the report now. (Mr. Elmer Logan reads report). We have heard the report of the tribal council. It is a hard proposition to put this before you in the light it should be—it covers so much ground. The council is asking that, if the vote is favorable to go into the community program, the government allot $1500 for each homeless family and it is estimated that there are one hundred homeless families on this reservation. There are actually 88 families on this reservation at this time who are homeless.

WILLIAM METCALF: I have a good place. It is the only place I got income from. I had a chance to sell it but I didn't. I vote against this because I am not able to be under self-government. I got income coming from my land.

MR. LARSEN: How many acres of cultivated land have you?

WILLIAM METCALF: 47 acres.

ALFRED LANE: I would like to express my opinion on this self-government. In the first place, we have self-government today if we will only exercise it. At elections a person has the privilege of putting an "x" before the name of the man he wants to vote for. He has a right to vote "no" or "yes" to any amendment that is past and he has a chance to exercise his rights. We don't have to pass that right on to someone else to rule us. That is what I have to say about this self-government. Now about our schools. It is being argued on this platform that the government is trying to help us, but does it show it when they are trying to abolish one of our greatest institutions for the education of our children? I don't see how it will help the Indians when they abolish Chemawa. About this inheritance, I don't think they should abolish inheritance as it would be done in the Indian Community. I think a man feels that he would like to accumulate and build up some things that he might pass onto his children. These are the objections that I have to this program.

MR. LARSEN: The points that Mr. Lane has brought up are well taken. Now let us hear someone else.

WILBUR MARTIN: I think that the plan as it is drawn up now is no good. Let us amend it. There are things in it that are no good for me. The committee has made amendments and I am satisfied with them. Some of the old people do not look out for the young people that are homeless. The old people sold off the young people's allotment rights, therefore, they have nothing today. They sold it back to the government for eighty cents an acre. I think the young people have a right to demand a home because they have been cheated out of their allotment rights. About this self-government, the way the council has drawn it up, I do not see any harm in it. I was one that said that we should not give up Chemawa. Chemawa belongs to our Indian people. It is one of the greatest government institutions. I think our children should go to public schools and when they are fit to go to Chemawa they should go there. That is why I said: 'Make amendments for our benefit.' It is up to the old people to see that the young people got their homes.

NORMAN STRONG: There are many questions involved in this program. Before we can get the homes for these young people, it demands the right to this inheritance; it demands the right to this taxable lands; it demands everyone to accept this reservation. The government appropriates each family a home.

BENSELL ORTON: I would like to say a few words in regard to this organization. I know I am on the Federal side because I have my name in there in the Indian Office in Washington, D. C. I am going to turn back to the treaty. I am in favor of what Mr. Logan said. We have a right to call back the treaty and we want the government to settle up with the Siletz people. I am not working against the chance for the young people. Now I am in favor of this treaty. We want the money that Uncle Sam owes us. We want to be full citizens of the United States. I am glad that our young people can transact their business— they can read and write. Archie Johnson, he forgot the Indian language—he become a white man now.

MR. LARSEN: Mr. Bensell states that we are still wards of the government and that we are not citizens. Of course, you are all entitled to vote—there is no question about that.

ABE LOGAN: There is an old man here that wants to say something.

PETER COLLINS: (Through interpreter, Abe Logan). The old people are passed away when this thing come up. They call the Rogue River reservation. I am Rogue River Indian. They sent our people away. It's just the land that stands there now. You young people now talk. We notice same thing about the govern-ment.   The papers are here how they promised the Rogue River Indians. Now the young people growed up and now they talk. I went on steamers when we

come in here. When they moved the Rogue River Indians, they promised everything. Here's the bill that the government put up for the Indians. They promised horses and wagons and everything like that. The old Indians are gone now
today but the papers are in the government house. Somebody must do this
business, those that haven't got no land. I want my treaty money today. I don't
want anybody to step between me and the treaty. I don't want them to turn me
around. I want my money. The superintendent at Chemawa must know how
they will talk to the Indians. I want my money today. The government give me
the land I got and nobody will go there and cut my trees down. We got a council
down here and that's the way we want them to settle it. There are some that
haven't got no land—they sold their land already. What the government give
me I got it yet today. If I die my children will get it—my grand children. Even if
I die tomorrow, it will be the same thing. That is the way the government want
it. Somebody that hasn't got no land must write that's why everything turn up
like that. Mr. Larson, you make it right. Those that got land, let him stay on his
land. This is all I say.

ABRAHAM TOM: I would like to say something with respect to this program. We do not want to stand in the way of the younger generation in getting
rights. I think we should help the younger people out—the coming generation
and their children. We all know this and so does the government. I believe it
had been known forty years ago that this condition would come. The census
is taken every year and they know that we only have just a limited amount of
acreage to begin with and the population is increasing and we know the land is
decreasing. The young people can't do anything for themselves, it is up to the
older generation to help them. In determining the heirs of inherited land, we
know that some times it goes away from the trueblood relation. It seems like
whether the land is trust or fee-patented, we have the same trouble where there
are three or four or more interested. I missed out because of my grandmother
being the sole heir to a piece of land and when she died this land went to another lady because she had her dower right. They didn't listen to me because I
was young. So you could see the disadvantage of the younger race. We find even
in fee-patented land where there are one or more involved in a piece of land,
one would try to buy the other out and when he paid one share, he couldn't
back out, he had to go ahead, and before he knew it he paid more than the
thing was worth. I think the older people should see their responsibility to the
younger people who did not get allotments.

MR. LARSEN: Mr. Tom has touched on points of inherited interests. We
have something like 6,600 acres of inherited Indian lands being owned by 154

heirs. Some own almost three hundred acres each, some own 80 acres; some 20 and some 160.

ABE LOGAN: I want to say a few words about the treaty. I understand self-government has got nothing to do with the treaty. The treaty will stand just the way it is now, which I know the treaty stood for over seventy years and if we say nothing about it, maybe it will stand another seventy years or a hundred years. It is a true bill that ought to come to our old people. That is what we want now. If we are going to vote, we ought to vote for the treaty. I am in favor of the treaty. The younger generation when they get that treaty they will all have money if only $150 a piece. Some of them got nice farms. If they get that money they can get thoroughbred stock and they won't run out of money for the rest of their lifetime.

MR. LARSEN: This program will not effect your treaty rights. (Reads from Indian Office letter dated January 20, 1934). I think your claim was presented to Congress and was vetoed by President Hoover. It is still alive and we hope it will be presented at this session.

HOXIE SIMMONS: I want to say a few words. If I don't say anything you people might suspicion me. It looks that way right now. My heart bleeds for the old people. Everything that was promised them, they never got. The other night I stood solid for the treaty. The Indians have not had just treatment and I believe it is coming to them. Since the other day our delegate, George Wasson, came back from Washington, D. C. He had to borrow money to come back. I have got a lot of boys and girls and I am going to wait for that treaty. I feel like we ought to make a move today for the younger generation. Even if the older ones do not want to step in that community where we have $1500 homes and schools, we ought to think of the younger generation. I am an ignorant Indian but I have been a school director for twenty years. I had back bone and stood with the white men. You young Indian men ought to do the same thing. To-day you young men can be leaders if you got the education.

This program will not interfere with our treaty. We provided that in here. Maybe next year we will introduce that again. We have a good claim. The government bought our land back for eighty cents an acre. We can sue the government for that. That will amount of $300,000 or maybe more. Don't think that I deserted you people; don't take it that way. I am looking out for these young people. They can have a home if this goes through. You will have to make up your minds. You will have to decide this afternoon. (Mr. Elmer Logan reads.)

BENSELL ORTON: I would like to repeat this treaty again. Uncle Sam has to fulfill his promise and settle up with this treaty business, then we can look

Arthur Bensell (1909–88), Mack-a-no-tin Band, Siletz Tribe, gained All-American honors in 1934 as a football player, Heidelberg College, Tiffin, Ohio. A teacher, he returned to Siletz to operate the family store, serve six terms as mayor, and worked for restoration of tribal status achieved in 1977 (Beckham).

after out younger generation that have got no homes. It we give $1500 to these young people, they will go down to Toledo or Newport and buy whiskey and get drunk. I think we should put this off for a while and let them tend to this treaty business first.

AGNES ISAACSON: I still have my land and am capable of keeping it. I don't think I would want to put it into this community.

MR. LARSEN: I think the question of relinquishing the inherited land would most likely be brought up another time. With the limited time we have had to make a study of this, we have no been able to go into every detail.

HARRY JONES: I think, in justice to those who have inherited property and have thus far clung to it, that it should be included in the provisions that the government buy the property, and if the government will say "yes" to our provisions, we will say "yes" to theirs. I think that any one who contributes anything should be duly compensated and that should be included in the provisions before we accept the matter.

ROBERT SERVICE: That is if this property is sold, the money will go to the heirs.

MR. LARSEN: The government proposes in this to take all such land as they cannot use.

I want to thank you people for treating us the way you have in presenting this matter to you. We set out with the idea of conveying to you the wished of the Commissioner, although we have not had as much time as we should have had. I think the community as a whole has shown excellent ability. It is a sign of better times and better feeling amongst you. I want to give every member a chance to vote without any undue influence. We are not here to influence you one way or another. You are to render your own judgment.

COQUELLE THOMPSON: Along with this self-government is the sub-marginal land question that is very important.

MR. LARSEN: I will turn the meeting over to the chairman of this tribal council, Mr. John V. Adams, who will take charge.

JOHN ADAMS: We will vote according to our constitution and by-laws—by ballot. Wolverton Orton will be at the head of the table here and you will get your ballot from him. If you are in favor of accepting this self-government plan, you will write 'yea' on the ballot and if you are not in favor, you will write the word, 'no.' You will then take your ballot over here and put it in the basket. Norman Strong will be in charge of the ballots until turned over to the tellers. When you have deposited your ballot, Coquelle Thompson will call your name as voted and the secretary, Elmer Logan will register your name. I will appoint Alfred Lane, Mrs. Sophia Johnson and William Towner as tellers. (A recess was declared so that all could vote and after all had been given an opportunity to vote, the tellers came forward. Mrs. Johnson taking the votes from the basket and calling whether it was 'yes" or "no" and handing the ballot to Mr. Towner who verified the ballot and the count was recorded by Mr. Alfred Lane.)

The result of the vote shows that 37 voted in favor of accepting the self-government plan and 63 voted against the acceptance.

If there is no more business, we will hear a motion for adjournment.

STANLEY STRONG: I move that we adjourn.

JOHN ADAMS: Motion is made, seconded and carried that the meeting be adjourned.

(Meeting adjourned at 5:00 o'clock P.M.).

SOURCES

Bureau of Indian Affairs. Final Meeting Held at Siletz, Oregon, February 10, 1934. Records of the Indian Reorganization Division, Records Concerning the Wheeler-Howard Act, 1933–1937, Entry 1011, Part 2A, Box 2, RG 75, National Archives, Washington, D.C.

Siletz Tribal Council. Report of Siletz Tribal Council Recommendations to the General Assembly, February 10, 1934. Records of the Indian Reorganization Division, Records

Concerning the Wheeler-Howard Act, 1933–37, Entry 1011, Part 2A, Box 2, RG 75, National Archives, Washington, D.C.

RELATED READING

Kelly, Lawrence. *The Assault on Assimilation: John Collier and the Origins of Indian Policy Reform*. Albuquerque, NM: University of New Mexico Press, 1954.

———-. The Indian Reorganization Act: The Dream and the Reality, *Pacific Historical Review* 44 (August, 1975):291–312.

Youst, Lionel D., and William Seaburg. *Coquelle Thompson, Athabaskan Witness: A Cultural Biography*. Norman, OK: University of Oklahoma Press, 2002.

"We Do Not Know Where We Stand," Concerns from Warm Springs, 1934

Uncertainty gripped the members of the Confederated Tribes of Warm Springs in early 1934. The Tribal Business Council had met and wrestled for four hours with the proposals of the Indian Reorganization Act. Its members had held seven district meetings across the reservation both to explain the new law and to solicit ideas. Finally on February 10, 1934, Superintendent F. W. Boyd called to order a meeting attended by an estimated one hundred fifty Indians. John Powyowit served as interpreter. Odile Munter, agency clerk, recorded the proceedings.

Jerry Brunoe, chairman of the Tribal Business Council, opened the meeting. "We want to find out how you folks feel about it and so we will now open the meeting for discussion," he said. "This is very complicated and we cannot understand it as well as we might, but this is just a starting point. I believe we will have to take time and go over this thoroughly," Brunoe concluded.

In the following remarks, members of the Warm Springs tribes wrestled with the prospect of having to assume responsibilities of self-government. The tutelage of the Bureau of Indian Affairs and the difficulty of carrying out tribal agendas in a larger world outside the reservation—a place where experience was limited— seemed daunting.

The question about retaining ownership of individual allotments or passing all lands back into community property proved highly divisive. Some individuals and families had safeguarded their allotments and kept them in trust. Others had sold their lands and spent the proceeds; they were landless and dependent on tribal lands and income to cover what they could not earn. The IRA's proposal to reconstitute the reservation lands in tribal ownership thus appealed to some and caused consternation in others. When the vote was taken, the Business Council split: one voted in favor and six opposed accepting the provisions of the Indian Reorganization Act.

WILLIAM JACKSON: We have been told that we were to run our own reservation and everything that was run by the government now would be run by ourselves. Here for the past 50 years I have not improved, and I wonder how I am going to carry the present proposition. I feel that we are only little kids even if we are as old as we are. I know that you are running this reservation but I reserve this much that until our children, who are going to school and getting an education, let us know that they can carry on this self-government, we should not attempt to carry on this self-government. This is my theory, and it is all I have to say.

SUPERINTENDENT [F. W.] BOYD: The Indian Office does not propose to have you take over all the duties connected with the agency immediately. If you decided that you as a tribe would like to attempt the self-government plan, you would probably start with your tribal business council as you now have and assume the obligations of running the agency just as fast as you were able to handle them. The question now is whether or not you are willing to turn your lands to the tribe and handle it as community property.

CHARLEY STALAMETE: This is a puzzle to me. I do not know where the law comes from that we are to govern ourselves. Will it come to the time when all these employees would be out of here and these forestry office employees?

SUPERINTENDENT BOYD: In time I would say that all agency positions would be held by Indians.

CHARLEY STALAMETE: And if that is the case, I want to pick out my own men. There are lots of men here who can take these employees job.

DAN HOWARD: I heard you say we will have to give up our lands into the community and all us Indian race remembers that. I am waiting here for a just law as it appears in my mind; that same law that has caused me to live on this reservation. The Commissioner has proposed this out of his theory and you as Superintendent is working under him. You are to let me know everything that you know and here among us Indian tribe will put it up for argument and discussion. It may be that we will make big mistake by accepting this self-government, and it may be that the Commissioner of Indian Affairs will not think right of me for not coming to satisfactory agreement. And if we accept this self-government it may cause declaration of us being citizens. That is all I have to say.

JACKSON CULPS: You have heard some fellows getting up and stating they are in doubt of what you say about self-government. Most of the people are not desirable of what you suggest. Do you know, Mr. Boyd is making lots of money and it goes back to the Commissioner of Indian Affairs. There is lots of money that this reservation is making that is in Washington. That is why I feel this way and even if we have our schools and education, that money won't do us any good, and therefore, I advise you not to make mistake in this, as I am watching your lips move as you speak. I do not want you to cause me to be in debt. I am just starting and I am not going to turn back and be a back slider. When you stated that there will be a sale for inherited land, that hurt my feelings. That is a theory that I will not accept. I will not do it. I am telling you I will bring this up sometime. This is our reservation and it belongs to us Indians. It is just like a picture belonging to us and we do not care to give it up.

SUPERINTENDENT BOYD: You misunderstood about the sale of inherited lands—I said at your death all lands would revert back to the tribe.

LITTLE JAKE: What I heard Mr. Boyd, it is very fine what you said. The land belongs to us Indians and we surely prize it. It belongs to us and we know it. You started saying this, that we are to exist now in self-government. There are two laws that us Indians have to abide by, one belongs to the white people and one to the Indians. We are to go into self-government now and you interpret your ways and means of your laws but you have not interpreted the ways and means of our laws. When you suggest that we are to govern our own lands it might be that we can. We are to utilize our land to the best of our knowledge. We can do it and all our boys can do it. That is why I state that we shall be governed by our rulings and laws and not by yourselves.

SUPERINTENDENT BOYD: Of course, if you governed yourselves you would be subject to State and Federal laws. You should dismiss all fear of losing your lands because the present Commissioner is doing everything in his power to retain all land holdings for the Indian. It is evident that some of you, at least those who have expressed their views, do not understand the plan thoroughly. I will ask Mr. William McCorkle, a member of your tribal business council to explain further.

JAMES JOHNSON: As I have heard the interpretations brought out by that circular, I would not blame our superintendent about anything. We are to go into self-government. Referring to my people here and to this self-government, I do not think there is anyone among us who can take up and carry on this thing. We have sent our children to school but we have never seen any consequences of their education. This has been brought up so sudden that we do not know whether or not to accept as it refers to something we do not know about. We should be given a little more time to think this over so we can make our decisions. Of course, there are some words in the circular that is all well and fine, but I think we have had such a short time that we cannot speak our thoughts of how we feel now. I want to know why this is brought up at this time.

CHARLES HELLON: There is a lot of unallotted land that our children can have. We would be glad to accept it. But I would not be glad to relinquish certain portion of my holdings to the community. This land belonged to the

Indian and no other people should be brought to live here then those belonging to this reservation. Do not marry a white man or woman. I never took this into consideration before and never realized it. Nice white lady or nice white boy marries Indian boy and girl and they then lose their land. Any proposal that the Commissioner of Indian Affairs makes I will not accept it, for my part.

FRANK WINISHUT: This is too complicated to understand. Where Charley Hellon states that this allotted land is coming to existence, we Indians never asked for allotments to come to our reservation; it came to us this way: A government surveyor came to give us allotments. I heard the surveyor and my father and he asked how many children my father had and when my father told him, the surveyor said, 'I will give allotments to each one of them and that allotment shall remain in your possession until you die, and after you die your children will fall heir to all your allotment holdings.' I do not understand why the Commissioner of Indian Affairs wants to put this out of existence. It seems that it is too big a thing to be done. Also, it cannot be determined in so short a time. This is my opinion in brief in the matter. My theory about this self-government is that my race is not fit to do this big thing. We did not get enough education to compete with the white people. The white people administers their law but we cannot take up this thing and compete with them.

ELIJAH KISHWALK: I have never heretofore said anything that my people have been having and since this thing is brought up I am willing to express my opinion, and after hearing this thing about giving up our inherited lands, I have arrived at the point that I do not want to accept this thing. I know most of us Indians are residing on inherited lands, and if the white people agree that we are to give up our inherited lands, where we are residing, then I feel that we will be put off our reservation. My fellow men have brought to us the opinion that these allotments were given to us never to be given up. This land that we have, our children can have. That is why I have been thinking since I heard the interpretation of the circular, and I do not care to give it up. I do not understand this circular about self-government, but if we Indians are to make our own rules and by-laws, I do not feel that we are able to do it, and I feel that it will be some strange administration to us Indians. It is too complicated and too big a thing for us to understand and accept.

BIG FRANK QUEAHPAMA: We are talking of something that is fatal to our interests. We are in doubt of things that will effect our children in the future. I feel that our land that has been designated to us by our ancestors may go out of existence. We older Indians have allotments which is the best land on the reservation, but the land which is unallotted is not much good, although there is an area of land, quite rugged, which our Superintendent classes as submarginal land, but which would not be fit for our children.

It is true that this circular interprets where it says, the person having an allotment and where this person dies it becomes heirship land and there are three or four heirs holding interests in this land, it is better that this land be turned into the tribal community, where it would never be sold. I know of 30 or 40 allotments that have been sold and will never be redeemed until the government can do something. Upon selling their share in the deceased allottee's land, the Indian only derives just a little portion of the money and has a good time for about a year or so and then the money is all gone and the Indian is broke.

This is where my consideration arrives and where I feel that if we old Indians could consider this and go into a definite agreement and come to a conclusion to accept or not to accept it. Where it says, after you die it goes back to the community holdings and still your children will have the same amount of land. This is where my misunderstanding is. Since I do not understand this circular I cannot accept what is proposed to me.

Isaac McKinley: Regarding our council meeting, it started Saturday, and since then these older people brought out as to their existence of their race in the past. They have brought themselves by so stating by their existence to where this circular of the Commissioner's has come before us. Now, when I refuse this circular of the Commissioner's before me and look back to see just how we existed in the past, and as I realize my existence when we first existed on the reservation to this day; when this circular of the Commissioner's came before me as being explained to me, and upon deriving of the contents of this circular and find I am not able to carry out the contents of the circular proposed before me, and by being unable to handle the proposition, I say to my people, and the majority of my people say it is too big a thing to accept, and as it is in the minds of these people, when their boys and girls finish their education, maybe they can carry on and handle this thing. If we had boys and girls who could participate in the Federal offices, and the state and county offices and abide by their laws, perhaps we could ask them to take up our self-government, but we do not have them.

I know that I am unable to exist without the various rulings which applies to me as to my people. My people and I feel that we are not able to accept this self-government for a time yet. As I know, heretofore, we have been going to school and it seems just like yesterday. It may be that our children will get a better education than we have been getting and that they have this self-government in a few years. That is my reason for saying, 'Let us let it be as it is now.' It is the truth right here on this reservation to say that we are in doubt of everything.

In regards to land tenure and allotments, it may be that I am saying this land belongs to the government, in trust. I know this much, I am existing, I sleep sound—without any worry, even though my land is in trust with the government. On this inherited land, even our parents, our relatives died, leaving their allotments behind so that the children may fall heir to these allotments, I say that we should leave it as it is now. I say this, that I am better off with our present way of land tenure than by putting all our land into the community. While it says that you Indian people take all your land and put it into the community, I do not approve of this. For a few nights I have been meditating thoroughly and determining this, and I have decided to exist as we are now doing and that our land should remain as it is.

Here is another thing that we have for council matters. Here we have discussed this matter from time to time since we started this meeting. We decided that we would pass this subject of self-government on to the tribal council and let them empress themselves on it. We have been meeting all day and still nothing has been done.

JESSIE HEATH (woman): I have a few words to say. Where I feel as I hear some of the speakers present their ideas, I refer to my forefathers and what they had at one time. Where the government has promised them an education for their children and my chief has been promised by the Government a first-class schooling and amount of money in connection with the education of their children, that has never been fulfilled. Today, I stand before you because of the promises which have never been fulfilled and it is not that I have a desire for the money.

About these land holdings from the present way proposed to change to the community, I feel that I am not able to carry out that proposal either. At that time when the government made promises to my chief, he said, "We will take care of you people and educate you in order that you can go among the white people" but that has been said but never fulfilled. If the government carried out its promises to these Indians it may be that some would have been willing to carry out some of the proposals we have from the Commissioner, before us. This is why I speak this, because the government has broken its treaty and promises.

Our Superintendent has been here with us for only a short time since he has come and I go in person to him appealing that he has heard what we have revealed to him of our inability to carry out what has been proposed to us. After appealing to him, we want him to explain our appealing to the Commissioner of Indian Affairs. We will be proud of his help towards us Indians on this reservation.

JERRY BRUNOE (Representing the Wasco Tribe): I have tried to explain the meaning of this circular to the people I represent, the Wasco Tribe, and according to their opinions they felt that they should leave this up to the committee, but I told them that I would rather they express their own opinions at the general council, where some of the older men could have a chance to talk. We have looked into it and were given such a short notice that we do not know which way to turn. We feel about putting all land into the community, how are we going to come out of it. In another way, we are going to give up all our rights under the allotment system. I wonder if my provisions could be made to hold on longer.

About this self-government, it sounds good enough. Before the treaty of '55, the Indians were known to have self-government; they had land and worked their soil and made their living; then the government came along and set aside land for their use and called it a reservation. We were to live, fish and hunt, and have an education, but the government came along again and took this land away from us. We have children on this reservation who have no home to call their own, and have no one advanced far enough to handle their own affairs.

The Wascos object to this plan because they have not enough time to make their decisions. At present we do not know where we stand, and the more you explain the circular to us the less we know about it. We object because we have not had enough time to consider this.

JERRY BRUNOE: I move that we take a vote on it. (The motion was seconded and carried).

All in favor of accepting the self-government and land tenure plan please signify by raising your right hand:

Affirmative - 1	Negative - 6
Corbet Hote	Jerry Brunoe
	John Powyowit
	Frank Queahpama
	Paul Queahpama
	Sam Wewa
	Wm. McCorkle

SOURCE

Indians of the Warm Springs Reservation. Minutes of the General Council of the Indians of the Warm Springs Reservation of Oregon . . . February 10, 1934. Records of the Indian Reorganization Division, Records Concerning the Wheeler-Howard Act, 1933–1937, Entry 1011, Part 2A, Box 2, RG 75, National Archives, Washington, D.C.

RELATED READING

Baughman, Michael, and Charlotte Hadella. *Warm Springs Millenium: Voices from the Reservation.* Austin, TX: University of Texas Press, 2000.

Confederated Tribes of Warm Springs. *The People of Warm Springs.* Portland, OR: Confederated Tribes of Warm Springs, 1984,

Celilo: Fishery and Trade Depot of the Northwest, 1942

For more than ten thousand years salmon fueled the energies of human enterprise at Celilo and Five Mile Rapids. West of the mouth of the Deschutes River, the Columbia entered a setting of massive basalt flows. The river literally turned on edge, narrowing and rushing like a boiling cauldron over the ledges and through bluffs of volcanic rock. The setting slowed the passage of migrating salmon, sturgeon, and lampreys and served as a marvelous fishery for those willing to brave its dangers with nets, gaffs, spears, and wicker basketry traps. From time before memory this site drew the hungry and ambitious.

Because of its abundance of foods, the Celilo Falls region attracted an ebb and flow of human population. These included Uto-Aztecan-speakers from Northern Paiute country lying southerly in the Great Basin, Sahaptian-speakers from across the Plateau both to the east and north, and Chinookan-speakers from the west. Indeed, by the time of Euro-American contact in 1805, the Chinookans had thrust easterly from the estuary on the Columbia River to occupy both banks of the Columbia through the Gorge and east to Celilo. The falls was the site of extensive trade and exchange. War captives moved down the river as slaves to be bartered north along the coast for shells and maritime foodstuffs. Obsidian from quarries in central Oregon fanned out from Celilo for use in weapons throughout the Pacific Northwest. Fish, hides, dugout canoes, and paddles from west of the mountains, bear grass for basketry—these commodities also drew visitors to the falls and river narrows.

During the first half of the twentieth century Tommy Thompson, chief of the Wyams at Celilo, served as arbiter of disputes among the many tribes who came to exercise their rights of fishing at the falls. Thompson, a much admired and revered Indian leader, endured the assaults of operators of fishwheels, construction of railroad lines, and the blasting of The Dalles-Celilo Bypass Canal and Locks through his village. Ultimately construction of The Dalles Dam and its massive reservoir flooded Celilo Falls and the Wyams' village. The great voice of the river—roaring since the cataclysmic floods carved the Columbia's course through this region at the end of the Pleistocene ice ages—fell silent.

Following are the affidavits of Tommy Thompson (1863?-1959) and Isaac McKinley (1879–?) secured in 1942 by Edward G. Swindell, Jr., of the Bureau of Indian Affairs. Swindell toured the Pacific Northwest during the New Deal administration to gather data to buttress tribal rights. Thompson and his interpreter, Isaac McKinley, a Tenino, participated in the belated process of documenting the "usual and accustomed grounds and stations" reserved as Indian fisheries and protected by treaties with the United States. Thompson addressed the increase in the number of Indian fishermen, competition for locations, and falling off of the runs. McKinley discussed trading activities, commercial sale of fish to canneries, and use of the perpetual winds along the river to dry fish for subsistence use.

State of Oregon, County of Wasco.

TOMMY THOMPSON, being first duly sworn, upon his oath deposes and says:

That he is 79 years old, a full blooded member of the Wyam Tribe of Indians, and a citizen of the United States of America residing at Celilo, Oregon; that to the Indians, Celilo is known as Wyam and the people who lived there in the old days prior to the coming of the white people, were known as Wy-am-pum;

That he was born at Wyam and has lived there all his life; that his father and mother told him his ancestors had always lived and fished at that place; that the Chief or Headman of the Wyam Indians had always been a member of his family; as for example, his father's oldest brother was Stocket-ly who, representing the Wyam Indians at the treaty council with Governor Joel Palmer, signed the treaty on their behalf; that after Stocket-ly's death about 36 years ago, affiant became the Chief or Headman of the Indians still living at Wyam and that, as a consequence of the foregoing, and the things that were told him by his parents as well as his own personal knowledge of the situation, he is fully familiar with how the Wy-am-pum lived and fished at the falls of the Columbia River, which in Indian is known as Chee-wan'-a or "Big Water" in the white man's language.

Affiant further deposes that he first fished at Wyam when he was about 14 years old and that ever since then he has fished there each year although that was not the only place where he has caught fish; that when the water was too high at Wyam for good fishing, he would go to Tenino where water conditions would permit fishing even though fish could not be caught at Wyam at that time.

That he also fished at what is known as Skein, which in Indian means "cradle board" and which is located immediately below the railroad bridge crossing the Columbia River west of the falls; and that the name Skein was given to that place and the group of Indians who lived there because their camp grounds were shaped like the cradle board used by the Indians to carry their babies; that the Indians also called this place Wah-pykt and that they used to be able to get a good supply of drift wood on account of the currents of the river there. The Indians considered Wah-pykt their permanent home and they were about 180 or so in number;

That a long time ago he also fished above the mouth of Rock Creek, which the Indians called Tampanoe, where fishing was carried on by a different method than that used at Wyam and Skein; that at the latter two places fish were caught with spears and dip or bag nets, whereas at Tam-pance, the Indians were accustomed to catch their fish with a long net;

That his principal fishing activities, however, have always been at Wyam, and that when he and the other Indians from Wyam would visit the other Indian fishing camps along the river, they would do so primarily for the purpose of meeting the people who lived at those other fishing places since they were all friends and joined each other in participating in Indian ceremonial dances and games of skill and chance;

Affiant deposes that up until the time the Celilo Ship Canal was constructed [1908–14], the old Indian village and camping ground was located up near where the present upstream or intake end of the canal comes out of the river, and that the Indians did not move to their present location until after they were forced to move by reason of the construction of the canal; that when he was a small boy his parents as well as the other older people told him that Wyam was and always had been a permanent village and that Indians lived there all the year around;

That he was told that prior to the time he was born, there were a large number of Indians living at Wyam, probably as many as 600 or 700 individuals; that of this number about 200 were adults; that when he was a boy, there were not, however, nearly as many Indians living at Wyam because most of the inhabitants moved to the various reservations when he was a young man about 20 years old; that they did this in accordance with their treaty with the Government; that the greatest number of them went to the Warm Springs Reservation, a few went to the Yakima Reservation and probably less than 10 went to the Umatilla Reservation; that he did not want to leave his own home and this despite the fact that his relatives are reported to have selected an allotment for him at Warm Springs;

That the Wyam Indians were related to those living at Tenino, Skein, and Wah-pykt and there was a slight relationship between them and the Indians who lived at Rock Creek; that all these people were friends amongst themselves as well as with the Umatillas, Walla-Wallas, Cayuses, Wascoes and Yakimas, even before the white people first came to the Indians' country, although he understands there were times some of the smaller groups would have trouble amongst themselves but this did not last; that since he first began to remember things, it is his recollection that generally speaking all of the river Indians in the area around Wyam were good friends and the older people have told him this was true prior to the time he was born;

That in addition to being friends, some members of all of the Indians tribes he has named would visit Wyam for the purpose of trading roots, berries, and venison for dried salmon put up by the people who lived at Wyam; that if the visiting Indians did not have anything to trade for fish, the local people would either give them some of their own supply or else they would lend them the necessary equipment and permit them to catch all the fish they needed from one of the established fishing stations belonging to the local people; in other words, all the Indians were friends and shared their food and the means of obtaining same with those who were less fortunate.

Affiant further deposes that the fishing platform locations on the banks of the river and on the rocks and islands in the river by the falls, have been used by the local people from as long back as the Indians can remember; that these stations have been handed down from the older to the younger Indians of the same family from generation to generation; that the Chief of the local Indians was the one who would say who should use a place when there was no one in the family to whom it had belonged capable of making use of it and that the decision of the Chief was final and respected by all the other Indians;

That as he remembers it, when he was a boy there were only about 25 or 27 Indians actually who went out to the rocks for the purpose of catching fish, whereas today there are as many as 200 Indians fishing during the heaviest part of the summer run; that in the old days, there were not as many controversies concerning who should use a particular fishing rock as there were plenty of such places for the number of Indians who then fished; that the location of the fishing stations changed as the river would go down after the high water in the springtime; that although a number of new fishing sites have been discovered since the number of Indians fishing has increased, there are still not enough places for all those who wish to fish at Wyam; that on account of this, it is necessary to divide the use of some places among those Indians who do not have fishing rocks which have been handed down in their family from generation to generation as long back as the Indians remembered;

That the number of Indians who came to obtain fish at Wyam is quite large and that most of them come from the Umatilla, Yakima, and Warm Springs Reservations, although a very few come from the Nez Perce country and Montana; that some of those who come from the first three named places are descendants of the original owners of the local fishing stations prior to their removal to the reservations.

Affiant further deposes that when he was a boy he recalls the Indians lived in houses made of tulles for which the Indian name is Tee-koe and that the same material was used for their drying sheds; that in some of the large houses as many as five or six families would live and in other instances there would be only one family to a house; that in the old days some of the houses were partly built underground because they were easier to keep warm and that the people entered them through a small opening close to the ground, after which they descended to the floor *by* a small ladder put there for that purpose;

That the Indians nowadays and always have dried their fish in the open air in a shed which kept them from the rays of the sun, and that they did not cure their fish by smoking them over fires;

That in the old days, the Indians would dry some of the fish they caught at all times through the spring and fall runs, whereas today most of the drying for their own personal future use is done during the season when the Columbia River is closed to commercial fishing; that the reason for this is the fact that the Indians in order to survive under modern conditions, must sell the largest portion of their catch which is not eaten fresh in order to have money available for the purchase of medicines and commodities, such as coffee, sugar, flour, and like things; that each family of Indians, when he was a boy, would dry and put away for their own future use, about 30 sacks of fish, depending, of course, on the size of the family; that large families would dry more than the average or small sized families; that each sack would contain about 10 or 12 fish which weighed almost 100 pounds, since each fish after it had been cleaned, the head and tail removed, and then dried, would only weigh between 6 and 8 pounds, as he would judge their weight;

That the annual fish runs are not as large as they used to be because he feels the white commercial fishing takes most of the fish from the river before they have had a chance to come up to the Indians' fishing place; that for that reason, as well as the others previously explained, such as the increased number of

Indians fishing and the need to sell the major portion of their catch, the Indians as a whole do not obtain as much fish or revenue as they used to;

That the spring run of salmon in 1941 seemed to be quite small and not nearly as heavy as the spring runs of a few years ago; that the fall run for that year was very good and although he did not catch many fish because of personal sickness, his grandsons and other relatives were fairly successful in their fishing operations;

That during the 1941 season, he did not dry many fish and that up through the month of September the number he had thus put away for his own use was only about 27; that this was brought about by the fact that the commercial fishing season opened early and he needed the money from the fish he caught to purchase medicines and other necessities of life; that the amount he received for the fish he caught and sold during the spring run was only about $70; that due to his illness he could not fish to any large extent during the fall fun.

Affiant further deposes and says that the Indians do not fish with spears nowadays because it is harder to catch them with spears and the canneries will not buy fish that have been caught in that fashion;

That although the main article of food for the Indians in the old days was fish, both fresh and dried, they supplemented this diet with venison and roots and berries, which were obtained at places other than Wyam; that he used to hunt occasionally but ordinarily depended upon other Indians supplying him with such articles in return for fish that he caught while they were gathering the roots and berries.

Affiant further deposes and says that since the Indians were not able to record the history of their ancestors, the only way that they knew of the things that happened before they were born or their parents were born, was the custom of the older Indians of each generation to tell the younger members of the tribe about the things and events that had occurred in the past, and in that manner the history and events relating to the Indians have been handed down from generation to generation and the information set forth herein with regard to the things that happened before affiant was born was obtained in that fashion, that the information set forth herein with regard to the way the Indians lived, fished, and hunted since his birth are matters within his own personal knowledge and relate to things that he actually saw himself.

Affiant further deposes and says that the fishing rights, which were reserved to the Indians by the treaty with the United States, have a value to the Indians which cannot be measured in the terms of dollars and cents of the white man; that the subsistence value to the Indians as a whole is enormous and that were the Indians to be deprived of such rights they would be left without their principal means of support.

Further affiant sayeth not.

(Sgd.) Tommy Thompson (his mark)

Tommy Thompson

Subscribed and sworn to before me at The Dalles, Wasco County, Oregon, this 7th day of May, 1942.

(Sgd.) J. W. Elliot

Superintendent Warm Springs Indian Agency, Oregon

ISAAC McKINLEY, being first duly sworn, upon his oath deposes and says:

That he is 63 years old, a full blood member of the Tenino tribe of Indians, and a citizen of the United States of America, residing on the Warm Springs Indian Reservation, Oregon;

That he is thoroughly conversant with the English language and with the language spoken by the Indians residents of Wyam, otherwise known as Celilo, Oregon, and can translate the English language into the Wyam Indian language and the Wyam Indian language into the English language;

That on October 8, 1941, at The Dalles, Oregon, in the presence of Chief Tommy Thompson, deponent in the foregoing affidavit, and Edward G. Swindell, Jr., Associate Attorney, U. S. Indian Service, affiant did, at the request of Mr. Swindell, interrogate Chief Thompson with regard to certain matters concerning usual and accustomed fishing stations of the Indians along the Columbia River, as well as with regard to the way in which they and their ancestors obtained a living; that he translated the questions of Mr. Swindell from the English language into the Wyam Indian language, which Chief Tommy Thompson speaks and understands; that he translated from the Wyam Indian language into the English language and answers of Chief Thompson to Mr. Swindell's interrogatories; that at that time Mr. Swindell made written notes of the information given by the said Chief Thompson and reduced said information to the narrative form as given in the above and foregoing affidavit of the said Chief Tommy Thompson.

Affiant further deposes and says that on the 7th day of May, 1942, in the presence of Chief Thompson and Mr. Swindell, he translated the information contained in the aforesaid affidavit from the English language into the Wyam language, as said affidavit was read to affiant by Mr. Swindell; that the deponent, Chief Thompson, told affiant that the said narrative affidavit contained the information given by him to Mr. Swindell on October 8, 1941, and had,

Isaac McKinley, Warm Springs, served as
interpreter and important informant in
documenting the "usual and accustomed grounds
and stations" of the Indian fisheries on the
Columbia Plateau. In this 1942 photograph by
Al Monner, McKinley wore a plains-style
headdress, a beaded vest, and carried a wand of
eagle feathers (Oregon Historical Society 12,500)

therefore, signed said affidavit because the information contained therein was
true.

Further affiant sayeth not.

(Sgd.) Isaac McKinley

Isaac McKinley, Interpreter

Isaac McKinley personally appeared before me this 7th day of May, 1942, and
after having the foregoing affidavit read to him in my presence did acknowledge to me that the statements contained therein are true and that he executed
same as his voluntary act.

Subscribed and sworn to before me this 7th day of May, 1942.

(Sgd.) J. W. Elliott

Superintendent, Warm Springs
Indian Agency, Oregon
State of Oregon, County of Wasco.

ISAAC MCKINLEY, being first duly sworn, upon his oath depose and says:

That he is 63 years of age, a full blood Tenino Indian of the Tenino tribe of Indians, and a citizen of the United States of America residing on the Warm Springs Indian Reservation, Oregon;

That he was born on the Warm Springs Reservation and has an allotment there; that his mother was a Tenino Indian and his father was a Umatilla Indian from the Washington side of the Columbia River; that his father's home was a long way east of Rock Creek probably farther east than the present town of Alderdale, Washington; that both his parents took allotments on the Warm Springs Reservation when the Indians were moved there by the Government; that prior to their taking allotments, however, they had maintained a home at Wyam;

That two of his uncles, who were his mother's brothers, had always fished at Wyam on the Oregon side and Skein on the Washington side of the Columbia River, although both of them spent most of their lives living at Skein; that he first fished at Wyam in about the year 1894 after leaving school at Warm Springs; that from 1894 until 1917 he fished at Wyam at various times but not every year; that since 1917 he has fished each year at the usual and accustomed fishing stations belonging to his family;

That because of the foregoing he is personally familiar with the situation along the Columbia River and especially at Wyam; that in addition to his personal knowledge of the situation, he was told many things with regard thereto by his parents concerning same as it existed during his lifetime and as it was prior to their lifetime, such latter information being predicated on the things that had been told them by their parents.

Affiant further deposes and says that when he first visited Wyam the Indians were camped at several places along the present Celilo Ship Canal right-of-way, which was constructed about 1905; that there were three principal places in the area where the Indians lived and that although each of them had its own name, all three of them were known by the principal name of Wyam;

That when he first recalls visiting Wyam there were about 80 Indians living there; this included men, women, and children; that there were only about 10 Indian families who would visit Wyam each year for short periods; that these families consisted of Umatillas and Yakimas; that these families who visited Wyam were former residents of Wyam and that they returned each year for the purpose of visiting their relatives as well as to obtain a supply of fish;

That some members of the Indian tribes he has named would visit Wyam for the purpose of trading roots, berries, and venison for dried salmon put up by the people who lived at Wyam; that if the visiting Indians did not have anything to trade for fish, the local people would either give them some of their own supply or else they would lend them the necessary equipment and permit them to catch all the fish they needed from one of the established fishing stations belonging to the local people; that the local Indians would sometimes gather roots and berries but usually they fished at Wyam and depended upon trading for their supply of roots, berries, and other things;

That Skein and Wah-pykt were two names for the same place which was located on the Washington side of the Columbia River at a point just below the present railroad bridge which crosses the river about three quarters of a mile below Celilo Falls; that the Indians who lived at Skein and Wyam spoke the same language as did the Tenino Indians and those which are now known as the John Day Indians; that the language of these four groups was somewhat different from the language of the Wasco Indians who also used to come to the various places along the river to fish;

That when he first accompanied his uncles to fish on the Washington side of the river there were about 15 families of 90 people in all living at Skein; that aside from the Indians who live there all year around this place, as were the others along the Columbia River, was used by former residents who had removed to the reservation; that in the event these people were dead, their descendants would use their same places; that this was customary practice of the Indians along the Columbia River; that old Indian law and custom provided that the fishing stations at the various villages along the river belong to certain families and when the father died the places that belong to that family were passed along to his children; that this was customary practice and is still followed today although it is difficult to keep outside Indians from interfering with the owners of usual and accustomed places;

That his family over the years was accustomed to using two fishing places depending on the height of the water in the river; that in the spring of the year he fishes at Tenino from a station which has belonged to his family for many many years; that in the spring the water is too high to fish at his family station at Wyam but that after the spring runoff has passed by, the water is too low for good fishing at Tenino and he, therefore, for the summer and fall fishing, uses the family fishing station at Wyam located on what is known as Big Island;

That in addition to himself, his family fishing station is shared with four other Indians whose names are: Charley McKinley, Andrew David, Charley Pete and Wilford Sooksoit; that all five of them fish at this place as a partnership and that all share alike in the catch and the proceeds of that part of the catch sold to the cannery; that the two usual and accustomed places of his family are better than ordinary and that each member of the partnership made about $1,000 for the fishing season of 1941;

That, in addition to the partnership, that uses these places, other Indians who either do not have places to fish from or whose places are not as good, are permitted to use his family's places when no member of the partnership is using it; that some of the Indians to whom this privilege is extended are: Clarence Menias, William Moody, Gibson Moody, and Wilson Menias, all of whom are from the Warm Springs Reservation;

Affiant further deposes and says that, as he recalls it, each family, when he was a boy, dried about 25 sacks of fish, each of which would weigh approximately 50 pounds and that all of this quantity would be for his own use; that although this amounts to approximately 1000 or 1200 pounds per family and therefore, might seem large, the Indians in those days required much more fish than they do now because other commodities were not as readily available as they are now; that, in addition to the amount that the Indians dried for their own use, each family would dry about 400 or 500 pounds of salmon which they used for trading purposes when they needed roots, berries, and other like things;

That when he was a boy and a young man, the permanent population of Wyam would be increased by 40 or 50 Indians who would come up from the Warm Springs Reservation during the fishing season; that these were people or descendants of people who formerly fished at the place; that the same situation existed with regard to those few Indians living at Skein and Rock Creek who had moved to the Yakima Reservation;

That nowadays he would estimate that approximately 300 Indians actually fish at Wyam during the height of the fall season and that although he believes almost this many Indians fish during the spring season, they are spread out along the river at places like Tenino where the fishing is best when the water is high; that, as he recalls it, there would be only approximately 40 Indians who actually fished at Wyam when he was a boy; that there were not nearly as many fishing stations as there are today; that in those days the fishing stations then used were the "usual and accustomed places" mentioned in the treaty and that the same Indians could and did use their places year in and year out without any interference by or trouble from the other Indians; that when the people who had the right to use these places died, their right passed to their children regardless of whether they were male or female and that if they did not have any children, the local chief would decide who thereafter should be permitted to use the place in question.

Affiant further deposes and says that the Indians have always been accustomed to fish along the Columbia River and that the descendants of those Indians who moved to reservations are principally located either at Umatilla, Yakima, or Warm Springs; that he does not believe that the Nez Perce Indians ever came to Wyam for the purpose either of fishing or to trade with the residents of that place.

Affiant further deposes and says that fishing along the river in recent years has been principally good and that in 1941 it has been much better than usual; that he believes the fishing will continue to be good because the state people and others like the Federal Government are trying to protect the fish from being all killed off; that he does not believe that the Bonneville Dam has affected or will affect the fishing of the Indians at Wyam and other places above the dam;

That when he was a boy, he recalls the Indians selling quite a number of the fish they caught to the Seufert Brothers cannery for which they only received 1[cent] per pound; that nowadays most of the Indians sells the greater portion of their annual catch to the canneries in order that they can obtain money for things that they cannot acquire without having that money; that Seufert does not object to the Indians bringing fish across his land when such fish is to be used for their own subsistence but that he does object to Indians bringing fish across his land when they intended to sell same to other canneries or fish buyers;

That the Indians dry most of their fish from those caught during the fall run and during the season when fishing for commercial purposes is prohibited; that practically all of the fish caught during the closed season are either eaten fresh or dried; that although some fish caught during the spring run are dried and put away for future use, the amount is not large because the fish are then too oily and they do not dry as well as those caught later on in the year; that the oil causes them to spoil before they are fully cured in the air; that that is why the Indians prefer to obtain practically all of their supply of dried fish from the late summer and fall runs;

That in the year 1941, his wife dried about 800 pounds of fish as compared to 1,300 pounds dried during the previous year; that the smaller quantity put away this year is explained by the fact that his wife had been ill and not because they did not want to put away a larger quantity; that of their supply of dried fish, they ordinarily only kept between 400 and 500 pounds and the balance is given away to the old folks on the Warm Springs Reservation who are unable to fish for themselves and who must have this help so that they can live through the winter.

Further affiant sayeth not.

(Sgd.) Isaac McKinley
Isaac McKinley

Isaac McKinley having personally appeared before me and after having the foregoing affidavit read to him in my presence did acknowledge to me that the statements contained therein are true and that he executed same as his voluntary act.

Subscribed and sworn to before me this 7th day of May, 1942.

(Sgd.) J. W. Elliot
Superintendent, Warm Springs

Thompson vigorously opposed construction of The Dalles Dam and the federal government's decision to tear down his village and relocate the "river Indians" on the south side of Interstate 84 on a thirty-five-acre tract. Thompson and Charlie Quitalkin dictated the following letter to Mrs. Jim Wild Horse. She wrote it out in longhand and each signed the letter with their fingerprints. The letter said:

The Wyums speak:

Chief Tommy Thompson of the Wyums or mid-Columbia Indians presents their side of present controversy here at Celilo on housing and improvement on north side of highway.

We, the Wyums or permanent residents of Celilo, Or., have stated from the first meeting with Morgan Pryse, regional director, who we met with in The Dalles on July 9, 1948, that we wanted our improvements here at Celilo of water, sewerage, lights and permanent houses, but we wanted them on north side of the highway where many now reside. In the 7.4 acres set aside by congress on February 2, 1929, for the Wyums or permanent residents at Celilo, Or.

To which Morgan Pryse agreed at first meeting on July 9, 1948. After that meeting he changed his mind and insisted and still insists that we, the permanent residents on the 7.4 acres, have our permanent houses and dry sheds on south side of highway and railroad tracks. We do not want them there, as the air currents for drying fish is all wrong, which we tell Morgan Pryse.

But on north side of highway where air currents are right, fish dry good.

The women do all the cutting and drying fish, and are much opposed and most unhappy about the south side of highway as fish doesn't dry and won't keep. The women are asking for proper disposal of all fish offal to do away with the smell that is offensive to them as well as the public.

My people have repeatedly asked for help in regards to this problem and always with failure. The Wyums of mid-Columbia river Indians at Celilo have been blamed for things they have no power over. Much of this has been caused by outsiders coming in during fishing season.

I, Chief Tommy Thompson, and others of the tribe and our interpreter, Andrew Barnhart, called the United States federal attorney's office in Portland recently and talked over our troubles and he advised us not to consent to being moved until all of this ground has been surveyed or by a legal court procedure, because these my people have resided here for many years.

(Signed)

Chief Tommy Thompson.

(Signed)   (his mark).

Charlie Quitalkin.

                    (his mark).

SOURCE

Anonymous. Plans for New Celilo Falls Indians Village Attacked in Letter from Chief Thompson, *The Oregonian* (Portland, OR), May 23, 1949.

Swindell, Edward G., Jr. *Report on Source, Nature, and Extent of the Fishing, Hunting and Miscellaneous Related Rights of Certain Indian Tribes in Washington and Oregon Together with Affidavits Showing Locations of a Number of Usual and Accustomed Fishing Grounds and Stations.* Los Angeles, CA: U. S. Department of Interior, Office of Indian Affairs, Division of Forestry and Grazing, 1942.

RELATED READING

Allen, Cain. Replacing Salmon: Columbia River Indian Fishing Rights and the Geography of Fisheries Migration, *Oregon Historical Quarterly*, 104(2)(Summer 2003):196–227.

American Friends Service Committee. *Uncommon Controversy: Fishing Rights of the Muckleshoot, Puyallup, and Nisqually Indians.* Seattle, WA: University of Washington Press, 1970.

Cohen, Fay G. *Treaties on Trial: The Continuing Controversy Over Northwest Indian Fishing Rights.* Seattle, WA: University of Washington Press, 1986.

Dills, Barbara, and Paulette D'Auteuil-Robideau. *In Defense of Che Wana: Fishing Rights on the Columbia River.* Portland, OR: Columbia River Defense Project/Youth Project, 1987.

McKeown, Martha Ferguson. *Come to Our Salmon Feast.* Portland, OR: Binfords & Mort, 1959.

Ulrich, Roberta. Empty Promises, Empty Nets. *Oregon Historical Quarterly,* 100(2)(Summer 1999):134–57.

Wilkinson, Charles F. Chap. 5, "The River Was Crouded with Salmon," pp. 175–218, *Crossing the Next Meridian: Land, Water, and the Future of the West.* Washington, DC, and Covelo, CA: Island Press, 1992.

———, and Daniel Keith Conner. The Law of the Pacific Salmon Fishery: Conservation and Allocation of a Transboundary Common Property Resource. *The University of Kansas Law Review,* 32(1):17–109.

Related Video:

McCluskey, Ian, and Steve Mital. *Echo of Water Against Rocks: Remembering Celilo Falls.* Corvallis, OR: Oregon Sea Grant Communications, n.d. 13 minutes.

Usual and Accustomed Grounds and Stations, 1942

Ten Pacific Northwest treaties in the 1850s explicitly reserved rights to the tribes as a matter of federal law. The legal assumption in the treaties was that the Indians had possessed these rights from time immemorial and that, at the time they agreed to cede millions of acres of lands to the United States, they reserved the rights of fishing, hunting, gathering roots, nuts, and berries, preserving their catch, and grazing their livestock on unenclosed lands. They were to exercise these rights in common with the citizens of the United States.

Decades passed. Initially few contested or questioned the treaty rights, but with the increase in Euro-American population, founding of state fish and wildlife agencies, setting of seasons and limits on fish and game, and creation of national parks and forests, the pressure against Indian exercise of their treaty rights became more and more intense. Stockraisers enclosed meadows where Indian women dug camas, cous, and biscuit root. District rangers closed off access to huckleberry patches, arguing that in fire season they could not permit camping or open fires used by the Indians to help cure the berry harvests. The Taylor Grazing Act (1935) and other range measures seemed to spell an end to the open range and free tribal access to resources.

In 1941–42 Edward G. Swindell, Jr., of the Bureau of Indian Affairs, Division of Forestry and Grazing, visited tribes across the Plateau to seek information on their traditional, treaty-protected subsistence sites. In the following affidavits Gilbert Minthorn, George Red Hawk, and James Kash Kash of the Umatilla Reservation addressed the importance of the seasonal round in securing traditional foods and the use of commodities in trade with other tribes. The impact of dams and dislocations because of the spread of new communities echoed through these statements.

State of Oregon, County of Umatilla.

GILBERT MINTHORN, 66 years of age, and GEORGE RED HAWK, 80 years of age, each being first duly sworn and put upon oath, severally deposes and says:

That they are full blood members of the Cayuse Indian Tribe and citizens of the United States of America residing on the Umatilla Indian Reservation, Oregon; that they have spent their entire life in the country formerly owned by the Cayuse Indians before it was sold to the Government in accordance with the treaty of 1855; that they are personally familiar with the location of the usual and accustomed fishing grounds of the Cayuse Indians, as well as the location of the hunting districts and the root digging and berry gathering patches; that during the course of their lifetime they have visited these places, or practically all of them, and that as a result of the personal knowledge thus gained from actual observation and utilization of such places, they are in a position to give information with regard to the location thereof as well as how and when such places were used by the Cayuse Indians; that, in addition to the personal knowledge thus gained from actual observation, they were told when small boys and young men by their parents and the older members of the Cayuse Tribe that such places had always been used by the Indians of that tribe in obtaining their daily food throughout the year: that as a result of their age and position as leaders of their people, as well as for their personal knowledge of the situation, they were selected by the tribal council of the Umatilla Indian Reservation to give information with regard to such places in order that an appropriate record thereof could be made a part of the official Government records;

Affiants further depose and say that during the course of the summer of 1941, that in company with Gilbert Conner and David Temple, members of the staff of the Umatilla Indian Agency, they visited the various herein above referred to places for the purpose of pointing out the location thereof to said Gilbert Conner and David Temple and to advise them as to how the Indians were accustomed to using such places; that at that time the said Gilbert Conner and David Temple made a written record of the things they were told by affiants, and affiants understand that such record is now a part of the official agency records.

Affiants further depose and say that the Cayuse Indians prior to the coming of the white man, as well as thereafter until they had been permanently settled, on the Umatilla Reservation, in accordance with the provisions of the treaty with the Government, were accustomed to roam throughout vast areas of what is now the State of Oregon; that due to the fact that it was difficult for them to obtain a sufficient supply of food at any one of a few places, it was necessary each year that they visit many places throughout the country owned by them at those times when they knew that fish, game, roots, and berries were available at such places; that as a result, they had no permanent villages although they were accustomed to spend the winter at various places along the streams throughout their country where the snow was not as deep as up toward the mountains;

That in the spring of the year when the snows had melted, the people in the various villages broke up in small groups for the purpose of visiting the various food supply places; that each group followed a well-established routine going from one place to another as the conditions were right at each for either fish or game and that ultimately they would all meet in the root and berry patches for visits and entertainment prior to returning in the fall to their winter camping grounds;

That the Indians knew when the salmon would be running in the various streams at the places where they were accustomed to catching them; that they would go to those places at those times and catch sufficient fish for their immediate needs as well as for the purpose of drying some to be put away for future use; that generally speaking, it was not possible to obtain sufficient fish at any one or two places which would permit them to have a sufficient supply for the entire year;

That the Cayuse Indians were accustomed to catching their fish at the various usual and accustomed grounds by using spears or Indian fish traps consisting of weirs constructed across the streams; that when they had sufficient fish for the time being, they would remove the traps so that the fish would be permitted to go up to their spawning grounds; that in this manner there was sufficient fish each year at each of the places for the people who went there; that the salmon in the old days was much more plentiful than at the present time, and that for a number of years last past, the Indians have not been able to get as much fish for their food supply as they used to in the old days and which they would still like to obtain;

That the younger members of the tribe due to the change in the way they live, which has been brought about by reservation life, no longer fish like their ancestors did, although quite a few of them still go to Celilo for the purpose of fishing both for food and subsistence; that some Cayuse Indians had always been accustomed to visiting Celilo for the purpose of seeing their relatives and friends and either fishing for themselves or trading some of the things they had to the local people for fish which the local people at Celilo caught; that this was true even before the white man came to the country and that the trade amounted to quite a bit.

Affiants further depose and say that the Cayuse Indians were friends with the Indians of the Umatilla and Walla Walla tribes, which now reside on the reservation with them; that all three tribes have always intermingled and married amongst themselves and that the same is true with regard to the Indians that had permanent villages along the Columbia River.

Further affiants sayeth not.

(Sgd.) Gilbert Minthorn (his mark)
Gilbert Minthorn
(Sgd.) George Red Hawk (his mark)
George Red Hawk

Subscribed and sworn to before me this 8th day of May, 1942.

(Sgd.) Dan Ohlerking
Notary Public for Oregon
My commission expires Nov. 28,1943

State of Oregon, County of Umatilla.

JAMES KASH KASH, being first duly sworn, upon his oath deposes and says:

That he has spent his entire life on the Umatilla Indian Reservation, as well as traveling in the country formerly owned by the Cayuse Indians before it was sold to the Government; that he is personally familiar with the location of the usual and accustomed fishing grounds of the Cayuse Indians, as well as the location of the hunting districts and the root digging and berry gathering patches; that during the course of his lifetime he has visited most of these places and that as a result of the personal knowledge thus gained from actual observation of the way the Indians utilized such places, he feels that he is qualified to give information with regard thereto; that in addition to the personal knowledge thus gained he was told by his parents when he was a small boy, and the other members of the tribe that these places had always been used by the Cayuse Indians in their effort to obtain a livelihood each year; that he was selected by the Cayuse Indians to give information to Government representatives with regard to the way the Indians used to live prior to the establishment of the reservation and subsequent thereto;

Affiant further deposes and says that he understands there was approximately 2,000 members of the Cayuse Tribe at the time of the treaty with the United States; that the great majority of these Indians would spend the winters in camps located at about the place where the city of Walla Walla, Washington, is located; that large numbers of them also had winter camps along the Walla Walla River near the present town of Milton, Oregon; that when spring came these people would break up their winter camps for the purpose of visiting the

The fisheries along the Columbia River sustained native peoples for thousands of years. Until its flooding by The Dalles Dam in the 1950s, Celilo Falls was the tribal crossroads of the region, a site for fishing, trade, and social interaction (Oregon Department of Transportation).

various places where they knew they could obtain fish, game, roots, and berries; that when they left their winter camps, they followed the spring run of salmon as the run progressed upstream in the tributaries of the Columbia River; that the men would hunt and fish and the women would gather roots close to the hunting and fishing grounds; that as the year progressed, the Indians would have traveled further back toward the mountains and that ultimately and before returning once again to the winter camps, they would meet with the Nez Perce Indians for the purpose of trading the things that they had, such as roots and berries for buffalo robes and other things that the Nez Perce people had that could not be obtained by the Cayuse people; that this trade amounted to quite a bit.

Affiant further deposes and says that the Cayuse Indians cannot use their old fishing grounds for the reason that so many of the tributaries of the Columbia

River are no longer used by the fish because they cannot ascend to the spawning grounds because the white people have constructed dams which they cannot get over; that in other streams the waste materials from mines is such that fish life cannot be supported; that aside from that, the habits of the younger generations are changing in that they are gradually adopting the white man's way of living and obtaining a livelihood either through farming or working on the sheep and cattle ranches;

That in addition to the foregoing, affiant recalls that when he was a young man a number of Cayuse Indians would go to Celilo on the Columbia River for the purpose of fishing the big salmon runs which were available at that point; that some of the Cayuse Indians, he understands, had always been accustomed to fishing at Celilo; that they were friends of the local people who lived there all the year around and that they did not have difficulty with regard to the use of the fishing stations located at that place; that the Indians who did not fish at Celilo would go there for the purpose of trading things that they acquired during the journey throughout the summer for things that the Celilo residents had that could not be obtained in the Cayuse country; that this trading amounted to quite a bit.

Affiant further deposes and says that it was customary for the Indians not to catch the salmon in the tributaries until after they had spawned for the reason that they knew there would be no salmon in the future if they did not permit the females to lay their eggs to be hatched and available in future years; that salmon was an important part of the food supply of the Cayuse Indians in the old days as well as at the present time, although he has noticed that the younger generations do not use as much salmon as their parents and ancestors were reported to have used; that he believes that this is the result of education to the white man's way of living, and since there are so few fish now as compared to what there were when he was a boy and what he understands was available prior to his birth, it is probably a good thing.

Further affiant sayeth not.

(Sgd.)James Kash Kash
James Kash Kash

Subscribed and sworn to before me this 8th day of May, 1942.

(Sgd.) Dan Ohlerking
Notary Public for Oregon
My commission expires Nov. 28, 1943

SOURCE

Swindell, Edward G., Jr. *Report on Source, Nature, and Extent of the Fishing, Hunting and Miscellaneous Related Rights of Certain Indian Tribes in Washington and Oregon Together with Affidavits Showing Locations of a Number of Usual and Accustomed Fishing Grounds and Stations.* Los Angeles, CA: U. S. Department of Interior, Office of Indian Affairs, Division of Forestry and Grazing, 1942.

RELATED READING

Hilty, Ivy E., et al. *Nutritive Values of Native Foods of Warm Springs Indians.* Extension Circular 809. Corvallis, OR: Oregon State University, 1972.

Schlick, Mary Dodds. *Columbia River Basketry: Gift of the Ancestors, Gift of the Earth.* Seattle, WA: University of Washington Press, 1994.

Related Video:

Conford, Michael and Michele Zaccheo. *River People: Behind the Case of David Sohappy.* New York, NY: Filmakers Library, 1990. 50 minutes.

"On the Altar of My Country"

Thousands of Oregon Indians have served their country. This service commenced during the Mexican War when Peter Umpqua joined American military forces in California. It continued when Warm Springs, Nez Perce, and Umatilla scouts in the 1870s served the U.S. Army during the Modoc and Bannock wars. It increased dramatically when Oregon Indians—both men and women—served in World War I, World War II, the Korean War, Vietnam War, the Gulf War, and the Iraq War.

The commitment of a young man to his country—like that of millions of men and women who have served the United States in military duty—resounded eloquently in the lines penned by Griffin John, a member of the Confederated Tribes of Siletz. Penned during World War II while he was serving in Germany, the following statement, "I am a Soldier," was sent to his sister Aurilla Tom.

I am a mother's son.

I am the pride of a family and part of a home.

I love my life as you love yours.

I am a youth in years and experienced in life, yet I am a gambler, betting the highest stakes that man can wager . . . my life.

If I win, you win; if I lose, I have lost all.

The loss is mine, not yours, and there is a grieved mother, a saddened family, and a broken home to which I can never return.

I ask only the Godspeed and support of my nation in return for laying upon the altar of my Country my all.

For bravery and blood will you furnish bullets and bread?

Will you pawn your sheckles if I pawn myself?

SOURCE

John, Griffin. I am a Soldier, *Siletz Restoration Days*, 1st Annual, November, 1977. Siletz, OR: Confederated Tribes of Siletz, 1977.

George Bundy Wasson: Indian Rights Advocate

George Bundy Wasson (1880–1947) was of mixed Coos, Coquille, and Euro-American descent. Born on South Slough on Coos Bay, he grew up in a largely Indian community where his father, brothers, and neighbors worked as loggers. He thrived in school, and, when his elementary days were completed, attended Chemawa School at Salem. Later he and his sister, Daisy (Wasson) Codding, went east to study at Carlisle Indian School. Both returned to Coos County, where Daisy became one of the first registered nurses. George Wasson became a noted proponent of Indian rights.

In an era when the federal government had invoked sovereign immunity and stood exempt from lawsuit by Indian tribes, Wasson dared to mount a lobby to persuade Congress to pass jurisdictional acts to permit litigation. He was painfully aware that the federal government had seized the entire coast of Oregon without ratified treaty and that in other agreements had paid the tribes unconscionable sums, a few cents per acre for rich farmlands and timber. Wasson waged a decades-long battle to permit tribes to have their day in court. He took on the cases of the Cow Creek Band of Umpqua, the tribes of the Grand Ronde and Siletz reservations, the Coquille tribe, and the case of the Coos, Lower Umpqua, and Siuslaw.

His commitments ran for years. He began work in 1916 to try to obtain a jurisdictional act to permit the land claims case of the Coos, Lower Umpqua, and Siuslaw. The process took ten years; finally, in 1929, Congress authorized filing of the case. Wasson helped line up the witnesses who in 1932 gave hours of testimony. Many of the aged tribal members spoke in their native language. Frank Drew, a Coos from Florence, Oregon, translated into English for the court reporter. The case that Wasson championed for nearly twenty years ended tragically in 1935. The U.S. Claims Court ruled that the tribes could not prove "aboriginal use and occupancy." It rejected oral testimony as hearsay and would not accept the unratified treaty of 1855 defining the tribal territory as evidence of aboriginal ownership. The tribes received nothing for their 1.3 million acres taken by the federal government.

Wasson married Elizabeth Finley, a school teacher of part-Indian descent. "Bess" taught school, reared their five children, and supported her husband in his nearly continuous travels and speaking to tribal meetings. Wasson died on the eve of the beginning of the work of the Indian Claims Commission, established by Congress in 1946, and the ultimate success of the litigation of the Coquille Indian Tribe. His labors, however, had fixed a determination in tribes throughout the Pacific Northwest to press for equity in the taking of their lands.

The following biography was written by Wasson's longtime friend, Emil R. Peterson (1883–1961) of North Bend, Oregon.

"Some day, George, you get it back!"

"Get what back?"

The old Indian woman was referring to the lands along the Oregon coast. She was speaking to her little grandson as she said. "One time, George, your hy-as papas belong all this land. Some day, George, you get it back!"

And so the thought lingered in George's mind until it was nourished by reminders and finally germinated, grew and developed into the multimillion dollar case against the United States now being adjudicated in the court of claims.

Perhaps there is no better way to get the background of this story than to go along with George and glimpse a few of the things that he saw and experienced through the 60–odd years that followed.

So let us begin down on South slough, which empties its waters into Coos bay near the bar, and thence flows into the Pacific. On its banks in pioneer days there dwelt a family of ten children—five boys and five girls, with an Indian mother and a white father.

Near their own house the father had built a cabin for the old Indian grandmother—Gek-ka, the children called her. Gek-ka was a sort of historian among her people—a keeper of Indian lore and legends and tales that had come down through the generations.

Three times a week the children were permitted to call on old Gek-ka, to hear her tell and retell the tales of years gone by. It may have been on one of those visits when Gek-ka first said to her little grandson, "Some day, George, you get it back!"

George had been named after his father, with the middle name of Bundy added. After he learned to write he always signed his name, George Bundy Wasson. When he was old enough, he entered the local one-room school. In 1892, at the age of 12, he was sent to the school for Indians at Chemawa, near Salem, in the Willamette valley.

Graduates of Chemawa and Carlisle Indian schools, Daisy (Wasson) Codding (1874–1963) and George Bundy Wasson (1880–1947) were of Coquille and Coos descent. Daisy became a registered nurse in 1904; George worked from 1917 to 1947 for Oregon Indian land claims and rights (Beckham).

At Chemawa the boys and girls went to school half a day and worked half a day; and they were required to learn a trade. George's first work was to carry firewood to the different buildings for the heating stoves. It was winter and snow was on the ground. The tailor shop was always warm and cozy. Then and there George decided he would learn to be a tailor.

After school days were over and George had returned to Coos county, he opened a tailor shop in North Bend, and later in Marshfield. But the call of the open spaces beckoned him back to the woods, to bull punching and timber cruising. In later years his skill as a timber cruiser made his services much in demand in all parts of Western Oregon.

Then one day George received an official looking letter, with a government franking stamp. It stated he had been chosen for a scholarship at Carlisle, the college for Indians, way back in Pennsylvania. George was sure that someone was trying to play a joke on him. But his older brother assured him that it was no joke. And so George was off to Carlisle. His experiences there make an interesting story. But we must skip that and go on, except to say merely that he became a member of the noted 60–piece Carlisle band, joining at times with the famous [John Philip] Sousa's and other bands of world-wide fame.

Returning once more to Oregon, George's health demanded that he take to the out-of-doors. For sometime he camped out and them returned to his work as a timber cruiser.

Then one day in 1916 we see him at a gathering of Oregon coast Indians in the little town of Empire City, one-time county seat of Coos county. Those Indians were representatives of the Coos Bay, the Lower Umpqua and the

Siuslaw tribes. They had gathered for the purpose of considering ways and means of presenting their claims to Uncle Sam, for lands that had been taken from their ancestors.

Previous efforts had been made, but with little of no results except the periodic collection of retainer fees by attorneys in Washington, D.C.

At that Empire meeting in 1916 we see George Wasson as he stands up, saying: "Mr. Chairman, we have a lot of useless Indians among us. Why don't we send one of our number back to Washington to see what can be done about our claim?"

Mrs. Bob Burns, wife of Chief Bob Burns, living near Empire, springs to her feet. "Mr. Chairman," she says, "George Wasson is the most useless Indian that we have with us. I suggest that we choose him as our representative to take our claim to the Washington chief, and keep him on the job till he gets results!"

And thereupon George Bundy Wasson was started on the mission laid down for him by his old grandmother, Gek-ka, some 30–odd years before.

It was a tremendous job. But George was "raring" to go. He was in the prime of life—36 years old, physically fit by natural inheritance and outdoor activities, possessor of a better-than-average education; and above all he was fired by the inspiration springing from the memory of those words of his old grandmother: "Some day, George, you get it back!"

So George went to Washington. In the years that followed he made many trips across the continent to the national capital. A report of his intricate activities there would fill volumes. Let us sum up in a few brief lines: Evidence to substantiate the claim had to be obtained—evidence in the form of old documents, reports, journals, records, letters—papers that had lain buried and fading with age in dusty archives.

But before any of this evidence could be presented to the court of claims it had to be reviewed and passed upon by committees and by a reluctant congress, and then approved by the president.

For years the fight went on. One obstacle after another had to be overcome—unsympathetic officials in the department of Indian affairs, congressional committees and congress itself; then a presidential veto.

But through all his ups and downs, George found the senators and congressman from Oregon sympathetic and helpful.

Through all those years George had to get jobs on the side in order that he might eat, dress, have a place to sleep, and to be supplied with the right brand of cigars to make it easier to get by the doorkeeper and outer clerks to committee rooms.

And right here it is only fair to say that in later years, back in Oregon, George's wife, Bess, with five children, helped to keep the home fires burning by teaching in the public schools and by nursing in hospitals during school vacations.

But finally, in the court of claims, the case was lost due to lack of adequate proof of original Indian title. That adverse decision eliminated Coos Bay, the Lower Umpqua and the Siuslaw tribes from claims that came later.

So George Bundy Wasson returned to his old stamping grounds of Oregon, where he resumed his work as timber cruiser, for he loved the outdoor freedom, which also proved beneficial to his health.

This gave him an opportunity to think and reflect. He had learned much— how to find his way about the capital city; how to dig up and submit documentary evidence, the kind of proof that was lacking in the case of the defeated tribes.

So when he was approached by representatives of another group of Oregon coast tribes, those not included in the previous claim, he found his fighting spirit renewed once more. Competent attorneys were obtained to handle the case. It was this case that was successfully waged through congress in 1935, passed by the president, then through the court of claims, and finally, in 1946, received a favorable decision in the supreme court of the United States, and is now being adjudicated as to the amount due the Indian.[1]

In reviewing the story forming the background of this claim, we find that many of us are unfamiliar with an important but a most interesting chapter in the history of our Oregon coast. So let us take a glimpse at just a few bits of the volumes of evidence that George and his attorneys found to substantiate their claim.

Bearing upon the final decision, two vitally important points are outstanding:

First, that original Indian title must be reasonably proved and established to the satisfaction of the court.

Second, that the act of congress in 1848, establishing the territorial government of Oregon guaranteed the protection of person and property pertaining to the Indians of that territory.

As regards the original title the attorneys found most helpful a report that had been made by a noted ethnologist, Dr. John P. Harrington of the Smithsonian institution. Dr. Harrington had said in part: "My study of the Indians of the Oregon coast and their holdings convinced me beyond any shadow of doubt that these bands which fringed the coast were the ancient and original inhabitants . . . ."

Regarding the second point: when congress admitted Oregon as a territory in 1848, their act included the clause:

"That nothing in this act contained shall be construed to impair the rights of person or property now pertaining to the Indians in said territory, so long as such rights shall remain unextinguished by treaty between the United States and such Indians . . . ."

So let us keep these two points in mind—the original Indian title and the guarantee in the territorial government of Oregon that the rights of the Indians would be protected by the United States.

At the time of the creation of the territorial government of Oregon and in the years immediately following, the gold rush was on in full force in California, and was soon spilling over into Southern Oregon. Scottsburg was settled on the Umpqua river in 1850; Port Orford in 1851; Coos Bay in 1853. Gold was the principal incentive that goaded men onward. In such a rush there were bound to be some unscrupulous men.

Conflicts soon arose with the natives. Soldiers were sent in to quell the uprisings. U.S. agents came to negotiate treaties.

In the autumn of 1855 General Joel Palmer met with delegations of Oregon coast Indians at different places. Agreements were reached whereby the Indians were to cede all their lands of the Oregon coast, extending back to the crest of the coast range of mountains containing about five million acres of land.

The Indians were to receive a stipulated amount of money, payments to extend over a number of years; also a tract of land was to be set aside as a reservation for these and other Indians.

The agreement thus reached between General Palmer and the Indians was sent to Washington. It was lost or held up in the department of Indian affairs, but finally reached President Pierce, who promptly signed it and sent it to the senate for ratification. On February 18, 1857, upon motion of Mr. [William K.] Sebastian, the senate ". . . referred the treaty to the committee on Indian affairs, and ordered that it be printed in confidence for the use of the senate."

It appears that the treaty was kept very much in confidence, for it was filed away, pigeon-holed and forgotten. It never was ratified.

And so the Indian lived and suffered and died while new generations were being born. And out of the marriage of Gek-ka's daughter to George Wasson, a pioneer gold miner, lumberman, post master and justice of the peace, came the family of ten children mentioned in the beginning of this story. One of those children you will recall, was George Jr., known later as George Bundy Wasson, who, when he was a little boy, heard from the lips of his old grandmother, "One time, George, your hy-as papas belong all this land. Some day, George, you get it back!"

That was 60–odd years ago. Now compensation for the land is in sight but George Bundy Wasson won't see it. He dropped dead while working on the case, cruising in the field with other men for information to be submitted to the court of claims in the final adjudication.

SOURCE

Peterson, Emil R. George Bundy Wasson: He Spent His Life Seeking Justice, *The Oregonian* (Portland, OR), November 30, 1947.

RELATED READING

Beckham, Stephen Dow. *The Indians of Western Oregon: This Land Was Theirs.* Coos Bay, OR: Arago Books, 1974.

Hall, Roberta L. *The Coquille Indians: Yesterday, Today, and Tomorrow.* Lake Oswego, OR: Smith, Smith and Smith Publishing Company, 1984.

O'Callaghan, Jerry A. Extinguishing Indian Titles on the Oregon Coast. *Oregon Historical Quarterly* 52(3): 139–44.

NOTES

1. This case, known as *Alsea Band of Tillamooks v. United States*, was resolved in 1951 in a award of $3.1 million to the descendants of the selected tribes of Oregon's northwest coast.

Six

The Disastrous Policy of Termination

The condition of the hospital and doctor's residence, Government Hill, Siletz Agency, Oregon, June, 1974, confirmed the impact of two decades of termination that ended tribal recognition and government assistance in 1956 (Beckham).

THE AMBITIOUS EFFORTS of the New Deal to try to craft a new Indian policy gave way by the mid-1940s to changed thinking. Some viewed the programs envisioned and established by John Collier and Congress as too expensive. They scoffed at efforts to affirm tribalism. They were dubious about encouraging Native American arts, languages, and religions. They embraced the concept of Israel Zangwill's "melting pot," an America where all embraced common identity and purpose. Critics of the New Deal charged that it had engaged in too much social engineering and that its efforts to encourage pluralism should be stopped.

Some, especially owners of large tracts of property or holders of leases on the public domain, were fearful that a more sophisticated generation of Indians would seek restoration of lands taken by fraud and wars of aggression waged in violation of the assurances of the "utmost good faith" clause of the Northwest Ordinance, a guarantee embedded in most organic acts creating new territories across the American West. They were aware of the mounting efforts of pan-Indian organizations, tribes, and pro-Indian advocates to protect treaty rights and secure jurisdictional acts to permit tribes to go to court.

The route toward Termination began with passage of the Indian Claims Commission Act (1946). Congress waived the nation's sovereign immunity for five years to permit tribes, bands, and even families having standing to sue the United States for a variety of causes. Congress imposed some important conditions on those taking advantage of the opportunity to sue: (1) litigants could gain no land, only money; (2) those who sued had to prove exclusive aboriginal use and occupancy of the land; (3) there would be no interest on the award; (4) attorney fees were set at ten percent of the judgment; (5) the decision of the Claims Commission would be final; the matter could not be relitigated; and (6) litigants could tap an expert witness loan fund to hire professional assistance; if they won, the fee for the witness would be deducted from their award; if they lost, the litigant did not have to repay the witness loan.

In spite of these several constraints, most Oregon tribes filed complaints. They had endured too many years of frustration in efforts to try to secure jurisdictional acts, only to fail to get to court. By 1946 the situation had also changed: the Claims Commission was willing to accept oral testimony and un-ratified treaties as evidence of tribal ownership. The National Archives, estab-lished in 1934, had accessioned hundreds of thousands of letters, treaties, coun-cil minutes, and other materials that increased the ability of tribes to document their presence and use of the lands for which they sought claims awards. A new breed of witness—the ethnohistorian—emerged to meld anthropological information with historical documentation to craft reports for consideration by the Claims Commission.

When Congress abolished the Commission in 1978, it had processed 285 cas-es and awarded approximately $800 million to litigants. Its unfinished work was transferred to the U.S. Claims Court.

The Indian Claims Commission was a belated effort of the United States to salve the national conscience by offering modest monetary awards to Indians. Having settled this unfinished business, Congress was then ready to take the Interior Department out of the Indian business altogether. The arguments for Termination were driven by the increasing political power of the Republican Party in Congress. The party's philosophy stressed economy and efficiency in government; it advocated reducing taxes and bureaucracy. Some Republicans were ready to declare that the Bureau of Indian Affairs had served its purpose and no longer had a mission. All Congress needed to do was to set up a program to provide for a few months of job training, deed trust properties to heirs, and facilitate the disposal of tribal properties. In a short period the federal govern-ment could close reservations, agencies, boarding schools, and hospitals, and escape from the administration of Indian probate, heirships, and realty. Criminal jurisdiction would be turned over to the states, relieving the Justice Department from concerning itself with Indian matters.

The sentiments for Termination were shaped as well by suspicions that Indians living on reservations had not fully bought into American life. Some perceived them as coddled and cared for by a government that was too gener-ous. That government, they believed, was under dire threat from the specter of Communism. Indians needed to learn the basics of capitalism: working for a living, managing their own affairs, and coping like other Americans. When Secretary of State John Foster Dulles advocated liberating the peoples of Eastern Europe from behind the Iron Curtain, Senator Arthur Watkins of Utah cham-pioned a parallel policy of terminating Indian tribes. Watkins said: "Secluded reservation life is a deterrent to the Indian, keeping him apart in ways far beyond the purely geographic. Following in the footsteps of the Emancipation Proclamation of ninety-four years ago, I see the following words embellished in letters of fire above the heads of the Indians–THESE PEOPLE SHALL BE FREE!"[1] As chair of the Senate Subcommittee on Indian Affairs, Watkins was positioned to drive his agenda.

On August 1, 1953, Congress adopted House Concurrent Resolution No. 108. The resolution called for the creation of a final tribal roll, distribution of tribal assets to those on the roll, an end of trust responsibility for individual and tribal land, and a severing of federal relations. This measure was the predicate to a number of Termination acts in the 1950s. The shift toward Termination commenced in the Truman administration and took off when, in 1952, Dwight Eisenhower became president.

Oregon tribes were vulnerable targets for Termination. Part of their predicament was that Douglas O. McKay, former governor of the state, was Secretary of Interior. McKay wanted Oregon to be a showcase for the new federal Indian policies of the Eisenhower administration. The western Oregon tribes, it was true, had achieved a high degree of acculturation, but their levels of income, education, and general health remained low. They survived by working hard and engaging in subsistence activities: hunting, gathering crabs and clams, fishing, picking berries, and growing a garden. They lived modestly and, sometimes, desperately. Many men worked seasonally as loggers or in sawmills. Families labored in agricultural harvests in the western Oregon valleys. Often their homes were one- or two-room shacks; some lived in floathouses on logs on estuaries where they did not have to pay taxes on land. A number resided on non-taxed allotments.

The Indians of the Klamath Reservation were especially a target for Termination. The Klamath tribes had recently received a favorable judgment of $2.6 million in their long-pending land claims case. Senator Watkins offered his assistance to get that award funded by Congress, provided the Klamath agreed, in principle, to accept Termination. The inducement to the tribal members was per capita distribution of the judgment fund and the potential sale of the timber-rich reservation, a holding of hundreds of thousands of acres of fine stands of virgin timber in a region where most privately owned forests had been logged out by 1950. The Klamath General Council conditionally accepted termination in order to get Watkins's support for their claims award. Historian Patrick Haynal has remarked: "This coerced endorsement was the only official position taken by the Klamath tribes in favor of termination. The tribes were never allowed to vote on the final draft of the Klamath Termination Act as written by Congress."[2]

As part of the Termination process, Congress in 1953 passed Public Law 280. In several states, including Oregon, this law transferred criminal and civil jurisdiction on Indian lands to the states. The exception in Oregon was the Warm Springs Reservation. The law was an overt attack on Indian rights and sovereignty. On July 1, 1955, Congress authorized the Public Health Service to take over delivery of health care to Native Americans, removing the responsibility from the Bureau of Indian Affairs. This change suggested that the BIA had not fulfilled its trust mandate for medical services.

The following selections open with the Western Oregon Termination Act of 1954, effective in 1956. For twenty years after its passage neither the Bureau of Indian Affairs nor Congress showed any interest in the fate of the terminated tribes. By the late 1960s, however, terminated Indians were stirring. They formed non-profit organizations that filed grant applications to secure Comprehensive Employment Training Act (CETA) funds to operate job-training programs. Native American parents pressured local school districts to apply for Indian Education Act funds to develop curriculum and train teachers about Native American culture and history. Their leaders became part of a regional network working with the Small Tribes Organization of Western Washington (STOWW) and the Affiliated Tribes of Northwest Indians to pass resolutions and to lobby Congress about the situation of terminated and non-federally recognized tribes.

Several of the terminated tribes sought to publicize their situation. They collected contributions to send delegates to the annual meetings of the National Congress of the American Indian to lift up their situation. The Confederated Tribes of Siletz worked with film-maker Harry Dawson, Jr., to produce the documentary *The People Are Dancing Again*. Members of the Klamath Tribes formed the Organization of the Forgotten American to lobby for tribal restoration and educational programs. Terminated tribes on the south coast worked through the Willow River Benevolent Association to gain grant monies and operate a food bank. The State of Oregon opened the door for tribal representation—without regard to federal status—when it created the Oregon Commission on Indian Services. Native American Program, Oregon Legal Services (NAPOLS) provided advice and helped open political doors for the tribes.

The challenge to turn the direction set by Congress in the 1950s seemed almost insurmountable. The people persisted. They met, passed coffee cans at meetings to collect coins to pay for postage, and solicited assistance from a variety of organizations. They went to the Native American Rights Fund (founded in 1970), National Indian Lutheran Board, Jesuit Ministries, and the American Friends Service Committee, among other organizations. They forged relationships with county historical societies and initiated educational programs for the U.S. Forest Service and Bureau of Land Management about their cultural properties and history. They grasped the value of developing community awareness and support. They learned the intricacies of politics and the necessity of working with congressional staffers and attorneys on the east side of the continent.

In time, the hard work and determination of the terminated tribes of Oregon paid off. The "restoration" of federal relationships included the following:

Confederated Tribes of Siletz Indians of Oregon, November 18, 1977

Cow Creek Band of Umpqua Tribe of Indians, January 25, 1982

Confederated Tribes of the Grand Ronde Community of Oregon, January 3, 1983

Confederated Tribes of Coos, Lower Umpqua, and Siuslaw Indians, October 17, 1984

Klamath Tribe, August 27, 1986

Coquille Tribe of Indians, June 28, 1989

The following selections speak to Termination, its impacts, and the efforts of the tribes and individuals to change the course of federal Indian policy.

NOTES

1. Peter Iverson, 'We Are Still Here' American Indians in the Twentieth Century (Wheeling, IL: Harlan Davidson, Inc., 1998), p. 129.

2. Patrick Haynal, Termination and Tribal Survival: The Klamath Tribes of Oregon. Oregon Historical Quarterly, 101(3)(Fall, 2000), pp. 278–79.

Termination: Quick Route to Oblivion, 1954

"It is our belief that the Indians subject to the proposed bill no longer require special assistance from the Federal Government," wrote Orme Lewis, Assistant Secretary of the Interior, "and that they have sufficient skill and ability to manage their own affairs." Thus unfolded the rationale in 1954 to terminate federal relationships with every tribe and band in western Oregon and, ultimately, with the tribes of the Klamath Reservation in south-central Oregon.

Termination proponents did not examine the larger consequences of the program. The law called for sale of all tribal lands and fee patenting (issuing a deed) to individual trust lands. Multiple heirs to allotments would have to work out agreements on paying taxes; when they did not, counties would foreclose and take the land within four years. No longer were these Indians eligible for treatment from the Indian Health Service, yet many had no other means to secure adequate medical care. No longer were the younger Indians to receive BIA educational assistance or admittance to government schools. When "terminated" Oregon Indians continued to participate in regional and national Indian meetings, they fell to second-class status; their concerns and needs no longer accorded with those belonging to tribes recognized by the federal government. Termination became the quick road to oblivion.

Termination was driven by Senator Arthur V. Watkins (Republican, Utah) and Congressman E. Y. Berry (Republican, South Dakota). Both were notorious for their anxiety about the prospects of Indian tribes asserting claims to lands. Both wanted the federal government to get out of the "Indian business." Both were present and Watkins chaired the hearings on February 16, 1954, over S. 2746 and H.R. 7317. Douglas O. McKay, former governor of Oregon and by 1954 Secretary of Interior, strongly supported Termination. McKay wrote on August 21, 1951: "The termination of Federal supervision over the Oregon coast Indians is in line with the established policy of our State, and we will support this program."

No western Oregon Indians had the opportunity to testify on the proposed legislation. Watkins and Berry, instead, heard from three BIA officials: H. Rex Lee, F. Morgan Pryse, and Lewis Sigler. Each assured the Congress that Termination was desirable. Arthur Lazarus, Jr., counsel for the Association on American Indian Affairs, Inc., however, filed a statement challenging the legislation on several grounds. He perceived a violation of rights of hunting and fishing. He found the tribes awaiting land claims payments that would enable them to provide for community enterprises and protect their lands—if the funds were appropriated. The objections of Lazarus were entered into the record and ignored. The Western Oregon Termination Act passed as P.L. 588 on August 13, 1954. It went into effect on August 13, 1956.

To provide for the termination of Federal supervision over the property of certain tribes and bands of Indians located in western Oregon and the individual members thereof, and for other purposes.

Be it enacted by the Senate and House of Representatives of the United States of American in Congress assembled, That the purpose of this Act is to provide for the termination of Federal supervision over the trust and restricted property of certain tribes and bands of Indians located in western Oregon and the individual members thereof, for the disposition of federally owned property acquired or withdrawn for the administration of the affairs of such Indians, and for a termination of Federal services furnished such Indians because of their status as Indians.

Sec. 2 For the purposes of this Act:

(a) "Tribe" means any of the tribes, bands, groups, or communities of Indians located west of the Cascade Mountains in Oregon, including the following: Confederated Tribes of the Grand Ronde Community, Confederated Tribes of the Siletz Indians, Alsea, Applegate Creek, Calapooya, Chaftan, Chempho, Chetco, Chetlessington, Chinook, Clackamas, Clatskanie, Clatsop, Clowwewalla, Coos, Cow Creek, Euchees, Galic Creek, Grave, Joshua, Karok, Kathlamet, Kusotony, Kwatami or Sixes, Lakmiut, Long Tom Creek, Lower Coquille, Lower Umpqua, Maddy, Mackanotin, Mary's River, Multnomah, Munsel Creek, Naltunnetunne, Nehalem, Nestucca, Northern Molalla, Port Orford, Pudding River, Rogue River, Salmon River, Santiam, Scoton, Shasta, Shasta Costa, Siletz, Siuslaw, Skiloot, Southern Molalla, Takelma, Tillamook, Tolowa, Tualatin, Tututui, Upper Coquille, Upper Umpqua, Willamette, Tumwater, Yamhill, Yaquina, and Yoncalla;

(b) "Secretary" means the Secretary of the Interior.

(c) "Lands" means real property, interest therein, or improvements thereon, and includes water rights.

(d) "Tribal property" means any real or personal property, including water rights, or any interest in real or personal property, that belongs to the tribe and either is held by the United States in trust for the tribe or is subject to a restriction against alienation imposed by the United States.

Sec. 3. Within ninety days after the date of this Act, the Secretary shall publish in the Federal Register (1) a list of those tribes for which membership rolls will be required for the purposes of this Act, and (2) a list of those tribes for which no membership rolls will be required for the purposes of this Act. Each tribe on each list shall have a period of six months from the date of publication of the notice in which to prepare and submit to the Secretary a proposed roll of the members of the tribe living on the date of this Act, which shall be published in the Federal Register. In the absence of applicable law, or eligibility requirements in an approved constitution, bylaws, or membership ordinance, eligibility for enrollment shill be determined under such rules and regulations as the Secretary may prescribe. No person shall be enrolled on more than one tribal roll prepared pursuant to this Act. If a tribe on list one falls to submit such roll within the time specified in this section, the Secretary shall prepare a proposed roll for the tribe, which shall be published in the Federal Register. Any person claiming membership rights in the tribe or an interest in its assets, or a representative of the Secretary on behalf of any such person, may, within ninety days from the date of publication of the proposed roll, file an appeal with the Secretary contesting the inclusion or omission of the name of any person on or from such roll. The Secretary shall review such appeals and his decisions thereon shall be final and conclusive. After disposition of all such appeals the roll of the tribe shall be published in the Federal Register and such roll shall be final for the purposes of this Act.

Sec. 4. Upon publication in the Federal Register of the final roll as provided in section 3 of this Act, the rights or beneficial interests in tribal property of each person whose name appears on the roll shall constitute personal property which may be inherited or bequeathed, but shall not otherwise be subject to alienation or encumbrance before the transfer of title to such tribal property as provided in section 5 of this Act without the approval of the Secretary. Any contract made in violation of this section shall be null and void.

Sec. 5. (a) Upon request of a tribe, the Secretary is authorized within two years from the date of this Act to transfer to a corporation or other legal entity organized by the tribe in a form satisfactory to the Secretary title to all or any part

COME TO DENVER
THE CHANCE OF YOUR LIFETIME !

Good Jobs
Retail Trade
Manufacturing
Government-Federal,State, Local
Wholesale Trade
Construction of Buildings,Etc.

Happy Homes
Beautiful Houses
Many Churches
Exciting Community Life.
Over Half of Homes Owned by Residents
Convenient Stores-Shopping Centers

Training
Vocational Training
Auto Mech., Beauty Shop ,Drafting,
Nursing,Office Work,Watchmaking
Adult Education
Evening High School, Arts and Crafts
Job Improvement, Home- making

Beautiful Colorado
"Tallest" State, 48 Mt. Peaks Over 14,000 Ft.
350 Days Sunshine , Mild Winters
Zoos, Museums , Mountain Parks, Drives
Picnic Areas,Lakes, Amusement Parks
Big Game Hunting,Trout Fishing ,Camping

In the early 1950s the Bureau of Indian Affairs promoted "termination" through travel and job training in a six-month program to transform Indians into mainstream American. The BIA offered programs in Colorado, Minnesota, and California (National Archives, 75-N-REL-G-37).

of the tribal property, real and personal, or to transfer to one or more trustees designated by the tribe and approved by the Secretary, title to all or any part of such property to be held in trust for management or liquidation purposes under such terms and conditions as may be specified by the tribe and approved by the Secretary, or to sell all or any part of such property and make a pro rata distribution of the proceeds of sale among the members of the tribe after deducting, in Ills discretion, reasonable costs of sale and distribution.

(b) Title to any tribal property that is not transferred in accordance with the provisions of subsection (a) of this section shall be transferred by the Secretary to one or more trustees designated by him for the liquidation and distribution of assets among the members of the tribe under such terms and conditions as the Secretary may prescribe: *Provided,* That the trust agreement shall provide for the termination of the trust not more than three years from the date of such transfer unless the term of the trust is extended by order of a judge of a court of record designated in the trust agreement: *Provided further,* That the trust agreement shall provide that at any time before the sale of tribal property by the trustees the tribe may notify the trustees that it elects to retain such property and to transfer title thereto to a corporation, other legal entity, or trustee in accordance with the provisions of subsection (a) of this section, and that the trustees shall transfer title to such property in accordance with the notice from the tribe if it is approved by the Secretary.

(c) The Secretary shall not approve any form of organization pursuant to subsection (a) of this section that provides for the transfer of stock or an undivided share in corporate assets as compensation for the services of agents or attorneys unless such transfer is based upon an appraisal of tribal assets that is satisfactory to the Secretary.

(d) When approving or disapproving the selection of trustees in accordance with the provisions of subsection (a) of this section, and when designating trustees pursuant to subsection (b) of this section, the Secretary shall give due regard to the laws of the State of Oregon that relate to the selection of trustees.

Sec. 6. (a) The Secretary is authorized and directed to transfer within two years after the date of this Act to each member of each tribe unrestricted control of funds or other personal property held in trust for such member by the United States.

(b) All restrictions on the sale or encumbrance of trust or restricted land owned by members of the tribes (including allottees, purchasers, heirs, and devisees, either adult or minor) are hereby removed two years after the date of this Act and the patents or deeds under which titles are then held shall pass the titles in fee simple, subject to any valid encumbrance. The titles to all interests in trust or restricted land acquired by members of the tribes by devise or inheritance two years or more after the date of this Act shall vest in such members in fee simple, subject to any valid encumbrance.

(c) Prior to the time provided in subsection (d) of this section for the removal of restrictions on land owned by more than one member of a tribe, the Secretary may—

(1) upon request of any of the owners, partition the land and issue to each owner a patent or deed for his individual share that shall become unrestricted two years from the date of this Act;

(2) upon request of any of the owners and a finding by the Secretary that partition of all or any part of the land is not practicable, cause all or any part of the land to be sold at not less than the appraised value thereof and distribute the proceeds of sale to the owners: *Provided,* That any one or more of the owners may elect before a sale to purchase the other interests in the land at not less than the appraised value thereof, and the purchaser shall receive an unrestricted patent or deed to the land; and

(3) if the whereabouts of none of the owners can be ascertained, cause such lands to be sold and deposit the proceeds of sale in the Treasury of the United States for safekeeping.

Sec. 7. (a) The Act of June 25, 1910 (36 Stat. 855), the Act of February 14, 1913 (37 Stat. 678), and other Acts amendatory thereto shall not apply to the probate of the trust and restricted property of the members of the tribes who die six months, or more after the date of this Act.

(b) The laws of the several States, Territories, possessions, and the District of Columbia with respect to the probate of wills, the determination of heirs, and the administration of decedents' estates shall apply to the individual property of members of the tribes who die six months or more after the date of this Act.

Sec. 8. The Secretary is authorized, in his discretion, to transfer to any tribe or any member or group of members thereof any federally owned property acquired, withdrawn, or used for the administration of the affairs of the tribes subject to this Act which he deems necessary for Indian use, or to transfer to a public or nonprofit body any such property which he deems necessary for public use and from which members of the tribes will derive benefits.

Sec. 9. No property distributed under the provisions of this Act shall at the time of distribution be subject to Federal or State income tax. Following any distribution of property made under the provisions of this Act, such property and any income derived therefrom by the individual, corporation, or other legal entity shall be subject to the same taxes, State and Federal, as in the case of non-Indians: *Provided,* That for the purpose of capital gains or losses the base value of the property shall be the value of the property when distributed to the individual, corporation, or other legal entity.

Sec. 10. Prior to the transfer of title to, or the removal of restrictions from, property in accordance with the provisions of this Act, the Secretary shall protect the rights of members of the tribes who are minors, non compos mentis, or in the opinion of the Secretary in need of assistance in conducting their affairs by causing the appointment of guardians for such members in courts of competent jurisdiction, or by such other means as he may deem adequate.

Sec. 11. Pending the completion of the property dispositions provided for in this Act, the funds now on deposit, or hereafter deposited in the Treasury of the United States to the credit of a tribe shall be available for advance to the tribe, or for expenditure, for such purposes as may be designated by the governing body of the tribe and approved by the Secretary.

Sec. 12. The Secretary shall have authority to execute such patents, deeds, assignments, releases, certificates, contracts, and other instruments as may be necessary or appropriate to carry out the provisions of this Act, or to establish a marketable and recordable title to any property disposed of pursuant to this Act.

Sec. 13. (a) Upon removal of Federal restrictions on the property of each tribe and individual members thereof, the Secretary shall publish in the Federal Register a proclamation declaring that the Federal trust relationship to the affairs of the tribe and its members has terminated. Thereafter individual members of the tribe shall not be entitled to any of the services performed by the United States for Indians because of their status as Indians, all statutes of the United States which affect Indians because of their status as Indians, excluding statutes that specifically refer to the tribe and its members, shall no longer be applicable to the members of the tribe, and the laws of the several States shall apply to the tribe and its members in the same manner as they apply to other citizens or persons within their jurisdiction.

(b) Nothing in this Act shall affect the status of the members of a tribe as citizens of the United States.

(c) Prior to the issuance of a reclamation in accordance with the provisions of this section, the Secretary is authorized to undertake, within the limits of available appropriations, a special program of education and training designed to help the members of the tribe to earn a livelihood, to conduct their own affairs, and to assume their responsibilities as citizens without special services because of their status as Indians. Such programs may include language training, orientation in non-Indian community customs and living standards, vocational training and related subjects, transportation to the place of training or instruction, and subsistence during the course of training or instruction. For the purposes of such program the Secretary is authorized to enter into contracts or agreements with any Federal, State, or local governmental agency, corporation, association, or person. Nothing in this section shall preclude any Federal agency from undertaking any other program for the education and training of Indians with funds appropriated to it.

Sec. 14. (a) Effective on the date of the proclamation provided for in section 13 of this Act, the corporate charter of the Confederated Tribes of the Grand Ronde Community, Oregon, issued pursuant to the Act of June 18, 1934 (48 Stat. 984), as amended, and ratified by the Community on August 22, 1936, is hereby revoked.

(b) Effective on the date of the proclamation provided for in section 13 of this Act, all powers of the Secretary or other officer of the United States to take, review, or approve any action under the constitution and bylaws of the tribe are hereby terminated. Any powers conferred upon the tribe by such constitution which are inconsistent with the provisions of the Act are hereby terminated. Such termination shall not affect the power of the tribe to take any action under its constitution and bylaws that is consistent with this Act without the participation of the Secretary or other officer of the United States.

Sec. 15. The Secretary is authorized to set off against any indebtedness payable to the tribe or to the United States by an individual member of the tribe, or payable to the United States by the tribe, any funds payable to such individual or tribe under this Act and to deposit the amount set off to the credit of the tribe or the United States as the case may be.

Sec. 16. Nothing in this Act shall affect any claim heretofore filed against the United States by any tribe.

Sec. 17. Nothing in this Act shall abrogate any valid lease, permit, license, right-of-way, lien, or other contract heretofore approved. Whenever any such instrument places in or reserves to the Secretary any powers, duties, or other functions with respect to the property subject thereto, the Secretary may transfer such functions, in whole or in part, to any Federal agency with the consent of such agency.

Sec. 18. The Secretary is authorized to issue rules and regulations necessary to effectuate the purposes of this Act and may in his discretion provide for tribal referenda on matters pertaining to management or disposition of tribal assets.

Sec. 19. All Acts or parts of Acts inconsistent with this Act are hereby repealed insofar as they affect a tribe or its members. The Act of June 18, 1934 (48 Stat. 948), as amended by the Act of June 15, 1935 (49 Stat. 378), shall not apply to a tribe and its members after the date of the proclamation provided for in section 13 of this Act.

Sec. 20. If any provision of this Act, or the application thereof to any person or circumstances is held invalid, the remainder of the Act and the application of such provision to other persons or circumstances shall not be affected thereby.

Approved August 13, 1954.

SOURCE

U.S. Congress. *Termination of Federal Supervision Over Certain Tribes of Indians, Joint Hearings Before the Subcommittee of the Committees on Interior and Insular Affairs, 83 Cong., 2 Sess., on S. 2743 and H.R. 7317, Part 3, Western Oregon,* February 17. Washington, DC: Government Printing Office, 1954.

RELATED READING

Philp, Kenneth R. *Termination Revisited: American Indians on the Trail to Self-Determination, 1933–1953.* Lincoln, NE: University of Nebraska Press, 1999.

Lifting the Prohibition on Inter-Racial Marriage, 1955

Although hundreds of Euro-Americans in the fur trade and period of pioneer set-
tlement married Native Americans, unions recorded in parish registers and county
courthouses, the residents of Oregon had second thoughts about these relations.
On October 16, 1862, the legislature passed "An Act to Regulate Marriages." The
measure imposed a fine of not more than $500 and up to one year in prison for
those "who shall join persons in marriage contrary to the provisions of this act."
On October 24, 1866, in its enumeration of "Crimes Against Public Policy," the
legislature passed the following statute:

> *Hereafter it shall not be lawful within this state for any white person, male or female,*
> *to intermarry with any negro, Chinese, or any person having one-fourth or more*
> *negro, Chinese, or kanaka blood, or any person having more than one-half Indian*
> *blood; and all such marriages, or attempted marriages, shall be absolutely null and*
> *void.*

The law took effect on January 18, 1867. It provided that anyone who knowingly
intermarried, attempted to intermarry, issued a license for such a marriage, or
performed a marriage ceremony in violation of the law would face three months
to one year in jail.

Although largely ignored, the prohibition on intermarriage remained Oregon
law until 1955. On the eve of termination of federal supervision of Indian tribes,
the Oregon legislature finally addressed the discriminatory legislation on mar-
riages. The recision of the law was approved on May 24, 1955.

Chapter 694. AN ACT Relating to and Validating Certain Marriages.

Be It Enacted by the People of the State of Oregon:

Section 1. Any marriage in all other respects legal and regular but heretofore
void by reason of Oregon Laws of 1866, Section 1, page 10 (Section 23–1010
O.C.L.A.) prohibiting marriage between a white person and one having Negro,

Chinese, Kanaka or Indian blood; hereby is declared valid; and any child conceived or born of such marriage shall be deemed legitimate.

SOURCES

Hill, William Lair. *The Codes and General Laws of Oregon*, Vol. 1, pp. 967–68, San Francisco, CA: Bancroft-Whitney Company, 1877.

Newbry, Earl T. *Oregon Laws Enacted and Joint Resolutions Concurrent Resolutions and Memorials Adopted by the Forty-eighth Regular Session of the Legislative Assembly* . . . . Salem, OR: State Printing Office, 1955, p. 909.

No Rights of Sovereignty Were Surrendered, 1956

Repeatedly Oregon tribes have fought to maintain rights of self-governance and to work within the bounds of laws handed down by Congress. The messages they have received from Washington, D.C. have often been contradictory. With the calamity of Termination in 1956, a sense of desperation gripped Howard Barrett, Sr., chair of the Confederated Tribes of Coos, Lower Umpqua, and Siuslaw. The United States had affirmed aboriginal land title in the Organic Act of 1848; the Senate had not ratified his tribe's treaty of 1855; the United States had appropriated his tribal lands without warfare; the Claims Court had ruled in 1935 that the plaintiff tribes possessed "no right, title or claim whatsover to any part of the coast of Oregon."

Barrett weighed the prospects. Few options proved viable. Finally he filed a petition with the United Nations, a desperate action by a small tribal confederation seeking peaceful redress of grievance and membership under the organization's charter. Barrett's petition summarized pivotal events in Oregon Indian history and confirmed a legacy of antipathy by the Bureau of Indian Affairs. In writing of events at Termination, Barrett noted: "For decade upon decade, a swarm of calloused bureaucrats has fattened upon the life blood of these tribes." Barrett's petition, like that of other tribes to the United Nations or to the International Court of Justice, was ignored. While tribes are treated as "domestic, dependent nations" in the United States, they have not succeeded in securing affirmations of their sovereignty outside the country that holds them in wardship.

The Siuslaw, Lower Umpqua and Coos Bay Indian Tribes acting through Mr. Howard Barrett, their president and chairman of their committee, do herewith petition the United Nations for the exercise of its good offices in their behalf looking toward the peaceful redress of their grievance and their consideration for membership in the United Nations pursuant to the provisions of the preamble and charter of the United Nations.

The petitioning Indian tribes respectfully represent and show unto the United Nations that from time immemorial and countless centuries prior to the coming of the white man to the North American continent, the tribes were sovereign people having their own forms of self-government and having well defined and recognized territorial boundary lines within which they lived in peace with their neighbors. Their territory extended some seventy-five miles along the Pacific Coast near the central part of what is known an the State of Oregon, being bounded on the north by Ten Mile Creek, south of the City of Yachats, and on the south by a line extending westerly from the Crest of the Coast Range of mountains to the Pacific Ocean and including the South Coos River. The territory was bounded an the west by the Pacific Ocean and on the east by the Crest of the Coast Range of mountains, an approximate distance of forty miles. Within the territory there extended vast natural resources consisting, among other things, of great stands of virgin timber, minerals, berries, abundant fish and game and numerous rivers and harbors. Here the tribes dwelt in peace and simplicity, free of the burdens of war, unbearable taxation and the social and economic disease later visited upon them against their will by the so-called civilized white man in the name of progress and of Christianity. So did they exist for countless centuries, probably predating the birth of Christ.

Their sovereign rights to self-government and territorial integrity were recognized by the United States Government by the treaty of August 11, 1855, also known as the Treaty of Empire, which was negotiated with the tribes, despite the protest of tribal chiefs, by General Joel Palmer. Article I of that treaty provided for the cession of the Indian territory to the United States of America. Article IX provided for the consent of the Indians to be governed by the laws of the United States of America. Article XIII provided that the treaty should become obligatory upon its ratification by the President and Senate of the United States. This treaty was never and has not to this day been so 'ratified' and hence never became law. By reason thereof, no rights of sovereignty were surrendered and no conveyance of the Indian's land ever took place. Their sovereign rights, however, were further recognized by the Act of June 5, 1850, (9 Stats. 437). This was an act entitled "An act authorizing the Negotiation of Treaties with Indian Tribes in the Territory of Oregon, for extinguishment of their claim to lands lying west of the Cascade Mountains and for other purposes." Section 1 of this act authorized the President to appoint commissioners to negotiate treaties with the various tribes for the extinguishment of their claims to land west of the Cascade Mountains, and the President was also directed to obtain assent and submission to certain laws of the United States. It was pursuant to the provisions of this act that General Joel Palmer negotiated the Treaty of August 11, 1855.

Art. I, Sec. 10 of the United States Constitution prohibits the making of treaties by states and any such power was also made negative by the Act of August 14, 1848, (9 Stat. 323) which created the Territory of Oregon. Section 1 of that act provided that nothing therein contained "shall be construed to impair the rights of person or property now pertaining to the Indians in said territory, so long as such rights shall remain unextinguished by treaty between the United States and such Indians, or that affects the authority of the Government of the United States to make regulations respecting such Indians, their lands, property, or other rights, by treaty, law, or otherwise, which it would have been competent to the government to make if this act had never been passed." It follows, therefore, that by both the provision of the United States Constitution and the foregoing act, no rights of sovereignty over the Indians or their territory could have been acquired by Oregon.

Without awaiting any ratification of the Treaty of August 11, 1855, the administrative officers of the United States Government threw the lands of the Indians open to settlement by the whites and for a hundred years has been freely giving the Indians' lands and possessions away, under the pretenses that it has had some lawful right to do so, that its laws have extra-territorial effect, and that it has by the mere passing of legislation acquired sovereignty over the Indians and their territory.

Concerning the illegality of this land grab, the United States Attorney General on June 5, 1855, (7 Op. Atty. Gen. 293, 299) stated, "There is one other idea suggested by the Commissioner of Indian Affairs—that any white settler may rightfully take possession of any of the lands occupied by the Indians and oust them prior to the extinguishment of their occupancy-title by the United States. This idea is too absurd to admit of reasoned reply. Suffice it to say that a white settler has the same right thus to oust the Indians as he has to oust a white man, and no more; that is, the right to substitute robbery for purchase, and violence for law."

Pursuant to an unauthorized executive order of the President of the United States, a reservation was carved out of the land belonging to the Indians and armed forces were used to compel the Indians to remove to that reservation. This use of armed force proved to be somewhat abortive, since many Indians refused to remain there. At no time, despite the provocations of the white man, did these tribes ever resort to force in repelling their unlawful invasion. They were a peace loving people and they lived accordingly.

The treaty negotiated by General Joel Palmer was not only negotiated with these three tribes, but also with numerous neighboring tribes, including the

Tillamooks, Coquille, Too-Too-To-Neys and Chetcos, who will be hereinafter mentioned with respect to the Alcea Case. All these tribes were parties to the same unratified Treaty of 1855. Among the other duties of treaty negotiation imposed upon General Palmer was the duty to investigate and ascertain the several Indian tribes and to determine the areas and boundaries of the lands occupied by them. This he did with care and thoroughness, accumulating and submitting detailed data of the geographical location and names of the tribes, including the boundaries of their territories.

As inducement to the Indians to negotiate a treaty, many promises of benefits were contained therein, among which were approximately one hundred twenty thousand dollars in money, some of which was to be used for building, opening and fencing farms, breaking land, providing teams, stock, agricultural instruments, seeds, clothing, payment of mechanics and farmers and for arms and ammunition. In addition, the United States agreed to erect two sawmills, two flouring mills, four school houses, and two blacksmith shops, to one of which was to be attached a tin shop; also to provide for two sawyers, two millers, one superintendent of farming operations, three farmers, one physician, four school teachers and two blacksmiths, a dwelling house and the necessary outbuildings for each; and to purchase and keep in repair, for the time specified for furnishing employees, all necessary mill fixtures, mechanical tools, medicines, book, stationery for schools and furniture for employees. These promises were never kept for Article XIII provided "This treaty shall be obligatory on the contracting parties as soon as the same shall be ratified by the President and Senate of the United States." Throughout the years, the tribes continually protested the nonratification of the treaty, which eventually became buried in the dusty files of Washington. A member of the tribes spent some fourteen years searching for the treaty before it was finally exhumed from its forgotten resting place.

The unlawful seizure of the tribal lands without compensation and in total disregard of the promises made the Indians was climaxed by the Act of March 3, 1871, 16 Stat. 566, R. S. Sec. 2079, 25 F. C. A. Sec. 71., which provided "No Indian nation or tribe within the territory of the United States shall be acknowledged or recognized as an independent nation, tribe or power with whom the United States may contract by treaty; but no obligation of any treaty lawfully made and ratified with any such Indian nation or tribe prior to March 3, 1871, shall be hereby invalidated or impaired." Thus was the seal of approval set upon the unchristian, unlawful and larcenous treatment of these Indian tribes at the hand of the white man.

At no time have the Indians of these tribes ever bound themselves by law to the cession of their property to the government of that United States or consented to be governed by the laws thereof and they maintain that the laws of the United States with respect to them have no more effect than such laws would have over Canada, Africa or the British Isles and that no court of the United States has or ever has had lawful jurisdiction to pronounce a judgment upon them or with respect to their ancient tribal territory. Despite this fact, the United States Government has sought by its own legislative acts to appoint and anoint itself through its Indian agencies as Guardian and Trustee of these peoples. As a result of this pretended care, the so-called Guardian and Trustee has religiously despoiled, destroyed and given away the assets of its helpless wards, exploiting and destroying the forests, the fish and the game and befouling the streams with the white man's unprocessed raw sewage.

The members of these tribes, together with the voice of truth, have been wrongfully bound in chains and left penniless and prostrate in the dust. Every effort, throughout these many decades, to secure some measure of Justice, honesty and fair dealing by the government has gone for naught. Every interested bureau of the so-called Guardian has fought remedial legislation tooth and nail. While the government today claims these Indians to be citizens of the United States, it has deprived them of the fruits of citizenship, in that it has held them to be legal incompetents and has deprived them of the benefits or legal representation by lawyers of their own choosing. If the government is or ever has been the Guardian and Trustee, or either, of these Indians, it may well be asked why It has never accounted for its stewardship of these Indians and their property. Such an accounting has never been had and will never voluntarily be had nor have the tribes ever been compensated for the wrongful taking of their property without just compensation and without due process of law.

With the Act of Congress of February 13, 1929, 39 Stat. 149, the Siuslaw, Lower Umpqua and Coos Bay Tribes were authorized to sue the United States Government and did so. The maps, data and other materials in the hands and under the control of the government, pertaining to their claims, was not available to them at this time. Their attorney [Daniel B. Henderson] died during the course of the trial. They were obliged to rely chiefly upon oral testimony and they lost their suit, 85 Ct. Cl. 143 (1938).

By the Act of Congress August 26, 1935, 49 Stat. 801, the neighboring tribes were authorized to sue and did so, *Alcea Band of Tillamooks, et al. vs. United States of America*, 103 Ct. Cl., 494. In both cases, the parties were parties signatory to the same unratified treaty and the same facts were involved. However, new documentary and oral evidence was then available and offered, as a result of which these other tribes prevailed. In the Lower Court, they were awarded the value of their lands as of 1855, plus reasonable interest, less any offsets which may have been advanced to them. Upon appeal to the Supreme Court, they were denied the recovery of interest for the reason that the Enabling Act made no provision therefor, and the court held that it was not shown that there had been a taking without just compensation under the Fifth Amendment of the Constitution. As a result, those tribes recovered an approximate three million dollars but lost a hundred years of interest, which would have amounted to many times the sum recovered. A valuable review of the history of this entire matter is contained In the Court of Claims decision in the Alcea Case, supra and should be carefully considered, since it is thought by many to be the first recognition of Indian title by reason of exclusive possession from time immemorial.

The age of these tribes and their territorial location was carefully investigated by Dr. John P. Harrington of the Smithsonian Institute, an eminent ethnologist of a quarter of a century of service in the Bureau of American Ethnology, and led him to testify that he had been convicted, beyond any shadow of a doubt, that these tribes and bands of Indians, which fringed the Coast, were the ancient and original inhabitants and that if an investigation had been made centuries before the expedition of Lewis and Clark, the tribal holdings would have been to all intents and purposes where they were at the dawn of history. . . .

Public Law No. 726, 79th Congress, Ch. 959–2d Session created an Indian Claims Commission, before which claims of various Indian tribes and nations were to be filed within a five year period and thereafter adjudicated. With great difficulty, the tribes succeeded in persuading their former attorney [John Mullen], who was registered and approved by the Bureau of Indian Affairs, to file a claim before the Commission immediately preceding the deadline for such filing. Thereafter a hearing was hold in Seattle without the Indians being aware thereof and they were represented by their then attorney at that hearing. The government moved for a summary dismissal of their claim, pleading that the matter was res judicata, which is to say that they had once had their day in court and could not again be heard. It does not appear that any brief or argument was presented by the Indians' attorney in their behalf and that consent was given to such dismissal. The act creating the Commission provided that after disposition of a claim, it could not thereafter be heard. Thus did the Indians find themselves despoiled of their possessions, left without compensation for their losses and without any remedy in the courts of the United States. It might be noted that even though every court in the land were thrown open to them, they would by reason of their penniless condition be unable, financially, to avail themselves thereof. This is the result of the acts of their Guardian and Trustee, over a century of time.

Public Law No. 588–83d Congress, Ch. 733–2d Session provides for the termination of federal supervision over the property of certain tribes and bands of Indians located in Western Oregon and the individual members thereof, including the Siuslaw, Lower Umpqua and Coos Bay Indian tribes. The only property remaining in the tribal hands was a tract of some six acres on which stands a common meeting hall for the tribes. This was given by a private individual [Louis J. Simpson and William G. Robertson] for the use of the Coos and neighboring tribes. In the government liquidating proceedings, it displayed its usual tender care and mercy toward its wards by seeking to give away this property gratuitously to the City of Empire, despite the fact that theretofore the tribes at their meeting had unanimously voted against disposing of this property. It was abundantly clear that the Bureau of Indian Affairs desired to dispose of the last shred of economic flesh belonging to the tribes and thereafter to wash its hands of its crimes and forget them. If any proof were needed to the total lack of concern with respect to its Indian wards, it would need only to be pointed out that after a century of its unlawful supervision, it does not know who its own wards are and has been and is now demanding that the individual members of the various tribes come forward with proof that they are Indians and are descendants of the old Indian tribal members.

For decade upon decade, a swarm of calloused bureaucrats has fattened upon the life blood of these tribes with a complete disregard of the duties of a Guardian or Trustee or any principle of common honesty, justice or ethical decency. They have lobbied and caused to be passed many bills patterned to suit their own purposes. Were any private citizen to conduct himself in a position of trust in any degree after the manner in which the Guardian has dealt with these wards, no time would be lost in lodging him behind the bars of the nearest penitentiary. Various efforts have been made over the years to secure remedial legislation, but in each case it has been hatcheted to death behind the doors of committees in Washington at the hands of the representatives of such agencies as the Bureau of Indian Affairs, the Bureau of the Budget and the Department of Justice. These gentlemen holding high office in the nation have tamed thumbs down on every effort thus far expended in behalf of these tribes. They say that it might cost money and that it might establish a precedent. It not only world cost some money, but it should cost some money and the fact that these tribes are not located in Europe or the Middle East ought not to preclude them from receiving payment, either by way of reparation for the damage done or as payment of an honest debt long past due and owing. If the payment of an honest debt will establish a precedent, it would seem that after a hundred years, a precedent should be established. The claim, however, that it would establish a precedent is without merit.

It is a specious statement by reason of the fact that there is no known parallel case wherein a portion of the tribes signatory to an unratified treaty are paid, while other tribes signatory to the same treaty are left unpaid and without remedy. All these things are well known to the government and the efforts of United States Senators Wayne Morse and Richard Neuberger, through the introduction of Senate Bill No. 5136 of the 84th Congress, again proved to be of no avail. The course of conduct by the government toward these people is an affront to the conscience of every honorable man in the nation who knows what has transpired. Unless the government is called to account for actions of the bulbous bureaucrats, who for decades have misrepresented the citizens and taxpayers of the land in their unconscionable dealings with the Indians, it will forever remain a blot upon the record and a disgrace to the American people.

These matters were called long ago to the attention of the President of the United States, the then Secretary of the Interior and the United States Attorney General in an effort to secure their interest and efforts to correct this situation. This has not been forthcoming. For countless centuries and before the dawn of any recorded history, relative thereto, those tribes governed themselves without the civilized benefits of jails, madhouses, unbearable taxes, armies, navies and H-bombs and they did so without in any way destroying the natural resources of the earth, which would have been maintained as a heritage for ten thousand future generations of children. They would never have been guilty of having fed the maw of an insatiable, avaricious greed, such as has been demonstrated to be possessed by the white man in his mad pursuit of a so-called progress which, in reality, is a pursuit of the economic fallacy of "the ever expanding economy."

Being followers of the principles enunciated by such as Jesus and Ghandi, rather than devotees at the shrine of brute force, the tribes have stood ready to convey their property to the Government of the United States for a reasonable consideration, whether by treaty or by deed; to submit themselves to the government's laws and pick up the white man's burden of taxes and debts upon the condition that the local bonds and shackles be stricken from their limbs.

There are certain painful truths which the Government does not desire to face before the eyes of the world. Among these are that it has never acquired a just and lawful sovereignty over these tribes or their territory; that every statute ever passed by which these tribes have been oppressed is void and a nullity as to them for lack of lawful sovereignty; that all land grants within the territory of the tribes are likewise utterly void for the same reason. These are facts which the representative of the United States to the United Nations cannot face for there he stands in the purple robe of Royalty stolen from the back of the American Indian and he cannot justify: 1, the violation of the golden rule; or the violation of the commandments: 2, thou shalt not covet, 3, thou shalt not steal, or 4, thou shalt not bear false witness and lastly he cannot justify the violation of the sovereignty of weaker nations unless the sole rule of conduct among nations is brute force. If such is the case, we imitate the mad Roman Emperor Caligula, the charter of the United Nations and its preamble are a mockery and the members of the United Nations may as well disband.

Wherefore, the petitioning tribes seek the exercise of every aid and facility of the United Nations in their behalf and in accordance with its own laws to the end that truth and justice may be raised up and accorded their proper place.

Dated this 8th day of August, 1956, at Florence, Oregon,

Howard Barrett

Chairman of the Committee of the Siuslaw,

Lower Umpqua and Coos Bay Tribes.

Florence, Oregon.

SOURCE

Barrett, Howard, Sr. Petition to the United Nations from the Siuslaw, Lower Umpqua,and Coos Bay Indian Tribes. MS Typescript, August 8, 1956. Confederated Tribes of Coos, Lower Umpqua, and Siuslaw Files, Stephen Dow Beckham, Lake Oswego, OR.

RELATED READING

Philp, Kenneth R. *Termination Revisited: American Indians on the Trail to Self-Determination, 1933–1953.* Lincoln, NE: University of Nebraska Press, 1999.

The Case for Education of Indian Children, 1976

Termination meant cutting off educational assistance for Indian children in every tribe and band in western Oregon, as well as for the Klamath Tribe. No longer did students qualify for admission to Chemawa Indian School in Salem. No longer did local school districts receive funding under the Johnson-O'Malley Act to provide tutorial assistance for Indian children. As a matter of law, the Indian children of terminated tribes were technically no longer Indian.

Sister Francella Mary Griggs, a member of the Confederated Tribes of Siletz, addressed the crisis in preparing younger generations of her tribe when she submitted testimony on March 30, 1976, in the hearing on S. 2801. Senator Mark O. Hatfield chaired the session of the Senate Subcommittee on Indian Affairs of the Committee on Interior and Insular Affairs. A bill, the first for an Oregon tribe, proposed to undo the Termination Act of 1954. The Siletz witnesses gathered anxiously. Only the Menominee Tribe had succeeded in persuading Congress to overturn Termination. The quest embraced by Sister Griggs and others, however, proved successful. The witnesses and others submitting written testimony made the case. On November 18, 1977, Congress passed P.L. 95–195 and restored the Siletz to a federal relationship.

I am Sister Francella Mary Griggs, granddaughter of Mrs. Nettie West, an enrolled member of the Confederated Tribes of Siletz. I live and work in Portland, Oregon, and have been an active member of the Council of the Confederated Tribes of Siletz, Inc., so that our people might once again be recognized officially as tribal members of a proud Western Oregon group of first inhabitants of this country.

Through the passage of this Senate Bill (S. 2801), we hope to benefit from the educational opportunities so badly needed by our children and youth. The Johnson O'Malley Act funding, attendance at the Chemawa Indian School in Salem, Oregon, and availability of college scholarships are denied our young people because of the non-federal recognition status of our Siletz Confederated Tribal members.

Siletz School Statistics

During December, 1973 and January, 1974, school officials of Lincoln County School District met with representatives of the Indian Community in Siletz to discuss educational problems of Siletz children and in Siletz schools. They identified the following problems:

1. Forty-four (44) percent of the Indian young people in Siletz between the ages of 17 and 25 years did not finish high school. Undoubtedly this rate would be higher for older Tribal members.
2. Eight of 16 girls and 22 of 34 boys ages 17 to 25 among the Indian young people of Siletz have only one parent due to the death of the other parent. Twenty three (23) percent of the children in grades 1–12 in the Siletz schools come from broken homes. There is little assistance available for children in these circumstances.
3. History, culture, and traditions of the Indian peoples are being lost and are not being transmitted to their children.
4. The Indian children do not have a high self image of themselves.
5. There is a lack of understanding and a lack of ability to communicate among the community, the children and the school staff.
6. Little career planning is done with Indian students.

A listing of these problems should *not*, in any sense, be seen as an indictment of the Siletz schools. Most of us are convinced that the local teachers and administrators are, by and large, genuinely concerned about the special problems of Indian students.

The question, rather, is whether these serious educational conditions can be alleviated by the additional resources which restoration can provide. The primary benefits of restoration would be Johnson-O'Malley funds to the Siletz schools; the availability of BIA educational facilities such as Chemawa; access to BIA scholarships for post-secondary education; and the increased sense of pride and cultural identity which would accompany reorganization of the Tribe.

Johnson-O'Malley Funding

These problems might be lessened considerably were the Johnson-O'Malley funds available to the Siletz Schools to provide tutors for the Indian children and counselors to help them. Indian teachers and aides would be available to assist these young people over the difficult years when their interest in academic subjects lags. Being able to relate to their own people with prestige and authority in the school setting would encourage them to pursue even the elementary schooling.

Johnson-O'Malley funds can be used to help alleviate the very serious drop-out problems which plague our young people. When these children drop out of school, who can help them realize their own identity, give them some historical perspective, teach them about the culture and traditions of their ancestors. If these are not parents who understand the needs of these young people, if no Indian teachers, aides, or counselors are present in the local school or help them realize the worth of being an American Indian with a rich background, if the Chemawa Indian school is closed to them, where can they go?

Chemawa Indian School

At Chemawa—where many of the older Siletz Indian residents attended school—there are classes dealing with the culture of the Native American, there is an opportunity for young people to develop their talents in music, art, and in all academic subjects.

Chemawa Indian school has answers to meet the educational needs of the Siletz school drop out. Classes are geared to meet the individual needs of the young people. There is a reasonable percentage of Native American teachers, and administration—a great advantage over the local Siletz schools. Students are not scheduled to work half a day and to attend classes the other half day. Such was the situation when some of our older Siletz people went to Chemawa.

BIA (Bureau of Indian Affairs) Scholarships

Siletz students through federal recognition of the Confederated tribes of Siletz, Inc., would be eligible for BIA scholarships for post-secondary education. I have met a number of Siletz young people who are interested in college, in attending law school, and in pursuing some career in the medical profession. Without a family income to meet this educational need, without the assistance of the regular channels open to other Native American Indian students who are federally recognized, the educational doors are closed to these ambitious young people. Some have attempted to enter college and to pursue an academic program; however, the pressure of having to work either off campus or at the school through the work study program at the same time as fulfilling the class attendance and assignments became too much for them.

Tribal witnesses appeared before congressional committees in 1977 to make the case for restoration of the Confederated Tribes of Siletz. Left to right: Delores Pigsley, Joe Lane, Robert Rilatos, Arthur Bensell, Katherine Harrison, Robert Tom, and Pauline Ricks (Beckham).

Some young people are interested in college and higher education, but they are among that 44% drop out group from high school. They are not academically ready to enter college, to receive a scholarship, and to feel comfortable in a structured college or university setting.

Even colleges and universities with Indian Studies Programs can not accept them because of the entrance requirements. Even so, some enter but are obliged to take "watered down" courses, have special tutoring sessions and find the regular schedule of classes very hard. The drop out finds attending daily classes most difficult. The remedy could be a period of time at Chemawa where an Indian student can adjust to the academic world.

Increased Sense of Pride and Cultural Identity

Basically the most beneficial outcome for all members of the Siletz Confederated tribes is the increased sense of pride and cultural identity. For years on application forms I have marked OTHER where the form called for ethnic identity. Since I was not able to gain any recognition for being a Native American of the Siletz Confederated Tribes, I felt that at least on paper I was OTHER, whatever that might mean to the readers and the statistics experts requesting ethnic information.

For years when anthropologists were studying our American Indians, I did not feel comfortable being identified as an American Indian. Now that we have experienced our own people writing books, teaching on the college and university level, directing Indian health programs, Indian urban programs, and speaking our during these bicentennial preparatory months, we can be proud to be recognized as Native Americans. Yet, when our own relatives and friends of the Siletz Confederated Tribes are not recognized as Native Americans, the first citizens of this country, what can we do. We are a people without a land, we are a people without visible recognition, we are—some of us—dark-skinned, black haired, brown eyed—all of us, proud, sensitive, intelligent descendents of a noble race.

We speak the English language, though when we were young, as in my case, our great grand parents, our grand parents, parents, and relatives spoke our native languages. Before my sister and I went to an orphanage (the same day our mother went to the state TB hospital where she died within nine weeks) we understood and spoke two native languages, the Chinook jargon, Spanish, and English.

We Siletz Indians dance and sing our native songs, mostly at special occasions. We do not wish to be on display to perform these sacred activities at bicentennial celebrations.

During this bicentennial celebration year, we want only to be recognized for the people we are with rights as Native Americans. We need to be recognized as American Indians by this Restoration Act so that the educational level of our people can be raised.

On the national level the Indian Education Act has made provision for the absolute participation of the Indian people in programs under the act. In statistics used in gathering information for the Act and for the studies made on the programs under the Act, terminated Indians are not included. This should be considered in all such reports.

Oregon census does not include terminated Indians, nor the urban Indians from out of state reservations. Federal and state funding for Oregon Indians, therefore, must address the needs of all Oregon Indians including a large segment of us terminated Indians.

One other facet of Siletz Indian children is the idea of foster children. Many of our Siletz children are in foster homes. When these drop out of school, where can they go. If Chemawa were open to them, it would solve this problem by giving them a secure place to attend school. They would finish school, be able to gain scholarships, pursue a definite career and be an asset to themselves, be somebody, and consequently help others.

I cannot stress enough the fact that when we are given the opportunity to become students in the proper setting, we will function to our highest potential. We will be the leaders of our people, as my fellow Siletz people here today have proven.

Thank you very much.

SOURCE

U.S. Congress. *Siletz Restoration Act Hearings Before the Subcommittee on Indian Affairs of the Committee on Interior and Insular Affairs, 94th Cong., 2 Sess., on S. 1801,* March 30–31. Washington, DC: Government Printing Office, 1976, pp. 148–53.

Termination Impacts on the Grand Ronde
Community, 1976

*Merle Holmes, who died in 2004, expended years studying the history of the
Confederated Tribes of Grand Ronde. Of Santiam descent, Holmes appeared in
1976 before Task Force No. 10 of the American Indian Policy Review Commission
to speak to the situation of the peoples of Grand Ronde on their treatment by the
government and the impact of Termination.*

Now our reservation at Grand Ronde was set aside by an executive order of
June 30, 1857, and this officially signed by President Buchanan set apart the
Grand Ronde Indian Reservation, making official the 69,120 acres proposed
in an act in November 1855, to personally establish what was then called the
Coast Reservation—ended up being the Grand Ronde. And our feelings—we
feel that all the people sent on to the Grand Ronde Reservation seemed to be
discriminated from the word "Reservation" because there were more than 23
tribes and small bands residing together, and we feel that the chances of that
large mixed group like that could never get along with each others very well,
because in fact some of these people were enemies in the valley, protecting the
land and the campgrounds and the people they were expecting to be neigh-
borly with and get along with under the government supervision.

On these treaties—I have the six treaties and I think I've sent most of those
to the Task Force, packet no. 2. You have then and you know they are ratified. The reason I have the six is that most of these people referred to on the
six treaties, a good many of them ended up in the Grand Ronde Reservation.
Under the stipulations of these reservations and these treaties that you see, it
is our contention that possibly the Indian people should have been of the best
educated people here in the valley, in as much as the treaties bore some responsibility to the Indian—a school with teachers along with agriculture expert
opinion, a blacksmith, a sawmill, and other things to improve their lives as well
as breaking ground and fencing. But the school, like I said, just the six we're
going to refer to, they all had a provision for the education but at Grand Ronde

they only had one, the agency school there, and they closed early without ever accomplishing the things for which it was sent there to do. We know many of the elders—of course it was probably a target of the young people—but most of the elders if they had done or two years, they couldn't read or write. The government never got anything for those people and the duration of the school and dictated into the treaties they came in there under, and just as soon as the maximum time had elapsed on the treaties, even though there was much lapse in what they were sent there to do, a lot of uneducated people, just as soon as it was up, they closed the schools down. And there again, a matter of the record, instead of packing those up and getting Swan Island, which I understand was the next nearest place, everything was burned there. There was nothing moved. So we don't have a very documented record of what degree they did educate people and how much they knew when they supposedly closed that school down.

And then under legislative policy, the 1901 Act, ratified and executed April 28, 1904. This Act ceded back to the United States government 25,791 acres of prime timber and all the remaining unallotted lands on the Grand Ronde Reservation. The United States, we feel, acting as trustee for the Indian people, were pretty negligent and didn't act in the best interest of the people they were representing, as this particular section of land took away the wealth of our people, both past and present. Now this land running from our reservation right up to the top of the coast range, backing up to this Siletz Reservation, reputed in many written articles and books to be the finest stand of old growth timber in the world. Now we feel, if the Indian agent was Mr. [Andrew] Kershaw at the time, we feel that if he hadn't talked these older people into this, that we could have, as late a date as this, we could have probably had a sustained yield from this timber in as much as these trees, you could market it in a hundred years. But then again we lost our resources that could have taken us out of this poverty situation that the people of Grand Ronde live today. This timber, bought by large timber companies and some of this is still standing, producing timber yet today, it's in little pockets, but they still are making money on it. And it's valuable timber that you hear me talking about. The sale price of this was about $8 an acre. There again the government handling and the projection of what that would have become worth if we'd been able to hang on to it as the Klamath did, the people would have been in fine shape and we wouldn't be trying to find government funds to merely exist. And all this same cession of land also sold all the unalloted land on the reservation, and we feel that the reason that they kept the Indians cramped right around the agency is possibly for control.

But they kept everybody cramped up right around the Grand Ronde agency and we have a map. It was the personal property of Mr. Kershaw who was the agent right at the time and it keeps us right up in a little block so we're utilizing maybe not half of the reservation, in as much as there were three grants to white people who had large holdings already. But we feel they kept us centralized so they could declare the land around us as surplus and that went with the 1901 cession, and in accordance with that cession all the Indian children who were under the age of 18, the treaty said share and share alike. Every man, woman, and child on the reservation would get their per capita share. But the stipulation, if you were a minor, if you were 12 years old, you would not get your share until you were 18. So their money was sent directly into the U.S. treasury to draw 5% until the youngsters became young adults at the age of 18. Now this money to this very day has not been appropriated to the people. The treasury did release it to the Indian agent or the BIA, but it never got as far as the Indian people at Grand Ronde. And we have people in their 80s that can verify this in testimony.

Now we go into the Grand Ronde—the Indian Reorganization Act. That was 383 of the 73rd Congress. Now this was really a ball of fire on paper. These many, many sums of money described, a quarter of a million, at a time for reorganization and self government, another quarter of a million for loans, tuition and expenses, and a quarter of a million again for the revolving fund regulated by the Secretary of the Interior for purposes he prescribed. Again this really looked good on paper and it was selling the paper people right along to get us into the Wheeler-Howard Act which eventually lead to our termination. But the old elders that were running the tribes business at the time, they weren't looking ahead to the fact that all the sums of money were terrific to look at buy they were all subject to appropriation by Congress, and these people didn't weight this. So if Congress didn't see to appropriate to raise those sums of money, they were cut or disallowed, leaving the people on the receiving end with nothing, just what they got.

So we go from there to Wheeler-Howard. It was the same thing. It became law June 18th, 1934, and there again it was all drawn up. We have a draft of the original Wheeler-Howard in our possession and it really looks good. It looks like the United States government is really going to help the Indians reorganize and be self-governing and be able to handle their tribal affairs as they see fit. But there again, none of it ever materialized to the fact where these people got any of these benefits that looked so good in the Wheeler-Howard Act. And then again, getting back to this resource we lost again, coming under this in the 1901 cession, the Wheeler-Howard Act covered all this. It protected all the resources and they had little sticky things in there like you would only graze two head of cattle per acre, and, by the time all the protection came to be, all the resources were all gone. We had nothing left to protect. There again, they were way late with laws to protect the Indians who were their wards at the time, and this drastically affected the security of the Grand Ronde Indians as a whole.

And then of course we had 588, but there again we had a charter and by-laws drawn up by the BIA and in 588 there is a provision to revoke our charter and it breaks down our tribal council. They already discouraged, and so with the enactment of 588 there's an awful breakdown in our ability to govern our own affairs, because they had no way to go and no way to guide with this charter being revoked from them. And then again, under 588, Dr. [Stephen] Beckham stated here this morning, there's no express provision for the loss of hunting and fishing and a valuable resource to the Indian people. Now for years prior to '54, those people could hunt over there as long as you were on government land and there was a provision that said you could transport your game across the white man's land if you went directly to and from your place of hunting to home. And they had those licenses that you witnessed here this morning. People carried those, but there again, I say no loss or no provision. They never paid the Indians for a loss and it is a valuable resource.

And we get up a little closer to what we're looking at here today. As you people on the Task Force have heard us talk about, the trustee that was actually named by the Secretary of the Interior and BIA to be our trustee, to see to the sale of our land which was supposed to be executed very quickly. They figured not longer than two years to liquidate the last of the tribal property and get us out into society where we could function as individuals without government direction. Mr. Fuller—many discrepancies of his handling of our business and we're looking into these things yet. Also we're afraid we're way too late, and just as late as Wednesday of this week we were over talking to an attorney representing Mr. Fuller, and here 22 years have gone by and now we find out the trustee may not have in fact sold all of our land. Which we were delighted. So if we can find out where this land is, we will reclaim it. But the admission of this attorney by his own—he volunteered to us that our trustee was pretty lax. He lost a lot of his expertise and he wasn't at all sure that he would be able to find the records and get to the county courthouse and see in fact what land actually was ours yet today. But we're hoping that he can come up with something to give us a little more land based on our cemetery.

So we feel that ever since the first treaty was signed there's just been one breach upon the other as far as the government is concerned because the people there in Grand Ronde—even if you go there right today, you can see that they're way below poverty level and there is certainly no way they will ever get above it unless we get some recognition, and we hope to be restored one day. We hope that when they see fit to change the Indian policy that maybe we can receive the benefits that were promised years ago updated to meet our needs here today and now.

SOURCE

American Indian Policy Review Commission, Task Force No. 10. Hearing Record, March, 1976. Grand Ronde Tribal Council: Testimony of Mr. Merle Holmes, pp. 104–12. Typescript in possession of Stephen Dow Beckham, Lake Oswego, OR.

Consequences of Termination: The Klamath Tribe, 1976

Twenty years passed before some members of Congress decided that it was time to gather information about the impacts of Termination. When Congress created the American Indian Policy Review Commission in 1975, it set up Task Force No. 10 to prepare a report on terminated and non-federally recognized tribes. The Task Force came to the Pacific Northwest in March 1976.

Task Force No. 10, chaired by attorney Jo Jo Hunt, held hearings with tribes that had been administratively terminated by the Bureau of Indian Affairs in the state of Washington. The tribes dropped from federal recognition without statutory authority included the Chinook, Cowlitz, Steilacoom, Duwamish, and Snoqualmie. The task force was interested in the situation of these people who were treated individually as Indians (having trust allotments in several instances) but whose tribes were deemed not to exist.

In Oregon, Task Force No. 10 held hearings in March 1976, at the State Capitol. The witnesses lined up to give formal statements and to respond to questions from the fact-finding group. Joe Coburn, a longtime leader in educational programs, testified about the situation of the Klamath and other tribes formerly resident on the Klamath Reservation.

So what I'd like to do is just hit some of the highlights of the Klamath termination. By Klamath, I'm speaking of the Modoc, the Klamath, and the Yahooskin band of Snakes which was on our reservation in Southern Oregon. The reservation was started by treaty in 1864.

Our reservation consisted of approximately 1,200,000 acres. Nearly 12, a little over 11,000,000 acres were ceded, and prior to the 1864 treaty, termination with this started with the end of the allotments, the giving out of allotments, which was in 1935. At that time there was some 880,000 acres that was not alloted. Part of the allotment act was to dispose of any remaining tribal lands not used for allotment, and it was to be used for the benefit of the tribal members. There was a move to—well, they didn't know what to do with this 880,000 acres.

There was a lot of talk about selling and what to do with it—to give it to in-dividual members or to put it into some tribal type of enterprise. They really couldn't decide. Tribal government, of course at that time, was not strong. They were quite heavily dominated by the Bureau of Indian Affairs. So much so that the Bureau of Indian Affairs could veto any tribal government objective that they came up with.

There were several schemes as to how to handle this 880,000 acres. One of them, about two of them quite similar in nature, did become introduced into the Congress as bills. One of them was to form a Klamath Corporation and manage this land by the Tribe. There still is feeling that if an individual doesn't want to be part of this, he should be able to sell his share. Another bill was entered—that bill by the way died. Another bill was entered, 1220, and it was quite similar in nature. Some sort of a corporate body would govern this land. Among the Indians themselves there is a strong feeling against the Indian service, that they should be able to govern themselves. They were pushing in this area throughout this same time period. 1220 also died in committee but the ideas were there.

In council throughout this time period there was a push for those people that did not want to be governed by the Tribe or by the Indian Service, that they should be able to take their assets and do what they would with them. Finally the termination act was passed. It required that a special act be passed for the Klamaths. This resulted in public Law 587 which is the Klamath Termination Act and was passed in 1954. There is some question as to the legality of this. For instance, some of these previous acts talking about some sort of a liquidation. Three different times a referendum vote was made to this effect and each time it was defeated. The final acceptance was not by referendum. As a matter of fact, the referendum was by-passed. I'm not sure whether this was a business council or the executive council, and it was by-passed in their session.

There were seven hearings held at the reservation. People were not sure what they were talking about. Several senators were present. The only one that comes to mind was a Senator [Arthur] Watkins. He comes to mind because he lied to the Indian people at the committee hearings in that the people would ask, does this mean tribal assets would be liquidated. He told them no. This is a matter of record, and he did this more than once. He told them, 'No, we are interested in you governing yourselves. That's what this act is all about. And we're not, the government is not wanting to liquidate your reservation.' A title of the act included liquidations by the way.

Anyway, they went back to Congress. They also took a lot of testimony from people other than Indians. One was from the state Department of Education representative, Mr. Wright, who said that the state was prepared to provide education for the Klamaths, which they have not by the way, satisfactorily. The sheriff, Mr. Lloyd Low at that time stated that with an additional three deputies they could handle the law enforcement for the tribe, or for this they would now be citizens, regular citizens. This has not been satisfactory.

As recently as three years ago there was a vigilante committee set up because there was not enough law enforcement in one of the former areas of the reservation. People were than taking the law into their own hands because there was no law enforcement or very little. A Judge, I can't remember his name, a Judge from the local court said that in his belief the Klamaths were ready for termination. So the Congressional Committee went back to Washington and started working on a bill and it was introduced. There was a series of hearings back there prior to the final disposition of the bill. At those hearings, the Bureau of Indian Affairs area director from the Portland area office was called back for four weeks.

Some Department of Interior officials were there. They gave some misleading statements. Statements like family level of income was something like $5,000. The education level is high. I think something like 16 Klamaths had graduated in the previous 15 years, something like that, from high school. The income level was high but no one pointed out that most of this was from per capita income which would immediately cease upon termination and the income level would drop at a drastic rate. The income level was high at that time, however it was misconstrued to lead people to believe that this was the income level. So there was some at least misleading information given by the Department of the Interior.

The final night before passage of the bill there was an all-night meeting. There were three tribal representatives there. There was still some push for the individual taking his assets in money or land and becoming a non-member. And at this final night before passage, this was accepted. During the—prior to the voting on the bill, one of the senators asked if indeed the Indians did agree, if they knew about and did agree to the terms of the bill, and was answered by one of the congressional delegates, yes, both factions of the tribe do agree to this. This is based on three delegates being at this final meeting. There was a time period or a time schedule, I think it was 7 years. So after the passage of the termination act, Public Law 587, there was a big push to get things down in a hurry. A lot of things had to be down. 888,000 acres had to be disposed of. Most of the prime Ponderosa pine, much of it virgin timber valued at something like $9,000,000, buyers had to be found for this. All sorts of things. So there was a big push to get these things done.

There was an educational aspect. Some approximately 275 tribal members did enroll in school. Even before termination was completed in 1961, 75% of these had dropped out of school. Everything was real rush at that time.

It's generally stated that there was a vote taken and termination accepted by some 1600 members. The vote that's referred to was after the termination act, and each member, each adult member, received a form whereby you could elect to withdraw and take your assets in money or to remain and no one was quite sure what that meant. I was 19 at the time. I think it was two weeks to decide one way or the other. If you didn't answer, you remained. There was a lot of vague rumors going around. It wasn't set up in the law what remaining member, what that would mean. It was kind of assumed that, as I remember it, I went around to various people, most of them family members, asking them to advise. And the feeling was those that remained there will be a handful of people that will run it, would be sort of a corporation. They would get good jobs, be a lot of corruptness, this type of thing. If you withdraw, the figure that was being tossed around was $56,000 so you had to make up your mind within two weeks. Like I say, 1600 and some odd members did elect to withdraw. I might add that at the same time, this was in about 1956, at that time was the great paranoia of the threat of the bomb. This is when everyone was building bomb shelters. You didn't know how long before the whole world blew up. There was a feeling no one was looking to what's going to happen to my grandchildren. There was that type of feeling. Especially when you were 19 years old and eligible for the draft. This type of thing. So many people, over 1600, did withdraw. 437, 447, something like that, did remain. The remaining members were placed under a trust under a U.S. National Bank, one of the larger banks in Oregon. Very conservative. They were much stricter than the other service had been. As a result, recently those members have elected to dissolve that corporation. The remaining members—well, the whole tribe dissolved nearly all ties with the Bureau of Indian Affairs. Hunting and fishing was not something that was mentioned as such in the final termination act. Just recently through the District 9 court the tribe did win back, not win back, but justified that they did have hunting and fishing rights.

Since termination there has been an organization formed called "The Organization of Forgotten Americans." They have obtained a lot of grant monies. They've installed an educational program, a dental program, health program, manpower, several supported mostly by grant monies. With the hunting and fishing decision, we have secured a contract with the Bureau of Indian Affairs for $55,000. This came through our pressuring the Department of Justice. Kind of mandated that the Bureau of Affairs deal with us. With this $55,000, we are setting up studies of our former game herds, fishing resources, which had been depleted in the intervening 13 years. We're studying how to regulate our game and our fishing laws, this type of thing, with this $55,000.

We do have tribal government. We operate under old by-laws prior to '54 termination. We have several suits against the government. We have one—three I believe. We have a couple pending yet. And that's kind of where we are today, very brief.

SOURCE

American Indian Policy Review Commission, Task Force No. 10. Hearings Transcript, March, 1976, Salem, OR. Organization of the Forgotten American: Testimony of Joe Coburn, pp. 143–49. Typescript in possession of Stephen Dow Beckham, Lake Oswego, OR.

"What Were We to Do When We Were Terminated?"

Bill Brainard (1931–2003), longtime tribal chair of the Confederated Tribes of the Coos, Lower Umpqua, and Siuslaw, raised troubling questions with members of Congress when on June 4, 1984, he and other witnesses appeared before the House Committee on the Interior in support of H.R. 5540. The bill, sponsored by Rep. James Weaver and Sen. Mark O. Hatfield, proposed to overturn Termination and restore the Confederated Tribes to federal status.

The route to Congress for Bill Brainard was convoluted and difficult. A man who had "kept the faith" through the dismal years following Termination in 1956, he fought to maintain both tribal meetings and to keep the tribal hall an Indian property. Erected in 1940–41 on a 6.1–acre reservation in Empire, Oregon, the property lingered in limbo status when the tribe refused to cooperate with the Bureau of Indian Affairs in selling it. Brainard and his wife, Muriel, sometimes were the only persons attending the tribal meetings in the old hall. Rain seeped through the roof and ran down the inside of the walls. Vandals tore away shingles and brush encroached on all sides. In his testimony Brainard explained, however, that the small reservation and its meeting place became an anchor during the thirty years the federal government had nothing to do with his tribe.

The BIA opposed the restoration bill. On June 7 John W. Fritz, Deputy Assistant Secretary, wrote to Congress: "It is unclear at this time, due to conflicting information, whether these groups meet the requirements for restoration of federal recognition, or whether they were tribes at the time of Termination." Congress dismissed the BIA's objections and passed the restoration act, P.L. 98–481, for the Confederated Tribes of Coos, Lower Umpqua, and Siuslaw Indians on October 17, 1984.

My name is Bill Brainard, and I am Chairman of the Confederated Tribes of Coos, Lower Umpqua & Siuslaw Indians. I currently reside at 555 Cleveland, Coos Bay, Oregon, which is within the tribe's aboriginal and historic lands.

I vividly recall the events leading toward our Termination in 1956. I was born in 1931 and participated as an adult in the tribal meetings when the Bureau of Indian Affairs began pushing the "Termination" program in 1950–51. My tribe had very special and specific reasons for opposing what the Bureau tried to "sell" in a series of meetings with western Oregon Indians in the early 1950's:

1. We possessed a federal trust reservation and tribal hall erected in 1940 by the Bureau of Indian Affairs for our meetings and the health clinic operated by the Indian Health Service. The Hall contained facilities for food processing and preservation which were very important to us. Then, as now, our people depended heavily upon clams, mussels, fish, elk, duck and deer as basic foods, and we feared that losing BIA funds as a result of Termination would force us to close the food processing facility. And that is what happened within only a couple of years.

2. A number of our tribal members possessed allotments held in trust by the United States. Since these properties were covered with valuable old-growth timber, we anticipated that the taxes on them would be high and the pressures to sell the last of our aboriginal lands would be intense. Again, this happened, just as we feared.

3. We had not resolved our tribal land claims with the United States. During 1950–51, our case was pending before the Indian Claims Commission and we were hopeful that it would provide us with sufficient money to assist tribal projects. We feared that Termination would jeopardize our land claims case.

4. We knew that we were Indian, were perceived as Indians in the area where we lived, and that we intended to stay members of the tribe.

Even though several other western Oregon tribes, among them the Siletz and the Grand Ronde, passed resolutions in favor of Termination, we opposed Termination for the previously stated reasons.

When the BIA summoned us to its Termination meetings, we went. When we voiced our opposition, we were told to be quiet. I recall one meeting at which we were very vocal in our opposition to Termination, we were removed by the BIA from the meeting room, taken across the road, put in another building and kept isolated until the meeting was over. The BIA told us that our views were not helpful and were not wanted. We also were told that Termination would not apply to us in light of our intense opposition, yet we were included.

What were we to do when we were terminated?

Bill Brainard (1931-2003) kept the faith of his Indian heritage. A determined voice in opposing "termination" and a dedicated advocate of "restoration," he led his tribe through long, difficult years. His determination and stubborn tenacity paid off in Public Law 98–481, October 17, 1984, restoring the federal relationship for the Coos, Lower Umpqua, and Siuslaw (Beckham).

We were a small western Oregon tribe, and none of our members was well educated. We were desperate and tried to do anything we could. We hired an attorney in Florence, Oregon, who helped us draft a petition to the United Nations to present our case. We filed that petition in August 1956, an action reported by *The Oregonian* in Portland, Oregon.

Ultimately our efforts to prevent the imposition of Termination on our tribe were in vain.

Although individual tribal members were given allotments of Indian land from within our aboriginal territory under the Dawes Act of 1887, we did not have a tribal land base until 1940. The situation of our people was very desperate during the Depression. Our tribal members had made a living digging and selling clams, shooting and cleaning ducks for sale to local cafes and butcher shops, chopping wood, working in sawmills, working as cleaning ladies and washerwomen, and working in salmon canneries. Many of these jobs disappeared or were lost to us when we were displaced by non-Indian workers in the 1930's.

William Robertson and Louis J. Simpson, developers of the townsite of Empire, Oregon—where our tribe signed its treaty in 1855—were aware of the dire circumstances of our tribal members. These two men, as an humanitarian gesture, offered to the government of the United States a fine 6.1 acre tract of land as a reservation for the Coos Bay Tribe and "neighboring Indian tribes," which constituted the Lower Umpquas and Siuslaws. In response to this offer, the Bureau of Indian Affairs accepted this property in trust, and in 1940 erected for us the Tribal Hall where we continue to meet to this day. It is worthy to note that in 1953, the BIA reported that the land was in trust for the Coos, Lower Umpqua and Siuslaw Tribes.

The retention of the reservation and tribal hall through the period since Termination has been a worry and yet a sense of satisfaction for the tribe. We have had many difficulties over the administration and management of the hall. In August 1956, the BIA turned its operation over to the City of Empire, the oldest town in Coos County, as the trustee for the tribe. For reasons not clear to us, the Indenture between the United States and the City of Empire stated that the trusteeship was for the "Coos, Coquille, Lower Umpqua, and Siuslaw Tribes of Indians." There has never been any participation in ownership of the land or maintenance of the tribal hall by any group calling itself "Coquille," and we have at all times since 1940 exercised dominion and control over the property, other than as is described in the following paragraph.

The City, which generally was unresponsive to our needs, leased the hall to the U.S. Navy Reserve Unit which in turn failed to maintain the property and through neglect allowed the building to be heavily vandalized. In 1967, the City of Empire was annexed by the City of Coos Bay and went out of existence.

At this point, the Tribe petitioned for the return of the reservation and hall to its own control. Since the City of Empire no longer existed and could not serve as trustee, the tribe recorded the deed at the Coos County Courthouse in the name of Coos, Lower Umpqua and Siuslaw Tribes of Western Oregon, Inc., an Oregon corporation.

We have for 28 years maintained the tribal hall and grounds. This has been costly and time-consuming, but has been crucial as a focus of tribal activity. The hall has housed our CETA Manpower Program, tribal offices, the Oregon Coastal Indian Cultural Museum and the Tribal Trading Post, a food co-op which we operated through our membership in the Small Tribes Organization of Western Washington. Of the 66 tribes and bands of western Oregon terminated in 1956, we are the only one which has managed to preserve its tribal land base and tribal hall.

Our tribal government, as we often say, is the oldest government in Oregon. We have an unbroken record of tribal existence, affirmed by anthropological and historical records. The selection of new "chiefs" was duly noted in the historic period by newspapers in our home area. For example, 105 years ago, on May 7, 1879, the *Coos Bay News* noted: "Indian Jack, Chief of the Coos Bay Indians, died at Empire City, last week, the funeral was preached by Rev. J. McCormac and was well attended." Since then we have had a continuous succession of chiefs and councils. Our councils have entered into attorney contracts, led us in gaining legislation relating to our land claims, helped us manage our tribal property and have drafted our governing documents.

Although we have had a fully operative tribal council of elected members since 1917, like other Indian tribes we did not have a written constitution and bylaws. Rather, for many years we were governed by tradition and the advice of our elders. In 1938, however, we adopted our first constitution in anticipation of voting whether or not to become an I.R.A. tribe pursuant to the Indian Reorganization Act of 1934. Since that time we have revised our constitutions and bylaws in 1960, 1972, and 1983. We filed as an non-profit corporation in the State of Oregon on December 8, 1972.

Today our council consists of five members and a secretary. We meet the second Sunday of every month, with the Tribal Corporation meeting in May. The tribe's annual meeting is held on the second Sunday in August at our burial grounds at the old village of Baldiyasa ('Where the South Wind Blows") at the Cape Arago Lighthouse on the Pacific coast. We have always held our meetings and elections in accord with our governing documents, and I personally have participated in these meetings for a half century, first as a child and later as an officer of the tribe. At no time during my life has our tribal government ceased to function.

We have a tribal roll that shows the descent of each member from the aboriginal tribe alive at the time of our treaty of 1855. We have a base roll recorded in 1940 by the Bureau of Indian Affairs, and this roll is supported by a documented genealogical record of each tribal member. We prepared this documentation from government records in a special Status Clarification Project in 1982–83 in anticipation of this legislation. Copies of all of this material have been furnished to the Bureau of Indian Affairs for reference in conjunction with this legislation.

The tribe has been responsible for governing its members' hunting and fishing rights. Until Termination, we were issued Indian identification cards by the State of Oregon. Since then, we have maintained our own hunting and fishing regulations, issued identity cards to our members, and in August 1977 made a public declaration of our hunting and fishing rights. We have worked with the

Oregon Department of Fish and Wildlife and the Oregon Steelheaders on this matter. This legislation makes no claims to hunting and fishing rights beyond those now existing.

The Tribe collects annual dues from its members, coordinates information with members through a regular *Newsletter* and has maintained the tribal hall through special assessments and fund raising efforts among members. The tribal council has encouraged individual members to serve on Indian Parent Committees administering Indian Education Act funds in local school districts within the aboriginal area, has endorsed the Tribe's membership in Indian organizations such as National Congress of American Indians and the Northwest Affiliated Tribes, and has coordinated the tribe's role as Native American liaison under Oregon's Indian Burials Act. Tribal members serve on state commissions and boards of national organizations.

The tribe has continued its annual salmon ceremony and in 1981 won enactment of state legislation allocating salmon from Oregon hatcheries to assist in providing fish for this traditional event.

I have been a Coos Indian all of my life. My mother was Indian and so was my father. My father and one of his brothers attended the BIA's Greenville School near Fresno, California, because we were under the administration of the Greenville School following the closing of the Roseburg, Oregon, Agency in 1917. I have worked with the elders of my tribe and today, as chairman of the Council, am working to train a new generation of my people in our traditional tribal ways.

I earnestly ask you to pass this legislation. I have worked for this moment most of my adult life. I fought Termination in the early 1950's only to be forcibly removed with my people by the BIA from a public meeting. For our efforts, we still are terminated, though two other Oregon tribes which actively supported Termination have had their federal status restored. I have committed years of my life to the ongoing activities of my tribe. It is my greatest desire that this legislation pass, for we, as a tribe, can meet every test of "acknowledgment" by the federal government save one: we are terminated. It is in your hands to remove that bar to our full status as a tribe.

Thank you.

SOURCE

Brainard, Bill. Testimony of Bill Brainard In Support of H.R. 5540 Before the House Committee on the Interior, June 4, 1984. Confederated Tribes of Coos, Lower Umpqua, and Siuslaw, 1984 Files, Stephen Dow Beckham, Lake Oswego, OR.

RELATED READING

Philp, Kenneth R. Dillon S. Myer and the Advent of Termination, 1950–53. *Western Historical Quarterly* 19 (January, 1988), 37–59.

Wilkinson, Charles F., and Eric R. Biggs. The Evolution of the Termination Policy. *American Indian Law Review* 5(1977):139–84.

Seven

Restoration of Hope

The Confederated Tribes of Warm Springs blazed new directions in the mid-twentieth century by developing Kahneeta Hot Springs resort on a former allotment. The tribe also began logging and producing lumber from its own sawmill at Warm Springs (Oregon State Archives).

THE LAST THREE DECADES of the twentieth century were a turning point for the tribes of Oregon. Most of the terminated tribes gained restoration through acts of Congress on a case-by-case basis. The Columbia Plateau tribes, however, endured major assaults by the states of Oregon, Washington, and Idaho on their treaty-reserved rights to fish. The agenda of the states to abrogate treaties and block tribal use of natural resources mounted throughout the twentieth century and came to resolution in federal cases that ultimately upheld the treaty rights. Most significantly, an initially obscure case about the right of the Cabazon Indians in California to operate a bingo hall led to a Supreme Court decision and the Indian Gaming Regulatory Act, permitting gambling on Indian land, that catapulted Oregon tribes into a remarkable renaissance of revenues to foster self-governance, delivery of services to members, pride, and philanthropy.

The assaults on treaty rights by the states tested tribes for most of the twentieth century. The pivotal issues were the reserved rights of the tribes to fish "at usual and accustomed grounds and stations" and to hunt. Individuals and the states tried to check tribal exercise of these rights. The states first imposed restrictions on fishing gear: Washington did so in 1871 and Oregon in 1878. The states next set fishing seasons: Washington did so in 1877 and Oregon in 1878.[1]

In *U.S. v. Winans* (1905), a case involving access of members of the Yakama Nation to a traditional fishing site, a non-Indian property owner operating a state-licensed fishwheel argued that his technology was superior to that of the Indians and that he could prohibit tribal access to his property. The Supreme Court rejected Winans' contentions. It confirmed the right of tribal access to the fishing site, and the tribe's right to fish in the river and erect houses for curing fish; it rejected the argument of technological superiority or that the treaty was no longer binding. The case of *Seufert Brothers v. U.S.* (1919), litigation involving the Seufert fishing and canning operations in The Dalles, extended the protection of tribal treaty rights.[2]

In *State v. Towessnute* (1916) and *State v. Alexis* (1916), Washington courts ruled against the Indians. In the Towessnute case, the state prosecuted an Indian for fishing without a license, for using a gaff hook, and for catching fish with a hook within a mile of a dam. In the Alexis case the courts further treated an Indian under state law as merely another citizen. State Justice Bausman wrote: "The Indian was a child, and a dangerous child of nature, to be both protected and restrained. In his nomadic life, he was to be left, as long as civilization did not demand his region. When it did demand that region, he was to be allotted a more confined area with permanent subsistence."[3] The rulings in the Washington state court cases diminished tribal rights and elicited no response from the United States Department of Justice to uphold treaty rights of tribes.

In 1939 Sampson Tulee, a Washington Indian, used a dip net, caught fish, and sold them without a state license. He was arrested and prosecuted, losing his contentions of treaty-protected rights in both county court and state supreme court. In 1942 the Supreme Court heard the case of *State v. Tulee.* It ruled that Washington could regulate the Indian fishery for conservation but could not impose license fees.[4] This meant, for the interim, that Indians could fish without fees. In both Oregon and Washington, the states issued Indian "blue cards," certifying tribal enrollment and fishing entitlement. Oregon revoked the "blue cards" with Termination in 1956.

Conflicts between Indian and non-Indian fishermen accelerated in the 1970s with the decline in fish stocks. The construction of dams on Pacific Northwest rivers, stemming from major projects in the 1930s, had closed off thousands of miles of spawning areas. Turbines chewed up migrating fry and plunged them into waters super-saturated with nitrogen that killed them on contact. Logging removed the protective shade covering from creek waters, raised temperatures, and accelerated the flow of eroded material into spawning grounds. Agricultural and urban wastes as well as pesticides and herbicides polluted streams and killed fish. The diminishing runs of fish pitted sports and commercial fishers against Indians.

Tribal victories in the courts in the 1970s changed affairs dramatically. The rulings of federal judges Robert Belloni in Portland and George Boldt in Seattle affirmed the treaty rights of the Indians. In *Sohappy v. Smith* (1969), Judge Belloni ruled that the tribes were entitled to a "fair and equitable share of all fish which it [Oregon] permits to be taken from a given run." Belloni instructed the state to work with the tribes in developing regulations and set the stage for direct tribal involvement in the management of the resource to which their treaties affirmed entitlement. In *U.S. v. Washington* (1974) Boldt found that Pacific Northwest tribes were entitled to fifty percent of the harvestable fish run (less the escapement of spawning fish). The Supreme Court modified Boldt's decision but upheld the entitlement of tribal fishing to fifty percent of the run.[5]

As a consequence of the Boldt and Belloni decisions, the tribes became players at a table from which they had been previously excluded. They created the Columbia River Intertribal Fish Commission. They participated with the states in setting seasons, monitoring hatchery programs, and working to improve habitat for anadromous fish. Their role—buttressed by court decisions—furthered the government-to-government relationships they had with the Forest Service, Bureau of Land Management, Corps of Engineers, and Fish and Wildlife Service.

Tribal Self-Governance programs, created on October 25, 1994, by the Tribal Self-Governance Act, encouraged tribes to take charge of their own destinies. Tribal councils gained the authority to administer federal dollars to hire personnel and run their own programs. While some were critical of the transfer of operations from the Bureau of Indian Affairs to the tribe, many tribal leaders liked taking charge of their own affairs. They hired consultants to assist work on tribal housing projects with the Department of Housing and Urban Development. They hired staff to open tribal clinics or entered into cooperative agreements such as that with Pequot Pharmacy to provide health care and medications, and to interface with the Indian Health Service. They studied options for increasing tribal economic self-sufficiency.

The quest for jobs and sources of income for tribes proved challenging. One source was the Social and Economic Development Strategies grants from the Department of Health and Human Services. SEDS grants enabled Oregon tribes to try start-up programs such as the Cow Creek sale of cordwood—shipped by rail—to California or the Blue Earth Foods of the Confederated Tribes of Coos, Lower Umpqua, and Siuslaw. The Siletz tribes, for a number of years, prepared and marketed smoked salmon. These efforts, however, were labor intensive and mounted in a highly competitive business atmosphere. None provided a viable future for charting tribal economies.

With a land base of nearly 700,000 acres, the Confederated Tribes of Warm Springs became by the 1970s a showcase for tribal economic programs. These ranged from the hot springs resort, hotel, and golf course—Kah-nee-tah—to a range cattle enterprise and tribal sawmill. Smaller operations included contract work to assemble electronic equipment. Less significant for jobs but of great importance for income were contracts the tribe entered into with Pacific Power and Light for production of electricity at Pelton and Round Butte dams. That scale of enterprise required outlay of capital beyond the reach of tribes to borrow, but the development of leases and then shared ownership permitted the tribes at Warm Springs an increasing portion of the electricity revenues generated on their reservation.

Oregon tribes confronted several sorts of schemes as they came back into federal relationship after 1977. Developers promoted potential ventures. They offered derelict hotels as new Indian housing units, abandoned aquaculture facilities as sure-fire means to make money, warehouses on lands to be taken into trust to transform the sites into "duty-free ports-of-entry," and other projects. Tribal leaders found a new round of possible exploitation by those seeking to dump derelict and polluted properties or trying to promote hare-brained schemes that had failed to secure investment by more traditional lenders.

The decision of the U.S. Supreme Court in *California v. Cabazon Band of Mission Indians* (1987) became a major turning point in tribal fortunes. The court ruled that California regulatory laws over gambling did not apply on Indian trust lands. In the Indian Gaming Regulatory Act (1988) Congress laid out a program of permissible gambling on reservations. A number of tribes responded when they grasped the economic opportunities. The Cow Creek Band of Umpqua Tribe of Indians led the way in Oregon. Dennis J. Whittlesey, the tribal attorney, negotiated a "gaming compact" with Governor Barbara Roberts. Although Oregon's constitution barred casinos, no one had defined the term. The tribe's compact edged into unknown territory, but it was not challenged. The Cow Creeks moved swiftly from running a bingo hall into full-scale gaming at Seven Feathers Casino on their reservation at Canyonville.

In the 1990s other Oregon tribes also developed casinos: Wild Horse (Umatilla), Chinook Winds (Siletz), Spirit Mountain (Grand Ronde), The Mill (Coquille), Kah-nee-tah (Warm Springs), Old Camp (Burns Paiute), and Kla-Mo-Ya (Klamath). In 2004 the Confederated Tribes of Coos, Lower Umpqua, and Siuslaw opened Three Rivers at Florence, Oregon. The journey of the Coos, Lower Umpqua and Siuslaw to gaming required two federal court cases and a six-year struggle to prove that their gaming site—a former non-taxed allotment and the driveway to their cemetery (entered into trust in 1947)—met the "restored lands" provision of IGRA.

By 2003 Oregon tribes had earned $189 million in profits through casino operations. Their annual casino payrolls totaled $192.4 million for 5,328 workers.

Economic analysis in 2005 suggested that their enterprises had created another 5,640 jobs and annually pumped more than a $1 billion into Oregon's economy. A consequence of tribal gaming was a significant improvement in individual and family income for Oregon Indians, an estimated decline of 7.5 percent in the poverty rate between 1990 and 2000. The flow of revenues to tribes enabled them to invest in hotels, motels, service stations, convenience stores, restaurants, and parks for recreational vehicles. Tribal capital investments between 1992 and 2005 were approximately $245 million.[6]

Court affirmation of treaty-reserved rights to hunt, fish, and gather resources enabled a number of Oregon tribes to proceed—for the first time in decades—without threat of prosecution and prolonged litigation. Restoration of terminated tribes permitted Native American communities to resume their unique relationship with the federal government and regain the benefits of trust responsibility for land, delivery of health care, education, and funding for core tribal services. Gaming opened the door to jobs, capital to invest in diversified enterprises, and the opportunity to engage in philanthropy. Rather than receiving assistance, tribes were suddenly sought out as donors for civic projects. They had become major players in philanthropy.

The following selections speak to the changing political atmosphere of the late twentieth century. They suggest that hope, rather than despair, became a possibility for Oregon tribes.

NOTES

1. Charles F. Wilkinson and Daniel Keith Conner. The Law of the Pacific Salmon Fishery: Conservation and Allocation of a Transboundary Common Property Resource, *The University of Kansas Law Review*, 32(1)(Fall, 1983), p. 33.

2. Fay G. Cohen, *Treaties on Trial: The Continuing Controversy Over Northwest Indian Fishing Rights*. Seattle, WA: University of Washington Press, 1986, pp. 55–56.

3. Ibid., pp. 56–57.

4. Ibid., pp. 62–63.

5. Wilkinson and Conner, The Laws of the Pacific Salmon Fishery, p. 47.

6. Jeff Mapes, Tribes Press Case on Gaming, *The Oregonian* (Portland, OR), March 8, 2005.

"The Indian Never Has Been a Conservationist," 1976

Restoration of tribal status proved a daunting challenge to Oregon tribes. It soon became evident that Congress anticipated certain measures of a tribe's entitlement for restoration. Had it sustained a social community? Did it have elected officers and a governing document? Did it have a membership roll? Did it have community support external to the tribe? In order to respond to these questions, tribal leaders solicited letters and scrambled to find funds to take witnesses to Washington, D.C., for hearings on restoration bills.

The Confederated Tribes of Siletz proceeded first. Ably assisted by Charles Wilkinson, a law professor at the University of Oregon, and the staff of the Native American Rights Fund, Boulder, Colorado, the tribe gathered social statistics, background information, support letters, and witnesses. On March 30–31, 1976, Senator Mark O. Hatfield chaired hearings before the Subcommittee on Interior and Insular Affairs on S. 2801, a bill to repeal Termination and restore the Confederated Tribes of Siletz.

The lengthy hearing record included written testimony, oral testimony from the tribe, and the remarks of several who questioned the legislation. The following statement is that of Forrest L. Meuret, vice-president of Save Oregon's Resources Today, Inc. (SORT), who rejected the Indian role in fisheries management and conservation. He found nothing redeeming in Indian history or recent tribal activities. His views, shaped by the decisions of federal judges George Boldt and Robert Belloni affirming treaty fishing rights, confirmed the difficulties tribes faced. The terminated Siletz had no reserved rights treaties nor did they seek hunting and fishing rights as a condition for restoration.

I would like to say that many people may not realize the importance of salmon and steelhead in the Pacific Northwest. Oregon has more licensed sportsfishermen than it has people voting at elections. More than half of these pursue the magnificent salmon and steelhead. Annual license to fish for these anadramous fish costs $11, and yields an average catch of less than one fish per license.

Oregon sport fishermen actually average paying more than a dollar a pound in license fees for such fish as they are lucky enough to remove from the water. Although sportsfishing license fees make up 54.8 percent, substantially more than half, of Oregon's $22,565,000 bi-annual budget for support of the fishery, sportsmen take only about a fourth as many pounds of all kinds of fish, this is fresh and saltwater and shellfish and everything, as do the commercial fishermen who contribute only 11.2 percent of that budget.

And incidentally, the Indian contribute nothing. Fishing for salmon and steelhead in Oregon is big. Many have spent a month camped beside the Columbia without a bite. Outdoorsmen in Oregon and Washington support a billion dollar service and supply industry, and spend well over $100 per salmon caught. The last accurate figures we have were in 1964, the figure was supposed to be $64 per fish at that time.

Both the hours required to catch a fish and the cost per hour have gone up in the meantime, drastically.

The Department of the Interior and BIA public relations and legal batteries are trying to convince us that a fish is more important to an Indian than to anyone else, some say because he has been fishing longer. He has only been fishing here longer, as most of our ancestors fished wherever they were. Stripped of the romance and propaganda, the Indian fisherman is a commercial fisherman, fishing for income, and will not spend $100, and more than a week for one fish. He is not the highest bidder, and does not contribute to the support of the resource.

Now, I will move to the next paragraph. It is not the difference in the races that worries us about the Siletz Restoration bill, but the similarities. Those of use that get our picture of the Indian from day to day acquaintance rather than from the ennobling propaganda regard him as being as greedy as any other commercial fishing group, and definitely needing regulation. Contrary to ongoing PR programs, the Indian never has been a conservationist. This is not particularly surprising, since no one else was, either, until we missed the water in the well. It is, however, the history of the Indian that he depleted the game and moved on. This country is supporting nearly a thousand times as many people as it did before the coming of the white man, and the Indian is better clothed, fed, housed, and educated, and enjoys better medical care than at any time in history. He has earned little, if any, of these gains himself. He had no written language, no wheel, or beast of burden, and was not progressing.

Now I think at this point, it is time to mention that I live near the Warm Springs Reservation, and all these problems of alcoholism and unemployment are there, too, and that has never been terminated. I took the trouble to go down to watch people come off a shift from the Warm Springs Forest Products Industry where Federal money purchased that for the Indians to provide jobs for Indians and they have priority, and I watched 111 people come out of there to see two that I could visually identify as an Indian.

Unemployment is a matter of choice. They don't want the job and one of the most arrogant things that the Caucasian majority does is think all these minorities want to be made over in our image and they do not, and I don't quarrel with them for this and they have a more casual way of life and I sometimes envy them.

I don't quarrel with the Indian for this, I should say. We don't oppose even greater improvement in health and educational benefits for the Indian, but we do feel that that is enough, and that he should not seek a disproportionate share of finite or destructible resources, and especially should not seek unregulated pursuit of living resources, just as no other concerned citizen should. We wish to point out the relatively few Indians fish. Those who do, mostly do so with nets or other wholesale or commercial means. Washington's 36,000 Indians represent barely over 1 percent of that State's population, and only 794 of those are commercial fishermen. If and when the Boldt decision is fully implemented, those 794 will have the opportunity to harvest substantially more than half of the State's fishery. Since Washington has something like a million other citizens seeking the same fish, and adjudged by the court to be entitled to less than half, the individual Indian has been granted more than a thousand times as many fish as other citizens. Even after that, he pays no taxes. He has been handed a resource worth nearly $100,000 per individual participant at current prices. He claims he is discriminated against. We say, who is discriminated against? Can we not stop this discrimination pendulum somewhere in the middle?

. . . I want to thank you for the opportunity to speak for Oregon sportsmen. It must be obvious that it means a great deal for me to have traveled so far, and I hope equally obvious that we are not interested in denying the Siletz their recognition, but only in protecting Oregon's living resources. Hopefully, world civilization will advance to the point that anadramous fish will belong to the country of origin, and that fishing for personal use will be recognized as one of the oldest and highest traditions, and enjoy top priority, and all will have equal opportunity to participate, including the disadvantaged minority.

Meuret was not the only witness to contest the Siletz Restoration bill. Beverly B. Hall, an Assistant Attorney General representing the Oregon Fish and Wildlife

Commission, also testified. Hall proposed an amendment that included the following sentence: "Notwithstanding any other provision of law, the State shall have the authority to regulating hunting, fishing and trapping by the tribe and its members to the same extent and in the same manner as the State may regulate hunting, fishing and trapping by non-Indian persons." The Siletz act of 1977 restored the tribe; it extended no fishing, hunting, or trapping rights not previously held.

SOURCE

U.S. Senate. *Hearings Before the Subcommittee on Indian Affairs of the Committee on Interior and Insular Affairs, United States Senate, Ninety-Fourth Congress, Second Session, on S. 2801.* Washington, DC: U.S. Government Printing Office, 1976, pp. 102–15.

Kimball v. Callahan: A Landmark Court Ruling, 1976–79

The Klamath Treaty of October 14, 1864, created a reservation and ceded vast acreage to the United States; it also expressly stated that the Indians reserved "the exclusive right of taking fish in the streams and lakes included in said reservation." The courts subsequently expanded the meaning of this clause to include hunting and trapping, traditional subsistence activities of the tribe. Congress moved in the 1950s to terminate all federal relationships with the Klamath. The Termination Act took effect in 1961 and led to the curtailment of all services of the Bureau of Indian Affairs, withdrawal of federal trust responsibilities, and sale or transfer of much of the reservation either to timber companies or to the U. S. Forest Service.

The members of the Klamath Tribe believed Congress was clear when in 1954 it stated that nothing in the Termination Act "shall abrogate any fishing rights or privileges of the tribe or the members thereof enjoyed under Federal treaty." Exercise of these rights, however, proved difficult. Klamath Indians were arrested and charged with violations of state law. The state contended that when, for purposes of Termination, individual Indians withdrew from the tribe, they were no longer beneficiaries of the treaty protections in fishing, hunting, and trapping.

The following selections explore pivotal court rulings. First is the ruling handed down in 1976 by U.S. District Court Judge Gus J. Solomon. Reported in The Oregonian, *the judge's ruling affirmed tribal subsistence rights and the accommodation of the Klamaths to state regulations. The second article, complete with case citations, was shared with Klamath tribal members in* Mukluks Hemcunga, *their "Indian Talk" newsletter. It reported the decision of the Court of Appeals for the Ninth Circuit on January 26, 1979. In that ruling the appeals court found that treaty hunting, fishing, and trapping rights survived the Termination Act and that the State of Oregon had regulatory authority only to the extent necessary for conservation.*

Court Upholds Klamath Descendants' Game Rights

The right of the Klamath Indians to hunt, fish and trap on ancestral lands free of state regulation extends to descendants of persons on the final tribal roll, U.S. District Court Judge Gus J. Solomon has ruled.

Solomon also said he hopes the state and Indians will agree on regulations governing hunting, fishing and trapping on the former reservation.

Solomon issued his opinion in an action brought by four persons who were listed on the final tribal rolls and one who was not.

The five sought an injunction against the Oregon Fish and Wildlife Commission and Oregon State Police prohibiting them from enforcing state game regulations against Indians on the lands which made up the Klamath reservation.

Solomon had dismissed the suit in 1973 on grounds his court had no jurisdiction. The 9th U.S. Circuit Court of Appeals ruled, however, that the court did have jurisdiction and that the Indians retained rights to hunt, fish and trap on the land although the reservation had been sold.

Solomon heard arguments in February on new motions by the defendants to dismiss the suit. Solomon said both issues raised by the state agencies were decided by the appeals court and are "now the law of the case."

On the matter of descendants retaining tribal rights Solomon held, "if Congress intended the Klamath termination act to terminate all of the treaty rights of the Klamath Indians on the death of the last survivor whose name appeared on the final tribal roll, Congress could have so provided in clear and unambiguous language."

He said under another federal court ruling "the intention to abrogate or modify a treaty is not to be lightly imputed to the Congress."

The judge added, "I therefore hold that the rights of the Klamath Indians to hunt, fish and trap, free of state regulations, extend to the descendants of persons on the 1957 final tribal rolls."

Solomon noted, "Plaintiffs do not seek to exercise their treaty rights on land sold to private owners who prohibit hunting, fishing and trapping on the land. Neither do they seek to enforce exclusive rights on the remaining land, most of which is owned by the United States Government."

The Indians are willing to acquiesce in state regulation, Solomon said, if the regulations are essential to preserving a particular species, Indian tribal enforcement is inadequate and necessary conservation cannot be achieved by restricting hunting and fishing by non-treaty sportsmen.

Solomon said, "These conditions appear to conform with the current principles of state regulation of off-reservation fishing rights' established through other court actions."

The opinion said the general council of the Klamath tribe had recently approved comprehensive hunting regulations covering Klamaths on the former reservation providing for joint regulation with state agencies.

"Apparently the plaintiffs want me to approve their proposal," Solomon wrote. "Although their objectives appear to be commendable I have no authority to judicially approve their proposals. Nevertheless I hope that the Oregon Fish and Wildlife Commission will approve these proposals; or if the commission is unable to approve all of them that the commission will meet with representatives of the Klamath Indians and promulgate mutually satisfactory regulations for the management of fish and game resources on these lands."

He ordered attorneys to prepare a joint statement on remaining issues in the case within 30 days.

Federal supervision over the Klamath Indians was terminated in the 1950s and much of the tribe's reservation in Southern Oregon was sold with proceeds divided among Indians who withdrew from the tribe. Later the remaining lands were sold to the federal government and incorporated into the Winema National Forest.

Klamaths' Fishing and Hunting Case

On January 26, 1979, the United States Court of Appeals for the Ninth Circuit rendered its decision in *Kimball v. Callahan*, the hunting and fishing rights case. Below is the full text of the court's opinion with footnotes omitted.

Appellants, the members and directors of the Oregon State Game Commission and the director of the Oregon State Patrol and Oregon Game Enforcement Division, have appealed from a judgment declaring that appellees, five Klamath Indians and the Klamath Indian Game Commission and the members of the Klamath Indian Tribe are "entitled to rights, privileges and immunities afforded under the Treaty of October 14, 1864, between the Klamath Indian Tribe and the United States to hunt, trap and fish within their ancestral Klamath Indian Reservation as it existed at the time of termination in 1954, free from Oregon State game and fish regulations"; and enjoining appellants from "asserting hunting, fishing and trapping regulations against members of the Klamath Indian Tribe while hunting, fishing, and trapping on the former

Klamath Indian Reservation as it existed at the time of termination in 1954." The United States has filed an amicus brief in support of appellees.

I. Background

The treaty of October 14, 1864, 16 Stat. 707, which created the Klamath and Modoc Reservation, provided that the reservation "shall, until otherwise directed by the President of the United States, be set apart as a residence for said Indians, (and) held and regarded as an Indian reservation. . . ." The treaty secured for the Indians "the exclusive right of taking fish in the streams and lakes included in said reservation. . . ." On a prior appeal this court interpreted this provision to include *Kimball v. Callahan,* 493 F. 2d 564, 566 (9 Cir.) *cert. denied,* 419 U. S. 1019 (1974), (*Kimball I*). See also *Klamath and Modoc Tribes v. Maison,* 139 F. Supp. 634, 637 (D. Or. 1956).

In 1954 Congress passed the Klamath Termination Act, which became fully effective in 1961. Act of August 13, 1954, 25 U. S. C. §§ 564–564x. The purpose of the Act was to terminate federal supervision over the trust and restricted property of the Klamath Tribe of Indians, to dispose of federally owned property acquired or withdrawn for the administration of the Indians' affairs, and to terminate federal services furnished the Indians because of their status as Indians. 25 U. S. C. § 564.

Pursuant to the Termination Act the tribal roll was closed on August 13, 1954. No child born thereafter was eligible for enrollment. 25 U. S. C. § 564b. Each person whose name appeared on the final roll had to elect either to withdraw from the tribe and receive the money value of his interest in tribal property or to remain in the tribe and participate in a nongovernmental tribal management plan. § 564d(a)(2). All tribal property was to be appraised and a sufficient amount of it sold to pay those members who elected to withdraw from the tribe and have their interest converted into money. § 564d(a)(3). Members who received the money value of their interests in tribal property "thereupon cease[d] to be members of the tribe. . . ." § 564e(c). The Act expressly provided, however, that nothing in the Act "shall abrogate any fishing rights or privileges of the tribe or the members thereof enjoyed under Federal treaty." § 564m(b).

In February, 1973, the appellees, five Klamath Indians who either personally withdrew or whose ancestors withdrew from the Tribe and had their interest in tribal property converted into money and paid to them, filed suit seeking a declaration of their right to hunt, trap and fish within their ancestral Klamath

Indian Reservation free of Oregon fish and game regulation, pursuant to the Treaty of October 14, 1864. In a memorandum opinion dated March 15, 1973, the district court granted defendants' motion to dismiss for failure to state a claim. This court reversed. *Kimball v. Callahan, supra.* (*Kimball I*) Relying on *Menominee Tribe of Indians v. United States,* 391 U. S. 404 (1968), we held that the plaintiffs who elected to withdraw from the Tribe pursuant to the Klamath Termination Act nevertheless retained treaty rights to hunt, fish, and trap, "free of state fish and game regulations on the lands constituting their ancestral Klamath Indian Reservation, including that land now constituting United States national forest land and that privately owned land on which hunting, trapping, or fishing is permitted." 493 F. 2d at 569–70.

Following remand a supplemental complaint was filed in which the Klamath Indian Game Commission was joined as a plaintiff. In an opinion entered on September 10, court in *Kimball I* found jurisdiction and "that the Indians' rights to hunt, fish and trap on their ancestral court's holdings on these issues were the 'law of the case.'" The district court held further (1) that the rights of the Indians to fish, hunt, and trap, free of state regulations, extended to the descendants of persons on the final tribal roll; and (2) that the court had no authority to approve the plaintiffs-appellees' offer to permit state regulation under specified conditions for conservation purposes. The court did suggest that the defendants-appellants approve the Tribe's proposal or negotiate with representatives of the Klamath Indians in an effort to promulgate mutually satisfactory regulations.

Since the filing of the district court's opinion, the appellees have filed a motion for leave to file as an appendix to their brief their "Klamath Tribal Wildlife Management Plan," to which the district court referred in its opinion. Appellants oppose this motion.

II. Contentions on Appeal

Appellants do not seek review of the jurisdiction issue; nor do they "seek reconsideration of the conclusion reach in *Kimball I* that rights of the Klamath Tribe under the treaty of 1864 survived the Klamath Termination Act." They argue, however, that the 'law of the case' does not apply to the issues raised on this appeal. They contend that:

(1) Tribal rights can be exercised only be persons on the final tribal roll of August 13, 1954 who did not withdraw under the Klamath Termination Act,

and withdrawn members cannot exercise hunting, fishing, and trapping rights under the 1864 treaty.

(2) Persons born after August 13, 1954 are not entitled to exercise hunting, fishing and trapping rights.

(3) Treaty rights cannot be exercised on land disposed of to the federal government and private purchasers.

(4) The State can "directly regulate the exercise of treaty rights by members of the Klamath Tribe for conservation purposes."

III. Reconsideration of Kimball I

(a) Law of the Case

Preliminary to a consideration of the effect of specific holdings in *Kimball I*, we note that under the "law of the case" doctrine one panel of an appellate court will not as a general rule reconsider questions which another panel has decided on a prior appeal in the same case. As the court stated in *Lehrman v. Gulf Oil Corporation*, 500 F. 2d 659, 662–63 (5 Cir. 1974), *cert. denied*, 420 U. S. 929 (1975):

> This laudable and self-imposed restriction is grounded upon the sound public policy that litigation must come to an end. An appellate court cannot efficiently perform its duty to provide expeditious justice to all "if a question once considered and decided by it were to be litigated anew in the same case upon any and every subsequent appeal."

While the 'law of the case' doctrine is not "an inexorable command," the prior decision of legal issues should be followed on a later appeal "unless the evidence on a subsequent trial was substantially different, controlling authority has since made a contrary decision of the law applicable to such issues, or the decision was clearly erroneous and would work a manifest injustice." *White v. Murtha, supra*, 337 F. 2d at 431–32.

Appellants contend that *Kimball I* is inconsistent with two subsequent controlling decisions: this court's decision in *United States v. Washington*, 520 F. 2d 676 (9 Cir. 1975), *cert. denied*, 423 U. S. 1086 (1976), and the Supreme Court's decision in *Puyallup Tribe, Inc. v. Department of Game*, 433 U. S., 165 (1977) (*Puyallup III*).

They also argue that evidence of the legislative history of 1958 amendments to the Klamath Termination Act which was not before this court on the prior appeal, shows Congress intended the Klamath Termination Act to terminate the treaty hunting, fishing, and trapping rights of those Indians who withdrew from the Tribe pursuant to the Termination Act. We cannot agree with either contention.

(b) *United States v. Washington*

In *Kimball I* the court held that a Klamath Indian possessing treaty rights to hunt, fish, and trap on the former reservation at the time of the Act's enactment retained those rights even though he relinquished his tribal membership pursuant to the Act. 493 F. 2d at 569. Appellants argue that the basis of this holding was the court's conclusion that the Klamath treaty rights belonged to "individual Indians." This, they contend, is inconsistent with the court's decision in *United States v. Washington, supra,* as well as the Court of Claims' decision in *Whitefoot v. United States,* 293 F. 2d 658 (Ct. Cl. 1961), *cert. denied,* 369 U. S. 818 (1962), that treaty rights are communal in nature and are owned by the tribe, not by the members who exercise them. Neither of these cases, however, was concerned, as was *Kimball I,* with the tribal rights of individual Indians upon the termination of a tribe.

The court in *Kimball I* did not base its decision that withdrawn tribal members retained their treaty rights to hunt and fish upon any rights to tribal property. On the contrary, the court expressly recognized that withdrawn members relinquished all interests in tribal property. The court's decision was based on the express provision in the Termination Act that nothing in the Act 'shall abrogate any fishing rights or privileges of the tribe or the members thereof enjoyed under Federal treaty.' Moreover, the court's statement that treaty rights to hunt and fish are rights of the individual Indian must be understood within the context of the two cases cited in its support, *McClanahan v. Arizona State Tax Comm'n,* 411 U. S. 164, 181 (1973), and *Mason v. Sams,* 5 F. 2d 255, 258 (W. D. Wash. 1925).

In *McClanahan,* the State of Arizona attempted to impose its personal income tax on a reservation Indian whose entire income derived from reservation sources. In upholding the tax the Arizona court focused not on whether the tax infringed upon the appellant's rights as an individual Navajo Indian, but on whether the tax infringed upon the rights of the Navajo Tribe to be self-governing. *McClanahan v. Arizona State Tax Comm'n,* 484 F. 2d 221, 223 (1971). The United States Supreme Court rejected the notion that it was irrelevant whether the state income tax infringed upon appellant's rights as an individual Navajo Indian. Recognizing that when Congress has legislated on

Indian matters, it has most often dealt with the tribes as collective entities, the Court reasoned that those entities were composed of individual Indians and the legislation conferred individual rights. The court held that appellant's rights as a reservation Indian were violated. 411 U. S. at 181.

In *Mason* the district court considered whether in light of treaty provision with the Quinaielt Tribe which the court construed as giving the Quinaielt Indians the exclusive right of fishing upon their reservation, the Commissioner of Indian Affairs could enforce regulations made by him without tribal consent which required the plaintiffs, members of the Quinaielt Tribe, to pay a royalty for the fish they caught in reservation streams to be used by the Tribe for the care of the aged and destitute members of the Tribe and for general agency purposes. Because a limited number of fishing locations were available, not all tribal members were assigned fishing locations. Failure to sell fish to licensed buyers and to pay the royalty could result in imposition of a fine and withdrawal of fishing privileges for a whole season. Although the treaty giving exclusive fishing rights to the Quinaielts was with the Tribe, the court held that the right of taking fish was a right common to the members of the Tribe and that "a right to a common in the right of an individual of the community." 5 F. 2d at 258.

From *Mason* it is clear that an individual Indian enjoys a right of user in tribal property derived from the legal or equitable property right of the tribe of which he is a member. See also F. Cohen, *Handbook of Federal Indian Law* 185 (1945). This was the basis for the court's statement in *Kimball I*. Prior to the Termination Act, the Klamath Tribe held treaty hunting, fishing, and trapping rights within its reservation in which the individual members of the Tribe held rights of user. The Termination Act did not affect those rights. That an individual member withdrew from the tribe for purposes of the Termination Act did not change his relationship with the tribe as to matters unaffected by the Act, e.g., treaty hunting, fishing, and trapping rights. We find nothing in *United States v. Washington* and *Whitefoot v. United States* to the contrary.

(c) *Puyallup III*

In *Kimball I* this court held that the appellees could exercise their treaty hunting, fishing, and trapping rights on former reservation lands which had been sold pursuant to the Termination Act. Appellants contend this holding is inconsistent with the Supreme Court's subsequent decision in *Puyallup Tribe, Inc. v. Department of Game, supra* (*Puyallup III*), which they read as sustaining this court's decision in *Klamath and Modoc Tribes v. Maison*, 338 G. 2d 620 (9

Cir. 1964), limiting the exercise of treaty hunting, fishing, and trapping rights to unsold lands on the reservation. We do not find *Kimball I* inconsistent with *Puyallup III*.

In *Puyallup III* the Puyallup Tribe asserted an exclusive right to take steelhead fish which passed through its reservation. The State of Washington sought to regulate the Puyallup Indians' on-reservation exercise of their treaty fishing rights in the interest of conservation. The Tribe argued that a treaty which provided that the Puyallup Reservation was to be "set apart, and, so far as necessary, surveyed and marked out for their exclusive use" and that no "white man (was to) be permitted to reside upon the same without permission of the tribe and the superintendent or agent," amounted to a reservation of a right to fish free of State interference on the Puyallup River. The Supreme Court found that such an interpretation clashed with the subsequent history of the reservation and that neither the Tribe nor its members continued to hold the Puyallup River fishing grounds for their exclusive use. The tribal members' treaty right to fish "at all usual and accustomed grounds and stations," however, continued 'to protect their right to fish on ceded lands within the confines of the reservation.' 433 U. S. at 174, n. 13.

Because the treaty with the Klamaths did not contain a similar treaty provision, appellants argue that there is no basis for limiting state regulation of Indian hunting, fishing and trapping on the sold-off reservation lands to conservation measures. The Treaty of October 14, 1864, however, secured for the Indians "the exclusive right of taking fish in the streams and lakes in said reservation. . . ." The Klamath Termination Act expressly provided that nothing in the Act would abrogate the fishing rights secured by the treaty. As this court held in *Kimball I*, these two provisions protect the exercise of those treaty rights on the lands constituting the ancestral Klamath Indian Reservation. We find nothing contrary to this conclusion in *Puyallup III*. Both cases recognize that the transfer of reservation lands and modification of reservation boundaries may affect treaty rights by converting the exercise of those rights from exclusive to non-exclusive. The Klamaths do not claim an *exclusive* right to hunt, fish and trap on the lands sold pursuant to the Termination Act. See *supra*, n. 8.

(d) Legislative History of Termination Act and 1958 Amendment

In 1958 Congress amended the 1954 Termination Act to prevent potential destruction from over-harvesting of tribal forest lands which were to be sold to pay withdrawing tribal members the cash value of their interest in tribal property. Act of August 23, 1958, P. L. No. 85–731, 72 Stat. 816 (codified at 25

U. S. C. § 564w-1). The American Law Division of the Library of Congress sub-mitted a report during the hearings on the bill which concluded that withdrawn tribal members would lose their treaty hunting and fishing rights and that res-ervation land sold pursuant to the Termination Act would not be subject to the treaty rights of the Indians. Hearings before the Subcommittee on Indians Affairs of the Senate Committee on Interior and Insular Affairs of the Senate Committee on Interior and Insular Affairs, 85th Cong., 2d Sess., Pt. 2, on S. 2047 and S. 3051, at 492–93 (Senate Hearings) (R. 587–88). In a letter to the Subcommittee chair-man, the Acting Secretary of Interior took a similar position. Senate Hearings, at 397–98, 491–92 (R. 584–87); see also 62 I. D. 186, 202–03 (1955). Appellants claim this legislative history shows Congress did not intend that withdrawn tribal members should retain their treaty hunting, fishing, and trapping rights.

In concluding that withdrawn tribal members retained these rights, the court in *Kimball I* relied in part upon legislative history of the 1954 Termination Act. Recognizing that treaty obligations existed, Senator Watkins suggested that the Government 'buy out' the Indians' hunting and fishing rights rather than pre-serve them after termination. The court found it telling that Congress did not heed this suggestion. *Kimball I*, 493 F. 2d at 568–69 n. 9; see also Joint Hearings, Subcommittees of the Committees on Interior and Insular Affairs, 83d Cong., 2d Sess., Pt. 4, on S. 2745 and H. R. 7320, at 245–55.

Other portions of the legislative history of the 1958 amendments indicate that the Subcommittee members themselves were not certain what effect, if any, the Termination Act had upon the tribal treaty rights. Senate Hearings, at 397–98, 491–93 (R. 584–87). The Acting Secretary of Interior also recognized that different interpretations of its effect were possible, and advised Congress to clearly state its intentions. Letter to Hon. Richard L. Neuberger, Senate Hearings, at 491 (R. 586–87). Congress did not do so. The 1958 amendments to the Termination Act related solely to preservation of tribal lands as forests after their sale. If Congress intended the Termination Act to abrogate the Klamaths' treaty rights, it did not so indicate. As the Court recognized in *Menominee Tribe of Indians v. United States*, 391 U. S. at 413, "the intention to abrogate or modify a treaty is not to be lightly imputed to the Congress."

We conclude that the decision in *Klamath I* that withdrawn tribal members retained their treaty rights to hunt, fish, and trap on the lands constituting their ancestral Klamath Indian Reservation, including land constituting United States forest lands and privately owned land on which hunting, fishing, and trapping is permitted, is the "law of the case."

IV. Exercise of Treaty Rights by Descendants

Appellants' contention that persons born after August 13, 1954, are not entitled
to exercise treaty hunting, fishing, and trapping rights rests upon two points:
(1) the Klamath Termination Act closed the tribal roll as of August 13, 1954 and
expressly provided that children not alive on that date could not subsequently
be included on that roll, 25 U. S. C. § 564b; and (2) to share in tribal property,
a participant ordinarily has to have tribal membership status in his own right,
not through his ancestors. This question was not decided by *Kimball I.*

Appellants' argument is based upon the premise that the tribal roll provided
for by the Termination Act was final for purposes of determining who could
exercise tribal treaty rights. We reject that premise. Although the act terminated
federal supervision over trust and restricted property of the Klamath Indians,
disposed of federally owned propertty, and terminated federal services to the
Indians, it specifically contemplated the continuing existence of the Klamath
tribe. It did not affect the power of the tribe to take any action under its constitution and bylaws consistent with the Act. § 564r. The Klamaths still maintain a tribal constitution and tribal government, which among other things
establishes criteria for membership in the tribe. The tribal roll created by the
Act was for purposes of determining who should share in the resulting distribution of property. *Kimball I* held that the Act did not abrogate tribal treaty
rights of hunting, fishing, and trapping. Neither did the Act effect the sovereign
authority of the tribe to regulate the exercise of those rights. The District Court
properly held that the Termination Act did not limit treaty hunting, fishing
and trapping rights to persons on the 1957 final tribal roll, but those rights also
extended to the descendants of persons on the final roll.

V. State Regulation of Treaty Rights for Conservation Purposes

In holding that off-reservation fishing may be regulated by the State for conservation purposes, the Court in *Puyallup I* said:

The right to fish "at all usual and accustomed" places may, of course, not be
qualified by the State, even though all Indians born in the United States are now
citizens of the United States. . . .But the manner of fishing, the size of the take,
the restriction of commercial fishing, and the like may be regulated by the State
in the interest of conservation, provided the regulation meets appropriate standards and does not discriminate against the Indians. 391 U. S. at 398.

In *Puyallup II* the Court held that the State of Washington's regulation barring net fishing of steelhead trout discriminated against the Indians and remanded the case for determination of a fair apportionment between Indian net fishing and non-Indian sports fishing. 414 U. S. at 48–49. In *Puyallup III* the Court found that the state court on remand from the decision in *Puyallup II*, had conducted a trial and from expert testimony and exhibits had applied a proper standard of conservation necessity and fashioned appropriate relief. 433 U. S. at 177.

Antoine v. Washington, 420 U. S. 194, 207 (1975), applied the rule set forth in *Puyallup I, supra*, with respect to land on a former Indian reservation which had been ceded to the Government. The Court said in part: "The 'appropriate standards' requirement means that the State must demonstrate that its regulation is a reasonable and necessary conservation measure (citing *Puyallup II* and *Tulee v. Washington*, 315 U. S. 681, 684 (1943)), *and* that its application to the Indians is necessary in the interest of conservation."

The district court in its opinion noted that appellees "do not seek to exercise their treaty rights on land sold to private owners who prohibit hunting, fishing, and trapping on that land"; nor "do they seek to enforce exclusive rights on the remaining land, most of which is owned by the United States Government." The court referred to conditions under which appellees were willing to permit State regulation and found that these conditions appeared 'to conform with the current principles of State regulation of off-reservation fishing rights set forth in *United States v. Washington*, 520 F. 2d 676 (9th Cir. 1975), and *Sohappy v. Smith*, 302 F. Supp. 899 (D. Or. 1969).'

The court also noted that the General Council of the Klamath Tribe had recently approved comprehensive regulations for the hunting of game by Klamath Indians on the former Klamath Indian Reservation, which provided for joint regulation with State agencies. While it found their objectives commendable, the court concluded that it had no authority to judicially approve the proposals. The court expressed the hope that the Oregon Fish and Wildlife Commission would approve the proposal; or if the Commission were unable to approve all of them, that the Commission would meet with representatives of the Klamath Indians to promulgate mutually satisfactory regulations.

Appellees recognize that the State of Oregon has authority to reasonable regulate the exercise of their treaty hunting, fishing and trapping rights for conservation purposes. The parties disagree with respect to (1) the scope of the State's authority and (2) whether this court should decide upon appropriate regulations or remand to the district court for its initial determination.

Appellees contend that this court "should adopt limitations on state conservation authority which secures the right of Klamath Indians to exercise their treaty
rights while providing adequate protection for reservation wildlife." Both appellees and the United States as *amicus curiae* take the position that the extent of
state regulation presents legal issues which can be resolved by this court on this
appeal.

Appellants urge a remand to the district court for development of a factual
record which would serve as a basis for establishing regulations within the scope
of the State's right to regulate the Indians' treaty rights. We agree with the state
that a factual record should be developed in the district court, as was done on
remand in *Puyallup II*. In the event the parties are unable to agree upon mutually
satisfactory regulations, it will be necessary for the district court to determine the
scope of the State's authority and formulate appropriate standards in the light
of the evidence presented and the guidelines contained in *Puyallup I, II,* and *III,*
supra; *Antoine v. Washington,* supra; *United States v. Washington,* supra; and
Settler v. Lameer, 507 F. 2d 231 (9 Cir. 1974).

VI. CONCLUSION

We conclude that (1) Klamath I is the law of the case in its holding that mem-
bers of the Klamath Tribe who withdrew pursuant to the Klamath Termination
Act retain their treaty rights to hunt, fish, and trap on the former Klamath
Reservation; (2) the treaty hunting, fishing, and trapping rights survived the
Klamath Termination Act for all members on the final roll and their descendants; (3) the State of Oregon has authority, under appropriate standards to
regulate treaty fishing, hunting, and trapping rights on the former Klamath
Indian Reservation for conservation purposes; and (4) in the event the parties
are unable to agree upon mutually satisfactory regulations, the district court
shall determine the scope of the State's authority in the light of the evidence
presented and standards set forth in applicable cases.

Affirmed in part, and remanded for further proceedings consistent with this
opinion.

SOURCES

Anonymous. Court Upholds Klamath Descendants' Game Rights, *The Oregonian* (Portland, OR), [1976], reprinted in *Mukluks Hemcunga*, Vol. 4(2)(Summer 1976), p. 1.

Kimball v. Callahan: Klamaths' Hunting and Fishing Case, *Mukluks Hemcunga* (Klamath Falls, OR), Winter 1978/79, Vol. 6(1), pp. 1, 6–7, 11–12.

RELATED READING

American Friends Service Committee. *Uncommon Controversy: Fishing Rights of the Muckleshoot, Puyallup, and Nisqually Indians.* Seattle, WA: University of Washington Press, 1970.

Cohen, Fay. *Treaties on Trial: The Continuing Controversy Over Northwest Indian Fishing Rights.* Seattle, WA: University of Washington Press, 1986.

Hood, Susan. Termination of the Klamath Tribe in Oregon, *Ethnohistory* 19 (Fall, 1972): 379–92.

Peterson, Tom F. *Oregon Department of Fish and Wildlife v. Klamath Indian Tribe:* Diminishing Treaty Rights, *Oregon Law Review* 64(1986):701–26.

Legacy of Allotment: A Nightmare of Heirship Interests, 1977

The General Allotment Act of 1887 was premised on the conversion of Native Americans to citizenship through a program of agriculture. In a direct assault on tribalism, the law provided for the division of the tribal landed estate into parcels of land varying from 10 to 160 acres, depending on the condition of the reservation and the projected activity of the allottees. The law anticipated a minimum of twenty-five years of "trust," during which the allottee was to engage in farming or stock-raising. Once he or she had proven the ability to survive on this individual land parcel, the Bureau of Indian Affairs would certify "competency." The individual thus became simultaneously an American citizen and a taxpayer on the land shifted from trust to fee status.

The Bureau of Indian Affairs eagerly embraced the allotment program and subjected almost all reservations to its provisions. The law, however, proved calamitous. Indian land holdings plunged from 150 million acres in 1887 to 48 million acres by 1934. The Indian Reorganization Act of 1934 suspended the program and extended trust status indefinitely. Inexorably, however, allottees died, their children died, and their grandchildren died. The heirship interests in these individual trust lands multiplied, creating a nightmare of bookkeeping, especially when allotments produced oil, gas, timber, grazing fees, and lease income.

In 1977 Senator Mark O. Hatfield chaired hearings on S. 470 and S. 471, bills proposing to consolidate fractional lands and heirships of fractional interests on the Umatilla Reservation. Senator Hatfield described the context in which Congress considered this proposed legislation:

These hearings of the Senate Select Committee on Indian Affairs have been called to receive testimony on Senate bill 470, a, bill pertaining to land consolidation and development on the Umatilla Indian Reservation, and Senate bill 471, pertaining to the inheritance of trust allotments of the reservation. These bills were introduced with the cosponsorship of Senator Bob Packwood on January

26 of this year. Identical legislation was sponsored by Representative Al Ullman and was the subject of hearings before the House Interior Subcommittee on Indian Affairs on June 6.

A brief history of the reservation's development, I believe, is helpful in understanding why this legislation is needed. A reservation of 245,000 acres was created by the treaty of June, 9, 1855. By that treaty, the Indians agreed to cede vast tracts of lands to the whites and move to the area designated as their reservation, provided, among other things, that they were to be protected from white encroachment onto their reservation and provided that all their hunting and fishing rights would be preserved.

Thirty years later, by the act of March 3, 1885, Congress provided for the allotment of the reservation.

All heads of households were allotted 160 acres; each single person over the age of 18, 80 acres; each orphan child under 18, 80 acres; and to each child under 18 not otherwise provided for, 40 acres. Additional land was set aside for tribal purposes and for a school. The remainder, despite the treaty language forbidding encroachment by whites, was opened for sale and settlement by non-Indians. Some 74,000 acres were sold in this manner. When the allotment policy was applied nationwide by the Dawes Act of 1887, the detrimental effect on Indian landholdings was even more severe; by 1933, in the Nation at large, 91 million acres or two-thirds of the Indian land base had been lost.

Today, Umatilla Indian holdings consist of 68,434 acres of trust allotments held by individuals, 16,168 acres of tribal trust land, 830 acres owned by individuals in fee simple, and 22 acres owned by the tribe fee simple. A total of 86,688 acres on the reservation are owned by non-Indians.

These figures reveal that the majority of Indian holdings are in trust allotments that were originally made by the 1885 act. Over the years, as these lands have passed from generation to generation, ownership has become fractionated amongst several heirs. This multiple ownership frustrates economic development. For example, as many of you know, the consent of all shareholders in an allotment is required for the leasing of that land to a non-Indian, and all share in the rent paid according to that lease. Some of these rent shares are ridiculously small, but each requires a separate payment.

Therefore, the purpose of Senate bill 470 and Senate bill 471 is to respond to this situation by providing the Confederated Tribes of the Umatilla Indian Reservation with a means of creating a stable economic base and eliminating the fractionalized ownership on tribal lands.

Senate bill 471 is straightforward and, I believe, noncontroversial. It deals strictly with the inheritance of individual trust allotments when the owner dies without a valid will. It would return the inheritance of trust allotments to the method prescribed under Oregon law until it was changed in 1969. The bill was designed to prevent the fractionalization of ownership that has occurred over the years. Individual shares of an allotment are as small as 3/3888, an equivalent of six-hundredths of an acre. Senate bill 471 will help reverse this trend, and I hope it will be expeditiously approved.

Senate bill 470 authorizes the Secretary of the Interior, in accordance with a land consolidation and development plan drafted by the tribes and approved by the Secretary, to acquire additional trust lands for the Umatilla Indians through purchase, relinquishment, or exchange. These lands may be acquired both inside and outside the reservation boundaries. However, no lands may be acquired for individuals outside the boundaries and lands acquired outside the boundaries for the tribe cannot be exempted from taxation.

The bill also provides for the sale of tribal trust lands and allotments. Proceeds from these sales will be used for the purchase of other lands or for other purposes in keeping with the consolidation plan approved by the Secretary.

Section 8 of Senate bill 470 authorizes the Confederated Tribes, with the, approval of the Secretary, to execute a mortgage on trust land. This would give the tribes a valuable financial management tool which they do not now enjoy. Similar mortgage authority exists for other tribes, so this is no precedent.

Now, the Secretary may use tribal trust funds and whatever additional funds are made available by the tribes for the purposes of acquiring land. I am advised by the tribe that no funds are now available for these purposes. The Secretary may also use whatever Federal funds are appropriated under the authority of section 5 of the Indian Reorganization Act of 1934—25 U.S.C. 465. It should be pointed out, however, that no funds have been appropriated for more than 20 years, and there is little likelihood that funding will be renewed under this act.

Any and all land acquisition and sales authorized by this bill would be completely and only voluntary, between a willing buyer and a willing seller. No condemnation authority is given in this bill.

Many interested citizens have voiced concerns about the kind of consolidation and development contemplated by the tribe in anticipation of the bill's passage—the status of water rights, and the potential impact upon the tax revenues of Umatilla County. It is my hope that testimony received here today from tribal representatives, Federal, State and local officials, and interested citizens will serve to allay these concerns and fears.

In closing, I want to make clear that the subject of these hearings today is Senate bill 470 and Senate bill 471, only. The draft jurisdiction proposal that was the subject of considerable debate earlier this year has been dropped, and since it is unrelated to the two bills at hand, it will not be a matter of discussion here today. The Chair reserves the right to rule out of order testimony or comment on extraneous issues.

These bills produced an animated response. Both Indian and non-Indian stakeholders expressed their opinions. Leslie Minthorn, chairman of the Board of Trustees of the Confederated Tribes of Umatilla Indian Reservation, submitted written and oral testimony. "The land is the only thing, the water, the timber, that these people live by," he stated. "The land base is very critical to their survival for future generations. And it is by the enactment of this bill, if this bill is passed, that some of the fractionalized ownership patterns on the reservation will be minimized for those generations who are yet to come, who have now today nothing more than handfuls of dirt as their share of that piece of ground."

The following was Minthorn's written statement to Congress. His statement, while well argued, failed to persuade the Senate on these bills. Ultimately Congress passed the Indian Land Consolidation Act (1983, amended 1984), but in 1997 the Supreme Court held in Babbitt v. Youpee *that its provisions violated the "just compensation" clause of the Fifth Amendment. The land consolidation statute thus had fostered the illegal taking of individual Indian land. The fractionalization of lands continues daily and the bookkeeping nightmare grows exponentially.*

Mr. Chairman, members of the Committee, I am Leslie Minthorn, Chairman of the Board of Trustees of the Confederated Tribes of the Umatilla Indian Reservation. The bills that we are here to discuss today and indeed, this hearing, are milestones in the history and development of our tribe.

We have worked hard in recent years to develop programs that are beneficial to our tribe and to build a strong and capable tribal government. We feel that our membership is entitled to a tribal government that can serve and protect their interests. We are proud of what we have accomplished on our reservation. However, as in all major endeavors, progress can only be made to a certain point before obstacles are encountered that would be insurmountable without additional assistance.

We have found ourselves at that point recently. We have encountered two distinct problems that impede our further development and it is within the power and authority of Congress to remedy these problems. Thus, through these two pieces of legislation, we are asking your assistance in resolving matters relating to the inheritance of trust allotments and land consolidation on the Umatilla Indian Reservation. I would like to discuss each of the two matters separately.

However, before dealing with the specific bills, I would like to provide you with some background on both our reservation and tribal government since both will be affected by the passage of these measures.

The Umatilla Indian Reservation is situated in northeastern Oregon and is primarily within Umatilla County, there being approximately 1,000 acres situated in Union County. The Reservation was created by the Treaty of June 9, 1855, 12 Stat. 941. As created, it encompassed approximately 245,799 acres, all of it held pursuant to the tribe's aboriginal title.

The reservation contains a great diversity of climates and land. The northern portion is characterized by flat, fertile soils that are valuable for dry land farming. The Umatilla River bisects the reservation from east to west and connects with several tributaries within the boundaries. To the south, one encounters hillsides suitable for grazing purposes, and ultimately, in the Blue Mountains, timbered country.

By the Act of March 3, 1885, 23 Stat. 340, Congress provided for the allotment of the Reservation. Under this Act, all tribal members alive at that time were given a parcel of land to further the government's goal of "civilization" by encouraging farming as an occupation. Of course, many Indians at that time were not disposed to be farmers and some of the allotments were sold. One tract of land was set aside as a farm school. Some was reserved for the Tribe and the remainder was to be sold to non-Indians. The allotment process and subsequent opening of the Reservation to non-Indian settlement was brought about by pressure from non-Indians in the area who complained that Reservation land was 'lying waste' and that it would support some 1500 farming families. McNab, *A Century of News and People In The East Oregonian*, pp. 77–80 (1975). Approximately 74,000 acres were thus sold. The Act of August 10, 1939, 53 Stat. 1351 restored "to tribal ownership the undisposed of surplus lands of the Umatilla Indian Reservation, Oregon, heretofore opened to entry or other form of disposal under the public land laws. . . ."

As mentioned earlier, the Reservation encompassed 245,799 acres when created. Of that total today, 16,168 acres are tribal trust land and the tribe owns 22 acres in fee simply. Trust allotments total 68,434 acres and 830 acres are owned by tribal members in fee simple. The remainder is deeded land owned by other than individual Indians or the Tribe.

From 1855 to the present we have suffered significant losses of our land base. From the Reservation that was set aside for the Tribe and tribal purposes in 1855, that same Tribe is left today with the 'remains' of the allotment and settlement process. One of the bills to be discussed today provides a method by which we could reacquire some of the lands that have been lost and better manage that which we have.

A tribal government plays a key role in the administration and development of land resources on any reservation. I am proud to say that ours is a very active and progressive tribal government that has developed rapidly in the past few years. I would like to review for you the structure and scope of our tribal government.

We have a governing body which consists of nine members, known as the Board of Trustees which is elected by the General Council which consists of all tribal members of legal voting age. Our Constitution and By-Laws were adopted in 1949. One amendment to the Constitution was approved in November of 1976.

At the present time, we have some 24 committees, tribal departments and enterprises. Among these are committees that are responsible for a specific subject and report to the Board of Trustees on relevant matters. They include Enrollment, Building, Planning, Johnson O'Malley, Child Care, Fish, Credit, Senior Citizens, Celebration, Law and Order, Health, Education and Housing Committees. There are enterprises whose function is to engage in profit making activities for the Tribe. They include Farm, Forest and Range, Construction and Commercial Enterprises.

A source of particular pride is the Mission Market, a grocery store with an arts and crafts shop, gas sales and a laundromat that was recently opened on the Reservation and is operated by the Commercial Enterprise Committee.

Our Housing Authority has constructed and now manages 84 housing units. Fifty more are to be constructed in the near future.

Community health programs include community health representatives, alcohol and drug program, zoning office, adult basic education program and needs assessment. These programs have been developed to meet the needs of our people or to provide wise management and protection of our tribal interests.

It is through the operation of this tribal government structure that we have found the problems these bills are designed to correct.

Umatilla Inheritance Bill

The Bill that has been introduced as S. 471 in the Senate and H.R. 2540 in the House of Representative is the Umatilla Inheritance Bill. This bill represents our effort to have trust allotments that are not subject to the provisions of a valid will pass by intestate succession in a manner acceptable to the tribe.

As you are aware, the descent and distribution of Indian trust allotments is subject to federal law. That law provides that the descent and distribution of such property shall be in accordance with the laws of the state wherein it is located. In 25 USC 348, it is provided in part, ". . . that the law of descent and partition in force in the state or territory where such lands are situate shall apply thereto after patents therefore have been executed and delivered. . . ." Similarly, in 25 USC 373, which is derived from the Act of June 25, 1910, 36 Stat. 856, provision is made for the approval of wills involving trust allotments by the Secretary of the Interior. Where such a will is declared invalid, the statute provides that ". . . the property of the testator shall thereupon descent or be distributed in accordance with the laws of the state wherein the property is located." In accordance with these provisions, the intestate passing of trust allotments on the Umatilla Reservation has been subject to the laws of the State of Oregon which are found in Oregon Revised Statutes, Chapter 112, 112.015 - 112.115.

For many years this was satisfactory to us. However, in 1969, the State of Oregon revised its laws on intestate succession. A summary description of the evolution of Oregon's intestate succession laws is attached to this statement for your reference. After several years experience under the new laws, the members of our Tribe expressed dissatisfaction with the resulting distribution of property. Other problems with the new laws also became evident in that the distribution required, compounded the already difficult problem of fractionated ownership and lands began to go out of trust.

Fractionation of land ownership is a perplexing problem that plague many parcels of land on our Reservation. Both the Inheritance and Land Consolidation bills address this problem. I would like to graphically display this problem to you. It begins, as you know, when the owner of an allotment dies and each of his heirs acquires an undivided interest in the allotment. When they die, their heirs each obtain an undivided interest and the process continues in a pyramidal fashion. After many generations, the following situations, which represent actual examples of allotments on the Umatilla Indian Reservation result.

Allotment No.	Share	Acreage Equivalent	Rental Received	
			October	April
A	132/9600	1.09	$1.09	$.00
B	300/604800	.0647	.36	.36
C	30/38880	.0617	.28	.28
D	32/73444	.0348	.13	.13
E	48/24480	.1568	2.36	.00
F	9702/13608000	.0533	.36	.00
G	18/40320	.0357	.00	.02
H	1/70	.5714	.00	.08
I	1/30	2.6	.00	1.48
J	10/2160	.3703	.00	.30
K	15/8640	.0814	.21	.21

I believe these figures speak for themselves. This is one of the problems that this legislation would help us overcome.

The Inheritance Bill provides that trust or restricted land that is not the subject of a valid will shall descend to the lineal descendants of the Indian descent.

This varies from the intestate succession laws of the State of Oregon that provide the following line of succession. If a descent leaves a spouse and issue, the net estate is taken one-half by each. If there is a spouse and no issue, the spouse takes the entire estate. That portion of the estate that does not go to the spouse shall pass to the issue of the descendent. If there is no issue, then to surviving parents. If there are no surviving parents, then to brothers and sisters. If there are no brothers or sisters, then grandparents. Of course if there are no heirs at all, a person's net estate would escheat to the State under state law.

Federal laws of descent and distribution presently provide that where no heirs exist, the decendant's trust property will escheat to the tribe that owned the property at the time the allotment was made. 25 USC 373 (A), Act of November 14, 1942, 56 Stat. 1021. This supersedes state law under which an estate for which there were no heirs would escheat to the state.

Under the system prescribed by state law, it is readily seen how trust allotments would go out of trust by going to a non-Indian spouse or other relative who was not eligible to have property held in trust for them.

By having trust allotments descend only to lineal descendants, the property will pass to persons of Indian blood and the trust status can more regularly be maintained.

The spouse of the decedent is not ignored under our bill. Section 2 provides for a life estate for a surviving spouse in one-half of the trust or restricted property. Thus, a spouse, whether Indian or non-Indian, will have an interest in the property and a means of support during their life while the title to the remainder of the life estate and the other one-half of the property lies with the lineal descendants of the decedent. The interest thus created in the spouse is akin to the common law curtsey and dower estates that were provided under Oregon statutes prior to 1969. Likewise, the emphasis on lineal descendency provided under this bill is similar to the older state scheme of distribution.

Section 3 of the bill provides that a spouse who has received an interest in a trust or restricted allotment by the will of the decedent has an election as to whether to take the property pursuant to the will or the provisions of this bill.

This bill, if enacted, would supersede state law and allow affected lands on the reservation to pass in accordance with its terms. It will allow the intestate succession of trust or restricted property in a manner consistent with the wishes of the tribal members and will go far to minimize the fractionalized ownership of land and to maintain a base of land in trust and restricted status on the Umatilla Indian Reservation.

Land Consolidation Bill

It has been said many times before that one of the most important things to the integrity and economy of a tribal government is a sizeable and stable land base. I would like to reaffirm that premise here and emphasize that this is especially true where, as in northeastern Oregon, the economy of the whole area is based upon agriculture. As I related earlier, vast amounts of tribal land on our reservation were lost due to the allotment process, and the opening of the Reservation to settlement by non-Indians. That which remains in tribal hands represents a major factor in terms of tribal income and development. Farm lands are custom farmed and produce tribal income. Grazing lands are leased and timbered land is utilized through timber sales and recreation. Tribal land is also used for housing projects and for buildings housing tribal offices and Indian Health Service Facilities. These needs are expanding. The acquisition of land means room for expansion and increased tribal income which could reduce the current tribal reliance on federal grants and contracts. The consolidation and acquisition of lands under tribal operation could importantly mean more jobs and a stimulated reservation economy. We would like to be able to support more of our own programs, but we need the means to produce our own income.

Unfortunately, we cannot reverse history. We cannot now urge Congress not to pass the Allotment Act and point out the adverse effect this Act would have on our Tribe. We cannot now urge that the opening of our Reservation is inconsistent with the obligation of the federal government to protect our interests. We cannot now refute the urgings of the non-Indian community that the land on our Reservation was "lying waste" when, in fact, it was being "utilized" to the highest degree by our ancestors as they had "utilized" that land and more, for centuries before. We can demonstrate for you that the proposed Land Consolidation Bill which has been introduced as S. 470 in the Senate and H.R. 2539 in this House of Representatives is a method by which we can make the most of what we have today.

Of the land that is presently held by the Tribe, much is in the form of small parcels scattered throughout the Reservation. Such a situation is undesirable from both a managerial and economic point of view. We have a Farming Enterprise that manages our farm land and a Forest/Range Enterprise that manages timbered and grazing lands. However, with the small scattered parcels, the only viable method of utilization is to lease them to other agricultural interests.

We face a desperate need to consolidate these properties into large, useable tracts and to reacquire some of the good agricultural land that has been lost to tribal ownership. The proposed Land Consolidation bill is the vehicle by which this can be accomplished.

The concept of the United States holding property in trust for a tribe or individual is a good and necessary one. Problems are encountered, however, when one considers the sale of exchanges of such properties or the acquisition of deeded lands to be returned to trust states. The most obvious example is where the Tribe wishes to sell a piece of land that is of relatively little value to the Tribe due to its small size, remote location or type of land. Permission must be obtained from the legal owner, the United States, and this can be a burdensome process.

More commonly, a non-Indian owner of land on the Reservation wished to sell his property and offers it first to the Tribe. Because the United States can only take land into trust that has a clear title, it is impossible to purchase that land under a normal land sale contract and mortgage and have it immediately taken into trust. We are also precluded from pledging any other tribal trust land as security for any land purchase because such a pledge would be an encumbrance upon trust property. Even if the Tribe had the funds on hand to pay cash for the property that becomes available, such payment is not acceptable to the seller because of the resultant high income taxes. In most cases, cash payment in full is an impossibly since the tracts offered for sale are large and cost per acre is high.

A recent study conducted by our Tribal Development Office reflects that from 1973 to the present, lands totaling 4,911 acres were offered to us. Although prices per acre varied, the total cost of these lands was $2,013,680.00. For the reasons just stated, we were unable to purchase these lands.

When land is purchased by the Tribe, we have found many times that the ability to have the land held in trust makes the difference between economic feasibility and impossibility. This is especially true of grazing and timbered tracts where the possible annual returns would be less than annual payments. The inclusion of the property tax factor may reduce anticipated income to a point far below anticipated expenditures for that parcel.

The Land Consolidated bill addresses these problems in very straight-forward terms.

The bill begins by stating that its provisions are amendments to the Act which restored the lands not purchased by non-Indian settlers to the Tribe and Reservation. Act of August 10, 1939, 53 Stat. 1351, 25 USC 463 E, F, and G.

This Act is couched, in part, in terms of land consolidation. However, it simply authorized the Secretary, under such rules and regulations as he might prescribe, to acquire lands within the Reservation. The Act further authorized him to take title to such lands in trust and to utilize such funds as were appropriated pursuant to 25 USC 465.

This act did not provide the procedural format in which exchanges, sales and purchases could take place and importantly, did not authorize the taking of title in trust where property had been mortgaged. Further, insofar as I am aware, no rules or regulations were ever developed and no funds were appropriated. The Act of 1939 falls far short of our needs in terms of land consolidation today.

Section 2 of the bill states that for the purposes of effecting land consolidations of land on the Reservation into tribal and individual ownership; attaining and preserving an economic land base; alleviating Indian heirship problems and assisting in the acquisition, disposition and other use of tribal lands, the Secretary is authorized, under such regulations as he may develop, to take the following actions:

A. Acquire for the Tribe or individual members, lands, interests in lands, im-provements, water rights or surface rights to lands within, adjacent to or in close proximity to the Reservation boundaries through purchase, exchange or relinquishment. Any properties acquired for individuals must be within the Reservation boundaries.
B. Sell or approve sales of trust lands, interests therein or improvements there-on.
C. Exchange tribal lands, interests or improvements for like items provided that the exchanges are for equal value or are equalized by money.
D. Accept title to any lands or interests in land in trust for the Tribe.

Section 3 provides that lands or interests in lands acquired under this Act shall be taken in trust and shall have the same status as other trust lands on the Reservation. However, lands acquired beyond the Reservation shall be subject to none of the trust protections.

Section 4 authorizes the use of any funds available or that may hereafter be appropriated for the purpose of this Act.

Section 5 provides the safeguard of allowing action under this bill only when requested by the Board of Trustees and when consistent with a land consolidation and development plan approved by the Secretary. Planning in regard to land purchases and consolidation has been a long term matter for us. At the present time we have plans approved that were developed by the Farm Committee for farm lands and the Forest/Range Committee for grazing and timbered lands. We would expect that our overall Economic Development Plan and our Comprehensive Plan might serve as a general land consolida-tion and development plan. In addition, our Commercial Enterprise is in the process of developing such a plan as it specifically relates to our commercial operations.

Section 6 provides another safeguard in that it provides that monies or cred-its received through sales or exchanges under this bill can only be used for the acquisition of other lands or interests or other purposes consistent with the approved land consolidation and development plan.

A major provision is found in Section 7 wherein the sale, to either the Tribe or individual purchasers, of lands held in multiple ownership is authorized when the owners of a majority of trust interests in such a parcel authorize the sale in writing. This provision will be a major step toward remedying the com-plex fractionalized ownership of lands within the Reservation.

Section 8 authorizes the use of a mortgage or deed of trust as security when purchasing land and the taking of title in trust in that situation. The section also defines how foreclosures will proceed and the role of the United States in such proceedings. This one step will open a basic door and make available to the Tribe the most commonly used security device in land purchases that has never heretofore been available to us.

This bill, in short, fills those precise needs that we have identified over years of managing lands within our Reservation.

The problems encountered have made that management very frustrating. The passage of this bill would provide us with an operating basis and mechanism that would allow us to develop an economically and administratively sound land base.

SOURCE

U.S. Senate. *Umatilla Indian Reservation Land Consolidation, Development, and Inheritance of Trust, Hearing Before the U.S. Senate Select Committee on Indian Affairs, 95 Cong., 1 Sess., on S. 470 and S. 471, July 5, 1977*. Government Printing Office, Washington, D.C.

RELATED READING

Washburn, Wilcomb E. *The Assault on Indian Tribalism: The General Allotment Law (Dawes Act) of 1887*. Philadelphia, PA: Lippincott, 1975.

Lands Worth Only 2 ⅓ Cents Per Acre, 1979

Troubles threatened in the gold-mining districts of the interior of southwestern Oregon during the summer of 1853. Widespread filing on Donation Land Claims and mineral discoveries brought a rush of thousands of miners into the watersheds of the Klamath, Rogue, and Umpqua rivers. By late summer, unable to work the diggings because of lack of water, the miners turned on the Indians, forming military units and billing the government for their "services" in murdering native peoples.

To attempt to quell imminent hostilities and to provide for the orderly transfer from aboriginal title to government ownership of lands, Joel Palmer, Superintendent of Indian Affairs, on September 19, 1853, secured a treaty with the Cow Creek Band of Umpqua Tribe of Indians. Ratified on April 12, 1854, the treaty ceded nearly eight hundred square miles of the watershed of the South Umpqua River. The government promised two cheap dwellings for chiefs, a five-acre tilled field and seeds, a reservation on Council Creek, and $12,000 in annuity goods. The commodities, to be distributed over twenty years, included pants, shoes, shirts, caps, coats, vests, socks, cotton flags, yard goods, needles, thread, and blankets.

Palmer described the treaty in his diary on September 19: "Today the Indians assembled at an early hour where we explained to them the importance of preserving peace with the whites and our desire to treat them kindly and finally after learning their great desire to sell their country made them a proposition which after a consultation among themselves they agreed to and a treaty was drawn up and signed in the evening at an offerance of 2 bushels potatoes." The Cow Creek Treaty ceded timberlands, meadows, the billion-dollar nickel mine at Riddle, placer gold deposits, and mercury resources for two and one-third cents an acre and two bushels of potatoes.

Over the next 120 years the Cow Creeks contended their treaty, the second ratified from the Pacific Northwest, took their lands in clear violation of the "utmost good faith" promises of the Organic Act creating Oregon Territory. Five times the tribe secured bills to litigate its claim in the 1920s. When the legislation ultimately *passed both the House and Senate, President Herbert Hoover vetoed it. The tribe was never informed of its opportunity to file a complaint with the Indian Claims Commission. Finally in 1979 the tribe testified before Congress on a jurisdictional act to place its case before the U.S. Claims Court. The bill, passed by unanimous consent, permitted the tribe to sue and resulted in 1984 in a negotiated settlement of $1.5 million—the value of the lands at the "date of taking" in 1855.*

The following statements were made before a joint hearing of the U.S. Senate Select Committee on Indian Affairs and the House Committee on Interior and Insular Affairs, June 14, 1979, in Washington, D. C. Senator Mark O. Hatfield presided; Rep. James Weaver participated. Witnesses included Ellis Buschmann, chairman of the tribe, Susan Crispen Shaffer, treasurer, Charles Jackson, vice-chair, and Amaryllis LaChance (Dumont) Freeman, a council member. The Cow Creeks, unlike all other Northwest tribes, voted overwhelmingly to vest 100 percent of their judgment fund in an endowment and use only the interest to leverage social and economic development programs. The Bureau of Indian Affairs fought the tribal plan to vest the fund. On October 26, 1987, Congress mandated the tribal plan in the Cow Creek Band of Umpqua Tribe of Indians Distribution of Judgment Funds Act. Ultimately the BIA complied with the law.

ELLIS BUSCHMANN:

Mr. Chairman, and members of the committees, my name is Ellis Buschmann. I reside at 1291 Speaker Road, Wolf Creek, Oreg. I am the chairman of the Cow Creek Band of the Umpqua Indians. We have met as a tribe for as long as I can remember.

The older people lived in the hope that the Government would someday make a just settlement of their claim. Even the older ones, who held much to the old ways of our people, knew that what had happened to them was not right. Not only had they been pushed off their land in their youth, but many had to hide in the hills for fear of being shot.

History often records the Indian as dour and solemn. That was not their natural way. They were much interested in their games and dancing; and, among the Indians themselves, playing jokes on one another was a great sport. After they lost their homes and their very way of life, the sadness they carried in their hearts did make them solemn.

I would say, for all of my tribe, to sum it up in a few words that, as far as the Government was concerned, we were truly the forgotten people.

Had the Indians been aware that they were signing their land away—what could they have done? They had no choice. Bows and arrows could not compete with bullets. On the other hand, the people signing the treaty had experience in what it meant to buy and sell. The Indians were considered primitive; yet, they had love and respect for the land and realized the need to protect it. It does not seem that the white man has the same feeling.

Because of its great natural beauty, our treaty land provides a very desirable place to live: Hunting, fishing, camping are relaxations that all can enjoy. Some of the land has rich river-bottom soil for farming.

During the last week of May 1979, about 2,000 sheep were brought in by a California rancher to graze for the summer on what is now Forest Service land. Last year, when our people went to the huckleberry patch for our annual gathering, there was sheep manure all around, and the odor was terrible.

You might ask me, "What did the land mean to your people?" I could answer, "The very meaning of our life." I might ask you, "What is the most important thing that the white man's god has given you?" The Indians' belief is that the most meaningful thing the Great Spirit gave to us was our land. The removal of the Indians from this land was like the removal of the spirit from the body.

The English language has no word to describe the pain, the anguish, and the shock our people felt at being torn from their homeland. It is truly a miracle that they could adjust to such a different way of life. Could you and I?

This is the past. Now we must look to the future of this tribe. At the present time, our Tribal Council, along with the South Umpqua Historical Society, is trying to establish a museum in Canyonville. Mr. Lawrence Boyle, the grandson of Isaac Boyle, who was the first white man to trade with our people up the Umpqua, has generously donated a choice piece of real estate as the museum site. It is planned that this museum will be equally divided between the history of the pioneer white settler and the Indian history.

It is my hope and dream that this museum will become a reality so that the records and history of our people will be preserved for the generations to come. I am convinced that the future of this tribe as a group is secure. Our families have remained united through all the years of adversity. They will remain united in the future.

I feel that our ancestors, who have passed over the Great Divide, and the Great Spirit too will bless you for hearing our people today. I thank you.

Susan Crispen Shaffer:
Mr. Chairman and members of the committees, I wish to thank you for giving my people the chance to appear before you today. We have long strived for this day. I wish also to thank Senator Mark Hatfield, Senator Bob Packwood, and

Representative Jim Weaver, and all others who have put forth effort on behalf of this tribe.

My name is Sue Crispin Shaffer. I live at 581 Fairchild Street, Canyonville, Oreg. I am a director and treasurer of the Cow Creek Band of the Umpqua Indians. I am the daughter of Ellen Furlong Crispen, granddaughter of Mary Thomason Furlong, and great grand-daughter of Susan Nonta Thomason. I identify myself as I have been identified throughout my lifetime, as an Indian of southern Douglas County, Oreg.

My mother was the eldest grandchild of William P. and Susan Thomason and very close to her grandmother. Susan was a remarkable woman. She was a fullblood Cow Creek medicine woman and midwife. Grandmother Thomason, after she was married and returned to Elk Creek, which later became Drew, Oreg., doctored many families including the white pioneer families as well as the Indian people. She was proud of her heritage and the customs of her people, and she instilled this feeling in her children and her grandchildren.

During my mother's lifetime, she tried, with unending patience, to get the Bureau of Indian Affairs to recognize the rights of her people. She read and researched every bit of information she could find relative to our claim. Her letters and records show that she earned the support of such people as Congressman William C. Hawley and Senator Charles McNary. She solicited help from the U.S. Attorney General and wrote continuous letters to any source where she thought she might get helpful information.

When inquiries were made to the Bureau of Indian Affairs, the stock answer was, "No; you are not reservation Indians; this does not apply to you." How discouraging it must have been for her to have the Commissioner of Indian Affairs write and tell her that they could not find the treaty and we have the original letter in our files today. What a demoralizing effect it must have had on all our people when President Hoover vetoed our bill in 1932.

I remember all of the families gathering at my grandmother's house for the usual Sunday meeting. It was like a wake. Everyone was so discouraged. I was just a little girl then, but I remember them trying to comfort each other. They had had such high hopes, and then, nothing.

In conclusion, I would like to make it clear that, in spite of all the obstacles my people have known, they have always known their own history and who they were. They have remained unified in their efforts to have their treaty honored and have continued to meet with each other.

After working a lifetime to establish the rights of her people, my mother died with the faith that one day it would all be resolved.

The old records that we have to present to you today will bear this out.

During the time of the Indian Claims Commission in 1946 to 1951, the tribal groups continued to meet and went wherever meetings were held where they might get useful information.

In the old diaries of my aunt, Mamie Furlong Denny Archambeau, it shows several places where they went to meetings at this time. After all the long years of struggle, had they been aware that they could have presented their claim, could anyone doubt that they would not have done so?

In a plea for peace among the whites and the Indians in 1854, Mary Huntley Sawtelle, who settled on the North Umpqua in 1850, made this moving prayer:

> Oh Almighty God, Father alike to red and white man, Thou hast the power to compel the men of our mighty nation to keep the treaty now about to be signed between these two nations of red and white men. Grant, Oh, God, that my words may be kept—in letter and in deed, truthfully kept.

CHARLES JACKSON:

My name is Charles Jackson. I am a director and vice-chairman of the Cow Creek Band of Umpqua Indians.

I will start this statement of my Indian heritage as I was told by many of the older Indian people, friends and relatives of mine. It is the way I have lived my own life.

My first shoes were hand-tanned moccasins of deer skin, made by my grandmother, Dolla Thomason Larson. I was about 12 years old when I discovered that we were the only people in our neighborhood that used rocks to grind our dried meat on for cooking. It has been a common thing in my life to go along the creeks, rivers and mountains and see the old Indian villages, the impressions of the house pits, circular impressions, trails and artifacts still on the ground. My great uncles, Louis, and Robert Thomason and my grandmother would tell me, "These are the homes of your ancestors. Do not disturb their ground." I have asked many times, "Where did our people come from?" They would point to the East. Then, I would ask, "How long have our people lived here?" They would answer, "Always." This answer didn't always satisfy my curiosity, so I would, ask many more questions about how long our people had lived here in the Umpqua, Elk Creek and Cow Creek areas. The old Indian people told me our ancestors were here when the first tree grew. They said this was a cedar tree, put here for the Indians to use, the different parts of the bark for clothing, matting and material for houses, as well as a very fine soft wood for arrows and many other uses.

They said that they were here before the big mountain burned high into the sky, finally leaving a hole in the center which filled with beautiful, cold water. This mountain burning caused much trouble for the Indians. They said it was of a demon because the rocks ran as if they were water. This was the molten lava, covering up streams and lakes, also causing much land to be covered and ruined by the dust and ashes. Of course, this is Crater Lake. Our family has published articles of these legends.

I would go to the huckleberry patch when I was very young and listen to the old stories of how hundreds of Indians would gather there; camping, picking berries, killing grouse (which the Indians referred to as their "chickens"), killing deer or elk and drying the meat and berries for winter food. A lot of different tribes gathered there to trade their goods, play games, gamble and have a very good time. The Indians looked forward to going to the huckleberry patch as it was their big yearly event. One time when I was about seven years old, my grandmother stood on a rock point over looking the berry patches and she pointed to some very large trees and said, "Close to those trees, there are many things buried. There are stone bowls, pestles, tools, arrowheads, weapons and many trinkets." I asked her how long these things had been buried and she said our Indian people always kept those things here. I asked her if we could dig some of the things up and look at them. She said the things buried there were to use if we needed them but they were always to be buried back in their original place because someone else may want to use them. Nothing is ever to be taken away. You are always to add something of your own when you rebury the items. They are to stay in this ground forever. A few years ago, a man from Central Point, Oregon by the name of [Earl F.] Moore who has a small private museum, found one of these caches, close to this area and he removed over 1200 pieces of beautiful Indian stone work which may be seen in his collection today. The Indians would watch a white butterfly flying in the big, tall trees. When the white butterfly was flying around the tree about half way up, they would start getting ready for the berry patch. As time went on, the butterfly would fly higher, near the tops of the trees and this meant the huckleberries were ripe.

In the areas of these Indian people there are many gathering places, some we still use today. Camas Valley was a great place for many tribes to gather and camp, digging the camas roots for a source of food. Today, a person can walk along Camas Creek and find arrowheads from several different tribes, all in this one area.

We still use one of the old Indian cemeteries. It has always remained in our family. It was located on the land of my great grandmother, Susan Nonta (Longtain) Thomason, close to the place of her birth. In Jan., 1979 we had a re-burial of two Indian remains which were accidentally dug up by construction. The ceremony and re-burial took place in this very old family cemetery. While digging graves, we have found some stone clippings and ashes five foot deep. On Joe Hall Creek, close to the cemetery, one day my great uncle, Louis Thomason, showed my cousin and I where several old, unmarked Indian graves are. He said, "This is the resting place of some of your ancestors." One is under a tree, beside the creek, where Louis' mother, Susan, showed her children where an old chief is buried with his favorite possession, his tomahawk. The old chief was a relative of Susan. One day, I took an archeologist to the place of Susan's birth. He determined it to be a place of prehistoric existence. His name is Dr. Joseph Hopkins and he is a professor at Southern Oregon College, Ashland, Ore.

I have been shown how to make the original Indian artifacts by my people such as arrowheads, knives, spears of stone and bone, bowls, pestles, bows, arrows, fish and eel traps, deer traps and many other things. In my life I have used many of these. My grandmother carved pipes and animal figures from a white pipe stone which always seemed to be a very prized stone. She gave several pieces of her carvings away. Her son, my uncle Wesley Larson carved some pipes which he gave away. In my collection I have one horse that my grandmother carved. I asked her many times if she would show me where this white stone came from. She said it was located high up in the mountains and that the old Indians used this stone for their pipes. She said, 'Someday, I will tell you where to find it.' When I was about 30 years old, she told me where to go and stand high in the mountains on a bed rock knoll, then look all around from this point and it is not very far. This is all the directions that she would give me. She said that if I wanted to find it, I would have to work for it, then I would appreciate it more. She said, "It is buried. When you find it, dig out only what you need, then rebury it and it will always be there." From this point, with some help, I did locate the white stone about a mile away. Not very far, can mean up to two or three miles away, so I was very lucky to find the stone. I have carved several pipes and figures from this stone. One year, I won a blue ribbon at the Douglas County Fair for my Indian carvings.

I have a small museum in a log school house which was built in 1906 that I have restored and is on my property at Drew, Oregon. Each school year, I have students from as far as 60 miles away come to my museum. I give them demonstrations on arrowhead, knife and tool making. I also do this for the Cub and Boy Scouts and the Jaycees. Our Indian culture is now referred to as Folk Culture. I have had some interviews from news papers and the Douglas County Museum on our Indian culture and folk art. To me, this is my way of life, this is how I have lived. I live in a log house my mother and father built on their homestead. This land was once the home of great grandmother, Susan's people.

Our family have always been referred to as Indians. Sometimes, this was very hard, especially in school when I was young. In grade school when you were called an Indian, everyone else always thought that meant you were some kind of a primitive person. I have lived with this all of my life. On June 1, 1979, a neighbor of mine that I have known all of my life, told me that I shouldn't wear a wrist watch because if it weren't for the white man, I wouldn't have a watch. I have always heard things like this. I am not a full blood Indian but if I were, I don't believe my life would be any different.

I believe our people in the Cow Creek Band of the Umpqua Indians have a legitimate claim here. Our great ancestors have always been the Indians of this area, no matter what they have been called, no matter where they have gone, this area has always been their home. There are many documents telling of our people living here in the mountains and I will say that, so far, there is no one anywhere that has come within 1,000 years of accurately dating the existence of our people here.

Several of our people have gone to school under the B.I.A. I went to Oakland Jr. College, Oakland Calif. under the B.I.A. as an Umpqua Indian and then was terminated without a hearing or notification. I don't believe this termination was fair or just to any kind of people. After so many years of our people trying to get someone to listen to them, I have hope that through these Indian hearings, the U.S. Government will listen to the facts and make a fair and just settlement for our people. Our people have worked toward this since 1853. So many times, have been told that this or that doesn't apply to our people, or we don't qualify for some reason. This has been a constant uphill struggle for several life times of our people here in the United States of America, to be dealt with fair and just. There always seems to be several billion U.S. Dollars given away to foreign lands. Now, let us settle with our own people. Let us give the children a chance for a proper education. There is money available for education but it is very hard or impossible to get because we are not reservation Indians. This is the same old story our people have been told so many times in the past. Or, we are told that we can't qualify because we are terminated Indians.

My great uncle, Louis Thomason who was born in 1882, told me, when I was about 10 years old that some day in June the leaders of our great government of the United States would come to us and settle with us for what had been taken away and for the death and suffering that our people had gone through. He said our people at one time were very rich in land, water, fish, deer and berries but most of all rich in their way of life and had a whole world full of peace and contentment. He died in 1949 without seeing that day in June but still believing in the Great Government. I could go on for several pages but I realize other people want to speak and many things have to be heard.

I thank you for hearing my testimony.

AMARYLLIS LaCHANCE (DUMONT) FREEMAN:
Ladies and gentlemen: My name is Amaryllis LaChance (Dumont) Freeman. After this long wait of 125 years, I am glad to appear here today with other members of our tribe. All my life I have been known as an Indian ... sometimes at school as a "dirty half breed" or a "lousy Indian." I've been in plenty of fights at school because of this. Never because of being called an Indian, I fought only when I felt my mother was being insulted. Regardless of what names I was called, I have held my head up high. I have been proud of my heritage and glad that I was born in the land of my people along the Umpqua. I've been taught the old Indian customs that were handed down and I am, in turn, passing them on to my children.

I love and respect this land that was ours. I find it hard to believe that the so called forefathers of this United States of America, left their own lands across the sea to escape religious oppression and poverty, then, after coming here, they perpetrated the same crimes on the Native American. He was influenced through devious means to give up his land for practically nothing. If he didn't give it up, he was forced off of it. Not only did the Indian have to give up his land but his religious beliefs, his culture and his freedom to roam wherever he wanted to go. It has been a matter of losing his entire identity.

A federal ordinance was passed in 1787 which was one of the first laws that was passed to protect the Indians and in 1848, Oregon passed an act that was to insure a "standard of fairness" when dealing with the Indians. Of course, both of these acts had been passed before the signing of our treaty in 1854. The terms of that treaty allowed the Cow Creeks $0.023 per acre while Donation Land

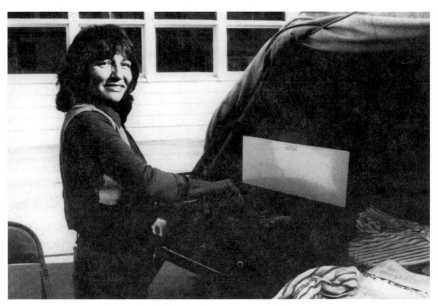

Amaryllis (LaChance) Dumont Freeman (1933–?) made fry-bread for a pow-wow of the Cow Creek Band of Umpqua. A mother of twelve children, she testified before congressional committees for the tribal land claims jurisdictional act (1979) and for the tribal restoration bill (1981)(Beckham).

Claims were being sold to the settlers for $1.25 per acre. Is this a "standard of fairness"? Not long ago it came to my attention that one of today's law makers, upon being presented information about our case said, "I am up to my neck in these old Indian treaties and cases." My answer to that is: "Maybe the Indians have had it up to their necks, too!"

I would like to give you a good example of the 'good' treatment our tribe always received from representatives of the B.I.A. At a meeting in Sutherlin in 1955 Mr. Clyde Busey who was the Director of the B.I.A. Portland office was present to help all the Indians establish permanent tribal rolls and to get our background. There was also another man and two women taking down information. My sister, Jane LaChance Heussner and I were standing by the table where Mr. Busey was interviewing Mrs. Nellie Crispen. We were the next in line so we heard the whole conversation. Mrs. Crispen had her documents and papers spread out on the table and she was trying to explain her family line. He talked so snotty to her and pushed her papers away and told her they didn't mean anything, that he did not want to look at them. His treatment was so rude and it made her so mad that she could not finish filling out her statement. I heard her say, "Listen here, young man, I know what I know." She was just furious. She said, "All of us here know the histories of our families." She was so upset that I had to help her out to the car so she could calm down and after the recess for lunch she was able to get her papers finished. My mother, Mary Gilbeaugh LaChance received the same treatment as did my uncle, Louie Gilbeaugh. He got so smart with Uncle Louie, that I heard Uncle Louie raise his voice and swear and that was the only time in all my life that I ever did hear him cuss. Later, that day my mother did finish filling out Uncle Louie's papers. You can talk to any of our people about that day. They remember it well. They were all talked to like they were a bunch of simple-minded idiots.

My mother, Mary Gilbeaugh LaChance, worked for many years for Judge Huron Clough and his sister, Bess, on their ranch. Their parents were Adeline Eliff Clough and Joseph Clough. The Eliffs were one of the oldest families of white settlers who lived on Upper Cow Creek and they had known Mama and her family all their lives. When I was about 6–8 years old, the Cloughs entertained as their honored guest at dinner, Sen. Wayne Morris [Morse], and George Neuner, Sr. who was a member of one of the oldest pioneer families at Riddle. That day, they talked to Mama about her Indian affairs and said they would try to help her. Neuner said that he would be willing to handle the case for 5 percent but that he would have to have a certain amount of money guaranteed. Of course, the situation was the same. We had no money for necessities and certainly no money to put up as a guarantee.

I will always feel that this land was ours and I feel hurt inside that the old people were deprived of their familiar way of life. Our tribe continues to meet and remain strong and firm in their belief that no matter how long it takes, right will prevail. Our parents and grand parents met with each other through the years and it is my hope that our children will do the same. Also that they will respect and protect this land.

When the merits of our case are weighed, please consider the heart break, tears and disappointment that we Indians have lived with through the years. We would have pleaded our case before this governing body thirty-three years ago, in 1946, had we known that we would have been allowed to be heard.

Before I close my statement, I would like to make it clear that Mr. Leonard Allen who was the Training Officer for the B.I.A. was the one person who was always kind and courteous to all of our people and tried to do all he could to help them.

Thank you.

SOURCE

U.S. Congress. *Joint Hearing Before the Select Committee on Indian Affairs, United States Senate, and the Committee on Interior and Insular Affairs, House of Representatives, Ninety-Sixth Congress on S. 668 and H.R. 2822 . . . June 14, 1979.* Washington, DC: Government Printing Office, 1979.

RELATED READING

Beckham, Stephen Dow. *Land of the Umpqua: A History of Douglas County, Oregon.* Roseburg, OR: Douglas County Commissioners, 1986.

Moore, Earl F. *Silent Arrows: Indian Lore and Artifact Hunting.* Klamath Falls, OR: Paul Tremaine Publishing, 1977.

Riddle, George. *Early Days in Oregon: A History of the Riddle Valley.* Riddle, OR: Riddle Parent Teachers Association, 1953.

The Importance of Congressional Leadership, 1983

Reversing the discredited program of Termination proved a tedious and challenging task. The route to "restoration" of Oregon Indian tribes was carried out on a case-by-case basis. Each tribe had to step forward, document the continuing existence of its community, argue from facts—particularly social and demographic statistics—and catch the ear of Congress. There was no blanket rescinding of Termination. Each tribe had to seek, fight for, and win its restoration to a federal relationship. Each had to seek its own Act of Congress.

In the following selection, Dennis J. Whittlesey of Washington, D.C., spoke to the singular role of two Oregon members of Congress, Mark O. Hatfield and James Weaver, who listened and responded when Oregon tribes sought to undo Termination. Whittlesey helped rewrite western Oregon Indian history. He was attorney for the Cow Creek Band of Umpqua in its Claims Court litigation, 1981– 84, and counsel during its restoration efforts. He was author of the first gaming compact—that of the Cow Creeks—with the State of Oregon under the Indian Gaming Regulatory Act of 1988. He was also counsel for the Confederated Tribes of Coos, Lower Umpqua, and Siuslaw and aided in their restoration effort, gaming compact, and acquisition of reservation lands. Whittlesey's remarks were shared on April 10, 1983, in Roseburg at the Cow Creek Band of Umpqua's "Federal Recognition Celebration."

If there are two people who deserve credit for the Cow Creek Band of Umpqua winning federal recognition, they are Senator Mark Hatfield and Congressman Jim Weaver. For it is they who were the chief supporters of the recognition legislation and who, along with staffs, carefully guided the legislation through the Congress and Presidential signature.

Congressman Weaver can be called the "father" of the Tribe's Federal Recognition, for it is he who encouraged the Tribe to seek full Recognition at a time when the Department of Interior was urging legislation which merely would have revoked Termination and permitted the Tribe to seek Federal

Recognition through an administrative process. Congressman Weaver felt that the Tribe should not have to wait for years and years (which would have been required under Interior's plan), and instead argued that the Tribe should be permitted to present its case to Congress *now* instead of waiting for Interior to review the same information and evidence at some future date.

With this, Congressman Weaver sponsored the legislation in June 1982, and pushed for early hearings, which were held only six weeks later. As you know, members of the Tribe traveled to Washington to testify at those hearings.

Once the Tribe had presented its case to the House Committee on Interior and Insular Affairs, Senator Hatfield—along with Oregon's junior Senator Bob Packwood—introduced the legislation before the United States Senate and began working for early action.

The staff aides to Weaver and Hatfield—David Jory and Jim Towey, respectively—were assigned to make the legislation "happen" and their effective work did just that. With the support of their bosses, they made certain that the legislation moved forward at all times. As a result, the legislation passed both the House of Representatives and the United States Senate *without a dissenting vote*—a most impressive achievement. Although the Administration had opposed the legislation, the fact that no member of Congress voted against the bill had to have influenced the President's decision to sign it.

The legislative skills of these two men, as well as their excellent staff, made the difference in the Cow Creek Band winning Federal Recognition. And they fully deserve all credit for the event which we today are celebrating.

SOURCE
Whittlesey, Dennis J. The Contributions of Senator Hatfield and Congressman Weaver, *Cow Creek Band of Umpqua Tribe of Indians Federal Recognition Celebration, April 10, 1983*. Roseburg, OR: Cow Creek Band of Umpqua Tribe of Indians, 1983.

RELATED READING
Beckham, Stephen Dow. Cow Creek Band of Umpqua, *Native America in the Twentieth Century: An Encyclopedia*, Mary B. Davis, ed. New York and London, Garland Publishing, Inc., 1994, pp. 145–47.
Beckham, Stephen Dow, and Sherri Shaffer. Patience and Persistence: The Cow Creek Band of Umpqua Tribe of Indians, *The First Oregonians*, Carolyn M. Buan and Richard Lewis, eds. Portland, OR: Oregon Council for the Humanities, 1992, pp. 89–94.

Sacramental Use of Peyote: A Matter Before the Courts

Peyote or mescal, a hallucinogenic button collected from the cactus Lophophora williamsii Lemaire, *spread widely among adherents to the Native American Church in the twentieth century. Moving from Mexico to the Southwest and the southern Plains, peyote is a sacrament consumed during hours of ritual, prayer, and singing. It is a non-addictive substance which induces vivid dreams and visionary experiences. It was not consumed or used by any aboriginal peoples in Oregon, but peyote use spread to the state by the 1960s.*

A landmark case, Employment Division, Department of Human Resources of Oregon v. Alfred L. Smith, et al., *raised significant questions about freedom of religion when argued in November, 1989, and decided on April 17, 1990, by the U.S. Supreme Court. At issue was the firing of Alfred L. Smith and Galen Black, employees of a private drug rehabilitation organization in Roseburg, Oregon, who had ingested peyote at a Native American Church ceremony. The dismissed workers sought unemployment compensation but were denied under a state law which disqualified anyone who had engaged in work-related "misconduct." The state contended that its controlled substance law made it a felony to possess peyote. The State Supreme Court held that the Free Exercise Clause of the Constitution permitted the state to prohibit sacramental peyote use and thus within its right to deny unemployment benefits.*

The matter went before the Supreme Court where the justices rendered a divided opinion. Dissenting were Justices Harry Blackmun, William Brennan, and Thurgood Marshall who observed: "... Oregon's interest in enforcing its drug laws against religious use of peyote is not sufficiently compelling to outweigh respondents' right to the free exercise of their religion. Since the State could not constitutionally enforce its criminal prohibition against respondents, the interests underlying the State's drug laws cannot justify its denial of unemployment benefits." To the distress of Smith, Black, Native American Church, and civil libertarians nationally, however, the opinion written by Justice Anthony Scalia prevailed. Smith and Black were denied benefits. The Native American Church suffered a major

setback in its effort to exercise its First Amendment rights of freedom of religion.
The following is Justice Scalia's opinion:

This case requires us to decide whether the Free Exercise Clause of the First Amendment permits the State of Oregon to include religiously inspired peyote use within the reach of its general criminal prohibition on use of that drug, and thus permits the State to deny unemployment benefits to persons dismissed from their jobs because of such religiously inspired use.

I

Oregon law prohibits the knowing or intentional possession of a 'controlled substance' unless the substance has been prescribed by a medical practitioner. Ore. Rev. Stat. § 475.992(4) (1987). The law defines 'controlled substance' as a drug classified in Schedules I through V of the Federal Controlled Substances Act, 21 U. S. C. §§811–812, as modified by the State Board of Pharmacy. Ore. Rev. Stat. §475.005(6) (1987). Persons who violate this provision by possessing a controlled substance listed on Schedule I are 'guilty of a Class B felony.' §475.992(4)(a). As compiled by the State Board of Pharmacy under its statutory authority, see §475.035, Schedule I contains the drug peyote, a hallucinogen derived from the plant *Lophophora williamsii Lemaire.* Ore. Admin. Rule 855–80–021(3)(s) (1988).

Respondents Alfred Smith and Galen Black (hereinafter respondents) were fired from their jobs with a private drug rehabilitation organization because they ingested peyote for sacramental purposes at a ceremony of the Native American Church, of which both are members. When respondents applied to petitioner Employment Division (hereinafter petitioner) for unemployment compensation, they were determined to be ineligible for benefits because they had been discharged for work-related 'misconduct.' The Oregon Court of Appeals reversed that determination, holding that the denial of benefits violated respondents' free exercise rights under the First Amendment.

On appeal to the Oregon Supreme Court, petitioner argued that the denial of benefits was permissible because respondents' consumption of peyote was a crime under Oregon law. The Oregon Supreme Court reasoned, however, that the criminality of respondents' peyote use was irrelevant to resolution of their constitutional claim—since the purpose of the 'misconduct' provision under which respondents had been disqualified was not to enforce the State's criminal laws but to preserve the financial integrity of the compensation fund, and since that purpose was inadequate to justify the burden that disqualification imposed on respondents' religious practice. Citing our decisions in *Sherbert* v. *Verner,* 374 U. S. 398 (1963), and *Thomas* v. *Review Bd. of Indiana Employment Security Div.,* 450 U. S. 707 (1981), the court concluded that respondents were entitled to payment of unemployment benefits. *Smith* v. *Employment Div., Dept. of Human Resources,* 301 Ore. 209, 217–219, 721 P. 2d 445, 449–450 (1986). We granted certiorari. 480 U. S. 916 (1987).

Before this Court in 1987, petitioner continued to maintain that the illegality of respondents' peyote consumption was relevant to their constitutional claim. We agreed, concluding that 'if a State has prohibited through its criminal laws certain kinds of religiously motivated conduct without violating the First Amendment, it certainly follows that it may impose the lesser burden of denying unemployment compensation benefits to persons who engage in that conduct.' *Employment Div., Dept. of Human Resources of Oregon* v. *Smith,* 485 U. S. 660, 670 (1988) *(Smith I).* We noted, however, that the Oregon Supreme Court had not decided whether respondents' sacramental use of peyote was in fact proscribed by Oregon's controlled substance law, and that this issue was a matter of dispute between the parties. Being 'uncertain about the legality of the religious use of peyote in Oregon,' we determined that it would not be 'appropriate for us to decide whether the practice is protected by the Federal Constitution.' *Id.,* at 673. Accordingly, we vacated the judgment of the Oregon Supreme Court and remanded for further proceedings. *Id.,* at 674.

On remand, the Oregon Supreme Court held that respondents' religiously inspired use of peyote fell within the prohibition of the Oregon statute, which 'makes no exception for the sacramental use' of the drug. 307 Ore. 68, 72–73, 763 P. 2d 146, 148 (1988). It then considered whether that prohibition was valid under the Free Exercise Clause, and concluded that it was not. The court therefore reaffirmed its previous ruling that the State could not deny unemployment benefits to respondents for having engaged in that practice.

We again granted certiorari. 489 U. S. 1077 (1989).

II

Respondents' claim for relief rests on our decisions in *Sherbert* v. *Verner, supra, Thomas* v. *Review Bd. of Indiana Employment Security Div., supra,* and *Hobbie v. Unemployment Appeals Comm'n of Florida,* 480 U. S. 136 (1987), in which we held that a State could not condition the availability of unemployment insurance on an individual's willingness to forgo conduct required by his religion. As we observed in *Smith I,* however, the conduct at issue in those cases was not prohibited by law. We held that distinction to be critical, for 'if Oregon does prohibit the religious use of peyote, and if that prohibition is consistent with the Federal Constitution, there is no federal right to engage in that conduct in Oregon,' and 'the State is free to withhold unemployment compensation from respondents for engaging in work-related misconduct, despite its religious motivation.' 485 U. S., at 672. Now that the Oregon Supreme Court has confirmed that Oregon does prohibit the religious use of peyote, we proceed to consider whether that prohibition is permissible under the Free Exercise Clause.

A

The Free Exercise Clause of the First Amendment, which has been made applicable to the States by incorporation into the Fourteenth Amendment, see *Cantwell* v. *Connecticut,* 310 U. S. 296, 303 (1940), provides that 'Congress shall make no law respecting an establishment of religion, or *prohibiting the free exercise thereof. . . .'* U. S. Const., Amdt. 1 (emphasis added). The free exercise of religion means, first and foremost, the right to believe and profess whatever religious doctrine one desires. Thus, the First Amendment obviously excludes all 'governmental regulation of religious *beliefs as* such.' *Sherbert* v. *Verner, supra,* at 402. The government may not compel affirmation of religious belief, see *Torcaso* v. *Watkins,* 367 U. S. 488 (1961), punish the expression of religious doctrines it believes to be false, *United States* v. *Ballard,* 322 U. S. 78, 86–88 (1944), impose special disabilities on the basis of religious views or religious status, see *McDaniel* v. *Paty,* 435 U. S. 618 (1978); *Fowler* v. *Rhode Island,* 345 U.S. 67, 69 (1953); cf. *Larson* v. *Valente,* 456 U. S. 228, 245 (1982), or lend its power to one or the other side in controversies over religious authority or dogma, see *Presbyterian Church in U. S.* v. *Mary Elizabeth Blue Hull Memorial Presbyterian Church,* 393 U. S. 440, 445–452 (1969); *Kedroff* v. *St. Nicholas Cathedral,* 344 U. S. 94, 95–119 (1952); *Serbian Eastern Orthodox Diocese* v. *Milivojevich,* 426 U. S. 696, 708–725 (1976).

  But the 'exercise of religion' often involves not only belief and profession but the performance of (or abstention from) physical acts: assembling with others for a worship service, participating in sacramental use of bread and wine, proselytizing, abstaining from certain foods or certain modes of transportation. It would be true, we think (though no case of ours has involved the point), that a State would be 'prohibiting the free exercise [of religion]' if it sought to ban such acts or abstentions only when they are engaged in for religious reasons, or only because of the religious belief that they display. It would doubtless be unconstitutional, for example, to ban the casting of 'statues that are to be used for worship purposes,' or to prohibit bowing down before a golden calf.

Respondents in the present case, however, seek to carry the meaning of 'prohibiting the free exercise [of religion]' one large step further. They contend that their religious motivation for using peyote places them beyond the reach of a criminal law that is not specifically directed at their religious practice, and that is concededly constitutional as applied to those who use the drug for other reasons. They assert, in other words, that 'prohibiting the free exercise [of religion]' includes requiring any individual to observe a generally applicable law that requires (or forbids) the performance of an act that his religious belief forbids (or requires). As a textual matter, we do not think the words must be given that meaning. It is no more necessary to regard the collection of a general tax, for example, as 'prohibiting the free exercise [of religion]' by those citizens who believe support of organized government to be sinful, than it is to regard the same tax as 'abridging the freedom . . . of the press' of those publishing companies that must pay the tax as a condition of staying in business. It is a permissible reading of the text, in the one case as in the other, to say that if prohibiting the exercise of religion (or burdening the activity of printing) is not the object of the tax but merely the incidental effect of a generally applicable and otherwise valid provision, the First Amendment has not been offended. Compare *Citizen Publishing Co.* v. *United States,* 394 U. S. 131, 139 (1969) (upholding application of antitrust laws to press), with *Grosjean* v. *American Press Co.,* 297 U. S. 233, 250–251 (1936) (striking down license tax applied only to newspapers with weekly circulation above a specified level); see generally *Minneapolis Star & Tribune Co.* v. *Minnesota Comm'r of Revenue,* 460 U. S. 575, 581 (1983).

Our decisions reveal that the latter reading is the correct one. We have never held that an individual's religious beliefs excuse him from compliance with an otherwise valid law prohibiting conduct that the State is free to regulate. On the contrary, the record of more than a century of our free exercise jurisprudence contradicts that proposition. As described succinctly by Justice Frankfurter in *Minersville School Dist. Bd. of Ed.* v. *Gobitis,* 310 U. S. 586, 594–595 (1940): "Conscientious scruples have not, in the course of the long struggle for religious toleration, relieved the individual from obedience to a general law not aimed at the promotion or restriction of religious beliefs. The mere possession of religious convictions which contradict the relevant concerns of a political

society does not relieve the citizen from the discharge of political responsibilities (footnote omitted)." We first had occasion to assert that principle in *Reynolds
v. United States,* 98 U. S. 145 (1879), where we rejected the claim that criminal laws
against polygamy could not be constitutionally applied to those whose religion
commanded the practice. "Laws," we said, "are made for the government of actions, and while they cannot interfere with mere religious belief and opinions,
they may with practices. . . . Can a man excuse his practices to the contrary
because of his religious belief? To permit this would be to make the professed
doctrines of religious belief superior to the law of the land, and in effect to permit
every citizen to become a law unto himself." *Id.,* at 166–167.

Subsequent decisions have consistently held that the right of free exercise
does not relieve an individual of the obligation to comply with a "valid and
neutral law of general applicability on the ground that the law proscribes (or
prescribes) conduct that his religion prescribes (or proscribes)." *United States
v. Lee,* 455 U. S. 252, 263, n. 3 (1982) (STEVENS, J., concurring in judgment);
see *Minersville School Dist. Bd. of Ed. v. Gobitis, supra,* at 595 (collecting cases).
In *Prince v. Massachusetts,* 321 U. S. 158 (1944), we held that a mother could be
prosecuted under the child labor laws for using her children to dispense literature in the streets, her religious motivation notwithstanding. We found no
constitutional infirmity in "excluding [these children] from doing there what
no other children may do." *Id.,* at 171. In *Braunfeld v. Brown* , 366 U. S. 599 (1961)
(plurality opinion), we upheld Sunday-closing laws against the claim that they
burdened the religious practices of persons whose religions compelled them to
refrain from work on other days. In *Gillette v. United States,* 401 U. S. 437, 461
(1971), we sustained the military Selective Service System against the claim that
it violated free exercise by conscripting persons who opposed a particular war
on religious grounds.

Our most recent decision involving a neutral, generally applicable regulatory law that compelled activity forbidden by an individual's religion was
United States v. Lee, 455 U. S., at 258–261. There, an Amish employer, on behalf
of himself and his employees, sought exemption from collection and payment
of Social Security taxes on the ground that the Amish faith prohibited participation in governmental support programs. We rejected the claim that an exemption was constitutionally required. There would be no way, we observed,
to distinguish the Amish believer's objection to Social Security taxes from the
religious objections that others might have to the collection or use of other
taxes. "If, for example, a religious adherent believes war is a sin, and if a cer-

tain percentage of the federal budget can be identified as devoted to war-related activities, such individuals would have a similarly valid claim to be exempt from paying that percentage of the income tax. The tax system could not function if denominations were allowed to challenge the tax system because tax payments were spent in a manner that violates their religious belief." *Id.*, at 260. Cf. *Hernandez* v. *Commissioner*, 490 U. S. 680 (1989) (rejecting free exercise challenge to payment of income taxes alleged to make religious activities more difficult).

The only decisions in which we have held that the First Amendment bars application of a neutral, generally applicable law to religiously motivated action have involved not the Free Exercise Clause alone, but the Free Exercise Clause in conjunction with other constitutional protections, such as freedom of speech and of the press, see *Cantwell* v. *Connecticut*, 310 U. S., at 304–307 (invalidating a licensing system for religious and charitable solicitations under which the administrator had discretion to deny a license to any cause he deemed nonreligious); *Murdock* v. *Pennsylvania*, 319 U. S. 105 (1943) (invalidating a flat tax on solicitation as applied to the dissemination of religious ideas); *Follett* v. *McCormick*, 321 U. S. 573 (1944) (same), or the right of parents, acknowledged in *Pierce* v. *Society of Sisters*, 268 U. S. 510 (1925), to direct the education of their children, see *Wisconsin* v. *Yoder*, 406 U. S. 205 (1972) (invalidating compulsory school-attendance laws as applied to Amish parents who refused on religious grounds to send their children to school).[1]

Some of our cases prohibiting compelled expression, decided exclusively upon free speech grounds, have also involved freedom of religion, cf. *Wooley* v. *Maynard*, 430 U. S. 705 (1977) (invalidating compelled display of a license plate slogan that offended individual religious beliefs); *West Virginia Bd. of Education* v. *Barnette*, 319 U. S. 624 (1943) (invalidating compulsory flag salute statute challenged by religious objectors). And it is easy to envision a case in which a challenge on freedom of association grounds would likewise be reinforced by Free Exercise Clause concerns. Cf. *Roberts* v. *United States Jaycees*, 468 U. S. 609, 622 (1984) ('An individual's freedom to speak, to worship, and to petition the government for the redress of grievances could not be vigorously protected from interference by the State [if] a correlative freedom to engage in group effort toward those ends were not also guaranteed').

The present case does not present such a hybrid situation, but a free exercise claim unconnected with any communicative activity or parental right. Respondents urge us to hold, quite simply, that when otherwise prohibitable conduct is accompanied by religious convictions, not only the convictions but the conduct itself must be free from governmental regulation. We have never held that, and decline to do so now. There being no contention that Oregon's drug law represents an attempt to regulate religious beliefs, the communication of religious beliefs, or the raising of one's children in those beliefs, the rule to which we have adhered ever since *Reynolds* plainly controls. "Our cases do not at their farthest reach support the proposition that a stance of conscientious opposition relieves an objector from any colliding duty fixed by a democratic government." *Gillette v. United States, supra*, at 461.

B

Respondents argue that even though exemption from generally applicable criminal laws need not automatically be extended to religiously motivated actors, at least the claim for a religious exemption must be evaluated under the balancing test set forth in *Sherbert* v. *Verner*, 374 U. S. 398 (1963). Under the *Sherbert* test, governmental actions that substantially burden a religious practice must be justified by a compelling governmental interest. See *id.*, at 402–403; see also *Hernandez* v. *Commissioner*, 490 U. S., at 699. Applying that test we have, on three occasions, invalidated state unemployment compensation rules that conditioned the availability of benefits upon an applicant's willingness to work under conditions forbidden by his religion. See *Sherbert* v. *Verner, supra; Thomas* v. *Review Bd. of Indiana Employment Security Div.,* 450 U. S. 707 (1981); *Hobbie* v. *Unemployment Appeals Comm'n of Florida,* 480 U. S. 136 (1987). We have never invalidated any governmental action on the basis of the *Sherbert* test except the denial of unemployment compensation. Although we have sometimes purported to apply the *Sherbert* test in contexts other than that, we have always found the test satisfied, see *United States* v. *Lee,* 455 U. S. 252 (1982); *Gillette* v. *United States,* 401 U. S. 437 (1971). In recent years we have abstained from applying the *Sherbert* test (outside the unemployment compensation field) at all. In *Bowen* v. *Roy,* 476 U. S. 693 (1986), we declined to apply *Sherbert* analysis to a federal statutory scheme that required benefit applicants and recipients to provide their Social Security numbers. The plaintiffs in that case asserted that it would violate their religious beliefs to obtain and provide a Social Security number for their daughter. We held the statute's application to the plaintiffs valid regardless of whether it was necessary to effectuate a compelling interest. See 476 U. S., at 699–701. In *Lyng* v. *Northwest Indian Cemetery Protective Assn.,* 485 U. S. 439 (1988), we declined to apply *Sherbert* analysis to the Government's logging and road construction activities on lands used for religious purposes by several Native American Tribes, even though it was undisputed that the activities "could have devastating effects on traditional Indian religious practices," 485 U. S., at 451. In *Goldman* v. *Weinberger*, 475 U. S. 503 (1986), we rejected application of the *Sherbert* test to military dress regulations that forbade the wearing of yarmulkes. In *O'Lone* v. *Estate of Shabazz*, 482 U. S. 342 (1987), we sustained, without mentioning the *Sherbert* test, a prison's refusal to excuse inmates from work requirements to attend worship services.

Even if we were inclined to breathe into *Sherbert* some life beyond the unemployment compensation field, we would not apply it to require exemptions from a generally applicable criminal law. The *Sherbert* test, it must be recalled, was developed in a context that lent itself to individualized governmental assessment of the reasons for the relevant conduct. As a plurality of the Court noted in *Roy*, a distinctive feature of unemployment compensation programs is that their eligibility criteria invite consideration of the particular circumstances behind an applicant's unemployment: "The statutory conditions [in *Sherbert* and *Thomas*] provided that a person was not eligible for unemployment compensation benefits if, 'without good cause,' he had quit work or refused available work. The 'good cause' standard created a mechanism for individualized exemptions." *Bowen* v. *Roy, supra*, at 708 (opinion of Burger, C. J., joined by Powell and REHNQUIST, JJ.). See also *Sherbert, supra*, at 401, n. 4 (reading state unemployment compensation law as allowing benefits for unemployment caused by at least some "personal reasons"). As the plurality pointed out in *Roy*, our decisions in the unemployment cases stand for the proposition that where the State has in place a system of individual exemptions, it may not refuse to extend that system to cases of "religious hardship" without compelling reason. *Bowen* v. *Roy, supra*, at 708.

Whether or not the decisions are that limited, they at least have nothing to do with an across-the-board criminal prohibition on a particular form of conduct. Although, as noted earlier, we have sometimes used the *Sherbert* test to analyze free exercise challenges to such laws, see *United States* v. *Lee, supra*, at 257–260; *Gillette* v. *United States, supra*, at 462, we have never applied the test to invalidate one. We conclude today that the sounder approach, and the approach in accord with the vast majority of our precedents, is to hold the test inapplicable to such challenges. The government's ability to enforce generally applicable prohibitions of socially harmful conduct, like its ability to carry out other aspects of public policy, "cannot depend on measuring the effects of a governmental action on a religious objector's spiritual development." *Lyng, supra*, at 451. To make an individual's obligation to obey such a law contingent upon the law's coincidence with his religious beliefs, except where the State's interest is "compelling"—permitting him, by virtue of his beliefs, "to become a law unto himself," *Reynolds v. United States,* 98 U. S., at 167—contradicts both constitutional tradition and common sense.[2]

The "compelling government interest" requirement seems benign, because it is familiar from other fields. But using it as the standard that must be met before the government may accord different treatment on the basis of race, see, *e. g., Palmore* v. *Sidoti,* 466 U. S. 429, 432 (1984), or before the government may regulate the content of speech, see, *e. g., Sable Communications of California v. FCC,* 492 U. S. 115, 126 (1989), is not remotely comparable to using it for the purpose asserted here. What it produces in those other fields—equality of treatment and an unrestricted flow of contending speech— are constitutional norms; what it would produce here—a private right to ignore generally applicable laws—is a constitutional anomaly.[3]

Nor is it possible to limit the impact of respondents' proposal by requiring a "compelling state interest" only when the conduct prohibited is "central" to the individual's religion. Cf. *Lyng* v. *Northwest Indian Cemetery Protective Assn.,* 485 U. S., at 474–476 (BRENNAN, J., dissenting). It is no more appropriate for judges to determine the "centrality" of religious beliefs before applying a "compelling interest" test in the free exercise field, than it would be for them to determine the "importance" of ideas before applying the "compelling interest" test in the free speech field. What principle of law or logic can be brought to bear to contradict a believer's assertion that a particular act is "central" to his personal faith? Judging the centrality of different religious practices is akin to the unacceptable "business of evaluating the relative merits of differing religious claims." *United States* v. *Lee,* 455 U. S., at 263 n. 2 (STEVENS, J., concurring). As we reaffirmed only last Term, "[i]t is not within the judicial ken to question the centrality of particular beliefs or practices to a faith, or the validity of particular litigants' interpretations of those creeds." *Hernandez* v. *Commissioner,* 490 U. S., at 699. Repeatedly and in many different contexts, we have warned that courts must not presume to determine the place of a particular belief in a religion or the plausibility of a religious claim. See, *e. g., Thomas* v. *Review Bd. of Indiana Employment Security Div.,* 450 U. S., at 716; *Presbyterian Church in U. S.* v. *Mary Elizabeth Blue Hull Memorial Presbyterian Church,* 393 U. S., at 450; *Jones* v. *Wolf,* 443 U. S. 595, 602–606 (1979); *United States* v. *Ballard,* 322 U. S. 78, 85–87 (1944).[4]

If the "compelling interest" test is to be applied at all, then, it must be applied across the board, to all actions thought to be religiously commanded. Moreover, if "compelling interest" really means what it says (and watering it down here would subvert its rigor in the other fields where it is applied), many laws will not meet the test. Any society adopting such a system would be courting anarchy, but that danger increases in direct proportion to the society's diversity of religious beliefs, and its determination to coerce or suppress none of them. Precisely because "we are a cosmopolitan nation made up of people of almost every conceivable religious preference," *Braunfeld* v. *Brown*, 366 U. S., at 606, and precisely because we value and protect that religious divergence, we cannot afford the luxury of deeming presumptively *invalid,* as applied to the religious objector, every regulation of conduct that does not protect an interest of the highest order. The rule respondents favor would open the prospect of constitutionally required religious exemptions from civic obligations of almost every conceivable kind—ranging from compulsory military service, see, *e. g., Gillette* v. *United States,* 401 U. S. 437 (1971), to the payment of taxes, see, *e. g., United States* v. *Lee, supra;* to health and safety regulation such as manslaughter and child neglect laws, see, *e. g., Funkhouser* v. *State,* 763 P. 2d 695 (Okla. Crim. App. 1988), compulsory vaccination laws, see, *e. g., Cude* v. *State,* 237 Ark. 927, 377 S. W. 2d 816 (1964), drug laws, see, *e. g., Olsen* v. *Drug Enforcement Administration,* 279 U. S. App. D. C. 1, 878 F. 2d 1458 (1989), and traffic laws, see *Cox* v. *New Hampshire,* 312 U. S. 569 (1941); to social welfare legislation such as minimum wage laws, see *Tony and Susan Alamo Foundation* v. *Secretary of Labor,* 471 U. S. 290 (1985), child labor laws, see *Prince* v. *Massachusetts,* 321 U. S. 158 (1944), animal cruelty laws, see, *e. g., Church of the Lukumi Babalu Aye Inc.* v. *City of Hialeah,* 723 F. Supp. 1467 (SD Fla. 1989), cf. *State* v. *Massey,* 229 N. C. 734, 51 S. E. 2d 179, appeal dism'd, 336 U. S. 942 (1949), environmental protection laws, see *United States* v. *Little,* 638 F. Supp. 337 (Mont. 1986), and laws providing for equality of opportunity for the races, see, *e. g., Bob Jones* University v. *United States,* 461 U. S. 574, 603–604 (1983). The First Amendment's protection of religious liberty does not require this.[5]

Values that are protected against government interference through enshrinement in the Bill of Rights are not thereby banished from the political process. Just as a society that believes in the negative protection accorded to the press by the First Amendment is likely to enact laws that affirmatively foster the dissemination of the printed word, so also a society that believes in the negative protection accorded to religious belief can be expected to be solicitous of that value in its legislation as well. It is therefore not surprising that a number of States have made an exception to their drug laws for sacramental peyote use. See, *e. g.,* Ariz. Rev. Stat. Ann. §§ 13–3402(B)(l)-(3) (1989); Colo. Rev. Stat. § 12–22–317(3) (1985); N. M. Stat. Ann. § 30–31–6(D) (Supp. 1989). But to say that a nondiscriminatory religious-practice exemption is permitted, or even that it is desirable, is not to say that it is constitutionally required, and that the appropriate occasions for its creation can be discerned by the courts. It may fairly be said that leaving accommodation to the political process will place at a relative disadvantage those religious practices that are not widely engaged in; but that unavoidable consequence of democratic government must be preferred to a system in which each conscience is a law unto itself or in which judges weigh the social importance of all laws against the centrality of all religious beliefs.

* * *

Because respondents' ingestion of peyote was prohibited under Oregon law, and because that prohibition is constitutional, Oregon may, consistent with the Free Exercise Clause, deny respondents unemployment compensation when their dismissal results from use of the drug. The decision of the Oregon Supreme Court is accordingly reversed.

It is so ordered.

1. Both lines of cases have specifically adverted to the non-free-exercise principle involved. *Cantwell,* for example, observed that "[t]he fundamental law declares the interest of the United States that the free exercise of religion be not prohibited and that freedom to communicate information and opinion be not abridged." 310 U. S., at 307. *Murdock* said:

> We do not mean to say that religious groups and the press are free from all financial burdens of government. . . . We have here something quite different, for example, from a tax on the income of one who engages in religious activities or a tax on property used or employed in connection with those activities. It is one thing to impose a tax on the income or property of a preacher. It is quite another thing to exact a tax from him for the privilege of delivering a sermon. . . . Those who can deprive religious groups of their colporteurs can take from them a part of the vital power of the press which has survived from the Reformation. 319 U, S., at 112.

Yoder said that "the Court's holding in *Pierce* stands as a charter of the rights of parents to direct the religious upbringing of their children. And, when the interests of parenthood are combined with a free exercise claim of the nature revealed by this record, more than merely a 'reasonable relation to some purpose within the competency of the State' is required to sustain the validity of the State's requirement under the First Amendment." 406 U. S., at 233.

2. JUSTICE O'CONNOR seeks to distinguish *Lyng* v. *Northwest Indian Cemetery Protective Assn.*, 485 U. S. 439 (1988), and *Bowen* v. *Roy*, 476 U. S. 693 (1986), on the ground that those cases involved the government's conduct of "its own internal affairs," which is different because, as Justice Douglas said in *Skerbert*, "the Free Exercise Clause is written in terms of what the government cannot do to the individual, not in terms of what the individual can exact from the government." *Post*, at 900 (O'CONNOR, J., concurring in judgment), quoting *Sherbert* v. *Verner*, 374 U. S. 398, 412 (1963) (Douglas, J., concurring). But since Justice Douglas voted with the majority in *Sherbert*, that quote obviously envisioned that what the government cannot do to the individual includes not just the prohibition of an individual's freedom of action through criminal laws but also the running of its programs (in *Sherbert*, state unemployment compensation) in such fashion as to harm the individual's religious interests. Moreover, it is hard to see any reason in principle or practicality why the government should have to tailor its health and safety laws to conform to the diversity of religious belief, but should not have to tailor its management of public lands, *Lyng, supra*, or its administration of welfare programs, *Roy, supra*.

3. JUSTICE O'CONNOR suggests that "[t]here is nothing talismanic about neutral laws of general applicability," and that all laws burdening religious practices should be subject to compelling-interest scrutiny because "the First Amendment unequivocally makes freedom of religion, like freedom from race discrimination and freedom of speech, a 'constitutional nor[m],' not an 'anomaly.'" *Post*, at 901 (opinion concurring in judgment). But this comparison with other fields supports, rather than undermines, the conclusion we draw today. Just as we subject to the most exacting scrutiny laws that make classifications based on race, see *Palmore* v. *Sidoti*, 466 U. S. 429 (1984), or on the content of speech, see *Sable Communications of California* v. *FCC*, 492 U. S. 115 (1989), so too we strictly scrutinize governmental classifications based on religion, see *McDaniel* v. *Paty*, 435 U. S. 618 (1978); see also *Torcaso* v. *Watkins*, 367 U. S. 488 (1961). But we have held that race-neutral laws that have the *effect* of disproportionately disadvantaging a particular racial group do not thereby become subject to compelling-interest analysis under the Equal Protection Clause, see *Washington* v. *Davis*, 426 U. S. 229 (1976) (police employment examination); and we have held that generally applicable laws unconcerned with regulating speech that have the *effect* of interfering with speech do not thereby become subject to compelling-interest analysis under the First Amendment, see

Citizen Publishing Co. v. *United States,* 394 U. S. 131, 139 (1969) (antitrust laws). Our conclusion that generally applicable, religion-neutral laws that have the effect of burdening a particular religious practice need not be justified by a compelling governmental interest is the only approach compatible with these precedents.

4. While arguing that we should apply the compelling interest test in this case, JUSTICE O'CONNOR nonetheless agrees that "our determination of the constitutionality of Oregon's general criminal prohibition cannot, and should not, turn on the centrality of the particular religious practice at issue," *post,* at 906–907 (opinion concurring in judgment). This means, presumably, that compelling-interest scrutiny must be applied to generally applicable laws that regulate or prohibit *any* religiously motivated activity, no matter how unimportant to the claimant's religion. Earlier in her opinion, however, JUSTICE O'CONNOR appears to contradict this, saying that the proper approach is "to determine whether the burden on the specific plaintiffs before us is constitutionally significant and whether the particular criminal interest asserted by the State before us is compelling." *Post,* at 899. "Constitutionally significant burden" would seem to be "centrality" under another name. In any case, dispensing with a "centrality" inquiry is utterly unworkable. It would require, for example, the same degree of "compelling state interest" to impede the practice of throwing rice at church weddings as to impede the practice of getting married in church. There is no way out of the difficulty that, if general laws are to be subjected to a "religious practice" exception, both the importance of the law at issue and the centrality of the practice at issue must reasonably be considered.

Nor is this difficulty avoided by JUSTICE BLACKMUN's assertion that "although . . . courts should refrain from delving into questions whether, as a matter of religious doctrine, a particular practice is 'central' to the religion, . . . I do not think this means that the courts must turn a blind eye to the severe impact of a State's restrictions on the adherents of a minority religion." *Post,* at 919 (dissenting opinion). As JUSTICE BLACKMUN'S opinion proceeds to make clear, inquiry into "severe impact" is no different from inquiry into centrality. He has merely substituted for the question "How important is X to the religious adherent?" the question "How great will be the harm to the religious adherent if X is taken away?" There is no material difference.

5. JUSTICE O'CONNOR contends that the "parade of horribles in the text only demonstrates . . . that courts have been quite capable of . . . strik[ing] sensible balances between religious liberty and competing state interests." *Post,* at 902

(opinion concurring in judgment). But the cases we cite have struck "sensible balances" only because they have all applied the general laws, despite the claims for religious exemption. In any event, JUSTICE O'CONNOR mistakes the purpose of our parade: it is not to suggest that courts would necessarily permit harmful exemptions from these laws (though they might), but to suggest that courts would constantly be in the business of determining whether the "severe impact" of various laws on religious practice (to use JUSTICE BLACKMUN'S terminology, *post*, at 919) or the "constitutiona[l] significan[ce]" of the "burden on the specific plaintiffs" (to use JUSTICE O'CONNOR'S terminology, *post*, at 899) suffices to permit us to confer an exemption. It is a parade of horribles because it is horrible to contemplate that federal judges will regularly balance against the importance of general laws the significance of religious practice.

SOURCE

U.S. Supreme Court. *United States Reports, Volume 494: Cases Adjudged in the Supreme Court at October Term, 1989, February 21 Through April 17, 1990*. Washington, D.C.: Government Printing Office, 1994, pp. 847–190.

RELATED READING

Anderson, Edward F. *Peyote: The Divine Cactus*. Tucson, AZ.: University of Arizona Press, 1980.

Slotkin, James S. *The Peyote Religion: A Study in Indian-White Relations*. Glencoe, IL.: The Free Press, 1956.

Stewart, Omer C. *Peyote Religion: A History*. Norman, OK.: University of Oklahoma Press, 1987.

Tepker, Harry F., Jr., "Hallucinations of Neutrality in the Oregon Peyote Case," *American Indian Law Review* 16 (1991): 1–56.

"A Better Day for Our People," 1996–97

Susan Crispen Shaffer has held one of the longest tenures of a tribal chair in modern times in Oregon. She came by her commitments through leadership and heritage. Her mother, Ellen (Furlong) Crispen, was longtime tribal secretary and treasurer. Her grandmother, Mary (Thomason) Furlong, was a tribal leader and civic figure for whom the Oregon State Highway Commission named Furlong Bridge on the South Umpqua River. Her great-grandmother, Susan (Nonta) Thomason, was born in a rock shelter deep in the western Cascades on the upper headwaters of the South Umpqua River.

In 1996 Shaffer, chair of the Cow Creek Band of Umpqua Tribe of Indians, addressed a large audience of tribal members and the general public in the tribe's 90,000–square-foot convention center at its Seven Feathers casino and hotel complex in Canyonville. In those remarks she reviewed briefly the tribe's search for "a better day" and its steady progress in achieving its hopes.

On July 17, 1997, Shaffer spoke to the heads of Oregon state departments and agencies. She did so at a time of increasing efforts of state and federal agencies to engage in "government-to-government" consultative relationships with tribes. Shaffer's perspectives were shaped by decades of involvement in tribal affairs and more than forty years experience as a business owner and as a civic leader in Douglas County, where she has served on the board of the community college and the historical society, and in numerous other capacities.

Using its own resources, the tribe, since 1986, has purchased its reservation, developed businesses, and invested significantly in its future and its community. The Cow Creeks by 2005 had a casino, a hotel, three motels, a convention center, a truck and travel center, a recreational vehicle park, a cattle ranch, a vineyard, a business park, an internet delivery company, a public relations firm, and other enterprises. The tribe dared to dream and build its future. Repeatedly it did so by forging relationships and engaging in active community involvement.

In November 2004, Susan Crispen Shaffer was elected to another three-year term as tribal chair. She was eighty-four years old.

"A Better Day for Our People," 1996

After the signing of our treaty in 1853, and the Rogue Indian Wars that followed, the Cow Creeks were ignored by the federal government and its treaty obligations for 128 years. Tribal families continued to meet and function together for the common good. Our parents and grandparents never lost the faith that a 'better tomorrow' would come. In the early 1970s, with no financial assets, present-day members held to the dream that there would be a better day for our people.

What we did have was dedication to the cause and determination that somehow we would be capable of reaching our goal. Perhaps we could equal the dedication that had carried our elders through all of those barren decades.

Where we are meeting this evening is the culmination, in part, of the tribal dream of providing a better future for our members. Cow Creeks are here as a tribe today because of the tenacity of many lifetimes that were invested in the struggle to keep our tribal families together, in spite of continued hardship and adversity. Our faith did not waiver . . . and here we are this evening in this elegant Seven Feathers complex.

All land in tribal ownership has been acquired by purchase.

We meet here as friends, co-workers, partners, and neighbors who share a common goal. That goal is, for all of us, to do what is right for our communities, for Douglas County, and for Oregon. The tribe is in a unique position to be a significant force in pulling the train of economic development into the future. We have brought together the mostly highly accomplished management team who have succeeded in training the 650+ people hired here to be professionals in the hospitality industry, many who have never had the opportunity before and who can now go anywhere and have successful careers.

The tribe provides health insurance for all employees. We have removed several from the Oregon Health Plan. Accommodations are made in working schedules, as much as possible, so that people can work and at the same time attend Umpqua Community College to further their education. The Cow Creek board takes the position that we must invest in the future through education.

We endeavor to encourage, inspire, and motivate. We intend to create incentive, not dependence. The tribe's focus is on education, not only for tribal members but the community as well. Each year the tribe provides a scholarship to U.C.C. for each high school in Douglas County.

The past year the Cow Creeks have entered into an aggressive building campaign—here and in the building of the tribal government offices on North

Stephens Street in Roseburg. All Cow Creek building is done according to code.

In 1996 the tribe has gross wages of $6.5 million, employer taxes/workmen's compensation of $900,000, employee benefits of nearly $1.0 million, over $40 million in construction projects, and has spent over $2.0 million with local vendors.

Sometimes, the journey seems such a long one, but the rewards are great. Every time I come here to Seven Feathers, I count my blessings for the tribe and for myself. For the tribe the rewards have been in the good things we have been able to do; for myself, my rewards have been the wonderful people that I have met along the way of the journey.

Address to Oregon State Department and Agency Heads, September 1, 1997

As are other elected tribal officials, I am here today as the Cow Creek tribal government. You folks are here representing government. No doubt what I say will be somewhat different from what other tribal leaders will present. We are here supposedly on a "government-to-government" meeting. I can no longer believe in that as reality.

I have served as an elected official on various levels of government unrelated to the tribe. After a lifetime of knowing the atrocities that tribal governments endured at the will of a stronger government, and because many people in government had been of great help to the Cow Creeks, I was lulled into believing in the "government-to-government" concept. However, the experience of the past year have taught me that I was a fool. It was only a charade. It can't be an equal playing field between an individual tribal government and a powerful state or federal government.

The strength in tribes is in strong leadership and believing in ourselves and the rights of our people, though time and experience have taught us that Indian people will have to fight all the way. Our strength will be in our support of each other, even if it only amounts to encouragement. I know that I, as a longtime leader, have depended on advice and often the "how to" of other tribal leaders.

It is my hope that we will all leave this meeting today with respect for each other and a better understanding of how we can start anew and built a stronger relationship here in the state of Oregon than we have ever had before. In order to do that we must face reality and begin with a solid foundation and a set of goals that are reachable.

About twenty-five years ago, I reached a time in my life where I decided that if there was one thing I wanted to do, it was to promulgate truth in Indian history—truth that is not in the textbooks. With that in mind, there are several pieces of information that I wish to present, including the history of my own people. Please bear with me.

THE DOCTRINE OF TRIBAL SOVEREIGNTY ... Indian government powers, with some exceptions, are not delegated powers, *but are inherent powers of a limited sovereignty that have never been extinguished.* This doctrine was first articulated in this country by Chief Justice John Marshall in *Worcester v. Georgia* in 1832. This relationship is marked by peculiar and cardinal distinctions which exist nowhere else. These obligations of the government promise to create a *"duty of protection"* toward the Indians—the trust responsibilities.

The purpose behind the trust doctrine is and always has been to ensure the survival and well-being of the tribes. This includes the obligation to provide services, to protect and enhance Indian lands, resources, and self-government. The Supreme Court has used such terms as "solemn," "special," and "trust" to describe the government-to-government relationship with Indian tribes.

LEGAL CONCEPTS OF FEDERAL INDIAN LAW ... There is a relatively consistent body of law whose origins flow from pre-colonial America to the present day. This body of law is neither well-known nor well understood by the American public. Federal Indian law—or, more accurately, United States constitutional law concerning Indian tribes and individuals—is unique and separate from the rest of American jurisprudence. Analogies to general constitutional law, civil rights law, public land law, and the like are misleading and often erroneous.

Indian law is distinct—it encompasses Western European international law, specific provisions of the United States Constitution, pre-colonial treaties, treaties of the United States, an entire volume of the United States Code, and numerous decisions of the United States Supreme Court and lower federal courts.

Indian tribes are governmental units that have a "special" political (trust) relationship with the government of the United States.

Indian treaties provide the clearest evidence of the sovereign nature of Native American tribal governments. They are documents of national and international law. They are legally binding contracts and solemn agreements that stand as canons of federal law in which tribes ceded their lands to the federal government for which they receive certain services (the trust responsibility).

Negotiations with tribes, from historic times to present, took place under the highest authority of the federal government. *No other sector of the American population has this unique relationship and these historic rights.*

HISTORY FROM DISCOVERY . . . From the earliest contact period European nations recognized the sovereignty of Indian tribes. Laws of discovery and conquest had been applied in different fashion throughout human history. Those who discovered lands were entitled to them—their riches and their spoils. The conquered people could be treated as slaves of the conquering people. But the discovery of America in 1492 was different. New continents had not been conquered before.

Tracing the historical antecedents of Indian legal history back to 1532, a mere 40 years after the discovery, the king of Spain sought the advice of Francisco de Vitoria, a prominent theologian, who reached the conclusion that the natives were *the true owners of the land* and that the Spanish could not claim title through discovery, for *title by discovery could only be justified where property was ownerless.* On that basis, the Indian tribes were recognized as legitimate entities capable of dealing with the European nations by treaty.

Some Indian tribes had highly complicated forms of government that could be traced back into pre-contact days, and according to some tribal traditions, back as far as their creation. It is interesting to note that the first written constitution drafted in North America appeared before Columbus ever embarked on his famous journey. The "Great Binding Law of the Five Nations" was a written constitution created by the Iroquois. It provided for a type of central government and was written on the sacred wampum belts made of seashells. This type of central government, based on the Iroquois Confederacy, would later be suggested to the colonies by Benjamin Franklin as an institution worthy of emulation.

INDIAN RIGHTS AND THE FORMING OF A NATION . . . The Northwest Ordinance (July 13, 1787) affirmed: "The utmost good faith shall always be observed toward the Indians; their lands and property shall never be taken from them without their consent; and, in their property, rights, and liberty, they shall never be invaded or disturbed, unless in just and lawful wars authorized by congress; but laws founded in justice and humanity shall, from time to time, be made, for preventing wrongs being done to them, and for preserving peace and friendship with them."

How ludicrous it is that the original owners of our homeland were not, in most instances, recognized as citizens until the Indian Citizenship Act of 1924 with many states not allowing them to vote until several years later . . . .

Shaffer concluded her remarks with a brief review of the tribe's difficult history during the Rogue River Indian Wars and years of isolation and living at the fringes of a federal relationship until terminated by Congress in 1956. Shaffer contended that Oregon tribes were not on an even playing field with the state and federal government. She also asserted, however, that tribal identities and rights are defined in law: by treaty, legislation, and judicial decision. Only when there is understanding of the unique nature of Indian tribes can there emerge an effective government-to-government relationship.

SOURCES

Shaffer, Susan Crispen. "A Better Day for Our People," 1996, Canyonville, OR. Copy in files of Stephen Dow Beckham, Lake Oswego, OR.

———. "Speech to Oregon State Department and Agency Heads," July 17, 1997, Canyonville, OR. Copy in files of Stephen Dow Beckham, Lake Oswego, OR.

Ancient One: Kennewick Man

Many issues surround the deep history of Native American residency in the Americas. Controversies about sacred sites, burials, and evidence of material culture have pitted tribes against real-estate developers, amateur collectors, archaeologists, and state and federal agencies. These tensions have been long felt, but the tribal ability to do anything about its cultural heritage was limited by lack of legal authority, financial resources, and support of the surrounding community. These matters slowly began to shift with the Antiquities Act (1906) and a series of post-World War II statutes that fostered protection for cultural resources. These measures included the Reservoir Salvage Act (1960), the National Historic Preservation Act (1966), National Environmental Protection Act (1969), and the Archaeological Resources Protection Act (1979).

The Native American Graves Protection and Repatriation Act (NAGPRA) (1990) compelled museums, state and federal agencies, and archaeologists to return human remains and religious objects to tribes. The law, however, created some complications: to whom should the remains be returned if more than one tribe sought them? What would be the fate of cultural objects if the tribe did not have the resources to curate and protect them? What would be done with remains so old that tribal affiliation might be unclear or challenged?

In spite of the problems that arose, tribes found the new direction of NAGPRA encouraging. Many opened consultations with museums to assess the materials and remains held in collections. The process enabled Oregon tribes to discover their "captured heritage," the recorded voices, works of art, objects of material culture, and human remains that had been collected decades before or removed without knowledge of the modern tribal communities.

One of the most lively national debates about the fate of human remains in the United States erupted with the discovery of a burial, believed to date to about 9,400 years before the present, at a site on the banks of the Columbia River near its confluence with the Snake River. The several tribes in that area requested return of the remains for internment. A determined contingent of physical anthropologists countered with the demand that they have the opportunity to study the skeletal materials to add to the understanding of the deep prehistory of the Americas. Mediation failed and the matter became entangled in years of litigation in federal court.

The following voices from the Confederated Tribes of Umatilla, one of the tribes determined to rebury "Ancient One" without scientific analysis, confirm the determination of tribes today to speak their views and chart their course. Armand Minthorn, a tribal religious leader, has frequently addressed cultural resource concerns for his tribe. Donald Sampson, a graduate of the University of Idaho, served as tribal chair from 1993 to 1997.

Armand Minthorn, "Human Remains Should be Reburied," September, 1996

In the summer of 1996 a human burial, believed to be about 9,000 years old, was discovered near Columbia Park in Kennewick, Washington. Scientists and others want to study this individual. They believe that he should be further desecrated for the sake of science, and for their own personal gain. The people of my tribe, and four other affected tribes, strongly believe that the individual must be re-buried as soon as possible.

My tribe has ties to this individual because he was uncovered in our traditional homeland—a homeland where we still retain fishing, hunting, gathering, and other rights under our 1855 Treaty with the U.S. Government.

Like any inadvertent discovery of ancestral human remains, this is a very sensitive issue for me and my tribe. Our religious beliefs, culture, and our adopted policies and procedures tell us that this individual must be re-buried as soon as possible. Our elders have taught us that once a body goes into the ground, it is meant to stay there until the end of time.

It is note our practice to publicize these types of discoveries, both for the protection of the individual as well as sensitivity to our tribal members. In this case, however, we must take the opportunity this incident has created to help educate the general public about the laws governing these discoveries and what these discoveries meant to us, as Indians. We also hope to give people a better understanding of why this is such a sensitive issue.

The Native American Graves Protection and Repatriation Act (NAGPRA) and Archaeological Resources Protection Act (ARPA), as well as other federal and state laws, are in place to prevent the destruction of, and to protect, human burials and cultural resources. The laws also say that authorities must notify affected Tribes and consult with tribal officials on how to handle the discovery, as well as protection and preservation. Our Tribe was not properly notified and if we had been, this difficult situation might have been avoided.

Under the Native American Graves Protection and Repatriation Act, tribes are allowed to file a claim to have ancestral human remains reburied. My tribe has filed a claim for this individual and when it is approved, we will rebury him and put him back to rest.

In filing this claim, we have the support of the four other tribes who potentially have ties to this individual. These tribes are the Yakama, Nez Perce, Colville, and Wanapum. We share the same religious belief, traditional practices, as well as oral histories that go back 10,000 years.

If this individual is truly over 9,000 years old, that only substantiates our belief that he is Native American. From our oral histories, we know that our people have been part of this land since the beginning of time. We do not believe that our people migrated here from another continent, as the scientists do.

We also do not agree with the notion that this individual is Caucasian. Scientists say that because the individual's head measurement does not match ours, he is not Native American. We believe that humans and animals change over time to adapt to their environment. And, our elders have told us that Indian people did not always look the way we look today.

Some scientists say that if this individual is not studied further, we, as Indians, will be destroying evidence of our own history. We already know our history. It is passed on to us through our elders and through our religious practices.

Scientists have dug up and studied Native Americans for decades. We view this practice as desecration of the body and a violation of our most deeply held religious beliefs. Today thousands of native human remains sit on the shelves of museums and institutions, waiting for the day when they can return to the earth, and waiting for the day that scientists and others pay them the respect they are due.

Our tribal policies and procedures, and our own religious beliefs, prohibit scientific testing on human remains. Our beliefs and policies also tell us that this individual must be re-buried as soon as possible.

Our religion and our elders have taught us that we have an inherent responsibility to care for those who are no longer with us. We have a responsibility to protect all human burials, regardless of race. We are taught to treat them all with the same respect.

Many people are asking if there's any chance for a compromise in this issue. We remind them that not only has this individual already been compromised, but our religious beliefs have once again been compromised. Many non-Indians are looking for a compromise—a compromise that fits their desires.

And, many non-Indians are trying to bend the laws to fit their desires. The Native American Graves Protection and Repatriation Act was passed by Congress in 1990 to protect Native American burials and set in place a mechanism to have human remains and artifacts returned to the tribes.

We are trying to ensure that the federal government lives up to its own laws, as well as honoring our policies, procedures, and religious beliefs. We understand that non-Indian cultures have different values and beliefs than us, but I ask the American people to please understand our stance on this issue. We are not trying to be troublemakers, we are doing what our elders have taught us—to respect people, while they're with us and after they've become part of the earth.

Don Sampson, "[Former] Tribal Chair Questions Scientists' Motives and Credibility," November 21, 1997

Most American Indians do not appreciate having the graves of our ancestors disturbed and their remains dissected and studied in the name of science. This practice, generally supported by non-Indian society, has come to the forefront over the past year and a half with the unearthing of a skeleton near present-day Kennewick, Washington. The media and the public have come to know this individual as Kennewick Man.

We have tried to explain to the public and scientists that our religious and cultural beliefs mandate that we rebury the remains of this individual as soon as possible. Many people don't seem to care about, or respect, our religious beliefs. So, rather than present those points again, I will take this opportunity to briefly address some of the scientific issues of this case.

We do not believe the issues surrounding this case are, in any manner, related to scientific facts. Rather, the issues are the result of an effort of a small group of scientists, through a media campaign, to lay claim to materials which Congress did not intend they have.

In their media campaign, the scientists have led the public to believe they can produce considerable data by studying this individual, including knowledge of the earliest peoples of this continent. In an article published last summer in *The New Yorker* magazine, scientists claim they already know a great deal about Kennewick Man. They think he may have been a fisherman who ate lots of salmon, that he was probably a tall, good-looking man, slender and well proportioned, that he was part of a small band of people who moved about, hunting, fishing, and gathering wild plants, that he may have lived in a simple sewn tent or mat hut, and that he may have worn tailored clothing.

The federal court, the Corps of Engineers, and the public should be asking the scientists to demonstrate how they can tell these things. These descriptions of the scientific "knowledge" obtained by the scientists is purely speculation and hypothesis, and do not advance our knowledge of this person, or mankind, a single bit. Almost anyone seeing an old skeleton in that area could have reached the same conclusions without destructive tests like the scientists want to perform.

These scientists are alleging that racial origins can be determined by examining the skeleton. But it is common knowledge among good anthropologists that it is impossible to determine the so-called "race" of an individual. A sample group is needed so that common traits can be determined.

The Kennewick Man remains were examined by Dr. Grover Krantz and there have been indications, using outdated techniques, that the skull has some "Caucasoid" features, some "Native American" features and a "Negroid" feature. Even following the 19th century science used by Dr. Krantz, there are 3 possible origins.

Dr. Grover Krantz has been regarded primarily as an expert on the "Big Foot" or "Sasquatch." From what we understand, his research is regarded by many of his colleagues as far from the mainstream of anthropology.

We also question the credibility and methodology of other scientists involved in the initial studies of Kennewick Man. Why hasn't a detailed report been compiled from those initial studies? Where is the statement of work and description of the methodology used? Were the studies conducted in accordance with the Archaeological Resources Protection Act (ARPA) as they should have been?

The "scientific case" for requiring the U.S. Army Corps of Engineers to allow testing of these remains is, in our viewpoint, shaky to non-existent.

We want the public and scientists to understand that we do not reject science. In fact, we have anthropologists and other scientists on staff, and we use science every day to help in protecting our people and the land. However, we do reject the notion that science is the answer to everything and therefore it should take precedence over the religious rights and beliefs of American citizens.

During protracted litigation, the remains of the "Ancient One" were transferred to the custody of the Burke Museum, University of Washington, Seattle. On February

4, 2004, the Ninth Circuit Court of Appeals ruled that the physical anthropologists seeking to study the remains had standing to challenge the federal government's application of NAGPRA to Kennewick Man. The Ninth Circuit also ruled that the record did not support the federal government's determination that the "Ancient One" was a Native American.

The efforts of the tribes to block scientific study and facilitate reburial of the remains of the "Ancient One" took time and considerable money. On July 19, 2004, the Board of Trustees of the Confederated Tribes of the Umatilla Reservation announced their decision not to appeal the case of "Kennewick Man" to the Supreme Court. Instead, they decided to expend their energies and resources to secure amendments to NAGPRA. Armand Minthorn commented: "NAGPRA needs to be strengthened so that it fulfills Congress' original intent, which was to protect Tribal burials and return sacred items to the Tribes."

SOURCES

Minthorn, Armand. Human Remains Should Be Reburied, www.umatilla.nsn.us/kman1.html. [Viewed 17 February 2005]

Sampson, Don. [Former] Tribal Chair Questions Scientists' Motives and Credibility, www.umatilla.nsn.us/kman.html. [Viewed 17 February 2005]

RELATED READING

Chatters, James C. Ancient Encounters: Kennewick Man and the First Americans. New York: Simon & Schuster, 2001.

Morrell, Virginia. Kennewick Man's Trials Continue. Science 280:190–92.

Bibliography

Beckham, Stephen Dow. History of Western Oregon Since 1846. *Handbook of North American Indians. Vol. 7, Northwest Coast,* Wayne Suttles, ed. Washington, DC: Smithsonian Institution, 1990.

Bensell, Royal A. *All Quiet on the Yamhill, the Civil War in Oregon: The Journal of Corporal Royal A. Bensell.* Gunter Barth, ed. Eugene, OR: University of Oregon Books, 1959.

Boyd, Robert. *The Coming of the Spirit of Pestilence: Introduced Infectious Diseases and Population Decline Among Northwest Coast Indians, 1774–1874.* Seattle, WA: University of Washington Press, 1999.

Cohen, Fay G. *Treaties on Trial: The Continuing Controversy Over Northwest Indian Fishing Rights.* Seattle, WA: University of Washington Press, 1986.

Collins, Cary C. The Broken Crucible of Assimilation: Forest Grove Indian School and the Origins of Off-Reservation Boarding School Education in the West. *Oregon Historical Quarterly,* 101(4)(Winter, 2000):466–507.

Cook, Warren L. *Flood Tide of Empire: Spain and the Pacific Northwest, 1543–1819.* New Haven, CT: Yale University Press, 1973.

Commissioner of Indian Affairs, *Annual Report of the Commissioner of Indian Affairs . . . 1870.* Washington, DC: Government Printing Office, 1870.

———. *Annual Report of the Commissioner of Indian Affairs . . . 1892.* Washington, DC: Government Printing Office, 1892.

Haynal, Patrick. Termination and Tribal Survival: The Klamath Tribes of Oregon. *Oregon Historical Quarterly,* 101(3)(Fall, 2000): 270–301.

Iverson, Peter. *'We Are Still Here' American Indians in the Twentieth Century.* Wheeling, IL: Harlan Davidson, Inc., 1998.

Johansen, Dorothy O. The Roll of Land Laws in the Settlement of Oregon, *Genealogical Material in Oregon Donation Land Claims,* Vol. 1. Portland, OR: Genealogical Forum of Portland, OR., 1957.

Kappler, Charles J., ed. *Indian Laws and Treaties.* Vol. 2, *Treaties.* Washington, DC: Government Printing Office, 1904.

Kelly, Lawrence C. The Indian Reorganization Act: The Dream and the Reality. *Pacific Historical Review,* 44(August, 1975):291–312.

Lea, Luke. Letter of July 20, 1850, to Anson Dart. *Annual Report of the Commissioner of Indian Affairs . . . 1850*. Washington, DC: Office of the Commissioner of Indian Affairs, 1850, pp. 117–20.

"News Clippings," *Plaindealer* (Roseburg, OR), 21 July 1871.

Nokes, J. Richard. *Columbia's River: The Voyages of Robert Gray, 1787–1793*. Tacoma, WA: Washington State Historical Society, 1991.

"Passing of the Red Man: An Aged Siletz Chief Declaims Against the White Man's Injustice," *The Oregonian* (Portland, OR), May 5, 1891.

Puter, Stephen A. D. *Looters of the Public Domain*. Portland, OR: The Portland Printing House, Publishers, 1908.

Reddick, SuAnn M. The Evolution of Chemawa Indian School: From Red River to Salem, 1825–1885. *Oregon Historical Quarterly*, 101(4)(Winter, 2000):444–65.

Smith, Michael T., The History of Indian Citizenship, *Great PlainsJournal*, 10 (Fall, 1970):25–35.

Statutes of Oregon, Enacted and Continued in Force by the Legislative Assembly at the Session Commencing 5th December 1853. Salem, OR: Asahel Bush, Public Printer, 1854.

Swan, E[dmund] A. Letter of September 11, 1880, to Carl Shurz. Department of Interior Appointment Papers, Oregon, 1849–1907, Microcopy —814, Roll 9, National Archives, Washington, D.C.

"Treatment of the Indian," *The Oregonian* (Portland, OR), April 14, 1886.

"The Umatilla Reservation," *Plaindealer* (Roseburg, OR), August 18, 1871.

Unruh, John D., Jr. *The Plains Across: The Overland Emigrations and the Trans-Mississippi West, 1840–60*. Urbana, IL: University of Illinois Press, 1979.

Wilkinson, Charles F., and Daniel Keith Conner. The Law of the Pacific Salmon Fishery: Conservation and Allocation of a Transboundary Common Property Resource. *The University of Kansas Law Review*, 32(1)(Fall, 1983):17–109.

Index

Confederated Tribes of Grand Ronde, xiv, 376, 437, 439, 445, 464–68, 475

Confederated Tribes of Siletz, 376, 384–92, 423, 436–37, 439, 458–63, 485, 488. *See also Siletz Indians*

Confederated Tribes of Umatilla, 218, 507, 555–59. *See also Umatilla Indians*

Confederated Tribes of Warm Springs, 393–400, 482, 485. *See also Warm Springs Indians*

Congregational Church, 294

Congress. *See U.S. Congress*

Connor, Gilbert, 417

The Conquest, 371

Cook, C. W., 71

Cook, James, 18

Coolidge, Calvin, 373

Coolidge, Mr., 24–26

Cooper, Jacob Calvin, 292, 367, 371

Coos, Lower Umpqua, and Siuslaw Reservation, 270, 474–77

Coos Bay, 131, 222–23, 269–70, 424–5, 429, 474

Coos County, OR, 424, 426, 477

Coos Head, 270

Coos Indians, 160, 259–70, 424, 426–27, 439, 449–57, 474–79

Coos River, 450

Coos Tom, 268

Coose County Volunteers, 131–39

Coquille Indians, 132–39, 424–25, 437, 477

Coquille River, 131, 241

Corney, Peter, 34–35

Cornoyer, Peter Kinai (Tualatin), 318, 320–21

Corps of Engineers, 375

Corvallis, OR, 232

Cosmashpello (Cayuse), 70

Couchey, John, 324

Council Creek, 220

Council Fire, 303

Cow Creek, 91, 228, 523, 529

Cow Creek Band of Umpqua, xiv, 91–100, 131, 183, 219–20, 374, 424, 437, 439, 485–86, 519–32, 548–53

Cow Creek Reservation, 220, 548

Cowles, R. A., 95

Coyote Creek, 228

Craig, William, 71, 79–80, 149

Cranks, Joseph/Nathaniel, 123

Crater Lake National Park, 222, 523

Crawley, Dennis, 251

Cree, T. K., 318–19

Crete, Edouard, 87

Crispen, Ellen (Nellie) Furlong (Cow Creek), 522, 528, 548

Crooked River, 172, 174, 177, 181

Crooks Point, 349, 353–54

Croquet, Adrian, 108, 320

Culps, Jackson, 394

Cultee, Charles (Chinook), 9

Cultus Jim (Rogue River), 184

Culver, Samuel H., 106, 225

Curl, Tom, 325–27

Curley Headed Jack, 283, 285

Currey, William, 277

Curry, George, 165–66

Curry County, OR, 31, 34, 348–58

Curtis, Edward Sheriff, 151

Curtis, H. P., 250, 257

Cush-Kella (Wasco), 201, 206

Cushman School (BIA), 374

Dagelma, 225

Dart, Anson, 105, 123, 220

Dave (Modoc), 250

David, Allen (Klamath), 300–302

David, Andrew, 410

Davidson, L. G., 365

Dawes Act. *See General Allotment Act*

Dawson, Catherine, 9

Dawson, Harry, Jr., 436